AUTOMOTIVE BRAKE SYSTEMS

FOURTH EDITION

James D. Halderman

PEARSON
Prentice
Hall

Upper Saddle River, New Jersey
Columbus, Ohio

Library of Congress Cataloging-in-Publication Data

Halderman, James D.
  Automotive brake systems / James D. Halderman. — 4th ed.
     p. cm.
  Includes index.
  ISBN-13: 978-0-13-174803-3
  ISBN-10: 0-13-174803-3
  1. Automobiles—Brakes. I. Title.
  TL269.H35 2008
  629.2'46—dc22

                              2007014904

Editor in Chief: Vernon Anthony
Associate Managing Editor: Christine Buckendahl
Editorial Assistant: Lara Dimmick
Production Coordination: Judy Ludowitz, Carlisle Publishing Services
Production Editor: Holly Shufeldt
Design Coordinator: Diane Ernsberger
Text and Cover Designer: Candace Rowley
Cover Art: Jeff Hinckley
Senior Production Manager: Deidra Schwartz
Director of Marketing: David Gesell
Marketing Assistant: Les Roberts

This book was set in Weidemann by Carlisle Publishing Services. It was printed and bound by Edwards Brothers. The cover was printed by Phoenix Color Corp.

Thanks to Byers Chevrolet, Dublin, Ohio, for allowing us to shoot the cover image in their showroom.

Pearson Prentice Hall™ is a trademark of Pearson Education, Inc.
Pearson® is a registered trademark of Pearson plc
Prentice Hall® is a registered trademark of Pearson Education, Inc.

Pearson Education Ltd.
Pearson Education Singapore Pte. Ltd.
Pearson Education Canada, Ltd.
Pearson Education—Japan

Pearson Education Australia Pty. Limited
Pearson Education North Asia Ltd.
Pearson Educación de Mexico, S.A. de C.V.
Pearson Education Malaysia Pte. Ltd.

10 9 8 7 6 5 4 3 2
ISBN-13: 978-0-13-174803-3
ISBN-10:   0-13-174803-3

PREFACE

PROFESSIONAL TECHNICIAN SERIES

Part of Prentice Hall Automotive's Professional Technician Series, the fourth edition of *Automotive Brake Systems* presents students and instructors with a practical, real-world approach to automotive technology and service. The series includes textbooks that cover all eight ASE certification test areas of automotive service: Engine Repair (A1), Automotive Transmissions/Transaxles (A2), Manual Drive Trains and Axles (A3), Suspension and Steering (A4), Brakes (A5), Electrical/Electronic Systems (A6), Heating and Air Conditioning (A7), and Engine Performance (A8).

Current revisions are written by an experienced author and peer reviewed by automotive instructors and experts in the field to ensure technical accuracy.

UPDATES TO THE FOURTH EDITION

- All content is correlated to the latest ASE and NATEF tasks for Brakes (A5).
- New chapters have been added on regenerative braking systems used on hybrid-electric vehicle systems (HEV).
- New content is added on electronic stability control (ESC).
- New information on brake assist system (BAS) has been added.
- Many additional photographs and line drawings help students understand the content material and bring the subject alive.
- Expanded content is presented on brake hydraulics and ABS and traction control systems (TCS).
- Many new photo sequences help explain service procedures.
- Unlike other textbooks, this book is written so that the theory, construction, diagnosis, and service of a particular component or system is presented in one location. There is no need to search through the entire book for other references to the same topic.

ASE AND NATEF CORRELATED

NATEF-certified programs need to demonstrate that they use course materials that cover NATEF and ASE tasks. This textbook has been correlated to the ASE and NATEF task lists and offers comprehensive coverage of all tasks. An NATEF TASK CORRELATION CHART and an ASE CERTIFICATION TEST CORRELATION CHART are included in the appendices to the book.

A COMPLETE INSTRUCTOR AND STUDENT SUPPLEMENTS PACKAGE

This textbook is accompanied by a full package of instructor and student supplements. See page vi for a detailed list of all supplements available with this book.

A FOCUS ON DIAGNOSIS AND PROBLEM SOLVING

The Professional Technician Series has been developed to satisfy the need for a greater emphasis on problem diagnosis. Automotive instructors and service managers agree that students and beginning technicians need more training in diagnostic procedures and skill development. To meet this need and demonstrate how real-world problems are solved, the "Real World Fix" features that appear in this textbook are included throughout and highlight how real-life problems are diagnosed and repaired.

The following pages highlight the unique core features that set the Professional Technician Series book apart from other automotive textbooks.

IN-TEXT FEATURES

OBJECTIVES and KEY TERMS appear at the beginning of each chapter to help students and instructors focus on the most important material in each chapter. The chapter objectives are based on specific ASE and NATEF tasks.

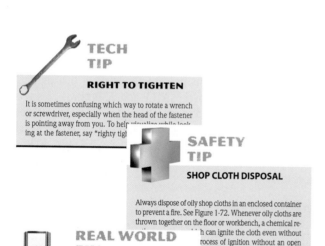

TECH TIP

RIGHT TO TIGHTEN

It is sometimes confusing which way to rotate a wrench or screwdriver, especially when the head of the fastener is pointing away from you. To help visualize while looking at the fastener, say "righty tigh...

SAFETY TIP

SHOP CLOTH DISPOSAL

Always dispose of oily shop cloths in an enclosed container to prevent a fire. See Figure 1-72. Whenever oily cloths are thrown together on the floor or workbench, a chemical re... ...h can ignite the cloth even without ... ...rocess of ignition without an open ...neous combustion.

REAL WORLD FIX

THE SINKING BRAKE PEDAL

This author has experienced what happens when brake fluid is not changed regularly. Just as many technicians will tell you, we do not always do what we know should be done to our own vehicles.

While driving a four-year-old vehicle on vacation in very hot weather in mountainous country, the brake pedal sank to the floor. When the vehicle was cold, the brakes were fine. But after several brake applications, the pedal became soft and spongy and sank slowly to the floor if pressure was maintained on the brake pedal. Because the brakes were OK when cold, I knew it had to be boiling brake fluid. Old brake fluid (four years old) often has a boiling point under 300°F (150°C). With th... 100°F (38°C), it does not tak... start boiling the brake flui... quart (1 liter) of new brake flui... the brakes worked normally. I'... replace the brake fluid as reco... cle manufacturer. See Figure 7-... be used to measure the boiling...

FREQUENTLY ASKED QUESTION

HOW MANY TYPES OF SCREW HEADS ARE USED IN AUTOMOTIVE APPLICATIONS?

There are many, including Torx, hex (also called Allen), plus many others used in custom vans and motorhomes. See Figure 1-10.

TECH TIPS feature real-world advice and "tricks of the trade" from ASE-certified master technicians.

SAFETY TIPS alert students to possible hazards on the job and how to avoid them.

REAL WORLD FIXES present students with actual automotive service scenarios and show how these common (and sometimes uncommon) problems were diagnosed and repaired.

FREQUENTLY ASKED QUESTIONS are based on the author's own experience and provide answers to many of the most common questions asked by students and beginning service technicians.

NOTES provide students with additional technical information to give them a greater understanding of a specific task or procedure.

NOTE: Most of these "locking nuts" are grouped together and are commonly referred to as *prevailing torque nuts*. This means that the nut will hold its tightness or torque and not loosen with movement or vibration. Most prevailing torque nuts should be replaced whenever removed to ensure that the nut will not loosen during service. Always follow the manufacturer's recommendations. Anaerobic sealers, such as Loctite, are used on the threads where the nut or cap screw must be both locked and sealed.

CAUTIONS alert students about potential damage to the vehicle that can occur during a specific task or service procedure.

CAUTION: Never use hardware store (nongraded) bolts, studs, or nuts on any vehicle steering, suspension, or brake component. Always use the exact size and grade of hardware that is specified and used by the vehicle manufacturer.

WARNINGS alert students to potential dangers to themselves during a specific task or service procedure.

WARNING: Hazardous waste disposal laws include serious penalties for anyone responsible for breaking these laws.

Hoisting the Vehicle Step-by-Step

STEP 1 The first step in hoisting a vehicle is to properly align the vehicle in the center of the stall.

STEP 2 Most vehicles will be correctly positioned when the left front tire is centered on the tire pad.

STEP 3 Most pads at the end of the hoist arms can be rotated to allow for many different types of vehicle construction.

STEP 4 The arms of the lifts can be retracted or extended to accommodate vehicles of many different lengths.

STEP-BY-STEP photo sequences show in detail the steps involved in performing a specific task or service procedure.

SUMMARY

1. Bolts, studs, and nuts are commonly used as fasteners in the chassis. The sizes for fractional and metric threads are different and are not interchangeable. The grade is the rating of the strength of a fastener.
2. Whenever a vehicle is raised above the ground, it must be supported at a substantial section of the body or frame.
3. Wrenches are available in open end, box end, and combination open and box end.
4. An adjustable wrench should only be used where the proper size is not available.
5. Line wrenches are also called flare-nut wrenches, fitting wrenches, or tube-nut wrenches and are used to remove fuel or refrigerant lines.
6. Sockets are rotated by a ratchet or breaker bar, also called a flex handle.
7. Torque wrenches measure the amount of torque applied to a fastener.
8. Screwdriver types include straight blade (flat tip) and Phillips.
9. Hammers and mallets come in a variety of sizes and weights.
10. Pliers are a useful tool and are available in many different types, including slip-joint, multigroove, lineman's, diagonal, needle nose, and locking pliers.
11. Other common hand tools include snap-ring pliers, files, cutters, punches, chisels, and hacksaws.

REVIEW QUESTIONS

1. List three precautions that must be taken whenever hoisting (lifting) a vehicle.
2. Describe how to determine the grade of a fastener, including how the markings differ between fractional and metric bolts.
3. List four items that are personal protective equipment (PPE).
4. List the types of fire extinguishers and their usage.
5. Why are wrenches offset 15 degrees?
6. What are the other names for a line wrench?
7. What are the standard automotive drive sizes for sockets?
8. Which type of screwdriver requires the use of a hammer or mallet?
9. What is inside a dead-blow hammer?
10. What type of cutter is available in left and right cutters?

CHAPTER QUIZ

1. The correct location for the pads when hoisting or jacking the vehicle can often be found in the _____.
   a. Service manual
   b. Shop manual
   c. Owner's manual
   d. All of the above
2. For the best working position, the work should be _____.
   a. At neck or head level
   b. At knee or ankle level
   c. Overhead by about 1 foot
   d. At chest or elbow level
3. A high-strength bolt is identified by _____.
   a. A UNC symbol
   b. Lines on the head
   c. Strength letter codes
   d. The coarse threads
4. A fastener that uses threads on both ends is called a _____.
   a. Cap screw
   b. Stud
   c. Machine screw
   d. Crest fastener

The **SUMMARY, REVIEW QUESTIONS,** and **CHAPTER QUIZ** at the end of each chapter help students review the material presented in the chapter and test themselves to see how much they've learned.

SUPPLEMENTS

The comprehensive **INSTRUCTOR'S MANUAL** includes chapter outlines, answers to all questions from the book, teaching tips, and additional exercises.

An **INSTRUCTOR'S RESOURCE CD-ROM** features:

- A complete text-specific **TEST BANK WITH TEST CREATION SOFTWARE**
- A comprehensive, text-specific **POWERPOINT PRESENTATION** featuring all of the art from the text as well as video clips and animations
- An **IMAGE LIBRARY** featuring additional images to use for class presentations
- Additional student activities including **CROSSWORD PUZZLES** and **WORD SEARCHES**
- A **SAMPLE ASE TEST** as well as the complete **ASE TASK LIST**
- **ASE TASK CORRELATION** Chart with checklist. The chart correlates the NATEF tasks to the text and the task sheets in the worktext.
- English and Spanish glossaries
- A Spanish translation of the entire text

- A **NATEF CORRELATION CHART**
- **NATEF CORRELATED TASK SHEETS**

Included with every copy of the book, the **STUDENT RESOURCE CD-ROM** features:

- A comprehensive, text-specific **POWERPOINT PRESENTATION** featuring all of the art from the text, as well as video clips and animations
- Additional activities including **CROSSWORD PUZZLES** and **WORD SEARCHES**
- A **NATEF CORRELATION CHART**
- A **SAMPLE ASE TEST** as well as the complete **ASE TASK LIST**
- English and Spanish glossaries
- A Spanish translation of the entire text

Available to be packaged with the book, the **STUDENT WORKTEXT (NATEF CORRELATED TASK SHEETS)** includes dozens of job sheets tied to specific NATEF tasks. Contact your local Prentice Hall representative for information on ordering the textbook packaged with the student worktext.

ACKNOWLEDGMENTS

A large number of people and organizations have cooperated in providing the reference material and technical information used in this text. The author wishes to express sincere thanks to the following organizations for their special contributions:

Allied Signal Automotive Aftermarket
Arrow Automotive
ASE
Automotion, Inc.
Automotive Parts Rebuilders Association (APRA)
Bear Automotive
Bendix
British Petroleum (BP)
Cooper Automotive Company
CR Services
DaimlerChrysler Corporation
Dana Corporation
Fluke Corporation
FMC Corporation
Ford Motor Company
General Motors Corporation Service Technology Group
Hennessy Industries
Hunter Engineering Company
John Bean Company
Lee Manufacturing Company
Monroe Shock Absorbers
Moog Automotive Inc.
Northstar Manufacturing Company, Inc.
Perfect Hofmann-USA
Shimco International, Inc.
SKF USA, Inc.
Society of Automotive Engineers (SAE)
Specialty Products Company
Tire and Rim Association, Inc.
Toyota Motor Sales, USA, Inc.
TRW Inc.
Wurth USA, Inc.

Technical and Content Reviewers

The following people reviewed the manuscript before production and checked it for technical accuracy and clarity of presentation. Their suggestions and recommendations were included in the final draft of the manuscript. Their input helped make this textbook clear and technically accurate while maintaining the easy-to-read style that has made other books from the same author so popular.

Jim Anderson
Greenville High School

Victor Bridges
Umpqua Community College

Robert Costanzo
Gateway Community College

Dr. Roger Donovan
Illinois Central College

A. C. Durdin
Moraine Park Technical College

Herbert Ellinger
Western Michigan University

Al Engeldahl
College of Dupage

Larry Hagelberger
Upper Valley Joint Vocational School

Oldrick Hajzler
Red River College

Betsy Hoffman
Vermont Technical College

Steve Levin
Columbus State Community College

Steven T. Lee
Lincoln Technical Institute

Carlton H. Mabe, Sr.
Virginia Western Community College

Roy Marks
Owens Community College

John McCormack
American River College

Kerry Meier
San Juan College

Fritz Peacock
Indiana Vocational Technical College

Dennis Peter
NAIT (Canada)

Kenneth Redick
Hudson Valley Community College

Peter Robert
Lansing Community College

Mitchell Walker
St. Louis Community College at Forest Park

Jennifer Wise
Sinclair Community College

Photo Sequences

I wish to thank Chuck Taylor, Mike Garblik, Blaine Heeter, and Frank Clay of Sinclair Community College, Dayton, Ohio, who helped with many of the photos.

Special thanks to Richard Reaves for all of his help. Most of all, I wish to thank Michelle Halderman for her assistance in all phases of manuscript preparation.

James D. Halderman

BRIEF CONTENTS

CONTENTS

CHAPTER **1**

SERVICE INFORMATION, TOOLS, AND SAFETY

OBJECTIVES

After studying Chapter 1, the reader should be able to:

1. Prepare for ASE knowledge content for vehicle identification and the proper use of tools and shop equipment.
2. Retrieve vehicle service information.
3. Explain the strength ratings of threaded fasteners.
4. Describe how to safely hoist a vehicle.
5. Discuss how to safely use hand tools.
6. List the personal protective equipment (PPE) that all service technicians should wear.

7. Describe what tool is the best to use for each job.
8. Discuss how to safely use hand tools.
9. Explain the difference between the brand name (trade name) and the proper name for tools.
10. Explain how to maintain hand tools.
11. Describe what precautions need to be followed when working on hybrid-electric vehicles.

KEY TERMS

VEHICLE IDENTIFICATION

All service work requires that the vehicle, including the engine and accessories, be properly identified. The most common identification is knowing the make, model, and year of the vehicle.

Make: e.g., Chevrolet
Model: e.g., Trailblazer
Year: e.g., 2003

The year of the vehicle is often difficult to determine exactly. A model may be introduced as the next year's model as soon as January of the previous year. Typically, a new model year starts in September or October of the year prior to the actual new year, but not always. This is why the **vehicle identification number,** usually abbreviated **VIN,** is so important. See Figure 1-1.

Since 1981, all vehicle manufacturers have used a VIN that is 17 characters long. Although every vehicle manufacturer assigns various letters or numbers within these 17 characters, there are some constants, including:

- The first number or letter designates the country of origin.

1 = United States	6 = Australia	L = China	V = France
2 = Canada	8 = Argentina	R = Taiwan	W = Germany
3 = Mexico	9 = Brazil	S = England	X = Russia
4 = United States	J = Japan	T = Czechoslovakia	Y = Sweden
5 = United States	K = Korea	U = Romania	Z = Italy

- The fourth or fifth character is the car line/series.
- The sixth character is the body style.
- The seventh character is the restraint system.

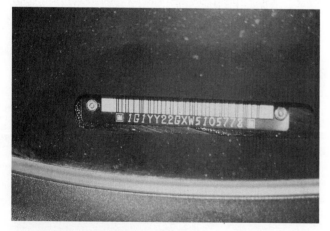

FIGURE 1-1 Typical vehicle identification number (VIN) as viewed through the windshield.

- The eighth character is often the engine code. (Some engines cannot be determined by the VIN number.)
- The tenth character represents the year on all vehicles. See the following chart.

VIN Year Chart (The pattern repeats every 30 years.)

A = 1980/2010	J = 1988/2018	T = 1996/2026	4 = 2004/2034
B = 1981/2011	K = 1989/2019	V = 1997/2027	5 = 2005/2035
C = 1982/2012	L = 1990/2020	W = 1998/2028	6 = 2006/2036
D = 1983/2013	M = 1991/2021	X = 1999/2029	7 = 2007/2037
E = 1984/2014	N = 1992/2022	Y = 2000/2030	8 = 2008/2038
F = 1985/2015	P = 1993/2023	1 = 2001/2031	9 = 2009/2039
G = 1986/2016	R = 1994/2024	2 = 2002/2032	
H = 1987/2017	S = 1995/2025	3 = 2003/2033	

Vehicle Safety Certification Label

A vehicle safety certification label is attached to the left side pillar post on the rearward-facing section of the left front door. This label indicates the month and year of manufacture as well as the **gross vehicle weight rating (GVWR),** the **gross axle weight rating (GAWR),** and the vehicle identification number (VIN).

VECI Label

The **vehicle emissions control information (VECI)** label under the hood of the vehicle shows informative settings and emission hose routing information. See Figure 1-2.

The VECI label (sticker) can be located on the bottom side of the hood, the radiator fan shroud, the radiator core support, or on the strut towers. The VECI label usually includes the following information:

- Engine identification
- Emissions standard that the vehicle meets
- Vacuum hose routing diagram
- Base ignition timing (if adjustable)
- Spark plug type and gap
- Valve lash
- Emission calibration code

Calibration Codes

Calibration codes are usually located on power train control modules (PCMs) or other controllers. Whenever diagnosing an engine operating fault, it is often necessary to know the calibra-

FIGURE 1-2 The vehicle emission control information (VECI) sticker is placed under the hood.

FIGURE 1-3 A typical calibration code sticker on the case of a controller. The information on this sticker is often needed when ordering parts or a replacement controller.

tion code to be sure that the vehicle is the subject of a technical service bulletin or other service procedure. See Figure 1-3.

Casting Numbers

Whenever an engine part such as a block is cast, a number is put into the mold to identify the casting. See Figure 1-4. These **casting numbers** can be used to check dimensions such as the cubic inch displacement and other information such as the year of manufacture. Sometimes changes are made to the mold, yet the casting number is not changed. Most often the casting number is the best piece of identifying information that the service technician can use for identifying an engine.

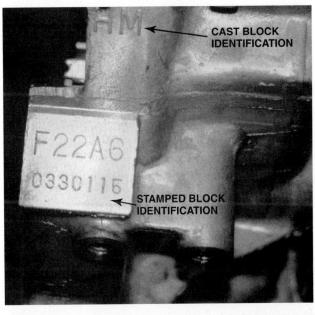

FIGURE 1-4 Engine block identification can be either cast or stamped or both.

SERVICE INFORMATION

Service information is needed by the service technician to determine specifications and service procedures, as well as learn about any necessary special tools.

Service Manuals

Factory and aftermarket service manuals contain specifications and service procedures. While factory service manuals cover just one year and one or more models of the same vehicle, most aftermarket service manufacturers cover multiple years and/or models in one manual. See Figure 1-5.

Included in most service manuals are the following:

- Capacities and recommended specifications for all fluids
- Specifications including engine and routine maintenance items
- Testing procedures
- Service procedures including the use of special tools when needed

Electronic Service Information

Electronic service information is available mostly by subscription and provides access to an Internet site where service manual-type information is available. See Figure 1-6. Most vehicle manufacturers also offer electronic service information to their dealers and to most schools and colleges that offer corporate training programs.

Technical Service Bulletins

Technical service bulletins, often abbreviated **TSBs,** are issued by the vehicle manufacturer to notify service technicians of a problem and include the necessary corrective action. Technical service bulletins are designed for dealership technicians but are republished by aftermarket companies and made available along with other service information to shops and vehicle repair facilities. See Figure 1-7.

Internet

The Internet has opened the field for information exchange and access to technical advice. One of the most useful websites is the International Automotive Technician's Network at

www.iatn.net. This is a free site but service technicians need to register to join. If a small monthly sponsor fee is paid, the shop or service technician can gain access to the archives, which include thousands of successful repairs in the searchable database.

Recalls and Campaigns

A **recall** or **campaign** is issued by a vehicle manufacturer and a notice is sent to all owners in the event of a safety-related fault or concern. While these faults may be repaired by shops, it is generally handled by a local dealer. Items that have created recalls in the past have included potential fuel system leakage problems, exhaust leakage, or electrical malfunctions that could cause a possible fire or the engine to stall. Unlike

FIGURE 1-6 Electronic service information is available from aftermarket sources such as All-Data and Mitchell-on-Demand as well as on websites hosted by the vehicle manufacturer.

FIGURE 1-5 A factory service manual contains all specifications and procedures for a particular vehicle or model in one or more volumes.

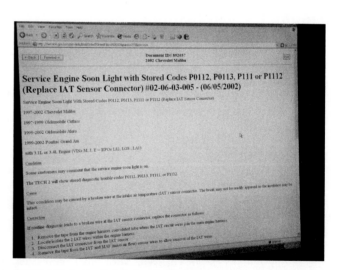

FIGURE 1-7 Technical service bulletins are issued by vehicle manufacturers when a fault occurs that affects many vehicles with the same problem.

technical service bulletins whose cost is only covered when the vehicle is within the warranty period, a recall or campaign is always done at no cost to the vehicle owner.

THREADED FASTENERS

Most of the threaded fasteners used on vehicles are cap screws. They are called *cap screws* when they are threaded into a casting. Automotive service technicians usually refer to these fasteners as **bolts,** regardless of how they are used. In this chapter, they are called bolts. Sometimes, studs are used for threaded fasteners. A **stud** is a short rod with threads on both ends. Often, a stud will have coarse threads on one end and fine threads on the other end. The end of the stud with coarse threads is screwed into the casting. A nut is used on the opposite end to hold the parts together.

The fastener threads *must* match the threads in the casting or nut. The threads may be measured either in fractions of an inch (called fractional) or in metric units. The size is measured across the outside of the threads, called the *crest* of the thread. See Figure 1-8.

Fractional threads are either coarse or fine. The coarse threads are called **Unified National Coarse (UNC),** and the fine threads are called **Unified National Fine (UNF).** Standard combinations of sizes and number of threads per inch (called **pitch**) are used. Pitch can be measured with a thread

pitch gauge as shown in Figure 1-9. Bolts are identified by their diameter and length as measured from below the head, and not by the size of the head or the size of the wrench used to remove or install the bolt.

Fractional thread sizes are specified by the diameter in fractions of an inch and the number of threads per inch. Typical

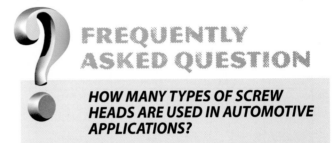

FREQUENTLY ASKED QUESTION

HOW MANY TYPES OF SCREW HEADS ARE USED IN AUTOMOTIVE APPLICATIONS?

There are many, including Torx, hex (also called Allen), plus many others used in custom vans and motorhomes. See Figure 1-10.

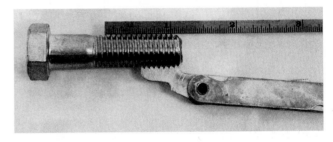

FIGURE 1-9   Thread pitch gauge used to measure the pitch of the thread. This bolt has 13 threads to the inch.

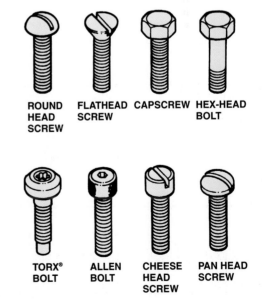

FIGURE 1-10   Bolts and screws have many different heads, which determine what tool must be used.

FIGURE 1-8   The dimensions of a typical bolt showing where sizes are measured. The major diameter is also called the crest.

UNC thread sizes would be 5/16-18 and 1/2-13. Similar UNF thread sizes would be 5/16-24 and 1/2-20. See Figure 1-11.

Metric Bolts

The size of a **metric bolt** is specified by the letter *M* followed by the diameter in millimeters (mm) across the outside (crest) of the threads. Typical metric sizes would be M8 and M12.

Size	Threads per inch		Outside Diameter Inches
	NC UNC	NF UNF	
0	. .	80	0.0600
1	64	. .	0.0730
1	. .	72	0.0730
2	56	. .	0.0860
2	. .	64	0.0860
3	48	. .	0.0990
3	. .	56	0.0990
4	40	. .	0.1120
4	. .	48	0.1120
5	40	. .	0.1250
5	. .	44	0.1250
6	32	. .	0.1380
6	. .	40	0.1380
8	32	. .	0.1640
8	. .	36	0.1640
10	24	. .	0.1900
10	. .	32	0.1900
12	24	. .	0.2160
12	. .	28	0.2160
1/4	20	. .	0.2500
1/4	. .	28	0.2500
5/16	18	. .	0.3125
5/16	. .	24	0.3125
3/8	16	. .	0.3750
3/8	. .	24	0.3750
7/16	14	. .	0.4375
7/16	. .	20	0.4375
1/2	13	. .	0.5000
1/2	. .	20	0.5000
9/16	12	. .	0.5625
9/16	. .	18	0.5625
5/8	11	. .	0.6250
5/8	. .	18	0.6250
3/4	10	. .	0.7500
3/4	. .	16	0.7500
7/8	9	. .	0.8750
7/8	. .	14	0.8750
1	8	. .	1.0000
1	. .	12	1.0000
1 1/8	7	. .	1.1250
1 1/8	. .	12	1.1250
1 1/4	7	. .	1.2500
1 1/4	. .	12	1.2500
1 3/8	6	. .	1.3750
1 3/8	. .	12	1.3750
1 1/2	6	. .	1.5000
1 1/2	. .	12	1.5000
1 3/4	5	. .	1.7500
2	4 1/2	. .	2.0000
2 1/4	4 1/2	. .	2.2500
2 1/2	4	. .	2.5000
2 3/4	4	. .	2.7500
3	4	. .	3.0000
3 1/4	4	. .	3.2500
3 1/2	4	. .	3.5000
3 3/4	4	. .	3.7500
4	4	. .	4.0000

FIGURE 1-11   The American National System is one method of sizing fasteners.

Fine metric threads are specified by the thread diameter followed by X and the distance between the threads measured in millimeters (M8 X 1.5). See Figure 1-12.

Grades of Bolts

Bolts are made from many different types of steel, and for this reason some are stronger than others. The strength or classification of a bolt is called the **grade.** The bolt heads are marked to indicate their grade strength.

The actual grade of bolts is two more than the number of lines on the bolt head. Metric bolts have a decimal number to indicate the grade. More lines or a higher grade number indicate a stronger bolt. Higher grade bolts usually have threads that are rolled rather than cut, which also makes them stronger. See Figure 1-13. In some cases, nuts and machine screws have similar grade markings.

CAUTION: *Never* use hardware store (nongraded) bolts, studs, or nuts on any vehicle steering, suspension, or brake component. Always use the exact size and grade of hardware that is specified and used by the vehicle manufacturer.

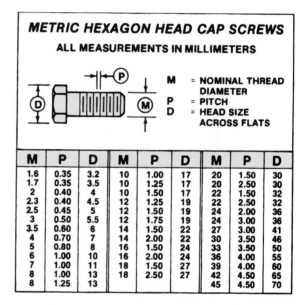

FIGURE 1-12   The metric system specifies fasteners by diameter, length, and pitch.

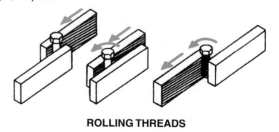

ROLLING THREADS

FIGURE 1-13   Stronger threads are created by coldrolling a heat-treated bolt blank instead of cutting the threads using a die.

Tensile Strength

Graded fasteners have a higher tensile strength than non-graded fasteners. **Tensile strength** is the maximum stress used under tension (lengthwise force) without causing failure of the fastener. Tensile strength is specified in pounds per square inch (psi). See the chart that shows the grade and specified tensile strength.

The strength and type of steel used in a bolt is supposed to be indicated by a raised mark on the head of the bolt. The type of mark depends on the standard to which the bolt was manufactured. Most often, bolts used in machinery are made to SAE standard J429.

SAE Bolt Designations

SAE Grade No.	Size Range	Tensile Strength, psi	Material	Head Marking
1	1/4 through 1 1/2	60,000	Low or medium carbon steel	
2	1/4 through 3/4	74,000		
	7/8 through 1 1/2	60,000		
5	1/4 through 1	120,000	Medium carbon steel, quenched and tempered	
	1-1/8 through 1 1/2	105,000		
5.2	1/4 through 1	120,000	Low carbon martensite steel,* quenched and tempered	
7	1/4 through 1 1/2	133,000	Medium carbon alloy steel, quenched and tempered	
8	1/4 through 1 1/2	150,000	Medium carbon alloy steel, quenched and tempered	
8.2	1/4 through 1	150,000	Low carbon martensite steel,* quenched and tempered	

* Martensite steel is steel that has been cooled rapidly, thereby increasing its hardness. It is named after a German metallurgist, Adolf Martens.

Metric bolt tensile strength property class is shown on the head of the bolt as a number, such as 4.6, 8.8, 9.8, and 10.9; the higher the number, the stronger the bolt. See Figure 1-14.

Nuts

Most **nuts** used on cap screws have the same hex size as the cap screw head. Some inexpensive nuts use a hex size larger than the cap screw head. Metric nuts are often marked with dimples to show their strength. More dimples indicate stronger nuts. Some nuts and cap screws use interference fit threads to keep them from accidentally loosening. This means that the shape of the nut is slightly distorted or that a section

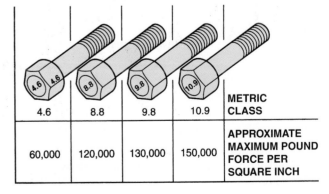

4.6	8.8	9.8	10.9	METRIC CLASS
60,000	120,000	130,000	150,000	APPROXIMATE MAXIMUM POUND FORCE PER SQUARE INCH

FIGURE 1-14   Metric bolt (cap screw) grade markings and approximate tensile strength.

TECH TIP

A 1/2-INCH WRENCH DOES NOT FIT A 1/2-INCH BOLT

A common mistake made by persons new to the automotive field is to think that the size of a bolt or nut is the size of the head. The size of the bolt or nut (outside diameter of the threads) is usually smaller than the size of the wrench or socket that fits the head of the bolt or nut. Examples are given in the following table:

Wrench Size	Thread Size
7/16 in.	1/4 in.
1/2 in.	5/16 in.
9/16 in.	3/8 in.
5/8 in.	7/16 in.
3/4 in.	1/2 in.
10 mm	6 mm
12 mm or 13 mm*	8 mm
14 mm or 17 mm*	10 mm

* European (Systeme International d'Unites-SI) metric.

NOTE: An open-end wrench can be used to gauge bolt sizes. A 3/8-in. wrench will closely fit the threads of a 3/8-in. bolt.

of the threads is deformed. Nuts can also be kept from loosening with a nylon washer fastened in the nut or with a nylon patch or strip on the threads. See Figure 1-15.

NOTE: Most of these "locking nuts" are grouped together and are commonly referred to as *prevailing torque nuts*. This means that the nut will hold its tightness or torque and not loosen with movement or vibration. Most prevailing torque nuts should be replaced whenever removed to ensure that the nut will not loosen during service. Always follow the manufacturer's recommendations. Anaerobic sealers, such as Loctite, are used on the threads where the nut or cap screw must be both locked and sealed.

Washers

Washers are often used under cap screw heads and under nuts. See Figure 1-16. Plain flat washers are used to provide an even clamping load around the fastener. Lock washers are added to prevent accidental loosening. In some accessories, the washers are locked onto the nut to provide easy assembly.

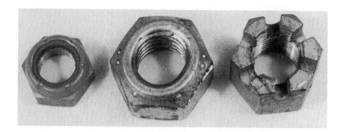

FIGURE 1-15 Types of lock nuts. On the left, a nylon ring; In the center, a distorted shape; and on the right, a castle for use with a cotter key.

FIGURE 1-16 Various types of nuts (top) and washers (bottom) serve different purposes and all are used to secure bolts or cap screws.

HAND TOOLS

Wrenches

Wrenches are the most used hand tool by service technicians. **Wrenches** are used to grasp and rotate threaded fasteners. Most wrenches are constructed of forged alloy steel, usually chrome-vanadium steel. See Figure 1-17.

After the wrench is formed, the wrench is hardened, and then tempered to reduce brittleness, and then chrome plated. There are several types of wrenches.

Open-End Wrench

An open-end wrench is usually used to loosen or tighten bolts or nuts that do not require a lot of torque. Because of the *open end*, this type of wrench can be easily placed on a bolt or nut with an angle of 15 degrees, which allows the wrench to be flipped over and used again to continue to rotate the fastener. The major disadvantage of an open end wrench is the lack of torque that can be applied due to the fact that the open jaws of the wrench only contact two flat surfaces of the fastener. An open end wrench has two different sizes; one at each end. See Figure 1-18.

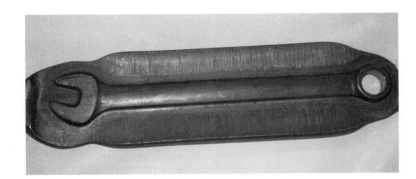

FIGURE 1-17 A forged wrench after it has been forged but before the flashing, extra material around the wrench, has been removed.

FIGURE 1-18 A typical open end wrench. The size is different on each end and notice that the head is angled 15 degrees at end.

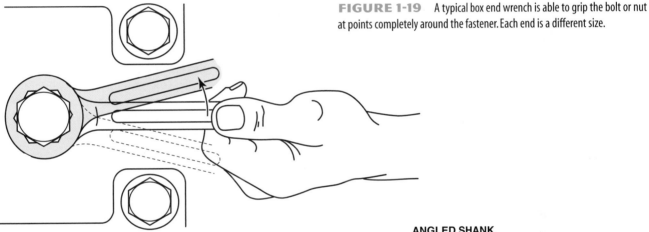

FIGURE 1-19 A typical box end wrench is able to grip the bolt or nut at points completely around the fastener. Each end is a different size.

Box-End Wrench

A *box-end wrench* also called a closed-end wrench is placed over the top of the fastener and grips the points of the fastener. A box end wrench is angled 15 degrees to allow it to clear nearby objects. See Figure 1-19.

Therefore, a box end wrench should be used to loosen or to tighten fasteners because it grasps around the entire head of the fastener. A box end wrench has two difference sizes; one at each end. See Figure 1-20.

Most service technicians purchase *combination wrenches*, which have the open end at one end and the same size box end on the other end. See Figure 1-21.

A combination wrench allows the technician to loosen or tighten a fastener using the box end of the wrench, turn it around, and use the open end to increase the speed of rotating the fastener.

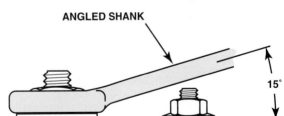

FIGURE 1-20 The end of a box-end wrench is angled 15 degrees to allow clearance for nearby objects or other fasteners.

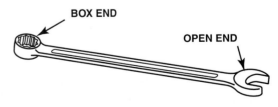

FIGURE 1-21 A combination wrench has an open end at one end and a box end at the other end.

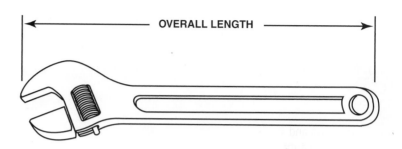

FIGURE 1-22 An adjustable wrench. Adjustable wrenches are sized by the overall length of the wrench and not by how far the jaws open. Common sizes of adjustable wrenches include 8, 10, and 12 inch.

Adjustable Wrench

An *adjustable wrench* is often used where the exact size wrench is not available or when a large nut, such as a wheel spindle nut, needs to be rotated but not tightened. An adjustable wrench should not be used to loosen or tighten fasteners because the torque applied to the wrench can cause the moveable jaws to loosen their grip on the fastener, causing it to become rounded. See Figure 1-22.

Line Wrenches

Line wrenches are also called *flare-nut wrenches*, *fitting wrenches* or *tube-nut wrenches* and are designed to grip almost all the way around a nut used to retain a fuel or refrigerant line, and yet, be able to be installed over the line. See Figure 1-23.

FIGURE 1-23 The end of a typical line wrench, which shows that it is capable of grasping most of the head of the fitting.

Safe use of wrenches. Wrenches should be inspected before use to be sure they are not cracked, bent, or damaged. All wrenches should be cleaned after use before being returned to the tool box. Always use the correct size of wrench for the fastener being loosened or tightened to help prevent the rounding of the flats of the fastener. When attempting to loosen a fastener, pull a wrench—do not push a wrench. If a wrench is pushed, your knuckles can be hurt when forced into another object if the fastener breaks loose or if the wrench slips.

Ratchets, Sockets, and Extensions

A **socket** fits over the fastener and grips the points and/or flats of the bolt or nut. The socket is rotated (driven) using either a long bar called a **breaker bar** (*flex handle*) or a **ratchet**. See Figures 1-24 and 1-25.

FIGURE 1-25 A typical flex handle used to rotate a socket, also called a breaker bar because it usually has a longer handle than a ratchet and therefore, can be used to apply more torque to a fastener than a ratchet.

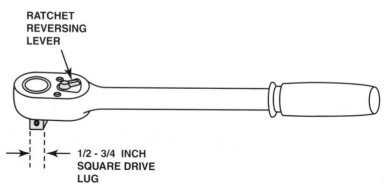

RATCHET REVERSING LEVER

1/2 - 3/4 INCH SQUARE DRIVE LUG

FIGURE 1-24 A typical ratchet used to rotate a socket. A ratchet makes a ratcheting noise when it is being rotated in the opposite direction from loosening or tightening. A knob or lever on the ratchet allows the user to switch directions.

A **ratchet** is a tool that turns the socket in only one direction and allows the rotating of the ratchet handle back and forth in a narrow space. Socket **extensions** and **universal joints** are also used with sockets to allow access to fasteners in restricted locations.

Sockets are available in various **drive sizes,** including 1/4-in., 3/8-in., and 1/2-in. sizes for most automotive use. See Figures 1-26 and 1-27.

Many heavy duty truck and/or industrial applications use 3/4-in. and 1-in. sizes. The drive size is the distance of each side of the square drive. Sockets and ratchets of the same size are designed to work together.

TECH TIP

RIGHT TO TIGHTEN

It is sometimes confusing which way to rotate a wrench or screwdriver, especially when the head of the fastener is pointing away from you. To help visualize while looking at the fastener, say "righty tighty, lefty loosey."

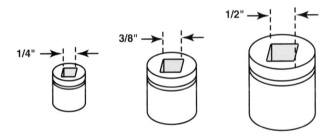

FIGURE 1-26 The most commonly used socket drive sizes include 1/4-in., 3/8-in., and 1/2-in. drive.

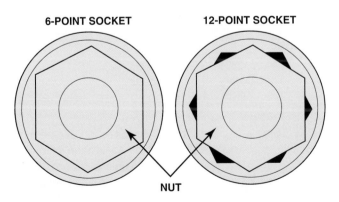

FIGURE 1-27 A 6-point socket fits the head of the bolt or nut on all sides. A 12-point socket can round off the head of a bolt or nut if a lot of force is applied.

Torque Wrenches

Torque wrenches are socket turning handles that are designed to apply a known amount of force to the fastener. There are two basic types of torque wrenches including:

1. Clicker type. This type of torque wrench is first set to the specified torque and then it "clicks" when the set torque value has been reached. When force is removed from the torque wrench handle, another click is heard. The setting on a clicker-type torque wrench should be set back to zero after use and checked for proper calibration regularly. See Figure 1-28.
2. A Beam-type. This type of torque wrench is used to measure torque, but instead of presenting the value, the actual torque is displayed on the dial of the wrench as the fastener is being tightened. Beam-type torque wrenches are available in 1/4-in., 3/8-in., and 1/2-in. drives and both English and Metric units. See Figure 1-29.

FIGURE 1-28 Using a torque wrench to tighten connecting rod nuts on an engine.

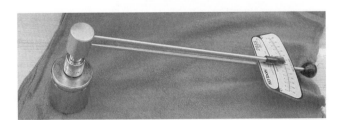

FIGURE 1-29 A beam-type torque wrench that displays the torque reading on the face of the dial. The beam display is read as the beam deflects, which is in proportion to the amount of torque applied to the fastener.

TECH TIP

CHECK TORQUE WRENCH CALIBRATION REGULARLY

Torque wrenches should be checked regularly. For example, Honda has a torque wrench calibration setup at each of their training centers. It is expected that a torque wrench be checked for accuracy before every use. Most experts recommend that torque wrenches be checked and adjusted as needed at least every year and more often if possible. See Figure 1-30.

FIGURE 1-30   Torque wrench calibration checker.

Safe use of sockets and ratchets.   Always use the proper size socket that correctly fits the bolt or nut. All sockets and ratchets should be cleaned after use before being placed back into the tool box. Sockets are available in short and deep well designs. See Figure 1-31.

Also select the appropriate drive size. For example, for small work, such as on the dash, select a 1/4-in. drive. For most general service work, use a 3/8-in. drive and for suspension and steering and other large fasteners, select a 1/2-in. drive. When loosening a fastener, always pull the ratchet toward you rather than push it outward.

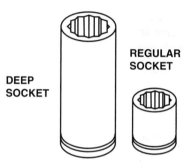

FIGURE 1-31   Deep sockets allow access to the nut that has a stud plus other locations needing great depth, such as spark plugs.

TECH TIP

USE SOCKET ADAPTERS WITH CAUTION

A **socket adapter** allows the use of one size of socket and another drive size ratchet or breaker bar. Socket adaptors are available and can be used for different drive size sockets on a ratchet. Combinations include:

1/4 in. drive—3/8 in. sockets
3/8 in. drive—1/4 in. sockets
3/8 in. drive—1/2 in. sockets
1/2 in. drive—3/8 in. sockets

Using a larger drive ratchet or breaker bar on a smaller size socket can cause the application of too much force to the socket, which could crack or shatter. Using a smaller size drive tool on a larger socket will usually not cause any harm, but would greatly reduce the amount of torque that can be applied to the bolt or nut.

TECH TIP

AVOID USING "CHEATER BARS"

Whenever a fastener is difficult to remove, some technicians will insert the handle of a ratchet or a breaker bar into a length of steel pipe sometimes called a **cheater bar.** The extra length of the pipe allows the technician to exert more torque than can be applied using the drive handle alone. However, the extra torque can easily overload the socket and ratchet, causing them to break or shatter, which could cause personal injury.

Screwdrivers

Many smaller fasteners are removed and installed by using a **screwdriver.** Screwdrivers are available in many sizes and tip shapes. The most commonly used screwdriver is called a *flat tip* or *straight blade.*

Flat tip screwdrivers are sized by the width of the blade and this width should match the width of the slot in the screw. See Figure 1-32.

CAUTION: Do not use a screwdriver as a pry tool or as a chisel. Screwdrivers are hardened steel only at the tip and are not designed to be pounded on or used for prying because they could bend easily. Always use the proper tool for each application.

Another type of commonly used screwdriver is called a Phillips screwdriver, named for Henry F. Phillips, who invented the crosshead screw in 1934. Due to the shape of the crosshead

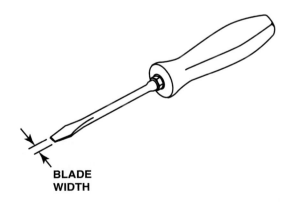

FIGURE 1-32   A flat-tip (straight blade) screwdriver. The width of the blade should match the width of the slot in the fastener being loosened or tightened.

screw and screwdriver, a Phillips screw can be driven with more torque than can be achieved with a slotted screw.

A Phillips head screwdriver is specified by the length of the handle and the size of the point at the tip. A #1 tip has a sharp point, a #2 tip is the most commonly used, and a #3 tip is blunt and is only used for larger sizes of Phillips head fasteners. For example, a #2 x 3 in. Phillips screwdriver would typically measure 6 in. from the tip of the blade to the end of the handle (3-in. long handle and 3-in. long blade) with a #2 tip.

Both straight blade and Phillips screwdrivers are available with a short blade and handle for access to fasteners with limited room. See Figure 1-33.

Offset Screwdrivers

Offset screwdrivers are used in places where a conventional screwdriver cannot fit. An offset screwdriver is bent at the ends and is used similar to a wrench. Most offset screwdrivers have a straight blade at one end and a Phillips end at the opposite end. See Figure 1-34.

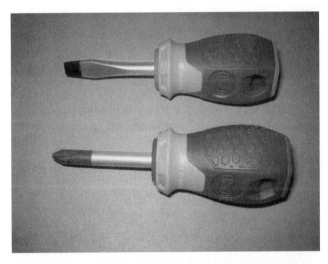

FIGURE 1-33   Two stubby screwdrivers that are used to access screws that have limited space above. A straight blade is on top and a #2 Phillips screwdriver is on the bottom.

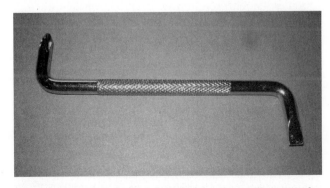

FIGURE 1-34   An offset screwdriver is used to install or remove fasteners that do not have enough space above to use a conventional screwdriver.

Impact Screwdriver

An *impact screwdriver* is used to break loose or tighten a screw. A hammer is used to strike the end after the screwdriver holder is placed in the head of the screw and rotated in the desired direction. The force from the hammer blow does two things: It applies a force downward holding the tip of the screwdriver in the slot and then applies a twisting force to loosen (or tighten) the screw. See Figure 1-35.

FIGURE 1-35   An impact screwdriver used to remove slotted or Phillips head fasteners that cannot be broken loose using a standard screwdriver.

FREQUENTLY ASKED QUESTION

WHAT IS A ROBERTSON SCREWDRIVER?

A Canadian named P. L. Robertson invented the Robertson screw and screwdriver in 1908, which uses a square-shaped tip with a slight taper. The Robertson screwdriver uses color-coded handles because different size screws required different tip sizes. The color and sizes include:

Orange (#00) – Number 1 and 2 screws
Yellow (#0) – Number 3 and 4 screws
Green (#1) – Number 5, 6, and 7 screws
Red (#2) – Number 8, 9, and 10 screws
Black (#3) – Number 12 and larger screws

The Robertson screws are rarely found in the United States but are common in Canada.

Safe use of screwdrivers.   Always use the proper type and size screwdriver that matches the fastener. Try to avoid pressing down on a screwdriver because if it slips, the screwdriver tip could go into your hand, causing serious personal injury. All screwdrivers should be cleaned after use. Do not use a screwdriver as a pry bar; always use the correct tool for the job.

Hammers

Hammers and mallets are used to force objects together or apart. The shape of the back part of the hammer head (called the *peen*) usually determines the name. For example, a ball peen hammer has a rounded end like a ball and it is used to straighten oil pans and valve covers using the hammer head and for shaping metal using the ball peen. See Figure 1-36.

NOTE: A claw hammer has a claw used to remove nails and is not used for automotive service.

A hammer is usually sized by the weight of the head of the hammer and the length of the handle. For example, a commonly used ball peen hammer has an 8-ounce head with an 11-in. handle.

Mallets

Mallets are a type of hammer with a large striking surface, which allows the technician to exert force over a larger area than a hammer, so as not to harm the part or component. Mallets are made from a variety of materials including rubber, plastic, or wood. See Figure 1-37.

FIGURE 1-36   A typical ball peen hammer.

FIGURE 1-37   A rubber mallet used to deliver a force to an object without harming the surface.

A shot-filled plastic hammer is called a *dead-blow hammer*. The small lead balls (shot) inside a plastic head prevent the hammer from bouncing off of the object when struck. See Figure 1-38.

Safe use of hammers and mallets. All mallets and hammers should be cleaned after use and not exposed to extreme temperatures. Never use a hammer or mallet that is damaged in anyway and always use caution to avoid doing damage to the components and the surrounding area. Always follow the hammer manufacturer's recommended procedures and practices.

Slip-Joint Pliers

Pliers are capable of holding, twisting, bending, and cutting objects and are an extremely useful classification of tools. The common household type of pliers is called the *slip-joint pliers*. There are two different positions where the junction of the handles meets to achieve a wide range of sizes of objects that can be gripped. See Figure 1-39.

Multigroove Adjustable Pliers

For gripping larger objects, a set of *multigroove adjustable pliers* is a commonly used tool of choice by many service technicians. Originally designed to remove the various size nuts holding rope seals used in water pumps, the name *water pump pliers* is also used. See Figure 1-40.

Linesman's Pliers

Linesman's pliers are specifically designed for cutting, bending, and twisting wire. While commonly used by construction workers and electricians, linesman's pliers are a very useful tool for the service technician who deals with wiring. The center parts of the jaws are designed to grasp round objects such as pipe or tubing with slipping. See Figure 1-41.

Diagonal Pliers

Diagonal pliers are designed to cut only. The cutting jaws are set at an angle to make it easier to cut wires. Diagonal pliers are also called *side cuts* or *dikes*. These pliers are constructed of hardened steel and they are used mostly for cutting wire. See Figure 1-42.

Needle Nose Pliers

Needle nose pliers are designed to grip small objects or objects in tight locations. Needle nose pliers have long pointed jaws, which allow the tips to reach into narrow openings or groups of small objects. See Figure 1-43.

Most needle nose pliers have a wire cutter located at the base of the jaws near the pivot. There are several variations of needle nose pliers, including right angle jaws or slightly angled to allow access to certain cramped areas.

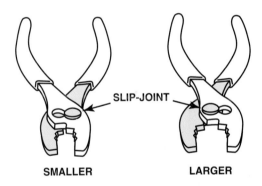

FIGURE 1-39 Typical slip-joint pliers are common household pliers. The slip joint allows the jaws to be opened to two different settings.

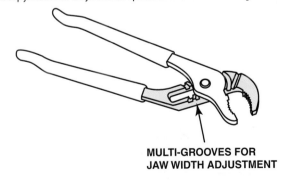

FIGURE 1-40 Multigroove adjustable pliers are known by many names, including the trade name Channel Locks.

FIGURE 1-38 A dead blow hammer that was left outside in freezing weather. The plastic covering was damaged, which destroyed this hammer. The lead shot is encased in the metal housing and then covered.

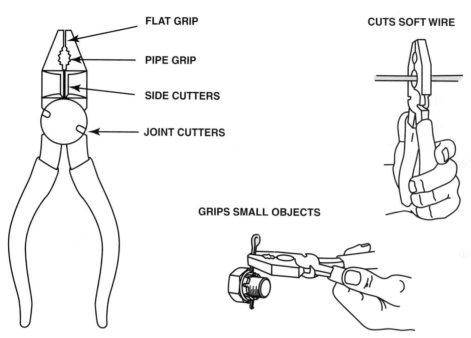

FLAT GRIP

PIPE GRIP

SIDE CUTTERS

JOINT CUTTERS

CUTS SOFT WIRE

GRIPS SMALL OBJECTS

FIGURE 1-41   Linesman's pliers are very useful because they can help perform many automotive service jobs.

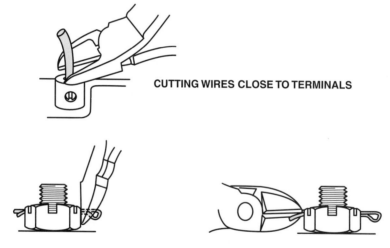

CUTTING WIRES CLOSE TO TERMINALS

PULLING OUT AND SPREADING COTTER PIN

FIGURE 1-42   Diagonal-cut pliers is another common tool that has many names.

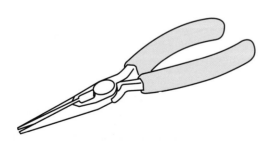

FIGURE 1-43   Needle nose pliers are used where there is limited access to a wire or pin that needs to be installed or removed.

Locking Pliers

Locking pliers are adjustable pliers that can be locked to hold objects from moving. Most locking pliers also have wire cutters built into the jaws near the pivot point. Locking pliers come in a variety of styles and sizes and are commonly referred to by the trade name *Vise Grip*®. The size is the length of the pliers, not how far the jaws open. See Figure 1-44.

Safe use of pliers.   Pliers should not be used to remove any bolt or other fastener. Pliers should only be used when specified for use by the vehicle manufacturer.

TECH TIP

BRAND NAME VERSUS PROPER TERM

Technicians often use slang or brand names of tools rather than the proper term. This results in some confusion for new technicians. Some examples are given in the following table.

Brand Name	Proper Term	Slang Name
Crescent wrench	Adjustable wrench	Monkey wrench
Vise Grips	Locking pliers	
Channel Locks	Water pump pliers or multigroove adjustable pliers	Pump pliers
	Diagonal cutting pliers	Dikes or side cuts

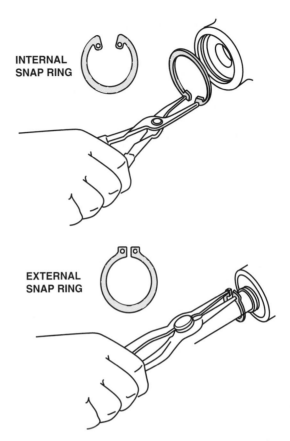

FIGURE 1-45 Snap ring pliers are also called lock ring pliers and most are designed to remove internal and external snap rings (lock rings).

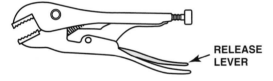

FIGURE 1-44 Locking pliers are best known by their trade name Vise-Grips.

Snap Ring Pliers

Snap ring pliers are used to remove and install snap rings. Many snap ring pliers are designed to be able to remove and install both inward, as well as outward, expanding snap rings. Snap ring pliers can be equipped with serrated tipped jaws for grasping the opening in the snap ring, while others are equipped with points, which are inserted into the holes in the snap ring. See Figure 1-45.

Files

Files are used to smooth metal and are constructed of hardened steel with diagonal rows of teeth. Files are available with a single row of teeth called a *single cut file,* as well as two rows of teeth cut at an opposite angle called a *double cut file.* Files are available in a variety of shapes and sizes from small flat files, half-round files, and triangular files. See Figure 1-46.

Safe use of files.   Always use a file with a handle. Because files only cut when moved forward, a handle must be attached to prevent possible personal injury. After making a forward strike, lift the file and return the file to the starting position; avoid dragging the file backward.

Snips

Service technicians are often asked to fabricate sheet metal brackets or heat shields and need to use one or more types of cutters available called **snips.** The simplest is called *tin snips* and are designed to make straight cuts in a variety of materials, such as sheet steel, aluminum, or even fabric. A variation of the tin snips is called *aviation tin snips.* There are three designs of aviation snips including one designed to cut straight (called a *straight cut aviation snip*), one designed to cut left (called an *offset left aviation snip*), and one designed to cut right (called an *offset right aviation snip*). See Figure 1-47.

Utility Knife

A *utility knife* uses a replaceable blade and is used to cut a variety of materials such as carpet, plastic, wood, and paper products, such as cardboard. See Figure 1-48.

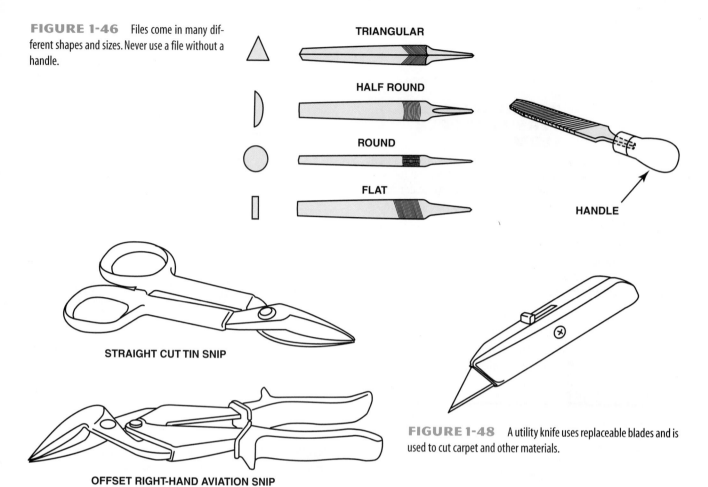

FIGURE 1-46 Files come in many different shapes and sizes. Never use a file without a handle.

TRIANGULAR

HALF ROUND

ROUND

FLAT

HANDLE

STRAIGHT CUT TIN SNIP

OFFSET RIGHT-HAND AVIATION SNIP

FIGURE 1-47 Tin snips are used to cut thin sheets of metal or carpet.

FIGURE 1-48 A utility knife uses replaceable blades and is used to cut carpet and other materials.

Safe use of cutters. Whenever using cutters, always wear eye protection or a face shield to guard against the possibility of metal pieces being ejected during the cut. Always follow recommended procedures.

Punches

A **punch** is a small diameter steel rod that has a smaller diameter ground at one end. A punch is used to drive a pin out that is used to retain two components. Punches come in a variety of sizes, which are measured across the diameter of the machined end. Sizes include 1/16 in., 1/8 in., 3/16 in., and 1/4 in. See Figure 1-49.

Chisels

A **chisel** has a straight sharp cutting end that is used for cutting off rivets or to separate two pieces of an assembly. The most common design of chisel used for automotive service work is called a *cold chisel*.

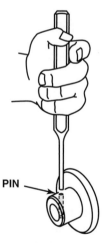

PIN

FIGURE 1-49 A punch used to drive pins from assembled components. This type of punch is also called a pin punch.

Safe use of punches and chisels. Always wear eye protection when using a punch or a chisel because the hardened steel is brittle and parts of the punch could fly off and cause serious personal injury. See the warning stamped on the side of this automotive punch in Figure 1-50.

The tops of punches and chisels can become rounded off from use, which is called "mushroomed." This material must be ground off to help avoid the possibility of the overhanging material being loosened and becoming airborne during use. See Figure 1-51.

Hacksaws

A **hacksaw** is used to cut metals, such as steel, aluminum, brass, or copper. The cutting blade of a hacksaw is replaceable and the sharpness and number of teeth can be varied to meet the needs of the job. Use 14 or 18 teeth per inch (TPI) for cutting plaster or soft metals, such as aluminum and copper. Use 24 or 32 teeth per inch for steel or pipe. Hacksaw blades should be installed with the teeth pointing away from the handle. This means that a hacksaw only cuts while the blade is pushed in the forward direction. See Figure 1-52.

FIGURE 1-50   Warning stamped in the side of a punch warning that goggles should be worn when using this tool. Always follow safety warnings.

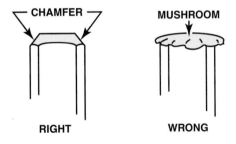

FIGURE 1-51   Use a grinder or a file to remove the mushroom material on the end of a punch or chisel.

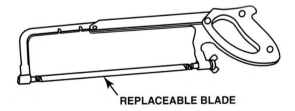

FIGURE 1-52   A typical hacksaw that is used to cut metal. If cutting sheet metal or thin objects, a blade with more teeth should be used.

Safe use of hacksaws.   Check that the hacksaw is equipped with the correct blade for the job and that the teeth are pointed away from the handle. When using a hacksaw, move the hacksaw slowly away from you, then lift slightly and return for another cut.

BASIC HAND TOOL LIST

The following is a list of hand tools every automotive technician should possess. Specialty tools are not included.

Safety glasses
Tool chest
1/4-in. drive socket set (1/4-in. to 9/16-in. standard and deep sockets; 6-mm to 15-mm standard and deep sockets)
1/4-in. drive ratchet
1/4-in. drive 2-in. extension
1/4-in. drive 6-in. extension
1/4-in. drive handle
3/8-in. drive socket set (3/8-in. to 7/8-in. standard and deep sockets; 10-mm to 19-mm standard and deep sockets)
3/8-in. drive Torx set (T40, T45, T50, and T55)
3/8-in. drive 13/16-in. plug socket
3/8-in. drive 5/8-in. plug socket
3/8-in. drive ratchet
3/8-in. drive 1 1/2-in. extension
3/8-in. drive 3-in. extension
3/8-in. drive 6-in. extension
3/8-in. drive 18-in. extension
3/8-in. drive universal
1/2-in. drive socket set (1/2-in. to 1-in. standard and deep sockets)
1/2-in. drive ratchet
1/2-in. drive breaker bar
1/2-in. drive 5-in. extension
1/2-in. drive 10-in. extension
3/8-in. to 1/4-in. adapter
1/2-in. to 3/8-in. adapter
3/8-in. to 1/2-in. adapter
Crowfoot set (fractional in.)
Crowfoot set (metric)
3/8-in. through 1-in. combination wrench set
10-mm through 19-mm combination wrench set
1/16-in. through 1/4-in. hex wrench set
2-mm through 12-mm hex wrench set
3/8-in. hex socket
13-mm to 14-mm flare nut wrench
15-mm to 17-mm flare nut wrench
5/16-in. to 3/8-in. flare nut wrench
7/16-in. to 1/2-in. flare nut wrench
1/2-in. to 9/16-in. flare nut wrench
Diagonal pliers
Needle pliers
Adjustable-jaw pliers

Locking pliers
Snap-ring pliers
Stripping or crimping pliers
Ball-peen hammer
Rubber hammer
Dead-blow hammer
Five-piece standard screwdriver set
Four-piece Phillips screwdriver set
#15 Torx screwdriver
#20 Torx screwdriver
Center punch
Pin punches (assorted sizes)
Chisel
Utility knife
Valve core tool
Filter wrench (large filters)
Filter wrench (smaller filters)
Test light
Feeler gauge
Scraper
Magnet

TOOL SETS AND ACCESSORIES

A beginning service technician may wish to start with a small set of tools before spending a lot of money on an expensive, extensive toolbox. See Figures 1-54 and 1-55.

FIGURE 1-54　A typical beginning technician tool set that includes the basic tools to get started.

TECH TIP

THE WINTERGREEN OIL TRICK

Synthetic wintergreen oil, available at drugstores everywhere, makes an excellent penetrating oil. So the next time you can't get that rusted bolt loose, use penetrating oil or head for the drugstore. See Figure 1-53.

FIGURE 1-53　Synthetic wintergreen oil can be used as a penetrating oil to loosen rusted bolts or nuts.

FIGURE 1-55　A typical large tool box, showing just one of many drawers.

TECH TIP

HIDE THOSE FROM THE BOSS

An apprentice technician started working for a dealership and put his top tool box on a workbench. Another technician observed that, along with a complete set of good-quality tools, the box contained several adjustable wrenches. The more experienced technician said, "Hide those from the boss." If any adjustable wrench is used on a bolt or nut, the movable jaw often moves or loosens and starts to round the head of the fastener. If the head of the bolt or nut becomes rounded, it becomes that much more difficult to remove.

TECH TIP

NEED TO BORROW A TOOL MORE THAN TWICE? BUY IT!

Most service technicians agree that it is okay for a beginning technician to borrow a tool occasionally. However, if a tool has to be borrowed more than twice, then be sure to purchase it as soon as possible. Also, whenever a tool is borrowed, be sure that you clean the tool and let the technician you borrowed the tool from know that you are returning the tool. These actions will help in any future dealings with other technicians.

TECH TIP

THE VALVE GRINDING COMPOUND TRICK

Apply a small amount of valve grinding compound to a Phillips or Torx screw or bolt head. The gritty valve grinding compound "grips" the screwdriver or tool bit and prevents the tool from slipping up and out of the screw head. Valve grinding compound is available in a tube from most automotive parts stores.

ELECTRICAL HAND TOOLS

Test Light

A test light is used to test for electricity. A typical automotive test light consists of a clear plastic screwdriver-like handle that contains a light bulb. A wire is attached to one terminal of the bulb, which the technician connects to a clean metal part of the vehicle. The other end of the bulb is attached to a point that can be used to test for electricity at a connector or wire. When there is power at the point and a good connection at the other end, the light bulb lights. See Figure 1-56.

Soldering Guns

- **Electric soldering gun.** This type of soldering gun is usually powered by 110-volt AC and often has two power settings expressed in watts. A typical electric soldering gun will produce from 85 to 300 watts of heat at the tip, which is more than adequate for soldering. See Figure 1-57.
- **Electric soldering pencil.** This type of soldering iron is less expensive and creates less heat than an electric soldering gun. A typical electric soldering pencil (iron) creates 30 to 60 watts of heat and is suitable for soldering smaller wires and connections.
- **Butane-powered soldering iron.** A butane-powered soldering iron is portable and very useful for automotive service work because an electrical cord is not needed. Most butane-powered soldering irons produce about 60 watts of heat, which is enough for most automotive soldering.

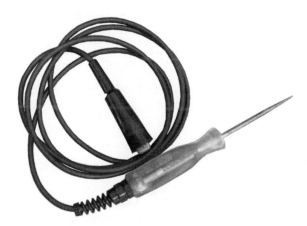

FIGURE 1-56 A typical 12-volt test light.

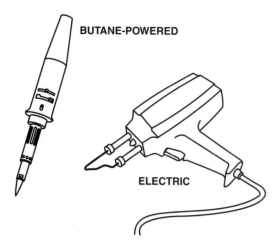

FIGURE 1-57 An electric soldering gun used to make electrical repairs. Soldering guns are sold by the wattage rating. The higher the wattage, the greater amount of heat created. Most solder guns used for automotive electrical work usually fall within the 60 to 160 watt range.

TECH TIP

IT JUST TAKES A SECOND

Whenever removing any automotive component, it is wise to screw the bolts back into the holes a couple of threads by hand. This ensures that the right bolt will be used in its original location when the component or part is put back on the vehicle. Often, the same diameter of fastener is used on a component, but the length of the bolt may vary. Spending just a couple of seconds to put the bolts and nuts back where they belong when the part is removed can save a lot of time when the part is being reinstalled. Besides making certain that the right fastener is being installed in the right place, this method helps prevent bolts and nuts from getting lost or kicked away. How much time have you wasted looking for that lost bolt or nut?

In addition to a soldering iron, most service technicians who do electrical-related work should have the following:

- Wire cutters
- Wire strippers
- Wire crimpers
- Heat gun for heat shrink tubing

A digital meter is a necessary tool for any electrical diagnosis and troubleshooting. A digital multimeter, abbreviated DMM, is usually capable of measuring the following units of electricity:

- DC volts
- AC volts
- Ohms
- Amperes

SAFETY TIPS FOR USING HAND TOOLS

The following safety tips should be kept in mind whenever you are working with hand tools:

- Always *pull* a wrench toward you for best control and safety. Never push a wrench.
- Keep wrenches and all hand tools clean to help prevent rust and to allow for a better, firmer grip.
- Always use a 6-point socket or a box-end wrench to break loose a tight bolt or nut.
- Use a box-end wrench for torque and an open-end wrench for speed.
- Never use a pipe extension or other type of "cheater bar" on a wrench or ratchet handle. If more force is required, use a larger tool or use penetrating oil and/or heat on the frozen fastener. (If heat is used on a bolt or nut to remove it, always replace it with a new part.)
- Always use the proper tool for the job. If a specialized tool is required, use the proper tool and do not try to use another tool improperly.
- Never expose any tool to excessive heat. High temperatures can reduce the strength ("draw the temper") of metal tools.
- Never use a hammer on any wrench or socket handle unless you are using a special "staking face" wrench designed to be used with a hammer.
- Replace any tools that are damaged or worn.

HAND TOOL MAINTENANCE

Most hand tools are constructed of rust-resistant metals but they can still rust or corrode if not properly maintained. For best results and long tool life, the following steps should be taken:

- Clean each tool before placing it back into the tool box.
- Keep tools separated. Moisture on metal tools will start to rust more readily if the tools are in contact with another metal tool.
- Line the drawers of the tool box with a material that will prevent the tools from moving as the drawers are opened and closed. This helps to quickly locate the proper tool and size.

WHAT IS AN "SST?"

Vehicle manufacturers often specify a **special service tool (SST)** to properly disassemble and assemble components, such as transmissions and other components. These tools are also called special tools and are available from the vehicle manufacturer or their tool supplier, such as Kent-Moore and Miller tools. Many service technicians do not have access to special service tools so they use generic versions that are available from aftermarket sources.

- Release the tension on all "clicker-type" torque wrenches.
- Keep the tool box secure.

AIR AND ELECTRICALLY OPERATED TOOLS

Impact Wrench

An impact wrench, either air or electrically powered, is a tool that is used to remove and install fasteners. The air-operated 1/2-in. drive impact wrench is the most commonly used unit. See Figure 1-58.

The direction of rotation is controlled by a switch. See Figure 1-59.

FIGURE 1-58   A typical 1/2-in. drive air impact wrench.

Electrically powered impact wrenches commonly include:

- Battery-powered units. See Figure 1-60.
- 110 volt AC-powered units. This type of impact is very useful, especially if compressed air is not readily available.

CAUTION: Always use impact sockets with impact wrenches, and always wear eye protection in case the socket or fastener shatters. Input sockets are thicker walled and constructed with premium alloy steel. They are hardened with a black oxide finish to help prevent corrosion and distinguish them from regular sockets. See Figure 1-61.

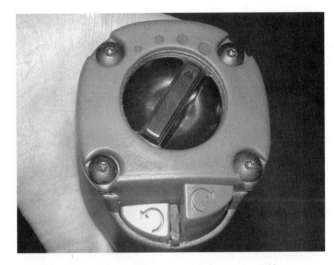

FIGURE 1-59   This air impact wrench features a variable torque setting using a rotary knob; the direction of rotation can be changed by pressing the buttons at the bottom.

FIGURE 1-60   A typical battery-powered 3/8-in. drive impact wrench.

Air Ratchet

An air ratchet is used to remove and install fasteners that would normally be removed or installed using a ratchet and a socket. See Figure 1-62.

Die Grinder

A die grinder is a commonly used air-powered tool which can also be used to sand or remove gaskets and rust. See Figure 1-63.

Bench- or Pedestal-Mounted Grinder

These high-powered grinders can be equipped with a wire brush wheel and/or a stone wheel.

FIGURE 1-61   A black impact socket. Always use impact-type sockets whenever using an impact wrench to avoid the possibility of shattering the socket, which can cause personal injury.

FIGURE 1-62   An air ratchet is a very useful tool that allows fast removal and installation of fasteners, especially in areas that are difficult to reach or do not have room enough to move a hand ratchet wrench.

- Wire brush wheel.   This type is used to clean threads of bolts as well as to remove gaskets from sheet metal engine parts.
- Stone wheel.   This type is used to grind metal or to remove the mushroom from the top of punches or chisels. See Figure 1-64.

CAUTION: Always wear a face shield when using a wire wheel or a grinder.

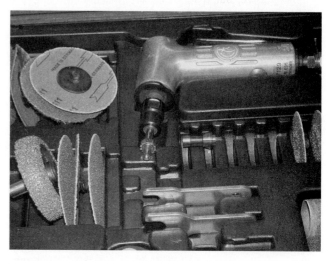

FIGURE 1-63   This typical die grinder surface preparation kit includes the air-operated die grinder as well as a variety of sanding disks for smoothing surfaces or removing rust.

FIGURE 1-64   A typical pedestal grinder with a wire wheel on the left side and a stone wheel on the right side. Even though this machine is equipped with guards, safety glasses or a face shield should always be worn whenever working using a grinder or wire wheel.

TECH TIP

WEARING GLOVES SAVES YOUR HANDS

Many technicians wear gloves not only to help keep their hands clean but also to help protect their skin from the effects of dirty engine oil and other possibly hazardous materials. Several types of gloves and their characteristics include:

- *Latex surgical gloves.* These gloves are relatively inexpensive, but tend to stretch, swell, and weaken when exposed to gas, oil, or solvents.
- *Vinyl gloves.* These gloves are also inexpensive and are not affected by gas, oil, or solvents.
- *Polyurethane gloves.* These gloves are more expensive, yet very strong. Even though these gloves are also not affected by gas, oil, or solvents, they do tend to be slippery.
- *Nitrile gloves.* These gloves are exactly like latex gloves, but are not affected by gas, oil, or solvents, yet they tend to be expensive.
- *Mechanic's gloves.* These gloves are usually made of synthetic leather and spandex and provide thermo protection, as well as protection from dirt and grime. See Figure 1-65.

FIGURE 1-65   Protective gloves such as these vinyl gloves are available in several sizes. Select the size that allows the gloves to fit snugly. Vinyl gloves last a long time and often can be worn all day to help protect your hands from dirt and possible hazardous materials.

PERSONAL PROTECTIVE EQUIPMENT

Service technicians should wear protective devices to prevent personal injury. The personal protection devices include the following:

- *Safety glasses that meet standard ANSI Z87.1 should be worn at all times while servicing any vehicle.* See Figure 1-66.

- Watch your toes—always keep your toes protected with steel-toed safety shoes. See Figure 1-67. If safety shoes are not available, then leather-topped shoes offer more protection than canvas or cloth.
- Wear gloves to protect your hands from rough or sharp surfaces. Thin rubber gloves are recommended when working around automotive liquids such as engine oil, antifreeze, transmission fluid, or any other liquids that may be hazardous.

FIGURE 1-66 Safety glasses should be worn at all times when working on or around any vehicle or servicing any component.

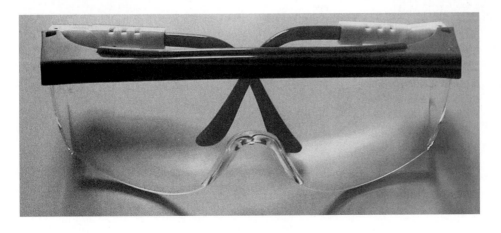

- Service technicians working under a vehicle should wear a **bump cap** to protect the head against under-vehicle objects and the pads of the lift. See Figure 1-68.
- Ear protection should be worn if the sound around you requires that you raise your voice (sound level higher than 90 dB). (A typical lawnmower produces noise at a level of about 110 dB. This means that everyone who uses a lawnmower or other lawn or garden equipment should wear ear protection.)

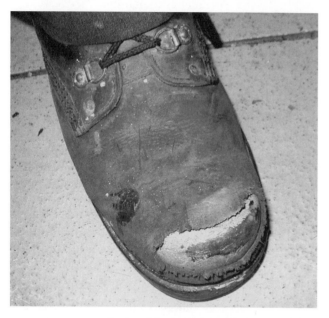

FIGURE 1-67 Steel-toed shoes are a worthwhile investment to help prevent foot injury due to falling objects. Even these well-worn shoes can protect the feet of this service technician.

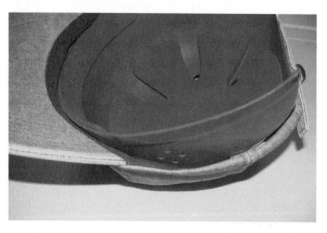

FIGURE 1-68 One version of a bump cap is this padded plastic insert that is worn inside a regular cloth cap.

SAFETY PRECAUTIONS

Besides wearing personal safety equipment, there are also many actions that should be performed to keep safe in the shop. These actions include:

- Remove jewelry that may get caught on something or act as a conductor to an exposed electrical circuit. See Figure 1-69.
- Take care of your hands. Keep your hands clean by washing with soap and hot water that is at least 110°F (43°C).
- Avoid loose or dangling clothing.
- When lifting any object, get a secure grip with solid footing. Keep the load close to your body to minimize the strain. Lift with your legs and arms, not your back.
- Do not twist your body when carrying a load. Instead, pivot your feet to help prevent strain on the spine.
- Ask for help when moving or lifting heavy objects.
- Push a heavy object rather than pull it. (This is opposite to the way you should work with tools—never push a wrench! If you do and a bolt or nut loosens, your entire weight is used to propel your hand(s) forward. This usually results in cuts, bruises, or other painful injury.)
- Always connect an exhaust hose to the tailpipe of any running vehicle to help prevent the build-up of carbon monoxide inside a closed garage space. See Figure 1-70.
- When standing, keep objects, parts, and tools with which you are working between chest height and waist height. If seated, work at tasks that are at elbow height.
- Always be sure the hood is securely held open. See Figure 1-71.

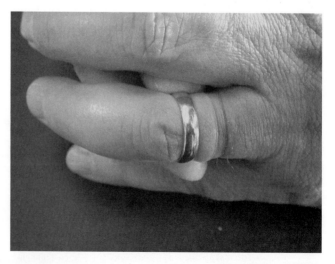

FIGURE 1-69 Remove all jewelry before performing service work on any vehicle.

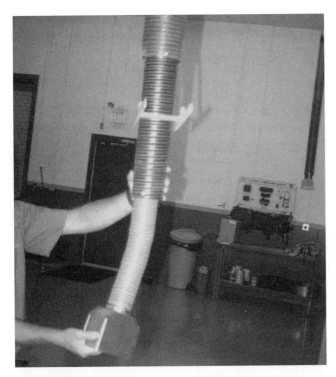

FIGURE 1-70   Always connect an exhaust hose to the tailpipe of the engine of a vehicle to be run inside a building.

SAFETY TIP

SHOP CLOTH DISPOSAL

Always dispose of oily shop cloths in an enclosed container to prevent a fire. See Figure 1-72. Whenever oily cloths are thrown together on the floor or workbench, a chemical reaction can occur, which can ignite the cloth even without an open flame. This process of ignition without an open flame is called **spontaneous combustion**.

TECH TIP

SHOCK CONTROL

To avoid impact damage from your impact wrench on your hand, take the rubber covering from an old electric fuel pump and fit it on the handle of the gun. This tremendously softens the blow.

(a)

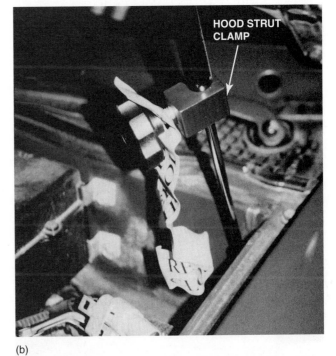

HOOD STRUT CLAMP

(b)

FIGURE 1-71   (a) A crude but effective method is to use locking pliers on the chrome-plated shaft of a hood strut. Locking pliers should only be used on defective struts, because the jaws of the pliers can damage the strut shaft. (b) A commercially available hood clamp. This tool uses a bright orange tag to help remind the technician to remove the clamp before attempting to close the hood. The hood could be bent if force is used to close the hood with the clamp in place.

FIGURE 1-72 All oily shop cloths should be stored in a metal container equipped with a lid to help prevent spontaneous combustion.

SAFETY IN LIFTING (HOISTING) A VEHICLE

Many chassis and underbody service procedures require that the vehicle be hoisted or lifted off the ground. The simplest methods involve the use of drive-on ramps or a floor jack and safety (jack) stands, whereas in-ground or surface-mounted lifts provide greater access. *Setting the pads is a critical part of the hoisting procedure.* All automobile and light-truck service manuals include recommended locations to be used when hoisting (lifting) a vehicle. Newer vehicles have a triangle decal on the driver's door indicating the recommended lift points. The recommended standards for the lift points and lifting procedures are found in SAE Standard JRP-2184. See Figure 1-73.

These recommendations typically include the following points:

1. The vehicle should be centered on the lift or hoist so as not to overload one side or put too much force either forward or rearward. See Figure 1-74.

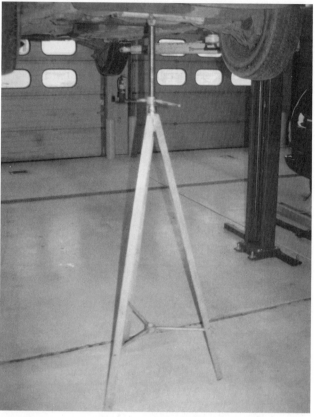

(a)

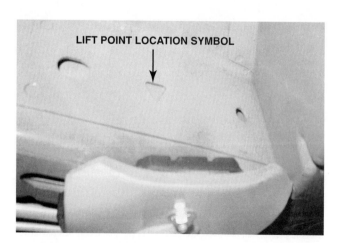

FIGURE 1-73 Most newer vehicles have a triangle symbol indicating the recommended hoisting lift points.

(b)

FIGURE 1-74 (a) Tall safety stands can be used to provide additional support for a vehicle while on a hoist. (b) A block of wood should be used to avoid the possibility of doing damage to components supported by the stand.

2. The pads of the lift should be spread as far apart as possible to provide a stable platform.

3. Each pad should be placed under a portion of the vehicle that is strong and capable of supporting the weight of the vehicle.

   a. Pinch weld seams at the bottom edge of the body are generally considered to be strong.

   CAUTION: Even though **pinch weld seams** are the recommended location for hoisting many vehicles with unitized bodies (unit-body), care should be taken not to place the pad(s) too far forward or rearward. Incorrect placement of the vehicle on the lift could cause the vehicle to be imbalanced, and the vehicle could fall. This is exactly what happened to the vehicle in Figure 1-75.

   b. Boxed areas of the body are the best places to position the pads on a vehicle without a frame. Be careful to note whether the arms of the lift might come into contact with other parts of the vehicle before the pad touches the intended location. Commonly damaged areas include the following:
      1. Rocker panel moldings
      2. Exhaust system (including catalytic converter)
      3. Tires or body panels (See Figures 1-76 and 1-77.)

4. The vehicle should be raised about a foot (30 centimeters [cm]) off the floor, then stopped and shaken to check for stability. If the vehicle seems to be stable when checked at a short distance from the floor, continue raising the vehicle and continue to view the vehicle until it has reached the desired height. The hoist should be lowered onto the mechanical locks, and then raised off of the locks before lowering.

   CAUTION: Do not look away from the vehicle while it is being raised (or lowered) on a hoist. Often one side or one end of the hoist can stop or fail, resulting in the vehicle being slanted enough to slip or fall, creating physical damage not only to the vehicle and/or hoist but also to the technician or others who may be nearby.

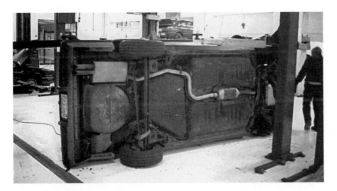

FIGURE 1-75   This vehicle fell from the hoist because the pads were not set correctly. No one was hurt, but the vehicle was a total loss.

NOTE: Most hoists can be safely placed at any desired height. For ease while working, the area in which you are working should be at chest level. When working on brakes or suspension components, it is not necessary to work on them down near the floor or over your head. Raise the hoist so that the components are at chest level.

5. Before lowering the hoist, the safety latch(es) must be released and the direction of the controls reversed. The speed downward is often adjusted to be as slow as possible for additional safety.

(a)

(b)

FIGURE 1-76   (a) An assortment of hoist pad adapters that are often necessary to safely hoist many pickup trucks vans, and sport utility vehicles. (b) A view from underneath a Chevrolet pickup truck showing how the pad extensions are used to attach the hoist lifting pad to contact the frame.

(a)

(b)

FIGURE 1-77   (a) In this photo the pad arm is just contacting the rocker panel of the vehicle. (b) This photo shows what can occur if the technician places the pad too far inward underneath the vehicle. The arm of the hoist has dented in the rocker panel.

JACKS AND SAFETY STANDS

Floor jacks properly rated for the weight of the vehicle being raised are a common vehicle lifting tool. Floor jacks are portable and relatively inexpensive and must be used with safety (jack) stands. The floor jack is used to raise the vehicle off the ground and safety stands should be placed under the frame on the body of the vehicle. The weight of the vehicle should never be kept on the hydraulic floor jack because a failure of the jack could cause the vehicle to fall. See Figure 1-78. The jack is then slowly released to allow the vehicle weight to be supported on the safety stands. If the front or rear of the vehicle is being raised, the opposite end of the vehicle must be blocked.

CAUTION: Safety stands should be rated higher than the weight they support.

(a)

(b)

FIGURE 1-78   (a) A typical 3-ton (6,000-pound) capacity hydraulic floor jack. (b) Whenever a vehicle is raised off of the ground a safety stand should be placed under the frame, axle, or body to support the weight of the vehicle.

DRIVE-ON RAMPS

Ramps are an inexpensive way to raise the front or rear of a vehicle. See Figure 1-79. Ramps are easy to store, but they can be dangerous because they can "kick out" when driving the vehicle onto the ramps.

CAUTION: Professional repair shops do not use ramps because they are dangerous to use. Use only with extreme care.

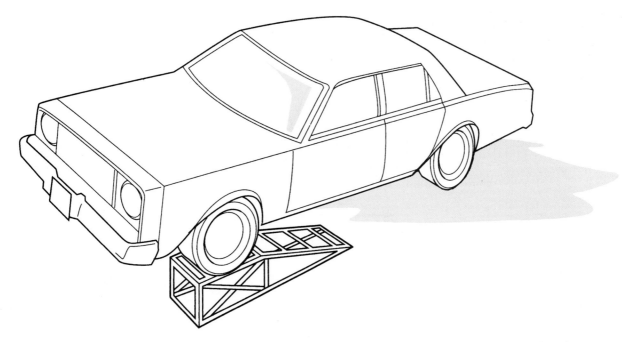

FIGURE 1-79   Drive-on type ramps. The wheels on the ground level *must* be chocked (blocked) to prevent accidental movement down the ramp.

TECH TIP

POUND WITH SOMETHING SOFTER

If you must pound on something, be sure to use a tool that is softer than what you are about to pound on to avoid damage. Examples are given in the following table.

The Material Being Pounded	What to Pound With
Steel or cast iron	Brass or aluminum hammer or punch
Aluminum	Plastic or rawhide mallet or plastic-covered dead-blow hammer
Plastic	Rawhide mallet or plastic dead-blow hammer

ELECTRICAL CORD SAFETY

Use correctly grounded three-prong sockets and extension cords to operate power tools. Some tools use only two-prong plugs. Make sure these are double insulated and repair or replace any electrical cords that are cut or damaged to prevent the possibility of an electrical shock. When not in use, keep electrical cords off the floor to prevent tripping over them. Tape the cords down if they are placed in high foot traffic areas.

JUMP STARTING AND BATTERY SAFETY

To jump start another vehicle with a dead battery, connect good quality copper jumper cables as indicated in Figure 1-80 or a jump box. The last connection made should always be on the engine block or an engine bracket as far from the battery as possible. It is normal for a spark to be created when the jumper cables finally complete the jumping circuit, and this spark could cause an explosion of the gases around the battery. Many newer vehicles have special ground connections built away from the battery just for the purpose of jump starting. Check the owner's manual or service information for the exact location.

Batteries contain acid and should be handled with care to avoid tipping them greater than a 45-degree angle. Always remove jewelry when working around a battery to avoid the possibility of electrical shock or burns, which can occur when the metal comes in contact with a 12-volt circuit and ground, such as the body of the vehicle.

FIGURE 1-80   Jumper cable usage guide.

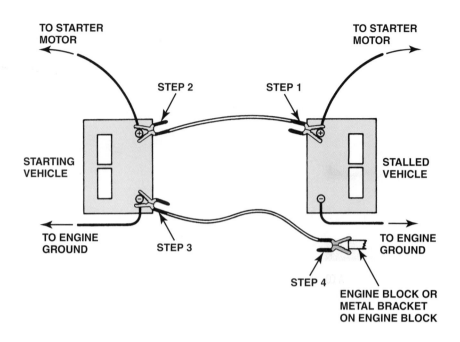

SAFETY TIP

AIR HOSE SAFETY

Improper use of an air nozzle can cause blindness or deafness. Compressed air must be reduced to less than 30 psi (206 kPa). See Figure 1-81. If an air nozzle is used to dry and clean parts, make sure the air stream is directed away from anyone else in the immediate area. Coil and store air hoses when they are not in use.

FIRE EXTINGUISHERS

There are four **fire extinguisher classes.** Each class should be used on specific fires only:

- **Class A** is designed for use on general combustibles, such as cloth, paper, and wood.
- **Class B** is designed for use on flammable liquids and greases, including gasoline, oil, thinners, and solvents.
- **Class C** is used only on electrical fires.
- **Class D** is effective only on combustible metals such as powdered aluminum, sodium, or magnesium.

The class rating is clearly marked on the side of every fire extinguisher. Many extinguishers are good for multiple types of fires. See Figure 1-82.

FIGURE 1-81   The air pressure going to the nozzle should be reduced to 30 psi or less.

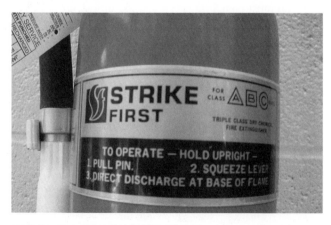

FIGURE 1-82   A typical fire extinguisher designed to be used on type A, B, or C fires.

FIGURE 1-83 A CO_2 fire extinguisher being used on a fire set in an open steel drum during a demonstration at a fire department training center.

FIGURE 1-84 A treated wool blanket is kept in this easy-to-open wall-mounted holder and should be placed in a centralized location in the shop.

When using a fire extinguisher, remember the word "PASS."

P = Pull the safety pin.
A = Aim the nozzle of the extinguisher at the base of the fire.
S = Squeeze the lever to actuate the extinguisher.
S = Sweep the nozzle from side-to-side.

See Figure 1-83.

Types of Fire Extinguishers

Types of fire extinguishers include the following:

- Water. A water fire extinguisher, usually in a pressurized container, is good to use on Class A fires by reducing the temperature to the point where a fire cannot be sustained.
- Carbon dioxide (CO_2). A carbon dioxide fire extinguisher is good for almost any type of fire, especially Class B or Class C materials. A CO_2 fire extinguisher works by removing the oxygen from the fire and the cold CO_2 also helps reduce the temperature of the fire.
- Dry chemical (yellow). A dry chemical fire extinguisher is good for Class A, B, or C fires by coating the flammable materials, which eliminates the oxygen from the fire. A dry chemical fire extinguisher tends to be very corrosive and will cause damage to electronic devices.

FIRE BLANKETS

Fire blankets are required to be available in the shop areas. If a person is on fire, a fire blanket should be removed from its storage bag and thrown over and around the victim to smother the fire. See Figure 1-84 showing a typical fire blanket.

FIRST AID AND EYE WASH STATIONS

All shop areas must be equipped with a first aid kit and an eye wash station centrally located and kept stocked with emergency supplies. See Figure 1-85.

First Aid Kit

A first aid kit should include:

- Bandages (variety)
- Gauze pads
- Roll gauze
- Iodine swab sticks
- Antibiotic ointment
- Hydrocortisone cream
- Burn gel packets
- Eye wash solution
- Scissors
- Tweezers
- Gloves
- First aid guide

Every shop should have a person trained in first aid. If there is an accident, call for help immediately.

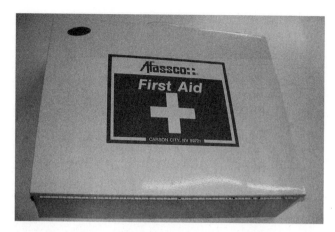

FIGURE 1-85   A first aid box should be centrally located in the shop and kept stocked with the recommended supplies.

EYE WASH STATION

An **eye wash station** should be centrally located and used whenever any liquid or chemical gets into the eyes. If such an emergency does occur, keep eyes in a constant stream of water and call for professional assistance. See Figure 1-86.

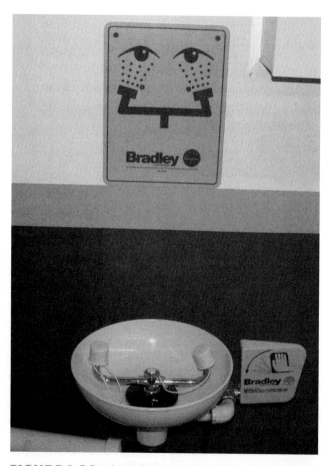

FIGURE 1-86   A typical eye wash station. Often a thorough flushing of the eyes with water is the best treatment in the event of eye contamination.

TECH TIP

MARK OFF THE SERVICE AREA

Some shops rope off the service bay area to help keep traffic and distractions to a minimum, which could prevent personal injury. See Figure 1-87.

SAFETY TIP

INFECTION CONTROL PRECAUTIONS

Working on a vehicle can result in personal injury including the possibility of being cut or hurt enough to cause bleeding. Some infections such as hepatitis B, HIV (which can cause acquired immunodeficiency syndrome, or AIDS), hepatitis C virus, and others are transmitted in the blood. These infections are commonly called blood-borne pathogens. Report any injury that involves blood to your supervisor and take the necessary precautions to avoid coming in contact with blood from another person.

FIGURE 1-87   This area has been blocked off to help keep visitors from the dangerous work area.

HYBRID ELECTRIC VEHICLE SAFETY ISSUES

Hybrid electric vehicles (HEV) use a high-voltage battery pack and an electric motor(s) to help propel the vehicle. See Figure 1-88 for an example of a typical warning label on a hybrid electric vehicle. The gasoline or diesel engine also is equipped with a generator or a combination starter and an integrated starter generator (ISG) or integrated starter alternator (ISA). To safely work around a hybrid electric vehicle, the high-voltage (HV) battery and circuits should be shut off following these steps:

Step 1   Turn off the ignition key (if equipped) and remove the key from the ignition switch. (This will shut off all high-voltage circuits if the relay[s] is [are] working correctly.)

Step 2   Disconnect the high-voltage circuits.

CAUTION: Some vehicle manufacturers specify that rubber insulated *lineman's gloves* be used whenever working around the high-voltage circuits to prevent the danger of electrical shock.

Toyota Prius

The cutoff switch is located in the trunk. To gain access, remove three clips holding the upper left portion of the trunk side cover. To disconnect the high-voltage system, pull the orange handled plug while wearing insulated rubber lineman's gloves. See Figure 1-89.

FIGURE 1-89   The high-voltage disconnect switch is in the trunk area on a Toyota Prius. High-voltage linemen's gloves should be worn when removing this plug. (Courtesy of Tony Martin)

Ford Escape/Mercury Mariner

Ford and Mercury specify that the following steps should be included when working with the high-voltage (HV) systems of a hybrid vehicle:

- Four orange cones are to be placed at the four corners of the vehicle to create a buffer zone.
- High-voltage insulated gloves are to be worn with an outer leather glove to protect the inner rubber glove from possible damage.
- The service technician should also wear a face shield and a fiberglass hook should be in the area and used to move a technician in the event of electrocution.

The high-voltage shut-off switch is located in the rear of the vehicle under the right side carpet. See Figure 1-90. Rotate the handle to the "service shipping" position, lift it out to disable the high-voltage circuit, and wait 5 minutes before removing high-voltage cables.

Honda Civic

To totally disable the high-voltage system on a Honda Civic, remove the main fuse (labeled number 1) from the driver's side underhood fuse panel. This should be all that is necessary to shut off the high-voltage circuit. If this is not possible, then remove the rear seat cushion and seat back. Remove the metal switch cover labeled "up" and remove the red locking cover. Move the "battery module switch" down to disable the high-voltage system.

FIGURE 1-88   A warning label on a Honda hybrid warns that a person can be killed due to the high-voltage circuits under the cover.

FIGURE 1-90   The high-voltage shut off switch on a Ford Escape hybrid. The switch is located under the carpet at the rear of the vehicle.

Chevrolet Silverado/GMC Sierra Pickup Truck

The high-voltage shut-off switch is located under the rear passenger seat. Remove the cover marked "energy storage box" and turn the green service disconnect switch to the horizontal position to turn off the high-voltage circuits. See Figure 1-91.

FIGURE 1-91   The shut-off switch on a GM parallel hybrid truck is green because this system uses 42 volts instead of higher, and possible fatal, voltages used in other hybrid vehicles.

CAUTION: Do not touch any orange wiring or component without following the vehicle manufacturer's procedures and wearing the specified personal protective equipment.

HOISTING THE VEHICLE   Step-by-Step

STEP 1 The first step in hoisting a vehicle is to properly align the vehicle in the center of the stall.

STEP 2 Most vehicles will be correctly positioned when the left front tire is centered on the tire pad.

STEP 3 Most pads at the end of the hoist arms can be rotated to allow for many different types of vehicle construction.

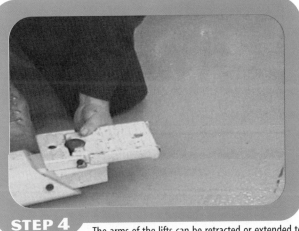

STEP 4 The arms of the lifts can be retracted or extended to accommodate vehicles of many different lengths.

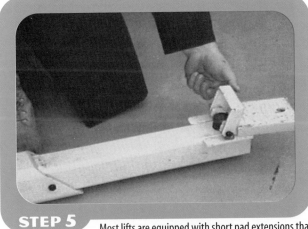

STEP 5 Most lifts are equipped with short pad extensions that are often necessary to use to allow the pad to contact the frame of a vehicle without causing the arm of the lift to hit and damage parts of the body.

STEP 6 Tall pad extensions can also be used to gain access to the frame of a vehicle. This position is needed to safely hoist many pickup trucks, vans, and sport utility vehicles.

(continued)

HOISTING THE VEHICLE continued

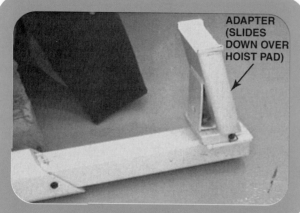

ADAPTER
(SLIDES
DOWN OVER
HOIST PAD)

STEP 7
An additional extension may be necessary to hoist a truck or van equipped with running boards to give the necessary clearance.

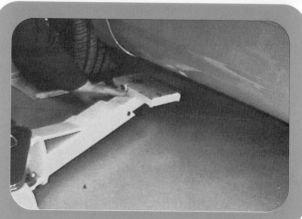

STEP 8
Position the front hoist pads under the recommended locations as specified in the owner's manual and/or service information for the vehicle being serviced.

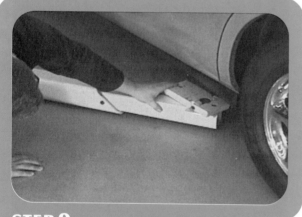

STEP 9
Position the rear pads under the vehicle under the recommended locations.

STEP 10
This photo shows an asymmetrical lift where the front arms are shorter than the rear arms. This design allows the driver to enter and leave the vehicle easier.

STEP 11
After being sure all pads are correctly positioned use the electromechanical controls to raise the vehicle.

STEP 12
Raise the vehicle about one foot (30 cm) and stop to double-check that all pads contact the body or frame in the correct positions.

HOISTING THE VEHICLE continued

STEP 13 With the vehicle raised about one foot off the ground, push down on the vehicle to check to see if it is stable on the pads.

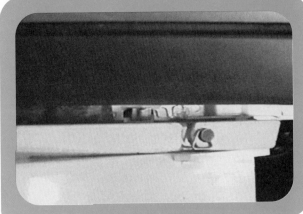

STEP 14 This photo shows the pads set flat and contacting the pinch welds of the body. This method spreads the load over the entire length of the pad.

PINCH WELD

STEP 15 Where additional clearance is necessary for the arms to clear the rest of the body, the pads can be raised and placed under the pinch weld area as shown.

PUSH BUTTON TO RAISE VEHICLE

SAFETY RELEASE

LEVER TO LOWER VEHICLE

STEP 16 When the service work is completed, the hoist should be raised slightly and the safety released before using the hydraulic lever to lower the vehicle.

STEP 17 After lowering the vehicle, be sure all arms of the lift are moved out of the way before driving the vehicle out of the work stall.

STEP 18 Carefully back the vehicle out of the stall. Notice that all of the lift arms have been neatly moved out of the way to provide clearance so that the tires will not contact the arms when the vehicle is driven out of the stall.

SUMMARY

1. Bolts, studs, and nuts are commonly used as fasteners in the chassis. The sizes for fractional and metric threads are different and are not interchangeable. The grade is the rating of the strength of a fastener.

2. Whenever a vehicle is raised above the ground, it must be supported at a substantial section of the body or frame.

3. Wrenches are available in open end, box end, and combination open and box end.

4. An adjustable wrench should only be used where the proper size is not available.

5. Line wrenches are also called flare-nut wrenches, fitting wrenches, or tube-nut wrenches and are used to remove fuel or refrigerant lines.

6. Sockets are rotated by a ratchet or breaker bar, also called a flex handle.

7. Torque wrenches measure the amount of torque applied to a fastener.

8. Screwdriver types include straight blade (flat tip) and Phillips.

9. Hammers and mallets come in a variety of sizes and weights.

10. Pliers are a useful tool and are available in many different types, including slip-joint, multigroove, lineman's, diagonal, needle nose, and locking pliers.

11. Other common hand tools include snap-ring pliers, files, cutters, punches, chisels, and hacksaws.

REVIEW QUESTIONS

1. List three precautions that must be taken whenever hoisting (lifting) a vehicle.

2. Describe how to determine the grade of a fastener, including how the markings differ between fractional and metric bolts.

3. List four items that are personal protective equipment (PPE).

4. List the types of fire extinguishers and their usage.

5. Why are wrenches offset 15 degrees?

6. What are the other names for a line wrench?

7. What are the standard automotive drive sizes for sockets?

8. Which type of screwdriver requires the use of a hammer or mallet?

9. What is inside a dead-blow hammer?

10. What type of cutter is available in left and right cutters?

CHAPTER QUIZ

1. The correct location for the pads when hoisting or jacking the vehicle can often be found in the _____.
   a. Service manual
   b. Shop manual
   c. Owner's manual
   d. All of the above

2. For the best working position, the work should be _____.
   a. At neck or head level
   b. At knee or ankle level
   c. Overhead by about 1 foot
   d. At chest or elbow level

3. A high-strength bolt is identified by _____.
   a. A UNC symbol
   b. Lines on the head
   c. Strength letter codes
   d. The coarse threads

4. A fastener that uses threads on both ends is called a _____.
   a. Cap screw
   b. Stud
   c. Machine screw
   d. Crest fastener

5. When working with hand tools, always _____.
   a. Push the wrench — don't pull toward you
   b. Pull a wrench — don't push away from you

6. The proper term for Channel Locks is _____.
   a. Vise Grips
   b. Crescent wrench
   c. Locking pliers
   d. Multigroove adjustable pliers

7. The proper term for Vise Grips is _____.
   a. Locking pliers
   b. Slip-joint pliers
   c. Side cuts
   d. Multigroove adjustable pliers

8. Two technicians are discussing torque wrenches. Technician A says that a torque wrench is capable of tightening a fastener with more torque than a conventional breaker bar or ratchet. Technician B says that a torque wrench should be calibrated regularly for the most accurate results. Which technician is correct?

   a. Technician A only
   b. Technician B only
   c. Both Technicians A and B
   d. Neither Technician A nor B

9. What type of screwdriver should be used if there is very limited space above the head of the fastener?
   a. Offset screwdriver
   b. Stubby screwdriver
   c. Impact screwdriver
   d. Robertson screwdriver

10. What type of hammer is plastic coated, has a metal casing inside, and is filled with small lead balls?
    a. Dead-blow hammer
    b. Soft-blow hammer
    c. Sledge hammer
    d. Plastic hammer

ENVIRONMENTAL AND HAZARDOUS MATERIALS

OBJECTIVES

After studying Chapter 2, the reader should be able to:

1. Prepare for the ASE assumed knowledge content required by all service technicians to adhere to environmentally appropriate actions and behavior.

2. Define the Occupational Safety and Health Act (OSHA).

3. Explain the term Material Safety Data Sheet (MSDS).

4. Identify hazardous waste materials in accordance with state and federal regulations and follow proper safety precautions while handling hazardous waste materials.

5. Define the steps required to safely handle and store automotive chemicals and waste.

KEY TERMS

Above ground storage tank (AGST) (p. 46)
Asbestosis (p. 44)
Battery Council International (BCI) (p. 49)
Clean Air Act (CAA) (p. 44)
Code of Federal Regulations (CFR) (p. 43)
Environmental Protection Agency (EPA) (p. 43)
Hazardous waste materials (p. 43)
High efficiency particulate air (HEPA) vacuum (p. 45)
Material Safety Data Sheets (MSDS) (p. 44)

Mercury (p. 51)
Occupational Safety and Health Act (OSHA) (p. 43)
Resource Conservation and Recovery Act (RCRA) (p. 43)
Right-to-know laws (p. 43)
Solvent (p. 45)
Underground storage tank (UST) (p. 46)
Used oil (p. 46)
Workplace Hazardous Materials Information Systems (WHMIS) (p. 44)

OCCUPATIONAL SAFETY AND HEALTH ACT

The United States Congress passed the **Occupational Safety and Health Act (OSHA)** in 1970. This legislation was designed to assist and encourage the citizens of the United States in their efforts to assure safe and healthful working conditions by providing research, information, education, and training in the field of occupational safety and health, as well as to assure safe and healthful working conditions for working men and women by authorizing enforcement of the standards developed under the Act. Since approximately 25% of workers are exposed to health and safety hazards on the job, the OSHA standards are necessary to monitor, control, and educate workers regarding health and safety in the workplace.

HAZARDOUS WASTE

CAUTION: When handling hazardous waste material, one must always wear the proper protective clothing and equipment detailed in the right-to-know laws. This includes respirator equipment. All recommended procedures must be followed accurately. Personal injury may result from improper clothing, equipment, and procedures when handling hazardous materials.

Hazardous waste materials are chemicals, or components, that the shop no longer needs that pose a danger to the environment and people if they are disposed of in ordinary garbage cans or sewers. However, one should note that no material is considered hazardous waste until the shop has finished using it and is ready to dispose of it. The **Environmental Protection Agency (EPA)** publishes a list of hazardous materials that is included in the **Code of Federal Regulations (CFR)**. The EPA considers waste hazardous if it is included on the EPA list of hazardous materials, or it has one or more of the following characteristics:

Reactive. Any material which reacts violently with water or other chemicals is considered hazardous.

Corrosive. If a material burns the skin, or dissolves metals and other materials, a technician should consider it hazardous. A pH scale is used, with the number 7 indicating neutral. Pure water has a pH of 7. Lower numbers indicate an acidic solution and higher numbers indicate a caustic solution. If a material releases cyanide gas, hydrogen sulfide gas, or similar gases when exposed to low pH acid solutions, it is considered hazardous.

Toxic. Materials are hazardous if they leak one or more of eight different heavy metals in concentrations greater than 100 times the primary drinking water standard.

Ignitable. A liquid is hazardous if it has a flash point below 140°F (60°C), and a solid is hazardous if it ignites spontaneously.

Radioactive. Any substance that emits measurable levels of radiation is radioactive. When individuals bring containers of a highly radioactive substance into the shop environment, qualified personnel with the appropriate equipment must test them.

WARNING: Hazardous waste disposal laws include serious penalties for anyone responsible for breaking these laws.

RESOURCE CONSERVATION AND RECOVERY ACT (RCRA)

Federal and state laws control the disposal of hazardous waste materials. Every shop employee must be familiar with these laws. Hazardous waste disposal laws include the **Resource Conservation and Recovery Act (RCRA)**. This law states that hazardous material users are responsible for hazardous materials from the time they become a waste until the proper waste disposal is completed. Many shops hire an independent hazardous waste hauler to dispose of hazardous waste material. The shop owner, or manager, should have a written contract with the hazardous waste hauler. Rather than have hazardous waste material hauled to an approved hazardous waste disposal site, a shop may choose to recycle the material in the shop. Therefore, the user must store hazardous waste material properly and safely, and be responsible for the transportation of this material until it arrives at an approved hazardous waste disposal site, where it can be processed according to the law. The RCRA controls these types of automotive waste:

- Paint and body repair products waste
- Solvents for parts and equipment cleaning
- Batteries and battery acid
- Mild acids used for metal cleaning and preparation
- Waste oil and engine coolants or antifreeze
- Air-conditioning refrigerants and oils
- Engine oil filters

The **right-to-know laws** state that employees have a right to know when the materials they use at work are hazardous. The right-to-know laws started with the Hazard Communication Standard published by the Occupational Safety and Health Administration (OSHA) in 1983. Originally, this document was intended for chemical companies and manufacturers that required employees to handle hazardous materials in their work situation. Meanwhile, the federal courts have decided to apply these laws to all companies, including automotive service shops. Under the right-to-know laws, the employer has responsibilities regarding the handling of hazardous materials by their employees. All employees must be trained about the types of hazardous materials they will encounter in the workplace. The employees must be informed about their rights under legislation regarding the handling of hazardous materials.

CLEAN AIR ACT

Air-conditioning (A/C) systems and refrigerant are regulated by the **Clean Air Act (CAA),** Title VI, Section 609. Technician certification and service equipment is also regulated. Any technician working on automotive A/C systems must be certified. A/C refrigerants must not be released or vented into the atmosphere, and used refrigerants must be recovered.

MATERIAL SAFETY DATA SHEETS (MSDS)

All hazardous materials must be properly labeled, and information about each hazardous material must be posted on **Material Safety Data Sheets (MSDS)** available from the manufacturer. See Figure 2-1. In Canada, MSDS sheets are called **Workplace Hazardous Materials Information Systems (WHMIS).**

The employer has a responsibility to place MSDS sheets where they are easily accessible by all employees. The MSDS

sheets provide the following information about the hazardous material: chemical name, physical characteristics, protective handling equipment, explosion/fire hazards, incompatible materials, health hazards, medical conditions aggravated by exposure, emergency and first-aid procedures, safe handling, and spill/leak procedures.

The employer also has a responsibility to make sure that all hazardous materials are properly labeled. The label information must include health, fire, and reactivity hazards posed by the material, as well as the protective equipment necessary to handle the material. The manufacturer must supply all warning and precautionary information about hazardous materials. This information must be read and understood by the employee before handling the material.

THE DANGERS OF EXPOSURE TO ASBESTOS

Friction materials such as brake and clutch linings often contain asbestos. While asbestos has been eliminated from most original equipment friction materials, the automotive service technician cannot know whether or not the vehicle being serviced is or is not equipped with friction materials containing asbestos. It is important that all friction materials be handled as if they do contain asbestos.

Asbestos exposure can cause scar tissue to form in the lungs. This condition is called **asbestosis.** It gradually causes increasing shortness of breath, and the scarring to the lungs is permanent.

Even low exposures to asbestos can cause *mesothelioma,* a type of fatal cancer of the lining of the chest or abdominal cavity. Asbestos exposure can also increase the risk of *lung cancer* as well as cancer of the voice box, stomach, and large intestine. It usually takes 15 to 30 years or more for cancer or asbestos lung scarring to show up after exposure. (Scientists call this the *latency period.*)

Government agencies recommend that asbestos exposure should be eliminated or controlled to the lowest level possible. These agencies have developed recommendations and standards that the automotive service technician and equipment manufacturer should follow. These U.S. federal agencies include the National Institute for Occupational Safety and Health (NIOSH), Occupational Safety and Health Administration (OSHA), and Environmental Protection Agency (EPA).

ASBESTOS OSHA STANDARDS

The **Occupational Safety and Health Administration (OSHA)** has established three levels of asbestos exposure. Any vehicle service establishment that does either brake or

FIGURE 2-1   Material Safety Data Sheets (MSDS) should be readily available for use by anyone in the area who may come into contact with hazardous materials.

clutch work must limit employee exposure to asbestos to less than 0.2 fibers per cubic centimeter (cc) as determined by an air sample.

If the level of exposure to employees is greater than specified, corrective measures must be performed and a large fine may be imposed.

NOTE: Research has found that worn asbestos fibers such as those from automotive brakes or clutches may not be as hazardous as first believed. Worn asbestos fibers do not have sharp flared ends that can latch onto tissue, but rather are worn down to a dust form that resembles talc. Grinding or sawing operations on unworn brake shoes or clutch discs *will* contain *harmful* asbestos fibers. To limit health damage, always use proper handling procedures while working around any component that may contain asbestos.

FIGURE 2-2   All brakes should be moistened with water or solvent to help prevent brake dust from becoming airborne.

ASBESTOS EPA REGULATIONS

The federal **Environmental Protection Agency (EPA)** has established procedures for the removal and disposal of asbestos. The EPA procedures require that products containing asbestos be "wetted" to prevent the asbestos fibers from becoming airborne. According to the EPA, asbestos-containing materials can be disposed of as regular waste. Only when asbestos becomes airborne is it considered to be hazardous.

ASBESTOS HANDLING GUIDELINES

The air in the shop area can be tested by a testing laboratory, but this can be expensive. Tests have determined that asbestos levels can easily be kept below the recommended levels by using a liquid or a special vacuum.

NOTE: Even though asbestos is being removed from brake and clutch lining materials, the service technician cannot tell whether or not the old brake pads, shoes, or clutch disc contain asbestos. Therefore, to be safe, the technician should assume that all brake pads, shoes, or clutch discs contain asbestos.

HEPA Vacuum

A special **high-efficiency particulate air (HEPA) vacuum** system has been proven to be effective in keeping asbestos exposure levels below 0.1 fibers per cubic centimeter.

Solvent Spray

Many technicians use an aerosol can of brake cleaning solvent to wet the brake dust and prevent it from becoming airborne. A **solvent** is a liquid that is used to dissolve dirt, grime, or solid particles. Commercial brake cleaners are available that use a concentrated cleaner that is mixed with water. See Figure 2-2.

The waste liquid is filtered, and when dry, the filter can be disposed of as solid waste.

CAUTION: Never use compressed air to blow brake dust. The fine talclike brake dust can create a health hazard even if asbestos is not present or is present in dust rather than fiber form.

Disposal of Brake Dust and Brake Shoes

The hazard of asbestos occurs when asbestos fibers are airborne. Once the asbestos has been wetted down, it is then considered to be solid waste, rather than hazardous waste. Old brake shoes and pads should be enclosed, preferably in a plastic bag, to help prevent any of the brake material from becoming airborne. *Always follow current federal and local laws concerning disposal of all waste.*

USED BRAKE FLUID

Most brake fluid is made from polyglycol, is water soluble, and can be considered hazardous if it has absorbed metals from the brake system.

- Collect brake fluid in containers clearly marked to indicate that it is dedicated for that purpose.
- If your waste brake fluid is hazardous, manage it appropriately and use only an authorized waste receiver for its disposal.
- If your waste brake fluid is nonhazardous (such as old, but unused), determine from your local solid waste collection provider what should be done for its proper disposal.
- Do not mix brake fluid with used engine oil.
- Do not pour brake fluid down drains or onto the ground.
- Recycle brake fluid through a registered recycler.

USED OIL

Used oil is any petroleum-based or synthetic oil that has been used. During normal use, impurities such as dirt, metal scrapings, water, or chemicals can get mixed in with the oil. Eventually, this used oil must be replaced with virgin or re-refined oil. The EPA's used oil management standards include a three-pronged approach to determine if a substance meets the definition of *used oil*. To meet the EPA's definition of used oil, a substance must meet each of the following three criteria:

- **Origin.** The first criterion for identifying used oil is based on the oil's origin. Used oil must have been refined from crude oil or made from synthetic materials. Animal and vegetable oils are excluded from the EPA's definition of used oil.
- **Use.** The second criterion is based on whether and how the oil is used. Oils used as lubricants, hydraulic fluids, heat transfer fluids, and for other similar purposes are considered used oil. Unused oil, such as bottom clean-out waste from virgin fuel oil storage tanks or virgin fuel oil recovered from a spill, does not meet the EPA's definition of used oil because these oils have never been "used." The EPA's definition also excludes products used as cleaning agents, as well as certain petroleum-derived products like antifreeze and kerosene.
- **Contaminants.** The third criterion is based on whether or not the oil is contaminated with either physical or chemical impurities. In other words, to meet the EPA's definition, used oil must become contaminated as a result of being used. This aspect of the EPA's definition includes residues and contaminants generated from handling, storing, and processing used oil.

NOTE: The release of only one gallon of used oil (a typical oil change) can make a million gallons of fresh water undrinkable.

If used oil is dumped down the drain and enters a sewage treatment plant, concentrations as small as 50 to 100 PPM (parts per million) in the waste water can foul sewage treatment processes. Never mix a listed hazardous waste, gasoline, waste water, halogenated solvent, antifreeze, or an unknown waste material with used oil. Adding any of these substances will cause the used oil to become contaminated, which classifies it as hazardous waste.

DISPOSAL OF USED OIL

Once oil has been used, it can be collected, recycled, and used over and over again. An estimated 380 million gallons of used oil are recycled each year. Recycled used oil can sometimes be used again for the same job or can take on a completely different task. For example, used engine oil can be re-refined and sold at the store as engine oil or processed for furnace fuel oil. After collecting used oil in an appropriate container (e.g., a 55-gallon steel drum), the material must be disposed of in one of two ways:

- Shipped offsite for recycling
- Burned in an onsite or offsite EPA-approved heater for energy recovery

USED OIL STORAGE

Used oil must be stored in compliance with an existing **underground storage tank (UST)** or an **aboveground storage tank (AGST)** standard, or kept in separate containers. See Figure 2-3. Containers are portable receptacles, such as a 55-gallon steel drum.

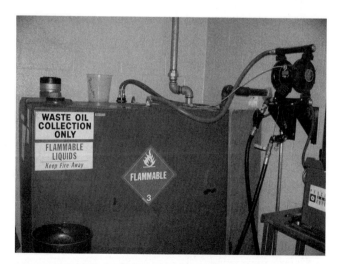

FIGURE 2-3   A typical aboveground oil storage tank.

Keep Used Oil Storage Drums in Good Condition

This means that they should be covered, secured from vandals, properly labeled, and maintained in compliance with local fire codes. Frequent inspections for leaks, corrosion, and spillage are an essential part of container maintenance.

Never Store Used Oil in Anything Other Than Tanks and Storage Containers

Used oil may also be stored in units that are permitted to store regulated hazardous waste.

Used Oil Filter Disposal Regulations

Used oil filters contain used engine oil that may be hazardous. Before an oil filter is placed into the trash or sent to be recycled, it must be drained using one of the following hot draining methods approved by the EPA:

- Puncture the filter antidrain back valve or filter dome end and hot drain for at least 12 hours
- Hot drain and crushing
- Dismantling and hot draining
- Any other hot draining method, which will remove all the used oil from the filter

After the oil has been drained from the oil filter, the filter housing can be disposed of in any of the following ways:

- Sent for recycling
- Pickup by a service contract company
- Disposed of in regular trash

SOLVENTS

The major sources of chemical danger are liquid and aerosol brake cleaning fluids that contain chlorinated hydrocarbon solvents. Several other chemicals that do not deplete the ozone, such as heptane, hexane, and xylene, are now being used in nonchlorinated brake cleaning solvents. Some manufacturers are also producing solvents they describe as environmentally responsible, which are biodegradable and noncarcinogenic.

Sources of Chemical Poisoning

The health hazards presented by brake cleaning solvents occur from three different forms of exposure: ingestion, in-halation, or physical contact. It should be obvious that swallowing brake cleaning solvent is harmful, and such occurrences are not common. Still, brake cleaning solvents should always be handled and stored properly, and kept out of the reach of children. The dangers of inhalation are perhaps the most serious problem, as even very low levels of solvent vapors are hazardous.

Allowing brake cleaning solvents to come in contact with the skin presents a danger because these solvents strip natural oils from the skin and cause irritation of the tissues, plus they can be absorbed through the skin directly into the bloodstream. The transfer begins immediately upon contact, and continues until the liquid is wiped or washed away.

There is no specific standard for physical contact with chlorinated hydrocarbon solvents or the chemicals replacing them. All contact should be avoided whenever possible. The law requires an employer to provide appropriate protective equipment and ensure proper work practices by an employee handling these chemicals.

Effects of Chemical Poisoning

The effects of exposure to chlorinated hydrocarbon and other types of solvents can take many forms. Short-term exposure at low levels can cause headache, nausea, drowsiness, dizziness, lack of coordination, or unconsciousness. It may also cause irritation of the eyes, nose, and throat, and flushing of the face and neck. Short-term exposure to higher concentrations can cause liver damage with symptoms such as yellow jaundice or dark urine. Liver damage may not become evident until several weeks after the exposure.

Health Care Rights

The OSHA regulations concerning on-the-job safety place certain responsibilities on the employer, and give employees specific rights. Any person who feels there might be unsafe conditions where he or she works, whether asbestos exposure, chemical poisoning, or any other problem, should discuss the issue with fellow workers, their union representative (where applicable), and their supervisor or employer. If no action is taken and there is reason to believe the employer is not complying with OSHA standards, a complaint can be filed with OSHA and it will investigate.

The law forbids employers from taking action against employees who file a complaint concerning a health or safety hazard. However, if workers fear reprisal as the result of a complaint, they may request that OSHA withhold their names from the employer.

SAFETY TIP

HAND SAFETY

Service technicians should wash their hands with soap and water after handling engine oil or differential or transmission fluids, or wear protective rubber gloves. Another safety hint is that the service technician should not wear watches, rings, or other jewelry that could come in contact with electrical or moving parts of a vehicle. See Figure 2-4.

FIGURE 2-4 Washing hands and removing jewelry are two important safety habits all service technicians should practice.

SOLVENT HAZARDOUS AND REGULATORY STATUS

Most solvents are classified as hazardous wastes. Other characteristics of solvents include the following:

- Solvents with flash points below 140°F are considered flammable and, like gasoline, are federally regulated by the Department of Transportation (DOT).
- Solvents and oils with flash points above 140°F are considered combustible and, like engine oil, are also regulated by the DOT. See Figure 2-5.

It is the responsibility of the repair shop to determine if its spent solvent is hazardous waste. Waste solvents that are considered hazardous waste have a flash point below 140°F

FIGURE 2-5 Typical fireproof flammable storage cabinet.

(60°C). Hot water or aqueous parts cleaners may be used to avoid disposing of spent solvent as hazardous waste. Solvent-type parts cleaners with filters are available to greatly extend solvent life and reduce spent solvent disposal costs. Solvent reclaimers are available that clean and restore the solvent so it lasts indefinitely.

USED SOLVENTS

Used or spent solvents are liquid materials that have been generated as waste and may contain xylene, methanol, ethyl ether, and methyl isobutyl ketone (MIBK). These materials must be stored in OSHA-approved safety containers with the lids or caps closed tightly. These storage receptacles must show no signs of leaks or significant damage due to dents or rust. In addition, the containers must be stored in a protected area equipped with secondary containment or a spill protector, such as a spill pallet. Additional requirements include the following:

- Containers should be clearly labeled "Hazardous Waste" and the date the material was first placed into the storage receptacle should be noted.
- Labeling is not required for solvents being used in a parts washer.
- Used solvents will not be counted toward a facility's monthly output of hazardous waste if the vendor under contract removes the material.
- Used solvents may be disposed of by recycling with a local vendor, such as SafetyKleen®, to have the used solvent removed according to specific terms in the vendor agreement. See Figure 2-6.

FIGURE 2-6 All solvents and other hazardous waste should be disposed of properly.

FIGURE 2-7 Used antifreeze coolant should be kept separate and stored in a leakproof container until it can be recycled or disposed of according to federal, state, and local laws. Note that the storage barrel is placed inside another container to catch any coolant that may spill out of the inside barrel.

- Use aqueous-based (nonsolvent) cleaning systems to help avoid the problems associated with chemical solvents.

COOLANT DISPOSAL

Coolant is a mixture of antifreeze and water. New antifreeze is not considered to be hazardous even though it can cause death if ingested. Used antifreeze may be hazardous due to dissolved metals from the engine and other components of the cooling system. These metals can include iron, steel, aluminum, copper, brass, and lead (from older radiators and heater cores).

1. Coolant should be recycled either onsite or offsite.
2. Used coolant should be stored in a sealed and labeled container. See Figure 2-7.
3. Used coolant can often be disposed of into municipal sewers with a permit. Check with local authorities and obtain a permit before discharging used coolant into sanitary sewers.

LEAD-ACID BATTERY WASTE

About 70 million spent lead-acid batteries are generated each year in the United States alone. Lead is classified as a toxic metal and the acid used in lead-acid batteries is highly corrosive. The vast majority (95% to 98%) of these batteries are re-

cycled through lead reclamation operations and secondary lead smelters for use in the manufacture of new batteries.

BATTERY HAZARDOUS AND REGULATORY STATUS

Used lead-acid batteries must be reclaimed or recycled in order to be exempt from hazardous waste regulations. Leaking batteries must be stored and transported as hazardous waste. Some states have more strict regulations, which require special handling procedures and transportation. According to the **Battery Council International (BCI),** battery laws usually include the following rules:

1. Lead-acid battery disposal is prohibited in landfills or incinerators. Batteries are required to be delivered to a battery retailer, wholesaler, recycling center, or lead smelter.
2. All retailers of automotive batteries are required to post a sign that displays the universal recycling symbol and indicates the retailer's specific requirements for accepting used batteries.

CAUTION: Battery electrolyte contains sulfuric acid, which is a very corrosive substance capable of causing serious personal injury, such as skin burns and eye damage. In addition, the battery plates contain lead, which is highly poisonous. For this reason, disposing of batteries improperly can cause environmental contamination and lead to severe health problems.

BATTERY HANDLING AND STORAGE

Batteries, whether new or used, should be kept indoors if possible. The storage location should be an area specifically designated for battery storage and must be well ventilated (to the outside). If outdoor storage is the only alternative, a sheltered and secured area with acid-resistant secondary containment is strongly recommended. It is also advisable that acid-resistant secondary containment be used for indoor storage. In addition, batteries should be placed on acid-resistant pallets and never stacked!

FUEL SAFETY AND STORAGE

Gasoline is a very explosive liquid. The expanding vapors that come from gasoline are extremely dangerous. These vapors are present even in cold temperatures. Vapors formed in gasoline tanks on many vehicles are controlled, but vapors from gasoline storage may escape from the can, resulting in a hazardous situation. Therefore, place gasoline storage containers in a well-ventilated space. Although diesel fuel is not as volatile as gasoline, the same basic rules apply to diesel fuel and gasoline storage. These rules include the following:

1. Approved gasoline storage cans have a flash-arresting screen at the outlet. These screens prevent external ignition sources from igniting the gasoline within the can when someone pours the gasoline or diesel fuel.
2. Technicians must always use red approved gasoline containers to allow for proper hazardous substance identification. See Figure 2-8.
3. Do not fill gasoline containers completely full. Always leave the level of gasoline at least one inch from the top of the container. This action allows expansion of the gasoline at higher temperatures. If gasoline containers are completely full, the gasoline will expand when the temperature increases. This expansion forces gasoline from the can and creates a dangerous spill. If gasoline or diesel fuel containers must be stored, place them in a designated storage locker or facility.
4. Never leave gasoline containers open, except while filling or pouring gasoline from the container.
5. Never use gasoline as a cleaning agent.
6. Always connect a ground strap to containers when filling or transferring fuel or other flammable products from one container to another to prevent static electricity that could result in explosion and fire. These ground wires prevent the buildup of a static electric charge, which could result in a spark and disastrous explosion.

AIRBAG HANDLING

Airbag modules are pyrotechnic devices that can be ignited if exposed to an electrical charge or if the body of the vehicle is

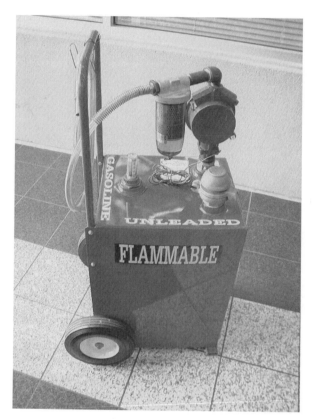

FIGURE 2-8 This red gasoline container holds about 30 gallons of gasoline and is used to fill vehicles used for training.

subjected to a shock. Airbag safety should include the following precautions:

1. Disarm the airbag(s) if you will be working in the area where a discharged bag could make contact with any part of your body. Consult service information for the exact procedure to follow for the vehicle being serviced. The usual procedure is to deploy the airbag using a 12-volt power supply, such as a jump start box, using long wires to connect to the module to ensure a safe deployment.
2. Do not expose an airbag to extreme heat or fire.
3. Always carry an airbag pointing away from your body.
4. Place an airbag module facing upward.
5. Always follow the manufacturer's recommended procedure for airbag disposal or recycling, including the proper packaging to use during shipment.
6. Wear protective gloves if handling a deployed airbag.
7. Always wash your hands or body well if exposed to a deployed airbag. The chemicals involved can cause skin irritation and possible rash development.

USED TIRE DISPOSAL

Used tires are an environmental concern because of several reasons, including the following:

1. In a landfill, they tend to "float" up through the other trash and rise to the surface.
2. The inside of tires traps and holds rainwater, which is a breeding ground for mosquitoes. Mosquito-borne diseases include encephalitis and dengue fever.
3. Used tires present a fire hazard and, when burned, create a large amount of black smoke that contaminates the air.

Used tires should be disposed of in one of the following ways:

1. Used tires can be reused until the end of their useful life.
2. Tires can be retreaded.
3. Tires can be recycled or shredded for use in asphalt.
4. Derimmed tires can be sent to a landfill (most landfill operators will shred the tires because it is illegal in many states to landfill whole tires).
5. Tires can be burned in cement kilns or other power plants where the smoke can be controlled.
6. A registered scrap tire handler should be used to transport tires for disposal or recycling.

AIR-CONDITIONING REFRIGERANT OIL DISPOSAL

Air-conditioning refrigerant oil contains dissolved refrigerant and is therefore considered to be hazardous waste. This oil must be kept separated from other waste oil or the entire amount of oil must be treated as hazardous. Used refrigerant oil must be sent to a licensed hazardous waste disposal company for recycling or disposal. See Figure 2-9.

FIGURE 2-9   Air-conditioning refrigerant oil must be kept separated from other oils because it contains traces of refrigerant and must be treated as hazardous waste.

TECH TIP

REMOVE COMPONENTS THAT CONTAIN MERCURY

Some vehicles have a placard near the driver's side door that lists the components that contain the heavy metal, mercury. **Mercury** can be absorbed through the skin and is a heavy metal that once absorbed by the body does not leave. See Figure 2-10.

These components should be removed from the vehicle before the rest of the body is sent to be recycled to help prevent releasing mercury into the environment.

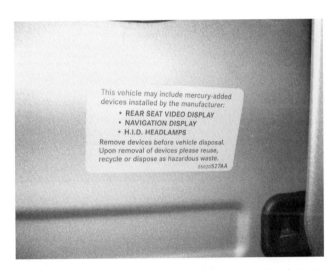

FIGURE 2-10   Placard near driver's door, including what devices in the vehicle contain mecury.

TECH TIP

WHAT EVERY TECHNICIAN SHOULD KNOW

The Hazardous Material Identification Guide (HMIG) is the standard labeling for all materials. The service technician should be aware of the meaning of the label. See Figure 2-11.

Hazardous Materials Identification Guide (HMIG)

TYPE HAZARD		DEGREE	
○	HEALTH	4	- Extreme
○	FLAMMABILITY	3	- Serious
○	REACTIVITY	2	- Moderate
○	PROTECTIVE EQUIPMENT	1	- Slight
		0	- Minimal

HAZARD RATING AND PROTECTIVE EQUIPMENT

Health	Flammable	Reactive
Type of Possible Injury	Susceptibility of materials to burn	Susceptibility of materials to release energy
4 Highly Toxic. May be fatal on short term exposure. Special protective equipment required.	4 Extremely flammable gas or liquid. Flash Point below 73°F.	4 Extreme. Explosive at room temperature.
3 Toxic. Avoid inhalation or skin contact.	3 Flammable. Flash Point 73°F to 100°F.	3 Serious. May explode if shocked, heated under confinement or mixed w/ water.
2 Moderately Toxic. May be harmful if inhaled or absorbed.	2 Combustible. Requires moderate heating to ignite. Flash Point 100°F to 200°F.	2 Moderate. Unstable, may react with water.
1 Slightly Toxic. May cause slight irritation.	1 Slightly Combustible. Requires strong heating to ignite.	1 Slight. May react if heated or mixed with water.
0 Minimal. All chemicals have a slight degree of toxicity.	0 Minimal. Will not burn under normal conditions.	0 Minimal. Normally stable, does not react with water.

Protective Equipment

A	Safety Glasses	E	Safety Glasses + Gloves + Dust Respirator	I	Safety Glasses + Gloves + Combination Dust & Vapor Respirator
B	Safety Glasses + Gloves	F	Safety Glasses + Gloves + Apron + Dust Respirator	J	Chemical Goggles + Gloves + Apron + Combination Dust & Vapor Respirator
C	Safety Glasses + Gloves + Apron	G	Safety Glasses + Gloves + Vapor Respirator	K	Apron + Gloves + Full Protection Suit + Boots
D	Faceshield + Gloves + Apron	H	Chemical Goggles + Gloves + Apron + Vapor Respirator	X	Ask your supervisor for guidance.

FIGURE 2-11 The Environmental Protection Agency (EPA) Hazardous Materials Identification Guide is a standardized listing of the hazards and the protective equipment needed.

WASTE CHART

All automotive service facilities create some waste and while most of it is handled properly, it is important that all hazardous and nonhazardous waste be accounted for and properly disposed. See the chart for a list of typical wastes generated at automotive shops, plus a checklist for keeping track of how these wastes are handled.

Typical Wastes Generated at Auto Repair Shops and Typical Category (Hazardous or Nonhazardous) by Disposal Method

Waste Stream	Typical Category If Not Mixed with Other Hazardous Waste	If Disposed in Landfill and Not Mixed with a Hazardous Waste	If Recycled
Used Oil	Used Oil	Hazardous Waste	Used Oil
Used Oil Filters	Nonhazardous Solid Waste, if Completely Drained	Nonhazardous Solid Waste, if Completely Drained	Used Oil, if Not Drained
Used Transmission Fluid	Used Oil	Hazardous Waste	Used Oil
Used Brake Fluid	Used Oil	Hazardous Waste	Used Oil
Used Antifreeze	Depends on Characterization	Depends on Characterization	Depends on Characterization
Used Solvents	Hazardous Waste	Hazardous Waste	Hazardous Waste
Used Citric Solvents	Nonhazardous Solid Waste	Nonhazardous Solid Waste	Hazardous Waste
Lead Acid Automotive Batteries	Not a Solid Waste if Returned to Supplier	Hazardous Waste	Hazardous Waste
Shop Rags Used for Oil	Used Oil	Depends on Used Oil Characterization	Used Oil
Shop Rags Used for Solvent or Gasoline Spills	Hazardous Waste	Hazardous Waste	Hazardous Waste
Oil Spill Absorbent Material	Used Oil	Depends on Used Oil Characterization	Used Oil
Spill Material for Solvent and Gasoline	Hazardous Waste	Hazardous Waste	Hazardous Waste
Catalytic Converter	Not a Solid Waste if Returned to Supplier	Nonhazardous Solid Waste	Nonhazardous Solid Waste
Spilled or Unused Fuels	Hazardous Waste	Hazardous Waste	Hazardous Waste
Spilled or Unusable Paints and Thinners	Hazardous Waste	Hazardous Waste	Hazardous Waste
Used Tires	Nonhazardous Solid Waste	Nonhazardous Solid Waste	Nonhazardous Solid Waste

Consolidated Screening Checklist for Automotive Repair Facilities

1. Waste Management

Waste Management	Has the facility determined which wastes are hazardous wastes?	Yes/No
	Does facility generate more than 100 kg (220 lb) of hazardous waste per month?	Yes/No
	If yes, does facility have a U.S. EPA hazardous waste generator I.D. number?	Yes/No
Used Oil	Are used oil containers and piping leak free, segregated, and labeled "used oil"?	Yes/No
	Are hazardous waste fluids mixed with used oil?	Yes/No
	Is used oil collected and sent offsite for recycling, or burned in an onsite heater?	Recycle/Onsite heater/Burned offsite/Other
	Does the facility accept household used oil?	Yes/No
	If yes, is it tested for hazardous waste (solvent/gasoline) contamination?	Yes/No
Used Oil Filters	Are used oil filters completely drained before disposal?	Yes/No
	How are used oil filters disposed?	Scrap metal/Service/Trash/Other
Used Antifreeze	Is used antifreeze properly contained, segregated, and labeled?	Yes/No
	Does the facility generate any antifreeze that is a hazardous waste (>5 ppm lead)?	Yes/No/Do not know
	If yes, is it recycled onsite in a closed-loop system?	Yes/No
	If no, is it counted toward facility generator status?	Yes/No
	If used antifreeze is not recycled onsite, how is it disposed?	Recycled offsite/Mixed w/other fluids/Landfill/Other
Used Solvents	Are used solvents stored in proper containers and properly labeled?	Yes/No/N/A
	How are used solvents disposed?	Service/Mixed w/other fluids/Other
	Does the facility have hazardous waste manifests for shipping papers on file?	Yes/No/N/A
Batteries	Does the facility return used batteries to new battery supplier?	Yes/No/N/A
	If not, how are used automotive batteries disposed?	Recycle/Hazardous waste landfill/Other
	Are used batteries contained and covered prior to disposal?	Yes/No
Rags	How are used rags and towels disposed?	Laundry service/Burned for heat/Trash
	How are used rags stored while onsite?	Separate container/Shop trash can/Floor
Tires	How are used tires disposed?	Resale/Retreading/Landfill/Customer/N/A/Other

Consolidated Screening Checklist for Automotive Repair Facilities

Absorbents	Does the facility use sawdust or other absorbents for spills or leaks?	Yes/No
	Does the facility determine whether used absorbents are considered hazardous before disposal?	Yes/No
	How are absorbents used for oil spills disposed?	N/A/Burned for energy/Disposed of as hazardous waste/Characterized as nonhazardous and land filled

2. Wastewater Management		
Floor Drains Wastewater Management	How does the facility clean shop floor and surrounding area?	Uses dry cleanup/ Uses water
	Are fluids (oil, antifreeze, solvent) allowed to enter floor drains for disposal?	Yes/No/No floor drains onsite
	How are fluids disposed?	Municipal sanitary sewer/Storm sewer/Street/Other
	If floor drains discharge to municipal sanitary sewer, to storm sewer system, or the street, has the facility notified Public Owned Treatment Works (POTW) about potential contamination in wash water?	Yes/No
	If drains discharge directly to surface waters or to an underground injection well, does the facility have an National Pollutant Discharge Elimination System (NPDES) (surface) or UIC (underground) permit?	Yes/No/N/A
Storm Water	Does the facility store parts, fluids, and/or other materials outside?	Yes/No
	Are materials protected from rain/snow in sealed containers or under tarp or roof?	Yes/No/N/A

3. Air Pollution Control

Parts Cleaners	If facility uses parts-cleaning sinks with halogenated solvents, has the facility submitted a notification report to the EPA?	Yes/No/N/A
	Are sinks kept closed and sealed except when actually cleaning parts?	Yes/No
	Does the facility follow required work and operational practices?	Yes/No
Motor Vehicle Air Conditioning (CFCs)	Are MVAC technicians trained and certified by an accredited program?	Yes/No/N/A
	If yes, are certificates on file?	Yes/No
	Is CFC recovery and/or recycling equipment EPA approved?	Yes/No/N/A
	Is equipment recovery/recycling or recovery only? (circle one)	Recover/recycling/ Recovery only/N/A
	If recovery only, is refrigerant reclaimed by an EPA-approved reclaimer?	Yes/No
Catalytic Converters (CCs)	Does the facility replace CCs that are the correct type based on vehicle requirements?	Yes/No/N/A
	Does the facility replace CCs on vehicles covered under original manufacturer's warranty?	Yes/No
	If yes, was original CC missing or due to state/local inspection program requirement?	Yes/No
	Does facility properly mark and keep replaced CCs onsite for at least 15 days?	Yes/No
	Does facility completely fill out customer paperwork and maintain onsite for at least 6 months?	Yes/No
Fuels	Is Stage I vapor recovery equipment operated properly during unloading of gasoline?	Yes/No/N/A
	Is Stage II vapor recovery equipment installed and working at pumps?	Yes/No/N/A
	Do fuel delivery records indicate compliance with appropriate fuel requirements?	Yes/No/Records not available
	Are pumps clearly labeled with the product they contain?	Yes/No
	Do gasoline pump nozzles comply with the 10 gallon per minute flow rate?	Yes/No/Don't know
	Is dyed, high-sulfur diesel/kerosene available for sale to motor vehicles?	Yes/No

Paints and Thinners	Are paints and thinners properly contained and marked when not in use?	Yes/No/N/A
	Does the facility use low VOC paints?	Yes/No/N/A
	Does the facility determine whether paints are considered hazardous before disposal?	Yes/No
	How are used paints, thinners, and solvents disposed?	reuse/recycle/Mix w/other fluids/Landfill
	Does the facility mix paint amounts according to need?	Yes/No
	Does the facility use newer, "high transfer efficiency" spray applications?	Yes/No
	If hazardous paints are used, are spray paint booth air filters disposed of properly as hazardous waste?	Yes/No
	If filters are not hazardous, how are they disposed?	Recycled/Landfill

4. UST/SPCC/Emergency Spill Procedures

Underground Storage Tanks (USTs)	Has the State UST program been notified of any USTs located onsite?	Yes/No/N/A
	Does the facility conduct leak detection for tank and piping of all onsite UST systems?	Yes/No/N/A
	Do USTs at the facility meet requirements for spill, overfill, and corrosion protection?	Yes/No/N/A
	Are records and documentation readily available (as applicable) for installation, leak detection, corrosion protection, spill/overfill protection, corrective action, financial responsibility, and closure?	Yes/No/N/A
Spill Emergency Response	Does the facility have a gasoline, fuel oil, or lubricating oil storage capacity total greater than 1,320 gallons (or greater than 660 gallons in any one tank) in above ground tanks or total underground tank storage capacity greater than 42,000 gallons?	Yes/No
	If yes, could spilled gasoline fuel oil or lubricating oil conceivably reach navigable waters?	Yes/No
	If yes, does the facility have an SPCC plan signed by a Professional Engineer?	Yes/No
	Are phone numbers of the national, station, and local emergency contact available onsite for immediate reporting of oil or chemical spills?	Yes/No

SUMMARY

1. Hazardous materials include common automotive chemicals, liquids, and lubricants, especially those whose ingredients contain *chlor* or *fluor* in their name.

2. Right-to-know laws require that all workers have access to Material Safety Data Sheets (MSDS).

3. Asbestos fibers should be avoided and removed according to current laws and regulations.

4. Used engine oil contains metals worn from parts and should be handled and disposed of properly.

5. Solvents represent a serious health risk and should be avoided as much as possible.
6. Coolant should be recycled.
7. Batteries are considered to be hazardous waste and should be discarded to a recycling facility.

REVIEW QUESTIONS

1. List five common automotive chemicals or products that may be considered hazardous materials.

2. List five precautions to which every technician should adhere when working with automotive products and chemicals.

CHAPTER QUIZ

1. Hazardous materials include all of the following *except* _____.
   a. Engine oil
   b. Asbestos
   c. Water
   d. Brake cleaner

2. To determine if a product or substance being used is hazardous, consult _____.
   a. A dictionary
   b. An MSDS
   c. SAE standards
   d. EPA guidelines

3. Exposure to asbestos dust can cause what condition?
   a. Asbestosis
   b. Mesothelioma
   c. Lung cancer
   d. All of the above are possible

4. Wetted asbestos dust is considered to be _____.
   a. Solid waste
   b. Hazardous waste
   c. Toxic
   d. Poisonous

5. An oil filter should be hot drained for how long before disposing of the filter?
   a. 30 to 60 minutes
   b. 4 hours
   c. 8 hours
   d. 12 hours

6. Used engine oil should be disposed of by all *except* the following methods.
   a. Disposed of in regular trash
   b. Shipped offsite for recycling
   c. Burned onsite in a waste oil-approved heater
   d. Burned offsite in a waste oil-approved heater

7. All of the following are the proper ways to dispose of a drained oil filter *except* _____.
   a. Sent for recycling
   b. Picked up by a service contract company
   c. Disposed of in regular trash
   d. Considered to be hazardous waste and disposed of accordingly

8. Which is *not* considered to be a hazardous solvent?
   a. Nonchlorinated hydrocarbon solvent
   b. Tetrachloroethylene
   c. MIBK
   d. Chlorinated hydrocarbon solvent

9. Gasoline should be stored in approved containers that include what color(s)?
   a. A red container with yellow lettering
   b. A red container
   c. A yellow container
   d. A yellow container with red lettering

10. What automotive devices may contain mercury?
    a. Rear seat video displays
    b. Navigation displays
    c. HID headlights
    d. All of the above

CHAPTER 3

BRAKING SYSTEM COMPONENTS AND PERFORMANCE STANDARDS

OBJECTIVES

After studying Chapter 3, the reader should be able to:

1. Prepare for the Brakes (A5) ASE certification test.
2. List the parts and terms for disc and drum brakes.
3. Describe brake design requirements.
4. List the six brake system categories.
5. Discuss federal braking and stopping standards.

KEY TERMS

Adjustable pedals (p. 64)
Antilock braking system (ABS) (p. 64)
Apply system (p. 63)
Base brakes (p. 60)
Boost system (p. 63)
Brake balance control system (p. 63)
Brake pedal (p. 63)
Brake warning lights (p. 64)
Department of Transportation (DOT) (p. 65)
Disc brakes (p. 61)
Drum brakes (p. 61)

Electric adjustable pedals (EAP) (p. 64)
Federal Motor Vehicle Safety Standards (FMVSS) (p. 65)
Foundation brakes (p. 60)
Gross vehicle weight rating (GVWR) (p. 66)
Hydraulic system (p. 63)
Lightly loaded vehicle weight (LLVW) (p. 66)
Parking brake (p. 63)
Red brake warning lamp (p. 64)
Service brakes (p. 60)
Snub (p. 66)
Wheel brakes (p. 63)

Brakes are by far the most important mechanism on any vehicle because the safety and lives of those riding in the vehicle depend on proper operation of the braking system. It has been estimated that the brakes on the average vehicle are applied 50,000 times a year!

HOW BRAKES STOP VEHICLES

Brakes are an energy-absorbing mechanism that converts vehicle movement into heat while stopping the rotation of the wheels. All braking systems are designed to reduce the speed and stop a moving vehicle and to keep it from moving if the vehicle is stationary. **Service brakes** are the main driver-operated brakes of the vehicle. See Figure 3-1.

Service brakes are also called **base brakes** or **foundation brakes.**

Most vehicles built since the late 1920s use a brake on each wheel. To stop a wheel, the driver exerts a force on a brake pedal. The force on the brake pedal pressurizes brake fluid in a master cylinder. This hydraulic force (liquid under pressure) is transferred through steel lines and flexible brake lines to a wheel cylinder or caliper at each wheel. Hydraulic pressure to each wheel cylinder or caliper is used to force friction materials against the brake drum or rotor. The friction between the stationary friction material and the rotating drum or rotor (disc) causes the rotating part to slow and eventually stop. Since the wheels are attached to the drums or rotors, the wheels of the vehicles also stop.

The heavier the vehicle and the higher the speed, the more heat the brakes have to be able to absorb. Long, steep hills can cause the brakes to overheat, reducing the friction necessary to slow and stop a vehicle. See Figures 3-2 and 3-3.

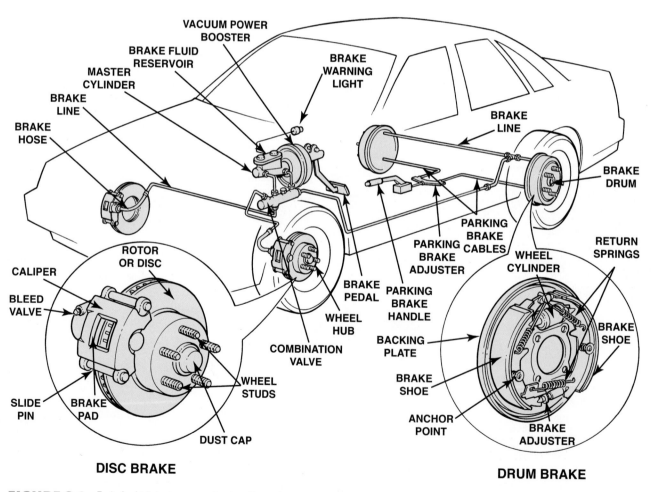

FIGURE 3-1 Typical vehicle brake system showing all typical components.

FIGURE 3-2   Brakes change the energy of the moving vehicle into heat. Too much heat and brakes fail, as indicated on this sign coming down from Pike's Peak in Colorado at 14,000 ft (4,300 m).

FIGURE 3-3   When driving down long, steep grades, select a lower transmission gear to allow the engine compression to help maintain vehicle speed.

DRUM BRAKES

Drum brakes are used on the rear of many rear-wheel-drive, front-wheel-drive, and four-wheel-drive vehicles. When drum brakes are applied, brake shoes are moved outward against a rotating brake drum. The wheel studs for the wheels are attached to the drum. When the drum slows and stops, the wheels also slow and stop.

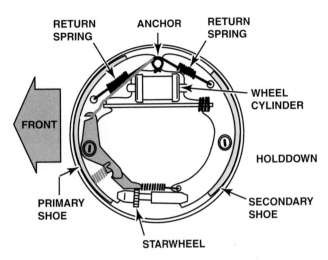

FIGURE 3-4   Typical drum brake assembly.

Drum brakes are economical to manufacture, service, and repair. Parts for drum brakes are generally readily available and reasonably priced. On some vehicles, an additional drum brake is used as a parking brake on vehicles equipped with rear disc brakes. See Figures 3-4 and 3-5.

DISC BRAKES

Disc brakes are used on the front of most vehicles built since the early 1970s and on the rear wheels of many vehicles. A disc brake operates by squeezing brake pads on both sides of a rotor or disc that is attached to the wheel. See Figure 3-6.

Type of Brake	Rotating Part	Friction Part
Drum brakes	Brake drum	Brake shoes
Disc brakes	Rotor or disc	Brake pads

Due to the friction between the road surface and the tires, the vehicle stops. To summarize, the events necessary to stop a vehicle include the following:

1. The driver presses on the brake pedal.
2. The brake pedal force is transferred hydraulically to a wheel cylinder or caliper at each wheel.
3. Hydraulic pressure inside the wheel cylinder or caliper presses friction materials (brake shoes or pads) against rotating brake drums or rotors.
4. The friction slows and stops the drum or rotor. Since the drum or rotor is bolted to the wheel of the vehicle, the wheel also stops.
5. When the wheels of the vehicle slow and stop, the tires must have friction (traction) with the road surface to stop the vehicle.

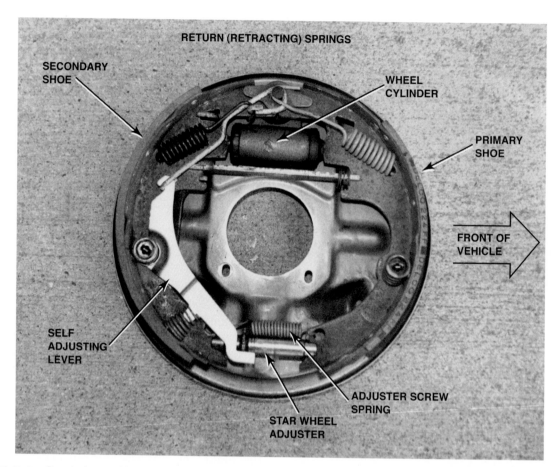

FIGURE 3-5   Drum brake assembly as used on the right rear wheel.

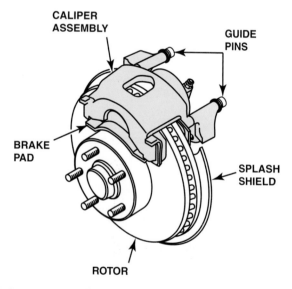

FIGURE 3-6   Typical disc brake assembly.

BRAKE DESIGN REQUIREMENTS

All braking forces must provide for the following:

1. Equal forces must be applied to both the left and right sides of the vehicle to assure straight stops.
2. Hydraulic systems must be properly engineered and serviced to provide for changes as vehicle weight shifts forward during braking. Hydraulic valves must be incorporated into the hydraulic system to permit the maximum possible braking forces but still prevent undesirable wheel lockup. Antilock braking systems (ABS) are specifically designed to prevent wheel lockup under all driving conditions, including wet or icy road conditions.
3. The hydraulic system must use a fluid that will not evaporate or freeze. The fluid has to withstand extreme temperatures without boiling and must not damage rubber or metal parts of the braking system.

4. The friction material (braking lining or brake pads) must be designed to provide adequate friction between the stationary axles and the rotating drum or rotor. The friction material should be environmentally safe. Nonasbestos lining is generally considered to be safe for the environment and the technician.

5. The design of the braking system should secure the brake lining solidly to prevent the movement of the friction material during braking.

NOTE: It is this movement of the friction material that causes brake noise (squeal). Various movement dampers are used by the vehicle manufacturers to help control any movement that does occur. It is important that every technician restore the operation of all aspects of the braking system whenever they are serviced, even the noise dampers.

---

6. Most braking systems incorporate a power assist unit that reduces the driver's effort but does not reduce stopping distance. The most commonly used brake booster is vacuum operated. The vacuum from the intake manifold is the most commonly used source of vacuum for power brake boosters. Therefore, the engine itself must be functioning correctly for proper operation of the power vacuum booster.

BRAKE SYSTEM CATEGORIES

Brake system components can be classified and placed into six subsystem categories, depending on their function. See Figure 3-7.

Apply System. The driver starts the operation of the braking system by pressing on the **brake pedal** or applying the **parking brake.** The apply system includes all the levers, pedals, or linkage needed to activate a braking force.

Boost System. The boost system is used on most vehicles to increase the brake pedal force.

Hydraulic System. The brake pedal force is transferred to the hydraulic system, where the force is directed through pipes and hoses to the wheel brakes.

Wheel Brakes. Hydraulic pressure from the hydraulic system moves a piston, in either a disc or drum brake system, that uses friction to press material against a rotating drum or rotor. The resulting friction slows the rotation of the wheels.

Brake Balance Control System. Mechanical, electrical, and hydraulic components are used to ensure that brakes are applied quickly and with balanced pressure for safe operation. Components in this category include metering valves, proportioning valves, and antilock braking system components.

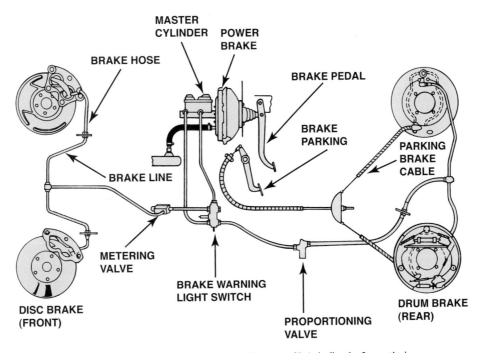

FIGURE 3-7 Typical brake system components. *(Courtesy of DaimlerChrysler Corporation)*

FREQUENTLY ASKED QUESTION

HOW DO ADJUSTABLE PEDALS WORK?

Adjustable pedals, also called **electric adjustable pedals (EAP),** place the brake pedal and the accelerator pedal on movable brackets that are motor operated. A typical adjustable pedal system includes the following components:

1. *Adjustable pedal position switch,* which allows the driver to position the pedals.
2. *Adjustable pedal assembly,* which includes the motor, threaded adjustment rods and a pedal position sensor. See Figure 3-8.

The position of the pedals, as well as the position of the seat system, is usually included as part of the memory seat function and can be set for two or more drivers.

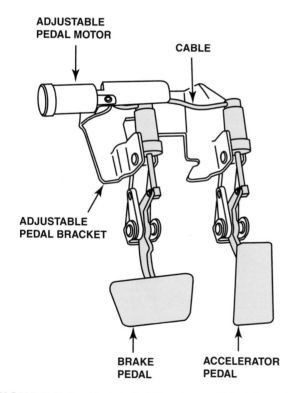

FIGURE 3-8   A typical adjustable pedal assembly. Both the accelerator and the brake pedal can be moved forward and rearward by using the adjustable pedal position switch.

FIGURE 3-9   The red brake warning lamp alerts the driver to a possible brake system fault.

Brake Warning Lights. The **red brake warning lamp** lights whenever a hydraulic system failure occurs. The amber ABS warning lamp or dim red brake light indicates an ABS self-test and/or a possible problem in the ABS system. See Figures 3-9 and 3-10.

ANTILOCK BRAKE SYSTEM OPERATION

The purpose of an **antilock braking system (ABS)** is to prevent the wheels from locking during braking, especially on low-friction surfaces such as wet, icy, or snowy roads. Remember, it is the friction between the tire tread and the road that does the actual stopping of the vehicle. Therefore, ABS does not mean that a vehicle can stop quickly on all road surfaces. ABS uses sensors at the wheels to measure the wheel speed. If a wheel is rotating slower than the others, indicating possible lockup (for example, on an icy spot), the ABS computer will control the brake fluid pressure to that wheel for a fraction of a second. *A locked wheel has less traction to the road surface than a rotating wheel.*

The ABS computer can reapply the pressure from the master cylinder to the wheel a fraction of a second later. Therefore, if a wheel starts to lockup, the purpose of the ABS system is to pulse the brakes on and off to maintain directional stability with maximum braking force. Many ABS units will cause the brake pedal to pulse if the unit is working in the ABS mode. The pulsating brake pedal is a cause

FIGURE 3-10   The ABS dash warning lamp alerts the driver to a possible antilock brake system fault.

for concern for some drivers. However, the pulsing brake pedal informs the driver that the ABS is being activated. Some ABS units use an isolator valve in the ABS unit to prevent brake pedal pulsations during ABS operation. With these types of systems, it is often difficult for the driver to know if and when the ABS unit is working to control a locking wheel. See Figure 3-11 for an overview of a typical ABS on a rear-wheel-drive vehicle.

Another symptom of normal ABS unit operation is the activation of the hydraulic pressure pump used by many ABS units. In some ABS units, the hydraulic pump is run every time the vehicle is started and moved. Other types of units operate randomly or whenever the pressure in the system calls for the pump to operate. See Chapters 19, 20, and 21 for additional details on antilock braking systems.

FEDERAL BRAKE STANDARDS

The statutes pertaining to automotive brake systems are part of the **Federal Motor Vehicle Safety Standards (FMVSS)** established by the United States **Department of Transportation (DOT).** Several standards apply to specific components within the brake system. The overall service and parking brake systems are dealt with in standard 135.

FMVSS 135 was first mandated on September 1, 2000, for passenger vehicles, and September 1, 2002, for multipurpose vehicles, trucks, and buses with a gross vehicle weight rating (GVWR) of 7,716 pounds (3,500 kilograms). Its purpose is to "ensure safe braking performance under normal and emergency conditions." FMVSS 135 applies "to passenger vehicles, multipurpose passenger vehicles, trucks, and buses."

FMVSS 135 deals with brake system safety by establishing specific brake performance requirements. It does not dictate the *design* of the system, although some

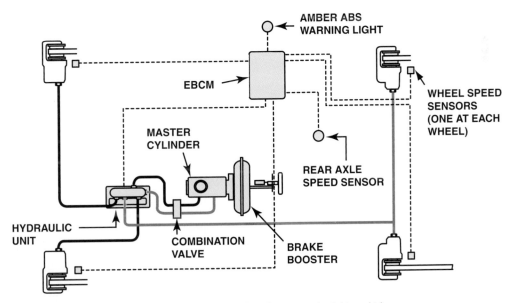

FIGURE 3-11   Typical components of an antilock braking system (ABS) used on a rear-wheel-drive vehicle.

requirements may make older technologies impractical or obsolete. Only four parts of the brake system are specifically regulated:

- Fluid reservoir and labeling
- Dashboard warning lights
- A method of automatic adjustment
- A mechanically engaging, friction-type parking brake system

The majority of FMVSS 135 consists of a comprehensive test procedure designed to reveal any weakness in a vehicle's braking system. The test is used by manufacturers to certify the braking performance of all new vehicles available for public purchase.

FMVSS 135 Brake Test

The overall FMVSS 135 brake test procedure consists of up to 24 steps, depending on the vehicle's configuration and braking system. The actual performance tests are made with the vehicle loaded to both the manufacturer's specified **gross vehicle weight rating (GVWR)** and the **lightly loaded vehicle weight (LLVW),** with certain applied brake forces. There are precise instructions for every step of the test, including the number of times the tests must be repeated, the sequence of the testing, and the allowable stopping distance for the particular type of vehicle. Some highlights of the testing procedure include:

- Burnish Procedure.   The brakes are burnished by making 200 stops from 50 mph (80 km/h) at a fixed rate of deceleration with a controlled cool-down period after each stop. This procedure conditions the friction material. Afterward, the brakes are adjusted manually according to the vehicle manufacturer's recommendations.
- Adhesion Utilization (torque wheel method).   For vehicles not equipped with ABS, this test is performed at LLVW and GVWR to determine if the brake system will make adequate use of the road surface in stopping the vehicle.
- Cold Effectiveness.   This test is performed at both GVWR and LLVW, to determine if the vehicle will have sufficient stopping power when the brake lining materials are not preheated by previous stops.
- High Speed Effectiveness.   This test is performed only on vehicles capable of exceeding 78 mph (125 km/h) to determine if the brake system will provide adequate stopping power for all loading conditions. The allowable stop-

ping distance is calculated from the maximum speed the vehicle can attain.

- Stops with the Engine Off.   This test is for vehicles equipped with brake power assist units. The vehicle, loaded to GVWR, must stop within 230 ft (70 m), from a speed of 62 mph (100 km/h). This test must be repeated six times.
- Antilock Functional Failure.   This test ensures that service brakes will function correctly in the event of an antilock functional failure, and the brake system warning indicator is activated when an ABS electrical function failure occurs.
- Variable Brake Proportioning System.   This test is performed on vehicles equipped with either a mechanical or an electrical variable proportioning system. It ensures that, in the event of a failure, the vehicle can still come to a stop in an acceptable distance. In addition, if the vehicle uses an electrically operated variable brake proportioning system, the brake warning system must immediately alert the driver of any electrical functional failure.
- Hydraulic Circuit Failure.   This test is performed to ensure that the driver will be alerted via the brake warning system indicator that a failure has occurred, and that the vehicle can still be stopped in an acceptable distance.
- Brake Power Assist Unit Inoperative.   This test makes sure the service brake can stop the vehicle in an acceptable distance with the brake power assist unit in an inoperative state. It is performed on vehicles with brake power assist units turned off or inoperative.
- Parking Brake.   The parking brake alone will hold the vehicle stationary in either the forward or reverse direction on a 20% grade for a period of at least 5 minutes.
- Heating Snubs.   This procedure heats the brake system by making a series of fifteen stops from a high speed. A **snub** is a controlled brake application. The vehicle is loaded to GVWR, with rapid acceleration between each stop to minimize cooling the brakes.
- Hot Performance.   After the brake system has been heated by a series of heating snubs, the hot performance test is immediately performed. The vehicle is loaded to GVWR and two stops are made. The stopping distance must be within acceptable limits as specified in the test. This test ensures that the brake system on the vehicle will not fade following a series of high speed stops at GVWR.

Although these tests may seem extreme, remember that they are only a minimum standard of performance. Any brake repair work should also leave the brake system capable of meeting FMVSS 135.

FREQUENTLY ASKED QUESTION

DO THE FMVSS 135 STANDARDS APPLY TO REPLACEMENT BRAKE PART PERFORMANCE?

No. The Federal Motor Vehicle Safety Standard 135 applies to new vehicles. Replacement parts used during a brake repair or replacement may or may not permit the vehicle to achieve the same standards as when new.

To help ensure like-new braking performance, the service technician should always use quality brake parts from a known manufacturer.

tive technicians to service their brake systems. Many states have laws that regulate brake work to help ensure safe repairs. These laws vary from one area to another, but they may require special licensing for brake technicians, or special business practices when selling brake work. In some cases, the laws provide the consumer with specific warranties and the right to outside arbitration in cases of defective or substandard repairs.

Regardless of whether there are specific laws governing brake repair, a technician is always liable for damage or injuries resulting from repairs performed in an unprofessional or unworkmanlike manner. Considering the lives and property that depend on good brakes, there is only one acceptable goal when making brake system repairs: to restore the system and its component parts so they perform to original specifications. In other words, *the purpose of any repair is to restore like-new performance.*

BRAKE REPAIR AND THE LAW

Once an automobile leaves the factory, the responsibility for maintaining the designed-in level of braking performance falls on the owner of the vehicle. Owners look to trained automo-

SUMMARY

1. Drum brakes are used on the rear of most vehicles.
2. Disc brakes are used on the front of most vehicles.
3. The six brake subsystems include: apply system, boost system, hydraulic system, wheel brakes, brake balance control system (which includes ABS), and brake warning lights.

4. An antilock braking system (ABS) pulses the hydraulic force to the wheels to prevent the tires from locking up. A locked tire has lower friction than a rolling tire.
5. The federal brake standards covered in FMVSS 135 regulate specific brake performance requirements, but not the actual design of the braking system.

REVIEW QUESTIONS

1. List the differences between drum brakes and disc brakes.
2. List the six brake subsystem categories.
3. Explain how ABS units prevent wheel lockup.

4. List ten of the brake tests performed under the Federal Motor Vehicle Safety Standard (FMVSS) 135.

CHAPTER QUIZ

1. Disc brakes use replaceable friction material called _____.
   a. Linings
   b. Pads
   c. Core
   d. Web

2. Drum brakes use replaceable friction material called _____.
   a. Linings
   b. Pads
   c. Core
   d. Web

3. Technician A says that a power-assisted brake reduces stopping distances compared with a nonpower-assisted brake system. Technician B says that the power-assisted brake system reduces the force that the driver must exert on the brake pedal. Which technician is correct?
   a. Technician A only
   b. Technician B only
   c. Both Technicians A and B
   d. Neither Technician A nor B

4. A locked wheel _____ to the road surface than a rolling wheel.
   a. Has less traction
   b. Has greater traction

5. Technician A says that all vehicles equipped with ABS will experience a pulsating brake pedal even during normal braking. Technician B says that some ABS units only control the rear wheel brakes. Which technician is correct?
   a. Technician A only
   b. Technician B only
   c. Both Technicians A and B
   d. Neither Technician A nor B

6. The FMVSS 135 standards determine _____.
   a. The design of the braking system
   b. The performance of the braking system
   c. The materials used in the braking system
   d. All of the above

7. An owner of a vehicle equipped with ABS brakes complained that whenever he tried to stop on icy or slippery roads, the brake pedal would pulse up and down rapidly. Technician A says that this is normal for many ABS units. Technician B says that the ABS unit is malfunctioning. Which technician is correct?
   a. Technician A only
   b. Technician B only
   c. Both Technicians A and B
   d. Neither Technician A nor B

8. A brake snub is _____.
   a. An event that results in an ABS stop
   b. A brake event that causes the tires to slide on the pavement
   c. A controlled brake application
   d. A parking brake test procedure

9. All of the following are specified by FMVSS 135 *except*:
   a. Brake burnish procedure
   b. Variable brake proportioning system
   c. Brake noise levels
   d. Cold effectiveness

10. What is the purpose of any brake repair?
    a. Reduce noise during braking
    b. Replace pads and linings
    c. Restore proper brake pedal height
    d. Restore like-new performance

CHAPTER **4**

BRAKING SYSTEM PRINCIPLES

OBJECTIVES

After studying Chapter 4, the reader should be able to:

1. Prepare for the Brakes (A5) ASE certification test.
2. Explain kinetic energy and why it is so important to brake design.
3. Discuss mechanical advantage and how it relates to the braking system.
4. Explain the coefficient of friction.
5. Describe how brakes can fade due to excessive heat.

KEY TERMS

Brake fade (p. 76)
Coefficient of friction (p. 73)
Energy (p. 70)
First-class lever (p. 72)
Friction (p. 73)
Fulcrum (p. 72)
Gas fade (p. 77)
Inertia (p. 71)
Kinetic energy (p. 70)
Kinetic friction (p. 74)
Leverage (p. 72)

Lining fade (p. 76)
Mechanical advantage (p. 72)
Mechanical fade (p. 76)
Pedal ratio (p. 72)
Second-class lever (p. 72)
Static friction (p. 74)
Third-class lever (p. 72)
Weight bias (p. 71)
Weight transfer (p. 71)
Work (p. 70)

ENERGY PRINCIPLES

Energy is the ability to do work. There are many forms of energy, but chemical, mechanical, and electrical energy are the most familiar kinds involved in the operation of an automobile. See Figure 4-1.

For example, when the ignition key is turned to the "Start" position, chemical energy in the battery is converted into electrical energy to operate the starter motor. The starter motor then converts the electrical energy into mechanical energy that is used to crank the engine.

In the example above, energy is being used to perform work. **Work** is the transfer of energy from one physical system to another—especially the transfer of energy to an object through the application of force. This is precisely what occurs when a vehicle's brakes are applied: The *force* of the actuating system *transfers* the energy of the vehicle's motion to the brake drums or rotors where friction *converts* it into heat energy and stops the vehicle.

KINETIC ENERGY

Kinetic energy is a fundamental form of mechanical energy. It is the energy of mass in motion. Every moving object possesses kinetic energy, and the amount of that energy is determined by the object's mass and speed. The greater the mass of an object and the faster it moves, the more kinetic energy it possesses. Even at low speeds, a moving vehicle has enough kinetic energy to cause serious injury and damage. The job of the brake system is to dispose of that energy in a safe and controlled manner.

Engineers calculate kinetic energy using the following formula:

$$\frac{mv^2}{29.9} = E_k$$

where:

m = mass or weight of the vehicle in pounds (lb)
v = velocity of the vehicle in miles per hour
E_k = kinetic energy in foot-pounds (ft-lb)

Another way to express this equation is as follows.

$$\frac{weight \times speed^2}{29.9} = kinetic\ energy$$

If a 3,000-lb vehicle traveling at 30 mph is compared with a 6,000-lb vehicle also traveling at 30 mph as shown in Figure 4-2, the equations for computing their respective kinetic energies look like this:

$$\frac{3,000\ lb \times 30^2\ mph}{29.9} = 90,301\ ft\text{-}lb$$

$$\frac{6,000\ lb \times 30^2\ mph}{29.9} = 180,602\ ft\text{-}lb$$

The results show that when the weight of a vehicle is doubled from 3,000 to 6,000 lb, its kinetic energy is also doubled from 90,301 ft-lb to 180,602 ft-lb. In mathematical terms, kinetic energy increases *proportionally* as weight increases. In other words, if the weight of a moving object doubles, its kinetic energy also doubles. If the weight quadruples, the kinetic energy becomes four times as great.

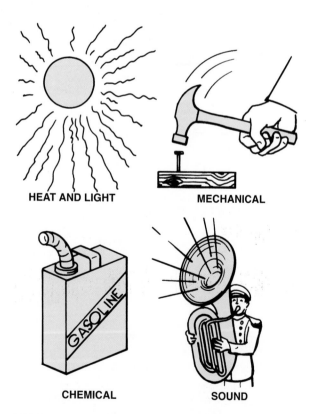

HEAT AND LIGHT   MECHANICAL

CHEMICAL   SOUND

FIGURE 4-1   Energy, which is the ability to perform work, exists in many forms.

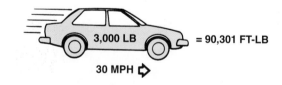

3,000 LB   = 90,301 FT-LB

30 MPH ▷

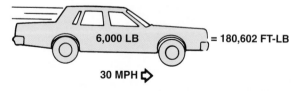

6,000 LB   = 180,602 FT-LB

30 MPH ▷

FIGURE 4-2   Kinetic energy increases in direct proportion to the weight of the vehicle.

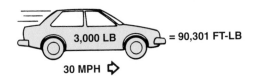

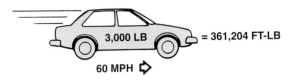

FIGURE 4-3   Kinetic energy increases as the square of any increase in vehicle speed.

If a 3,000-lb vehicle traveling at 30 mph is compared with the same vehicle traveling at 60 mph (Figure 4-3), the equations for computing their respective kinetic energies look like this:

$$\frac{3{,}000 \text{ lb} \times 30^2 \text{ mph}}{29.9} = 90{,}301 \text{ ft-lb}$$

$$\frac{3{,}000 \text{ lb} \times 60^2 \text{ mph}}{29.9} = 361{,}204 \text{ ft-lb}$$

The results show that the vehicle traveling at 30 mph has over 90,000 ft-lb of kinetic energy, but at 60 mph the figure increases to over 350,000 ft-lb. In fact, at twice the speed, the vehicle has exactly four times as much kinetic energy. If the speed were doubled again to 120 mph, the amount of kinetic energy would grow to almost 1,500,000 ft-lb! In mathematical terms, kinetic energy increases as the *square of its speed*. In other words, if the speed of a moving object doubles (2), the kinetic energy becomes four times as great ($2^2 = 4$). And if the speed quadruples (4), say from 15 to 60 mph, the kinetic energy becomes 16 times as great ($4^2 = 16$). This is the reason speed has such an impact on kinetic energy.

Kinetic Energy and Brake Design

The relationships between weight, speed, and kinetic energy have significant practical consequences for the brake system engineer. If vehicle A weighs twice as much as vehicle B, it needs a brake system that is twice as powerful. But if vehicle C has twice the speed potential of vehicle D, it needs brakes that are, not twice, but four times more powerful.

INERTIA

Although brake engineers take both weight and speed capability into account when designing a brake system, these are not the only factors involved. Another physical property, inertia,

also affects the braking process and the selection of brake components. **Inertia** is defined by Isaac Newton's first law of motion, which states that a body at rest tends to remain at rest, and a body in motion tends to remain in motion in a straight line unless acted upon by an outside force.

Weight Transfer and Bias

Inertia, in the form of **weight transfer,** plays a major part in a vehicle's braking performance. Newton's first law of motion dictates that a moving vehicle will remain in motion unless acted upon by an outside force. The vehicle brakes provide that outside force, but when the brakes are applied at the wheel friction assemblies, only the wheels and tires begin to slow immediately. The rest of the vehicle, all of the weight carried by the suspension, attempts to remain in forward motion. The result is that the front suspension compresses, the rear suspension extends, and the weight is transferred toward the front of the vehicle. See Figure 4-4.

The total weight of the vehicle does not change, only the amount supported by each axle.

To compound the problem of weigh transfer, most vehicles also have a forward **weight bias,** which means that even when stopped, more than 50% of their weight is supported by the front wheels. Front-wheel-drive (FWD) vehicles, in particular, have a forward weight bias. This occurs because the engine, transmission, and most other heavy parts are located toward the front of the vehicle. See Figure 4-5.

Whenever the brakes are applied, weight transfer and weight bias greatly increase the load on the front wheels, while the load on the rear wheels is substantially reduced. This requires the front brakes to provide 60% to 80% of the total braking force. To deal with the extra load, the front brakes are much more powerful than the rear brakes. They are able to convert more kinetic energy into heat energy.

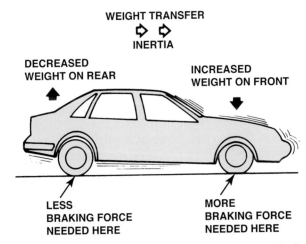

FIGURE 4-4   Inertia creates weight transfer that requires the front brakes to provide most of the braking power.

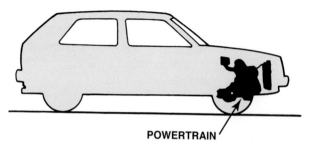

FIGURE 4-5 Front-wheel-drive vehicles have much of their weight over the front wheels.

TECH TIP

BRAKES CANNOT OVERCOME THE LAWS OF PHYSICS

No vehicle can stop on a dime. The energy required to slow or stop a vehicle must be absorbed by the braking system. All drivers should be aware of this fact and drive at a reasonable speed for the road and traffic conditions.

MECHANICAL PRINCIPLES

The primary mechanical principle used to increase application force in every brake system is **leverage.** In the science of mechanics, a lever is a simple machine that consists of a rigid object, typically a metal bar that pivots about a fixed point called a **fulcrum.** There are three basic types of levers, but the job of all three is to change a quantity of energy into a more useful form.

A **first-class lever** increases the force applied to it and also changes the direction of the force. See Figure 4-6.

With a first-class lever, the weight is placed at one end while the lifting force is applied to the other. The fulcrum is positioned at some point in between. If the fulcrum is placed twice as far from the long end of the lever as from the short end, a 10-lb weight on the short end can be lifted by only a 5-lb force at the long end. However, the short end of the lever will travel only half as far as the long end. Moving the fulcrum closer to the weight will further reduce the force required to lift it, but it will also decrease the distance the weight is moved.

A **second-class lever** increases the force applied to it and passes it along in the same direction. See Figure 4-7.

With a second-class lever, the fulcrum is located at one end while the lifting force is applied at the other. The weight is positioned at some point in between. If a 10-lb weight is

placed at the center of the lever, it can be lifted by only a 5-lb force at the end of the lever. However, the weight will only travel half the distance the end of the lever does. As the weight is moved closer to the fulcrum, the force required to lift it, and the distance it travels, are both reduced.

A **third-class lever** actually reduces the force applied to it, but the resulting force moves farther and faster. See Figure 4-8.

With a third-class lever, the fulcrum is located at one end and the weight is placed at the other. The lifting force is applied at some point in between. If a 10-lb weight is placed at the end of the lever, it can be lifted by a 20-lb force applied at the middle of the lever. Although the force required to move the weight has doubled, the weight is moved twice as far and twice as fast as the point on the lever where the force was applied. The closer to the fulcrum the lifting force is applied, the greater the force required by the weight and the further and faster the weight will move.

The levers in brake systems are used to increase force, so they are either first- or second-class. Second-class levers are the most common, and the service brake pedal is a good example. In a typical suspended brake pedal, the pedal arm is the lever, the pivot point is the fulcrum, and the force is applied at the foot pedal pad. See Figure 4-9.

The force applied to the master cylinder by the pedal pushrod attached to the pivot is much greater than the force applied at the pedal pad, but the pushrod does not travel nearly as far.

Leverage creates a **mechanical advantage** that, at the brake pedal, is called the **pedal ratio.** For example, a pedal ratio of 5 to 1 is common for manual brakes, which means that

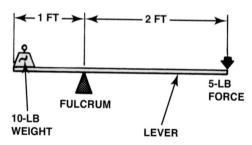

FIGURE 4-6 A first-class lever increases force and changes the direction of the force.

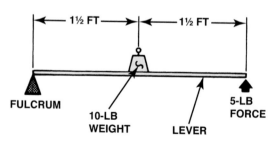

FIGURE 4-7 A second-class lever increases force in the same direction as it is applied.

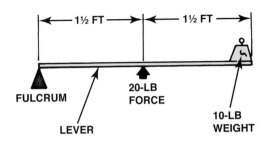

FIGURE 4-8 A third-class lever reduces force but increases the speed and travel of the resulting work.

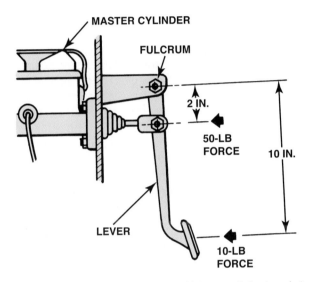

FIGURE 4-9 This brake pedal assembly is a second-class lever design that provides a 5 to 1 mechanical advantage.

a force of 10 lb at the brake pedal will result in a force of 50 lb at the pedal pushrod. In practice, leverage is used at many points in both the service and parking brake systems to increase braking force while making it easier for the driver to control the amount of force applied.

FRICTION PRINCIPLES

The wheel friction assemblies use friction to convert kinetic energy into heat energy. **Friction** is the resistance to movement between two surfaces in contact with one another. Brake performance is improved by increasing friction (at least to a point), and brakes that apply enough friction to use all the grip the tires have to offer will always have the potential to stop a vehicle faster than brakes with less ability to apply friction.

Coefficient of Friction

The amount of friction between two objects or surfaces is commonly expressed as a value called the **coefficient of friction**

and is represented by the Greek letter mu (μ). The coefficient of friction, also referred to as the friction coefficient, is determined by dividing tensile force by weight force. The tensile force is the pulling force required to slide one of the surfaces across the other. The weight force is the force pushing down on the object being pulled. The equation for calculating the coefficient of friction is as follows.

$$\frac{F_t}{G} = \mu$$

where:

F_t = tensile force in pounds
G = weight force in pounds
μ = coefficient of friction

Another way to express the equation is as follows.

$$\frac{\text{Tensile force}}{\text{Weight force}} = \text{Coefficient of friction}$$

This equation can be used to show the effect different variables have on the coefficient of friction. At any given weight (application) force there are three factors that affect the friction coefficient of vehicle brakes:

- Surface finish
- Friction material
- Heat

For reasons that will be explained later, the friction coefficient of the wheel friction assemblies of vehicle brake systems is always less than one.

Surface Finish Effects

The effect of surface finish on the friction coefficient can be seen in Figure 4-10.

In this case, 100 lb of tensile force is required to pull a 200-lb block of wood across a concrete floor. The equation for computing the coefficient of friction is as follows:

$$\frac{100 \text{ lb}}{200 \text{ lb}} = 0.5$$

The friction coefficient in this instance is 0.5. Now take the same example, except assume that the block of wood has been sanded smooth, which improves its surface finish and reduces the force required to move it to only 50 lb. In this case the equation reads as follows:

$$\frac{50 \text{ lb}}{200 \text{ lb}} = 0.25$$

The friction coefficient drops by half, and it would decrease even further if the surface finish of the floor were changed from rough concrete to smooth marble.

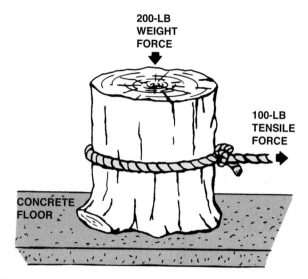

200-LB WEIGHT FORCE

100-LB TENSILE FORCE

CONCRETE FLOOR

FIGURE 4-10 The coefficient of friction (μ) in this example is 0.5.

It is obvious that the *surface finish* of two connecting surfaces has a major effect on their coefficient of friction. See Chapter 16 for details on achieving the proper surface finish on brake drums and rotors.

Friction Material Effects

Taking the example above one step further, consider the effect if a 200-lb block of ice, a totally different type of material, is substituted for the wood block. In this case, it requires only a 10-lb force to pull the block across the concrete. See Figure 4-11.

The equation reads as follows:

$$\frac{10 \text{ lb}}{200 \text{ lb}} = 0.05$$

The coefficient of friction in this example decreases dramatically to only 0.05, and once again, even further reductions would be seen if the floor surface were changed to polished marble or some other similar smooth surface.

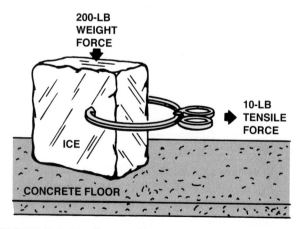

200-LB WEIGHT FORCE

10-LB TENSILE FORCE

ICE

CONCRETE FLOOR

FIGURE 4-11 The types of friction materials affect the friction coefficient, which is only 0.05 in this example.

It is obvious that the *type* of materials being rubbed together have a very significant effect on the coefficient of friction. The choice of materials for brake drums and rotors is limited. Iron and steel are used most often because they are relatively inexpensive and can stand up under the extreme friction brake drums and rotors must endure.

The brake lining material, however, can be replaced relatively quickly and inexpensively, and therefore does not need to have as long a service life. Brake shoe and pad friction materials play a major part in determining coefficient of friction. There are several fundamentally different materials to choose from, and each has its own unique friction coefficient and performance characteristics.

Friction Contact Area

For *sliding* surfaces, such as those in wheel friction assemblies, the amount of contact area has no effect on the amount of friction generated. This fact is related to the earlier statement that brake friction materials always have a friction coefficient of less than 1.0. To have a friction coefficient of 1.0 or more, material must be *transferred* between the two friction surfaces. The amount of contact area does not affect the coefficient of friction, but it does have significant effects on lining life and the dissipation of heat that can lead to brake fade.

Tires are an example where contact area makes a difference. All other things being equal, a wide tire with a large contact area on the road has a higher coefficient of friction than a narrow tire with less contact area. This occurs because the tire and road *do not* have a sliding relationship. A tire conforms to and engages the road surface, and during a hard stop, a portion of the breaking force comes from shearing or tearing away the tire tread rubber. The rubber's tensile strength, its internal resistance to being pulled apart, adds to the braking efforts of friction. A racing tire making a hard stop on dry pavement, for example, has a friction coefficient of 1.0 or better. The transfer of material between the two surfaces can be seen as skid marks on the pavement.

Static and Kinetic Friction

There are actually two measurements of the coefficient of friction, the **static friction** coefficient and the **kinetic friction** coefficient. The static value is the coefficient of friction with the two friction surfaces at rest. The kinetic value is the coefficient of friction while the two surfaces are sliding against one another.

The coefficient of static friction is always higher than that of kinetic friction, which explains why it is harder to *start* an object moving than to *keep* it moving. In the example shown in Figure 4-12, it takes 100 lb of tensile force to start the wooden block sliding, but once in motion, it takes only 50 lb to keep it sliding. The relatively high static friction is harder to overcome than the somewhat lower kinetic friction. The static and kinetic friction coefficients for several combinations of materials are shown in Figure 4-13.

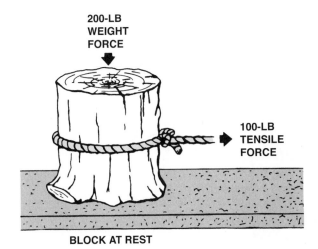

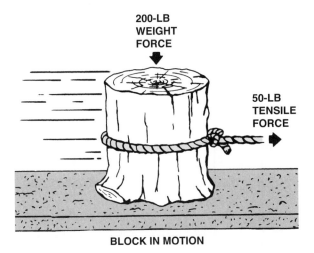

FIGURE 4-12 The static friction coefficient of an object at rest is higher than its kinetic friction coefficient once in motion.

FRICTION AND HEAT

The function of the brake system is to convert kinetic energy into heat energy through friction. But just how much heat is created by this conversion process? Although there are too many variables to obtain the exact temperature increase of any

The difference between static and kinetic friction explains why parking brakes, although much less powerful than service brakes, are still able to hold a vehicle in position on a hill. The job of the parking brakes is relatively easy because the stationary vehicle has no kinetic energy, and the brake lining and drum or disc are not moving when they are applied. To start the vehicle moving, enough force would have to be applied to overcome the relatively high static friction of the parking brakes. The service brakes, however, have a much more difficult job. The moving vehicle has a great deal of kinetic energy, and the fact that the brake friction surfaces are in relative motion means that kinetic friction makes them less efficient.

CONTACTING SURFACES	COEFFICIENT OF FRICTION	
	STATIC	KINETIC
STEEL ON STEEL (DRY)	0.6	0.4
STEEL ON STEEL (GREASY)	0.1	0.05
TEFLON ON STEEL	0.04	0.04
BRASS ON STEEL (DRY)	0.5	0.4
BRAKE LINING ON CAST IRON	0.4	0.3
RUBBER TIRES		
ON SMOOTH PAVEMENT (DRY)	0.9	0.8
METAL ON ICE	—	0.02

FIGURE 4-13 Every combination of materials has different static and kinetic friction coefficients.

specific component, the *average* temperature rise of the brakes during a single stop can be computed as follows:

$$\frac{K_c}{77.8 \, W_b} = T_r$$

where:

K$_c$ = kinetic energy change in ft-lb
W$_b$ = weight of all the rotors and drums in pounds
T$_r$ = temperature rise in Fahrenheit degrees

Another way to express this equation is as follows:

$$\frac{\text{Energy change}}{77.8 \times \text{drum/rotor weight}} = \text{Temperature rise}$$

To see how this works, consider a 3,000-lb vehicle with a combined brake drum and rotor weight of 20 lb that is brought to a complete stop from 30 mph. See Figure 4-14.

In the first section of this chapter we calculated that this vehicle has 90,301 ft-lb of kinetic energy, and since the vehicle is coming to a full stop, the change in kinetic energy during the stop will equal the entire 90,301 ft-lb. Based on this information, the equation for computing the rise in brake temperature reads as follows:

$$\frac{90,301 \text{ ft-lb}}{77.8 \times 20 \text{ lb}} = 58°F \, (32°C)$$

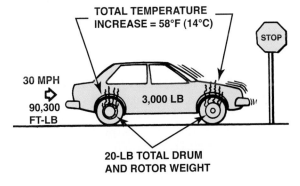

FIGURE 4-14 Brake temperature increase is determined mostly by vehicle weight, drum and rotor weight, and the change in kinetic energy.

The total brake temperature increase in this case is 58°F (32°C). This increase is relatively small, but the weight and speed of the vehicle are also rather low. It is the *change* in kinetic energy that determines the amount of temperature increase, and kinetic energy increases proportionately with increases in weight, and as the square of any increase in speed. If the weight of the vehicle is doubled to 6,000 lb, the change in kinetic energy required to bring it to a full stop will be 180,602 ft-lb.

The temperature increase computed with this equation is the average of all the friction generating components. Some of the heat is absorbed by the brake drums and rotors, some goes into the shoes and pads, and some is conducted into the wheel cylinders, calipers, and brake fluid. In addition, the front brakes provide 60% to 80% of the total braking force and they receive a similar percentage of the average temperature increase. The increase at each axle is divided evenly between the two wheel friction assemblies unless there is unequal traction from one side to the other, or there is a problem within the brake system itself.

HEAT-CAUSED BRAKE FADE

The temperature of a brake drum or rotor may rise more than 100°F (55°C) in only seconds during a hard stop, but it could take 30 seconds or more for the rotor to cool to the temperature that existed before the stop. If repeated hard stops are performed, the brake system components can overheat and lose effectiveness, or possibly fail altogether. This loss of braking power is called **brake fade.**

The point at which brakes overheat and fade is determined by a number of factors including the brake design, its cooling ability, and the type of friction material being used. There are three primary types of brake fade caused by heat:

- Mechanical fade
- Lining fade
- Gas fade

Mechanical fade occurs when a brake drum overheats and expands away from the brake lining. See Figure 4-15.

To maintain braking power, the brake shoes must move farther outward, which requires additional brake pedal travel. When the drum expands to a point where there is not enough pedal travel to keep the lining in contact with the drum, brake fade occurs. Sometimes, partial braking power can be restored by rapidly pumping the brake pedal to move the brake shoes farther outward and back into contact with the drums. Mechanical fade in drum brakes is reduced by using larger or heavier drums that can absorb more heat before they expand too far. Cooling fins are also added to the drums or make them partially of aluminum to help speed heat transfer to the passing air. Mechanical fade is not a problem with disc brakes because as a brake rotor heats up it expands *toward* the brake pads rather than away from them.

Lining fade affects both drum and disc brakes, and occurs when the friction material overheats to the point where its coefficient of friction drops off. See Figure 4-16.

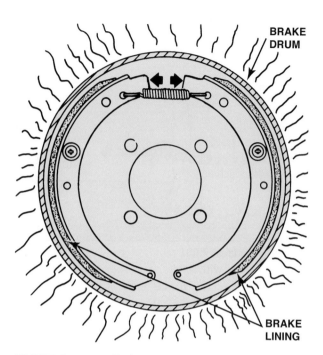

FIGURE 4-15   Mechanical fade occurs when the brake drums become so hot they expand away from the brake lining.

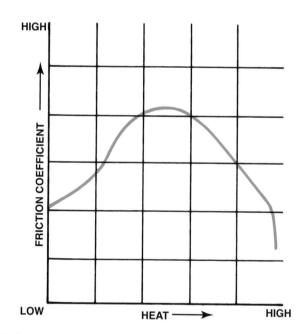

FIGURE 4-16   Some heat increases the coefficient of friction, but too much heat can cause it to drop off sharply.

When lining fade occurs on drum brakes, partial braking power can sometimes be restored by increasing pressure on the brake pedal, although this may only make matters worse since the extra pressure increases the amount of heat and fade. With disc brakes, lining fade is possible, but less of a problem because of disc brakes' superior ability to dissipate heat. The rotor friction surfaces are exposed to the passing air, and most rotors have internal ventilation passages that further aid in cooling.

Gas fade is a relatively rare type of brake fade that occurs under very hard braking when a thin layer of hot gases and dust particles builds up between the brake drum or rotor and linings. The gas layer acts as a lubricant and reduces friction. See Figure 4-17.

As with lining fade, greater application force at the brake pedal is required to maintain a constant level of stopping power. Gas fade becomes more of a problem as the size of the brake lining increases because gases and particles have a harder time escaping from under a drum brake shoe than a disc brake pad. Some high-performance brake shoes and pads have slotted linings to provide paths for gas and particles to escape.

In most cases brake fade is a temporary condition. The brakes will return to normal once they have all been allowed to cool. This is true in all except extreme situations where the heat has been so great it has damaged the friction material or melted rubber seals within the hydraulic system.

NOTE: The possibility of brake fade caused by heat can be reduced if the transmission gear selector is placed in a lower gear when descending a steep or long hill to reduce the amount of braking needed to maintain a safe road speed. Engine braking will help keep the vehicle speed under control.

WATER-CAUSED BRAKE FADE

If a vehicle is driven through deep water or during a severe rainstorm, water can get between the brake drum and the linings. When this occurs, no stopping power is possible until the water is pushed out and normal friction is restored. While water fade is most likely to occur with drum brakes, it can also occur on disc brakes. After driving through deep water, the wise driver should lightly apply the brakes to check the operation and to help remove any water trapped between the friction material and the rotor or drum.

DECELERATION RATES

Deceleration rates are measured in units of "feet per second per second" (No, this is not a misprint). What it means is that

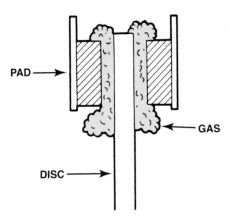

FIGURE 4-17   One cause of brake fade occurs when the phenolic resin, a part of the friction material, gets so hot that it vaporizes. The vaporized gas from the disc brake pads gets between the rotor (disc) and the friction pad. Because the friction pad is no longer in contact with the rotor, no additional braking force is possible.   *(Courtesy of Raybestos Brake Parts Inc.)*

the vehicle will change in velocity during a certain time interval divided by the time interval. Deceleration is abbreviated "ft/sec^2" (pronounced "feet per second per second" or "feet per second squared") or meters per sec^2 (m/sec^2) in the metric system. Typical deceleration rates include the following:

- Comfortable deceleration is about 8.5 ft/sec^2 (3 m/sec^2).
- Loose items in the vehicle will "fly" above 11 ft/sec^2 (3.5 m/sec^2).
- Maximum deceleration rates for most vehicles and light trucks range from 16 to 32 ft/sec^2 (5 to 10 m/sec^2).

An average deceleration rate of 15 ft/sec^2 (3 m/sec^2) can stop a vehicle traveling at 55 mph (88 km/h) in about 200 ft (61 m) in less than 4 seconds. During a standard brake system test, a vehicle is braked at this rate 15 times. Temperatures at the front brake pads can reach 1,300°F (700°C) or higher, sometimes reaching as high as 1,800°F (980°C). Brake fluid and rubber components may reach 300°F (150°C) or higher.

SUMMARY

1. Energy is the ability to do work. A vehicle in motion represents kinetic energy, which must be absorbed by the braking system during a stop.

2. The front brakes must provide a higher percentage of the braking force due to weight bias and weight transfer.

3. The brake pedal uses mechanical advantage to increase the force applied by the driver to the master cylinder.

4. Coefficient of friction represents the amount of friction between two surfaces.

5. Friction creates heat during a stop and the braking system must be able to absorb this heat.

6. Brake fade results when the heat generated by the brakes causes changes in the friction materials that reduce the braking force or by water that can get between the brake drum and the linings.

7. Deceleration rates are expressed in feet per second per second or ft/sec^2 or m/sec^2.

REVIEW QUESTIONS

1. What is kinetic energy?

2. How is mechanical advantage used in the braking system?

3. What is the coefficient of friction?

4. Why do brakes fade due to excessive heat or water?

CHAPTER QUIZ

1. All of the following are correct statements about braking *except*:
   a. Kinetic energy must be absorbed by the braking system.
   b. Kinetic energy of a vehicle doubles when the speed doubles.
   c. The heavier the vehicle, the greater the kinetic energy when moving.
   d. If the vehicle weight is doubled, the kinetic energy of a moving vehicle is doubled.

2. Technician A says that the front brakes do most of the braking because the front brakes are larger. Technician B says that due to weight transfer, most of the braking force needs to be done by the front brakes. Which technician is correct?
   a. Technician A only
   b. Technician B only
   c. Both Technicians A and B
   d. Neither Technician A nor B

3. The brake pedal assembly uses a mechanical lever to _____.
   a. Increase the driver's force on the brake pedal applied to the master cylinder
   b. Increase the distance the brake pedal needs to be depressed by the driver
   c. Decrease the driver's force on the brake pedal applied to the master cylinder
   d. Allow for clearance between the brake pedal and the floor when the brakes are applied

4. The friction between two surfaces is affected by all *except* _____.
   a. Speed difference between the two surfaces
   b. Surface finish
   c. Frictional material
   d. Heat

5. Technician A says that the thicker or heavier the disc brake rotor, the more heat can be absorbed. Technician B says that the faster the vehicle is traveling when the brakes are applied, the greater the amount of heat created in the brake system. Which technician is correct?

   a. Technician A only
   b. Technician B only
   c. Both Technicians A and B
   d. Neither Technician A nor B

6. All of the following are types of brake fade *except* _____.
   a. Mechanical fade
   b. Lining fade
   c. Gas fade
   d. Rotor fade

7. Brake fade caused by water can occur _____.
   a. Only if the vehicle is driven in water above the centerline of the axle
   b. Whenever it rains and the roads are wet or damp
   c. Due to moisture in the air on a humid day
   d. Whenever driving through water puddles or during a severe rainstorm

8. What can the driver do to reduce the possibility of brake fade caused by heat?
   a. Ride the brakes to keep the shoes and pads against the drum or rotor
   b. Pump the brake pedal while descending a steep hill
   c. Select a lower transmission gear
   d. Shift the transmission into neutral and allow the vehicle to coast down long or steep hills

9. Maximum deceleration rates for a typical passenger car or light truck is _____.
   a. 1 to 3 ft/sec
   b. 5 to 10 ft/sec
   c. 16 to 32 ft/sec²
   d. 200 to 250 ft/sec²

10. Disc brake pads can reach temperatures as high as _____.
   a. 300°F (150°C)
   b. 1,000°F (540°C)
   c. 1,300°F (700°C)
   d. 1,800°F (980°C)

CHAPTER **5**

BRAKE HYDRAULIC SYSTEMS

OBJECTIVES

After studying Chapter 5, the reader should be able to:

1. Prepare for the Brakes (A5) ASE certification test content area "A" (Hydraulic System Diagnosis and Repair).

2. State Pascal's Law.

3. Describe the function, purpose, and operation of the master cylinder.

4. Explain how hydraulic force can be used to supply high pressures to each individual wheel brake.

5. Describe the process of troubleshooting master cylinders and related brake hydraulic components.

6. Explain how a quick take-up master cylinder works.

KEY TERMS

HYDRAULIC PRINCIPLES

In addition to the mechanical advantage provided by leverage, all vehicles use hydraulic pressure to help increase brake application force.

All braking systems require that a driver's force is transmitted to the drum or rotor attached to each wheel. See Figure 5-1.

The force that can be exerted on the brake pedal varies due to the strength and size of the driver. Engineers design braking systems to require less than 150 lb of force (68 kg) from the driver, yet provide the force necessary to stop a heavy vehicle from high speed.

NONCOMPRESSIBILITY OF LIQUIDS

Hydraulic systems use liquids to transmit motion. For all practical purposes, a liquid cannot be compressed. No matter how much pressure or force is placed on a quantity of liquid, its volume will remain the same. This fact enables liquids in a closed system to transmit motion. See Figure 5-2.

If piston A is moved a distance of 1 in., the liquid will be displaced ahead of it and piston B will move 1 in. as well.

Liquids cannot be compressed, but any air trapped in the system can be compressed. The simple hydraulic system has been contaminated with air. See Figure 5-3.

Even though piston A is moved a distance of 1 in., piston B will not move if the load on it is greater than the pressure of the air in the system. For example, if the load on piston B is 50 pounds per square inch (psi), the movement of piston A must compress the air in the system to that same pressure before piston B will begin to move. A brake hydraulic system must be air free or there will be serious problems.

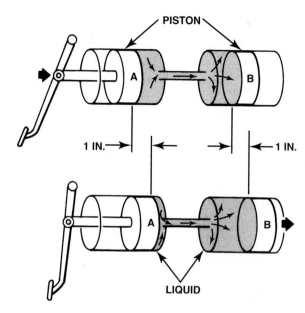

FIGURE 5-2   Because liquids cannot be compressed, they are able to transmit motion in a closed system.

PASCAL'S LAW

The hydraulic principles that permit a brake system to function were discovered by a French physicist, Blaise Pascal (1632–1662). **Pascal's Law** states that "when force is applied to a liquid confined in a container or an enclosure, the pressure is transmitted equal and undiminished in every direction." To help understand this principle, assume that a force of 10 lb is exerted on a piston with a surface area of 1 square inch (sq. in.). Since this *force* measured in lb or Newtons (N) is applied to a piston with an area measured in square inches (sq. in.), the *pressure* is the force divided by the area or "10

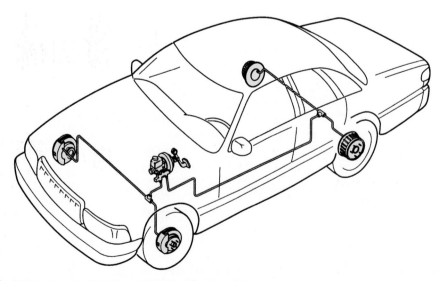

FIGURE 5-1   Hydraulic brake lines transfer the brake effort to each brake assembly attached to all four wheels.

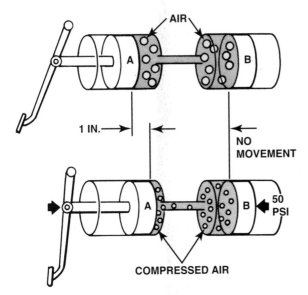

FIGURE 5-3 Hydraulic system must be free of air to operate properly.

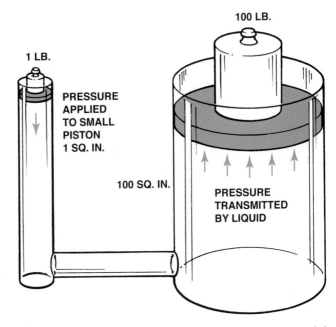

FIGURE 5-4 A one-pound force exerted on a small piston in a sealed system transfers the pressure to each square inch throughout the system. In this example, the 1-lb force is able to lift a 100-lb weight because it is supported by a piston that is 100 times larger in area than the small piston.

pounds per square inch" (psi). It is this "pressure" that is transmitted, without loss, throughout the entire hydraulic system. See Figure 5-4.

If you know two out of the three factors, you can calculate the other one by using this formula:

F = force (lb) (Newtons)
P = pressure in lb per sq. in. (kilo Pascals [kPa])
A = area in sq. in. (cm²)
F = P × A (force is equal to the pressure multiplied by the area)
P = F ÷ A (pressure is equal to the force divided by the area)
A = F ÷ P (area is equal to the force divided by the pressure)

A practical example involves a master cylinder with a piston area of 1 sq. in., and one wheel cylinder with an area of 1 sq. in., and one wheel cylinder with a piston area of 2 sq. in. See Figure 5-5.

The real "magic" of a hydraulic brake system is the fact that different forces can be created at different wheel cylinders. More force is necessary for front brakes than for rear brakes because, as the brakes are applied, the weight of the vehicle moves forward.

Larger (area) pistons are used in wheel cylinders (calipers, if disc brakes) on the front wheels to increase the force used to apply the front brakes.

Not only can hydraulics act as a "force machine" (by varying piston size), but the hydraulic system also can be varied to change piston stroke distances.

On a typical vehicle, a driver-input force of 150 lb (660 Newtons) is boosted both mechanically (through the brake pedal linkage) and by the power booster to a fluid pressure of about 1700 psi (11,700 kPa).

NOTE: During a typical brake application, only about *1 teaspoon (5 ml or cc) of brake fluid* actually is moved from the master cylinder and into the hydraulic system to cause the pressure build-up to occur.

With a drum brake, the wheel cylinder expands and pushes the brake shoes against a brake drum. *The distance the shoes move is only about 0.005–0.012 in. (5 to 12 thousandths of an inch) (0.015–0.30 mm).* See Figure 5-6.

With a disc brake, brake fluid pressure pushes on the piston in the caliper a small amount and causes a clamping of the disc brake pads against both sides of a rotor (disc). See Figure 5-7.

The typical distance the pads move is only about 0.001–0.003 in. (1 to 3 thousandths of an inch) (0.025–0.076 mm).

Hydraulic Pressure and Piston Size

If a mechanical force of 100 lb is exerted by the brake pedal pushrod onto a master cylinder piston with 1 sq. in. of surface area, the equation reads as follows:

$$\frac{100 \text{ lb}}{1 \text{ sq. in.}} = 100 \text{ psi}$$

The result in this case is 100 psi of brake system hydraulic pressure. See Figure 5-8.

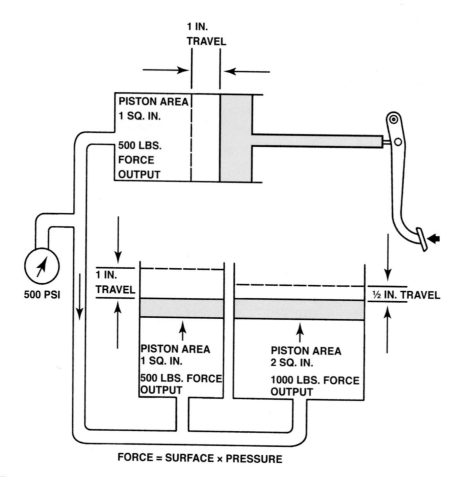

FIGURE 5-5 The amount of force on the piston is the result of pressure multiplied by the surface area.

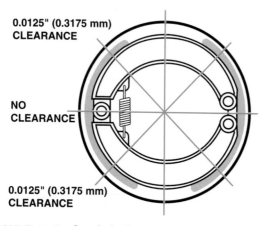

FIGURE 5-6 Drum brake illustrating the typical clearance between the brake shoes (friction material) and the rotating brake drum represented as the outermost black circle.

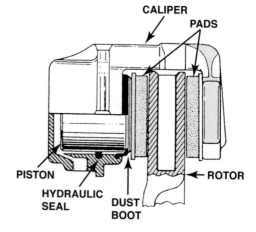

FIGURE 5-7 The brake pad (friction material) is pressed on both sides of the rotating rotor by the hydraulic pressure of the caliper. *(Courtesy of EIS Brake Parts)*

However, if the same 100-lb force is applied to a master cylinder piston with twice the area (2 sq. in.), the equation will read as follows:

$$\frac{100 \text{ lb}}{2 \text{ sq. in.}} = 50 \text{ psi}$$

Doubling the area of the master cylinder piston cuts the hydraulic system pressure in half. Conversely, if the same 100-lb force is applied to a master cylinder piston with only half the area (0.5 or 1/2 sq. in.), the equation will show that the system pressure is doubled:

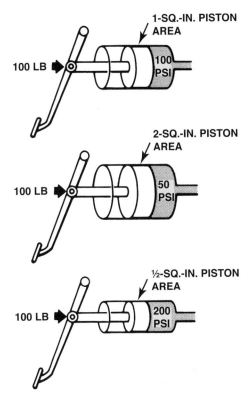

FIGURE 5-8 Mechanical force and the master cylinder piston area determine the hydraulic pressure in the brake system.

$$\frac{100\ \text{lb}}{0.5\ \text{sq. in.}} = 200\ \text{psi}$$

Application Force and Piston Size

While the size of the master cylinder piston affects the hydraulic pressure of the entire brake system, weight shift and bias require that the heavily loaded front brakes receive much higher application force than the lightly loaded rear brakes. These differences in force are obtained by using different-sized pistons in the wheel cylinders and brake calipers. Pascal's law states that a pressurized liquid in a confined space acts with equal pressure on equal *areas* and as long as the pistons in a hydraulic system have the same area, 100 psi from the master cylinder will result in 100 psi of friction assembly application force. See Figure 5-9.

However, when equal pressure acts on *unequal* areas, as with different-sized pistons, the brake application force will differ as well.

The mechanical *force* (F) at the brake pedal pushrod is applied to the master cylinder piston *area* and converted into brake system hydraulic *pressure* (P). Brake calipers and wheel cylinders perform exactly the opposite. Hydraulic *pressure* applied to the wheel cylinder or brake caliper piston *area* (A) is converted back into mechanical *force* that is used to apply the

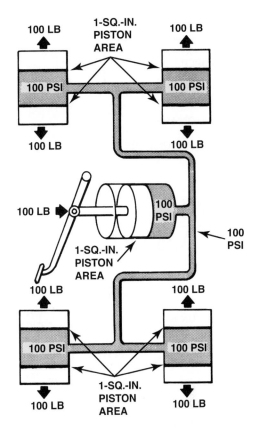

FIGURE 5-9 Hydraulic pressure is the same throughout a closed system and acts with equal force on equal areas.

wheel friction assemblies. Because the variables are identical, the same equation can be rewritten to explain how changes in piston size affect brake application force:

$$p \times A = F$$

It is piston surface *area*, not diameter, that affects force.

In the simple brake system, the pedal and linkage apply a 100-lb force on a master cylinder piston with an area of 1 sq. in. See Figure 5-10.

This results in a pressure of 100 psi throughout the hydraulic system. At the front wheels, the 100 psi is applied to a brake caliper piston that has an area of 4 sq. in. The equation for this example is as follows:

$$100\ \text{psi} \times 4\ \text{sq. in.} = 400\ \text{lb}$$

In this case the difference in piston areas (1 sq. in. compared with 4 sq. in.) results in the 100-psi brake pedal pushrod force being increased for 400 lb of application force at the wheel friction assembly. The hydraulic pressure is still 100 psi at all points within the system and the increase in application pressure is solely the result of 100 psi acting on a 4-sq.-in. piston. The 400 lb is a mechanical force, not hydraulic pressure.

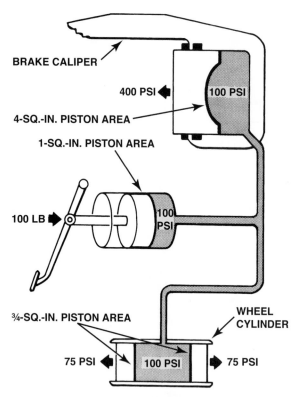

FIGURE 5-10 Differences in brake caliper and wheel cylinder piston area have a major effect on brake application force.

The drum brakes at the rear wheels of the same brake system use wheel cylinders whose pistons have three-quarters (3/4 or 0.75) of an inch of surface area. If the hydraulic system pressure remains 100 psi, the equation for this example is as follows:

$$100 \text{ psi} \times 0.75 \text{ sq. in.} = 75 \text{ lb}$$

Just as larger pistons increase application force, this example shows that smaller pistons decrease it. The system hydraulic pressure remains 100 psi at all points, but the smaller piston is unable to transmit all of the available pressure. As a result, the mechanical application force is reduced to only 75 lb.

Piston Size versus Piston Travel

In disc brakes, the mechanical force available to apply the brakes is four times greater because of the size difference between the master cylinder and caliper pistons. Some of the hydraulic energy is converted into *increased* mechanical force. The tradeoff is that the larger caliper piston with the greater force will not move as far as the smaller master cylinder piston. The amount of hydraulic energy converted into mechanical motion is *decreased*. The relative movement of pistons within the brake system can be calculated with the following equation:

$$\frac{A_1}{A_2} \times S = M$$

where:

 A_1 = the area of the master cylinder piston
 A_2 = the area of the wheel cylinder or caliper piston
 S = the master cylinder piston stroke length
 M = the wheel cylinder or caliper piston movement

Another way to express this equation is as follows:

$$\frac{\text{Area}_1}{\text{Area}_2} \times \text{Stroke} = \text{Movement}$$

In the case of the disc brake example above, the equation would read as follows:

$$\frac{1 \text{ sq. in.}}{4 \text{ sq. in.}} \times 1 \text{ in.} = {}^1\!/_4 \text{in.}$$

The results show that, in this example, if the master cylinder piston stroke is 1 in., the caliper piston will move only 1/4 inch. See Figure 5-11.

If the caliper piston area were reduced to only 2 sq. in., the application force would increase to only 200 lb, but the caliper piston would travel 1/2 inch for a 1 in. master cylinder stroke.

The equation for computing the difference in piston movement works for wheel cylinders as well. In the drum brake example above, the amount of force transmitted by the wheel cylinder is less than the 100 psi that exists within the hydraulic system. If energy cannot be destroyed, the extra 25 psi of pressure must be converted into another form. The equation for this problem reveals where the energy goes:

$$\frac{1 \text{ sq. in.}}{0.75 \text{ sq. in.}} \times 1 \text{ in.} = 1.333 \text{ in.}$$

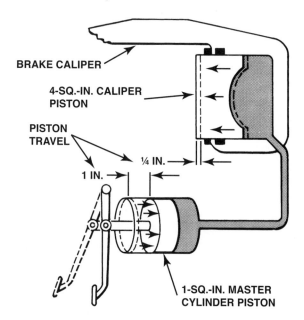

FIGURE 5-11 The increase in application force created by the large brake caliper piston is offset by a decrease in piston travel.

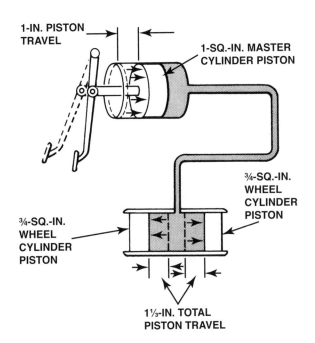

FIGURE 5-12 The decrease in application force created by a small wheel cylinder piston is offset by an increase in piston travel.

The answer shows that if the master cylinder again travels 1 in., the wheel cylinder piston will travel 1.333 in. With a dual-piston wheel cylinder like that shown in Figure 5-12, the total travel is divided between the two pistons.

If the wheel cylinder piston area were reduced to only 0.5 or 1/2 inch, the application force would be further reduced to only 50 lb, but the wheel cylinder piston would travel 2 in. for a 1-in. master cylinder stroke.

Hydraulic Principles and Brake Design

When a brake system is designed, the hydraulic relationships discussed above play a major part in determining the sizes of the many pistons within the system. The piston sizes selected must move enough fluid to operate the wheel cylinder and brake caliper pistons through a wide range of travel, while at the same time they must create enough application force to lock the wheel friction assemblies. The piston sizes chosen should also provide the driver with good brake pedal "feel" so the brakes are easy to apply in a controlled manner.

For example, a very small master cylinder piston can provide a lot of hydraulic pressure with light pedal effort, but it will not move enough fluid to operate brake calipers with large pistons. In addition, a small piston will give the brake pedal a very "touchy" feel that makes modulation difficult and leads to premature brake lockup. A large piston, however, provides less pressure and requires higher pedal effort, but it provides

plenty of fluid volume and results in a less-sensitive pedal feel that makes the brakes easier to control. Most vehicles with disc brakes have large master cylinder pistons to move the required volume of fluid, and a power booster to reduce the required brake pedal force.

MASTER CYLINDERS

The **master cylinder** is the heart of the entire braking system. No braking occurs until the driver depresses the brake pedal. The brake pedal linkage is used to apply the force of the driver's foot into a closed hydraulic system.

Master Cylinder Reservoirs

Most vehicles built since the early 1980s are equipped with see-through master cylinder reservoirs, which permit owners and service technicians to check the brake fluid level without having to remove the top of the reservoir. Some countries have laws that require this type of reservoir. See Figure 5-13.

The reservoir capacity is great enough to allow for the brakes to become completely worn out and still have enough reserve for safe operation. The typical capacity of the entire braking system is usually 2 to 3 pints (1 to 1.5 liters). Vehicles equipped with four-wheel disc brakes usually hold 4 pints (2 liters) or more.

Master Cylinder Reservoir Diaphragm

The entire brake system is filled with brake fluid up to the "full" level of the master cylinder reservoir.

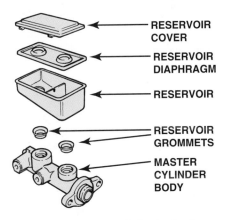

FIGURE 5-13 Typical master cylinder showing the reservoir and associated parts. The reservoir diaphragm lays directly on top of the brake fluid, which helps keep air from the surface of the brake fluid because brake fluid easily absorbs moisture from the air. *(Courtesy of Allied Signal Automotive Aftermarket)*

REAL WORLD FIX

IS BIGGER BETTER?

A vehicle owner wanted better braking performance from his off-road race vehicle. Thinking that a larger master cylinder would help, a technician replaced the original 1-in.-bore-diameter master cylinder with a larger master cylinder with a 1 1/8 in. bore-diameter master cylinder.

After bleeding the system, the technician was anxious to test drive the "new" brake system. During the test drive the technician noticed that the brake pedal "grabbed" much higher than with the original master cylinder. This delighted the technician. The owner of the vehicle was also delighted until he tried to stop from highway speed. *The driver had to use both feet to stop!*

The technician realized, after the complaint, that the larger master cylinder was able to move more brake fluid, but with *less* pressure to the wheel cylinders. The new master cylinder gave the impression of better brakes because the fluid was moved into the wheel cylinders (and calipers) quickly, and the pads and shoes contacted the rotor and drums sooner because of the greater volume of brake fluid moved by the larger pistons in the master cylinder.

To calculate the difference in pressure between the original (stock) master cylinder and the larger replacement, the technician used Pascal's Law with the following results:

Original Master Cylinder (1 in. bore)

$$\text{Pressure} = \frac{\text{Force}}{\text{Area}}$$

$$\text{psi} = \frac{450 \text{ lb}}{\text{Area}} \text{ (typical)}$$

$\text{Area} = \pi r^2 = 3.14 \times .5^2 \text{ (1/2 of 1 in.)}$

$\text{Area} = 3.14 \times .25$

$\text{Area} = .785 \text{ sq. in.}$

$$\text{Pressure} = \frac{450}{.785} = 573 \text{ psi}$$

Replacement Master Cylinder (1 1/8 in. bore)

$$\text{Pressure} = \frac{\text{Force}}{\text{Area}}$$

$$\text{psi} = \frac{450 \text{ lb}}{\text{Area}} \text{ (typical)}$$

$\text{Area} = \pi r^2 = 3.14 \times .5625^2 \text{ (1/2 of 1 1/8 in.)}$

$\text{Area} = 3.14 \times .316$

$\text{Area} = .992 \text{ sq. in.}$

$$\text{Pressure} = \frac{450}{.992} = 454 \text{ psi}$$

The difference in pressure is 119 psi less with the larger master cylinder ($573 - 454 = 119$).

The stopping power of the brakes was reduced because the larger diameter master cylinder piston produced lower pressure (the same force was spread over a larger area and this means that the pressure [psi] is less).

All master cylinders are sized correctly from the factory for the correct braking effort, pressure, pedal travel, and stopping ability. *A technician should never change the sizing of any hydraulic brake component on any vehicle!*

CAUTION: The master cylinder should never be filled higher than the recommended full mark to allow for brake fluid expansion that occurs normally when the brake fluid gets hot due to the heat generated by the brakes.

The reservoir is vented to the atmosphere so the fluid can expand and contract without difficulty as would be the case if the reservoir were sealed.

Being open to the atmosphere, however, allows the possibility of moisture-laden air coming in contact with the brake fluid! This moisture in the air is readily and rapidly absorbed into the brake fluid because brake fluid has an affinity (attraction) to moisture (water).

Master cylinders use a rubber diaphragm or floating disc to help seal outside air from direct contact with brake fluid and still allow the brake fluid to expand and contract as the fluid heats up and cools down during normal brake system operation. This rubber diaphragm is vented between the steel cap and diaphragm. As the brake fluid level drops due to normal disc brake pad wear, the rubber diaphragm also lowers to remain like a second skin on top of the brake fluid.

Whenever adding brake fluid, push the rubber diaphragm back up into the cover. Normal atmospheric pressure will allow the diaphragm to return to its normal position on top of the brake fluid. Whenever servicing a brake system, be sure to check that the vent hole is clear on the cover to allow air to get between the cover and the diaphragm. See Figure 5-14.

VENT PASSAGE AS VIEWED FROM UNDERNEATH COVER

EXTERNAL VENT PASSAGE AS VIEWED FROM OUTSIDE OF COVER

FIGURE 5-14 All master cylinders should have a vent hole on the outside cover that allows air between the cover and the rubber diaphragm.

FIGURE 5-15 Master cylinder with brake fluid level at the "min" (minimum) line.

TECH TIP

DON'T FILL THE MASTER CYLINDER WITHOUT SEEING ME!

The boss explained to the beginning technician that there are two reasons why the customer should be told not to fill the master cylinder reservoir when the brake fluid is down to the "minimum" mark, as shown in Figure 5-15.

1. If the master cylinder reservoir is low, there may be a leak that should be repaired.
2. As the brakes wear, the disc brake piston moves outward to maintain the same distance between friction materials and the rotor. Therefore, as the disc brake pads wear, the brake fluid level goes down to compensate.

If the customer notices that the brake fluid is low in the master cylinder reservoir, the vehicle should be serviced—either for new brakes or to repair a leak.

MASTER CYLINDER OPERATION

The master cylinder is the heart of any hydraulic braking system. Brake pedal movement and force are transferred to the brake fluid and directed to wheel cylinders or calipers. See Figure 5-16.

The master cylinder is also separated into two pressure-building chambers (or circuits) to provide braking force to one-half of the brake in the event of a leak or damage to one circuit. See Figure 5-17.

Both pressure-building sections of the master cylinder contain two holes from the reservoir. The Society of Automotive Engineers' (SAE) term for the forward (tapered) hole is the **vent port,** and the rearward straight drilled hole is called the **replenishing port.** See Figure 5-18.

Various vehicle and brake component manufacturers call these ports by various names. For example, the vent port is the high-pressure port. This tapered forward hole is also called the **compensating port.**

The replenishing port is the low-pressure rearward, larger diameter hole. The inlet port is also called the **bypass port, filler port,** or **breather port.**

The function of the master cylinder can be explained from the at-rest, applied, and released positions.

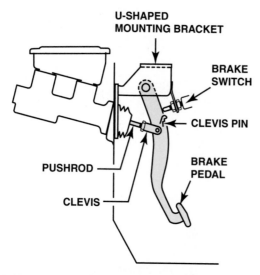

FIGURE 5-16   The typical brake pedal is supported by a mount and attached to the pushrod by a U-shaped bracket. The pin used to retain the clevis to the brake pedal is usually called a clevis pin.

At-Rest Position

The primary sealing cups are between the compensating port hole and the inlet port hole. In this position, the brake fluid is free to expand and move from the calipers, wheel cylinders, and brake lines up into the reservoir through the vent port (compensation port) if the temperature rises and the fluid expands. If the fluid was trapped, the pressure of the brake fluid would increase with temperature, causing the brakes to **self-apply.** See Figure 5-19.

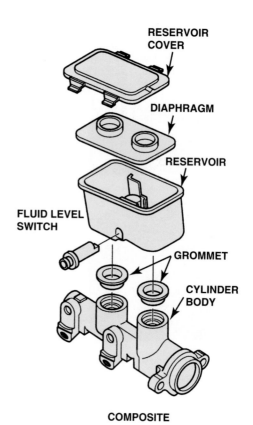

COMPOSITE

FIGURE 5-17   The composite master cylinder is made from two different materials—aluminum for the body and plastic materials for the reservoir and reservoir cover. This type of reservoir feeds both primary and secondary chambers, and therefore uses a fluid level switch that activates the red dash warning lamp if the brake fluid level drops.

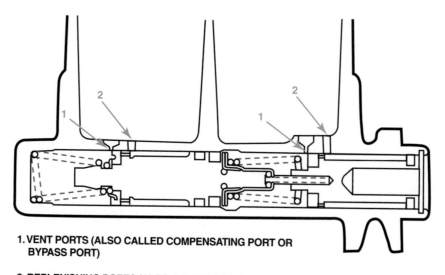

1. VENT PORTS (ALSO CALLED COMPENSATING PORT OR BYPASS PORT)

2. REPLENISHING PORTS (ALSO CALLED INLET PORT, BYPASS PORT, FILLER PORT, OR BREATHER PORT)

FIGURE 5-18   Note the various names for the vent port (front port) and the replenishing port (rear port). Names vary by vehicle and brake component manufacturer. The names vent port and replenishing port are the terms recommended by the Society of Automotive Engineers (SAE).

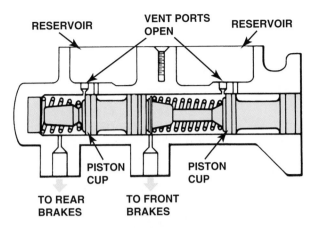

MASTER CYLINDER UNAPPLIED

FIGURE 5-19   The vent ports must remain open to allow brake fluid to expand when heated by the friction material and transferred to the caliper and/or wheel cylinder. As the brake fluid increases in temperature, it expands. The heated brake fluid can expand and flow back into the reservoir through the vent ports.   *(Courtesy of DaimlerChrysler Corporation)*

TECH TIP

TOO MUCH IS BAD

Some vehicle owners or inexperienced service people may fill the master cylinder to the top. Master cylinders should only be filled to the "maximum" level line or about 1/4 in. (6 mm) from the top to allow room for expansion when the brake fluid gets hot during normal operation. If the master cylinder is filled to the top, the expanding brake fluid has no place to expand and the pressure increases. This increased pressure can cause the brakes to "self-apply," shortening brake friction material life and increasing fuel consumption. Overheated brakes can result and the brake fluid may boil, causing a total loss of braking.

The pistons (primary and secondary) are retained by a clip at the push-rod end and held in position by return springs.

Applied Position

When the brake pedal is depressed, the pedal linkage forces the push rod and primary piston down the bore of the master cylinder. See Figure 5-20.

As the piston moves forward, the primary sealing cup covers and blocks off the vent port (compensating port). Hydraulic pressure builds in front of the primary seal as the pushrod moves forward. The back of the piston is kept filled through the replenishing port. See Figure 5-21.

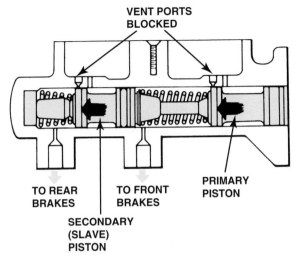

MASTER CYLINDER APPLIED

FIGURE 5-20   As the brake pedal is depressed, the pushrod moves the primary piston forward, closing off the vent port. As soon as the port is blocked, pressure builds in front of the primary sealing cup which pushes on the secondary piston. The secondary piston also moves forward, blocking the secondary vent port and building pressure in front of the sealing cup.   *(Courtesy of DaimlerChrysler Corporation)*

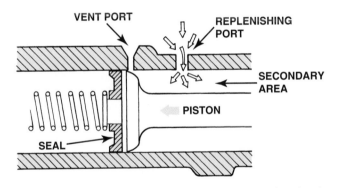

FIGURE 5-21   The purpose of the replenishing port is to keep the volume behind the primary piston filled with brake fluid from the reservoir as the piston moves forward during a brake application.

This stops any suction (vacuum) from forming behind the piston. The secondary piston is moved forward as pressure is exerted by the primary piston. If, for any reason, such as a leak, the primary piston cannot build pressure, a mechanical link on the front of the primary piston will touch the secondary piston and move it forward, as the primary piston is pushed forward by the pushrod and brake pedal.

Released Position

Releasing the brake pedal removes the pressure on the pushrod and master cylinder pistons. A spring on the brake pedal linkage returns the brake pedal to its normal at-rest

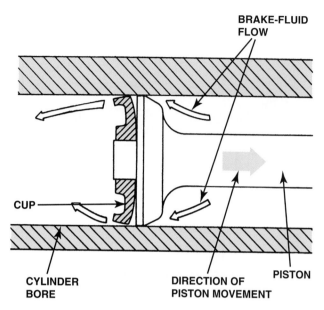

FIGURE 5-22 When the brake pedal is released, the master cylinder piston moves rearward. Some of the brake fluid is pushed back up through the replenishing port, but most of the fluid flows past the sealing cup. Therefore, when the driver pumps the brake pedal, the additional fluid in front of the pressure-building sealing cup is available quickly.

(up) position. The spring in front of the master cylinder piston expands, pushing the pistons rearward. At the same time, pressure is released from the entire braking system and the released brake fluid pressure is exerted on the master cylinder pistons, forcing them rearward. As the piston is pushed back, the lips of the seal fold forward allowing fluid to quickly move past the piston, as shown in Figure 5-22.

Some pistons have small holes that allow the fluid to move more quickly. Once the primary seal passes the vent port, the remaining hydraulic pressure forces any excess fluid into the reservoir.

DUAL SPLIT MASTER CYLINDERS

Dual split master cylinders use two separate pressure-building sections. One section operates the front brakes and the other section operates the rear brakes on vehicles equipped with a front/rear-split system. See Figure 5-23.

The *nose end* of the master cylinder is the closed end toward the front of the vehicle. The open end is often called the *pushrod end* of the master cylinder. See Figure 5-24.

Some manufacturers operate the front brakes (which do the most braking) from the "nose end" section (secondary piston end) of the master cylinder. The secondary piston has only one pressure-building seal. The primary piston (pushrod end) requires two (2) seals to build pressure.

TECH TIP

ALWAYS CHECK FOR VENTING (COMPENSATION)

Whenever diagnosing any braking problem, start the diagnosis at the master cylinder—the heart of any braking system. Remove the reservoir cover and observe the brake fluid for spurting while an assistant depresses the brake pedal.

Normal operation (movement of fluid observed in the reservoir)

There should be a squirt or movement of brake fluid out of the vent port of both the primary and secondary chambers. This indicates that the vent port is open and that the sealing cup is capable of moving fluid upward through the port before the cup seals off the port as it moves forward to pressurize the fluid.

No movement of fluid observed in the reservoir in the primary piston

This indicates that brake fluid is not being moved as the brake pedal is depressed. This can be caused by the following.

a. Incorrect brake pedal height—brake pedal or pushrod adjustment could be allowing the primary piston to be too far forward, causing the seal cup to be forward of the vent port. Adjust the brake pedal height to a higher level and check for a too long pushrod length.

b. A defective or swollen rubber sealing cup on the primary piston could cause the cup itself to block the vent port.

NOTE: If the vent port is blocked for any reason, the brakes of the vehicle may *self-apply* when the brake fluid heats up during normal braking. Since the vent port is blocked, the expanded hotter brake fluid has no place to expand and instead increases the pressure in the brake lines. The increase in pressure causes the brakes to apply. Loosening the bleeder valves and releasing the built-up pressure is a check that the brakes are self-applying. Then check the master cylinder to see if it is "venting."

Therefore, the nose end of the master cylinder is considered the more reliable of the two master cylinder pressure-building sections.

If the rear section of the hydraulic system fails, the primary piston will not build pressure to operate the secondary piston. To permit the operation of the secondary piston (nose end piston) in the event of a hydraulic failure of the rear section, the primary piston extension will mechanically contact and push on the secondary piston. See Figure 5-25.

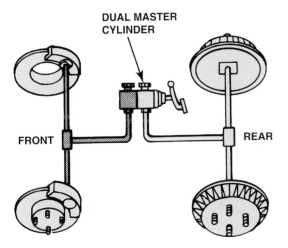

FIGURE 5-23   Rear-wheel-drive vehicles use a dual-split master cylinder.

FIGURE 5-24   The primary outlet is the outlet closest to the pushrod end of the master cylinder and the second outlet is closest to the nose end of the master cylinder.

If there is a failure of the front section hydraulic system, the primary piston (pushrod end) operates normally and exerts pressure on the secondary piston. The secondary piston, however, will not be able to build pressure because of the leak in the system.

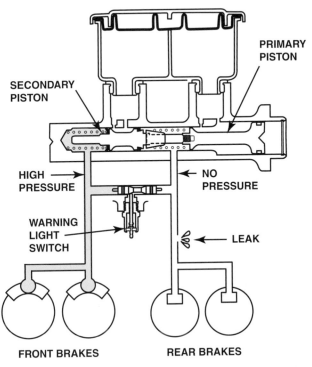

FIGURE 5-25   In the event of a primary system failure, no hydraulic pressure is available to push the second piston forward. As a result, the primary piston extension contacts the secondary piston and pushes on the secondary piston mechanically rather than hydraulically. The loss of pressure in the primary system is usually noticed by the driver by a lower-than-normal brake pedal and the lighting of the red brake warning lamp.

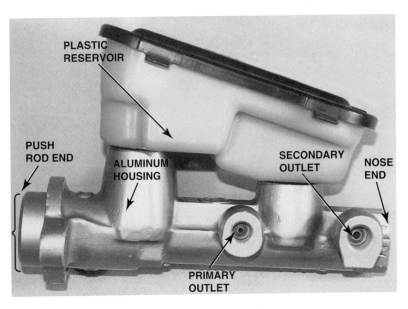

DIAGONAL SPLIT MASTER CYLINDERS

With front-wheel drive vehicles, the weight of the entire power train is on the front wheels and 80% to 90% of the braking force is achieved by the front brakes. This means that only 10% to 20% of the braking force is being handled by the rear brakes. If the front brakes fail, the rear brakes alone would not provide adequate braking force. The solution is the use of a **diagonal split master cylinder.** See Figures 5-26 and 5-27.

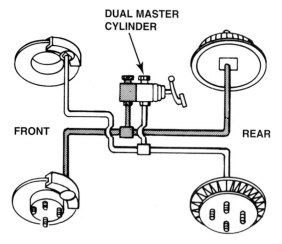

FIGURE 5-26   Front-wheel-drive vehicles use a diagonal split master cylinder. In this design one section of the master cylinder operates the right front and the left rear brake and the other section operates the left front and right rear. In the event of a failure in one section, at least one front brake will still function.

FIGURE 5-27   Typical General Motors diagonal split master cylinder. Notice the two aluminum proportioner valves. These valves limit and control brake fluid pressure to the rear brakes to help eliminate rear wheel lockup during a rapid stop.

In a diagonal split braking system, the left front brake and the right rear brake are on one circuit, and the right front with the left rear is another circuit of the master cylinder. If one circuit fails, the remaining circuit can still stop the vehicle in a reasonable fashion because each circuit has one front brake. To prevent this one front brake from causing the vehicle to pull toward one side during braking, the front suspension is designed with negative scrub radius geometry. This effectively eliminates any handling problem in the event of a brake circuit failure.

QUICK TAKE-UP MASTER CYLINDERS

Many newer vehicles use low drag disc brake calipers to increase fuel economy. However, due to the larger distance between the rotor and the friction pads, excessive brake pedal travel would be required before the pads touched the rotor. The solution to this problem is a master cylinder design that can take up this extra clearance.

The design of a **quick take-up master cylinder** includes a larger diameter primary piston (low-pressure chamber) and a quick take-up valve. This type of master cylinder is also called **dual-diameter bore, step-bore,** or **fast-fill master cylinders.**

A spring-loaded check ball valve holds pressure on the brake fluid in the large diameter rear chamber of the primary piston. When the brakes are first applied, the movement of the rear larger piston forces this larger volume of

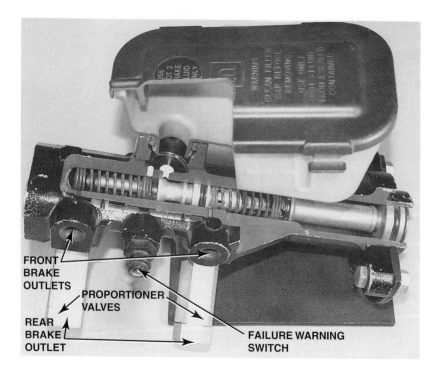

FRONT BRAKE OUTLETS

PROPORTIONER VALVES

REAR BRAKE OUTLET

FAILURE WARNING SWITCH

brake fluid forward past the primary piston seal and into the primary high-pressure chamber. This extra volume of brake fluid "takes up" the extra clearance of the front disc brake calipers without increasing the brake pedal travel distance. See Figure 5-28.

At 70 to 100 psi, the check ball valve in the quick take-up valve allows fluid to return to the brake fluid reservoir. Because the quick take-up "works" until 100 psi is reached, a metering valve is not required to hold back the fluid pressure to the front brakes. See Figures 5-29 through 5-31.

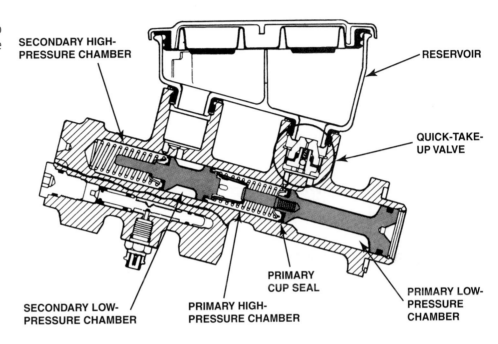

FIGURE 5-28 Quick take-up master cylinder can be identified by the oversize primary low-pressure chamber.

SECONDARY HIGH-PRESSURE CHAMBER

RESERVOIR

QUICK-TAKE-UP VALVE

PRIMARY CUP SEAL

PRIMARY LOW-PRESSURE CHAMBER

SECONDARY LOW-PRESSURE CHAMBER

PRIMARY HIGH-PRESSURE CHAMBER

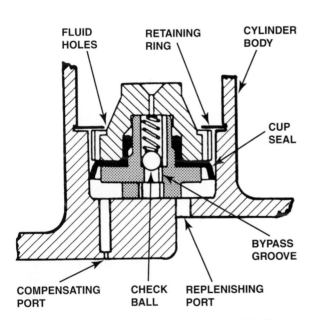

FLUID HOLES

RETAINING RING

CYLINDER BODY

CUP SEAL

BYPASS GROOVE

COMPENSATING PORT

CHECK BALL

REPLENISHING PORT

FIGURE 5-29 The quick take-up valve controls fluid flow to and from the primary low-pressure chamber.

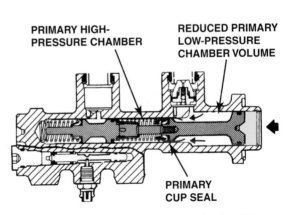

PRIMARY HIGH-PRESSURE CHAMBER

REDUCED PRIMARY LOW-PRESSURE CHAMBER VOLUME

PRIMARY CUP SEAL

FIGURE 5-30 As the brakes are applied, reduced low-pressure chamber volume results in a pressure increase that causes fluid to bypass the primary cup seal.

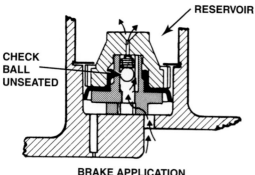

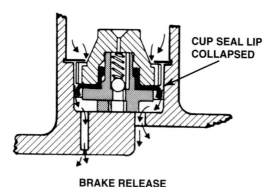

FIGURE 5-31   The one-way sealing abilities of both a spring-loaded check ball and a cup seal are used in the quick take-up valve.

THE BRAKE PEDAL DEPRESSOR TRICK

The master cylinder can be used to *block* the flow of brake fluid. Whenever any hydraulic brake component is removed, brake fluid tends to leak out because the master cylinder is usually higher than most other hydraulic components such as wheel cylinders and calipers.

To prevent brake fluid loss that can easily empty the master cylinder reservoir, simply *depress* the brake pedal slightly or prop a stick or other pedal depressor to keep the brake pedal down. When the brake pedal is depressed, the piston sealing cups move forward, blocking off the reservoir from the rest of the braking system. The master cylinder stays full and the brake fluid stops dripping out of brake lines that have been disconnected. See Figure 5-32.

NOTE: Try this—put a straw into a glass of water. Use a finger to seal the top of the straw and then remove the straw from the glass of water. The water remains in the straw because air cannot get into the top of the straw. This is why the brake pedal depressor trick works to prevent the loss of brake fluid from the system even if the brake line is totally disconnected.

DIAGNOSING AND TROUBLESHOOTING MASTER CYLINDERS

A thorough visual inspection is important when inspecting any master cylinder. The visual inspection should include checking the following items:

1. Check the brake fluid for proper level and condition. (Brake fluid should not be rusty, thick, or contaminated.)
2. Check that the vent holes in the reservoir cover are open and clean.
3. Check that the reservoir cover diaphragm is not torn or enlarged.

NOTE: If the cover diaphragm is enlarged, this is an indication that a mineral oil, such as automatic transmission fluid or engine oil, has been used in or near the brake system, because rubber that is brake fluid resistant expands when exposed to mineral oil.

FIGURE 5-32   A brake pedal depressor like this, normally used during a wheel alignment, can be used to block the flow of brake fluid from the master cylinder during service work on the hydraulic system.

4. Check for any external leaks at the lines or at the pushrod area. See Figure 5-33.

   After a thorough visual inspection, check for proper operation of **pedal height, pedal free play,** and **pedal reserve distance.** See Figures 5-34 and 5-35.

Proper brake pedal height is important for the proper operation of the stop (brake) light switch. If the pedal is not correct, the pushrod may be in too far forward, preventing the master cylinder cups from uncovering the compensation port. If the pedal is too high, the free play will be excessive. Pedal reserve height is easily checked by depressing the brake pedal with the right foot and attempting to slide your left foot under the brake pedal. See Figure 5-36.

Free play is the distance the brake pedal travels before the primary piston in the master cylinder moves. *Most vehicles*

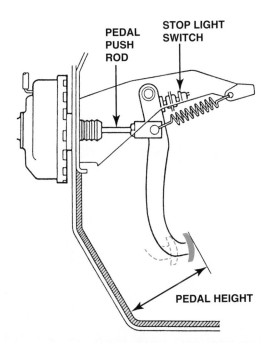

FIGURE 5-33 Some seepage is normal when a trace of fluid appears on the vacuum booster shell. Excessive leakage, however, indicates a leaking secondary (end) seal. *(Courtesy of Ford Motor Company)*

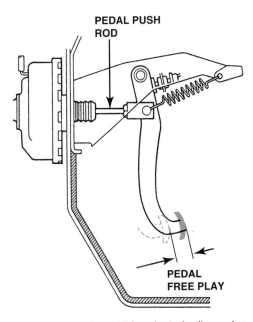

FIGURE 5-35 Brake pedal free play is the distance between the brake pedal fully released and the position of the brake pedal when braking resistance is felt. *(Courtesy of Toyota Motor Sales, U.S.A., Inc.)*

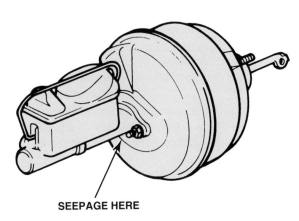

FIGURE 5-34 Pedal height is usually measured from the floor to the top of the brake pedal. Some vehicle manufacturers recommend removing the carpet and measure from the asphalt matting on the floor for an accurate measurement. Always follow the manufacturer's recommended procedures and measurements. *(Courtesy of Toyota Motor Sales, U.S.A., Inc.)*

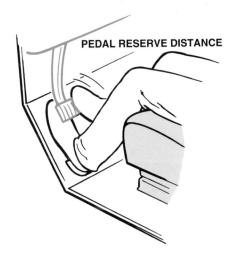

FIGURE 5-36 Brake pedal reserve is usually specified as the measurement from the floor to the top of the brake pedal with the brakes applied. A quick-and-easy test of pedal reserve is to try to place your left toe underneath the brake pedal while the brake pedal is depressed with your right foot. If your toe will *not* fit, then pedal reserve *may* not be sufficient.

require brake pedal free play between 1/8 to 1 1/2 in. (3 to 38 mm). Too little or too much free play can cause braking problems that can be mistakenly contributed to a defective master cylinder.

Spongy Brake Pedal

A spongy pedal with a larger than normal travel indicates air in the lines. Check for leaks and bleed the air from the system as discussed later in this chapter.

Lower Than Normal Brake Pedal

A brake pedal that travels downward more than normal and then gets firm is an indication that one circuit of the dual-circuit hydraulic system is probably not working. Check for leaks in the system and repair as necessary. Another possible reason is an out-of-adjustment drum brake allowing too much pedal travel before the shoes touch the brake drum.

NOTE: A lower than normal brake pedal may also be an indication of air in the hydraulic system.

Sinking Brake Pedal

If the brake pedal sinks all the way to the floor, suspect a defective master cylinder that is leaking internally. This internal leakage is often called **bypassing** because the brake fluid is leaking past the sealing cup. See the Tech Tip, "Check for Bypassing" later in this chapter.

NOTE: A sinking brake pedal, on a vehicle equipped with an antilock braking system (ABS), could be caused by a defective dump valve. See Chapter 20 for details.

DISASSEMBLY OF THE MASTER CYLINDER

Many master cylinders can be disassembled, cleaned, and restored to service.

NOTE: Check the vehicle manufacturer's recommendation before attempting to overhaul or service a master cylinder. Many manufacturers recommend replacing the master cylinder as an assembly.

Step 1   Remove the master cylinder from the vehicle, being careful to avoid dripping or spilling brake fluid onto painted surfaces of the vehicle. Dispose of all old brake fluid and clean the outside of the master cylinder.

Step 2   Remove the reservoir, if possible, as shown in Figure 5-37.

Step 3   Remove the retaining bolt that holds the secondary piston assembly in the bore.

Step 4   Depress the primary piston with a *blunt* tool such as a Phillips screwdriver, a rounded wooden dowel, or an engine pushrod. Use of a straight blade screwdriver or other nonrounded tool can damage and distort the aluminum piston.

CAUTION: If holding the master cylinder in a vise, use the flange area. Never clamp the body of the master cylinder.

Step 5   Remove the snap ring and slowly release the pressure on the depressing tool. Spring pressure should push the primary piston out of the cylinder bore. See Figure 5-38.

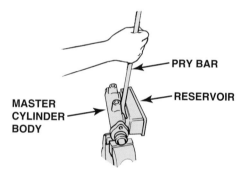

FIGURE 5-37   Using a pry bar to remove the reservoir from the master cylinder. *(Courtesy of Allied Signal Automotive Aftermarket)*

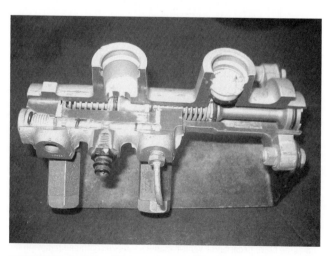

FIGURE 5-38   Whenever disassembling a master cylinder, note the exact order of parts as they are removed. Master cylinder overhaul kits (when available) often include entire piston assemblies rather than the individual seals.

Step 6   Remove the master cylinder from the vise and tap the open end of the bore against the top of a workbench to force the secondary piston out of the bore. If necessary, use compressed air in the outlet to force the piston out.

CAUTION: Use extreme care when using compressed air. The piston can be shot out of the master cylinder with a great force.

INSPECTION AND REASSEMBLY OF THE MASTER CYLINDER

Inspect the master cylinder bore for pitting, corrosion, or wear. Most cast iron master cylinders cannot be honed because of the special bearingized surface finish that is applied to the bore during manufacturing. Slight corrosion or surface flaws can usually be removed with a hone or crocus cloth. Otherwise, the master cylinder should be replaced as an assembly. Always follow the recommended procedures for the vehicle being serviced.

Aluminum master cylinders cannot be honed. Aluminum master cylinders have an anodized surface coating applied that is hard and wear resistant. Honing would remove this protective coating. See Figure 5-39.

Thoroughly clean the master cylinder and any other parts to be reused (except for rubber components) in clean denatured alcohol. If the bore is okay, replacement **piston assemblies** can be installed into the master cylinder after dipping them into clean brake fluid.

NOTE: While most master cylinder overhaul kits include the entire piston assemblies, some kits just contain the sealing cups and/or O-rings. Always follow the installation instructions that accompany the kit and always use the installation tool that is included to prevent damage to the replacement seals.

Step 1   Install the secondary (smaller) piston assembly into the bore, spring end first. See Figure 5-40.

Step 2   Install the primary piston assembly, spring end first.

Step 3   Depress the primary piston and install the snap ring.

Step 4   Install the stop bolt.

Step 5   Reinstall the plastic reservoir, if equipped, as shown in Figure 5-41.

Step 6   Bench bleed the master cylinder. This step is very important. See Figure 5-42.

FIGURE 5-39   Nylon brush used to clean the bore of aluminum master cylinders by a national remanufacturer. The soft nylon will not harm the anodized surface coating.

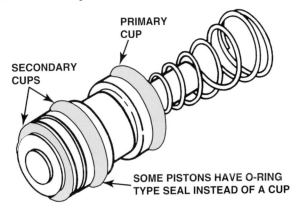

FIGURE 5-40   Piston assembly. *(Courtesy of Allied Signal Automotive Aftermarket)*

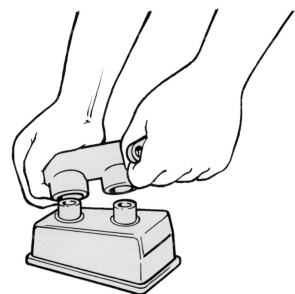

FIGURE 5-41   To reinstall the reservoir onto a master cylinder, place the reservoir on a clean flat surface and push the housing down onto the reservoir after coating the rubber seals with brake fluid. *(Courtesy of Allied Signal Automotive Aftermarket)*

FIGURE 5-42 Bleeding a master cylinder before installing it on the vehicle. The master cylinder is clamped into a bench vise while using the rounded end of a breaker bar to push on the pushrod end with bleeder tubes down into the brake fluid. Master cylinders should be clamped on the mounting flange as shown to prevent distorting the master cylinder bore.

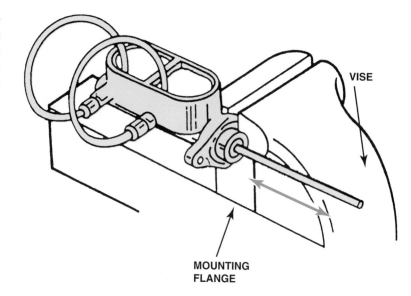

VISE

MOUNTING
FLANGE

TECH TIP

CHECK FOR BYPASSING

If a master cylinder is leaking internally, brake fluid can be pumped from the rear chamber into the front chamber of the master cylinder. This internal leakage is called **bypassing**. When the fluid bypasses, the front chamber can overflow while emptying the rear chamber. Therefore, whenever checking the level of brake fluid, do not think that a low rear reservoir is always due to an external leak. Also, a master cylinder that is bypassing (leaking internally) will usually cause a lower than normal brake pedal.

Tighten the fasteners to factory specifications. See Figure 5-43. Bleed the system as needed. See Chapter 8 for details on brake bleeding.

INSTALLING THE MASTER CYLINDER

After the master cylinder has been bench bled, it can be installed in the vehicle.

NOTE: Brake fluid can drip from the outlet of the master cylinder and could drip onto the vehicle. Brake fluid is very corrosive and can remove paint. Use fender covers and avoid letting brake fluid touch any component of the vehicle.

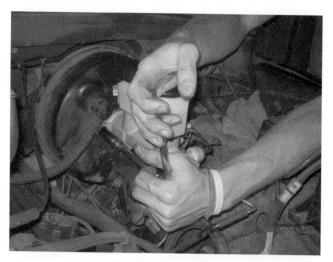

FIGURE 5-43 Installing a master cylinder. Always tighten the retaining fastener and brake lines to factory specifications.

SUMMARY

1. During a typical brake application, only about 1 teaspoon (5 ml or cc) of brake fluid actually is moved from the master cylinder and into the hydraulic system.
2. Pascal's Law states that: "When a force is applied to a liquid confined in a container or enclosure, the pressure is transmitted equally and undiminished in every direction."
3. Master cylinder reservoirs are large enough for the brakes to be worn completely down and still have a small reserve.
4. The front port of the master cylinder is called the compensating port and the rear port is called the inlet port.
5. Brake system diagnosis should always start with checking for venting (compensation).

6. Dual split master cylinders that separate the front brakes from the rear brakes are used on rear-wheel-drive vehicles.
7. Diagonal split master cylinders that separate right front and left rear from the left front and right rear brakes are used on front-wheel-drive vehicles.
8. Some master cylinders can be rebuilt, but the cylinder bore should not be honed unless recommended by the manufacturer.

REVIEW QUESTIONS

1. Explain Pascal's Law.
2. Describe how a master cylinder works.
3. Discuss the difference between a dual split and a diagonal split master cylinder.
4. What is the difference between checking for venting (compensation) and bypassing?

CHAPTER QUIZ

1. Two technicians are discussing master cylinders. Technician A says that it is normal to see fluid movement in the reservoir when the brake pedal is depressed. Technician B says a defective master cylinder can cause the brake pedal to slowly sink to the floor when depressed. Which technician is correct?
   a. Technician A only
   b. Technician B only
   c. Both Technicians A and B
   d. Neither Technician A nor B

2. If the brake pedal linkage is not adjusted correctly, brake fluid may not be able to expand back into the reservoir through the _____ port of the master cylinder when the brakes get hot.
   a. Vent port (forward hole)
   b. Replenishing port (rearward hole)

3. The primary brake circuit fails due to a leak in the lines, leaving the rear section of a dual split master cylinder. Technician A says that the driver will notice a lower than normal brake pedal and some reduced braking power. Technician B says that the brake pedal will "grab" higher than normal. Which technician is correct?
   a. Technician A only
   b. Technician B only
   c. Both Technicians A and B
   d. Neither Technician A nor B

4. Two technicians are discussing a problem where the brake pedal travels too far before the vehicle starts to slow. Technician A says that the brakes may be out of adjustment. Technician B says that one circuit from the master cylinder may be leaking or defective. Which technician is correct?
   a. Technician A only
   b. Technician B only
   c. Both Technicians A and B
   d. Neither Technician A nor B

5. Air in the lines will cause what type of problem?

   a. Vibration in the brake pedal during stops

   b. Low spongy brake pedal

   c. Brake noise

   d. Hard brake pedal

6. The master cylinder is able to move about how much brake fluid during each brake application?

   a. One tablespoon

   b. One teaspoon

   c. One cu. in.

   d. 50 ml

7. Brake fluid pressure is measured in what unit?

   a. Sq. in.

   b. Pounds

   c. Inches

   d. psi

8. How much brake fluid is in a typical master cylinder reservoir?

   a. One gallon

   b. Enough to allow all brakes to become completely worn

   c. 15 to 20 liters

   d. One pint

9. What part in the master cylinder helps keep air from contacting the brake fluid yet allows the fluid level to drop as the disc brakes wear?

   a. Vent valve

   b. Compensating valve

   c. Residual valve

   d. Rubber diaphragm or floating disc

10. The brakes on a vehicle work okay for a while, then the vehicle slows because the brakes self-applied. Technician A says that an overfilled master cylinder could be the cause. Technician B says that a blocked vent port (compensating port) could be the cause. Which technician is correct?

   a. Technician A only

   b. Technician B only

   c. Both Technicians A and B

   d. Neither Technician A nor B

CHAPTER 6

HYDRAULIC VALVES AND SWITCHES

OBJECTIVES

After studying Chapter 6, the reader should be able to:

1. Prepare for the Brakes (A5) ASE certification test content area "A" (Hydraulic System Diagnosis and Repair).
2. Describe the operation of a residual check valve.
3. Explain how a proportioning valve works.
4. Discuss the need and use of a metering valve.
5. List testing procedures used to test hydraulic valves.
6. Describe how the brake fluid level and brake light switches work.

KEY TERMS

RESIDUAL CHECK VALVE

A **residual check valve** has been used on some drum brake systems to keep a slight amount of pressure on the entire hydraulic system for drum brakes (5 to 12 psi). See Figure 6-1.

This residual check valve is located in the master cylinder at the outlet for the drum brakes. The check ball and spring in the residual check valve permit all the brake fluid to return to the master cylinder until the designated pressure is reached.

This slight pressure prevents air leaks from entering into the hydraulic system in the event of a small hole or leak. With a low pressure kept on the hydraulic system, any small hole will cause fluid to leak out rather than permit air to enter the system. This slight pressure also keeps the wheel cylinder sealing cups tight against the inside wall of the wheel cylinder. See Figure 6-2.

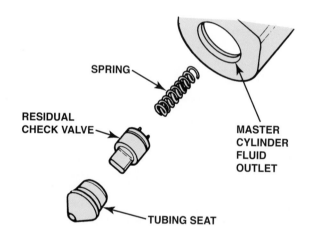

FIGURE 6-1 Most residual check valves are located under the tubing seals in the master cylinder outlet ports.

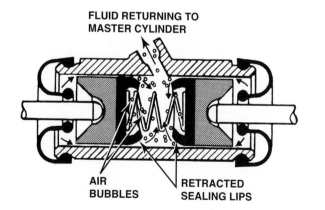

FIGURE 6-2 The momentary drop in pressure created when the brakes are released can draw air into the hydraulic system.

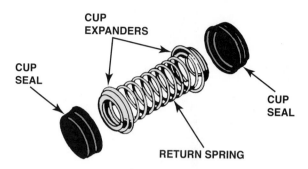

FIGURE 6-3 The use of cup expanders is the main reason why residual check valves are not used in most braking systems today.

Residual check valves are often *not* used on late model vehicles equipped with front disc/rear drum brakes. The residual check valve has been eliminated by equipping the wheel cylinder internal spring with a sealing cup **expander** to prevent sealing cup lip collapse. See Figure 6-3.

PRESSURE-DIFFERENTIAL SWITCH (BRAKE WARNING SWITCH)

A **pressure-differential switch** is used on all vehicles built after 1967 with dual master cylinders to warn the driver of a loss of pressure in one of the two separate systems by lighting the dashboard red brake warning indicator lamp. See Figures 6-4 and 6-5.

The brake lines from both the front and the rear sections of the master cylinder are sent to this switch, which lights the brake warning indicator lamp in the event of a "difference in pressure" between the two sections. See Figure 6-6.

A failure in one part of the brake system does not result in a failure of the entire hydraulic system. After the hydraulic system has been repaired and bled, moderate pressure on the brake pedal will center the piston in the switch and turn off the warning lamp.

If the lamp remains on, it may be necessary to do the following:

1. Apply light pressure to the brake pedal.
2. Momentarily open the bleeder valve on the side that did not have the failure.

This procedure should center the pressure-differential switch valve in those vehicles that are not equipped with self-centering springs. See Figure 6-7.

FIGURE 6-4   A red brake warning lamp.

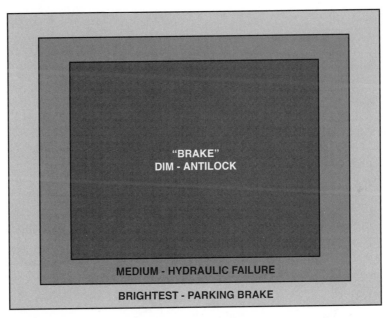

"BRAKE"
DIM - ANTILOCK

MEDIUM - HYDRAULIC FAILURE

BRIGHTEST - PARKING BRAKE

FIGURE 6-5   Most red brake warning lamps indicate only hydraulic or brake fluid level. However, some, such as those on older General Motors light trucks, can indicate ABS, parking, or hydraulic failure depending on their brightness. This can be confusing to vehicle owners as well as technicians, especially if the brightness level is not noticed.

BRAKE FLUID LEVEL SENSOR SWITCH

Many master cylinders, especially systems that are a diagonal split, usually use a **brake fluid level sensor** or switch in the master cylinder reservoir. This sensor will light the red "brake" warning lamp on the dash if low brake fluid level is detected. A float-type sensor or a magnetic reed switch are commonly used and provide a complete electrical circuit when the brake fluid level is low. After refilling the master cylinder reservoir to the correct level, the red "brake" warning lamp should go out. See Figures 6-8 and 6-9 on page 105.

BRAKE MALFUNCTION

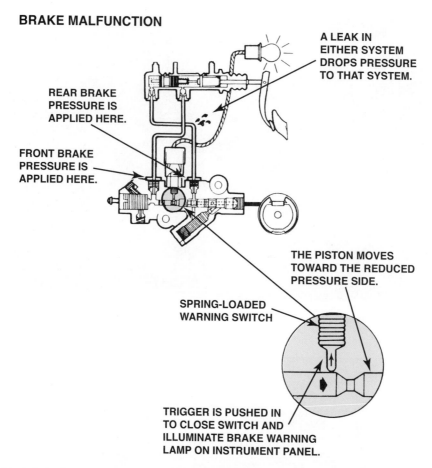

A LEAK IN EITHER SYSTEM DROPS PRESSURE TO THAT SYSTEM.

REAR BRAKE PRESSURE IS APPLIED HERE.

FRONT BRAKE PRESSURE IS APPLIED HERE.

THE PISTON MOVES TOWARD THE REDUCED PRESSURE SIDE.

SPRING-LOADED WARNING SWITCH

TRIGGER IS PUSHED IN TO CLOSE SWITCH AND ILLUMINATE BRAKE WARNING LAMP ON INSTRUMENT PANEL.

FIGURE 6-6 A leak in the hydraulic system causes unequal pressures between the two different brake circuits. This difference in pressures causes the plunger inside the pressure-differential switch to move, which completes the electrical circuit for the red brake warning lamp. *(Courtesy of Ford Motor Company)*

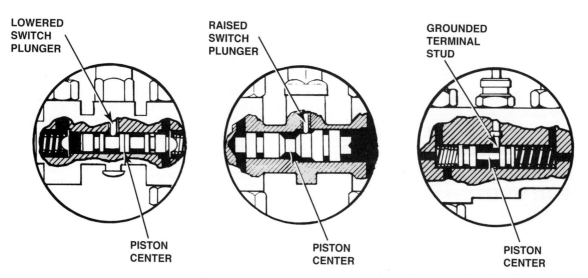

LOWERED SWITCH PLUNGER

RAISED SWITCH PLUNGER

GROUNDED TERMINAL STUD

PISTON CENTER

PISTON CENTER

PISTON CENTER

FIGURE 6-7 The pressure-differential switch piston is used to provide the electrical ground for the red brake warning light circuit.

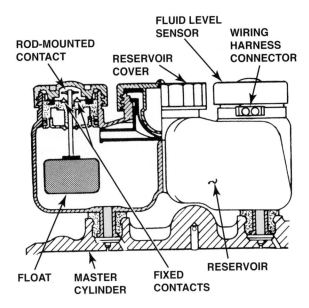

FIGURE 6-8 A movable contact brake fluid level switch.

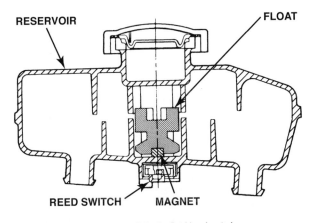

FIGURE 6-9 A magnetic brake fluid level switch.

DIAGNOSING A RED "BRAKE" DASH WARNING LAMP

Activation of the red brake dash warning lamp can be for any one of several reasons:

1. Parking Brake "On." The same dash warning lamp is used to warn the driver that the parking brake is on.
2. Low Brake Fluid. This lights the red dash warning lamp on vehicles equipped with a master cylinder reservoir brake fluid level switch.
3. Unequal Brake Pressure. The pressure-differential switch is used on most vehicles with a front/rear brake split system to warn the driver whenever there is low brake pressure to either the front or rear brakes.

NOTE: Brake systems use *either* a pressure-differential switch *or* a low brake fluid switch to light the dash red "brake" lamp, but not both.

The most likely cause of the red "brake" warning lamp being on is low brake fluid caused by a leaking brake line, wheel cylinder, or caliper. Therefore, the first step in diagnosis is to determine the cause of the lamp being on, then to repair the problem.

Step 1   *Check the Level of the Brake Fluid.* If low, carefully inspect the entire hydraulic brake system for leaks and repair as necessary.

Step 2   *Disconnect the Wire from the Pressure-Differential Switch.* If the lamp is still "on," the problem is due to the parking brake lever switch being "on" or grounded, or the wire going to the switch is shorted to ground. If the red brake warning lamp is "off" after being disconnected from the pressure-differential switch, then the problem is due to a hydraulic failure (a low pressure in either the front or the rear system that creates a difference in pressure of at least 150 psi).

NOTE: Many Japanese vehicles energize the relay that turns off the red "brake" warning lamp from the output terminal of the alternator. If a quick inspection of the brake system seems to indicate that everything is okay, check for correct charging voltage before continuing a more detailed brake system inspection.

PROPORTIONING VALVE

A **proportioning valve** improves brake balance during hard stops by limiting hydraulic pressure to the rear brakes. See Figure 6-10.

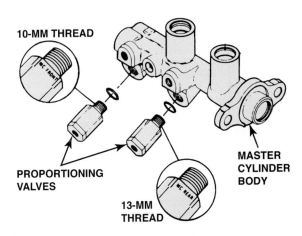

FIGURE 6-10 Many proportioning valves are mounted directly to the master cylinder in the outlet to the rear brakes.

A proportioning valve is necessary because inertia creates weight shift toward the front of the vehicle during braking. The weight shift unloads the rear axle, which reduces traction between the tires and the road, and limits the amount of stopping power that can be delivered. Unless application pressure to the rear wheels is limited, the brakes will lock, making the vehicle unstable and likely to spin. The best overall braking performance is achieved when the front brakes lock just before the rear brakes.

Vehicles with front disc and rear drum brakes require a proportioning valve for two reasons:

1. Disc brakes require higher hydraulic pressure for a given stop than do drum brakes. In a disc/drum system, the front brakes always need more pressure than the rear brakes.
2. Once braking has begun, drum brakes require less pressure to *maintain* a fixed level of stopping power than they did to *establish* that level. In a disc/drum system, the rear brakes will always need less pressure than the front brakes.

A proportioning valve is used to compensate for these differences because it is easier to reduce pressure to the rear brakes than to increase pressure to the front brakes.

The proportioning valve does not work at all times. During light or moderate braking, there is insufficient weight transfer to make rear wheel locking a problem. Before proportioning action will begin, brake system hydraulic pressure must reach a minimum level called the **split point**. Below the split point full system pressure is supplied to the rear brakes. See Figure 6-11.

Above the split point, the proportioning valve allows only a portion of the pressure through to the rear brakes.

The proportioning valve gets its name from the fact that it regulates pressure to the rear brakes *in proportion* to the pressure applied to the front brakes. Once system hydraulic pressure exceeds the split point, the rear brakes receive a fixed percentage of any further increase in pressure. Brake engineers refer to the ratio of front to rear brake pressure proportioning as the **slope.** Full system pressure to the rear brakes equals a slope of 1, but if only half the pressure is allowed to reach the rear brakes, the proportioning valve is said to have a slope of 0.50. The proportioning valves on most vehicles have a slope between 0.25 and 0.50. See Figures 6-12 and 6-13.

Proportioning Valve Operation

A simple proportioning valve consists of a spring-loaded piston that slides in a stepped bore. See Figure 6-14.

The piston is exposed to pressure on both sides. The smaller end of the piston is acted on by pressure from the master cylinder, while the larger end reacts to pressure in the rear brake circuit. The actual proportioning valve is located in the center of the piston and is opened or closed depending on the position of the piston in the stepped bore.

When the brakes are first applied, hydraulic pressure passes through the proportioning valve to the rear brakes. Hy-

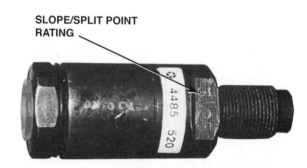

FIGURE 6-12   A Chrysler proportioning valve. Note that slope and split point are stamped on the housing.

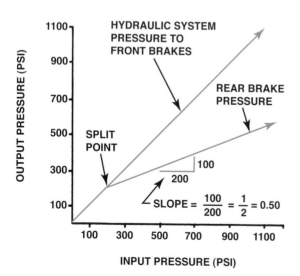

FIGURE 6-11   Typical proportioner valve pressure relationship. Note that, at low pressures, the pressure is the same to the rear brakes as is applied to the front brakes. After the split point, only a percentage (called the slope) of the master cylinder pressure is applied to the rear brakes.

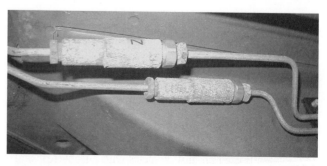

FIGURE 6-13   These two proportioning valves are found under the vehicle on this Dodge minivan.

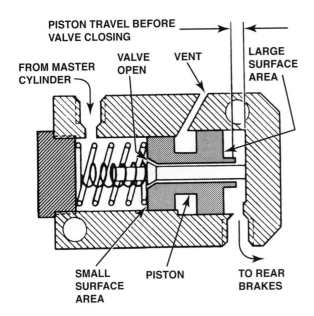

FIGURE 6-14 The proportioning valve piston can travel within the range shown without reducing pressure to the rear brakes.

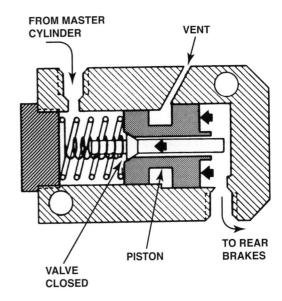

FIGURE 6-15 At the split point, the proportioning valve piston closes the fluid passage through the valve.

draulic pressure is the same on both sides of the piston, but because the side facing the rear brakes has more surface area than the side facing the master cylinder, greater force is developed and the piston moves to the left against the spring tension. At pressures below the split point, the proportioning valve is open, and pressure to both the front and rear brakes is the same.

As the vehicle is braked harder, increased system pressure forces the piston so far to the left that the proportioning valve is closed. See Figure 6-15.

This seals off the brake line and prevents any additional pressure from reaching the rear brakes. The pressure at the moment the proportioning valve first closes is the split point of the valve. From this point on, the rear brakes receive only a portion of the pressure supplied to the front brakes.

As system pressure (the pressure to the front brakes) increases, enough force is developed on the master cylinder side of the piston to overcome the pressure trapped in the rear brake circuit. This forces the piston back to the right and opens the proportioning valve. Some of the higher pressure enters the rear brake circuit, but before pressure in the two circuits can equalize, the force developed on the larger piston area in the rear circuit moves the piston back to the left and closes the valve. The difference in surface area between the two ends of the piston determines the slope of the valve, and thus the percentage of system pressure allowed to reach the rear brakes.

As long as system pressure continues to increase, the piston will repeatedly cycle back and forth, opening and closing the proportioning valve, and maintaining a fixed proportion of full system pressure to the rear brakes. When the brakes are released, the spring returns the piston all the way to the right, which opens the valve and allows fluid to pass in both directions.

TECH TIP

ALWAYS INSPECT BOTH FRONT AND REAR BRAKES

If a vehicle tends to lock up the rear brakes during a stop, many technicians may try to repair the problem by replacing the proportioning valve or servicing the rear brakes. Proportioning valves are simple spring-loaded devices that are usually trouble free. If the rear brakes lock up during braking, carefully inspect the rear brakes looking for contaminated linings or other problems that can cause the rear brakes to grab. Do not stop there—always inspect the front brakes, too. If the front brakes are rusted or corroded, they cannot operate efficiently and greater force must be exerted by the driver to stop the vehicle. Even if the proportioning valve is functioning correctly, the higher brake pedal pressure by the driver could easily cause the rear brakes to lock up.

A locked wheel has less traction with the road than a rotating wheel. As a result, if the rear wheels become locked, the rear of the vehicle often "comes around" or "fishtails," causing the vehicle to skid. Careful inspection of the *entire* braking system is required to be assured of a safe vehicle.

HEIGHT-SENSING PROPORTIONING VALVES

Many vehicles use a proportioning valve that varies the amount of pressure that can be sent to the rear brakes depending on the height of the rear suspension. This type of valve is called a **height-sensing proportioning valve**. If the vehicle is lightly loaded, the rear suspension is high, especially during braking. In this case, the amount of pressure allowed to the rear brakes is reduced. This *helps* prevent rear wheel lockup and possible skidding. Besides, a lightly loaded vehicle requires less braking force to stop than a heavily loaded vehicle.

When the vehicle is loaded, the rear suspension is forced downward. The lever on the proportioning valve moves and allows a greater pressure to be sent to the rear brakes. See Figures 6-16 and 6-17. This greater pressure allows the rear brakes to achieve more braking force, helping to slow a heavier vehicle. When a vehicle is heavily loaded in the rear, the chances of rear wheel lockup are reduced.

CAUTION: Some vehicle manufacturers warn that service technicians should never install replacement air lift shock absorbers or springs that may result in a vehicle height difference than specified by the vehicle manufacturer.

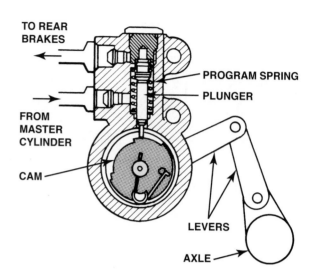

FIGURE 6-17   A stepped cam is used to alter the split point of this height-sensing proportioning valve.

PROPORTIONING VALVE ADJUSTMENT

Height-sensing proportioning valves should be adjusted when replaced. The proper adjustment ensures that the proper pressure is applied to the rear brakes in relation to the loading of the vehicle.

Procedures vary from one vehicle to another. Always consult the factory service information for the exact procedure. Some trucks require the use of special plastic gauges available from the dealer.

PROPORTIONING VALVE DIAGNOSIS AND TESTING

A defective proportioning valve usually allows rear brake pressure to increase too rapidly, causing the rear wheels to lock up during hard braking. When the rear brakes become locked, the traction with the road surface decreases and the vehicle often skids. Whenever rear brakes tend to lock during braking, the proportioning valve should be checked for proper operation. If the proportioning valve is height sensing, verify the proper vehicle ride (trim) height and adjustment of the operating lever. See Figure 6-18.

Pressure gauges can also be used to check for proper operation. Install one gauge into the brake line from the master cylinder and the second gauge to the rear brake outlet of the proportioning valve. While an assistant depresses the brake pedal, observe the two gauges. Both gauges should register an increasing pressure as the brake pedal is depressed until the split point. After the split point, the gauge connected to the proportioning valve (rear brakes) should increase at a slower

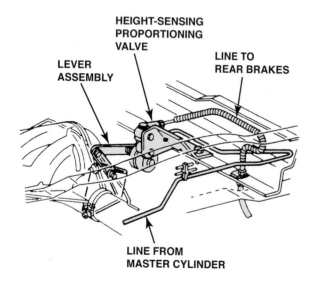

FIGURE 6-16   A height-sensing proportioning valve provides the vehicle with variable brake balance. The valve allows higher pressure to be applied to the rear brakes when the vehicle is heavily loaded and less pressure when the vehicle is lightly loaded.

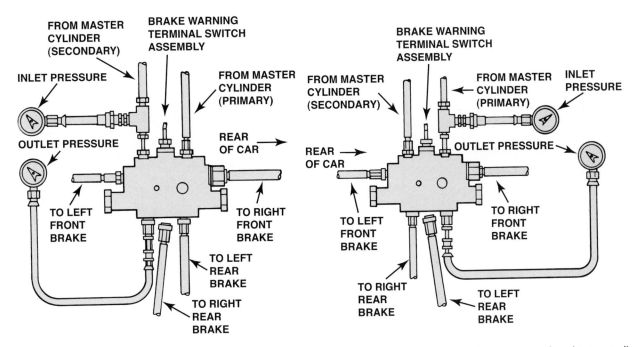

FIGURE 6-18   A proportioning valve pressure test can be performed using two pressure gauges —one to register the pressure from the master cylinder and the other gauge to read the pressure being applied to the rear brakes. This test has to be repeated in order to read the pressure to each rear wheel.   *(Courtesy of DaimlerChrysler Corporation)*

rate than the reading on the gauge connected to the master cylinder.

If the pressures do not react as described, the proportioning valve should be *replaced*. The same procedure can be performed on a diagonal split-type system as used on most front-wheel-drive vehicles.

ELECTRONIC BRAKE PROPORTIONING

The Delphi DBC-7 eliminates the need for a conventional brake proportioning valve. A proportioning valve is usually necessary to reduce pressure to the rear brakes to keep them from locking up. This is because there is less weight over the rear wheels, and weight shifts forward when braking. Proportioning is needed most when a vehicle is lightly loaded or braking from a high speed. Most proportioning valves are calibrated to reduce pressure to the rear brakes by a fixed amount, which may increase the risk of rear-wheel lockup if the vehicle is loaded differently or is braking on a wet or slick surface. Dynamic rear proportioning is overcome by adjusting brake balance to match the need of the vehicle to changing road and load conditions.

Electronic brake proportioning in the DBC-7 system is accomplished by monitoring front- and rear-wheel speeds, and reducing pressure to the rear brakes as needed using the ABS solenoids when there is a difference in wheel decelera-

tion rates. The controller energizes the inlet valve solenoids for both rear brakes to hold pressure in the lines, and then energizes both rear outlet valve solenoids to release pressure as needed. The pump may also run to clear the accumulators if a sufficient number of release cycles are required.

The dynamic rear proportioning function is enabled at all times unless there is a failure of the EBCM or two wheel speed sensors on the same axle both fail simultaneously. But as long as there is at least one functional speed sensor on the front and rear axles, the Electronic Brake Control Module (EBCM) can compare the relative speeds of the front and rear wheels.

METERING VALVE (HOLD-OFF) OPERATION

A **metering valve** is used on all front-disc, rear-drum-brake-equipped vehicles. The metering valve prevents the full operation of (holds off) the disc brakes until between 75 to 125 psi is sent to the rear drum brakes to overcome rear-brake return spring pressure. This allows the front and rear brakes to apply at the same time for even stopping. Most metering valves also allow for the pressure to the front brakes to be gradually blended up to the metering valve pressure to prevent front brake locking under light pedal pressures on icy surfaces.

A metering valve consists of a piston controlled by a strong spring and a valve stem controlled by a weak spring. See Figure 6-19.

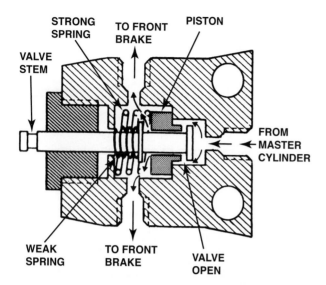

FIGURE 6-19   A metering valve when the brakes are not applied. Notice the brake fluid can flow through the metering valve to compensate for brake fluid expansion and contraction that occurs with changes in temperature.

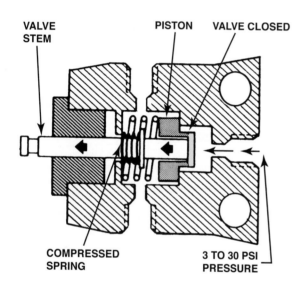

FIGURE 6-20   A metering valve under light brake pedal application.

When the brakes are not applied, the strong spring seats the piston and prevents fluid flow around it. At the same time, the weak spring holds the valve stem to the right and opens a passage through the center of the piston. Brake fluid is free to flow through this passage to compensate for changes in system fluid volume.

When the brakes are applied and pressure in the front brake line reaches 3 to 30 psi (20 to 200 kPa), the tension of the weak spring is overcome and the metering valve stem moves to the left, which closes the passage through the piston and prevents fluid flow to the front brakes. See Figure 6-20.

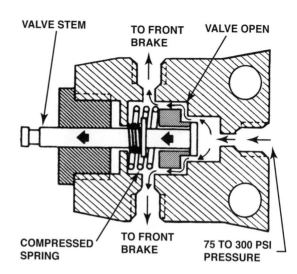

FIGURE 6-21   A metering valve during a normal brake application.

The small amount of pressure applied to the calipers before the metering valve closes is enough to take up any clearance, but not enough to generate braking force.

While the fluid flow to the front calipers is shut off, the rear brake shoes move into contact with the drums, braking begins, and hydraulic pressure throughout the brake system increases. When the pressure at the metering valve reaches 75 to 300 psi, the tension of the strong spring is overcome and the valve stem and piston move farther to the left. See Figure 6-21.

This opens a passage around the outside of the piston and allows fluid to flow through the valve to the front brake calipers.

When the brakes are released, the strong spring seats the piston and prevents fluid flow around it. At the same time, the weak spring opens the fluid passage through the center of the piston. Excess fluid returns to the master cylinder through this passage and the valve is ready for another brake application.

TECH TIP

NO VALVES CAN CAUSE A PULL

When diagnosing a pull to one side during braking, some technicians tend to blame the metering valve, proportional valve, the pressure differential switch, or the master cylinder itself.

Just remember that if a vehicle pulls during braking that the problem *has* to be due to an individual wheel brake or brake line. The master cylinder and all the valves control front or rear brakes together or diagonal brakes and cannot cause a pull if not functioning correctly.

NOTE: Braking systems that are diagonal split, such as those found on most front-wheel-drive vehicles, do *not* use a metering valve. A metering valve is only used on front/rear split braking systems such as those found on most rear-wheel-drive vehicles.

SYSTEMS WITHOUT METERING VALVES

There are three reasons front-wheel-drive vehicles do not use metering valves:

1. Front-wheel-drive vehicles usually have a diagonally split dual braking system that would require a separate metering valve for each hydraulic circuit. This would make the brake system more costly and complicated.
2. Front-wheel-drive vehicles have a forward weight bias that requires the front brakes to supply up to 80% of the total braking power. Since the front brakes do most of the work, it is desirable to apply them as soon as possible when the brake pedal is depressed. A metering valve would create a slight delay.
3. Until all the clearance in the brake system is taken up, there will not be enough pressure in the brake hydraulic system for the front disc brakes to overcome the engine torque applied to the driven front wheels.

Engine torque and a heavy front weight bias help prevent front wheel lockup from being a problem during light braking or when the brakes are first applied.

Most rear-wheel-drive vehicles without metering valves are equipped with four-wheel disc brakes. Because the clearance between the pads and rotors is approximately the same at all four wheels, there is no need to delay front brake actuation. Some of these vehicles also have antilock brake systems that prevent the wheels from locking at any time. Other rear-wheel-drive vehicles without metering valves have a predominantly forward weight bias, like front-wheel-drive vehicles, and therefore benefit from having the front brakes applied sooner.

METERING VALVE DIAGNOSIS AND TESTING

A defective metering valve can leak brake fluid and/or cause the front brakes to apply before the rear brakes. This is most commonly noticed on slippery surfaces such as on snow or ice or on rain-slick roads. If the front brakes lock up during these conditions, the front wheels cannot be steered. Inspect the metering for these two conditions:

1. Look around the bottom of the metering valve for brake fluid leakage. (Ignore slight dampness.) Replace the metering valve assembly if it is leaking.
2. As the pressure builds to the front brakes, the metering valve stem should move. If it does not, replace the valve.

More accurate testing of the metering valve can be accomplished using pressure gauges. Install two gauges, one in the pressure line coming from the master cylinder and the other in the outlet line leading to the front brakes. When depressing the brake pedal, both gauges should read the same until about 3 to 30 psi (20 to 200 kPa) when the metering valve shuts, thereby delaying the operation of the front brakes. The master cylinder outlet gauge should show an increase in pressure as the brake pedal is depressed further.

Once 75 to 300 psi is reached, the gauge showing pressure to the front brakes should match the pressure from the master cylinder. If the pressures do not match these ranges, the metering valve assembly should be replaced.

NOTE: Neither the metering valve nor the proportioning valve can cause a pull to one side if defective. The metering valve controls *both* front brakes, and the proportioning valve controls *both* rear brakes. A defective master cylinder cannot cause a pull either. Therefore, if a vehicle pulls to one side during a stop, look for problems in the individual wheel brakes, hoses, or suspension.

TECH TIP

PUSH-IN OR PULL-OUT METERING VALVE?

Whenever bleeding the air out of the hydraulic brake system, the metering valve should be bypassed. The metering valve stops the passage of brake fluid to the front wheels until pressure exceeds about 125 psi (860 kPa). It is important not to push the brake pedal down with a great force so as to keep from dispersing any trapped air into small and hard-to-bleed bubbles. To bypass the metering valve, the service technician has to push or pull a small button located on the metering valve. An easy way to remember whether to push in or to pull out is to inspect the button itself. *If the button is rubber coated, then you push in. If the button is steel, then pull out.*

Special tools allow the metering valve to be held in the bypass position. Failure to remove the tool after bleeding the brakes can result in premature application of the front brakes before the rear drum brakes have enough pressure to operate.

COMBINATION VALVE

Most vehicle manufacturers combine the function of a proportioning valve with one or more other valves into one unit called a **combination valve.** See Figures 6-22 and 6-23.

On a typical rear-wheel-drive vehicle, a typical combination valve consists of the following components all in one replaceable unit:

- Metering valve
- Proportioning valve
- Pressure-differential switch

Some combination valves have only two functions and contain the pressure-differential and the metering valve, while others combine the pressure-differential with the proportioning valve.

BRAKE LIGHT SWITCH

The job of the **brake light switch** is turn on the brake lights at the back of the vehicle when the brakes are applied. A properly adjusted light switch will activate the brake lights as soon as the brake pedal is applied and before braking action actually begins at the wheels.

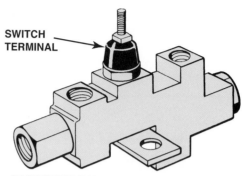

PROPORTIONING—PRESSURE DIFFERENTIAL

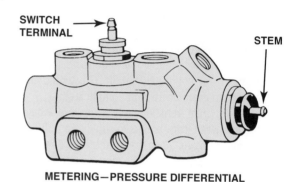

METERING—PRESSURE DIFFERENTIAL

FIGURE 6-22   Typical two-function combination valves.

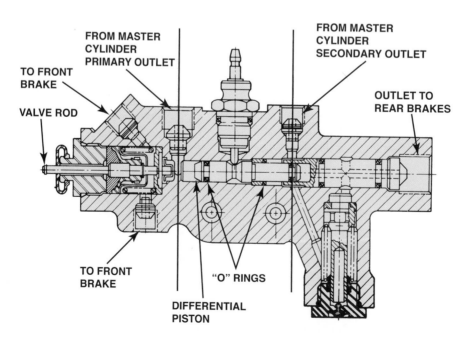

FIGURE 6-23   Combination valve containing metering, pressure-differential (warning switch), and proportioning valves all in one unit. This style is often called a "pistol grip" design because the proportioning valve section resembles the grip section of a hand gun.   *(Courtesy of DaimlerChrysler Corporation)*

Mechanical switches that operate directly off the brake pedal arm are most often used. See Figure 6-24.

Brake light switches are normally open. When the brakes are applied, the switch closes, which completes the brake light circuit.

CAUTION: Always check service information for the specified procedures to follow when replacing and/or adjusting a brake switch to ensure proper operation.

FIGURE 6-24   Typical brake light switches.

SUMMARY

1. Residual check valves are used in older vehicles to keep a slight amount of pressure on the system to help prevent air from entering the system when the brake pedal is released.
2. A pressure-differential switch is used to turn on the red brake warning lamp in the event of a hydraulic pressure failure.
3. Brake fluid level sensors are used in many vehicles to warn the driver that the brake fluid level is low.
4. Proportioning valves are used to limit the maximum fluid pressure sent to the rear wheel brakes during heavy braking to help prevent rear wheel lockup.
5. Metering valves are used on some vehicles to keep the front disc brakes from locking up on slippery surfaces.
6. Combination valves include two or more hydraulic valves in one assembly.

REVIEW QUESTIONS

1. Why are residual check valves not used in most vehicles?
2. List the three possible reasons that could cause the red brake warning lamp to come on during driving.
3. Explain why metering valves are not used on all vehicles.
4. Explain the split point and the slope of a proportioning valve.

CHAPTER QUIZ

1. Technician A says a pull to the right during braking could be caused by a defective metering valve. Technician B says a pull to the left could be caused by a defective proportioning valve. Which technician is correct?
   a. Technician A only
   b. Technician B only
   c. Both Technicians A and B
   d. Neither Technician A nor B
2. The rear brakes lock up during a regular brake application. Technician A says the metering valve could be the cause. Technician B says that stuck front disc brake calipers could be the cause. Which technician is correct?
   a. Technician A only
   b. Technician B only
   c. Both Technicians A and B
   d. Neither Technician A nor B

3. The rear wheels lock up during hard braking. Technician A says that a defective metering valve could be the cause. Technician B says that a defective proportioning valve could be the cause. Which technician is correct?

   a. Technician A only

   b. Technician B only

   c. Both Technicians A and B

   d. Neither Technician A nor B

4. A combination valve includes _____.

   a. Metering and proportioning valves

   b. Proportioning and pressure-differential valves

   c. Proportioning, metering, and pressure-differential valves

   d. Any of the above depending on the make and model of the vehicle

5. A residual check valve is used to _____.

   a. Maintain a slight pressure on the hydraulic system

   b. Prevent front wheel lockup during hard braking

   c. Prevent rear wheel lockup during hard braking

   d. Speed brake release to reduce brake wear

6. Technician A says that the red brake warning light can be turned on if a difference in pressure is detected by the pressure-differential switch. Technician B says that the red brake warning light can be turned on if the brake fluid level sensor detected low brake fluid level. Which technician is correct?

   a. Technician A only

   b. Technician B only

   c. Both Technicians A and B

   d. Neither Technician A nor B

7. Which type of vehicles most often do not use metering valves?

   a. Rear-wheel drive

   b. Four-wheel drive

   c. Front-wheel drive

   d. All-wheel drive

8. A spongy brake pedal is being diagnosed. Technician A says that air in the hydraulic system could be the cause. Technician B says a defective pressure-differential switch could be the cause. Which technician is correct?

   a. Technician A only

   b. Technician B only

   c. Both Technicians A and B

   d. Neither Technician A nor B

9. The button on the _____ valve should be held when pressure bleeding the brakes.

   a. Metering

   b. Proportioning

   c. Pressure-differential

   d. Residual check

10. A typical brake light is electrically _____.

   a. Normally open

   b. Normally closed

CHAPTER 7

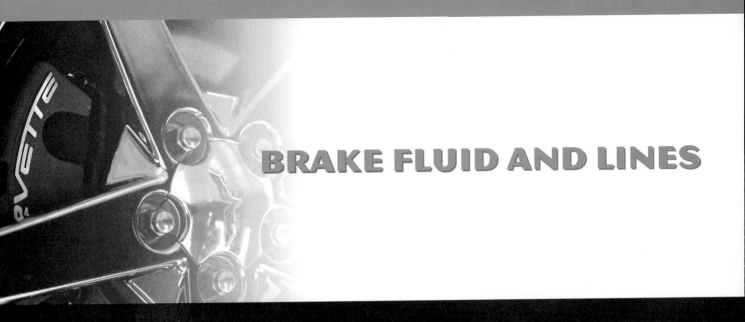

BRAKE FLUID AND LINES

OBJECTIVES

After studying Chapter 7, the reader should be able to:

1. Prepare for the Brakes (A5) ASE certification test.
2. List the types of brake fluids.
3. Describe where armored brake line is used.
4. Discuss the differences between double-flare and ISO flare.
5. Explain how flexible brake lines should be handled during service.
6. List the precautions necessary when handling or disposing of brake fluid.
7. Discuss the types of rubber that are used in brake system components.

KEY TERMS

Armored brake line (p. 126)
Brake fluid (p. 116)
Brake lines (p. 122)
Brake pipes (p. 122)
Brake tubing (p. 122)
DOT 3 (p. 116)
DOT 4 (p. 116)
DOT 5 (p. 117)
DOT 5.1 (p. 117)

Double flare (p. 123)
Elastomers (p. 121)
Flexible brake hoses (p. 127)
Hydraulic System Mineral Oil (HSMO) (p. 118)
Hygroscopic (p. 116)
International Standards Organization (ISO) (p. 123)
Nonhygroscopic (p. 117)
Polyglycol (p. 116)
Silicone brake fluid (p. 117)

BRAKE FLUID

Brake fluid is designed to function in the hydraulic brake system under all operating conditions. Brake fluid boiling point is one of the most critical aspects and ratings for brake fluid. As brake fluid ages, it absorbs moisture, which lowers its boiling point and causes increased corrosion of the brake system components.

All automotive experts agree that brake fluid should be changed regularly as part of normal routine service. Even through the driver may not notice an immediate improvement, the reduced corrosion will eventually result in less money being spent for brake system component replacement in the future. Getting the old low-boiling-point brake fluid out of the system could prevent a total loss of brakes due to brake fluid boiling!

All brake fluids must be able to pass tests for the following:

1. Fluidity at low temperatures
2. Controlled percentage loss due to evaporation at high temperatures (tested at 212°F [100°C])
3. Compatibility with other brake fluids
4. Resistance to oxidation
5. Specific effects on rubber, including:
   a. No disintegration
   b. No increase in hardness of the rubber tested
   c. Limited amount of decrease in hardness of the rubber

BRAKE FLUID TYPES

Brake fluid is made from a combination of various types of glycol, a non-petroleum-based fluid. Brake fluid is a polyalkylene–glycol–ether mixture called **polyglycol** for short. *All polyglycol brake fluid is clear to amber in color.* Brake fluid has to have the following characteristics:

- A high boiling point
- A low freezing point
- No ability to damage rubber parts in the brake system

BRAKE FLUID SPECIFICATIONS

All automotive brake fluid must meet federal Motor Vehicle Safety Standard 116. The Society of Automotive Engineers (SAE) and the Department of Transportation (DOT) have established brake fluid specification standards as shown in the following chart.

	DOT 3	DOT 4	DOT 5.1	DOT 5
Dry boiling point				
°F	401	446	500	500
°C	205	230	260	260
Wet Boiling Point				
°F	284	311	356	356
°C	140	155	180	180

The wet boiling point is often referred to as ERBP, or equilibrium reflux boiling point. ERBP refers to the method in the specification (SAE J1703) by which the fluid is exposed to moisture and tested.

DOT 3

DOT 3 brake fluid is the type most often used. There are, however, certain important characteristics.

1. DOT 3 absorbs moisture. According to SAE, DOT 3 can absorb 2% of its volume in water per year. Moisture is absorbed by the brake fluid through microscopic seams in the brake system and around seals. See Figure 7-1. Over time, the water will corrode the system and thicken the brake fluid. The moisture can also cause a spongy brake pedal, due to reduced vapor-lock temperature. See Figure 7-2.
2. DOT 3 must be used from a sealed (capped) container. If allowed to remain open for any length of time, DOT 3 will absorb moisture from the surrounding air, which is called **hygroscopic**.
3. Always check the brake fluid recommendations on the top of the master cylinders of imported vehicles before adding DOT 3.

CAUTION: DOT 3 brake fluid is a very strong solvent and can remove paint! Care is required when working with DOT 3 brake fluid to avoid contact with the vehicle's painted surfaces. It also takes the color out of leather shoes.

DOT 4

DOT 4 brake fluid is formulated for use by all vehicles, imported or domestic. DOT 4 is polyglycol based but has borate esters added to provide an extra buffer for the fluid against acids that can form in the moisture that has been absorbed in the fluid when it is heated. DOT 4 is approximately double the cost of DOT 3. DOT 4 can often be used where DOT 3 is used and even though the two types of brake fluid are compatible and miscible (able to be mixed), some vehicle manufacturers

FIGURE 7-1 Brake fluid can absorb moisture from the air even through plastic, so many experts recommend that brake fluid be purchased in metal containers.

recommend that DOT 3 and DOT 4 not be mixed. If DOT 4 is to be used, the system should be purged of all of the old DOT 3 and replaced with DOT 4.

NOTE: Because brake fluid absorbs moisture over time, many vehicle manufacturers recommend changing the brake fluid as part of the standard services to be performed routinely. The typical recommended brake fluid change interval is every two years or every 30,000 miles (48,000 km), whichever comes first. This is particularly important for vehicles equipped with an antilock braking system (ABS) because of the problem of expensive brake component wear or corrosion caused by contaminated brake fluid.

DOT 5.1

DOT 5.1 brake fluid is a non-silicone-based polyglycol fluid and is clear to amber in color. This severe duty fluid has a boiling point of over 500°F equal to the boiling point of silicone-based DOT 5 fluid. Unlike DOT 5, DOT 5.1 can be mixed with either DOT 3 or DOT 4 according to brake fluid manufacturer's recommendations.

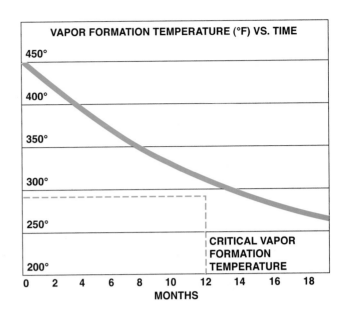

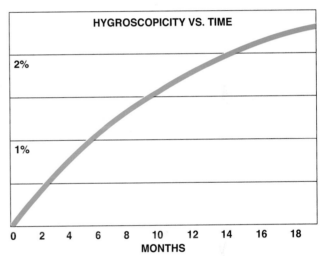

FIGURE 7-2 Brake fluid absorbs moisture from the air at the rate of about 2% per year. As the brake fluid absorbs water, its boiling temperature decreases.

CAUTION: Some vehicle manufacturers such as DaimlerChrysler do not recommend the use of or the mixing of other types of polyglycol brake fluid and specify the use of DOT 3 brake fluid only. Always follow the vehicle manufacturer's recommendation.

DOT 5

DOT 5 brake fluid is commonly called **silicone brake fluid** and is made from polydimethylsiloxanes. It does not absorb any water, and is therefore called **nonhygroscopic**.

NOTE: Even though DOT 5 does not normally absorb water, it is still tested using standardized SAE procedures in a humidity chamber. After a fixed amount of time, the brake fluid is measured for boiling point. Since it has had a chance to absorb moisture, the boiling point after this sequence is called the minimum wet boiling point.

DOT 5 brake fluid is purple (violet) in color to distinguish it from DOT 3 or DOT 4 brake fluid. Silicones have about three times the amount of dissolved air as glycol fluids (about 15% of dissolved air versus only about 5% for standard glycol brake fluid). It is this characteristic of silicone brake fluid that causes the most concern about its use.

1. Silicone brake fluid has an affinity for air; therefore, it is more difficult to bleed the hydraulic system of trapped air.
2. The trapped air expands with increasing temperature. This causes the brake pedal to feel "mushy" because the pressure exerted on the hydraulic system simply compresses the air in the system and does not transfer the force to the wheel cylinders and calipers as it should.

NOTE: The characteristics of DOT 5 silicone brake fluid to absorb air is one of the major reasons why it is not recommended for use with an antilock braking system (ABS). In an ABS, valves and pumps are used which can aerate the brake fluid. Brake fluid filled with air bubbles cannot properly lubricate the ABS components and will cause a low, soft brake pedal.

3. The air trapped in the silicone brake fluid can also "off-gas" at high altitudes, causing a mushy brake pedal and reduced braking performance. DOT 5 brake fluid has

been known to create a braking problem during high-altitude (over 5,000 ft. [1,500 m]) and high-temperature driving. The high altitude tends to vaporize (off-gassing) some parts of the liquid, creating bubbles in the brake system, similar to having air in the brake system.
4. DOT 5 brake fluid should not be mixed with any other type of brake fluid. Therefore, the entire braking system must be completely flushed and refilled with DOT 5.
5. DOT 5 does not affect rubber parts and will not cause corrosion.
6. DOT 5 is expensive. It is approximately four times the cost of DOT 3 brake fluid.

HYDRAULIC SYSTEM MINERAL OIL

Some French-built Citroen and British-designed Rolls-Royce vehicles use **hydraulic system mineral oil (HSMO)** as part of their hydraulic control systems. The systems in these vehicles use a hydraulic pump to pressurize hydraulic oil for use in the suspension leveling and braking systems.

REAL WORLD FIX

THE SINKING BRAKE PEDAL

This author has experienced what happens when brake fluid is not changed regularly. Just as many technicians will tell you, we do not always do what we know should be done to our own vehicles.

While driving a four-year-old vehicle on vacation in very hot weather in mountainous country, the brake pedal sank to the floor. When the vehicle was cold, the brakes were fine. But after several brake applications, the pedal became soft and spongy and sank slowly to the floor if pressure was maintained on the brake pedal. Because the brakes were OK when cold, I knew it had to be boiling brake fluid. Old brake fluid (four years old) often has a boiling point under 300°F (150°C). With the air temperature near 100°F (38°C), it does not take much more heat to start boiling the brake fluid. After bleeding over a quart (1 liter) of new brake fluid through the system, the brakes worked normally. I'll never again forget to replace the brake fluid as recommended by the vehicle manufacturer. See Figure 7-3 for a tester that can be used to measure the boiling point of brake fluid.

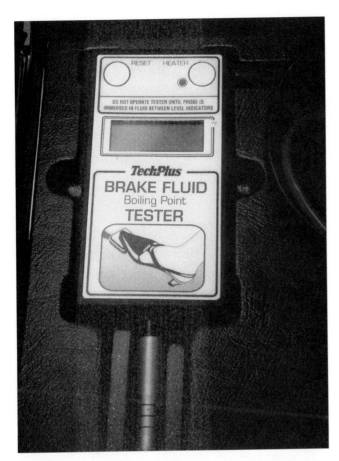

FIGURE 7-3 A brake fluid tester can test brake fluid for boiling point.

CAUTION: Mineral hydraulic oil should never be used in a braking system that requires DOT 3 or DOT 4 polyglycol-based brake fluid. If any mineral oil, such as engine oil, transmission oil, or automatic transmission fluid (ATF), gets into a braking system that requires glycol brake fluid, every rubber part in the entire braking system must be replaced. Mineral oil causes the rubber compounds that are used in glycol brake fluid systems to swell (see Figure 7-4).

To help prevent hydraulic system mineral oil from being mixed with glycol brake fluid, *hydraulic mineral oils are green.*

FIGURE 7-4 Both rubber sealing cups were exactly the same size. The cup on the left was exposed to mineral oil. Notice how the seal greatly expanded.

BRAKE FLUID INSPECTION AND TESTING

The brake fluid should be inspected regularly, including the following items:

1. Proper Level. The brake fluid level should be above the minimum level (labeled MIN) and below the maximum (labeled MAX) on the side of the master cylinder reservoir. Do not add brake fluid unless the entire brake system is carefully inspected for worn brake pads and shoes and for signs of any external leakage.
2. Color/Condition. New brake fluid is clear or amber in color, as seen in Figure 7-5. If the brake fluid is black or discolored as shown in Figure 7-6, the fluid should be changed.

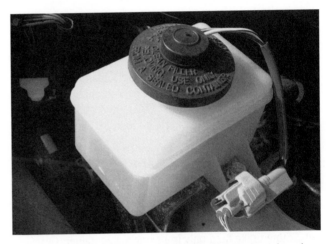

FIGURE 7-5 New brake fluid is clear or amber in color as shown here.

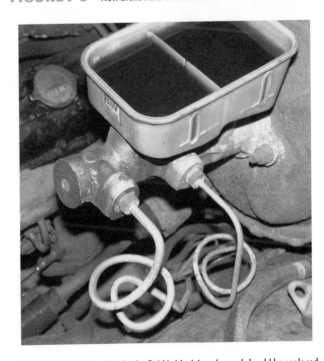

FIGURE 7-6 This brake fluid is black in color and should be replaced.

NOTE: Some experts recommend replacing the brake fluid if it looks like coffee, either black coffee or coffee with cream.

3. **Tested Using a Tester or Test Strips.** Often, brake fluid does not look as if it is bad but has absorbed moisture enough to reduce its effectiveness. See Figure 7-7.

4. **Brake Fluid Contamination Test.** If brake fluid is mixed with any mineral oil, such as engine oil, power steering fluid, or automatic transmission fluid, rubber components will swell and cause brake system failure. To check for possible contamination, remove the reservoir cover from the master cylinder. If the rubber diaphragm is swelled or distorted, brake fluid contamination is likely. To check the brake fluid, use a Styrofoam cup filled with water. Place a teaspoon (1 ml) of brake fluid from the master cylinder into the water. Pure brake fluid will completely dissolve in the water. Petroleum or mineral oil fluids will float on the surface of the water and retain their color. Petroleum fluids will also dissolve the Styrofoam cup at the waterline. If the brake fluid is contaminated, the entire braking system must be drained and flushed and all rubber components replaced.

BRAKE FLUID SERVICE PROCEDURES AND PRECAUTIONS

1. Store brake fluid only in its original container.

   NOTE: To help prevent possible contamination with moisture, air, or other products, purchase brake fluid in small containers. Keep all brake fluid containers tightly closed to prevent air (containing moisture) from being absorbed.

2. Before opening a brake fluid container, remove any dirt, moisture, or other contamination from the top and outside of the container.

3. When a brake fluid container is empty, it should be discarded—the container should never be used for anything except brake fluid.

4. Do not transfer brake fluid to any other container that may have contained oil, kerosene, gasoline, antifreeze, water, cleaners, or any other liquids or chemicals.

5. Do not reuse brake fluid that has been siphoned from another vehicle or drawn out during a brake bleeding operation. (Brake bleeding means to open special bleeder valves in the hydraulic system to rid the system of any trapped air.)

6. Use only fresh new brake fluid for flushing the hydraulic brake system.

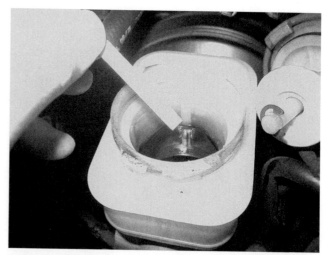

(a)

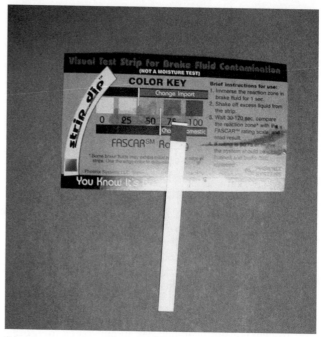

(b)

FIGURE 7-7 (a) A brake fluid test strip is being used to test the condition of the brake fluid. (b) The color of the test strip is then compared with a chart on the package, which indicates the condition.

CAUTION: Alcohol or flushing fluids should not be used because they cannot be totally removed and will contaminate the system. Disassembled parts, however, can and should be cleaned with denatured alcohol or spray brake cleaner where the parts can be visually inspected to be free of cleaning solutions.

REAL WORLD FIX

THE PIKE'S PEAK BRAKE INSPECTION

All vehicles must stop about halfway down Pike's Peak mountain in Colorado (14,110 ft. [4300 m]) for a "brake inspection." When this author stopped at the inspection station, a uniformed inspector simply looked at the right front wheel and waved us on. I pulled over and asked the inspector what he was checking. He said that when linings and drums/rotors get hot, the vehicle loses brake effectiveness. But if the brake fluid boils, the vehicle loses its brakes entirely. The inspector was listening for boiling brake fluid at the front wheel and feeling for heat about 1 ft. (30 cm) from the wheel. If the inspector felt heat 1 ft. away from the brakes, the brakes were definitely too hot to continue, and you would be instructed to pull over and wait for the brakes to cool. The inspector recommended placing the transmission into a lower gear, which uses the engine to slow the vehicle during the descent without having to rely entirely on the brakes.

BRAKE FLUID HANDLING AND DISPOSAL

Polyglycol brake fluid presents little toxicity hazard, but for some individuals, brake fluid may produce moderate eye and skin irritation. For good safety practice, protective clothing and safety glasses or goggles should be worn.

Brake fluid spilled on the floor should be cleaned up using absorbent material and the material disposed of in the regular trash. Brake fluid becomes a hazardous waste if spilled onto open ground, where it can seep into groundwater. The disposal requirements for brake fluid spilled onto open ground vary with the exact amount spilled and other factors. Refer to local EPA guidelines and requirements for the exact rules and regulations in your area.

RUBBER TYPES

Vehicles use a wide variety of rubber in the braking system, suspension system, steering system, and engine. Rubber products are called **elastomers.** Some are oil- and grease-resistant elastomers and can be harmed by brake fluid, while others are brake-fluid resistant and can swell or expand if they come in contact with oil or grease. See the chart for types and compatible fluids.

Rubber Compatibility Chart

Name	Abbreviations	OK	Not OK	Uses
Ethylene propylene diene (developed in 1963)	EPM, EPDM, EPR	Brake fluid, silicone fluids	Petroleum fluids	Most brake system seals and parts
Styrene, butadiene (developed in 1920s)	SBR, BUNA S, GRS	Brake fluid, silicone fluids, alcohols	Petroleum fluids	Some drum brake seals, O-rings
Nitrile (nitrile butadiene rubber)	NBR, BUNA N	Petroleum fluids, ethylene glycol (antifreeze)	Brake fluid	Engine seals, O-rings
Neoprene (polychloroprene)	CR	Refrigerants (Freons: R-12 and R-134a), petroleum fluids	Brake fluids	Refrigerant, O-rings
Polyacrylate	ACM	Petroleum fluids, automatic transmission fluids	Brake fluids	Automatic transmission and engine seals
Viton (fluorocarbon)	FKM	Petroleum fluids	Brake fluid, 134a refrigerant	Engine seals, fuel system parts
Natural rubber	NR	Water, brake fluid	Petroleum fluids	Tires

See Figures 7-8 through 7-10 for examples of where rubber is used in the braking system.

Brake fluid (DOT 3 or DOT 4 glycol brake fluid) affects all elastomers and causes a slight swelling effect (about 5%). This swelling action is necessary for the seals to withstand high hydraulic pressures. Silicone (DOT 5) brake fluid does not cause rubber to swell; therefore, a rubber swell additive is used in silicone brake fluid. While these additives work well for EPDM rubber, it can cause SBR rubber to swell too much. Although most seals today use EPDM, many drum brakes still use SBR seals. This is a major reason that DOT 5 brake fluid is not recommended by many vehicle manufacturers.

BRAKE LINES

High-pressure double-walled steel brake lines or high-strength flexible lines are used to connect the master cylinder to each wheel. The steel **brake lines** are also called **brake pipes** or **brake tubing.** Brake lines carry brake fluid from the master cylinder to the wheel cylinder and brake calipers. The brake lines contain and direct the pressure of the brake hydraulic system.

Most of the total length of the brake line consists of rigid tubing. For maximum strength and durability, all brake systems

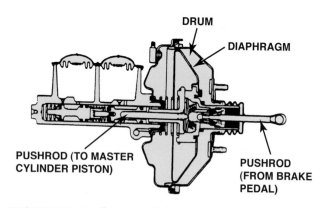

FIGURE 7-8   The master cylinder piston seals are usually constructed from EPDM rubber, and the diaphragm of the vacuum power brake booster is usually made from SBR.

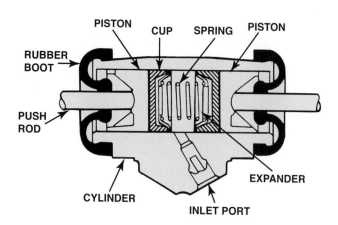

FIGURE 7-9   Cross-sectional view of a typical drum brake wheel cylinder. Most wheel cylinder boots and cups are either SBR or EPDM rubber.

FIGURE 7-10   Exploded view of a typical disc brake caliper. Both the caliper seal and dust boot are constructed of EPDM rubber.

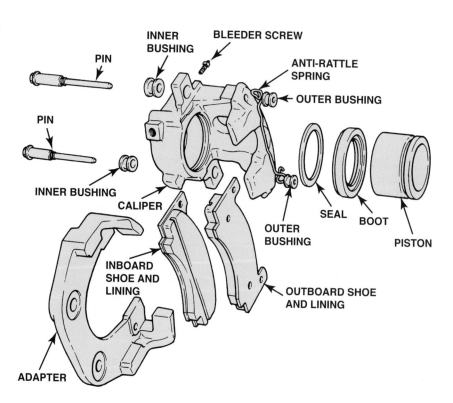

use double-walled brake tubing made from plated steel sheet. There are two types of double-walled tubing (See Figure 7-11):

- Seamless
- Multiple ply

All double-walled brake tubing is plated with tin, zinc, or other similar substances for protection against rust and corrosion. The Society of Automotive Engineers (SAE) has guidelines for brake tubing. SAE standard J1047 specifies that a sample section of brake line must be able to withstand 8,000 psi (55,000 kPa) plus other standards for resistance to fatigue, heat, rust, and corrosion.

CAUTION: Copper tubing should *never* be used for brake lines. Copper tends to burst at a lower pressure than steel.

All steel brake lines have one of two basic types of ends:

- **Double Flare.** See Figure 7-12.
- **ISO,** which stands for **International Standards Organization** (also called a *ball flare* or *bubble flare*). See Figure 7-13.

When replacing steel brake line, new steel tubing should be used and a double lap flare or an ISO flare completed at each end using a special flaring tool. See Figures 7-14 and 7-15.

Brake line can also be purchased in selected lengths already correctly flared. They are available in different diameters, the most commonly used being 3/16 in. (4.8 mm), 1/4 in. (6.4 mm), and 5/16 in. (7.9 mm) outside diameter (O.D.).

CAUTION: According to vehicle manufacturers' recommended procedures, compression fittings should never be used to join two pieces of steel brake line. Only use double flare ends and connections, if necessary, when replacing damaged steel brake lines.

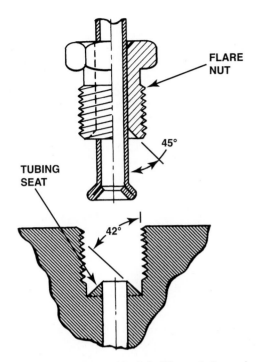

FIGURE 7-12 Because of the slight difference in flare angle, double-flare fitting seals cause a wedging action.

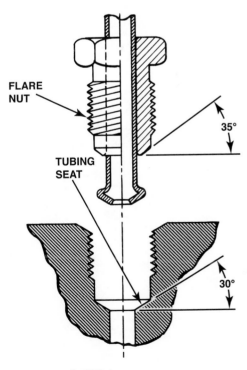

FIGURE 7-13 An ISO fitting.

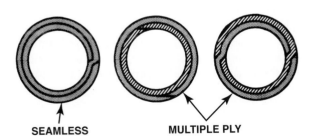

FIGURE 7-11 Steel brake tubing is double-walled for strength and plated for corrosion resistance.

(a)

(b)

(c)

(d)

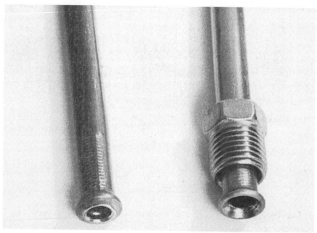

(e)

FIGURE 7-14 Double flaring the end of a brake line. (a) Clamp the line at the correct height above the surface of the clamping tool using the shoulder of the insert as a gauge. (b) The insert is pressed into the end of the tubing. This creates the first bend. (c) Remove the insert and use the pointed tool to complete the overlap double flare. (d) The completed operation as it appears while still in the clamp. (e) The end of the line as it appears after the first operation on the left and the completed double flare on the right.

(a)

(b)

FIGURE 7-15 Making an ISO flare requires this special tool. (a) Position the brake line into the two-part tool at the correct height using the gauge end of the tool. (b) Assemble the two blocks of the tool together and clamp in a vise. Turn the tool around and thread it into the tool block. The end of the threaded part of the tool forms the "bubble" or ISO flare.

Brake line diameter is also very important and replacement lines should be the same as the original. Many vehicle manufacturers use larger diameter brake lines for the rear brakes because the larger line decreases brake response time. *Response time is the amount of time between the pressure increase at the master cylinder and the pressure increase at the brakes.* On most vehicles, the brake lines to the front wheels are shorter. To help assure that the rear brakes apply at the same time as the front brakes, the diameter of the brake

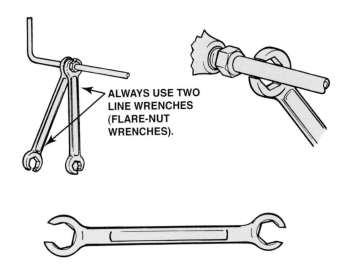

ALWAYS USE TWO LINE WRENCHES (FLARE-NUT WRENCHES).

FIGURE 7-16 Whenever disconnecting or tightening a brake line, always use the correct size flare nut wrench. A flare nut wrench is also called a tube nut wrench or a line wrench.

lines is increased to the rear brakes. Brake engineers size each line to keep the time lag to less than 0.2 second (200 milliseconds). Fast response time is critical for the proper operation of the antilock braking system (ABS). Also, as brake fluid ages, its viscosity (resistance to flow) increases, resulting in longer response time.

CAUTION: The exhaust system near brake lines should be carefully inspected for leaks when diagnosing a "lack of brakes" complaint. Exhaust gasses can hit the brake line going to the rear brakes, causing the brake fluid to boil. Since brake fluid vapors are no longer liquid, they can be compressed, resulting in a total loss of brakes. After the vehicle is stopped and allowed to cool, the brakes often return to normal.

Always use two line wrenches when disconnecting or reattaching brake lines. See Figure 7-16.

COILED BRAKE LINE

Steel brake line is often coiled, as shown on a race car in Figure 7-17.

The purpose of the coils is to allow movement between the brake components without stress that could lead to metal fatigue and brake line breakage. The typical master cylinder attaches to the bulkhead of the vehicle and the combination valve is often attached to the frame. Because the body and frame are usually insulated from each other using rubber isolators, some movement occurs while driving.

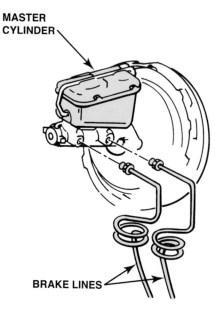

FIGURE 7-17   The coils in the brake line help prevent cracks caused by vibration.

ARMORED BRAKE LINE

In many areas of the brake system, the steel brake line is covered with a wire coil wrap, as shown in Figure 7-18. This type of brake line is called **armored brake line.**

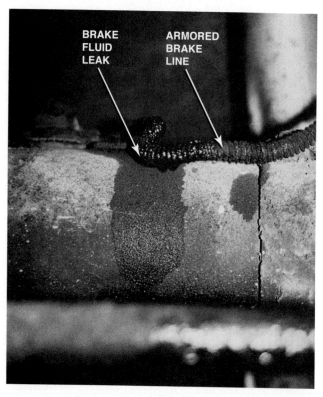

FIGURE 7-18   Armored brake line is usually used in the location where the line may be exposed to rock or road debris damage. Even armored brake line can leak and a visual inspection is an important part of any brake service.

TECH TIP

BEND IT RIGHT THE FIRST TIME

Replacing rusted or damaged brake line can be a difficult job. It is important that the replacement brake line be located in the same location as the original to prevent possible damage from road debris or heat from the exhaust. Often this means bending the brake line with many angles and turns. To make the job a lot easier, use a stiff length of wire and bend the wire into the exact shape necessary. Then use the wire as a pattern to bend the brake line. Always use a tubing bender to avoid kinking the brake line. A kink not only restricts the flow of brake fluid, but also weakens the line. To bend brake line without a tubing bender tool, use an old V-belt pulley. Clamp the pulley in a vise, lay the tubing in the groove, and smoothly bend the tubing. Different diameter pulleys will create various radius bends. See Figure 7-19.

NOTE: Always use a tubing cutter instead of a hacksaw when cutting brake line. A hacksaw will leave a rough and uneven end that will not flare properly except when forming. An ISO flare and a hacksaw is used to provide a rough surface to allow the flaring tool to grip the line during the procedure.

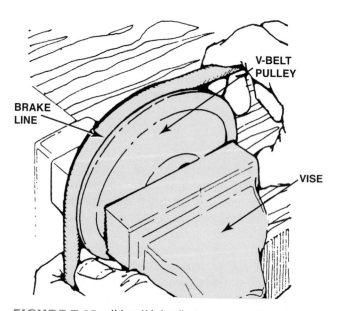

FIGURE 7-19   Using a V-belt pulley in a vise to bend brake line.

This armor is designed to prevent damage from stones and other debris that could dent or damage the brake line. If a section of armored brake line is to be replaced, armored replacement line should be installed.

FLEXIBLE BRAKE HOSE

Flexible brake hoses are used on each front wheel to allow for steering and suspension movement and at the rear to allow for rear suspension travel. See Figure 7-20.

These rubber high-strength hoses can crack, blister, or leak, and should be inspected at least every six months. See Figure 7-21.

Flexible brake hose is made from synthetic yarn (poly vinyl alcohol, abbreviated PVA) that is braided into position from multiend yarn spindles. By braiding the yarn, all of the strands operate in tension and, therefore, have great strength to withstand braking system pressure over 1,000 psi (6,900 kPa). See Figure 7-22.

A typical brake hose has an inner tube for conveying the brake fluid and a cushion liner that is between the braided layers to prevent the braids from chafing. All three layers use ethylene-propolyene-diene-monomer (EPDM)-type thermosetting polymers, which help prevent the hose from absorbing moisture from the outside air. An outside jacket is made

from rubber and protects the reinforcement fabric from moisture and abrasion. The outside covering is also ribbed as part of the manufacturing process to hide surface blemishes. These ribs also make it easy for the technician to see if the hose is twisted. It is not unusual for flexible brake lines to become turned around and twisted when the disc brake caliper is removed and then replaced during a brake pad change. See Figures 7-23 and 7-24.

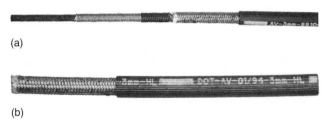

(a)

(b)

FIGURE 7-21   (a) Typical flexible brake hose showing the multiple layers of rubber and fabric. (b) The inside diameter (ID) is printed on the hose (3 mm).

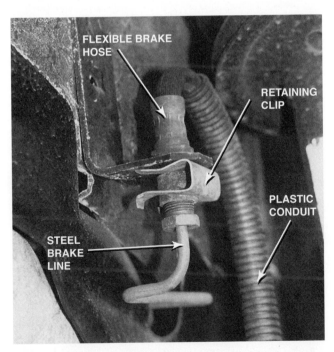

FIGURE 7-20   Flexible brake hoses are used between the frame or body of the vehicle and the wheel brakes. Because of suspension and/or steering movement, these flexible brake lines must be strong enough to handle high brake fluid pressures, yet remain flexible. Note that this flexible brake hose is further protected against road debris with a plastic conduit covering.

FIGURE 7-22   Brake hose fabric being woven at the Delco Chassis plant in Dayton, Ohio, USA.

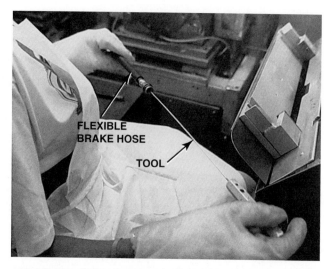

FIGURE 7-23 All brake hose is carefully inspected and a 3-mm-diameter gauging tool is inserted through the hose to make sure the hose is not restricted. Notice the small diameter of the tool compared to the outside diameter of the hose. Seeing how small the inside diameter of the hose actually is makes it easier to visualize how easy it would be to have a restricted or blocked flexible hose.

A constricted brake hose can cause the brakes to remain applied, thereby causing excessive brake pad wear and unequal braking. A constricted flexible brake line can also cause the vehicle to pull to one side. See Figure 7-25.

CAUTION: Never allow a disc brake caliper to hang by the flexible brake line. Damage to the line can result. Always use a wire to support the weight of the caliper.

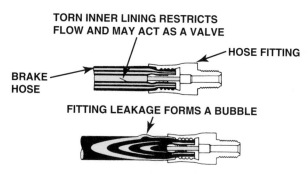

FIGURE 7-24 Typical flexible brake hose faults. Many faults cannot be seen, yet can cause the brakes to remain applied after the brake pedal is released.

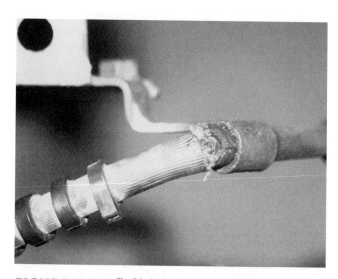

FIGURE 7-25 Flexible brake hose should be carefully inspected for cuts or other damage, especially near sections where the brake hose is attached to the vehicle. Notice the crack and cut hose next to the mounting bracket.

SUMMARY

1. Most brake fluid is amber in color and polyglycol based.
2. DOT 3 is the type of brake fluid most often recommended for use.
3. Brake fluid absorbs moisture over time and can remove paint.
4. DOT 4 and DOT 5.1 are also polyglycol-based fluids, whereas DOT 5 is silicone based.
5. Brake fluid should be checked for proper level and color and tested for condition or for contamination.
6. Brake fluid should be disposed of according to local and state guidelines.
7. Most brake systems use EPR or SBR-type rubber that is compatible with brake fluid but they can swell in size if exposed to mineral oil such as power steering fluid, engine oil, or automatic transmission fluid.
8. Brake lines are double-walled steel with a rust prevention coating with either a double lap flare or an ISO flare end.
9. Flexible brake hose is constructed of braided synthetic yarn and EPDM rubber.

REVIEW QUESTIONS

1. What is the difference between DOT 3, DOT 4, DOT 5.1, and DOT 5 brake fluid?

2. List four things that should be done during a thorough inspection of the brake fluid.

3. List four precautions that should be followed when handling brake fluid.

4. What are the two types of flares used on brake lines?

5. Why are some brake lines coiled?

CHAPTER QUIZ

1. The type of brake fluid most often recommended by vehicle manufacturers is _____.
   a. DOT 3
   b. DOT 4
   c. DOT 5
   d. DOT 5.1

2. Which of the following is *not* a characteristic of conventional brake fluid?
   a. Absorbs moisture from the air
   b. Removes paint if spilled on vehicle surfaces
   c. Lasts the life of the vehicle unless there is a leak
   d. Is clear or amber in color

3. Technician A says that DOT 5 brake fluid can be added to DOT 3 brake fluid. Technician B says that it is wise to purchase brake fluid that is in metal rather than plastic containers. Which technician is correct?
   a. Technician A only
   b. Technician B only
   c. Both Technicians A and B
   d. Neither Technician A nor B

4. As brake fluid ages, what happens?
   a. The boiling temperature decreases
   b. The boiling temperature increases
   c. The viscosity (thickness) decreases
   d. The color changes to purple

5. Technician A says that glycol-based brake fluid causes the seals to swell slightly. Technician B says the DOT 5 (silicone-based) brake fluid causes rubber seals to swell slightly. Which technician is correct?
   a. Technician A only
   b. Technician B only
   c. Both Technicians A and B
   d. Neither Technician A nor B

6. The two types of flares used on brake lines are _____.
   a. SAE and DOT
   b. Double flare and ISO
   c. Ball flare and bubble flare
   d. SAE and double flare

7. Two technicians are discussing why the brake lines are coiled near the master cylinder on many vehicles. Technician A says that these coils help prevent moisture from flowing from the master cylinder to the calipers. Technician B says that they help prevent cracks that could be caused by vibrations. Which technician is correct?
   a. Technician A only
   b. Technician B only
   c. Both Technicians A and B
   d. Neither Technician A nor B

8. Flexible brake hose should be inspected for all of the following *except* _____.
   a. Cracks
   b. Leakage
   c. Twisted
   d. Worn outer ribs

9. Why should brake calipers be supported by a wire during brake service and not allowed to hang by the flexible brake hose?
   a. To keep air from getting into the system
   b. To help prevent damage to the brake hose
   c. To hold the caliper higher than the master cylinder to prevent fluid loss
   d. To prevent bending the hose support bracket

10. Used brake fluid should be _____.
    a. Mixed with and recycled with used oil
    b. Poured down the drain
    c. Absorbed with a cloth or absorbent material and disposed of in regular trash
    d. Poured onto open ground to reduce dust

BRAKE BLEEDING METHODS AND PROCEDURES

OBJECTIVES

After studying Chapter 8, the reader should be able to:

1. Prepare to take the Brakes (A5) ASE certification test content area "A" (Hydraulic System Diagnosis and Repair).
2. Explain how to bench bleed a master cylinder.

3. Describe the proper brake bleeding sequence.
4. Describe the single stroke manual brake bleeding procedure.
5. Discuss how to gravity bleed the hydraulic brake system.
6. List the steps needed to perform a pressure bleed procedure.

KEY TERMS

BRAKE BLEEDING

Brake bleeding is removing any trapped air from the hydraulic system. Air can get into the hydraulic system whenever any hydraulic brake line or unit is opened. Air can also be drawn into the hydraulic system through small holes or loose brake line connections during the release of the brake pedal. A common source of air in the brake system of this type can occur through very small holes in rubber flexible brake lines. Another source of air in the braking system is through the absorption of moisture by the brake fluid. When moisture is absorbed, the boiling point of the brake fluid is reduced. During severe braking, the heat generated can cause the brake fluid to boil and create air bubbles in the hydraulic brake system. Air eventually travels to the highest part of the brake system, if not restricted by pressure control valves. Air in the system results in a spongy brake pedal.

BLEEDING THE MASTER CYLINDER

Whenever the master cylinder is replaced or the hydraulic system has been left opened for several hours, the air may have to be bled from the master cylinder. Bleed the master cylinder "on the bench" before installing it on the vehicle. See Figure 8-1.

If bleeding the master cylinder after working on the hydraulic system, follow these steps:

Step 1 Fill the master cylinder with clean brake fluid from a sealed container up to the recommended "full" level.

Step 2 Have an assistant slowly depress the brake pedal as you "crack open" the master cylinder bleed screw starting with the section closest to the bulkhead. It is very important that the primary section of the master cylinder be bled before attempting to bleed the air out of the secondary section of the master cylinder. Before the brake pedal reaches the floor, close the bleeder valve.

NOTE: A proper manual bleeding of the hydraulic system requires that accurate communications occur between the person depressing the brake pedal and the person opening and closing the bleeder valve(s). The **bleeder valve** (also called a *bleed valve*) should be open only when the brake pedal is being depressed. The valve *must* be closed when the brake pedal is released to prevent air from being drawn into the system.

Step 3 Repeat the procedure several times until a solid flow of brake fluid is observed leaving the bleeder valve. If the master cylinder is not equipped with bleeder valves, the outlet tube nuts can be loosened instead.

BRAKE BLEEDER VALVE LOOSENING METHODS

Attempting to loosen a bleeder valve often results in breaking (shearing off) the bleeder valve. Several of these service procedures can be tried that help prevent the *possibility* of breaking a bleeder valve. Bleeder valves are tapered and become wedged in the caliper on the wheel cylinder housing. See Figures 8-2 and 8-3.

All of these methods use shock to "break the taper" and to loosen the stuck valve.

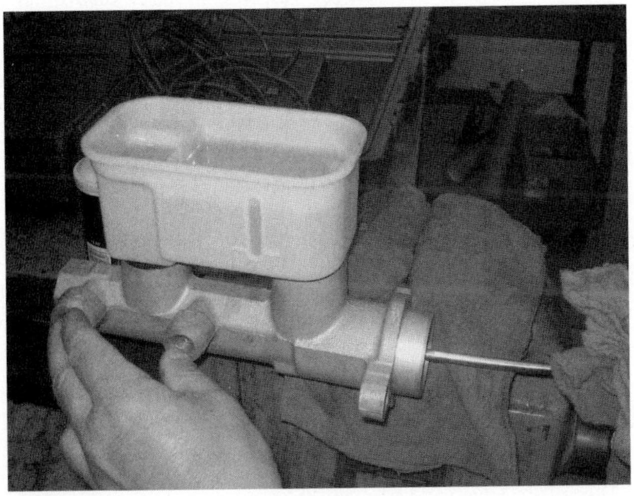

FIGURE 8-1 Always clamp a master cylinder in a vise by the mounting flange to prevent distortion of the cylinder bore.

FIGURE 8-2 Typical bleeder valve from a disc brake caliper. The arrows point to the taper section that does the actual sealing. It is this taper that requires a shock to loosen. If the bleeder is simply turned with a wrench, the bleeder usually breaks off because the tapered part at the bottom remains adhered to the caliper or wheel cylinder. Once loosened, brake fluid flows around the taper and out through the hole in the side of the bleeder valve.

FIGURE 8-3 Typical bleeder locations. Note that the combination valve and master cylinder shown do not have bleeder valves; therefore, bleeding is accomplished by loosening the brake line at the outlet parts. *(Courtesy of Allied Signal Automotive Aftermarket)*

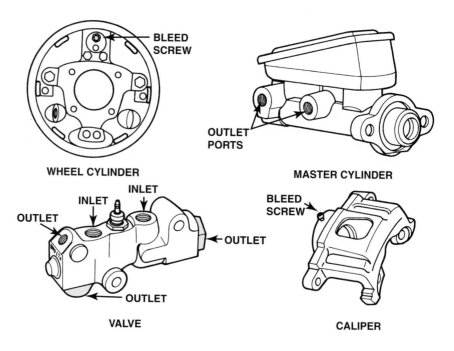

TECH TIP

DO IT RIGHT— REPLACE THE BRAKE FLUID

Often, used brake fluid looks like black coffee or coffee with cream. Both conditions indicate contaminated or moisture-laden brake fluid that should be replaced. The following steps will help assure a complete brake fluid change:

Step 1   Remove the old brake fluid from the master cylinder using a suction bulb. (Dispose of this old brake fluid properly.)

Step 2   Fill the master cylinder with new clean brake fluid from a sealed container.

Step 3   Bleed each wheel brake until the brake fluid is clean.

CAUTION: Do not allow the master cylinder to run out of brake fluid. Recheck and refill as necessary during the bleeding process.

This brake fluid replacement will fully restore the brake hydraulic system to as-new condition and help protect the system from rust and corrosion. Replacing only the friction pads and/or linings is not a complete and thorough brake system service. Customers should be educated as to the importance of this service procedure.

Air Impact Method

Use a 6-point socket for the bleeder valve and use the necessary adapters to fit an air impact wrench to the socket. Apply some penetrating oil to the bleeder valve and allow it to flow around the threads. Turn the pressure down on the impact wrench to limit the force. The hammering effect of the impact wrench loosens the bleeder valve without breaking it off.

Hit and Tap Method

Step 1   Tap on the end of the bleeder valve with a steel hammer. This shock often "breaks the taper" at the base of the bleeder valve. The shock also breaks loose any rust or corrosion on the threads.

Step 2   Using a 6-point wrench or socket, *tap* the bleeder valve in the clockwise direction (tighten).

Step 3   Using the same 6-point socket or wrench, *tap* the bleeder valve counterclockwise to loosen and remove the bleeder valve.

NOTE: It is the *shock* of the tap on the wrench that breaks loose the bleeder valve. Simply pulling on the wrench often results in breaking off the bleeder.

Step 4   If the valve is still stuck (frozen), repeat Step 1 through Step 3.

Air Punch Method

Use an air punch near the bleeder valve while attempting to loosen the bleeder valve at the same time. See Figure 8-4.

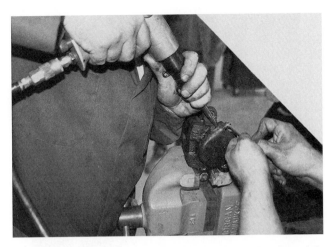

FIGURE 8-4   Using an air punch next to the bleeder valve to help "break the taper" on the bleeder valve.

The air punch creates a shock motion that often loosens the taper and threads of the bleeder valve from the caliper or wheel cylinder. It is also helpful to first attempt to turn the bleeder valve in the clockwise (tightening) direction, then turn the bleeder in the counterclockwise direction to loosen and remove the bleeder valve.

Heat and Tap Method

Heat the area around the bleeder valve with a torch. The heat expands the size of the hole and usually allows the bleeder to be loosened and removed.

CAUTION: The heat from a torch will damage the rubber seals inside the caliper or wheel cylinder. Using heat to free a stuck bleeder valve will *require* that all internal rubber parts be replaced.

Wax Method

Step 1   Heat the bleeder valve itself with a torch. The heat causes the valve itself to expand.

Step 2   Remove the heat from the bleeder valve. As the valve is cooling, touch paraffin wax or candle wax to the hot valve. The wax will melt and run down around the threads of the bleeder valve.

Step 3   Allow the bleeder valve to cool until it can be safely touched with your hand. This assures that the temperature is low enough for the wax to return to a solid and provide the lubricating properties necessary for the easy removal of the bleeder valve. Again, turn the bleeder valve clockwise before turning the valve counterclockwise to remove.

BLEEDING SEQUENCE

After bleeding the master cylinder, the combination valve should be bled if equipped. Follow the same procedure as when bleeding the master cylinder, being careful not to allow the master cylinder to run dry.

NOTE: The master cylinder is located in the highest section of the hydraulic braking system. Some master cylinders are equipped with bleeder valves. All master cylinders can be bled using the same procedure as that used for bleeding calipers and wheel cylinders. If the master cylinder is not equipped with bleeder valves, it can be bled by loosening the brake line fittings at the master cylinder.

Check the level in the master cylinder frequently and keep it filled with clean brake fluid throughout the brake bleeding procedure.

For most rear-wheel-drive vehicles equipped with a front/rear split system, start the bleeding with the wheel farthest from the master cylinder and work toward the closest. See Figure 8-5.

For most vehicles, this sequence is as follows:

1. Right rear
2. Left rear
3. Right front
4. Left front

NOTE: If the vehicle has two wheel cylinders on one brake, bleed the upper cylinder first.

For vehicles equipped with a diagonal split section or equipped with ABS, follow the brake bleeding procedure recommended in the service information for the vehicle.

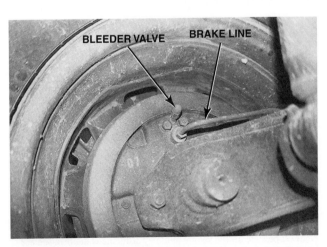

FIGURE 8-5   Most vehicle manufacturers recommend starting the brake bleeding process at the rear wheel farthest from the master cylinder.

MANUAL BLEEDING

Manual bleeding uses hydraulic pressure created by the master cylinder to pump fresh fluid through the brake system. This method is called the **single stroke bleeding method.**

It is extremely important when manually bleeding a brake system that the pedal be applied and released slowly and gently. Rapid pedal pumping can churn up the fluid and reduce the size of trapped air bubbles, making them more difficult to bleed from the system. There are, however, special situations where rapid pedal pumping may be helpful in brake system bleeding. These are covered in the "Surge Bleeding" section later in the chapter.

Manual bleeding requires an assistant to apply and release the brake pedal, a bleeder screw wrench, approximately two feet of clear, plastic hose with an inside diameter small enough to fit snugly over the bleeder screws, and a clear jar partially filled with clean brake fluid. To manually bleed the brake system, follow these steps:

1. Discharge the vacuum or hydraulic power booster (if equipped) by pumping the brake pedal with the ignition OFF until the pedal feels hard.
2. Fill the master cylinder reservoir with new brake fluid and make sure it remains at least half full throughout the bleeding procedure.
3. Attach the plastic hose over the bleeder screw of the first wheel cylinder or caliper in the bleeding sequence, and submerge the end of the tube in the jar of brake fluid. See Figure 8-6.
4. Loosen the bleeder screw approximately one-half turn, and have an assistant slowly depress the brake pedal. Air bubbles leaving the bleeder screw will be visible in the hose to the jar.
5. Tighten the bleeder screw, then have your assistant slowly release the brake pedal.
6. Wait at least 15 seconds to allow time for any small bubbles to form into larger bubbles. See the Tech Tip called, "Tiny Bubbles."
7. Repeat steps 4 and 5 until no more air bubbles emerge from the bleeder.
8. Transfer the plastic hose to the bleeder screw of the next wheel cylinder or caliper in the bleeding sequence, and repeat steps 4 through 7. Continue around the vehicle in the specified order until the brakes at all four wheels have been bled.

NOTE: Make certain all the brake components such as calipers and wheel cylinders are correctly installed with the bleeder valve located on the highest section of the part. Some wheel cylinders and calipers (such as many Ford calipers) can be installed upside down! This usually occurs whenever both front calipers are off the vehicle and they accidentally get reversed left to right. If this occurs, the air will never be completely bled from the caliper.

FIGURE 8-6   Bleeding brakes using clear plastic tubing makes it easy to see air bubbles. Submerging the hose in a container of clean brake fluid helps ensure that all of the air will be purged by the system.

VACUUM BLEEDING

Vacuum bleeding uses a special suction pump that attaches to the bleeder screw. The pump creates a low-pressure area at the bleeder screw, which allows atmospheric pressure to force brake fluid through the system when the bleeder screw is opened. Vacuum bleeding requires only one technician. To vacuum bleed a brake system follow these steps.

1. Fill the master cylinder reservoir with new brake fluid and make sure it remains at least half full throughout the bleeding procedure.
2. Attach the plastic tube from the vacuum bleeder to the bleeder screw of the first wheel cylinder or caliper in the bleeding sequence. See Figure 8-7. If necessary, use one of the adapters provided with the vacuum in the catch bottle.
3. Operate the pump handle to create a partial vaccum in the catch bottle.
4. Loosen the bleeder screw approximately one-half turn. Brake fluid and air bubbles will flow into the bottle. When the fluid flow stops, tighten the bleeder screw.
5. Repeat steps 3 and 4 until no more air bubbles emerge from the bleeder.

TECH TIP

TINY BUBBLES

Do not use excessive brake pedal force while bleeding and never bleed the brake with the engine running! The extra assist from the power brake unit greatly increases the force exerted on the brake fluid in the master cylinder. The trapped air bubbles may be dispersed into tiny bubbles that often cling to the inside surface of the brake lines. These tiny air bubbles may not be able to be bled from the hydraulic system until enough time has allowed the bubbles to reform. To help prevent excessive force, do *not* start the engine. Without power assistance, the brake pedal force can be kept from becoming excessive. If the dispersal of the air into tiny bubbles is suspected, try tapping the calipers or wheel cylinders with a plastic hammer. After this tapping, simply waiting for a period of time will cause the bubbles to re-form into larger and easier-to-bleed air pockets. Most brake experts recommend waiting *15 seconds or longer* between attempts to bleed each wheel. This waiting period is critical and allows time for the air bubbles to form.

NOTE: To help prevent depressing the brake pedal down too far, some experts recommend placing a 2 × 4 in. board under the brake pedal. This helps prevent the seals inside the master cylinder from traveling over unused sections inside the bore that may be corroded or rusty.

---

6. Transfer the vacuum bleeder to the bleeder screw of the next wheel cylinder or caliper in the bleeding sequence, and repeat steps 3 and 4. Continue around the vehicle in the specified order until the brakes at all four wheels have been bled.

GRAVITY BLEEDING

Gravity bleeding is a slow, but effective, method that will work on many vehicles to rid the hydraulic system of air. The procedure involves simply opening the bleeder valve and waiting until brake fluid flows from the open valve. Any air trapped in the part being bled will rise and escape from the port when the valve is opened. It may take several minutes before brake fluid escapes. If no brake fluid comes out, remove the bleeder valve entirely—it may be clogged. Remember, nothing but air and brake fluid will be *slowly* coming out of the wheel cylinder or caliper when the bleeder valve is removed. *Do not*

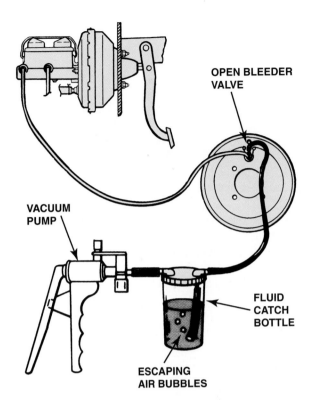

FIGURE 8-7 Vacuum bleeding uses atmospheric pressure to force brake fluid through the hydraulic system.

press on the brake pedal with the bleeder valve out while gravity bleeding.

Gravity bleeding works because any liquid tends to seek its own level. This means that the brake fluid in the master cylinder tends to flow downward toward the wheel cylinders or calipers. As long as the brake fluid level in the master cylinder is higher than the bleeder valve, the brake fluid will flow downward and out the open bleeder valve, as shown in Figure 8-8.

This flow of brake fluid can even get past the metering valve and proportioning valve. The proportioning valve is normally open to the rear brakes until the pressure reaches a predetermined level when it starts to limit increasing pressure to the rear brakes. The metering valve used to control or delay the operation of the front brakes is open to the front wheels until the pressure exceeds 10 to 15 psi (70 to 100 kPa). Therefore, as long as no one is pushing on the brake pedal, the metering valve remains open to the front wheels and the brake fluid from the master cylinder can easily flow downward through the valve and out the open bleeder valve.

Since no pressure is exerted on the brake fluid, the large air bubbles remain large air bubbles and are not separated into smaller, harder-to-bleed air bubbles that can occur with manual bleeding.

All four wheel brakes can be bled at one time using the gravity method. In this process, the bleeder screws at all four wheels are opened at the same time, and the system is allowed

TECH TIP

THE MASTER CYLINDER ONE-DRIP-PER-SECOND TEST

Excessive brake wear is often caused by misadjusted brake linkage or brake light switches keeping the brake pedal from fully releasing. If the brake pedal is not fully released, the primary piston sealing cup blocks the compensating port from the brake fluid reservoir. To test if this is the problem, loosen both lines from the master cylinder. Brake fluid should drip out of both lines about one drip per second. This is why this test is also called the "Master Cylinder Drip Test." If the master cylinder does not drip, the brake pedal may not be allowing the master cylinder to fully release. Have an assistant pull up on the brake pedal. If the dripping starts, the problem is due to a misadjusted brake light or speed (cruise) control switch or pedal stop. If the master cylinder still does not drip, loosen the master cylinder from the power booster. If the master cylinder now starts to drip, the pushrod adjustment is too long.

If the master cylinder still does not drip, the problem is in the master cylinder itself. Check for brake fluid contamination. If mineral oil, such as engine oil, power steering fluid, or automatic transmission fluid (ATF), has been used in the system, the rubber sealing cups swell and can block off the compensating port. If contamination is discovered, *every* brake component that contains rubber *must* be replaced.

to drain naturally until the fluid coming out of the bleeders is free of air.

Gravity bleeding is a slow process that can take an hour or more. In addition, this procedure cannot be used on brake systems with residual pressure check valves because the valves restrict the fluid flow. The advantage of gravity bleeding is that it can be done by a single technician, who is freed to attend to other jobs while the brakes bleed. When other bleeding procedures fail, gravity bleeding can sometimes be effective on brake systems that trap small pockets of air.

Gravity bleeding requires a bleeder wrench, four lengths of plastic hose that fit snugly over the bleeder screws, and four jars to catch the dripping fluid. Unless a plastic hose is used to "start a siphon" at each bleeder screw, it is possible that air may enter the system rather than be bled from it. This can occur because the total open area of the four bleeder screws is somewhat larger than that of the two compensating ports through which the fluid must enter the system. To gravity bleed the brake system, follow these steps.

1. Fill the master cylinder reservoir with new brake fluid. During the bleeding process, check the fluid level periodically to ensure that the reservoir remains at least half full.
2. Attach a length of plastic tubing to each bleeder screw, and place the ends of the tubes in jars to catch the drainage.
3. Open each bleeder screw approximately one full turn and make sure that fluid begins to drain. Allow the system to drain until the fluid flowing from the bleeder screws is free of air bubbles.
4. Close the bleeder screws and top up the fluid level in the master cylinder reservoir.

FIGURE 8-8 Gravity bleeding is simply opening the bleeder valve and allowing gravity to force the brake fluid out of the bleeder valve. Because air is lighter than brake fluid all of the air escapes before the brake fluid runs out.

TECH TIP

GRAVITY BLEED DURING AN OIL CHANGE

Brake fluid tends to absorb moisture near the wheel brakes through the flexible brake lines and other connections. Some service technicians open the bleeder valves whenever the vehicle is in for an oil change service. As the brake fluid slowly flows from the open bleeder valve, any trapped air is also released. After a few minutes, the bleeder valves are closed and the vehicle lowered. The brake fluid level is checked and the oil change is completed. This procedure not only helps provide the vehicle owner with an air-free brake system, but opening the bleeder at every oil change helps keep the bleeder free and easy to open.

PRESSURE BLEEDING

Pressure bleeding, sometimes called **power bleeding,** is a common method used to bleed the brake hydraulic system. In this process, a pressure bleeder attached to the master cylinder forces brake fluid through the system under pressure to purge any trapped air. Once the hydraulic system is pressurized, the technician simply opens the bleeder screws in the prescribed order and allows fluid to flow until it is free of air bubbles.

The tools required for pressure bleeding include a plastic hose and fluid catch jar as used in manual bleeding, as well as a pressure bleeder, a source of air pressure to charge the bleeder, and an adapter to attach the pressure bleeder to the master cylinder fluid reservoir. Cast-metal cylinders with integral reservoirs commonly use a flat, plate-type adapter that seals against the same surface as the reservoir cover. See Figure 8-9.

Some plastic master cylinder reservoirs also use plate-type adapters, but others require adapters that seal against the bottom of the reservoir. Pressure bleeder manufacturers offer many adapters to fit specific applications. See Figure 8-10.

METERING VALVE OVERRIDE TOOLS

In addition to the tools previously described, a metering valve override tool is required when pressure bleeding the front brakes of certain vehicles. The override tool is used to deacti-

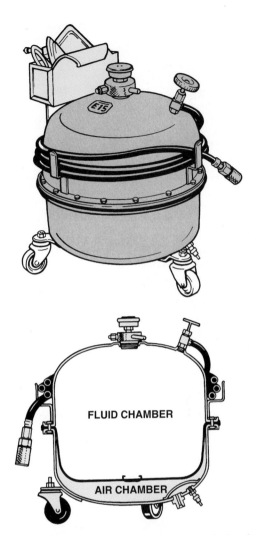

FIGURE 8-9   A typical pressure bleeder. The brake fluid inside is pressurized with air pressure in the air chamber. This air pressure is applied to the brake fluid in the upper section. A rubber diaphragm separates the air from the brake fluid.   *(Courtesy of EIS Brake Parts)*

vate the metering valve because the operating pressure of power bleeders is within the range where the metering valve blocks fluid flow to the front brakes. Metering valves that require an override tool have a stem or button on one end that is either pushed in or pulled out to hold the valve open. The override tool performs this service.

To install the override tool used on General Motors vehicles, loosen the combination valve mounting bolt and slip the slot in the tool under the bolt head. See Figure 8-11.

Push the end of the tool toward the valve body until it depresses the valve plunger, then tighten the mounting bolt to hold the tool in place.

FIGURE 8-10   Brake fluid under pressure from the power bleeder is applied to the top of the master cylinder. It is very important that the proper adapter be used for the master cylinder. Failure to use the correct adapter or failure to release the pressure on the brake fluid before removing the adapter can cause brake fluid to escape under pressure.

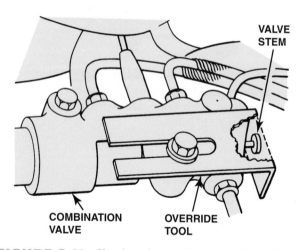

FIGURE 8-11   Metering valve override tool on a General Motors vehicle.

Some full-size Ford vehicles have a metering valve with a stem that must be pushed in to bleed the front brakes, but Ford does not offer a special tool for this purpose. An assistant is needed to override the valve when the front brakes are being bled.

To install the override tool used on older Chrysler and Ford vehicles, slip one fork of the tool under the rubber boot, and the other fork under the valve stem head. See Figure 8-12.

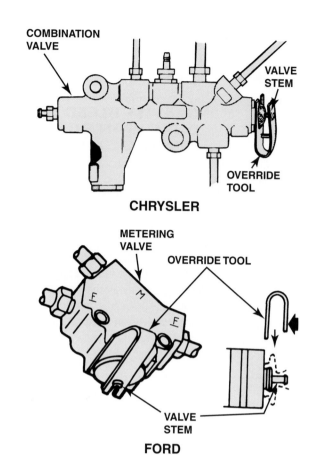

FIGURE 8-12   Pull-out-type metering valves being held out using a special override tool.

The spring tension of the tool holds the valve open, but allows the valve stem to move slightly when the system is pressurized. If the valve is held rigidly open, internal damage will result.

PRESSURE BLEEDING PROCEDURE

Just as in manual bleeding, it is important to follow the proper sequence when pressure bleeding a brake system. Some manufacturers recommend one sequence for manual bleeding and another for pressure bleeding. To pressure bleed a brake system, follow these steps:

1. If it has not already been done, consult the equipment manufacturer's instructions and fill the pressure bleeder with the proper type of brake fluid.
2. Make sure the bleeder is properly sealed and the fluid supply valve is closed, then use compressed air to pressurize the bleeder until approximately 30 psi (207 kPa) is indicated on the bleeder gauge.
3. If the vehicle is equipped with a metering valve, override it with the appropriate tool.

4. Clean the top of the master cylinder, then remove the master cylinder cover and clean around the gasket surface. Be careful not to allow any dirt to fall into the reservoir.

5. Fill the reservoir about half full with new brake fluid, then install the proper pressure bleeder adapter on the master cylinder.

6. Connect the pressure bleeder fluid supply hose to the adapter, making sure the hose fitting is securely engaged.

7. Open the fluid supply valve on the pressure bleeder to allow pressurized brake fluid to enter the system. Check carefully for fluid leaks that can damage the vehicle finish.

8. Slip the plastic hose over the bleeder screw of the first wheel cylinder or caliper to be bled, and submerge the end of the tube in the jar of brake fluid.

9. Open the bleeder screw approximately one-half turn, and let the fluid run until air bubbles no longer emerge from the tube. Close the bleeder screw.

10. Transfer the plastic hose to the bleeder screw of the next wheel cylinder or caliper in the bleeding sequence, and repeat steps 9 and 10. Continue around the vehicle in the specified order until the brakes at all four wheels have been bled.

11. Remove the metering valve override tool.

12. Close the fluid supply valve on the pressure bleeder.

13. Wrap the end of the fluid supply hose in a shop towel, and disconnect it from the master cylinder adapter. Do not spill any brake fluid on the vehicle finish.

14. Remove the master cylinder adapter, adjust the fluid level to the full point, and install the fluid reservoir cover.

SURGE BLEEDING

Surge bleeding is a supplemental bleeding method used to help remove air bubbles that resist other bleeding processes. In surge bleeding, the brake pedal is pumped rapidly to create turbulence in the hydraulic system. This agitation helps dislodge air bubbles that cling to the pores of rough castings, or become trapped at high points or turns in the brake lines. Surge bleeding is *not* recommended for systems filled with silicone DOT 5 brake fluids. These fluids tend to trap tiny air bubbles that are very difficult to bleed from the hydraulic system. The added agitation of surge bleeding only makes the problem worse.

Surge bleeding requires an assistant to pump the brake pedal, a bleeder screw wrench, approximately two feet of clear, plastic hose with an inside diameter small enough to fit snugly over the bleeder screw, and a jar partially filled with clean brake fluid. To surge bleed a brake system, follow these steps.

1. Slip the plastic hose over the bleeder screw of the wheel cylinder or caliper to be bled and submerge the end of the tube in the jar of brake fluid.

2. Open the bleeder screw approximately one-half turn.

3. With the bleeder screw *open*, have your assistant rapidly pump the brake pedal several times. Air bubbles should come out with the brake fluid.

4. While your assistant holds the brake pedal to the floor, close the bleeder screw.

5. Repeat steps 2 through 4 at each bleeder screw in the recommended order.

6. Re-bleed the system using one of the four other methods previously described.

FREQUENTLY ASKED QUESTION

WHAT IS REVERSE FLUID INJECTION?

Reverse fluid injection is a procedure that uses an air- or hand-operated injection gun that pushes brake fluid from the bleeder valve into the hydraulic system. See Figure 8-13.

By forcing brake fluid into the bleeder valve, any trapped air is forced upward into the master cylinder.

CAUTION: This procedure should only be done after a thorough flushing of the hydraulic system. Many experts warn that debris and sediment in the hydraulic system can be back-flushed into the ABS hydraulic unit and/or master cylinder. Many brake and ABS failures have been caused by forcing old brake fluid back into the system.

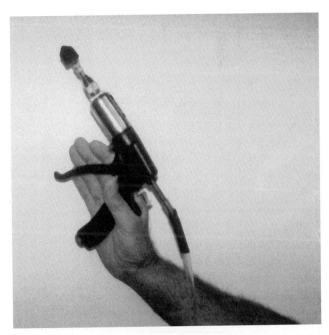

FIGURE 8-13   A reverse fluid injection unit that is used to bleed hydraulic brake and clutch systems by forcing brake fluid up from the bleeder valve into the master cylinder, thereby forcing any trapped air up and out of the system.

TECH TIP

QUICK AND EASY TEST FOR AIR IN THE LINES

If air is in the brake lines, the brake pedal will be low and will usually feel "spongy" or "mushy." To confirm that trapped air in the hydraulic system is the cause, perform this simple and fast test:

Step 1   Remove the cover from the master cylinder. Have an assistant pump the brake pedal several times and then hold the pedal down.

Step 2   Observe the squirts of brake fluid from the master cylinder when the brake pedal is quickly released. (This is best performed by allowing the foot to slip off the end of the brake pedal.)

Results

If the brake fluid squirts higher than 3 in. (8 cm) from the surface, then air is trapped in the hydraulic system. See Figure 8-14.

CAUTION: Always use a fender cover whenever performing this test. Brake fluid will remove paint if it gets onto the unprotected fender. See Figure 8-15 for an example of how to keep fender covers from slipping off.

Explanation

Air can be compressed; however, liquid cannot be compressed. When pumping the brake pedal, the assistant is compressing any trapped air. When the pedal is released quickly, the compressed air expands and takes up more volume, forcing the brake fluid upward through the compensation ports into the reservoir. Some upward movement is normal because of the return spring pressure on the valves in the master cylinder and springs in the wheel cylinders. If, however, the spurt is higher than normal, this is a sure sign of air being trapped in the system. This test is also called "the air entrapment test."

FIGURE 8-14   Note the large drops being squirted from the top of the master cylinder due to trapped air when the brakes were released.

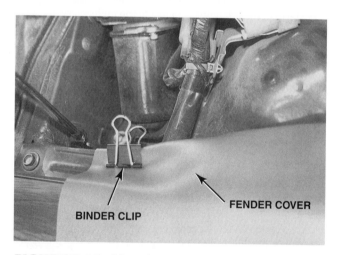

FIGURE 8-15   It is very important to use fender covers to protect the paint of the vehicle from being splashed with brake fluid. Use a binder clip available at local office supply stores to clip the fender cover to the lip of the fender, thereby preventing the fender cover from slipping.

FLUID CHANGING

In addition to removing air, brake systems need to be bled in order to clean out old and/or contaminated fluid. This process is called fluid changing or flushing. The hygroscopic (water attracting) nature of most brake fluid makes it necessary to flush the brake system periodically because moisture in the fluid drastically lowers the boiling point. Water also causes rust and corrosion of system components that can lead to brake failure. To avoid these problems, brake fluid should be changed yearly in humid climates and every other year in dry climates.

Brake fluid changing or flushing is done by bleeding the system until all of the old fluid is purged from the system. Because fluid changing requires the ability to flush out contamination and move a great deal of fluid, the best method to use is pressure bleeding. Other acceptable choices are manual bleeding and vacuum bleeding. Gravity bleeding is *not* recommended for fluid changing because it is slow, and without significant pressure behind the fluid flow, there is no guarantee that contamination will be completely flushed from the system.

To change a vehicle's brake fluid, remove all the old brake fluid from the master cylinder reservoir.

NOTE: A low-cost turkey baster can be used to draw the old brake fluid from the master cylinder reservoir. See Figure 8-16.

Fill the reservoir with new fluid, then follow the procedures outlined earlier in the chapter for the chosen method of bleeding. Continue to bleed at each wheel until the fluid that emerges from the bleeder screw is free of any discoloration and contamination.

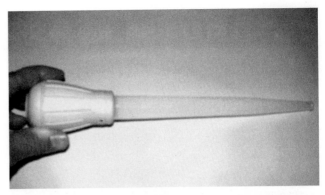

(a)

(b)

FIGURE 8-16   (a) A turkey baster can be used to remove the old brake fluid from the master cylinder reservoir. (b) Use care to avoid dripping brake fluid after drawing from the master cylinder reservoir.

BRAKE BLEEDING Step-by-Step

STEP 1

The first step in brake bleeding is to remove the protective rubber cap that covers the bleeder valve.

STEP 2

To help loosen the bleeder valve, use a hammer to tap on the end of it. The shock of the hammer blow helps free the bleeder valve.

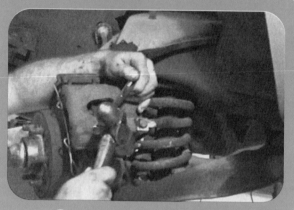

STEP 3

Place a 6-point box-end wrench onto the bleeder valve and use a hammer to lightly tap the wrench clockwise as if to tighten it. The shock of the hammer blow again helps loosen the bleeder valve.

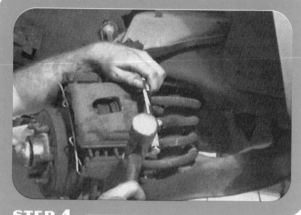

STEP 4

Use a hammer to tap the wrench to the counterclockwise position. This should loosen the bleeder valve.

STEP 5

The tapered portion of the bleeder valve is what seals the brake fluid in the caliper as shown. The repeated shock blows help break this taper.

STEP 6

A vacuum-type bleeder being used to draw brake fluid from the open bleeder valve into the hand-held unit.

BRAKE BLEEDING continued

STEP 7 Another method that can be used to bleed a caliper is called a manual method. To manually bleed a caliper, loosen the bleeder valve about one full turn.

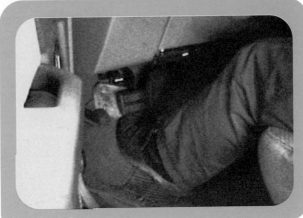

STEP 8 To prevent the possibility of harming the master cylinder, place a block of wood under the brake pedal.

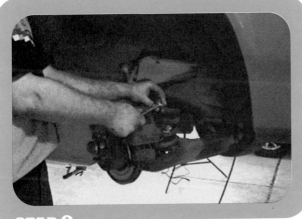

STEP 9 Tighten the bleeder valve.

STEP 10 After tightening the bleeder valve, release the brake pedal.

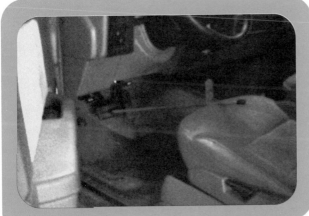

STEP 11 A commom trick that can be used to reduce the need to bleed the system after a component has been replaced is to use a brake pedal depressor to depress the brake pedal about 1 in. (25 mm).

STEP 12 With the brake pedal depressed, the primary seals inside the master cylinder block the fluid in the reservoir from dripping out of an open line.

SUMMARY

1. Bleeding the brakes means to pump the hydraulic system free of air.
2. A new or replacement master cylinder should be bled before installing it in the vehicle.
3. Bleeder valves are located on all disc brake calipers and drum brake wheel cylinders.
4. The most commonly used method of brake bleeding is the single stroke bleeding method.
5. Vacuum bleeding is used to draw the old fluid and any trapped air from the hydraulic system through the bleeder valve.
6. Gravity bleeding is an excellent but slow method.
7. Pressure bleeding requires adapters and special equipment, plus the metering valve must be held open to allow fluid to flow to the front brakes.
8. Surge bleeding is the least desirable method of bleeding, but is necessary at times.

REVIEW QUESTIONS

1. Describe how to bench bleed a master cylinder.
2. List the steps necessary to manually bleed a brake hydraulic system.
3. Discuss the equipment and the procedures needed to pressure bleed a brake hydraulic system.
4. Explain how to gravity bleed a brake hydraulic system.
5. Describe how to vacuum bleed a brake hydraulic system.
6. Discuss the surge method of brake bleeding.

CHAPTER QUIZ

1. The button on the _____ valve should be held when bleeding the brakes.
   a. Metering
   b. Proportioning
   c. Pressure-differential
   d. Residual check

2. The brake bleeding procedure usually specified for a rear-wheel vehicle with a dual split master cylinder is _____.
   a. RR, LR, RF, LF
   b. LF, RF, LR, RR
   c. RF, LR, LF, RR
   d. LR, RR, LF, RF

3. Two technicians are discussing bench bleeding a master cylinder. Technician A says that the front (nose end) of the master cylinder should be bled first. Technician B says that rear (brake pedal end) should be bled first. Which technician is correct?
   a. Technician A only
   b. Technician B only
   c. Both Technicians A and B
   d. Neither Technician A nor B

4. Two technicians are discussing how to loosen bleeder valves. Technician A says that a shock is usually necessary to break the taper at the base of the valve. Technician B says to apply steady, loosening torque to the bleeder valve using a 6-point wrench. Which technician is correct?
   a. Technician A only
   b. Technician B only
   c. Both Technicians A and B
   d. Neither Technician A nor B

5. Technician A says that the brake pedal should be depressed with as much force as possible during the normal bleeding procedure. Technician B says that the brake pedal should be pumped rapidly during this manual bleeding procedure to force the air down toward the bleeder valve(s). Which technician is correct?
   a. Technician A only
   b. Technician B only

c. Both Technicians A and B

d. Neither Technician A nor B

6. Vacuum is applied where during vacuum bleeding?

   a. At each wheel brake bleeder valve

   b. At the master cylinder reservoir

   c. At the vacuum booster check valve

   d. At the metering valve end of the combination valve

7. The bleeder is opened at a caliper and no brake fluid flows out. Technician A says that this is normal and that brake fluid should not flow or drip out of an open bleeder valve. Technician B says that the vent port in the master cylinder may be blocked. Which technician is correct?

   a. Technician A only

   b. Technician B only

   c. Both Technicians A and B

   d. Neither Technician A nor B

8. The usual maximum pressure that should be used when pressure bleeding a brake system is _____.

   a. 20 psi

   b. 30 psi

   c. 50 psi

   d. 70 psi

9. Why do many vehicle manufacturers recommend that brake fluid be changed regularly?

   a. Brake fluid absorbs moisture over time

   b. The boiling point of the brake fluid decreases

   c. Old brake fluid can cause rust and corrosion of brake system components

   d. All of the above

10. Air in the brake hydraulic system can cause all *except* _____.

   a. Spongy brake pedal

   b. Hard brake pedal

   c. Lower than normal brake pedal

   d. May require the driver to "pump up" the brakes before they will stop the vehicle

CHAPTER 9

WHEEL BEARINGS AND SERVICE

OBJECTIVES

After studying Chapter 9, the reader should be able to:

1. Prepare for Suspension and Steering (A4) ASE certification test content area "C" (Related Suspension and Steering Service).
2. Discuss the various types, designs, and parts of automotive antifriction wheel bearings.
3. Describe the symptoms of defective wheel bearings.
4. Explain wheel bearing inspection procedures and causes of spalling and brinelling.
5. List the installation and adjustment procedures for front wheel bearings.
6. Explain how to inspect, service, and replace rear wheel bearings and seals.

KEY TERMS

ANTIFRICTION BEARINGS

Bearings allow the wheels of a vehicle to rotate and still support the weight of the entire vehicle. **Antifriction bearings** use rolling parts inside the bearing to reduce friction. Four styles of rolling contact bearings include ball, roller, needle, and tapered roller bearings, as shown in Figure 9-1. All four styles convert sliding friction into rolling motion. All of the weight of a vehicle or load on the bearing is transferred through the rolling part. In a ball bearing, all of the load is concentrated into small spots where the ball contacts the *inner and outer race (rings)*. See Figure 9-2.

Ball Bearings

Ball bearings use hardened steel balls between the inner and outer race to reduce friction. While ball bearings cannot support the same weight as roller bearings, there is less friction in ball bearings and they generally operate at higher speeds. Ball bearings can control thrust movement of an axle shaft because the balls ride in grooves on the inner and outer races. The groove walls resist lateral movement of the wheel on the spindle. The most frequent use of ball bearings is at the rear wheels of a rear-wheel-drive vehicle with a solid rear axle. See Figure 9-3. These bearings are installed into the axle housing and are often press fitted to the axle shaft. Many front-wheel-drive vehicles use sealed double-row ball bearings as a complete sealed unit and are nonserviceable except as an assembly.

FIGURE 9-1   Rolling contact bearings include (left to right) ball, roller, needle, and tapered roller.

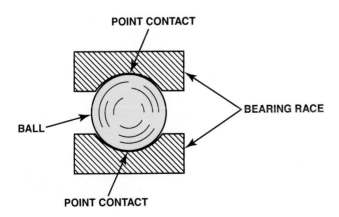

FIGURE 9-2   Ball bearing point contact.

Roller Bearings

Roller bearings use rollers between the inner and outer race to reduce friction. A roller bearing having a greater (longer) contact area can support heavier loads than a ball bearing. See Figure 9-4.

A needle bearing is a type of roller bearing that uses smaller rollers called needle rollers. The clearance between the diameter of the ball or straight roller is manufactured into the bearing to provide the proper *radial clearance* and is *not adjustable*.

Tapered Roller Bearings

The most commonly used automotive wheel bearing is the **tapered roller bearing.** Not only is the bearing itself tapered, but the rollers are also tapered. By design, this type of bearing can withstand **radial loads** (up and down) as well as **axial loads** (thrust) in one direction. See Figure 9-5.

Many non-drive-wheel bearings use tapered roller bearings. The taper allows more weight to be handled by the friction-reducing bearings because the weight is directed over the entire length of each roller rather than concentrated on a small

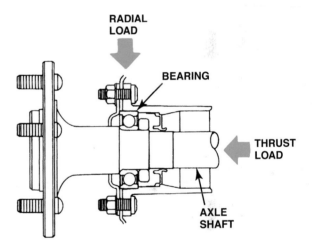

FIGURE 9-3   Radial load is the vehicle weight pressing on the wheels. The thrust load occurs as the chassis components exert a side force during cornering.

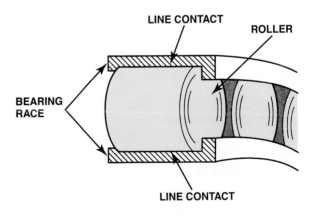

FIGURE 9-4   Roller bearing line contact.

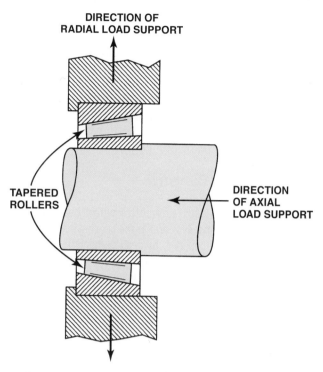

FIGURE 9-5 A tapered roller bearing will support a radial load and an axial load in only one direction.

spot, as with ball bearings. The rollers are held in place by a **cage** between the inner race (also called the **inner ring** or **cone**) and the outer race (also called the **outer ring** or **cup**). Tapered roller bearings must be loose in the cage to allow for heat expansion. Tapered roller bearings should always be adjusted for a certain amount of free play to allow for heat expansion. On non-drive-axle vehicle wheels, the cup is tightly fitted to the wheel hub and the cone is loosely fitted to the wheel spindle. New bearings come packaged with the rollers, cage, and inner race assembled together with the outer race wrapped with moisture-resistant paper. See Figure 9-6.

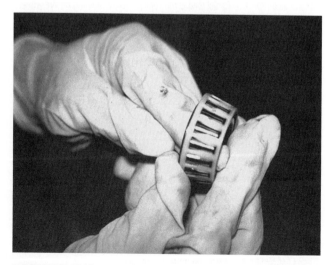

FIGURE 9-6 Many tapered roller bearings use a plastic cage to retain the rollers.

Inner and Outer Wheel Bearings

Many rear-wheel-drive vehicles use an inner and an outer wheel bearing on the front wheels. The inner wheel bearing is always the larger bearing because it is designed to carry most of the vehicle weight and transmit the weight to the suspension through to the spindle. See Figure 9-7. Between the inner wheel bearing and the spindle, there is a grease seal, which prevents grease from getting onto the braking surface and prevents dirt and moisture from entering the bearing.

Standard Bearing Sizes

Bearings use standard dimensions for inside diameter, width, and outside diameter. The standardization of bearing sizes helps interchangeability. The dimensions that are standardized include bearing bore size (inside diameter), bearing series (light to heavy usage), and external dimensions. When replacing a wheel bearing, note the original bearing brand name and number. Replacement bearing catalogs usually have cross-over charts from one brand to another. The bearing number is usually the same because of the interchangeability and standardization within the wheel bearing industry.

Sealed Front-Wheel-Drive Bearings

Most front-wheel-drive (FWD) vehicles use a sealed nonadjustable front wheel bearing. This type of bearing can include either two preloaded tapered roller bearings or a double row ball bearing. This type of sealed bearing is also used on the rear of many front-wheel-drive vehicles.

Double row ball bearings are often used because of their reduced friction and greater seize resistance. See Figures 9-8 and 9-9.

FIGURE 9-7 Non-drive-wheel hub with inner and outer tapered roller bearings. By angling the inner and outer in opposite directions, axial (thrust) loads are supported in both directions.

BALL-BEARING ASSEMBLY

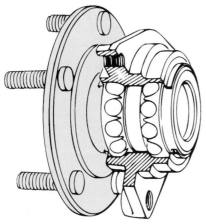

**TAPERED ROLLER
BEARING ASSEMBLY**

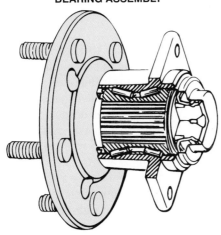

FIGURE 9-8 Sealed bearing and hub assemblies are used on the front and rear wheels of many vehicles.

WHEEL SPEED SENSOR CONNECTOR   SEALED BEARING ASSEMBLY

FIGURE 9-9 Sealed bearing and hub assemblies are serviced as a complete unit as shown. This assembly includes the wheel speed sensor.

BEARING GREASES

Vehicle manufacturers specify the type and consistency of grease for each application. The technician should know what these specifications mean. **Grease** is an oil with a thickening agent to allow it to be installed in places where a liquid lubricant would not stay. Greases are named for their thickening agent, such as aluminum, barium, calcium, lithium, or sodium.

Grease Additives

Commonly used additives in grease include the following:

- Antioxidants
- Antiwear agents
- Rust inhibitors
- Extreme pressure (EP) additives such as sulfurized fatty oil or chlorine

Grease also contains a dye to not only provide product identification but also to give the grease a consistent color.

The grease contains a solid such as graphite or molybdenum disulfide (moly), which acts as an antiseize additive.

FREQUENTLY ASKED QUESTION

WHAT DO DIFFERENT GREASE COLORS MEAN?

Nothing. According to grease manufacturers, grease is colored for identification, marketing, and for consistency color reasons.

- *Identification.* The color is often used to distinguish one type of grease from another within the same company. The blue grease from one company may be totally different from the blue grease produced or marketed by another company.
- *Marketing.* According to grease manufacturers, customers tend to be attracted to a particular color of grease and associate that color with quality.
- *Consistency of color.* All greases are produced in batches, and the color of the finished product often varies in color from one batch to another. By adding color to the grease, the color can be made consistent.

Always use the grease recommended for the service being performed.

NLGI Classification

The **National Lubricating Grease Institute (NLGI)** uses the penetration test as a guide to assign the grease a number. Low numbers are very fluid and higher numbers are more firm or hard. See the chart.

National Lubricating Grease Institute (NLGI) Numbers

NLGI Number	Relative Consistency
000	Very fluid
00	Fluid
0	Semi-fluid
1	Very soft
2	Soft (typically used for wheel bearings)
3	Semi-firm
4	Firm
5	Very firm
6	Hard

Grease is also classified according to quality. Wheel bearing classifications include the following:

- GA—mild duty
- GB—moderate duty
- GC—severe duty, high temperature (frequent stop and go service)

GC indicates the highest quality. Chassis grease, such as is used to lubricate steering and suspension components, include the following:

- LA—mild duty (frequent relubrication)
- LB—high loads (infrequent relubrication)

LB indicates the highest quality. Most multipurpose greases are labeled with both wheel bearing and chassis grease classifications such as **GC-LB.**

More rolling bearings are destroyed by over lubrication than by under lubrication because the heat generated in the bearings cannot be transferred easily to the air through the excessive grease. Bearings should never be filled beyond one-third to one-half of their grease capacity by volume.

SMOKING CAN KILL YOU

Some greases contain polymers such as Teflon® that turn to a deadly gas when burned. Always wash your hands thoroughly after handling grease that contains these ingredients before smoking. If some of the grease is on the cigarette paper and is burned, these polymers turn into nitrofluoric acid—a deadly toxin.

SEALS

Seals are used in all vehicles to keep lubricant, such as grease, from leaking out and to prevent dirt, dust, or water from getting into the bearing or lubricant. Two general applications of seals are static and dynamic. **Static seals** are used between two surfaces that do not move. **Dynamic seals** are used to seal between two surfaces that move. Wheel bearing seals are dynamic type seals that must seal between rotating axle hubs and the stationary spindles or axle housing. Most dynamic seals use a synthetic rubber lip seal encased in metal. The lip is often held in contact with the moving part with the aid of a **garter spring,** as seen in Figure 9-10.

The sealing lip should be installed toward the grease or fluid being contained. See Figure 9-11.

FIGURE 9-10   Typical lip seal with a garter spring.

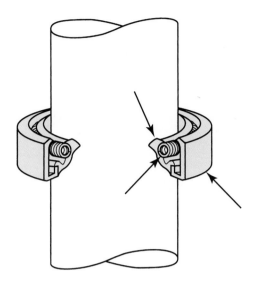

FIGURE 9-11 A garter spring helps hold the sharp lip edge of the seal tight against the shaft.

SYMPTOMS AND DIAGNOSIS OF DEFECTIVE BEARINGS

Wheel bearings control the positioning and reduce the rolling resistance of vehicle wheels. Whenever a bearing fails, the wheel may not be kept in position and noise is usually heard. Symptoms of defective wheel bearings include the following:

1. A hum, rumbling, or growling noise that increases with vehicle speed
2. Roughness felt in the steering wheel that changes with the vehicle speed or cornering
3. Looseness or excessive play in the steering wheel especially while driving over rough road surfaces
4. A loud grinding noise in severe cases of a defective front wheel bearing
5. Pulling during braking

With the vehicle off the ground, rotate the wheel by hand, listening and feeling carefully for bearing roughness. Grasp the wheel at the top and bottom and wiggle it back and forth, checking for bearing looseness.

NOTE: Excessive looseness in the wheel bearings can cause a low brake pedal. If any of the above symptoms are present, carefully clean and inspect the bearings.

TECH TIP

"BEARING OVERLOAD"

It is not uncommon for vehicles to be overloaded. This is particularly common with pickup trucks and vans. Whenever there is a heavy load, the axle bearings must support the entire weight of the vehicle, including its cargo. If a bump is hit while driving with a heavy load, the balls of a ball bearing or the rollers of a roller bearing can make an indent in the race of the bearing. This dent or imprint is called **brinelling,** named after Johann A. Brinell, a Swedish engineer who developed a process of testing for surface hardness by pressing a hard ball with a standard force into a sample material to be tested.

Once this imprint is made, the bearing will make noise whenever the roller or ball rolls over the indent. Continued use causes wear to occur on all of the balls or rollers and eventual failure. While this may take months to fail, the *cause* of the bearing failure is often overloading of the vehicle. Avoid shock loads and overloading for safety and for longer vehicle life.

NON-DRIVE-WHEEL BEARING INSPECTION AND SERVICE

The steps in a non-drive-wheel bearing inspection include the following:

1. Hoist the vehicle safely.
2. Remove the wheel.
3. Remove the brake caliper assembly and support it with a coat hanger or other suitable hook to avoid allowing the caliper to hang by the brake hose.
4. Remove the grease cap (dust cap). See Figure 9-12.
5. Remove the old cotter key and discard.

NOTE: The term *cotter,* as in cotter key or cotter pin, is derived from the old English verb meaning "to close or fasten."

---

6. Remove the spindle nut (castle nut).
7. Remove the washer and the outer wheel bearing. See Figure 9-13.

FIGURE 9-12   Removing the grease cap with grease cap pliers.

FIGURE 9-13   After wiggling the brake rotor slightly, the washer and outer bearing can be easily lifted out of the wheel hub.

FIGURE 9-14   Some technicians remove the inner wheel bearing and the grease seal at the same time by jerking the rotor off the spindle after reinstalling the spindle nut. While this is a quick-and-easy method, sometimes the bearing is damaged (deformed) from being jerked out of the hub using this procedure.

8. Remove the bearing hub from the spindle. The inner bearing will remain in the hub and may be removed (simply lifted out) after the grease seal is pried out. See Figure 9-14.
9. Most vehicle and bearing manufacturers recommend cleaning the bearing thoroughly in solvent or acetone. If there is no acetone, clean the solvent off the bearings with denatured alcohol to make certain that the thin solvent layer is completely washed off and dry. *All solvent must be removed or allowed to dry from the bearing because the new grease will not stick to a layer of solvent.*
10. Carefully inspect the bearings and the races for the following:
   a. The outer race for lines, scratches, or pits. See Figure 9-15.

b. The cage should be round. If the round cage has straight sections, this is an indication of an overtightened adjustment or a dropped cage.
   If either of the above is observed, then the bearing, including the outer race, must be replaced. Failure to

TECH TIP

BEARING NOISE— TIRE NOISE

A defective wheel bearing is often difficult to diagnose because the noise is similar to a noisy winter tire or a severely cupped tire. Customers often request that tires be replaced as a result of the noise when the real problem is a bad wheel bearing. To help determine if the noise is caused by a wheel bearing or a tire, try these tips:

Tip 1   Drive the vehicle over a variety of road surfaces. If the noise changes with a change in road surface, then the noise is caused by a tire(s). If the noise remains the same, then the cause is a defective wheel bearing.

Tip 2   Try temporarily overinflating the tires. If the noise changes, then the tires are the cause. If the noise is the same, then defective wheel bearings are the cause.

BENT CAGE

CAGE DAMAGE CAUSED BY IMPROPER HANDLING OR TOOL USE

GALLING

METAL SMEARS OR ROLLER ENDS CAUSED BY OVERHEATING, OVERLOADING, OR INADEQUATE LUBRICATION

STEP WEAR

NOTCHED WEAR PATTERN ON ROLLER ENDS CAUSED BY ABRASIVES IN THE LUBRICANT

ETCHING AND CORROSION

EATEN AWAY BEARING SURFACE WITH GRAY OR GRAY-BLACK COLOR CAUSED BY MOISTURE CONTAMINATION OF THE LUBRICANT

PITTING AND BRUISING

PITS, DEPRESSIONS, AND GROOVES IN THE BEARING SURFACES CAUSED BY PARTICULATE CONTAMINATION OF THE LUBRICANT

SPALLING

FLAKING AWAY OF THE BEARING SURFACE METAL CAUSED BY FATIGUE

MISALIGNMENT

SKEWED WEAR PATTERN CAUSED BY BENT SPINDLE OR IMPROPER BEARING INSTALLATION

HEAT DISCOLORATION

FAINT YELLOW TO DARK BLUE DISCOLORATION FROM OVERHEATING CAUSED BY OVERLOADING OR INADEQUATE LUBRICATION

BRINELLING

INDENTATIONS IN THE RACES CAUSED BY IMPACT LOADS OR VIBRATION WHEN THE BEARING IS NOT TURNING

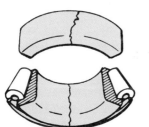

CRACKED RACE

CRACKING OF THE RACE CAUSED BY EXCESSIVE PRESS FIT, IMPROPER INSTALLATION OR DAMAGED BEARING SEATS

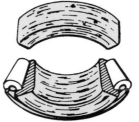

SMEARING

SMEARED METAL FROM SLIPPAGE CAUSED BY POOR FIT, POOR LUBRICAITON, OVERLOADING, OVERHEATING, OR HANDLING DAMAGE

FRETTAGE

ETCHING OR CORROSION CAUSED BY SMALL RELATIVE MOVEMENTS BETWEEN PARTS WITH NO LUBRICATION

FIGURE 9-15   Wheel bearing inspection chart.

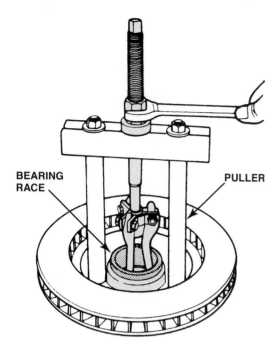

FIGURE 9-16   A wheel bearing race puller.

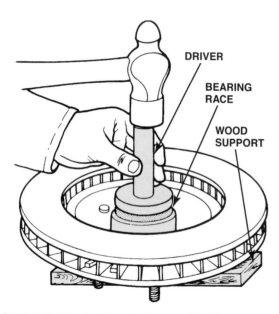

FIGURE 9-17   Installing a bearing race with a driver.

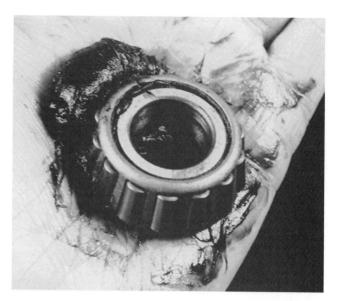

FIGURE 9-18   When packing grease into a cleaned bearing force grease around each roller as shown.

replace the outer race (which is included when purchasing a bearing) could lead to rapid failure of the new bearing. See Figures 9-16 and 9-17.

11. Pack the cleaned or new bearing thoroughly with clean, new, approved wheel bearing grease using hand packing or a wheel-bearing packer. Always clean out all of the old grease before applying the recommended type of new grease. *Because of compatibility problems,*

it is not recommended that greases be mixed. See Figure 9-18.

> **NOTE:** Some vehicle manufacturers do *not* recommend that "stringy-type" wheel bearing grease be used. Centrifugal force can cause the grease to be thrown outward from the bearing. Because of the stringy texture, the grease may not flow back into the bearing after it has been thrown outward. The final result is a lack of lubrication and eventual bearing failure.

12. Place a thin layer of grease on the outer race.
13. Apply a thin layer of grease to the spindle, being sure to cover the outer bearing seat, inner bearing seat, and shoulder at the grease seal seat.
14. Install a new **grease seal** (also called a *grease retainer*) flush with the hub using a seal driver.
15. Place approximately 3 tablespoons of grease into the grease cavity of the wheel hub. Excessive grease could cause the inner grease seal to fail, with the possibility of grease getting on the brakes. Place the rotor with the inner bearing and seal in place over the spindle until the grease seal rests on the grease seal shoulder.
16. Install the outer bearing and the bearing washer.
17. Install the spindle nut and, while rotating the tire assembly, tighten to about 12 to 30 lb. ft. with a wrench to "seat" the bearing correctly in the race (cup) and on the spindle. See Figure 9-19.
18. While still rotating the tire assembly, loosen the nut approximately one-half turn and then *hand tighten only* (about 5 lb. in.).

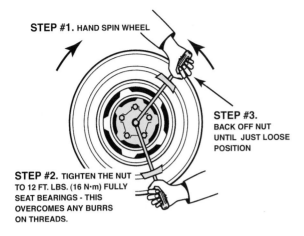

STEP #1. HAND SPIN WHEEL

STEP #3.
BACK OFF NUT
UNTIL JUST LOOSE
POSITION

STEP #2. TIGHTEN THE NUT
TO 12 FT. LBS. (16 N·m) FULLY
SEAT BEARINGS - THIS
OVERCOMES ANY BURRS
ON THREADS.

STEP #5. LOOSEN NUT UNTIL EITHER
HOLE IN THE SPINDLE LINES UP WITH
A SLOT IN THE NUT – THEN INSERT
COTTER PIN.

NOTICE: BEND ENDS OF COTTER
PIN AGAINST NUT, CUT OFF EXTRA
LENGTH TO PREVENT
INTERFERENCE WITH DUST CAP.

STEP #4.
HAND "SNUG-UP"
THE NUT

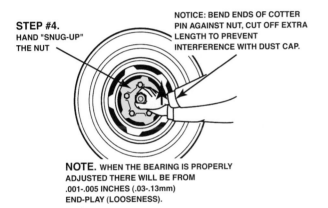

NOTE. WHEN THE BEARING IS PROPERLY
ADJUSTED THERE WILL BE FROM
.001-.005 INCHES (.03-.13mm)
END-PLAY (LOOSENESS).

FIGURE 9-19 The wheel bearing adjustment procedure as specified for rear-wheel-drive vehicles.

NOTE: If the wheel bearing is properly adjusted, the wheel will still have about 0.001 to 0.005 in. (0.03 to 0.13 mm) end play. This looseness is necessary to allow the tapered roller bearing to expand when hot and not bind or cause the wheel to lock up.

19. Install a new cotter key. (An old cotter key could break a part off where it was bent and lodge in the bearing, causing major damage.)

NOTE: Most vehicles use a cotter key that is 1/8 in. in diameter by 1 1/2 in. long.

20. If the cotter key does not line up with the hole in the spindle, loosen slightly (no more than 1/16 in. of a turn) until the hole lines up. Never tighten more than hand tight.

21. Bend the cotter key ends up and around the nut, not over the end of the spindle where the end of the cotter key could rub on the grease cap, causing noise. See Figure 9-20.

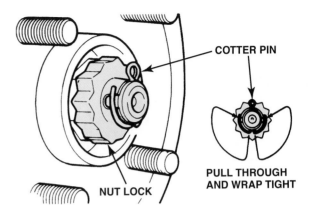

COTTER PIN

NUT LOCK

PULL THROUGH
AND WRAP TIGHT

FIGURE 9-20 A properly secured wheel bearing adjust nut.

TECH
TIP

WHEEL BEARING LOOSENESS TEST

Looseness in a front wheel bearing can allow the rotor to move whenever the front wheel hits a bump, forcing the caliper piston in, which causes the brake pedal to kick back and creates the feeling that the brakes were locking up.

Loose wheel bearings are easily diagnosed by removing the cover of the master cylinder reservoir and watching the brake fluid as the front wheels are turned left and right with the steering wheel. If the brake fluid moves while the front wheels are being turned, caliper piston(s) are moving in and out, caused by loose wheel bearing(s). If everything is OK, the brake fluid should not move.

NOTE: Loose wheel bearings can also cause the brake pedal to sink due to movement of the rotor, causing the caliper piston to move. This sinking brake pedal is usually caused by a defective master cylinder. Before replacing a master cylinder, check the wheel bearings.

22. Install the grease cap (dust cap) with a rubber mallet or soft-faced hammer to help prevent denting or distorting the grease cap. Install the wheel cover or hub cap.

CAUTION: Clean grease off the disc brake rotors or drums after servicing the wheel bearings. Use a brake cleaner and a shop cloth. Even a slight amount of grease on the friction surfaces of the brakes can harm the friction lining and/or cause brake noise.

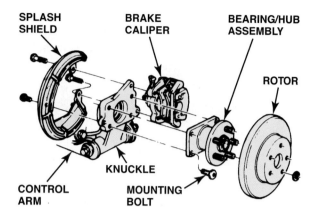

FIGURE 9-21   A rear wheel sealed bearing hub assembly.

SEALED BEARING REPLACEMENT

Most front-wheel-drive vehicles use a sealed bearing assembly that is bolted to the steering knuckle and supports the drive axle or the rear, as shown in Figure 9-21.

Many front-wheel-drive vehicles use a bearing that must be pressed off the steering knuckle. Special aftermarket tools are also available to remove many of the bearings without removing the knuckle from the vehicle. Check the factory service manual and tool manufacturers for exact procedures for the vehicle being serviced. See Figures 9-22 and 9-23.

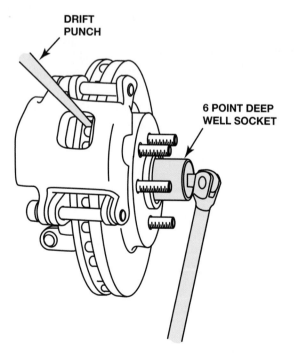

FIGURE 9-22   Removing the drive axle shaft hub nut. This nut is usually very tight and the drift (tapered) punch wedged into the cooling fins of the brake rotor keeps the hub from revolving when the nut is loosened.

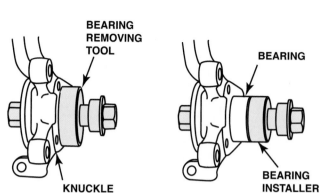

FIGURE 9-23   A special puller makes the job of removing the hub bearing from the knuckle easy without damaging any component.

Diagnosing a defective front bearing on a front-wheel-drive vehicle is sometimes confusing. A defective wheel bearing is usually noisy while driving straight, and the noise increases with vehicle speed (wheel speed). A drive axle shaft U-joint (CV joint) can also be the cause of noise on a front-wheel-drive vehicle, but usually makes *more noise* while turning and accelerating.

REAR-DRIVE-AXLE CLASSIFICATIONS

There are three rear-drive-axle classifications:

- Full-floating
- Three-quarter-floating
- Semi-floating

These classifications indicate whether the axle shafts or the axle housing supports the wheel. The category of a rear drive axle is determined by how the wheel and wheel bearing mount to the axle or housing.

FULL-FLOATING AXLE

On a full-floating axle, the bearings are mounted and retained in the hub of the brake drum or rotor. The hub and bearing mount onto the axle housing, and are held in place by a bearing retainer or adjustment nuts and safety locks. The flanged end of the drive axle is attached to the hub by bolts or nuts. The inner end of the axle splines into the differential side gears. The wheel mounts onto the hub, and lug bolts or nuts retain it. In this design, the axle shafts "float" in the axle housing and drive the wheels without supporting their weight. Because the

FIGURE 9-24 A typical full-floating rear axle
assembly.

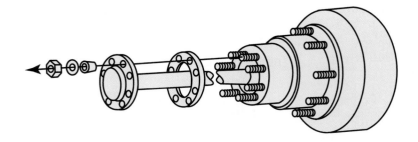

axle shafts do not retain the wheel, the axle shafts can usually
be removed from the vehicle while it is standing on the wheels.
Most three-quarter-ton pickups, all heavy-duty truck tractors,
and trailers use full-floating axles. See Figure 9-24.

Three-Quarter-Floating Axle

The bearings in a three-quarter-floating axle are mounted and
retained in the brake drum or rotor hub, which mounts onto
the axle housing. The outer extension of the hub fits onto the
end of the axle, which is usually splined and tapered, and a nut
and cotter pin secure the hub to the axle. The axle shaft splines
to the side gears inside the differential. The wheels are
mounted on the hub and retained by lug bolts or nuts. As in the
full-floating axle, the axle housing and bearings in the hub support the weight in a three-quarter-floating axle. Because of the
construction of a three-quarter-floating axle, the wheel must be
removed before removing the axle shaft from the vehicle.

Semi-Floating Axle

The wheel bearings in a semi-floating axle either press onto the
axle shaft or are installed in the outer end of the axle housing. A
retainer plate at the outer end of the axle shaft or a C-clip inside
the differential at the other end keeps the axle shaft in the housing. The brake drum or rotor fits onto the end of the axle, and
lug bolts or nuts fasten the wheel to the drum or rotor and to the
axle. These axles are called "semi-floating" because only the inboard ends of the axle shaft "float" in the housing. The outboard
end of the shaft retains the wheel and transmits the weight of
the wheel to the housing. Most solid-axle rear-wheel-drive cars
and light trucks use a semi-floating type of axle. See Figure 9-25.

REAR AXLE BEARING
AND SEAL REPLACEMENT

The rear bearings used on rear-wheel-drive vehicles are constructed and serviced differently from other types of wheel bearings. Rear axle bearings are either sealed or lubricated by the
rear-end lubricant. The rear axle must be removed from the vehicle to replace the rear axle bearing. There are two basic types
of axle retaining methods, **retainer plate-type** and the **C-lock.**

THREE-QUARTER-FLOATING

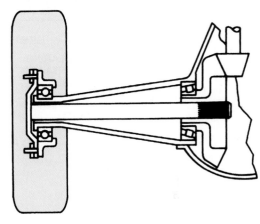

SEMI-FLOATING

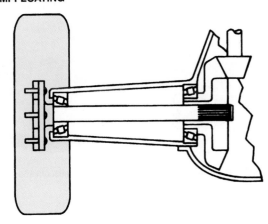

FIGURE 9-25 Rear axle shafts may be full-floating, three-quarter-
floating, or semi-floating, depending on whether the shafts or the axle housing
support the wheels.

RETAINER PLATE-TYPE
REAR AXLES

The retainer plate-type rear axle uses four fasteners that retain
the axle in the axle housing. To remove the axle shaft and the
rear axle bearing and seal, the retainer bolts or nuts must be
removed.

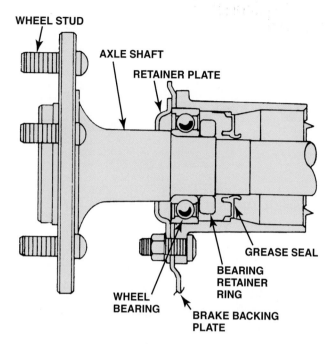

FIGURE 9-26   A retainer plate-type rear axle bearing. Access to the fasteners is through a hole in the axle flange.

FIGURE 9-27   A slide hammer-type axle puller can also be used.

NOTE: If the axle flange has an access hole, then a retainer plate-type axle is used.

The hole or holes in the wheel flange permit a socket wrench access to the fasteners. After the fasteners have been removed, the axle shaft must be removed from the rear axle housing. With the retainer plate-type rear axle, the bearing and the retaining ring are press fit onto the axle and the bearing cup (outer race) is also tightly fitted into the axle housing tube. See Figure 9-26. See Figure 9-27 for one way to remove the axle shaft. It is often necessary to remove the axle to per-

FIGURE 9-28   The ball bearings fell out onto the ground when this axle was pulled out of the axle housing. Diagnosing the cause of the noise and vibration was easy on this vehicle.

form a visual inspection especially if trying to diagnose driveline noises. See Figure 9-28.

C-Lock-Type Axles

Vehicles that use C-locks (clips) use a straight roller bearing supporting a semi-floating axle shaft inside the axle housing. The straight rollers do not have an inner race. The rollers ride on the axle itself. If a bearing fails, both the axle and the bearing usually need to be replaced. The outer bearing race holding the rollers is pressed into the rear axle housing. The axle bearing is usually lubricated by the rear-end lubricant and a grease seal is located on the outside of the bearing.

TECH TIP

THE BRAKE DRUM SLIDE HAMMER TRICK

To remove the axle from a vehicle equipped with a retainer plate-type rear axle, simply use the brake drum as a slide hammer to remove the axle from the axle housing. See Figure 9-29. If the brake drum does not provide enough force, a slide hammer can also be used to remove the axle shaft.

(a)

(b)

FIGURE 9-29 (a) To remove the axle from this vehicle equipped with a retainer-plate rear axle, the brake drum was placed back onto the axle studs backward so that the drum itself can be used as a slide hammer to pull the axle out of the axle housing. (b) A couple of pulls and the rear axle is pulled out of the axle housing.

NOTE: Some replacement bearings are available that are designed to ride on a fresh, unworn section of the old axle. These bearings allow the use of the original axle, saving the cost of a replacement axle.

The C-lock-type rear axle retaining method requires that the differential cover plate be removed. After removal of the cover, the differential pinion shaft has to be removed before the C-lock that retains the axle can be removed. See Figures 9-30 and 9-31.

NOTE: When removing the differential cover, rear axle lubricant will flow from between the housing and the cover. Be sure to dispose of the old rear axle lubricant in the environmentally approved way, and refill with the proper type and viscosity (thickness) of rear-end lubricant. Check the vehicle specifications for the recommended grade.

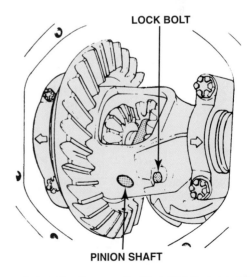

LOCK BOLT

PINION SHAFT

FIGURE 9-30 To remove the C-lock (clip), the lock bolt has to be moved before the pinion shaft.

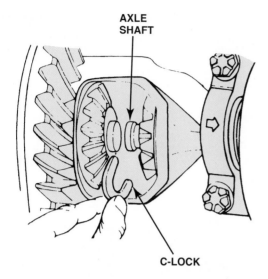

AXLE
SHAFT

C-LOCK

FIGURE 9-31   The axle must be pushed inward slightly to allow the C-lock to be removed. After the C-lock has been removed, the axle can be easily pulled out of the axle housing.

Once the C-lock has been removed, the axle simply is pulled out of the axle tube. Axle bearings with inner races are pressed onto the axle shaft and must be pressed off using a hydraulic press. A bearing retaining collar should be chiseled or drilled into to expand the collar, allowing it to be removed. See Figure 9-32.

Always follow the manufacturer's recommended bearing removal and replacement procedures. Always replace the

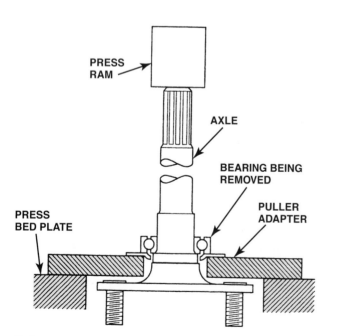

PRESS
RAM

AXLE

BEARING BEING
REMOVED

PULLER
ADAPTER

PRESS
BED PLATE

FIGURE 9-32   Using a hydraulic press to press an axle bearing from the axle. When pressing a new bearing back onto the axle, pressure should only be on the inner bearing race to prevent damaging the bearing.

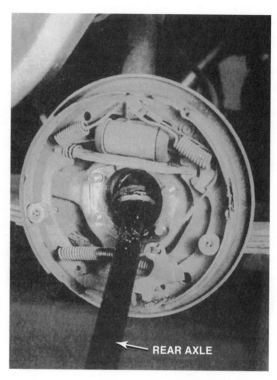

REAR AXLE

FIGURE 9-33   Removing an axle seal using the axle shaft as the tool.

rear axle seal whenever replacing a rear axle bearing. See Figure 9-33 for an example of seal removal.

Always check the differential vent to make sure it is clear. A clogged vent can cause excessive pressure to build up inside the differential and cause the rear axle seals to leak. If rear-end lubricant gets on the brake linings, the brakes will not have the proper friction and the linings themselves are ruined and must be replaced:

BEARING FAILURE ANALYSIS

Whenever a bearing is replaced, the old bearing must be inspected and the cause of the failure eliminated. See Figures 9-34 through 9-40 for examples of normal and abnormal bearing wear.

A wheel bearing may also fail for reasons, including the following:

Metal Fatigue.   Long vehicle usage, even under normal driving conditions, causes metal to fatigue. Cracks often appear, and eventually these cracks expand downward into the metal from the surface. The metal between the cracks can break out into small chips, slabs, or scales of metal. This process of breaking up is called **spalling.** See Figure 9-41.

FIGURE 9-34   This is a normally worn bearing. If it does not have too much play, it can be reused. *(Courtesy SKF USA Inc.)*

(a)   (b)

FIGURE 9-38   (a) Regular patterns of etching in the race are from corrosion. This bearing should be replaced. (b) Light pitting comes from contaminants being pressed into the race. Discard the bearing.   *(Courtesy SKF USA Inc.)*

(a)   (b)

FIGURE 9-35   (a) When corrosion etches into the surface of a roller or race, the bearing should be discarded. (b) If light corrosion stains can be removed with an oil-soaked cloth, the bearing can be reused.   *(Courtesy SKF USA Inc.)*

(a)   (b)

FIGURE 9-39   (a) This bearing is worn unevenly. Notice the stripes. It should not be reused. (b) Any damage that causes low spots in the metal renders the bearing useless.   *(Courtesy SKF USA Inc.)*

(a)   (b)

FIGURE 9-36   (a) When just the end of a roller is scored, it is because of excessive preload. Discard the bearing. (b) This is a more advanced case of pitting. Under load, it will rapidly lead to spalling.   *(Courtesy SKF USA Inc.)*

(a)   (b)

FIGURE 9-40   (a) In this more advanced case of pitting, you can see how the race has been damaged. (b) Discoloration is a result of overheating. Even a lightly burned bearing should be replaced.   *(Courtesy SKF USA Inc.)*

(a)   (b)

FIGURE 9-37   (a) Always check for faint grooves in the race. This bearing should not be reused. (b) Grooves like this are often matched by grooves in the race (above). Discard the bearing.   *(Courtesy SKF USA Inc.)*

(a)   (b)

FIGURE 9-41   (a) Pitting eventually leads to spalling, a condition where the metal falls away in large chunks. (b) In this spalled roller, the metal has actually begun to flake away from the surface.   *(Courtesy SKF USA Inc.)*

Shock Loading.   Dents can be formed in the race of a bearing, which eventually leads to bearing failure. See the Tech Tip titled "Bearing Overload" and Figure 9-42.

FIGURE 9-42 These dents resulted from the rollers "hammering" against the race, a condition called brinelling. *(Courtesy SKF USA Inc.)*

TECH TIP

WHAT'S THAT SOUND?

Defective wheel bearings usually make noise. The noise most defective wheel bearings make sounds like noisy off-road or aggressive tread, or mud and snow tires. Wheel bearing noise will remain constant while driving over different types of road surfaces while tire tread noise usually changes with different road surfaces. In fact, many defective bearings have been ignored by the vehicle owners and technicians because it was thought that the source of the noise was the aggressive tread design of the mud and snow tires. Always suspect defective wheel bearings whenever you hear what seems to be extreme or unusually loud tire noise.

SUMMARY

1. Wheel bearings support the entire weight of a vehicle and are used to reduce rolling friction. Ball and straight roller-type bearings are nonadjustable while tapered roller-type bearings must be adjusted for proper clearance.
2. Most front-wheel-drive vehicles use sealed bearings, either two pre-loaded tapered roller bearings or double row ball bearings.
3. Most wheel bearings are standardized sizes.
4. A defective bearing can be caused by metal fatigue that leads to spalling, shock loads that cause brinelling, or damage from electrical arcing due to poor body ground wires or improper electrical welding on the vehicle.
5. Bearing grease is an oil with a thickener. The higher the NLGI number of the grease, the thicker or harder the grease consistency.
6. Tapered wheel bearings must be adjusted by hand tightening the spindle nut after properly seating the bearings. A new cotter key must always be used.
7. Defective wheel bearings usually make more noise while turning because more weight is applied to the bearing as the vehicle turns.
8. All bearings must be serviced, replaced, and/or adjusted using the vehicle manufacturer's recommended procedures as stated in the service manual.

REVIEW QUESTIONS

1. List three common types of automotive antifriction bearings.
2. Explain the adjustment procedure for a typical tapered roller wheel bearing.
3. List four symptoms of a defective wheel bearing.
4. Describe how the rear axle is removed from a C-lock-type axle.

CHAPTER QUIZ

1. Which type of automotive bearing can withstand radial and thrust loads, yet must be adjusted for proper clearance?
   a. Roller bearing
   b. Tapered roller bearing
   c. Ball bearings
   d. Needle roller bearing

2. Most sealed bearings used on the front wheels of front-wheel-drive vehicles are usually which type?
   a. Roller bearing
   b. Single tapered roller bearing
   c. Double row ball bearing
   d. Needle roller bearing

3. On a bearing that has been shock loaded, the race (cup) of the bearing can be dented. This type of bearing failure is called _____.
   a. Spalling
   b. Arcing
   c. Brinelling
   d. Fluting

4. The bearing grease most often specified is rated NLGI _____.
   a. #00
   b. #0
   c. #1
   d. #2

5. A non-drive-wheel bearing adjustment procedure includes a final spindle nut tightening torque of _____.
   a. Finger tight
   b. 5 lb. in.
   c. 12 to 30 lb. ft.
   d. 12 to 15 lb. ft. plus 1/16 in. turn

6. After a non-drive-wheel bearing has been properly adjusted, the wheel should have how much end play?
   a. Zero
   b. 0.001 to 0.005 in.

c. 0.10 to 0.30 in.
d. 1/16 to 3/32 in.

7. The differential cover must be removed before removing the rear axle on which type of axle?
   a. Retainer plate
   b. C-lock
   c. Press fit
   d. Welded tube

8. What part(s) should be replaced when servicing a wheel bearing on a non-drive wheel?
   a. The bearing cup
   b. The grease seal
   c. The cotter key
   d. Both the grease seal and the cotter key

9. Technician A says that a defective wheel or axle bearing often makes a growling or rumbling noise. Technician B says that a defective wheel or axle bearing often makes a noise similar to a tire with an aggressive mud or snow design. Which technician is correct?
   a. Technician A only
   b. Technician B only
   c. Both Technicians A and B
   d. Neither Technician A nor B

10. Two technicians are discussing differentials. Technician A says all differentials are vented. Technician B says that a clogged vent can cause the rear axle seal to leak. Which technician is correct?
    a. Technician A only
    b. Technician B only
    c. Both Technicians A and B
    d. Neither Technician A nor B

DRUM BRAKES

OBJECTIVES

After studying Chapter 10, the reader should be able to:

1. Prepare for the Brakes (A5) ASE certification test content area "B" (Drum Brake Diagnosis and Repair).

2. Identify drum brake component parts.

3. Describe the operation of non-servo brakes.

4. Explain the operation of dual-servo brakes.

5. Discuss drum brake adjusters.

DRUM BRAKE ADVANTAGES

Drum brakes were the first type of brakes used on motor vehicles. Even today, over 100 years after the first "horseless carriages," drum brakes are still used on the rear of most vehicles, as shown in Figure 10-1.

The drum brake has been more widely used than any other automotive brake design. See Figure 10-2.

Although the disc brake has proven its superiority in extreme braking conditions, and has replaced the drum brake on the front axle of new vehicles, the drum brake continues to have a number of advantages that contribute to its widespread use on the rear axle of most automobiles.

Self-Energizing and Servo Action

The primary advantage of drum brakes is that they can apply more stopping power for a given amount of force applied to the brake pedal than can disc brakes. This is possible because the drum brake design offers a self-energizing action that helps force the brake linings tightly against the drum. In addition, some drum brake designs use an effect called servo action that enables one brake shoe to help apply the other for increased stopping power. Both self-energizing and servo action are explained in detail later in the chapter.

Parking Brake Service

One significant advantage that results from the superior banking power of drum brakes at low application forces is that they make excellent parking brakes. A simple linkage fitted to the brake assembly allows relatively low effort from the driver to hold a heavy vehicle in place when parked. Disc brakes, which do not benefit from self-energizing or servo action, require a complex set of extra parts to provide enough application force to work well as parking brakes.

DRUM BRAKE DISADVANTAGES

Drum brake disadvantages fall into three areas:

- Brake fade
- Brake adjustment
- Brake pull

Brake Fade

The greatest drawback of drum brakes is that they are susceptible to fade. **Brake fade** is the loss of stopping power that occurs when excessive heat reduces the friction between the brake shoe linings and the drum.

FIGURE 10-1 Typical brake system components showing disc brakes on the front and drum brakes on the rear. *(Courtesy of DaimlerChrysler Corporation)*

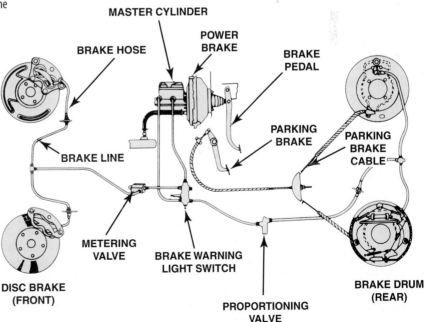

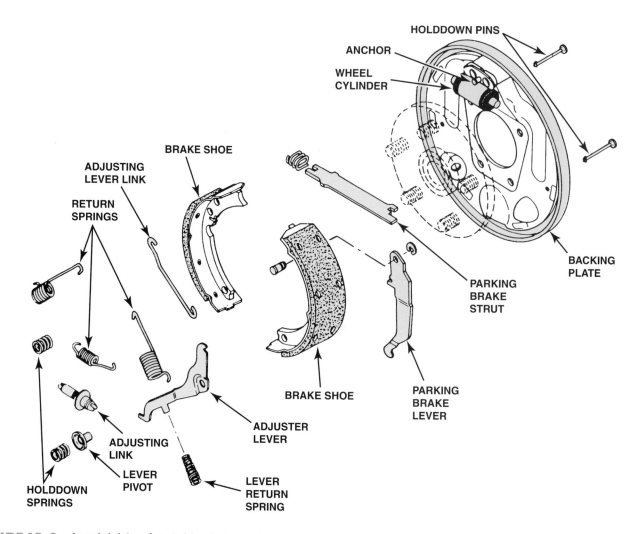

FIGURE 10-2   An exploded view of a typical drum brake assembly.

Mechanical Fade.   Drum brakes are not very efficient at dissipating heat. The brake drum shrouds the linings, and most of the heat produced when braking must pass through the drum, from the inside out, before it can be carried away by the passing airflow. **Mechanical fade** occurs when the brake drum gets so hot it expands away from the brake linings. The brake shoes then move outward to maintain contact with the drum, causing the brake pedal to drop toward the floor as additional brake fluid moves into the hydraulic system.

Lining Fade.   **Lining fade** occurs when the friction coefficient of the brake lining material drops off sharply because intense heat makes it "slippery." Unlike mechanical fade, brake pedal travel does not increase when lining fade occurs. Instead, the pedal becomes hard and there is a noticeable loss of braking power. The portions of the linings that do remain in contact with the drum become extremely hot and mechanical fade of the drum soon results.

Gas Fade.   A relatively rare type of brake fade is called **gas fade.** Under extended hard braking from high speeds, a thin layer of hot gasses and dust particles can build up between the brake shoe linings and drum. The gas layer acts as a lubricant and reduces friction. As with the lining fade, the brake pedal becomes hard, and greater application force is required to maintain a constant level of stopping power.

Water Fade.   Drum brakes are also affected by a problem called **water fade.** A drum brake friction assembly cannot be made waterproof because clearance is necessary between the rotating drum and the fixed backing plate. This clearance allows a small amount of air circulation that helps combat heat fade, but it can also allow water to enter the friction assembly. Water fade occurs when moisture is trapped between the shoes and drum, where it acts as a lubricant. This lowers braking efficiency until friction creates enough heat to evaporate the water.

QUICK-AND-EASY DRUM BRAKE ADJUSTMENT CHECK

Tap the brake drum lightly with a hammer or wrench. If the brake shoes are not contacting the drum, the drum will ring like a bell. If the shoes are contacting the drum, the sound will be muffled.

Brake Adjustment

Another disadvantage of the drum brake design is its need for an adjusting mechanism. As the brake shoe lining material wears, the clearance between the linings and drum increases, resulting in longer brake pedal travel. To maintain a high brake pedal, a mechanism must be included in the friction assembly for periodic adjustment of the clearance between the shoe and drum. Most vehicles have automatic adjusters that maintain the proper clearance between the brake linings and the drum.

Brake Pull

The final disadvantage of drum brakes is that they sometimes pull the vehicle to one side or the other during braking. Certain designs are more susceptible to this than others, but all drum brakes suffer from it to one degree or another. Brake pull occurs when the friction assemblies on opposite sides of the vehicle have different amounts of stopping power. These differences can be caused by brake fade or misadjustment of the clearance between the brake linings and drum.

DRUM BRAKE PARTS

A typical drum brake assembly consists of many parts, including the backing plate and springs, as well as the brake shoes and adjuster.

The foundation of every drum brake is the backing plate that mounts to the steering knuckle on the front brakes, or to the suspension or axle housing on the rear brakes. See Figure 10-3.

The backing plate serves as the mounting surface for all the other friction assembly parts. The backing plate also functions as a dust and water shield to keep contaminants out of the brake assembly. The edge of the backing plate curves out-

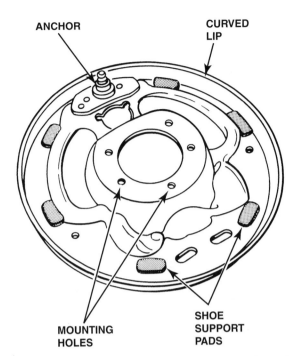

FIGURE 10-3 The backing plate is the foundation of every drum brake.

ward to form a lip that strengthens the backing plate and fits inside the brake drum to help prevent water entry. The lip fits into a machined groove in the open edge of the brake drum to provide an even better water barrier or seal. This is called a **labyrinth seal**. See Figure 10-4.

In addition to mounting holes for the various brake parts, the backing plate may also have openings that are used to inspect the wear of the brake linings, or adjust the lining-to-drum clearance. These openings are sometimes sealed with metal plugs that must be punched out the first time inspection or adjustment is needed. Rubber plugs are available to seal the holes and prevent water entry once the metal plugs have been removed.

Shoe Anchors

Shoe anchors prevent the brake shoes from rotating with the drum when the brakes are applied. The majority of drum brakes have a single anchor, but some drum brake designs use two or more.

Many anchors are a simple round post that is permanently mounted on the backing plate. The brake shoes have semicircular cutouts where they contact the anchor, and the anchor positively locates the shoe on the backing plate. Another type of anchor is the self-centering or keystone anchor. See Figure 10-5.

It is called a keystone anchor becausen of the angled shape similar to a keystone used on the top center of a stone arch.

FIGURE 10-4   The flange on the backing plate is designed to come close to a notch or groove on the brake drum, forming a type of seal that helps prevent debris and water from getting onto the drum brake.

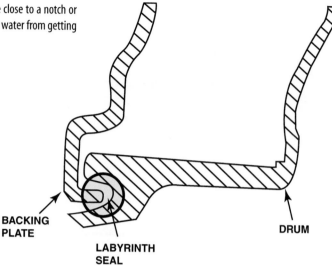

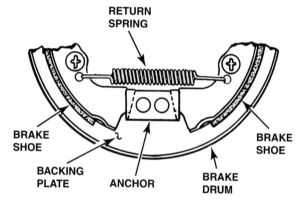

FIGURE 10-5   A keystone anchor allows the brake shoes to self-center in the drum.

Piston Stops

Some backing plates incorporate **piston stops** that prevent the wheel cylinder pistons from coming out of their bores when the friction assembly is disassembled for servicing. The stops may be part of a reinforcing plate positioned under the anchor or they can be stamped directly into the shape of the backing plate itself. See Figure 10-6.

When piston stops are used, the wheel cylinder must be removed from the backing plate before it can be taken apart for servicing.

Shoe Support Pads

The **shoe support pads** are stamped into the backing plate and contact the edges of the brake shoes to keep the linings properly aligned with the center of the friction surface inside the brake drum. These pads are also called **ledges** or **shoe contact areas**. The support pads are slightly coated with special high-temperature silicone brake grease to minimize wear, prevent rust, and eliminate squeaking that can occur when the shoes move slightly on the pads during a stop.

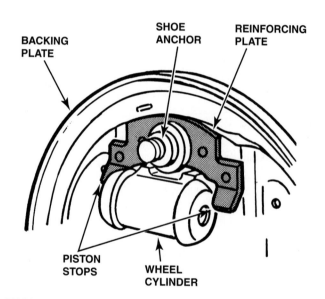

FIGURE 10-6   Piston stops prevent the wheel cylinder from coming apart.

Wheel Cylinders

Hydraulic pressure is transferred from the master cylinder to each wheel cylinder through brake fluid. The force exerted on the brake fluid by the driver forces the piston inside the wheel cylinder to move outward. See Figure 10-7. Through pushrods or links, this movement acts on the brake shoes, forcing them outward against the brake drum. See Figure 10-8.

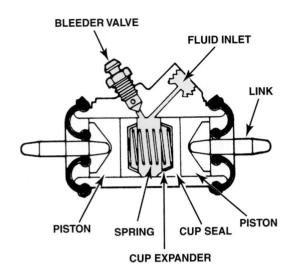

FIGURE 10-7   Cross-section of a wheel cylinder that shows all of its internal parts. The brake line attaches to the fluid inlet. The cup expander prevents the cup seal lip from collapsing when the brakes are released.

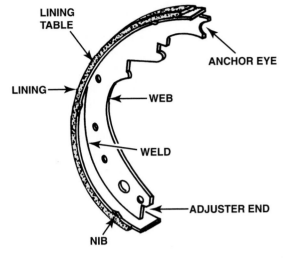

FIGURE 10-9   Steel brake shoes are made from two stampings welded together.

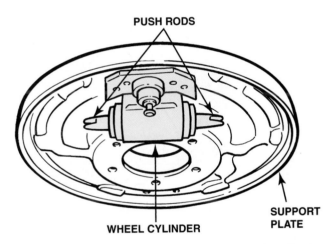

FIGURE 10-8   The pushrods are held in place by the rubber dust boots. As the wheel cylinder pistons move outward, the pushrods transfer the movement to the brake shoes.   *(Courtesy of DaimlerChrysler Corporation)*

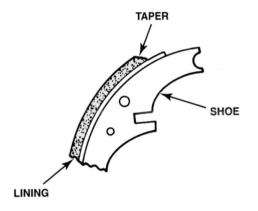

FIGURE 10-10   Tapered ends on the brake linings reduce noise.

DRUM BRAKE SHOES

The linings of drum brakes are attached to curved metal assemblies called **brake shoes.** Most shoes are made of two pieces of sheet steel welded together in a T-shaped cross section. See Figure 10-9.

While aluminum shoes are lighter than their steel counterparts, they are more expensive to make and not as durable at high temperatures. The outer edge is lined with a friction material that contacts the brake drum to generate the actual stopping power. The ends of the linings on most brake shoes are tapered to prevent vibration and brake noise as shown in Figure 10-10.

The curved metal piece on the outer portion of the shoe is called the **lining table,** the **shoe rim** or **platform.** The lining table supports the block of friction material that makes up the brake lining. On some shoes, the edge of the lining table contains small V- or U-shaped notches called **nibs.** The nibs rest against the shoe support pads on the backing plate when the shoe is installed.

The metal piece of the shoe positioned under the lining table and welded to it is called the **shoe web.** All of the application force that actuates the shoe is transferred through the web to the lining table. The web usually contains a number of holes in various shapes and sizes for the shoe return springs, hold-down hardware, parking brake linkage, and self-adjusting mechanism.

One end of the web usually has a notch or protrusion where the wheel cylinder touches the shoe, while the other end commonly has a flat or curved surface where the shoe meets an anchor or adjusting link. The upper ends of the webs on dual-servo brake shoes have semicircular **anchor eyes.** See Figure 10-11.

Brake shoes are sturdy parts that can be relined and reused many times if the web and lining table are not damaged. Brake shoes for any given application are usually available in both "new" and "relined" versions from suppliers. Relined brake shoes are usually sold on an exchange basis. At the time of purchase, a **core charge** is added to the cost of the relined parts. This charge is refunded when the old shoes are returned in rebuildable condition.

Primary and Secondary Brake Shoes

In many drum brake friction assemblies, the two shoes are interchangeable; one is a mirror image of the other. However, the shoes in a dual-servo brake perform very different jobs. The primary shoe (forward facing shoe) is self-energized by drum rotation to create a servo action that forces the secondary shoe more firmly against the drum. Because of this, the two shoes have definite physical differences and cannot be interchanged.

To help deal with the added friction, heat, and wear it undergoes, the lining of the secondary shoe extends nearly the full length of the shoe lining table. See Figure 10-12.

The secondary shoe lining material also has a high coefficient of friction to provide good stopping power. The primary shoe undergoes far less stress than the secondary shoe, and its lining is often shorter—sometimes less than half the length of the lining table. In addition, the lining material usually has a

lower coefficient of friction. This prevents the shoe from engaging the drum too quickly or harshly, which could cause the brakes to grab or lock. See Figure 10-13.

On most dual-servo brake primary shoes, the lining is positioned near the center of the lining table. However, in some cases, the lining may be positioned above or below the lining table centerline. Higher or lower lining positions provide better braking action, or prevent noise, in certain applications. See Figure 10-14.

Lining Assembly Methods

Before any type of brake lining can do its job, it must be firmly attached to the lining table of a drum brake shoe or the back-

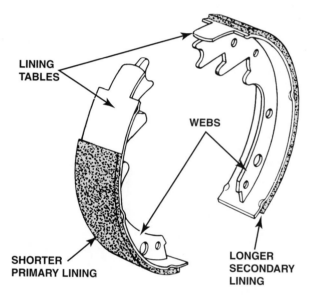

FIGURE 10-12 The primary (forward facing) brake shoe often has a shorter lining than the secondary shoe (rearward facing).

FIGURE 10-11 Typical drum brake shoe and the names of the parts. *(Courtesy of Allied Signal Automotive Aftermarket)*

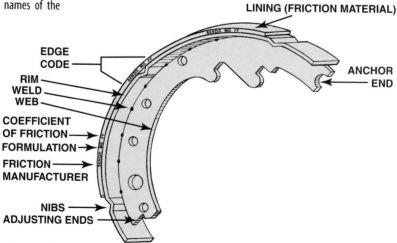

FIGURE 10-13   Brake lining on the assembly line at Delphi (Delco) brake systems. The darker color linings are the secondary shoes.

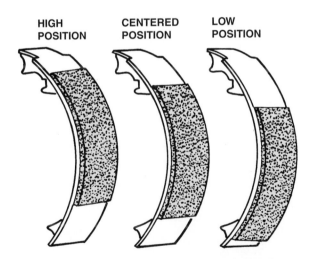

HIGH POSITION   CENTERED POSITION   LOW POSITION

FIGURE 10-14   Primary shoe lining may vary depending on the application.

ing plate of a disc brake pad. Several methods are used to mount brake linings; the most common are the following:

- Riveting
- Bonding
- Mold bonding

Riveting. **Riveted linings** take advantage of the oldest method of lining attachment still in use. In this system, the brake block is attached to the lining table or backing plate with copper or aluminum rivets. See Figure 10-15.

The major advantage of riveting is that it allows a small amount of flex between the brake block and lining table or backing plate. This play enables the assembly to absorb vibration, and the result is that riveted linings operate more quietly than bonded linings. Rivets are also very reliable and will not loosen at high temperatures.

Despite the benefit of quiet operation, riveted linings present a number of problems. In order to leave sufficient friction material for the rivets to clamp the brake block securely against the lining table or backing plate, the rivet holes are countersunk only about two-thirds to three-quarters of the way through the lining. This reduces the service life of the assembly because the shoes must be replaced before the rivet heads contact and score the drum.

The rivet holes themselves also present some unique problems. First, they trap abrasive brake dust and other grit that can score the drum or rotor. Some rivets are hollow to allow these materials to escape.

Rivet holes also create stress points in the lining where cracks are likely to develop. Some riveted semimetallic brake pads have a thin layer of asbestos bonded to the back of the brake block to provide a more crack resistant mounting surface.

In a process similar to riveting, heavy-duty truck and trailer brake linings are often bolted in place. See Figure 10-16. The lining is countersunk as in riveting, but the rivet is replaced by a brass bolt, nut, and washer.

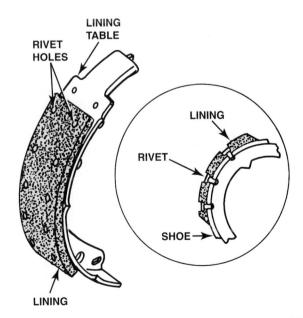

FIGURE 10-15   Riveted brake linings are quiet and reliable at high temperatures.

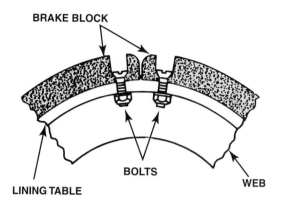

FIGURE 10-16   The brake line is bolted to the shoe on most heavy trucks and busses.

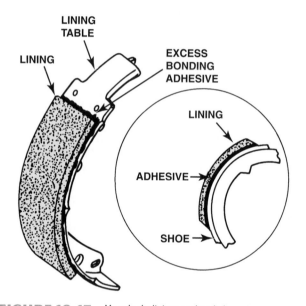

FIGURE 10-17   Many brake linings are bonded.

Bonded linings are also more prone to be noisy because they do not allow any vibration absorbing flex between the brake block and lining table or backing plate.

LINING EDGE CODES

The **lining edge codes** contain three groups of letters and numbers:

- The first group is a series of letters that identify the manufacturer of the lining.
- The second group is a series of numbers, letters, or both that identify the lining compound or formula. This code is usually known to the manufacturer of the lining material and helps identify the lining after manufacture.
- The third group is two letters that identify the coefficient of friction (see Figures 10-18 and 10-19).

The coefficient of friction is a pure number that indicates the amount of friction between two surfaces. A coefficient of friction will always be less than 1; the higher the number, the greater the amount of friction between two surfaces. (For example, a material with 0.55 coefficient of friction has more friction than a material with a coefficient of friction of 0.39.)

These codes were established by the SAE (Society of Automotive Engineers):

Code C	0.00 to 0.15
Code D	0.15 to 0.25
Code E	0.25 to 0.35
Code F	0.35 to 0.45
Code G	0.45 to 0.55
Code H	0.55 and above
Code Z	ungraded

Bonding.   **Bonded linings** use high-temperature adhesive to glue the brake block directly to the shoe lining table or pad backing plate as shown in Figure 10-17.

Heat and pressure are then applied to cure the assembly. Bonding is a common form of shoe and pad assembly, and is most often used to mount organic friction materials.

Bonding offers several advantages. Without rivets, bonded linings can wear closer to the lining table or backing plate and provide a longer service life. If the linings wear too far, bonding adhesive is not as destructive to drums or rotors as rivets. Bonded linings also have fewer problems with cracking because they have no rivet holes to weaken the brake block.

The primary disadvantage of bonded linings is a limited ability to withstand high temperatures. If a bonded lining gets too hot, the bonding adhesive will fail and allow the brake block to separate from the lining table or backing plate.

FIGURE 10-18   Typical drum brake lining edge codes.

FIGURE 10-19 Even the lining that cannot be seen is labeled. This drum brake lining has been formed and drilled and is ready to be assembled (riveted) to steel brake shoes. This photo was taken at the Delphi (Delco) Chassis Brake Division Plant in Dayton, Ohio.

The first letter, which is printed on the side of most linings, indicates its coefficient of friction when brakes are cold, and the second letter indicates the coefficient of friction of the brake lining when the brakes are hot. (For example, FF indicates that the brake lining material has a coefficient of friction between 0.35 and 0.45 when both cold and hot.)

These letters should not be interpreted to mean the relative quality of the lining material. Lining wear, fade resistance, tensile strength, heat recovery rate, wet friction, noise, and coefficient of friction must be considered when purchasing high-quality linings. Unfortunately, there are no standards that a purchaser can check regarding all of these other considerations. For best brake performance, always purchase the best-quality name-brand linings that you can afford.

NOTE: While many brands of replacement brake lining provide acceptable stopping power and long life, purchasing factory brake lining from a dealer is usually the best opportunity to get lining material that meets all vehicle requirements. Aftermarket linings are not required by federal law to meet performance or wear standards that are required of original factory brake linings.

Brake Shoe Return Springs

The **brake shoe return springs** retract the shoes to their unapplied positions when the brake pedal is released. This helps prevent brake drag, and aids the return of brake fluid to the master cylinder reservoir. Most brakes use closed-coil return springs to retract the brake shoes. See Figure 10-20.

The coils on these springs are very tightly wound and contact one another when the spring is relaxed. Some vehicles have a single, large, horseshoe-shaped return spring. See Figure 10-21.

The type, location, and number of return springs vary from one brake design to the next. All springs are installed in one of two ways. Some connect directly from shoe to shoe, while others connect from one shoe to the anchor post.

FIGURE 10-20 Typical drum brake showing support plate (backing plate), anchor pin, and shoe guide plate. *(Courtesy of DaimlerChrysler Corporation)*

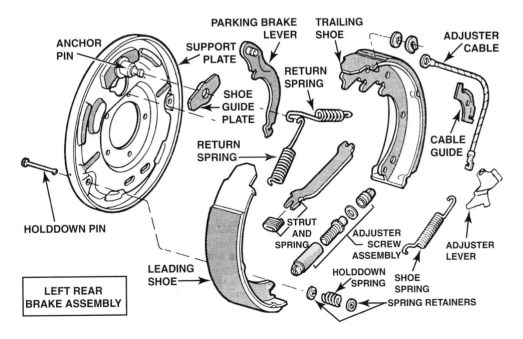

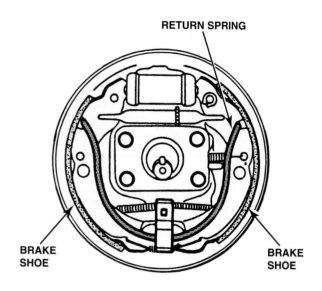

FIGURE 10-21   A single spring-steel return spring is used on some drum brakes.

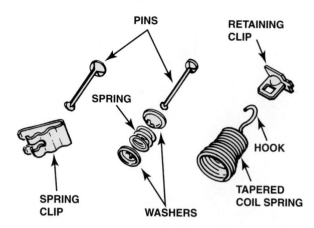

FIGURE 10-22   Various types and styles of holddown springs.

Brake Shoe Holddowns

While the return springs retract the brake shoes to their unapplied positions, the **brake shoe holddowns** keep the shoes securely against the support pads on the backing plate. The holddowns prevent noise, vibration, and wear, but still allow the shoes to move out and back as the brakes are applied and released. The holddowns also provide enough freedom of movement to allow adjustments of the shoes outward as the linings wear. Shoe holddowns take many forms, as shown in Figure 10-22.

The most common design is a steel pin installed through a hole in the backing plate and a corresponding hole in the brake shoe web. A spring fits over the end of the pin against the shoe web, and a special washer compresses the spring and locks onto the flattened end of the pin.

Another type of holddown is a taper-wound coil spring with a hook formed on its end. Because of its shape, this part is sometimes called a **beehive holddown.** The hook end of the spring is installed through a hole in the brake shoe web and attached into a retaining clip that fits into a corresponding hole in the backing plate.

Parking Brake Linkage

Most rear drum brake friction assemblies include a parking brake linkage. See Figure 10-23.

The linkage commonly consists of a cable, lever, and strut system that spread the brake shoes apart to apply the brake mechanically. The parking brake strut plays a large part in many of the automatic brake adjusters described later in this chapter.

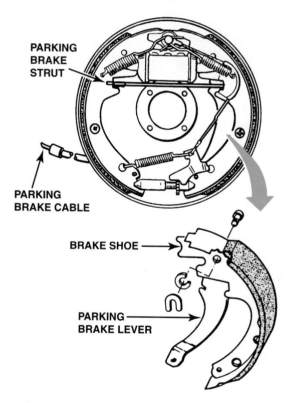

FIGURE 10-23   A mechanical parking brake linkage is part of most rear drum brakes.

Brake Drum

The last major component in a drum brake friction assembly is the brake drum. The brake drum is not connected to the backing plate, but turns with the wheel. The drum mounts on the hub or axle, and covers the rest of the friction assembly. Brake drums are made of cast iron or cast aluminum with a cast-iron liner. Many of these drum types may have

FIGURE 10-24 An aluminum brake drum with a cast iron friction surface. The cooling fins around the outside help dissipate the heat from the friction surface to the outside air.

ribs or fins on their outer edge to help dissipate heat. See Figure 10-24.

DRUM BRAKE DESIGN

Drum brake designs are classified by the way in which the shoes are applied, and how they react when the linings make contact with the drum. All drum brakes fall into two basic categories:

- Non-servo brakes
- Servo brakes

Early automotive drum brake friction assemblies were non-servo designs, and non-servo brakes are still in many rear-wheel applications. The more powerful servo drum brakes were developed later and are still used on some vehicles.

NON-SERVO BRAKES

The identifying feature of a **non-servo brake** is that each brake shoe is applied individually. The action of one shoe has no effect on the action of the other. Drum brakes have the advantage of a self-energizing action that can provide increased application force. Many non-servo drum brakes use this **self-energizing action** to improve their braking performance.

Self-Energizing Action

The simple drum brake assembly shown in Figure 10-25 shows how the self-energizing process works.

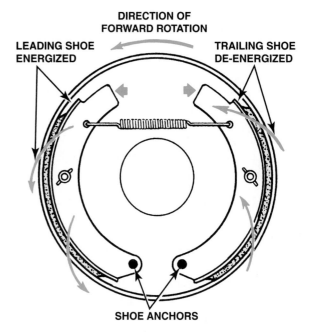

DIRECTION OF FORWARD ROTATION

LEADING SHOE ENERGIZED   TRAILING SHOE DE-ENERGIZED

SHOE ANCHORS

FIGURE 10-25 Self-energizing action can increase or decrease the stopping power of a brake shoe.

As the forward or **leading shoe** contacts the drum, the drum attempts to rotate the shoe along with it. However, the shoe cannot rotate because its far end (relative to drum rotation) is fixed in place by an anchor. As a result, drum rotation *energizes* the shoe by forcing it outward and wedging it tightly against the brake drum.

The drum also attempts to rotate the reverse or **trailing shoe** as it contacts the drum. However, in this case, the far end of the shoe (relative to drum rotation) is not solidly anchored. As a result, drum rotation *de-energizes* the shoe by forcing it inward away from the brake drum.

When this type of brake is applied with the vehicle backing up, the roles of the forward and reverse shoes are switched. The reverse shoe becomes the leading shoe, which is self-energized by drum rotation, while the forward shoe becomes the trailing shoe, which is de-energized. *A leading shoe is always energized by drum rotation. A trailing shoe is always de-energized by drum rotation.*

To identify the leading shoe on a non-servo brake with only one wheel cylinder, the first shoe from the wheel cylinder in the direction of drum rotation is the leading shoe. If the piston of a wheel cylinder moves in the same direction as drum rotation when the brakes are applied, the shoe it actuates is a leading shoe. If the piston moves opposite the direction of drum rotation, the shoe actuated is the trailing shoe.

Leading shoes generally wear at a faster rate than trailing shoes because they are applied with greater force. Where a brake uses one leading and one trailing shoe, the leading shoe will sometimes have a thicker lining or one with a larger surface area than that of the trailing shoe. The thicker or larger lining balances the wear between the two shoes so that they will both need replacement at about the same time.

Double-Trailing Brake

The least powerful non-servo drum brake is the **double-trailing brake.** See Figure 10-26. This design has two trailing shoes and does not use any self-energization. Both shoes have identically sized and shaped linings that are applied with equal force by a pair of single-piston wheel cylinders. Each shoe is anchored at the end opposite the wheel cylinder that applies it. In many double-trailing brakes, the backside of one wheel cylinder serves as the anchor for the brake shoe actuated by the other wheel cylinder.

The double-trailing brake is usually found only on the rear axles of vehicles with an extreme forward weight bias. In these applications its relative lack of stopping power aids brake balance and helps prevent rear lockup. Unfortunately, it also makes the double-trailing design a poor parking brake in the forward direction.

Leading–Trailing Brake Design

The non-servo **leading–trailing brake** has one leading shoe and one trailing shoe. See Figure 10-27.

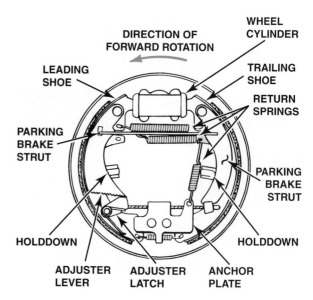

FIGURE 10-27   A leading–trailing non-servo drum brake.

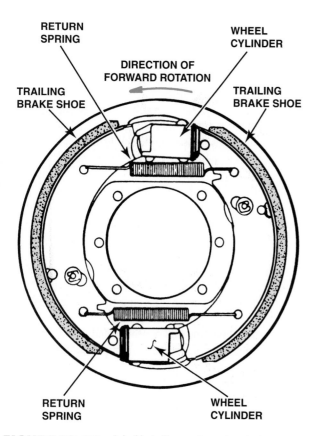

FIGURE 10-26   A double-trailing non-servo drum brake.

Typically, a single, two-piston wheel cylinder is mounted at the top of the backing plate and the two brake shoes are anchored at the bottom of the backing plate.

The brake design has one energized and one de-energized shoe regardless of whether it is applied while the vehicle is traveling forward or in reverse. This allows the leading–trailing brake to work equally well in either direction.

Leading–trailing brakes are popular on the rear wheels of many small and front-wheel-drive vehicles because, although they are not as powerful as a servo brake, they are also less prone to lockup. They have the further benefit of making a good parking brake in both directions.

Dual-Servo Brake Design

The **servo brake** is the most common drum brake design. It gets its name from the fact that one shoe "serves" the other to increase application force. One version of this brake, the uni-servo design, is used primarily on trucks and supplies additional stopping power in the forward direction only. All servo brakes used on automobiles, however, are of the duo- or dual-servo design that works with equal force in both directions.

The primary advantage of the dual-servo brake is that it is more powerful than any of the non-servo designs. Another advantage of the dual-servo brake is that it makes a good parking brake. Dual-servo action not only makes the brake very powerful, it allows the brake to hold equally well in both directions.

Dual-servo brakes are more susceptible to pull than other brake designs, and their greater application force can lead to faster fade under extreme braking conditions.

NOTE: Dual-servo brakes are also called **Duo-Servo**, which is a brand name of the Bendix Corporation.

Dual-Servo Brake Construction

The basic **dual-servo brake** uses one anchor and a single two-piston wheel cylinder. See Figure 10-28. The anchor is usually mounted at the top of the backing plate with the wheel cylinder directly beneath it. The tops of the brake shoes are held against the anchor by individual return springs. The bottoms of the shoes are spaced apart by an adjusting link held in position by a third return spring that connects the two shoes.

Adjusting Link

The adjusting link consists of a starwheel that is part of an adjusting screw, a pivot nut that one end of the adjusting screw threads into, and a socket that rotates freely on the opposite end of the adjusting screw. See Figure 10-29.

The outer ends of the pivot nut and socket are notched to fit over the brake shoe webs. Some adjusting links have a steel thrust washer and/or spring washer installed between the

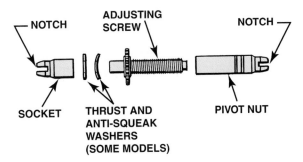

FIGURE 10-29 A dual-servo brake adjusting link.

socket and the starwheel. These washers allow easier rotation of the starwheel and help reduce brake squeal.

NOTE: Adjusting links generally have specific left- or right-hand threads, and must be installed on the correct side of the vehicle.

Primary and Secondary Brake Shoes

Although dual-servo brakes make use of self-energizing action to help provide servo action, the two brake shoes are not called leading and trailing parts as in non-servo brakes. Instead, they are identified as the **primary shoe** and the **secondary shoe.** To identify the primary shoe on a dual-servo brake with a single two-piston wheel cylinder, point to the wheel cylinder, and then move your finger in the direction of drum rotation. The first shoe reached is the primary shoe and the other shoe is the secondary shoe.

The secondary brake shoe provides approximately 70% of the total braking power in a dual-servo brake. For this reason, the lining is usually somewhat larger than that of the primary shoe. In addition, some manufacturers use different types of friction materials on the primary and secondary shoes to help equalize wear.

Dual-Servo Brake Operation

When a dual-servo brake is applied, the wheel cylinder attempts to force the tops of both brake shoes outward against the drum. See Figure 10-30.

As the primary shoe makes contact it rotates with the drum because its far end (relative to the direction of drum rotation) is not directly anchored to the backing plate. As the primary shoe rotates, it forces the adjusting link and the secondary shoe to also rotate until the secondary shoe seats firmly against the anchor.

Although the wheel cylinder attempts to push the top of the secondary shoe outward, the rotational force developed

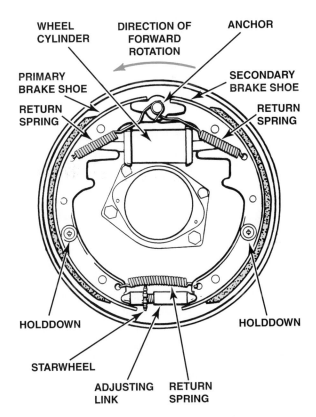

FIGURE 10-28 A typical dual-servo drum brake.

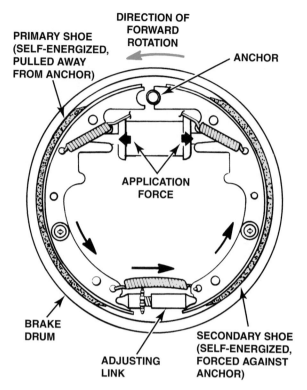

FIGURE 10-30   Dual-servo brake operation. The primary shoe on the left exerts a force on the secondary shoe on the right.

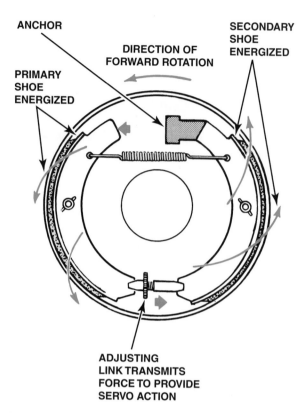

FIGURE 10-31   Servo action greatly increases the application force on the secondary shoe.

by friction between the brake shoes and drum is much greater than the application force developed by hydraulic pressure in the wheel cylinder. As a result, the secondary shoe is held solidly against the anchor. In effect, only one-half of the wheel cylinder is used to apply the brakes.

Servo-Action

Once all slack is taken up between the brake shoes, adjusting link, and anchor, both brake shoes become self-energized like the leading shoes in a non-servo brake. The anchor pin prevents the secondary shoe from rotating, and the adjusting link (held in position by the secondary shoe) serves as the anchor for the primary shoe. Servo action then occurs as a portion of the braking force generated by the primary shoe is transferred through the adjusting link to help apply the secondary shoe. See Figure 10-31.

When a dual-servo brake is applied with the vehicle moving in reverse, the primary and secondary shoes switch roles. The primary shoe is forced against the anchor while the secondary shoe moves outward and rotates with the drum to apply the primary shoe with a greater force.

TECH TIP

REAR WHEEL LOCKUP? CHECK THE ADJUSTMENT

Servo action enables a drum brake to provide increased stopping power, but it can also cause the brakes to grab and lock if they get too far out of adjustment. As clearance between the shoes and drum increases, the primary brake shoe is allowed a greater range of movement. The farther the shoe moves, the more speed it picks up from the rotating brake drum. At the moment the slack is taken up between the brake shoes, adjusting link, and anchor, the speed of the primary shoe is converted into application force by servo action. If the primary shoe is moving too quickly, it will apply the secondary shoe very hard and fast, causing the brakes to grab and possibly lock the wheels.

AUTOMATIC BRAKE ADJUSTERS

Automatic adjusters use the movement of the brake shoes to continually adjust lining-to-drum clearance as the brakes wear.

Servo Brake Starwheel Automatic Adjusters

Servo brakes use three styles of starwheel adjusters:

- Cable. See Figure 10-32.
- Lever. See Figure 10-33.
- Link. See Figure 10-34.

All three adjusters mount on the secondary brake shoe and adjust only when the brakes are applied while the vehicle is moving in reverse.

As the brakes are applied on a vehicle with a cable or link automatic adjuster, the wheel cylinder and drum rotation combine to move the secondary shoe away from the anchor. Movement of the shoe causes the cable or linkage to pull up on the adjuster **pawl**. See Figure 10-35.

If the brake lining has worn far enough, the pawl engages the next tooth on the starwheel. When the brakes are released, the pawl return spring pulls the pawl down, rotating the starwheel and moving the brake shoes apart to reduce the lining-to-drum clearance.

Some servo brakes with cable-actuated starwheel automatic adjusters have an **over-travel spring** assembly on the end of the cable. See Figure 10-36.

In this design, the adjuster pawl is mounted *under* the starwheel, and adjustment is made as the brakes are applied rather than released. The over-travel spring dampens the movements of the adjuster mechanism, and prevents over-adjustment if the brakes are applied very hard and fast. It also prevents damage to the adjusting mechanism if the starwheel seizes or is otherwise unable to rotate.

The lever starwheel adjuster makes the adjustment as the brakes are applied rather than released. As the secondary shoe moves away from the anchor, the solid link between the

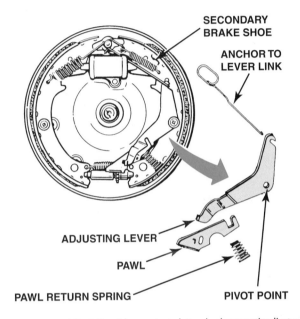

FIGURE 10-33   A lever-actuated starwheel automatic adjuster. This type of adjuster makes the adjustment as the brakes are applied.

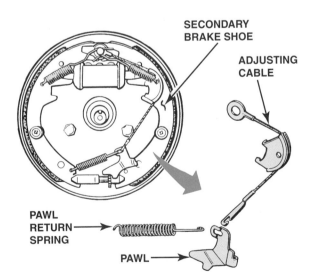

FIGURE 10-32   A cable-actuated starwheel automatic adjuster. This type of adjuster makes the adjustment as the brakes are released.

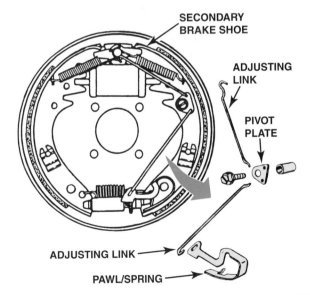

FIGURE 10-34   A link-activated starwheel automatic adjuster. This type of adjuster makes the adjustment as the brakes are released.

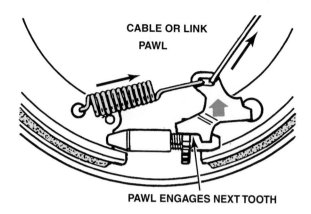

CABLE OR LINK

PAWL

PAWL ENGAGES NEXT TOOTH

BRAKES APPLIED

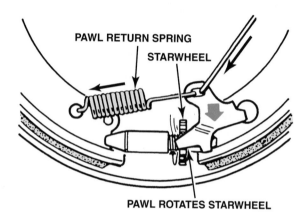

PAWL RETURN SPRING

STARWHEEL

PAWL ROTATES STARWHEEL

BRAKES RELEASED

FIGURE 10-35   The operation of a typical self-adjuster. Notice that the adjuster actually moves the starwheel.

anchor and the top of the adjuster lever forces the lever to rotate around the pivot point where it attaches to the brake shoe. This moves the bottom half of the lever downward, which causes the pawl to rotate the starwheel and make the adjustment. The separate pawl piece is free to pivot on the lever to prevent damage if the starwheel will not rotate. When the brakes are released, the return springs lift the lever. If the brakes have worn enough, the end of the lever engages the next tooth on the starwheel and additional adjustment will be made the next time the brakes are applied.

Non-Servo Starwheel Automatic Adjusters

The starwheel automatic adjusters used on non-servo brakes may be mounted on either the leading or trailing shoe. These types of adjusters work whenever the brakes are applied—in either the forward or reverse direction. A leading-shoe design is shown in Figure 10-37.

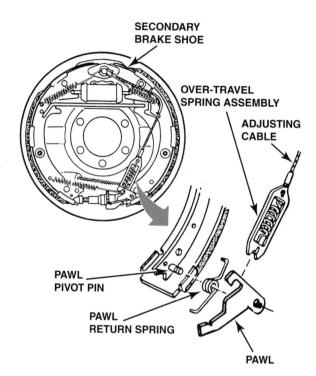

SECONDARY BRAKE SHOE

OVER-TRAVEL SPRING ASSEMBLY

ADJUSTING CABLE

PAWL PIVOT PIN

PAWL RETURN SPRING

PAWL

FIGURE 10-36   A cable-actuated starwheel automatic adjuster with an over-travel spring.

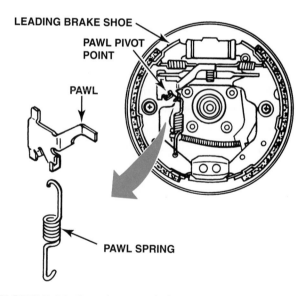

LEADING BRAKE SHOE

PAWL PIVOT POINT

PAWL

PAWL SPRING

FIGURE 10-37   A non-servo brake with a lever-activated starwheel automatic adjuster on the leading shoe. This type of adjuster makes the adjustment as the brakes are applied.

When the brakes are not applied, the adjuster pawl is held in position by the parking brake strut. When the brakes are applied and the primary shoe moves out toward the brake drum (away from the parking brake strut), the pawl spring pivots the pawl downward where it mounts on the brake shoe and rotates the starwheel to adjust the brake. When the brakes are released, the return springs retract the shoes and the pawl is levered back into its resting position by the parking brake strut. If the linings have worn far enough, the lever engages the next tooth on the starwheel and further adjustment will occur the next time the brakes are applied.

The trailing-shoe non-servo starwheel adjuster shown in Figure 10-38 works somewhat like the leading-shoe design, but it makes the adjustment as the brakes are released rather than applied.

The upper shoe return spring in this design returns the brake shoes and operates the automatic adjuster. When the brakes are not applied, spring tension holds the trailing shoe and the adjuster pawl tightly against the parking brake strut. When the brakes are applied, the trailing shoe moves out toward the drum and away from the parking brake strut. This allows the adjuster pawl, which is restrained by the return spring, to pivot where it attaches to the brake shoe, causing the adjuster arm to move upward. If the brakes have worn far enough, the arm will engage the next tooth of the starwheel. When the brakes are released, the return spring pulls the brake shoes back together and the parking brake strut levers the adjuster pawl downward to rotate the starwheel and adjust the brakes.

TECH TIP

COOL THE BRAKES BEFORE BACKING

Self-adjusters can over adjust the rear drum brakes if the brake drums are hot and have increased in diameter due to the heat. A typical example of how this can occur involves a pickup truck towing a boat down a long steep grade to reach the lake and the boat ramp. If the brakes are used to slow the truck and trailer, the rear brake drums can become larger in diameter due to the heat created during braking. Then when the truck is backing the boat trailer down the ramp, the brakes can over adjust if the driver repeatedly depresses and releases the brake pedal while backing. Then after the boat has been removed from the trailer and the rear brakes have cooled, the drums will shrink and keep the rear brakes from releasing preventing the movement of the truck up the ramp.

NOTE: Some drum brakes are equipped with a bimetallic heat sensor that prevents the self-adjusters from working if the brakes are hot.

Ratchet Automatic Adjusters

Most ratchet automatic adjusters use movement of the brake shoes to adjust the lining-to-drum clearance. The adjustment of a ratchet adjuster is carried out by two parts that have small interlocking teeth. As the adjustment is made, the two toothed elements ratchet across one another. Once adjustment is complete, the teeth lock together to hold the brake shoes in their new positions.

Lever-Latch Automatic Adjuster.   The lever-latch automatic adjuster installs on the leading shoe of a non-servo brake and operates whenever the brakes are applied. See Figure 10-39.

This design consists of a large lever and a smaller latch with interlocking teeth. A spring on the latch piece keeps it in contact with the lever to maintain the adjustment. One end of the parking brake strut hooks into an opening in the lever and the other end is held against the trailing brake shoe by a strong spring.

As the brakes are applied and the shoes move outward toward the drum, the parking brake strut pulls on the adjuster lever and forces it to pivot inward from where it attaches to the top of the leading shoe. If the brakes are sufficiently worn,

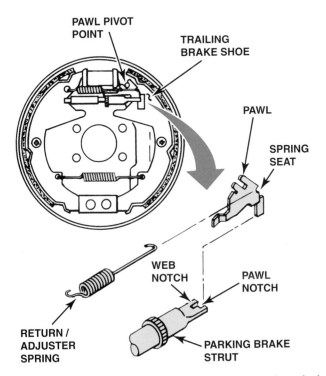

FIGURE 10-38   A non-servo brake with a lever-actuated starwheel automatic adjuster on the trailing shoe. This type of adjuster makes the adjustment as the brakes are released.

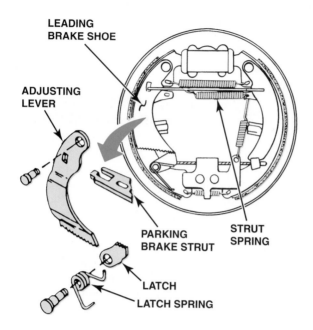

FIGURE 10-39 A lever-latch ratchet automatic adjuster.

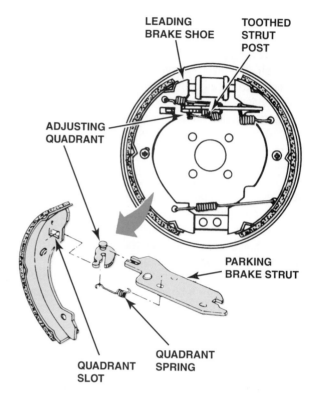

FIGURE 10-40 A strut-quadrant ratchet automatic adjuster.

the bottom of the lever will ratchet one or more teeth on the latch. When the brakes are released, the parking brake strut, which bottoms against the lever, will hold the shoes farther apart to reduce the lining-to-drum clearance.

Strut-quadrant automatic adjuster. The strut-quadrant automatic adjuster is used on some non-servo brakes. See Figure 10-40.

The strut-quadrant adjuster consists of three basic parts:

- The parking brake strut
- Adjusting quadrant
- A quadrant spring

The strut has a toothed post solidly mounted on its underside. The adjuster quadrant pivots on a pin that slips into a notch in the end of the strut, and the backside of the quadrant has a toothed, cam-shaped surface that interlocks with the toothed post on the strut. The quadrant also has an arm that extends through an opening in the web of the leading brake shoe. The outer side of this arm serves as the brake

shoe stop when the brakes are released. The quadrant spring holds the quadrant in contact with the post to maintain the adjustment.

When the brakes are applied, the leading shoe moves out toward the brake drum. If there is sufficient wear of the brake lining, the edge of the slot in the shoe web contacts the inner side of the adjuster quadrant arm and pulls it outward. When this happens, the toothed section of the quadrant is lifted away from the post on the parking brake strut. The quadrant spring then rotates the quadrant until its pivot pin is bottomed in the slot in the parking brake strut. When the brakes are released, the quadrant returns inward with the leading shoe. The toothed section of the quadrant then engages the teeth on the strut post, causing the quadrant arm to remain in its new extended position that holds the shoes farther apart and reduces the lining-to-drum clearance.

SUMMARY

1. Drum brake shoes include the lining table, shoe web plus holes for the springs to attach, and semicircular anchor eyes.

2. Brake linings can be attached using rivets or bonding.

3. Lining edge codes identify the manufacturer and include two letters at the end, which identify the coefficient of friction of the material. The first letter indicates the coefficient when the lining is cold and the second indicates the coefficient when the lining is hot.

4. Brake shoes are forced outward against a brake drum by hydraulic action working on the brake shoes by the piston of a wheel cylinder.

5. The curved arch of the brake shoe causes a wedging action between the brake shoe and the rotating drum. This wedging action increases the amount of force applied to the drum.

6. Dual-servo brakes use primary and secondary brake shoes that are connected at one end. The wedge action on the front (primary) shoe forces the secondary shoe into the drum with even greater force. This action is called servo self-energizing.

7. Leading–trailing brakes use two brake shoes that are not connected. Leading–trailing brakes operate on a more linear basis and are therefore more suited than dual-servo for ABS.

8. Most self-adjusting mechanisms usually operate from the secondary or rearward facing brake shoe and adjust the brakes as the brakes are released.

9. Some self-adjusters operate on the primary shoe and adjust the brakes as they are being applied.

REVIEW QUESTIONS

1. Describe the difference between a dual-servo and a leading–trailing drum brake system.

2. List all the parts of a typical drum brake.

3. Explain how a self-adjusting brake mechanism works.

4. What is the meaning of the last two letters of the lining or pad edge code?

CHAPTER QUIZ

1. Two technicians are discussing drum brake shoes. Technician A says that forward and rear-facing shoes are the same and can be installed in either position on any drum brake system. Technician B says that the darker color lining should always be placed toward the front of the vehicle. Which technician is correct?

   a. Technician A only

   b. Technician B only

   c. Both Technicians A and B

   d. Neither Technician A nor B

2. Two technicians are discussing brake lining edge codes. Technician A says that the code can identify the manufacturer. Technician B says that all friction material from the same manufacturer will have the same edge codes. Which technician is correct?

   a. Technician A only

   b. Technician B only

   c. Both Technicians A and B

   d. Neither Technician A nor B

3. Technician A says that starwheel adjusters use different threads (left- and right-handed) for the left and right sides of the vehicle. Technician B says that a pawl controls the teeth of the starwheel adjuster. Which technician is correct?

   a. Technician A only

   b. Technician B only

   c. Both Technicians A and B

   d. Neither Technician A nor B

4. Technician A says that drum brakes can fail to slow the vehicle if driven through deep water. Technician B says that when drum brakes get hot, the brake pedal will drop because the drum expands away from the shoes. Which technician is correct?

   a. Technician A only

   b. Technician B only

   c. Both Technicians A and B

   d. Neither Technician A nor B

5. Technician A says that self-adjusters used on most drum brakes work when the brakes are applied, then release while traveling in reverse. Technician B says that some adjusters can over adjust if the brake drums are hot. Which technician is correct?

   a. Technician A only

   b. Technician B only

   c. Both Technicians A and B

   d. Neither Technician A nor B

6. Drum brake shoes _____.

   a. Can have riveted linings

   b. Can have bonded linings

   c. Can have one shoe that is longer than the other on the same wheel brake

   d. All of the above are possible

7. Which lining does most of the braking on a dual-servo brake?

   a. Front (forward facing)

   b. Rear (rearward facing)

   c. Both contribute equally

   d. Depends on the speed of the vehicle

8. Which lining does most of the braking on a leading–trailing brake?

   a. Leading (forward facing)

   b. Trailing (rearward facing)

   c. Both contribute equally

   d. Depends on the speed of the vehicle

9. Two technicians are discussing drum brake self adjusters. Technician A says that a frozen starwheel adjuster can cause the brakes to lock up due to the adjusting lever being unable to move the adjuster causing the linkage to bind. Technician B says that some brakes self-adjust when the brakes are applied rather than when released. Which technician is correct?

   a. Technician A only

   b. Technician B only

   c. Both Technicians A and B

   d. Neither Technician A nor B

10. A typical drum brake backing-plate has how many shoe support pads (also called ledges)?

    a. 3

    b. 4

    c. 6

    d. 8

CHAPTER 11

DRUM BRAKE DIAGNOSIS AND SERVICE

OBJECTIVES

After studying Chapter 11, the reader should be able to:

1. Prepare for the Brakes (A5) ASE certification test content area "B" (Drum Brake Diagnosis and Repair).

2. Discuss the procedure recommended for brake drum removal.

3. Discuss the inspection and lubrication points of the backing plate.

4. Explain the importance of the proper drum brake hardware.

5. Disassemble and reassemble a drum brake assembly.

KEY TERMS

Bearingized (p. 191)
Brake hardware kits (p. 194)

Speed nuts (p. 186)
Tinnerman nuts (p. 186)

DRUM BRAKE DIAGNOSTIC PROCEDURE

Diagnosing brake concern includes the following steps:

Step 1   Verify the customer complaint (concern). For example, common drum brake concerns include:
- Low brake pedal
- Parking brake does not hold the vehicle on a hill
- Noise while braking
- Noise when the vehicle is moving, but the brakes are not applied

Step 2   Perform a visual inspection of the brakes and related parts, such as the wheels, tires, and suspension system.

Step 3   Determine the root cause. For example, this could include determining that the parking brake is corroded causing the brake shoes to wear. Replacing just the brake shoes will not correct the root cause.

Step 4   Restore the brake system to like-new operation, which is the purpose of any repair.

Step 5   Test drive the vehicle to verify that the service has corrected the customer's complaint.

Drum brake service usually involves the following steps:

Step 1   Removing the brake drums

Step 2   Inspect the brake drums for damage and measure the inside diameter and compare to specifications.

Step 3   Inspect brake linings and hardware for wear or damage.

Step 4   Inspect the wheel cylinder and brake lines for leakage.

Step 5   Check the backing plate for excessive rust or wear.

BRAKE DRUM REMOVAL

The drum has to be removed before inspection or repair of a drum brake can begin. There are two basic types of drums, and the removal procedure depends on which type is being serviced. With either type it is usually recommended that the drums be marked with an "L" for left or an "R" for right so that they can be replaced in the same location.

CAUTION: Proper precaution should be taken to prevent any asbestos that may be present in the brake system from becoming airborne. Removal of the brake drum should occur inside a sealed vacuum enclosure equipped with a HEPA filter or washed with water or solvent. See Figure 11-1.

Hub or Fixed Drums

A fixed or hub-mounted drum is often used on the rear of front-wheel-drive vehicles. The drum has a hub for inner and outer

FIGURE 11-1   Before removing the brake drum, a liquid soaking solvent, such as brake cleaner, should be used to wet the linings. The purpose of wetting the lining material while the drum is still on the vehicle is to prevent the possibility of asbestos from the lining from becoming airborne. Asbestos is only hazardous when asbestos dust is airborne and is breathed in during brake system service.

bearings and is retained by a spindle nut. To remove the brake drum, remove the dust cap and cotter key that is used to retain the spindle nut. Remove the spindle nut and washer and then the brake drum can be carefully pulled off the spindle.

Hubless or Floating Drums

Floating or hubless drums are usually used on the rear of a rear-wheel-drive vehicle. The drums are secured to the axle flange by the wheel and lug nuts. New vehicles have **tinnerman nuts** (clips), also called **speed nuts,** on the stud when the vehicle is being assembled. These thin sheet-metal nuts keep the brake drum from falling off during shipping and handling prior to installation of the rear wheels. See Figure 11-2.

The tinnerman nuts can be discarded because they are not needed after the vehicle leaves the assembly plant. After removing the wheels, the drum *should* move freely on the hub and slip off over the brake shoes. Some drum brakes have two threaded holes in the drum that allow bolts to be installed. See Figure 11-3.

By tightening the bolts, the drum is forced off of the hub. Two situations that can prevent the drum from being removed include the following:

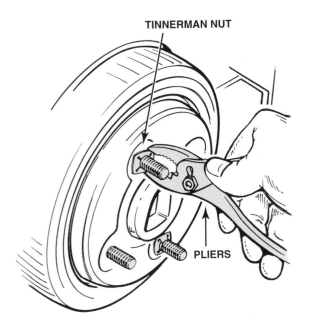

FIGURE 11-2 Tinnerman nuts are used at the vehicle assembly plant to prevent the brake drum falling off until the wheels can be installed. These sheet metal retainers can be discarded after removal.

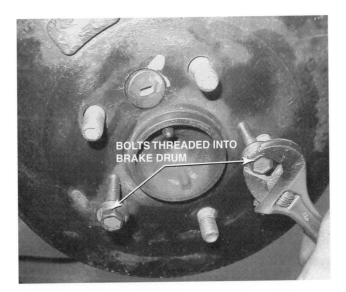

FIGURE 11-3 Turning the bolts that are threaded into the brake drum forces the drum off the hub.

1. **The Drum Is Rusted to the Hub.** The fit between the drum and the hub is very close because it is this center pilot hole in the drum that centers the drum on the axle. Rust and corrosion often causes the drum to seize to the hub. Striking the area inside the wheel studs will usually break the drum loose from the hub. Sometimes a torch has to be used to expand the pilot hole.

NOTE: Use of an air hammer with a flat-headed driver against the hub also works well to break the drum loose from the hub.

CAUTION: Overheating or not allowing the drum to cool slowly can cause the brake drum to distort. Using a puller can also damage a drum.

2. **The Brake Shoes Are Worn into the Drum.** Even if the pilot hole is loose, many brake drums cannot be removed because the inner edge of the brake drum catches on the lining. Pulling outward on the drum often bends the backing plate or breaks some of the mounting hardware. To prevent damage, remove the adjuster plug from the backing plate or drum and back off the adjuster. See Figures 11-4 and 11-5.

NOTE: Be sure to reinstall the adjuster opening plugs. These plugs help keep water and debris out of the brakes.

After removing the brake drums, they should be cleaned, inspected, measured, and possibly machined before being returned to service. See Chapter 15 for measuring and machining procedures.

FIGURE 11-4 Access to the starwheel adjuster is through adjuster plugs, often called knock-out plugs because they have to be knocked out to reach the adjuster. Sometimes these plugs are in the drum itself rather than in the backing plate.

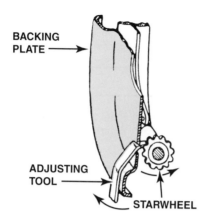

BACKING
PLATE

ADJUSTING
TOOL

STARWHEEL

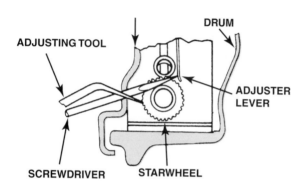

DRUM

ADJUSTING TOOL

ADJUSTER
LEVER

SCREWDRIVER   STARWHEEL

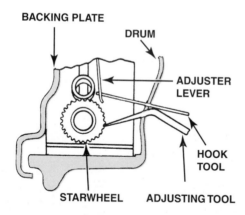

BACKING PLATE

DRUM

ADJUSTER
LEVER

HOOK
TOOL

STARWHEEL   ADJUSTING TOOL

FIGURE 11-5   If the brake shoes have worn into the brake drum, the adjuster can be backed in after removing the access plug. After removing the plug, use another wire or screwdriver to move the adjusting lever away from the starwheel, then turn the starwheel with a brake adjusting tool, often called a brake "spoon." *(Courtesy of Allied Signal Automotive Aftermarket)*

DRUM BRAKE DISASSEMBLY

After removal of the brake drum, the brake shoes and other brake hardware should be wetted down with a solvent or en-

TECH TIP

CUTTING THE NAILS TRICK

Many times a brake drum cannot be removed because the linings have worn a groove into the drum. Attempting to adjust the brakes inward is often a frustrating and time-consuming operation. The easy solution is to use a pair of diagonal side-cut pliers and cut the heads off the holddown pins (nails) at the backing plate. This releases the brake shoes from the backing plate and allows enough movement of the shoes to permit removal of the brake drum without bending the backing plate.

The holddown pins (nails) must obviously be replaced, but they are included in most drum brake hardware kits. Since most brake experts recommend replacing all drum brake hardware anyway, this solution does not cost any more than normal, may save the backing plate from damage, and saves the service technician lots of time. See Figure 11-6.

FIGURE 11-6   Using side-cut pliers to cut the heads off the holddown spring pins (nails) from the backing plate to release the drum from the shoes.

closed in an approved evacuation system to prevent possible asbestos release into the air. See Figure 11-7.

Usually, the first step in the disassembly of a drum brake system is removal of the return (retracting) springs. See Figure 11-8.

After the return springs have been removed, the holddown springs and other brake hardware can be removed. See Figure 11-9.

FIGURE 11-7 All brakes should be moistened with solvent or disassembled in an approved enclosure to prevent possible asbestos dust from becoming airborne.

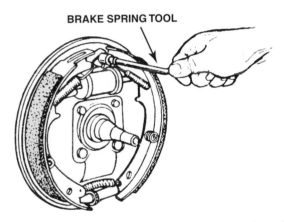

FIGURE 11-8 Using a brake spring tool to release a return (retracting) spring from the anchor pin.

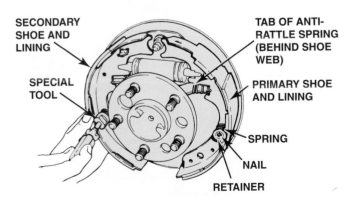

FIGURE 11-9 A special tool, called a holddown spring tool, being used to depress and rotate the retainer. *(Courtesy of DaimlerChrysler Corporation)*

NOTE: There are generally no "exact" disassembly or reassembly procedures specified by the manufacturer. The order in which the parts are disassembled or reinstalled is based on experience and the personal preference of the technician.

INSPECTING THE BACKING PLATE

The backing plate supports the parts of the drum brake and helps to keep water from getting onto the brake shoes. The backing plate bolts to the rear axle or spindle and is made from stamped steel. Backing plates are plated (usually cadmium) or painted to prevent rusting. When brakes are serviced, the six raised contact surfaces, called pads, ledges, or shoe contact areas, of the backing plate should be inspected because they rub against the sides of the shoes. See Figure 11-10.

If the pads are worn more than 1/16 in. (1.5 mm), the backing plate should be replaced. The backing plate must be inspected for looseness or bending. Backing plates should also be inspected to ensure that they are parallel with the axle flange. A simple gauge or dial indicator (gauge) can be used, as shown in Figure 11-11.

The raised pads should be cleaned and lubricated. Lithium high-temperature brake grease, synthetic brake grease, silicone grease, or antiseize should be used to lubricate drum brake parts. See Figure 11-12.

FIGURE 11-10 A typical rusting backing plate shoe pad. This can cause the brakes to squeak when the shoes move outward during a brake application and again when the brake pedal is released.

FIGURE 11-11   Because the backing plate is the foundation of the drum brake, it is important that it be square with the axle and flat. A homemade gauging tool can be made to check quickly how even the raised contact areas are to each other.

FIGURE 11-12   Lithium high-temperature brake grease is used by many service technicians to lubricate metal-to-metal contact surfaces of a drum brake. A small metal-handled acid brush is stuck through a hole cut into the lid of this container of grease to make the application of grease easy and less messy. Avoid using too much grease. Excessive grease can get onto the friction surfaces of the brake shoes or drum and affect braking performance.

DRUM BRAKE LINING INSPECTION

Both primary (front facing) and secondary (rear facing) lining material must be thicker than 0.060 in. (1.5 mm).

NOTE: Most vehicle and brake lining manufacturers recommend replacing worn brake lining when the thickness of the riveted lining reaches 0.060 in. or less. An American nickel is about 0.060 in. thick, so simply remember that you must always have at least "a nickel's worth of lining." See Figure 11-13.

The lining must be replaced if cracked, as shown in Figure 11-14.

Some vehicles are equipped with holes in the backing plate that allow for a visual inspection of the thickness of the lining. Most experts agree that the best possible inspection involves removing the brake drum and making a thorough visual inspection of the entire brake instead of just looking at the thickness of the remaining lining. If a riveted brake lining is cracked between rivets, the lining should be replaced. Some brake manufacturers recommend riveted replacement linings because of reduced brake noise. These manufacturers say that the recessed rivet holes allow brake dust to pocket away from the lining surface and thus help prevent the linings from glazing. Most experts agree that high-quality linings purchased from a known brake manufacturer will help assure that the brake performance is returned to original equipment standards.

SPRING INSPECTION

Return Springs

Each lining has a return spring (retracting spring) that returns the brake shoes back from the drums whenever the brakes are

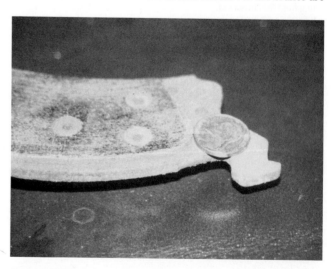

FIGURE 11-13   A rule of thumb is that the lining should be at least the thickness of a nickel.

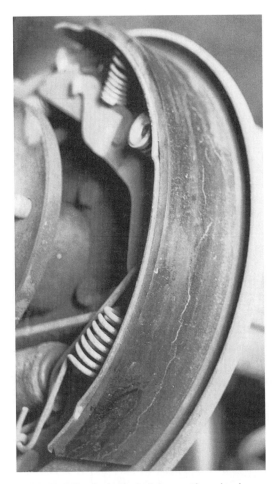

FIGURE 11-14   Cracked brake lining must be replaced.

FIGURE 11-15   Brake lining worn at the top edge near the anchor pin is one indication that the return (retracting) springs are weak.

TECH TIP

THE DROP TEST

Brake return (retracting) springs can be tested by dropping them to the floor. A good spring should "thud" when the spring hits the ground. This noise indicates that the spring has not stretched and that all coils of the springs are touching each other. If the spring "rings" when dropped, the spring should be replaced because the coils are not touching each other. See Figure 11-16.

Although this drop test is often used, many experts recommend replacing all brake springs every time the brake linings are replaced. Heat generated by the brake system often weakens springs enough to affect their ability to retract brake shoes, especially when hot, yet not "ring" when dropped.

released. The springs are called primary and secondary return springs. The primary return spring attaches to the primary brake shoe and the secondary return spring attaches to the secondary brake shoe. These springs should be tested prior to a brake overhaul, especially when uneven lining wear is discovered, as shown in Figure 11-15.

Some drum brakes use a spring that connects the primary and secondary shoes and is commonly called a shoe-to-shoe spring. Return springs can get weak due to heat and time and can cause the linings to remain in contact with the drum.

Holddown Springs

Holddown springs (one on each shoe) are springs used with a retainer and a holddown spring pin (or nail) to keep the linings on the backing plate. Other types of holddown springs include U-shape, flat spring steel type, and the combination return-and-hold spring. These springs still allow the freedom of movement necessary for proper braking operation.

Connecting Spring (Adjusting Screw Spring)

The connecting spring attaches to the lower portion and connects the two shoes together.

WHEEL CYLINDERS

Drum brake wheel cylinders are cast iron with a bore (hole) drilled and finished to provide a smooth finish for the wheel cylinder seals and pistons. This special finish is called **bearingized.** The final step in manufacture of the wheel cylinder is to force a

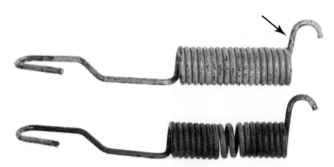

FIGURE 11-16 The top spring is a good-looking spring because all coils of the spring are touching each other. The bottom spring is stretched and should be discarded. The arrow points to the back side of the spring, which goes into a hole in the brake shoe. The open loop of the spring is not strong enough to keep from straightening out during use. Using the back side of the hook provides a strong, long-lasting hold in the brake shoe.

hardened steel ball through the bore to bend over the "grain" of the metal and to smooth the inner surface. This process provides a smooth porous-free surface for the sealing caps to travel over. It is this bearingized surface finish on the inside of the wheel cylinder that is often destroyed when a wheel cylinder is honed. The hone stone used to refinish the inside bore of a wheel cylinder often opens up the end grain of the cast iron. As a result, the sealing cups do not seal as well. The brake fluid can penetrate the porous cast iron. This porous condition can cause the brake fluid to seep through the wheel cylinder, causing the outside of the wheel cylinder to become wet with brake fluid.

CAUTION: It is because of this bearingized surface finish that most vehicle manufacturers do not recommend that wheel cylinders be honed. Be sure to follow the vehicle manufacturer's recommended procedures. Some manufacturers state that the wheel cylinders can be overhauled using new (replacement) sealing cups and dust shields after cleaning the cylinder bore only.

Outside each wheel cylinder piston are dust boots installed to keep dirt out of the cylinder bore. Between both piston seals, there is a spring with piston seal expanders to keep the seals from collapsing toward each other and to keep pressure exerted on the lips of both seals to ensure proper sealing. See Figure 11-17.

FIGURE 11-17 Exploded view of a typical wheel cylinder. Note how the flat part of the cups touch the flat part of the piston. The cup expander and spring go between the cups. *(Courtesy of DaimlerChrysler Corporation)*

On the back of each wheel cylinder there is a threaded hole for the brake line and a bleeder valve that can be loosened to remove (bleed) air from the hydraulic system. The wheel cylinder is bolted or clipped to the backing plate. See Figures 11-18 and 11-19.

TECH TIP

WET IS OK—DRIPPING IS NOT OK

When inspecting a wheel cylinder, use a blunt nose tool and pry up the dust boot. If the inside of the seal is wet, this means that some seepage has occurred, which is normal. If, however, brake fluid drips from the dust seal, this indicates that the wheel cylinder sealing cups have failed and the wheel cylinder should be replaced.

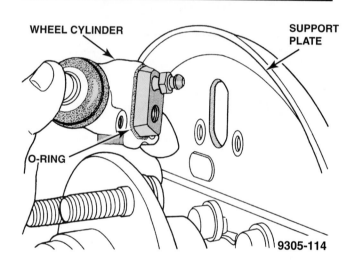

FIGURE 11-18 Many wheel cylinders are bolted to the support plate (backing plate). The O-ring seal helps keep water and dirt out of the drum brake. *(Courtesy of DaimlerChrysler Corporation)*

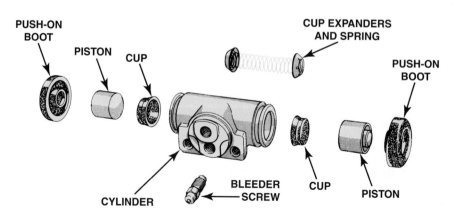

Overhaul of the Wheel Cylinders

If defective or leaking, wheel cylinders can be overhauled if recommended by the vehicle manufacturer. The following steps and procedures should be followed:

Step 1 Loosen the bleeder valve. If unable to loosen the bleeder valve without having it break off, a new replacement wheel cylinder is required. To help prevent broken bleeder valves, attempt to tighten the bleeder valve while tapping on the valve to loosen the rust before loosening the valve.

Step 2 To remove the wheel cylinder, the brake line must first be removed from the wheel cylinder. Unbolt or remove the wheel cylinder retainer clip. Be careful not to twist the brake line when removing the line from the wheel cylinder or the brake line will also require replacement.

Step 3 If the bleeder valve can be removed, remove all internal parts of the wheel cylinder.

NOTE: With some vehicles, the wheel cylinder must be unbolted from the backing plate to enable removal of the seals and piston.

Step 4 Clean and/or hone a wheel cylinder as specified by the manufacturer to remove any rust and corrosion. See Figure 11-20.

Step 5 Install the pistons (usually not included in a wheel cylinder overhaul kit), seals, spring, and dust boots. Install on the vehicle and bleed the system.

NOTE: Even though the wheel cylinder is not leaking, many brake experts recommend replacing or rebuilding the wheel cylinder every time new replacement linings are installed. Any sludge build-up in the wheel cylinder can cause the wheel cylinder to start to leak shortly after a brake job. When the new thicker replacement linings are installed, the wheel cylinder piston may be pushed inward enough to cause the cup seals to ride on a pitted or corroded section of the wheel cylinder. As the cup seal moves over this rough area, the seal can lose its ability to maintain brake fluid pressure and an external brake fluid leak can occur. See Figure 11-21.

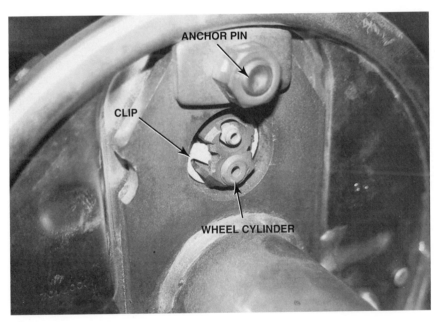

(a)

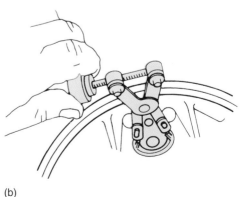

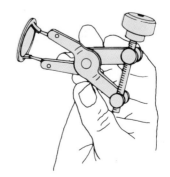

FIGURE 11-19 (a) Some wheel cylinders are simply clipped to the backing plate. (b) This special tool makes it a lot easier to remove the wheel cylinder clip. A socket (1 1/8 in., 12 point) can be used to push the clip back onto the wheel cylinder.   (b)

(a)

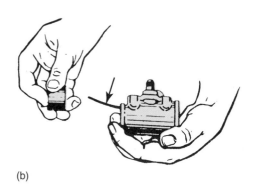

(b)

FIGURE 11-20   (a) A wheel cylinder hone being turned with an electric drill. Use brake fluid to lubricate the hone stones during the honing operation. Clean the wheel cylinder thoroughly using a soft cloth and clean brake fluid. (b) Use a narrow [1/4 in. (6 mm)] (feeler) gauge 0.005 in. (0.13 mm) thick held into the wheel cylinder. If the cylinder piston fits, the wheel cylinder bore is too large and the wheel cylinder must be replaced. Typical piston-to-wall clearance should range from 0.001 to 0.003 in. (0.03 to 0.08 mm).

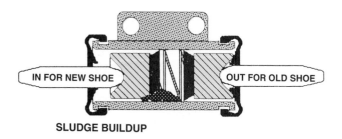

IN FOR NEW SHOE   OUT FOR OLD SHOE

SLUDGE BUILDUP

FIGURE 11-21   When new, thicker materials are installed, the pistons and cups are forced back into the wheel cylinder and pushed through the sludge that is present in every cylinder.

FIGURE 11-22   This starwheel adjuster is damaged and must be replaced. A lack of proper lubrication can cause the starwheel to become frozen in one place and not adjust properly.

DRUM BRAKE HARDWARE KIT

If any spring is found to be defective, it is possible to purchase most parts individually or in pairs. However, for best results, many brake suppliers sell drum **brake hardware kits.** These kits usually include the items listed below for two drum brakes (axle set):

1. Primary and secondary return springs
2. Connecting spring
3. Holddown springs
4. Holddown spring retainers
5. Holddown spring pins (nails)

Self-adjuster kits are available if needed. See Figure 11-22.

INSPECTING THE DRUM BRAKE SHOES

Carefully inspect the replacement brake shoes. Check all of the following:

1. Check that the replacements are exactly the same size (width and diameter) as the original. Hold the replacement shoes up against the old shoes to make the comparison.
2. Check for sound rivets (if rivet type). The friction material should also be snug against the metal brake shoe backing.

After checking that the replacement brake lining is okay, place the old shoes into the new linings' box. This helps ensure proper credit for the old shoes (called the core) as well as protection against asbestos contamination exposure.

TECH TIP

TIME—NOT MILEAGE— IS IMPORTANT

Many brake experts recommend rebuilding or replacing wheel cylinders at every other brake job. Some experts recommend that the wheel cylinders be overhauled or replaced every time the brake linings are replaced. If the wheel cylinders are found to be leaking, they must be replaced or overhauled. The most important factor is time, not mileage, when determining when to repair or replace hydraulic components.

The longer the time, the more moisture is absorbed by the brake fluid. The greater the amount of moisture absorbed by the brake fluid, the greater the corrosion to metal hydraulic components. For example, the brakes will probably wear out much sooner on a vehicle that is used all day every day than on a vehicle driven only a short distance every week. In this example the high-mileage vehicle may need replacement brake linings every year, whereas the short-distance vehicle will require several years before replacement brakes are needed. The service technician should try to determine the amount of time the brake fluid has been in the vehicle. The longer the brake fluid has been in the system, the greater the chances that the wheel cylinders need to be replaced or overhauled.

TECH TIP

BRAKE PARTS CLEANING TIPS

Denatured alcohol or "brake clean" should only be used to clean brake parts that are disassembled. When individual parts are cleaned, they can dry in the air before being assembled. Never clean or flush assembled brake components with denatured alcohol or brake clean. Often, the alcohol cannot evaporate entirely from an assembled component. This trapped alcohol will evaporate inside the brake system, causing contamination. The trapped alcohol vapors also act like trapped air in the braking system and can cause a spongy brake pedal. Always clean assembled brake components with brake fluid.

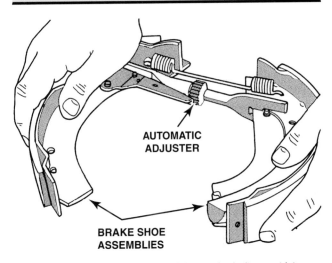

AUTOMATIC ADJUSTER

BRAKE SHOE ASSEMBLIES

FIGURE 11-23 Preassembly of the starwheel adjuster with its connecting spring often helps when reassembling a drum brake. *(Courtesy of DaimlerChrysler Corporation)*

REASSEMBLING THE DRUM BRAKE

Ressembling the drum brake includes the following steps:

Step 1   Carefully clean the backing plate.
Step 2   Check the anchor pin for looseness.
Step 3   Lubricate the shoe contact surfaces (shoe pads) with antiseize, brake grease, or synthetic grease.
Step 4   Reassemble the primary and secondary shoes and brake strut, along with all springs.
Step 5   Finish assembling the drum brake, being careful to note the correct location of all springs and parts.

NOTE: Many technicians preassemble the primary and secondary shoes with the connecting (lower retracting) spring as a unit before installing them onto the backing plate. See Figures 11-23 and 11-24.

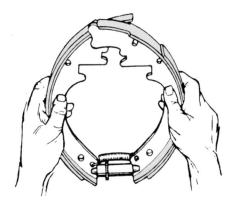

FIGURE 11-24 Sometimes it is necessary to cross the shoes when preassembling the starwheel adjuster and connecting spring. *(Courtesy of Allied Signal Automotive Aftermarket)*

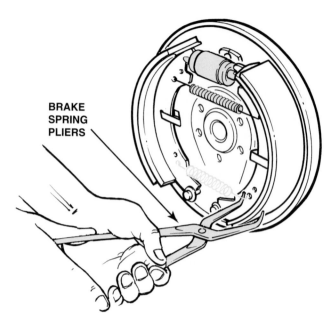

FIGURE 11-25   Installing a shoe-to-shoe spring using brake spring pliers.

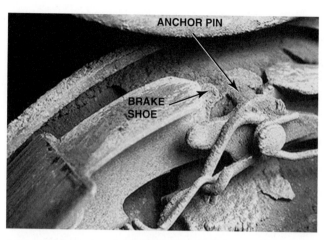

FIGURE 11-26   Notice that the brake shoe is not contacting the anchor pin. This often occurs when the parking brake cable is stuck or not adjusted properly.

Most self-adjusters operate off the rear (secondary) shoe and should therefore be assembled toward the rear of the vehicle. See Figure 11-25.

ADJUSTING DRUM BRAKES

Most drum brakes are adjusted by rotating a starwheel or rotary adjuster. As the adjuster is moved, the brake shoes move toward the drum. If the brakes have been assembled correctly and with the parking brake fully released, both brake shoes should make contact with the anchor pin at the top. See Figure 11-26 for an example where one shoe does not make contact with the anchor pin. See Chapter 14 for details on parking brake operation and adjustment procedures.

If the clearance between the brake shoes and the brake drum is excessive, a low brake pedal results. The wheel cylinder travel may not be adequate to cause the lining to contact the drums. Often, the driver has to pump the brakes to force enough brake fluid into the wheel cylinder to move it enough for braking action to occur.

Many technicians use a brake shoe clearance gauge to adjust the brake shoes before installing the drum. See Figures 11-27 and 11-28.

CAUTION: Before installing the brake drum, be sure to clean any grease off the brake lining. Some experts warn not to use sandpaper on the lining to remove grease. The sandpaper may release asbestos fiber into the air. Grease on the linings can cause the brakes to grab.

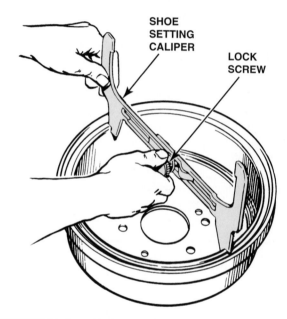

FIGURE 11-27   The first step in using a brake shoe clearance gauge is to adjust it to the drum inside diameter and tighten the lock screw.

TECH TIP

THE MASKING TAPE TRICK

Some technicians cover the friction material with masking tape to prevent contaminating the linings with dirt or grease during installation. After everything has been installed and double checked, the masking tape is removed and the brake drums are installed. See Figure 11-29.

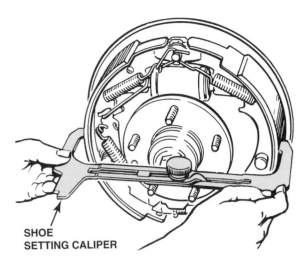

**SHOE
SETTING CALIPER**

FIGURE 11-28 Place the gauge over the shoes and adjust the brakes until they contact the inside of the gauge.

FIGURE 11-29 To prevent getting grease on the lining, the wise service technician covers the friction material with masking tape. The tape is removed after the brake shoes have been installed.

LUBRICATION CHECKLIST

For proper operation, the following points should be lubricated with approved brake lubricant:

CAUTION: Do not use wheel bearing or chassis grease on a braking system. Use only approved brake lubricant such as molybdenum disulfide (moly) grease, synthetic grease, lithium-based brake grease, or antiseize compound.

---

1. The starwheel adjuster threads and under end caps
2. The backing plate contact areas (pads or ledges)
3. Anchor pins

Also, be sure to check and lubricate the parking brake cable, if necessary. See Chapter 14 for details.

SYMPTOM-BASED TROUBLESHOOTING GUIDE

Low Pedal or the Pedal Goes to the Floor

Possible causes for low pedal include the following:

1. Excessive clearance between the linings and drum
2. Automatic adjusters not working
3. Leaking wheel cylinder
4. Air in the system

Springy, Spongy Pedal

Possible causes for springy, spongy pedal include the following:

1. Drums worn below specifications
2. Air in the system

Excessive Pedal Pressure Required to Stop the Vehicle

Possible causes for excessive pedal pressure include the following:

1. Grease or fluid-soaked linings
2. Frozen wheel cylinder pistons
3. Linings installed on wrong shoes

Light Pedal Pressure—Brakes Too Sensitive

Possible causes for light pedal pressure include the following:

1. Brake adjustment not correct
2. Loose backing plate
3. Lining loose on the shoe
4. Excessive dust and dirt in the drums
5. Scored, bell-mouthed, or barrel-shaped drum
6. Improper lining contact pattern

Brake Pedal Travel Decreasing

Possible causes for brake pedal travel decreasing include the following:

1. Weak shoe retracting springs
2. Wheel cylinder pistons sticking

Pulsating Brake Pedal (Parking Brake Apply Pulsates Also)

Possible causes for pulsating brake pedal include the following:

1. Drums out-of-round

Brakes Fade (Temporary Loss of Brake Effectiveness When Hot)

Possible causes for brake fade include the following:

1. Poor lining contact
2. Drums worn below the discard dimension
3. Charred or glazed linings

Shoe Click

Possible causes for shoe click include the following:

1. Shoes lift off the backing plate and snap back
2. Holddown springs weak
3. Shoe bent
4. Grooves in the backing plate pads

Snapping Noise in the Front End

Possible causes for snapping noise in the front end include the following:

1. Grooved backing plate pads
2. Loose backing plates

Thumping Noise When Brakes Are Applied

Possible causes for thumping noise include the following:

1. Cracked drum; hard spots in the drum
2. Retractor springs unequal—weak

Grinding Noise

Possible causes for grinding noise include the following:

1. Shoe hits the drum
2. Bent shoe web
3. Brake improperly assembled

One Wheel Drags

Possible causes for one wheel dragging include the following:

1. Weak or broken shoe retracting springs
2. Brake-shoe-to-drum clearance too tight—brake shoes not adjusted properly

3. Brake assembled improperly
4. Wheel cylinder piston cups swollen and distorted
5. Pistons sticking in the wheel cylinder
6. Drum out-of-round
7. Loose anchor pin/plate
8. Parking brake cable not free
9. Parking brake not adjusted properly

Vehicle Pulls to One Side

Possible causes for vehicle pulling to one side include the following:

1. Brake adjustment not correct
2. Loose backing plate
3. Linings not of specified kind; primary and secondary shoes reversed or not replaced in pairs
4. Water, mud, or other material in brakes
5. Wheel cylinder sticking
6. Weak or broken shoe retracting springs
7. Drums out-of-round
8. Wheel cylinder size different on opposite sides
9. Scored drum

Wet Weather: Brakes Grab or Will Not Hold

Possible causes for brakes grabbing or not holding include the following:

1. Bent backing plate flange
2. Incorrect or abused shoe and linings

Brakes Squeak

Possible causes for brakes squeaking include the following:

1. Backing plate is bent or shoes twisted
2. Shoes scraping on backing plate pads
3. Weak or broken holddown springs
4. Loose backing plate, anchor, or wheel cylinder
5. Glazed linings
6. Dry shoe pads and holddown pin surfaces

Brakes Chatter

Possible causes for brake chattering include the following:

1. Incorrect lining-to-drum clearance
2. Loose backing plate
3. Weak or broken retractor spring
4. Drums out-of-round
5. Tapered or barrel-shaped drums
6. Improper lining contact pattern

DRUM BRAKE SERVICE Step-by-Step

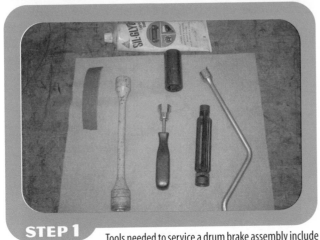

STEP 1 Tools needed to service a drum brake assembly include brake tools, silicone grease, wheel lug nut sockets, and torque limiting adapters or a torque wrench.

STEP 2 After safely hoisting the vehicle to chest height, remove the brake drum.

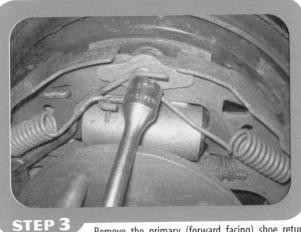

STEP 3 Remove the primary (forward facing) shoe return spring, using a brake tool. Then, remove the secondary return spring.

STEP 4 Remove the parking brake strut along with the anti-rattle spring.

STEP 5 Use a brake tool to depress the holddown spring, and then rotate it until the slot in the retainer lines up with the flattened part of the holddown pin.

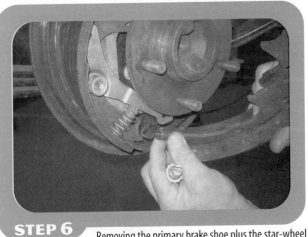

STEP 6 Removing the primary brake shoe plus the star-wheel adjuster and connecting spring.

(continued)

DRUM BRAKE SERVICE continued

STEP 7 When the secondary lining holddown spring is removed, the adjusting lever and pawl return spring can be removed.

STEP 8 The parking brake lever can now be disconnected from the secondary brake shoe.

STEP 9 Check the wheel cylinder for leakage. This wheel cylinder is relatively new and not leaking.

STEP 10 Clean all six brake shoe ledges. Lubricate the ledges with silicone brake grease.

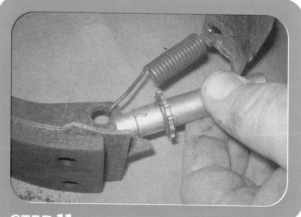

STEP 11 Many technicians prefer to assemble the connecting spring and star-wheel adjuster to both shoes to help in the reinstallation.

STEP 12 Attaching the parking brake lines to the secondary shoe. The assembled parts at the bottom help keep everything together.

DRUM BRAKE SERVICE continued

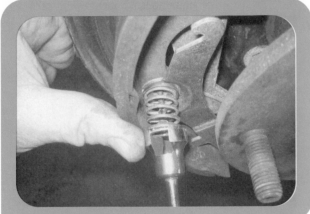

STEP 13 Installing the secondary shoe holddown spring.

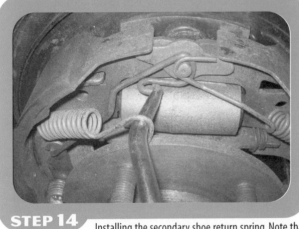

STEP 14 Installing the secondary shoe return spring. Note that the primary return spring has already been installed.

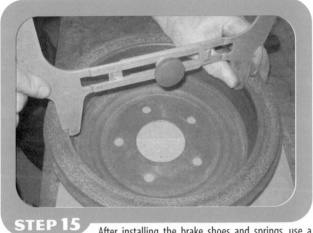

STEP 15 After installing the brake shoes and springs, use a drum/shoe clearance gauge and set it to the inside diameter of the drum.

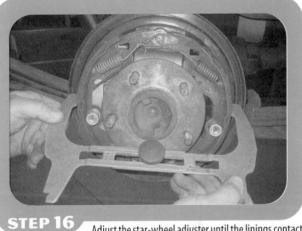

STEP 16 Adjust the star-wheel adjuster until the linings contact the drum brake shoe clearance gauge.

STEP 17 After installing the drum, it may be necessary to make the final adjustment using a brake adjusting tool (spoon).

STEP 18 After completing the brake service, be sure to cover the brake adjustment opening to prevent water from getting into the brake.

SUMMARY

1. Care should be exercised when removing a brake drum so as not to damage the drum, backing plate, or other vehicle components.

2. After disassembly of the drum brake component, the backing plate should be inspected and cleaned.

3. Most experts recommend replacing the wheel cylinder as well as all brake springs as part of a thorough drum brake overhaul.

4. Measure the brake drum and adjust the brake shoes to fit the drum.

5. Use care to prevent getting grease on brake linings. It can cause the brake to grab.

REVIEW QUESTIONS

1. Explain how to remove a brake drum.

2. List all items that should be lubricated on a drum brake.

3. List the steps necessary to follow when replacing drum brake linings.

4. Explain why many vehicle manufacturers do not recommend the wheel cylinder be honed.

CHAPTER QUIZ

1. Technician A says that the tinnerman nuts are used to hold the brake drum on and should be reinstalled when the drum is replaced. Technician B says that a drum should be removed inside a sealed vacuum enclosure or washed with water or solvent to prevent possible asbestos dust from being released into the air. Which technician is correct?

   a. Technician A only

   b. Technician B only

   c. Both Technicians A and B

   d. Neither Technician A nor B

2. The backing plate should be replaced if the shoe contact areas (pads or ledges) are worn more than _____.

   a. 1/2 in. (13 mm)

   b. 1/4 in. (7 mm)

   c. 1/8 in. (4 mm)

   d. 1/16 in. (2 mm)

3. Technician A says that silicone brake grease can be used to lubricate the shoe contact ledges. Technician B says that synthetic brake grease, lithium brake grease, or antiseize compound can be used as a brake lubricant. Which technician is correct?

   a. Technician A only

   b. Technician B only

   c. Both Technicians A and B

   d. Neither Technician A nor B

4. Most brake experts and vehicle manufacturers recommend replacing brake lining when the lining thickness is _____.

   a. 0.030 in. (0.8 mm)

   b. 0.040 in. (1.0 mm)

   c. 0.050 in. (1.3 mm)

   d. 0.060 in. (1.5 mm)

5. Technician A says that starwheel adjusters use different threads (left- and right-handed) for the left and right sides of the vehicle. Technician B says that the threads and end caps of the adjusters should be lubricated with brake grease before being installed. Which technician is correct?

   a. Technician A only

   b. Technician B only

   c. Both Technicians A and B

   d. Neither Technician A nor B

6. Technician A says that many vehicle manufacturers recommend that wheel cylinders not be honed because of the special surface finish inside the bore. Technician B says that seal expanders are used to help prevent the lip of the cup seal from collapsing when the brakes are released. Which technician is correct?

   a. Technician A only

   b. Technician B only

   c. Both Technicians A and B

   d. Neither Technician A nor B

7. Most manufacturers recommend that brake parts should be cleaned with _____.
   a. Clean water only
   b. Denatured alcohol
   c. Stoddard solvent
   d. Detergent and water

8. Old brake shoes are often returned to the manufacturer when new friction material is installed. These old shoes are usually called the _____.
   a. Core
   b. Web
   c. Rim
   d. Nib

9. After assembling a drum brake, it is discovered that the brake drum will not fit over the new brake shoes. Technician A says that the parking brake cable may not have been fully released. Technician B says to check to see if both shoes are contacting the anchor pin. Which technician is correct?
   a. Technician A only
   b. Technician B only
   c. Both Technicians A and B
   d. Neither Technician A nor B

10. Technician A says to use masking tape temporarily over the lining material to help prevent getting grease on the lining. Technician B says that grease on the brake lining can cause the brakes to grab. Which technician is correct?
    a. Technician A only
    b. Technician B only
    c. Both Technicians A and B
    d. Neither Technician A nor B

CHAPTER **12**

DISC BRAKES

OBJECTIVES

After studying Chapter 12, the reader should be able to:

1. Prepare for the Brakes (A5) ASE certification test content area "C" (Disc Brake Diagnosis and Repair).
2. Describe how disc brakes function.
3. Name the parts of a typical disc brake system.
4. Describe the construction of disc brake pads.
5. Describe the difference between fixed caliper and floating or sliding caliper.
6. Explain the difference between a standard caliper and a low-drag caliper.

KEY TERMS

DISC BRAKES

Disc brakes use a piston(s) to squeeze friction material (pads) on both sides of a rotating disc (rotor). Disc may be spelled *disk* by some manufacturers, but *disc* is the SAE (Society of Automotive Engineers) term and the most commonly used spelling in the industry. The rotor is attached to and stops the wheel.

Disc brakes are used on the front wheels of late-model vehicles, and on the rear wheels of an increasing number of automobiles. Disc brakes were adopted primarily because they can supply greater stopping power than drum brakes with less likelihood of fade. This makes disc brakes especially well suited for use as front brakes, which must provide 60% to 80% of the vehicle's total stopping power.

DISC BRAKE ADVANTAGES

Although increased federal brake performance standards hastened the switch to disc brakes, the front drum brakes would eventually have been eliminated anyway because disc brakes are superior in almost every respect. The disc brake friction assembly has several significant strong points, and only a few relatively minor weak points. See Figure 12-1.

The main advantages of the disc brake include the following:

- Fade resistance
- Self-adjustment
- Freedom from pull

Fade Resistance

When a disc brake is compared with a drum brake of similar diameter, its biggest advantage is a much greater ability to resist fade. In fact, disc brakes are more resistant to all kinds of fade, including the following:

- Mechanical fade
- Lining fade
- Gas fade
- Water fade

The main design features that help disc brakes avoid heat-induced fade is their cooling ability because all of the major parts of a disc brake are exposed to the air flowing over the friction assembly. Many brake rotors also have cooling passages cast into them to further reduce operating temperatures.

Another reason disc brakes have greater fade resistance than drum brakes is that they have greater **swept area.** Swept area is the amount of brake drum or rotor friction surface that moves past the brake linings every time the drum or rotor completes a rotation. A larger swept area allows the heat generated in braking to be transferred more rapidly into the rotor for better cooling. A disc brake has swept area on both sides of the rotor. A drum brake has swept area only on the inside of the drum. Large diameter rotors, however, require larger diameter wheels to provide the necessary clearance. This is one of the major reasons why high-performance vehicles use 17-inch diameter and larger wheels.

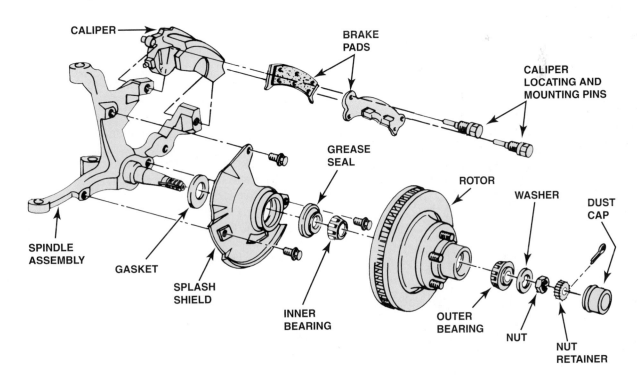

FIGURE 12-1   A typical disc brake assembly.

Mechanical Fade. **Mechanical fade** is not a problem with disc brakes because, unlike a brake drum, the disc brake rotor expands *toward* the brake linings as it heats up rather than *away* from them. This fundamental design difference makes it physically impossible for heat to cause the rotor to expand out of contact with the brake linings. Because of this, there is never the need to move the brake linings out to keep them in contact with the rotor, so brake pedal travel does not increase. If the brake pedal on a vehicle with disc brakes drops toward the floor, it is almost always a sign of vapor lock, a fluid leak, fluid bypassing the seals in the master cylinder, or mechanical fade of the rear *drum* brakes.

Lining Fade. **Lining fade** can and does occur if the brakes become overheated. A little bit of heat brings the brake pads to their operating temperature and actually increases the friction coefficient of the lining material. A warm brake performs better than a cold brake. However, when too much heat is generated by braking, the lining material overheats. Its friction coefficient drops, and lining fade occurs.

The primary symptom of lining fade is a hard brake pedal that requires the driver to apply greater force to maintain stopping power. Unlike the similar situation in a drum brake, however, increased application force will not distort the brake rotor because the caliper applies equal force to both sides. See Figure 12-2.

Increased pressure will, however, create even more heat, and if brake lining temperatures continue to increase, gas fade and vapor lock of the hydraulic system can occur.

If the pads are overheated to the point where the lining material is physically damaged, the brakes will not recover their full stopping power until the pads are replaced. See Figure 12-3.

FIGURE 12-3 Disc brakes can absorb and dissipate a great deal of heat. Druing this demonstration, the brakes were gently applied as the engine drove the front wheels until the rotor became cherry red. During normal braking, the rotor temperature can exceed 350°F (180°C), and about 1,500°F (800°C) on a race vehicle.

Gas Fade. **Gas fade** is a problem only under severe braking conditions when hot gasses and dust particles from the linings are trapped between the brake linings and rotor, where they act as lubricants. The symptoms of gas fade are the same as those for lining fade. The pedal becomes hard and increased force is required to maintain stopping power.

Even though disc brakes operate at higher temperatures than drum brakes, they have fewer problems with gas fade for a number of reasons.

1. Disc brakes do not have a drum to contain gasses and particles in the area around the brake linings.
2. The constant flow of air over the brake carries away contaminants that might otherwise build up.
3. The surface area of the brake lining material in a disc brake is smaller than that of a comparable drum brake and this allows gasses and particles to escape more easily.

To help prevent gas fade, many brake pads have slots cut in the lining material. These slots allow gasses and dust particles to escape. See Figure 12-4.

The holes required in riveted linings also perform this function. For even greater protection against gas fade, high-performance vehicles and motorcycles sometimes have holes or slots cut into the rotor. These openings allow gasses and water to escape, and their sharp edges continually wipe loose particles off the linings.

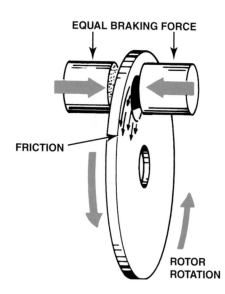

FIGURE 12-2 Braking force is applied equally to both sides of the brake rotor.

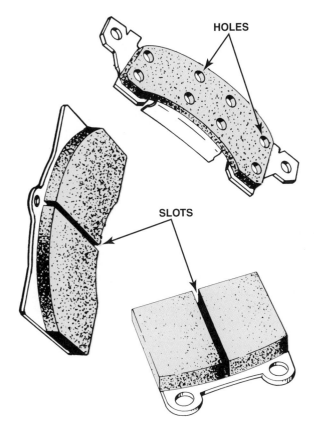

The surface finish on the piston must be clean to allow the piston to slide past this seal. Moisture accumulation inside the caliper often causes the piston to rust. These rust pits can cut or groove the caliper seal. Excessive friction between the caliper piston and the caliper bore can prevent the piston from retracting. If the force of the caliper seal is not strong enough, the piston stays in the applied position. Because the brake pads are still in contact with the rotor, one or both pads will show excessive wear.

Normal Operation.   The piston moves just enough to distort the caliper seal and returns to the original position when the brake pedal is released.

Wear Compensation.   The piston moves more than the caliper seal can distort. The piston moves through the seal until the pad contacts the rotor. The caliper piston returns to the released position by the seal distortion, the same as during normal operation, except now in a different, more applied position. See Figure 12-5.

As the wear occurs and the piston moves, additional brake fluid is needed behind the piston. This additional brake fluid comes from the master cylinder and the brake fluid level drops as the disc brake pads wear.

Freedom from Pull

A disc brake will stop straighter under a wider range of conditions than will a drum brake. A disc brake is self-cleaning, will throw off most water, and is less likely to pull.

Disc brakes do not have self-energizing or servo action. These actions increase the power of drum brakes, but depend

FIGURE 12-4   Slots and holes in the brake linings help prevent gas and water fade.

Water Fade.   **Water fade** is not a big problem with disc brakes because centrifugal force created by the spinning rotor throws off most moisture, and the brake pads positioned only a few thousandths of an inch away from the rotor continuously wipe it clean. When the brakes are applied, the leading edge of the brake pad lining material wipes the last bit of water from the disc. Once good lining-to-rotor contact is established, water is unable to enter the space between the linings and rotor until the brakes are released.

Although far more resistant to water fade than drum brakes, disc brakes are not entirely free from its effects. Splash shields and the vehicle's wheels help keep water off of the rotor, and the brake lining materials specified for most vehicles minimize the effects of water fade.

Self-Adjusting Ability

Disc brakes are self-adjusting because any wear of the linings is automatically compensated for by the action of the brake caliper.

When the brakes are applied the caliper pistons move out as far as needed to force the brake pads into contact with the rotor. When the brakes are released, the piston retracts only the small distance dictated by rotor runout and piston seal flex.

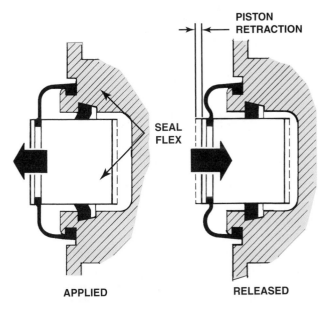

FIGURE 12-5   The square-cut O-ring not only seals hydraulic brake fluid, but also retracts the caliper piston when the brake pedal is released.

on friction between the linings and drum for their effect. This means that even a small loss of lining-to-drum friction causes a large loss of braking power and a significant side-to-side variation in the amount of braking force. Since disc brakes do not use friction between the linings and rotor to increase their braking power, the effects of a loss of friction on one side of the vehicle are far less pronounced than with drum brakes.

DISC BRAKE DISADVANTAGES

The most notable fact about the disadvantages of disc brakes is that there are so few. The weaknesses of disc brakes include the following:

- No self-energizing or servo action
- Brake noise
- Brake dust
- Poor parking brake performance

No Self-Energizing or Servo Action

The disc brake's lack of self-energizing or servo action is a disadvantage for two reasons. It contributes to poor parking brake performance and requires the driver to push harder on the brake pedal for a given stop. However, the problem of high pedal pressures has been virtually eliminated through the use of brake power boosters, since the disc brake responds more directly to pressure on the brake pedal. This makes it easier to modulate the brakes for the exact amount of stopping power desired.

Brake Noise

Probably the biggest complaint about disc brakes is that they sometimes make various squeaks and squeals during a brake application. As long as the brake linings are not worn down to the backing plate, these noises are usually caused by high-frequency rattling or vibration of the brake pads.

Several methods are used to quiet noisy disc brakes. Manufacturers use specific lining materials that damp vibrations, and most calipers have **anti-rattle clips** or springs that hold the pads in the caliper under tension to help prevent vibration. See Figure 12-6.

Some calipers use special shims between the brake pad backing plate and the caliper piston to damp vibrations. See Figure 12-7.

These shims may be made of metal or fiber.

Antinoise sprays and brush-on liquids are available and provide a cushion layer between the pad and the caliper piston. The bond lowers the **natural frequency** of the pad, and the cushion layer damps any vibration that may still occur.

Brake Dust

Because the lining is exposed on a disc brake, rather than being enclosed on a drum brake, some brake dust can accumulate on the wheels. This brake dust is often dark brown or black and can stain wheels if not cleaned often or protected from the dust.

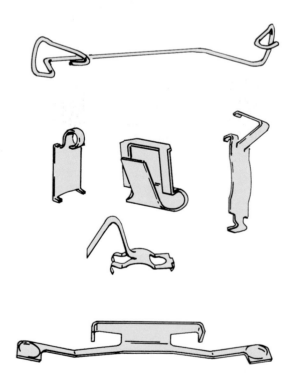

FIGURE 12-6   Anti-rattle clips reduce brake pad movement and vibration.

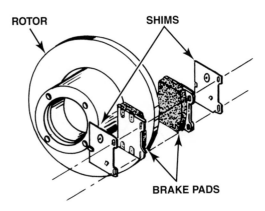

FIGURE 12-7   Anti-vibration shims are used behind the pads on many disc brake caliper designs.

WAX THE WHEELS

Brake dust from semimetallic brake pads often discolors the front wheels. Customers often complain to service technicians about this problem, but it is normal for the front wheels to become dirty because the iron and other metallic and nonmetallic components wear off the front disc brake pads and adhere to the wheel covers. A coat of wax on the wheels or wheel covers helps prevent damage and makes it easier to wash off the brake dust.

Poor Parking Brake Performance

The lack of self-energizing and servo action plays a large part in poor disc brake parking brake performance. The lining-to-rotor contact area of a disc brake is somewhat smaller than the lining-to-drum contact area of a drum brake. This causes the disc brake to have a lower static coefficient of friction, and therefore less holding power when the vehicle is stopped.

DISC BRAKE CONSTRUCTION

A disc brake is relatively simple compared with a drum brake. The major disc brake friction assembly components include the following:

- Caliper
- Splash shield
- Brake pads
- Brake rotor

Caliper

With the exception of the rotor, the caliper is the largest part of a disc brake friction assembly. The brake caliper uses hydraulic pressure to create the mechanical force required to move the brake pads into contact with the brake rotor. At the front axle, the caliper mounts to the spindle or steering knuckle. See Figure 12-8.

Rear disc brake calipers mount to a support bracket on the axle flange or suspension. See Figure 12-9.

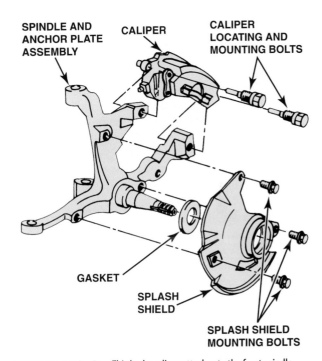

FIGURE 12-8   This brake caliper attaches to the front spindle.

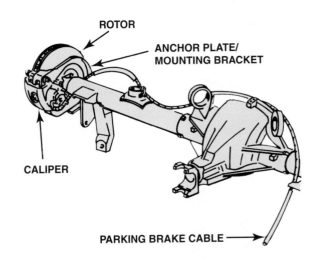

FIGURE 12-9   This brake caliper attaches to a mounting bracket on the rear axle housing.

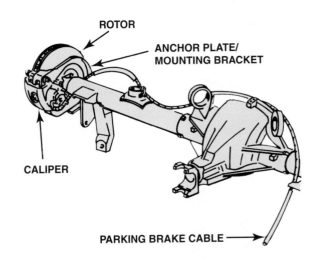

Disc Brakes   209

Splash Shield

The splash shield bolts to the front spindle or steering knuckle, or in rear disc brake applications, to the axle flange or a suspension adapter plate. The job of the splash shield is to protect the inner side of the brake rotor from water and other contaminants, whereas the outer side of the rotor is protected by the wheel. Most splash shields are made of stamped steel or plastic.

DISC BRAKE PADS

The lining of a disc brake is part of an assembly called the **brake pad**. See Figure 12-10.

Compared to a brake shoe, a brake pad is a relatively simple part that consists of a block of friction material attached to a stamped steel backing plate. Some pad backing plates have tabs that bend over the caliper to hold the pad tightly in place and help prevent brake noise. See Figure 12-11.

Other pad backing plates have tabs with holes in them as shown in Figure 12-12.

A pin slips through the holes and fastens to the caliper body to hold the pads in position. Still other pad backing plates have a retainer spring attached that locates the pad in the caliper by locking it to the caliper piston. See Figure 12-13.

As with brake shoes, the lining material of a disc pad can be any one of a number of products that can be fastened to the backing plate in several ways. The edges of the lining material on a brake pad are usually perpendicular to the rotor surface, although a few larger pads do have tapered edges to help combat vibration and noise. See Figure 12-14.

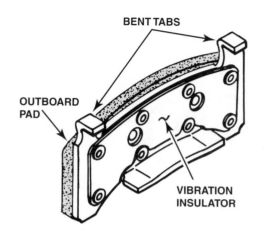

FIGURE 12-11   To prevent noise, bent tabs on the backing plate hold some brake pads to the caliper housing.

Pad Wear Indicators

Although not required by law, a growing number of vehicle manufacturers are fitting **pad wear indicators** to their brakes for safety reasons. Pad wear indicators are either mechanical or electrical, and signal the driver when the lining material has worn to the point where pad replacement is necessary.

A mechanical wear indicator is a small spring-steel tab riveted to the pad backing plate. When the friction material wears to a predetermined thickness, the tab contacts the rotor and makes a squealing or chirping noise (when the brakes are not applied) that alerts the driver to the need for service. See Figure 12-15.

Electrical wear indicators, such as those shown in Figure 12-16, use a coated electrode imbedded in the lining material to generate the warning signal.

The electrode is wired to a warning light in the instrument panel and when the lining wears sufficiently, the electrode grounds against the rotor to complete the circuit and turn on the warning light.

Pad Assembly Methods

As mentioned in Chapter 10, there are several methods used to mount brake linings, including:

- Riveting
- Bonding
- Mold bonding

Riveting.   Riveted linings take advantage of the oldest method of lining attachment still in use. In this system, the brake block is attached to the backing plate with copper or aluminum rivets.

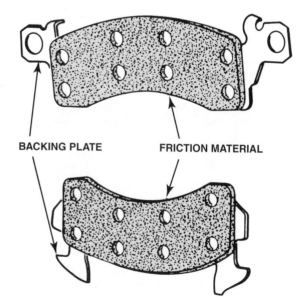

FIGURE 12-10   A typical disc brake pad.

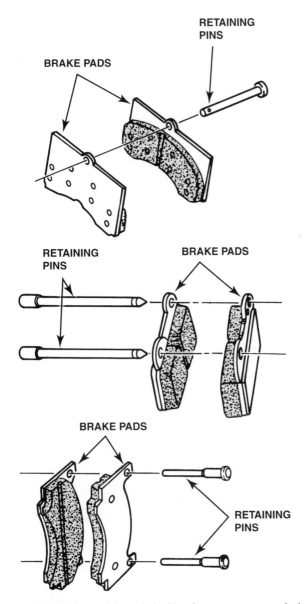

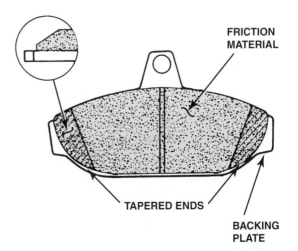

FIGURE 12-14   The lining edges of some brake pads are tapered to help prevent vibration.

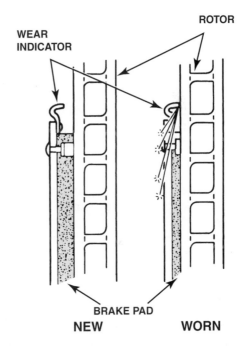

FIGURE 12-12   Holes in the backing plate are a common method of locating a pad in the caliper.

FIGURE 12-15   Typical pad wear sensor operation. It is very important that the disc brake pads are installed on the correct side of the vehicle to be assured that the wear sensor will make a noise when the pads are worn. If the pads with a sensor are installed on the opposite side of the vehicle, the sensor tab is turned so that the rotor touches it going the opposite direction. Usually the correct direction is where the rotor contacts the sensor before contacting the pads when the wheels are being rotated in the forward direction.

The major advantage of riveting is that it allows a small amount of flex between the brake block backing plate. This play enables the assembly to absorb vibration, and the result is that riveted linings operate more quietly than bonded linings. Rivets are also very reliable and will not loosen at high temperatures.

Despite the benefit of quiet operation, riveted pads present a number of problems. In order to leave sufficient

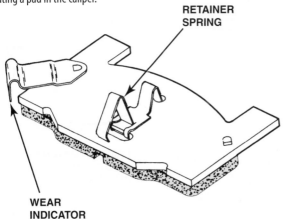

FIGURE 12-13   Retainer springs lock the pad to the caliper piston to prevent brake noise.

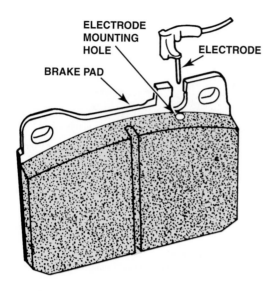

FIGURE 12-16 Electrical wear indicators ground a warning light circuit when the pads need replacement.

friction material for the rivets to clamp the brake block securely against the backing plate, the rivet holes are countersunk only about two-thirds to three-quarters of the way through the lining. This reduces the service life of the assembly because the shoes must be replaced before the rivet heads contact and score the rotor.

The rivet holes themselves also present some unique problems. First, they trap abrasive brake dust and other grit that can score the rotor. Some rivets are hollow to allow these materials to escape. Rivet holes also create stress points in the lining where cracks are likely to develop.

Bonding

Bonded linings use high-temperature adhesive to glue the brake block directly to the shoe pad backing plate. Heat and pressure are then applied to cure the assembly. Bonding is a common form of shoe and pad assembly, and is most often used to mount organic friction materials.

Bonding offers several advantages. Without rivets, bonded linings can wear closer to the backing plate and provide a longer service life. If the linings wear too far, bonding adhesive is not as destructive to rotors as rivets. Bonded linings also have fewer problems with cracking because they have no rivet holes to weaken the brake block.

The primary disadvantage of bonded linings is a limited ability to withstand high temperatures. If a bonded lining gets too hot, the bonding adhesive will fail and allow the brake block to separate from the backing plate. Bonded linings are also more prone to be noisy because they do not al-

low any vibration absorbing flex between the brake block and backing plate.

Mold Bonding

Mold bonded linings are found on some disc brake pads. Mold bonding is a manufacturing process that combines the advantages of bonding with some of the mechanical strength of riveting. Instead of riveting and/or bonding a cured brake block to a separate backing plate, the friction material in a mold bonded pad is cured on the backing plate during manufacture. This process is also called **integrally molded**. Most high-performance disc brake pads are made in this way.

To make a mold-bonded pad, one or more holes are punched in the pad backing plate, and a high-temperature adhesive is applied to it. The backing plate is then installed in a molding machine where uncured friction material is formed onto the plate and forced into the holes. See Figure 12-17.

Once the pad is cured under heat and pressure, the bonding adhesive combines with the portions of the lining that extend into the backing plate holes to solidly lock the brake block in place.

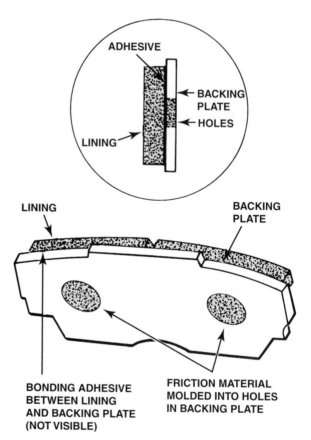

FIGURE 12-17 Mold-bonded linings are commonly used in many applications.

Brake Lining Composition

Shoes and pads operate under the most extreme conditions in the entire brake system and are subject to a great deal of wear. The replacement of worn brake shoes and pads is a common part of brake service.

Although they appear to be simple parts, brake shoes and pads are the result of years of engineering development. Often, two shoes or pads that look identical will not perform the same because different friction materials are used for their linings. When a brake system is designed, engineers test the performance characteristics of many friction materials and then specify those that will work best in the particular application.

Friction materials such as disc brake pads or drum brake shoes contain a mixture of ingredients. These materials include a binder such as a thermosetting resin, fibers for reinforcement, and friction modifiers to obtain a desired coefficient of friction (abbreviated μ—Greek letter mu). The various ingredients in brake lining are mixed and molded into the shape of the finished product. The fibers in the material are the only thing holding this mixture together. A large press is used to force the ingredients together to form a **brake block,** which eventually becomes the brake lining.

Typical Compositions for Asbestos (Organic) Lining

Ingredient	Typical Formula Range
Phenolic resin (binder)	9–15%
Asbestos fiber	30–50%
Organic friction modifiers (rubber scrap)	8–19%
Inorganic friction modifiers (barites, talc, whiting)	12–26%
Abrasive particles (alumina)	4–20%
Carbon	4–20%

SEMIMETALLIC FRICTION MATERIAL

The term *semimetallic* refers to brake lining material that uses metal rather than asbestos in its formulation. It still uses resins and binders and is, therefore, not 100% metal, but rather, semimetallic. Semimetallics are commonly called **semimets.** The metal in most metallic linings is made from metal particles that have been fused together without melting. This process is called **sintering** and the result is called **sintered metal** linings. See Figure 12-18.

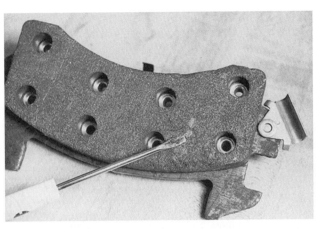

FIGURE 12-18   Poor-quality semimetallic disc brake pad. The screwdriver is pointing to large chunks of steel embedded in the lining.

Typical Compositions for Semimetallic Pads

Ingredient	Formula Range
Phenolic resin	15–40%
Graphite or carbon particles	15–40%
Steel fibers	0–25%
Ceramic powders	2–10%
Steel, copper, brass metal powders	15–40%
Other modifiers (rubber scrap)	0–20%

Most semimetallic linings do not contain asbestos. Semimetallic linings require a very smooth finish on the rotor because the metal in the lining does not conform to the surface of the rotor, as does asbestos lining.

Nonasbestos Friction Material

Brake pads and linings that use synthetic material such as aramid fibers instead of steel are usually referred to as **nonasbestos, nonasbestos organic (NAO),** or **nonasbestos synthetic (NAS).** Linings are called "synthetic" because synthetic (man-made) fibers are used. These linings use **aramid fiber** instead of metal as the base material. Aramid is the generic name for aromatic polyamide fibers. **Kevlar** is the Dupont brand name of aramid and a registered trademark of E.I. Dupont de Nemours and Company. Nonasbestos linings are often quieter than semimetallics and do not cause as much wear to brake rotors as do semimetallic pads.

Carbon Fiber Friction Material

Carbon fiber brake lining is the newest and most expensive of the lining materials. Carbon fiber material is often called

CFRC (carbon fiber–reinforced carbon). It is composed of a carbon mix into which reinforcing carbon fibers are embedded. CFRC is commonly used in the brakes of jet aircraft and racing cars. CFRC brakes provide constant friction coefficient whether cold or hot, low wear rates, and low noise development.

Ceramic Friction Material

Some vehicle manufacturers use friction materials that contain ceramic fibers. These ceramic fibers are usually potassium titanite. Some vehicle manufacturers do not recommend the use of ceramic friction material because they tend to wear the rotors more than NAO or semimetallic friction materials.

LINING EDGE CODES

As explained in Chapter 10, the lining edge codes help identify the coefficient of friction.

These codes were established by the SAE (Society of Automotive Engineers):

Code C	0.00 to 0.15
Code D	0.15 to 0.25
Code E	0.25 to 0.35
Code F	0.35 to 0.45
Code G	0.45 to 0.55
Code H	0.55 and above
Code Z	ungraded

FREQUENTLY ASKED QUESTION

WHAT DOES "D³EA" MEAN?

Original equipment brake pads and shoes are required to comply with the Federal Motor Vehicle Safety Standard (FMVSS) 135, which specifies maximum stopping distances. There is also a requirement for fade resistance, but no standard for noise or wear. Aftermarket (replacement) brake pads and shoes are not required to meet the FMVSS standard. However, several manufacturers of replacement brake pads and shoes are using a standardized test that closely matches the FMVSS standard and is called the "Dual Dynamometer Differential Effectiveness Analysis" or D³EA. This test is currently voluntary and linings that pass the test can have a "D³EA certified" seal placed on the product package.

FREQUENTLY ASKED QUESTION

WHAT IS A BRAKE PAD RECIPE?

The actual amount of each ingredient in a typical brake lining is varied for each application. Each vehicle has its own "recipe" based on vehicle weight and options. For example, a Chevrolet with a light four-cylinder engine and no air conditioning may use a different brake lining recipe than the same vehicle, but with the heavier V-6 engine, air conditioning, and other options that increase the vehicle weight. Both of these brake linings (shoes or pads) may physically fit other similar vehicles, yet their brake lining recipe is different.

Replacement linings are usually a compromise "generic" recipe that will give acceptable service. The brake lining recipe is just one of many factors that results in the fact that new brakes always seem to last longer than any replacement lining. Replacement lining should have the same friction code as the original. Although this will not guarantee the same braking performance, this edge code rating does help assure the service technician that the replacement brakes will give "as new" performance.

TECH TIP

COMPETITIVELY PRICED BRAKES

The term *competitively priced* means lower cost. Most brake manufacturers offer "premium" as well as lower-price linings, to remain competitive with other manufacturers or with importers of brake lining material produced overseas by U.S. or foreign companies. Organic asbestos brake lining is inexpensive to manufacture. In fact, according to warehouse distributors and importers, the box often costs more than the brake lining inside!

Professional brake service technicians should only install brake linings and pads that will give braking performance equal to that of the original factory brakes. "Competitive" asbestos linings should never be substituted for semimetallic or NAO original linings or pads. For best results, always purchase high-quality brake parts from a known brand-name manufacturer.

The first letter, which is printed on the side of most linings, indicates its coefficient of friction when brakes are cold, and the second letter indicates the coefficient of friction of the brake lining when the brakes are hot. (For example, FF indicates that the brake lining material has a coefficient of friction between 0.35 and 0.45 when both cold and hot.)

BRAKE ROTORS

The brake rotor provides the friction surfaces for the brake pads to rub against. The rotor, the largest and heaviest part of a disc brake, is usually made of cast iron because that metal has excellent friction and wear properties. There are two basic types of rotors: solid and vented. See Figure 12-19.

Vented rotors have radial cooling passages cast between the friction surfaces, whereas solid rotors are most often used on the rear of vehicles equipped with four-wheel disc brakes.

DISC BRAKE DESIGN

While the hydraulic operation of all brake calipers is similar, calipers differ in two important areas: how they attach to the vehicle, and how they apply the brake pads to the rotor. The manners in which these tasks are performed determine the design of a disc brake friction assembly. There are basically three types of calipers:

- Fixed
- Floating
- Sliding

Fixed calipers have several unique features, but sliding and floating calipers share similar features.

Fixed Caliper Design

The **fixed brake caliper** is the earliest design. See Figure 12-20. The fixed caliper has a body manufactured in two halves, and uses two, three, or four pistons to apply the brake pads. The fixed caliper gets its name from the fact that the caliper is rigidly mounted to the suspension. When the brakes are applied, the pistons extend from the caliper bores and apply the brake pads with equal force from both sides of the rotor. No part of the caliper body moves when the brakes are applied.

Fixed Caliper Advantages.   Fixed calipers are relatively large and heavy, which enables them to absorb and dissipate great amounts of heat. This allows the brake rotor and pads to run cooler, and reduce the amount of heat transferred to the brake fluid. Compared with other caliper designs, a fixed caliper is able to withstand a greater number of repeated hard stops without heat-induced fade or vapor lock of the hydraulic system.

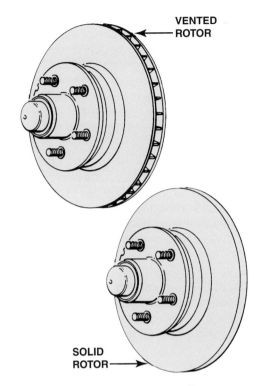

FIGURE 12-19   Disc brake rotors can be either solid or vented.

FIGURE 12-20   Four-piston fixed caliper assembly on a race vehicle.

The size and rigid mounting of a fixed caliper also means it does not flex as much as other designs. A caliper that is flexing is usually felt by the driver as a spongy brake pedal. Fixed calipers are very strong and provide a firm and linear brake pedal feel.

The strength and heat-dissipating abilities of fixed calipers make them best suited for heavy-duty use such as in most race vehicles.

Fixed Caliper Disadvantages.

The size and weight of fixed calipers are advantages in heavy-duty use, but they add weight to the vehicle. To obtain better fuel economy, manufacturers want to eliminate as much weight as possible from new vehicles.

Another disadvantage of fixed calipers is that, with multiple pistons and split bodies, service is more difficult and allows greater opportunity for leaks. The drilled passages that route fluid through the inside of the caliper body also contribute to cracking as miles accumulate and the caliper goes through hundreds of thousands of heating and cooling cycles. See Figure 12-21.

Fixed Caliper Alignment.

Because the caliper body is locked in position, a fixed caliper must be centered over the rotor and aligned so the pistons contact the brake pad backing plates parallel to the friction surface of the rotor. See Figure 12-22.

If the caliper is not properly aligned, the pistons will contact the pads at an angle and cause tapered wear of the brake linings. If the misalignment is bad enough, the pistons will cock into their bores, suffer increased wear, and possibly crack.

Whenever a fixed caliper is unbolted from its mounts, care should be taken to note the location and quantity of any shims so they can be replaced in the same positions during reassembly. If a different caliper is installed, its alignment must be checked and adjusted as necessary.

Floating and Sliding Caliper Design

The front brakes of most vehicles are fitted with either floating or sliding calipers, which are *not* rigidly mounted. The caliper is free to move within a limited range on an **anchor plate** that *is* solidly mounted to the vehicle suspension. The anchor plate may be cast into a suspension member (often the front spindle) or it can be a separate piece that bolts to the suspension. See Figure 12-23.

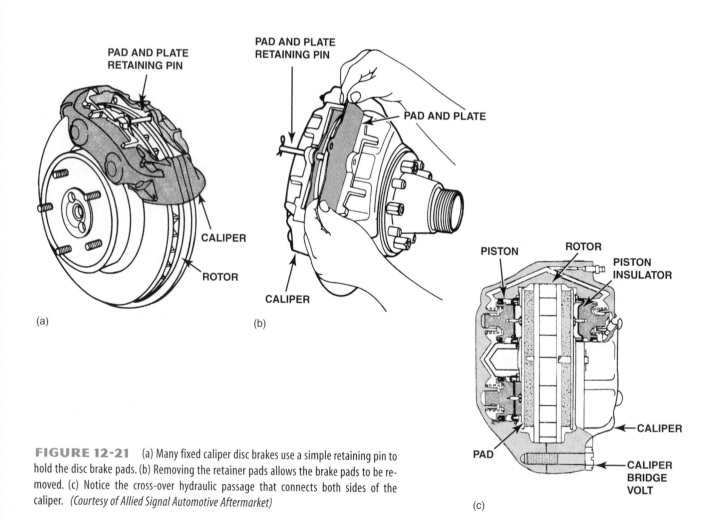

(a)   (b)   (c)

FIGURE 12-21   (a) Many fixed caliper disc brakes use a simple retaining pin to hold the disc brake pads. (b) Removing the retainer pads allows the brake pads to be removed. (c) Notice the cross-over hydraulic passage that connects both sides of the caliper. *(Courtesy of Allied Signal Automotive Aftermarket)*

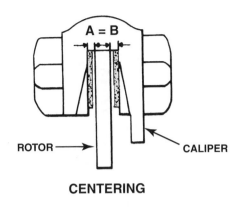

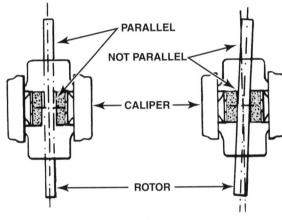

FIGURE 12-22 Fixed brake calipers must be centered over the rotor with their pistons parallel to the rotor friction surfaces.

When the brakes are applied the caliper piston moves out of its bore and applies the inner brake pad. At the same time, the caliper body moves in the opposite direction on the anchor plate and applies the outer brake pad. With a floating or sliding caliper, the caliper body moves every time the brakes are applied. See Figure 12-24.

Floating and Sliding Caliper Advantages. The biggest advantages of floating and sliding calipers are lower cost, simple construction, and compact size. Most floating and sliding calipers are single-piston designs. Because they have fewer pieces, floating and sliding calipers are cheaper to build and service, and have fewer places where leaks can develop.

The smaller size of floating and sliding calipers also allows better packaging of the caliper on the vehicle. A single-piston caliper with the piston located on the inboard side of the brake rotor fits easily within the diameter of a small wheel. The inboard position of the caliper piston also contributes to better cooling because the bulk of the caliper body is exposed to the passing airflow.

Like any disc brake, floating and sliding calipers have poor parking brake performance. Unlike a fixed caliper, a floating or

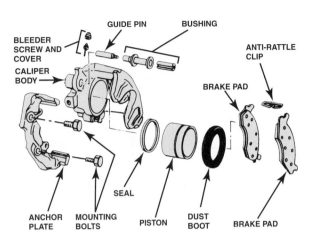

FIGURE 12-23 This floating caliper mounts on a separate anchor plate that bolts to the vehicle suspension.

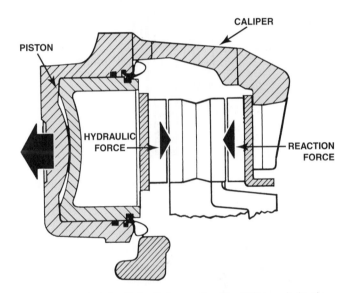

FIGURE 12-24 Hydraulic force on the piston (left) is applied to the inboard pad and the caliper housing itself. The reaction of the piston pushing against the rotor causes the entire caliper to move toward the inside of the vehicle (large arrow). Since the outboard pad is retained by the caliper, the reaction of the moving caliper applies the force of the outboard pad against the outboard surface of the rotor.

sliding caliper can be mechanically actuated by applying the single piston with a cable and lever mechanism.

Floating and Sliding Caliper Disadvantages. The movable caliper body allows a certain degree of flex, which can contribute to a spongy brake pedal. Caliper flex also allows the caliper body to twist slightly when the brakes are applied, causing tapered wear of the brake pad lining material. See Figure 12-25.

Although the inboard piston location of floating and sliding calipers provides good cooling, these designs can never absorb as much heat (and therefore have the fade resistance) as

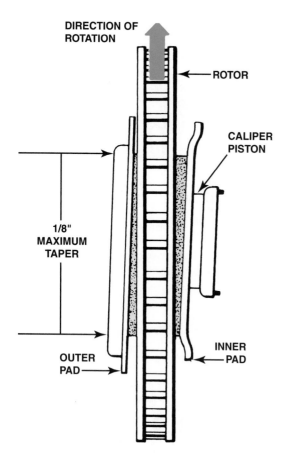

DIRECTION OF ROTATION

ROTOR

CALIPER PISTON

1/8" MAXIMUM TAPER

OUTER PAD

INNER PAD

FIGURE 12-25   Caliper flex can cause tapered wear of the brake lining.

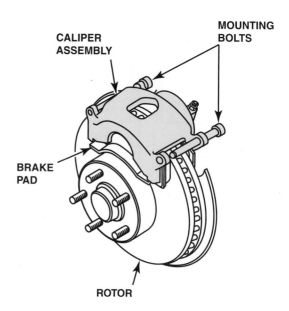

CALIPER ASSEMBLY

MOUNTING BOLTS

BRAKE PAD

ROTOR

FIGURE 12-26   A typical single-piston floating caliper. In this type of design, the entire caliper moves when the single piston is pushed out of the caliper during a brake application. When the caliper moves, the outboard pad is pushed against the rotor.

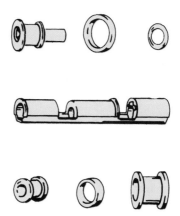

FIGURE 12-27   Floating calipers are supported by rubber O-rings or plastic bushings.

a fixed caliper with similar stopping power. Floating and sliding calipers simply do not have the mass of fixed calipers, and their flexible mounting systems slow the transfer of heat from the caliper body to the anchor plate and other suspension components that aid in the cooling process.

Floating Calipers

The body of a **floating caliper** does not make direct metal-to-metal contact with the anchor plate. See Figure 12-26.

Instead, the caliper body is supported by bushings and/or O-rings that allow it to "float" or slide on metal guide pins or locating sleeves attached to the anchor plate. For this reason, some automakers call the floating caliper a **pin-slider caliper.**

The bushings that support floating calipers are made from a number of materials including rubber, Teflon, and nylon. O-rings are generally made from high-temperature synthetic rubber. See Figure 12-27.

The guide pins and sleeves are made of steel and come in a variety of shapes and sizes for different caliper designs. See Figure 12-28.

Floating calipers depend on proper lubrication of their pins, sleeves, bushings, and O-rings for smooth operation. If these parts become rusted or corroded, the caliper will bind and stick, causing loss of braking power that is usually accompanied by rapid and unusual wear of brake pads. Special high-temperature brake grease must be used to lubricate these parts any time the caliper is disassembled. Many manufacturers recommend that floating caliper pins, sleeves, bushings, and O-rings be replaced whenever the caliper is serviced. These parts come in a "small parts kit" available from brake part suppliers.

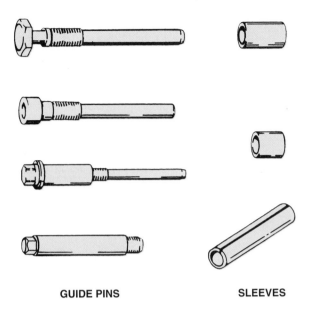

GUIDE PINS   **SLEEVES**

FIGURE 12-28 Metal guide pins and sleeves are used to retain and locate floating calipers.

FREQUENTLY ASKED QUESTION

WHAT IS A LOW-DRAG CALIPER?

A **low-drag caliper** differs from a standard caliper in the area of the square-cut O-ring. A V-shaped cutout allows the O-ring to deflect more and, as a result, is able to pull the caliper piston back into the bore when the brakes are released. Because of this further movement, the brake pads are pulled further from the rotor and are less likely to drag. The negative aspect of this design is that greater volume of brake fluid is needed to achieve a brake application. To compensate for this need for greater brake fluid volume, a quick-take-up master cylinder was designed and is used whenever low-drag calipers are used. See Figure 12-29.

Sliding Calipers

Unlike a floating caliper, the body of a **sliding caliper** mounts in direct metal-to-metal contact with the anchor plate. See Figure 12-30.

Instead of pins and bushings, sliding calipers move on **ways** cast and machined into the caliper body and anchor plate. See Figure 12-31.

Retaining clips and the design of the caliper prevent the body from coming out of the ways once the caliper is assembled.

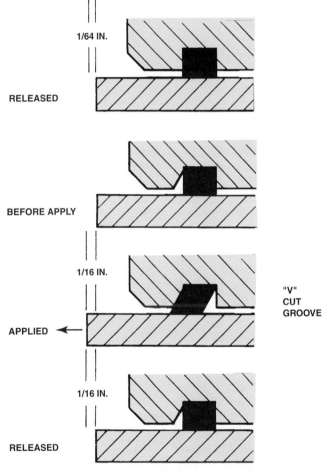

FIGURE 12-29 In a standard disc brake caliper, the square-cut O-ring deforms when the brakes are applied and returns the piston to its original (released) position due to the elastic properties of the rubber seal. In a low-drag caliper design, the groove for the square-cut O-ring is V-shaped, allowing for more retraction. When the brake pedal is released, the piston is moved away from the rotor, further resulting in less friction between the disc brake pads and the rotor when the brakes are released.

On some calipers, the ways may have to be filed for proper clearance between the caliper body and anchor plate if the caliper is replaced.

Like floating calipers, sliding calipers depend on good lubrication of their ways for proper operation. If not properly coated with high-temperature brake grease, the ways can rust or corrode, causing the caliper to drag or seize.

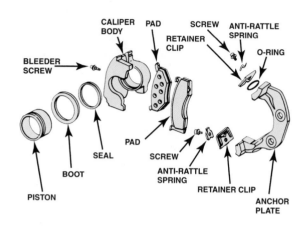

FIGURE 12-30   Exploded view of a typical sliding brake caliper.

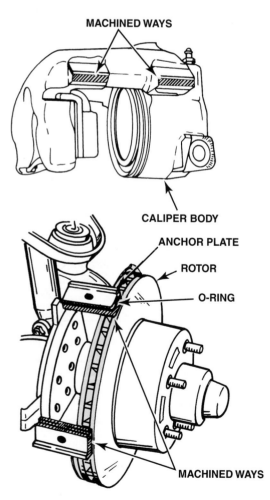

FIGURE 12-31   Sliding calipers move on machined ways.

REAR DISC BRAKES

In recent years, four-wheel disc brake systems have become more common. In most rear-wheel applications, drum brakes are adequate to provide the relatively small portion of a vehicle's total braking power required of them. Because rear drum brakes are lightly loaded, fade is a problem only in extreme conditions when the front brakes fade and force the rear brakes to take on a larger part of the braking load. The automatic adjusting ability of disc brakes is also less of an advantage in slow-wearing rear brakes.

Rear Disc Parking Brakes

There are two methods of providing parking brakes when rear discs are installed on a vehicle.

1. Adapt the disc brake to also function as the parking brake. This is done by installing a series of cables, levers, and internal parts to mechanically actuate the brake caliper. See Figures 12-32 and 12-33.
2. Use mechanically actuated drum brakes inside the rear rotors. See Figure 12-34.

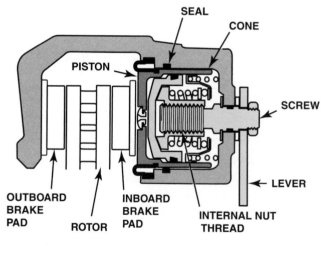

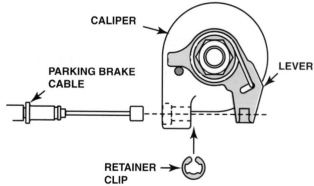

FIGURE 12-32   Exploded view of a typical rear disc brake with an integral parking brake. The parking brake lever mechanically pushes the calliper piston against the rotor.

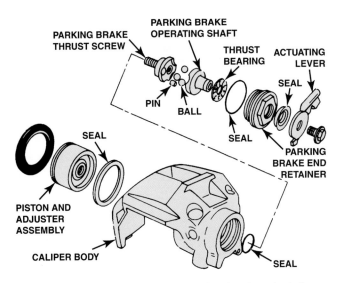

FIGURE 12-33   This single-piston brake caliper is mechanically actuated to serve as a parking brake.

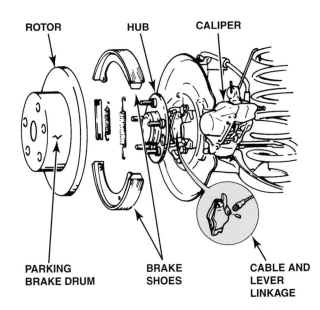

FIGURE 12-34   Drum parking brakes are fitted inside the rotors on this vehicle equipped with rear disc brakes.

SUMMARY

1. Disc brakes are superior to drum brakes because they are fade-resistant, self-adjusting, and are less likely to pull during braking.
2. Disc brakes, however, lack self-energization requiring greater force be applied to the brake pedal compared with the drum brakes.
3. Disc brakes are more prone to noise than drum brakes.
4. A typical disc brake assembly includes the caliper assembly, splash shield, brake pads, and brake rotor.
5. The three basic types of disc brake calipers include fixed, floating, and sliding designs.
6. A low drag caliper requires the use of a quick take-up master cylinder.
7. Some disc brakes are equipped with integral parking brakes.
8. Brake pads can be attached using rivets, bonding, or integrally molded.
9. Typical semimetallic brake linings contain phenolic resin, graphite or carbon particles, steel fibers, ceramic and metal powders plus other modifiers such as rubber scraps.
10. Other types of friction material include nonasbestos organic (NAO), nonasbestos synthetic (NAS), and carbon fiber-reinforced carbon (CFRC).
11. Lining edge codes identify the manufacturer and include two letters at the end, which identify the coefficient of friction of the material. The first letter indicates the coefficient when the lining is cold and the second indicates the coefficient when the lining is hot.

REVIEW QUESTIONS

1. What are the advantages and disadvantages of disc brakes?
2. What parts are included in a typical disc brake?
3. How does a low-drag caliper work?
4. What mechanism is used to apply the parking brake on a vehicle equipped with rear disc brakes?
5. What do the abbreviations NAO, NAS, and CFRC mean?

CHAPTER QUIZ

1. What part causes the disc brake caliper piston to retract when the brakes are released?
   a. Return (retracting) spring
   b. The rotating rotor (disc) that pushes the piston back
   c. The square-cut O-ring
   d. The caliper bushings

2. Two technicians are discussing the reason that the brake fluid level in the master cylinder drops. Technician A says that it may be normal due to the wear of the disc brake pads. Technician B says that a low brake fluid level may indicate a hydraulic leak somewhere in the system. Which technician is correct?
   a. Technician A only
   b. Technician B only
   c. Both Technicians A and B
   d. Neither Technician A nor B

3. Two technicians are discussing a floating-type disc brake caliper. Technician A says that if the caliper slides are corroded, one pad may wear more than the other pad on the same wheel brake. Technician B says that if a caliper slide is corroded, reduced braking may occur. Which technician is correct?
   a. Technician A only
   b. Technician B only
   c. Both Technicians A and B
   d. Neither Technician A nor B

4. Technician A says that disc brakes are self adjusting and the brake pedal height should not become lower as the disc brake pads wear. Technician B says that as the disc brake pads wear, the level of brake fluid in the master cylinder reservoir drops. Which technician is correct?
   a. Technician A only
   b. Technician B only
   c. Both Technicians A and B
   d. Neither Technician A nor B

5. Which type of disc brake caliper may require alignment for proper operation?
   a. Sliding
   b. Fixed
   c. Floating
   d. Single piston

6. A quick take-up master cylinder is required when what type of caliper design is used on a vehicle?
   a. Fixed
   b. Two-piston
   c. Sliding
   d. Low-drag

7. Technician A says that all vehicles equipped with rear disc brakes use a parking brake that is integrated in the caliper. Technician B says that all vehicles equipped with rear disc brakes use a small drum brake inside the rear rotor for a parking brake. Which technician is correct?
   a. Technician A only
   b. Technician B only
   c. Both Technicians A and B
   d. Neither Technician A nor B

8. The brake pad edge code letters "FF" mean _____.
   a. Brand name
   b. Coefficient of friction rating
   c. Quality factor
   d. Noise level rating

9. Semimetallic brake pads are made by a process called _____.
   a. Sintering
   b. Melting
   c. Grating
   d. Composition

10. The major ingredient in most brake lining is _____.
    a. Carbon
    b. Graphite
    c. Ceramic powders
    d. Phenolic resin

CHAPTER 13

DISC BRAKE DIAGNOSIS AND SERVICE

OBJECTIVES

After studying Chapter 13, the reader should be able to:

1. Prepare for the Brakes (A5) ASE certification test content area "C" (Disc Brake Diagnosis and Repair).
2. List the items that should be checked during a visual inspection.
3. Describe the caliper disassembly procedure.
4. Describe the caliper assembly procedure.
5. List the steps necessary to reduce brake noise.

KEY TERMS

Abutments (p. 233)
Antiseize compound (p. 237)
Bedded in (p. 235)
Brake assembly fluid (p. 230)
Burnished (p. 235)
Constrained layer shims (CLS) (p. 236)
Lithium-based brake grease (p. 237)
Loaded calipers (p. 231)

Minimum thickness (p. 224)
MOS$_2$ (molybdenum disulfide) grease (p. 237)
Polyalphaolefin (PAO) (p. 237)
Phenolic caliper pistons (p. 226)
Reaction pads (p. 233)
Silicone grease (p. 237)
Synthetic grease (p. 237)
Ways (p. 233)

DISC BRAKE DIAGNOSTIC PROCEDURE

When diagnosing disc brake concerns, the first step is to verify the customer complaint. This step usually includes test driving the vehicle to see if the complaint can be duplicated. If the problem cannot be duplicated, then the repair or service cannot be verified.

CAUTION: Do not test drive the vehicle on public roads if the red brake warning light is on.

After verifying the customer concern, the brake system should be carefully inspected and all parts and systems checked for proper operation. These steps include:

Step 1   Check the brake pedal height and verify proper operation. If the brake pedal is low, check the parking brake and count the number of "clicks." There should be 3 to 7 clicks. If there are over 10 clicks, check the rear brakes.

Step 2   Safely hoist the vehicle and remove the wheels. Visually check the following:
   ▪ Flexible brake lines for wear or damage
   ▪ Disc brake rotors for excessive rust or scoring
   ▪ Disc brake calipers for leakage or damage

Step 3   Remove disc brake calipers and check the disc brake pads for proper lining thickness and check for cracks or other damage.

Step 4   Replace all components that do not meet factory specifications.

Step 5   Test drive the vehicle to verify that the repairs did correct the customer concern.

TECH TIP

LET THE OWNER DRIVE

When verifying the customer complaint, ask the owner or driver of the vehicle to drive. Often, the problem is best discovered if the vehicle is being driven exactly the same way as when the complaint first occurred. For example, the technician may brake harder or softer than the driver so the problem may not be detected.

VISUAL INSPECTION

Even with operating wear-indicating sensors, a thorough visual inspection is very important. See Figure 13-1.

A lining thickness check alone should not be the only inspection performed on a disc brake. *A thorough visual inspection can only be accomplished by removing the friction pads.* See Figure 13-2 for an example of a disc brake pad that shows usable lining thickness, but is severely cracked and *must* be replaced.

NOTE: Some disc brake pads use a heat barrier (thermo) layer between the steel backing plate and the friction material. The purpose of the heat barrier is to prevent heat from transferring into the caliper piston where it may cause the brake fluid to boil. Do not confuse the thickness of the barrier as part of the thickness of the friction lining material. The barrier material is usually a different color and usually can be distinguished from the lining material.

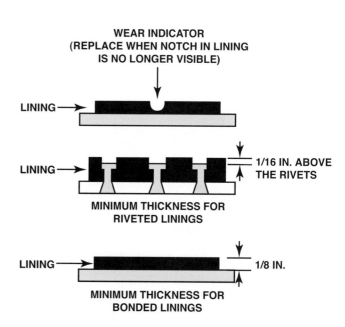

FIGURE 13-1   Minimum thickness for various types of disc brake pads. Disc brake pads can, of course, be replaced before they wear down to the factory-recommended *minimum* thickness.

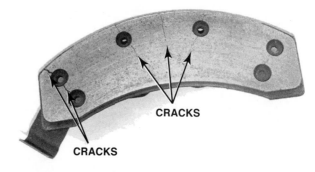

FIGURE 13-2   This cracked disc brake pad must be replaced even though it is thicker than the minimum allowed by the vehicle manufacturer.

Some disc brake pads may show more wear on the end of the pad that first contacts the rotor as compared to the trailing end of the pad. This uneven wear is caused by the force between the pad and the abutment (slide area). In designs that place the caliper piston exactly in the center of the leading edge of the pad that first contacts the rotor as it is revolving through the caliper, pressures are often one-third higher than the average pressure exerted on the entire pad. The result of this higher pressure is greater wear.

Brake engineers design brakes to minimize or eliminate tapered pad wear by offsetting the piston more toward the trailing edge of the shoe or by other caliper/pad mounting designs.

One method used to help reduce tapered pad wear is the design that offsets the friction material off center. Be certain to position the pads correctly or severe tapered pad wear will occur. See Figures 13-3 and 13-4.

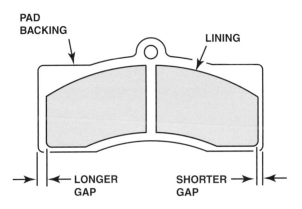

FIGURE 13-3   Be careful to observe the direction in which replacement linings are facing. Some vehicle manufacturers offset the friction material on the steel backing to help prevent or minimize tapered pad wear.

TECH TIP

THE BLEED AND SQUIRT TEST

If you suspect a brake is not being fully released, simply loosen the bleeder valve. If brake fluid squirts out under pressure, then the brake is being kept applied. Look for a defective flexible brake hose.

If the vehicle is off the ground, the wheels should be able to be rotated with the brakes off. If a wheel is difficult or hard to turn by hand and is easy to turn after opening the bleeder valve, then there is a brake fluid restriction between the master cylinder and the brake.

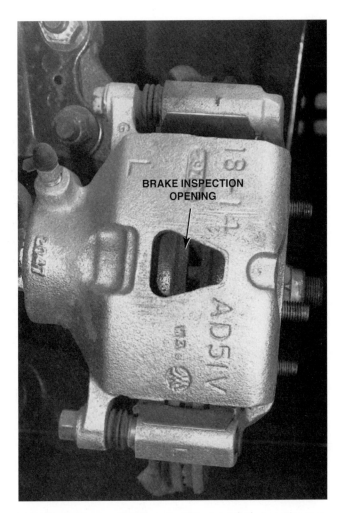

FIGURE 13-4   Most disc brake calipers have a brake inspection opening. For a thorough inspection, however, the caliper should be removed and the entire braking system thoroughly inspected.

DISC BRAKE CALIPER SERVICE

Removal

Hoist the vehicle and remove the wheel(s). Note the caliper mount position as shown in Figure 13-5 before removing the caliper.

Knowing whether the caliper is "rear mount" position or "forward mount" position is often needed when purchasing replacement calipers.

Remove the caliper following the steps in Figures 13-6 through 13-10.

Inspection and Disassembly

Check for brake fluid in and around the piston boot area. If the boot is damaged or a fluid leak is visible, then a caliper

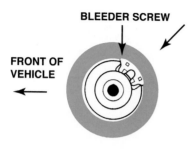

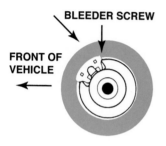

REAR-MOUNT CALIPER POSITION

(a)

FORWARD-MOUNT CALIPER POSITION

(b)

FIGURE 13-5 Both rear- and forward-mounted calipers have the bleeder valve at the top. Some calipers *will* fit on the wrong side of the vehicle, yet not be able to be bled correctly because the bleeder valve would point down, allowing trapped air to remain inside the caliper bore. If both calipers are being removed at the same time, mark them "left" and "right."

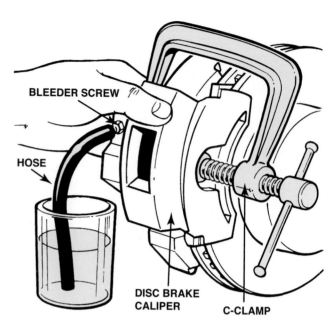

FIGURE 13-7 Most manufacturers recommend that the bleeder valve be opened and the brake fluid forced into a container rather than back into the master cylinder reservoir. This helps prevent contaminated brake fluid from being forced into the master cylinder where the dirt and contamination could cause problems.

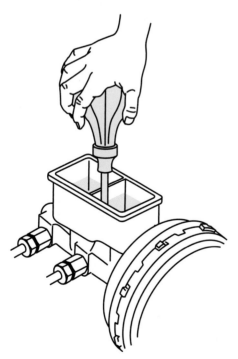

FIGURE 13-6 Many manufacturers recommend removing one-half of the brake fluid from the master cylinder before servicing disc brakes. Use a squeeze bulb and dispose of the used brake fluid correctly.

assembly repair or replacement is required. See Figures 13-11 and 13-12 on page 228.

Phenolic Caliper Pistons

Phenolic caliper pistons are made from a phenol-formaldehyde resin combined with various reinforcing fibers. When phenolic brake caliper pistons were first used, the results were not good and the problem was blamed on "those *darn* plastic pistons." What was happening was that the pistons were becoming stuck in the caliper, which caused the brake pads to remain applied. This caused the brake pads to wear out very rapidly. The problem occurred because the phenolic pistons absorbed moisture and swelled in size.

By reducing the diameter of the pistons 0.001 to 0.002 in. (0.025 to 0.050 mm) and improving the caliper boot seal, the sticking problem has been solved. Since the mid-1980s, phenolic caliper pistons have been used as original equipment by many vehicle manufacturers. Phenolic caliper pistons are natural thermal insulators and help keep heat generated by the disc brake pads from transferring through the caliper piston to the brake fluid. Phenolic brake caliper pistons are also lighter in weight than steel caliper pistons and are usually brown in color. See Figure 13-13 on page 228.

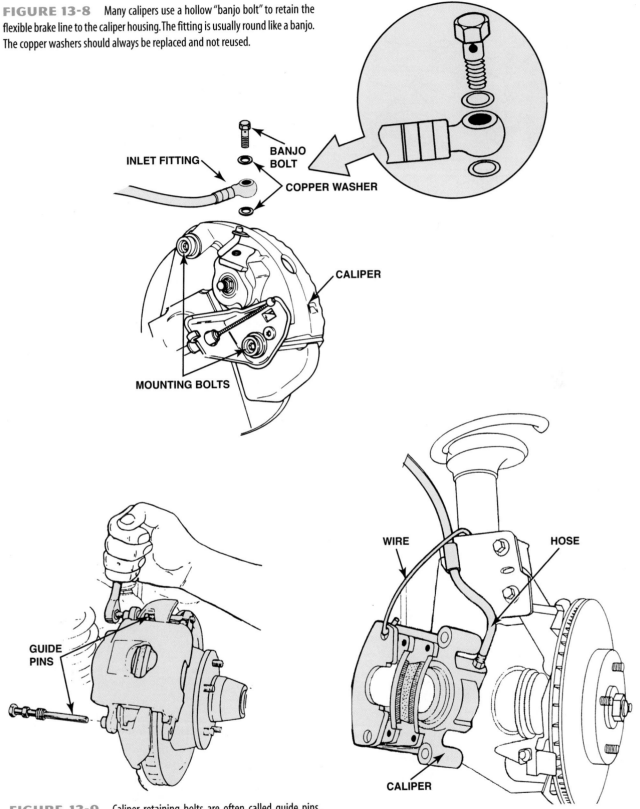

FIGURE 13-8 Many calipers use a hollow "banjo bolt" to retain the flexible brake line to the caliper housing. The fitting is usually round like a banjo. The copper washers should always be replaced and not reused.

INLET FITTING

BANJO BOLT

COPPER WASHER

CALIPER

MOUNTING BOLTS

GUIDE PINS

WIRE

HOSE

CALIPER

FIGURE 13-9 Caliper retaining bolts are often called guide pins. These guide pins are used to retain the caliper to the steering knuckle. These pins also slide through metal bushings and rubber O-rings. *(Courtesy of EIS Brake Parts)*

FIGURE 13-10 If the caliper is not being removed, it must be supported properly so that the weight of the caliper is not pulling on the flexible rubber brake line. A suitable piece of wire, such as a coat hanger, may be used.

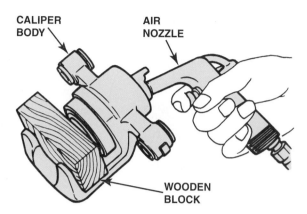

FIGURE 13-11   A wooden block or a folded shop cloth helps prevent damage when caliper pistons are removed.

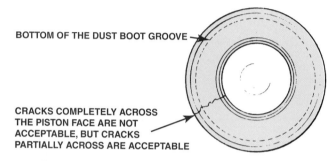

CRACKS, CHIPS, OR GOUGES MAY NOT ENTER THE PISTON SEAL GROOVE

CRACKS, CHIPS, OR GOUGES MAY BE ½ INCH LONG AND MAY GO INWARD ALMOST TO THE PISTON SEAL GROOVE

NO CRACKS, CHIPS, GOUGES, OR ANY OTHER SURFACE DAMAGE ON THE SEAL SURFACE ARE ACCEPTABLE

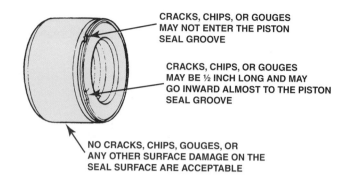

BOTTOM OF THE DUST BOOT GROOVE

CRACKS COMPLETELY ACROSS THE PISTON FACE ARE NOT ACCEPTABLE, BUT CRACKS PARTIALLY ACROSS ARE ACCEPTABLE

FIGURE 13-13   Phenolic (plastic) pistons should be carefully inspected.

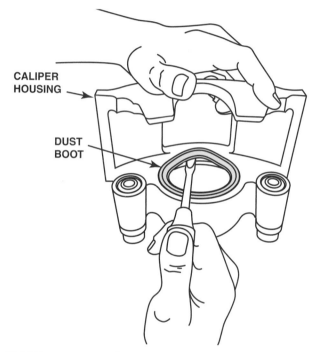

FIGURE 13-12   After the piston is removed from the caliper housing, the dust boot can often be removed using a straight-blade screwdriver.

Steel Caliper Pistons

Many manufacturers still use steel pistons. The stamped steel pistons are plated first with nickel, then chrome to achieve the desired surface finish. See Figure 13-14.

Unlike phenolic caliper pistons, steel pistons can transfer heat from the brake pads to the brake fluid. The surface finish on a steel piston is critical. Steel can rust and corrode. Any surface pitting can cause the piston to stick.

NOTE: Care should be taken when cleaning steel pistons. Use crocus cloth to remove any surface staining. Do not use sandpaper, emery cloth, or any other substance that may remove or damage the chrome surface finish.

REAL WORLD FIX

THREE BRAKE JOBS IN 40,000 MILES

A service technician was asked to replace the front disc brake pads on a Pontiac Grand Am because the sensors were touching the rotors and making a squealing sound. This was the third time that the front brakes needed to be replaced. Previous brake repairs had been limited to replacement of the front disc brake pads only.

When the caliper was removed and the pads inspected, it was discovered that a part of one pad had broken and a piece of the lining was missing. See Figure 13-15.

Then the technician spotted something at the rear of the vehicle that told the whole story—a trailer hitch. See Figure 13-16.

The owner confirmed that a heavy jet ski was towed in hilly terrain. The technician recommended overhauling the front disc brake calipers to prevent the possibility of the front pads dragging. The technician also recommended an inspection of the rear brakes. The rear brakes were glazed and out-of-adjustment. The technician received permission to replace the rear brakes, overhaul both front calipers, and install quality disc brake pads. When the customer returned, the technician advised the customer to use the transmission on long downhill roads to help keep the brakes from overheating and failing prematurely.

(a)

(b)

FIGURE 13-14   (a) The outside surface of caliper pistons should be carefully inspected. The square-cut O-ring inside the caliper rides on this outside surface of the piston. Sometimes dirty pistons can be cleaned and reused. (b) If there are any surface flaws such as rust pits on the piston, it should be replaced.

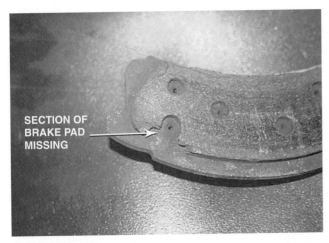

FIGURE 13-15   These pads were found to be cracked and a section was missing from a part of one pad.

FIGURE 13-16   The observant technician noticed the trailer hitch indicating that the owner may have been towing a trailer, which can cause more stress than normal on the braking system.

REASSEMBLING DISC BRAKE CALIPERS

After disassembly, the caliper should be thoroughly cleaned in denatured alcohol and closely examined. See Figure 13-17.

If the caliper bore is rusted or pitted, some manufacturers recommend that a special hone be used, as shown in Figure 13-18.

Some manufacturers do *not* recommend honing the caliper bore because the actual sealing surface in the caliper is between the piston seal and the piston itself. This is the reason why the surface condition of the piston is so important.

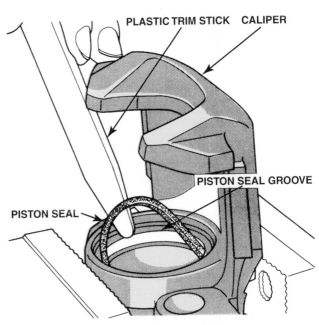

FIGURE 13-17   Removing the square-cut O-ring seal from the caliper bore. Use a wooden or plastic tool to prevent damage to the seal groove. *(Courtesy of DaimlerChrysler Corporation)*

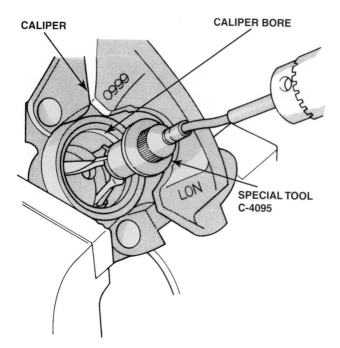

CALIPER   CALIPER BORE

LON   SPECIAL TOOL
C-4095

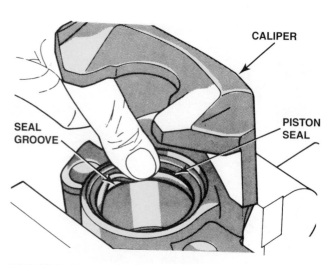

CALIPER

SEAL
GROOVE

PISTON
SEAL

FIGURE 13-19   Installing a new piston seal. Never reuse old rubber parts. *(Courtesy of DaimlerChrysler Corporation)*

FIGURE 13-18   Some manufacturers recommend cleaning the inside of the caliper bore using a honing tool as shown. Even though the caliper piston does not contact the inside of this bore, removing any surface rust or corrosion is important to prevent future problems. If the honing process cannot remove any pits or scored areas, the caliper should be replaced. *(Courtesy of DaimlerChrysler Corporation)*

To assemble the disc brake caliper, perform the following steps:

Step 1   Carefully clean the caliper bore with clean brake fluid from a sealed container. Coat a new piston seal with clean brake fluid and install it in the groove inside the caliper bore, as shown in Figure 13-19.

Step 2   Check the piston-to-caliper bore clearance. Typical piston-to-caliper bore clearance is as follows:

steel piston   0.002–0.005 in. clearance
                    (0.05–0.13 mm)
phenolic piston   0.005–0.010 in. clearance
                    (0.13–0.25 mm)

Step 3   Coat a new piston boot with brake fluid or **brake assembly fluid**. See Figure 13-20. Brake assembly fluid is similar to brake fluid but has antiwear additives.

Step 4   Install the piston into the caliper piston, as shown in Figures 13-21 and 13-22.

Step 5   Some caliper boots require a special boot-seating tool, as shown in Figure 13-23.

Step 6   Always lubricate caliper bushings, shims, and other brake hardware as instructed by the manufacturer. See Figure 13-24.

Step 7   The pads should also be securely attached to the caliper as shown in Figures 13-25 and 13-26 on page 233.

Raybestos
HYDRAULK
BRAKE CYLINDER
ASSEMBLY
FLUID
NET 12 FL. OZ. (.355 LITERS)

FIGURE 13-20   Brake assembly fluid or clean brake fluid from a sealed container can be used to lubricate the caliper seal and caliper pistons before assembly.

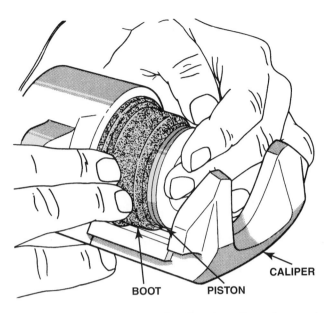

FIGURE 13-21   Installing the caliper piston. Many calipers require that the dust boot be installed in the groove of the piston and/or caliper before installing the piston.   *(Courtesy of DaimlerChrysler Corporation)*

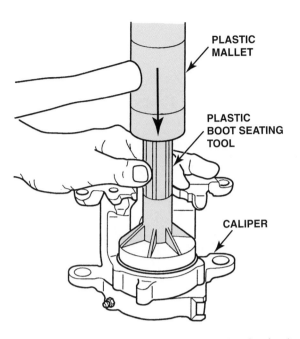

FIGURE 13-23   Seating the dust boot into the caliper housing using a special plastic seating tool.

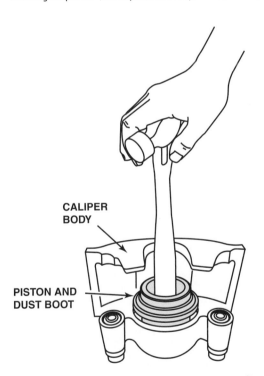

FIGURE 13-22   Installing a piston into a caliper. Sometimes a C-clamp is needed to install the piston. Both the piston and the piston seal should be coated in clean brake fluid before assembly.

CAUTION: Installing disc brake pads on the wrong side of the vehicle (left versus right) will often prevent the sensor from making noise when the pads are worn down.

TECH TIP

USING "LOADED CALIPERS" SAVES TIME

Many technicians find that disassembly, cleaning, and rebuilding calipers can take a lot of time. Often the bleeder valve breaks off or the caliper piston is too corroded to reuse. This means that the technician has to get a replacement piston, caliper overhaul kit (piston seal and boot), plus the replacement friction pads and hardware kit.

To save time (and sometimes money), many technicians are simply replacing the old used calipers with "loaded calipers." **Loaded calipers** are remanufactured calipers that include (come loaded) with the correct replacement friction pads and all the necessary hardware. See Figure 13-27 on page 233.

Therefore, only one part number is needed for each side of the vehicle for a complete disc brake overhaul.

Caliper Mounts

When the hydraulic force from the master cylinder applies pressure to the disc brake pads, the entire caliper tends to be forced in the direction of rotation of the rotor. All calipers are mounted to the steering knuckle or axle housing. See Figure 13-28 on page 234.

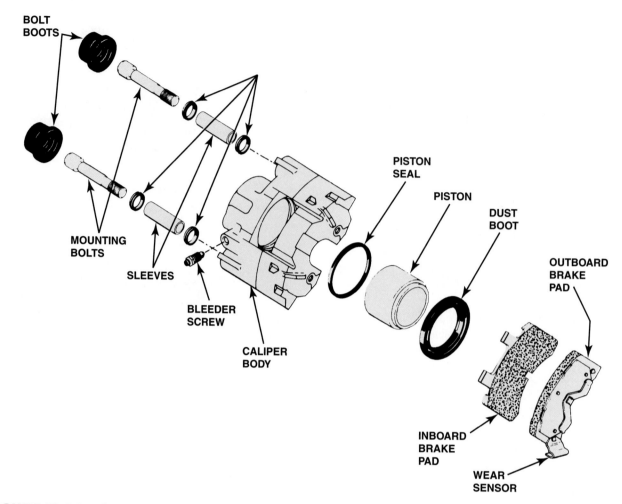

FIGURE 13-24   All rubber bushings should be lubricated with silicone brake grease for proper operation.

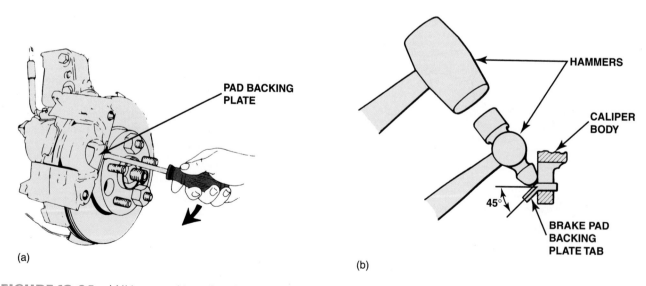

(a)

(b)

FIGURE 13-25   (a) Using a screwdriver to force the outboard pad into proper position before bending the retaining tabs. (b) Use two hammers to bend the tab where it extends through the hole in the caliper body.

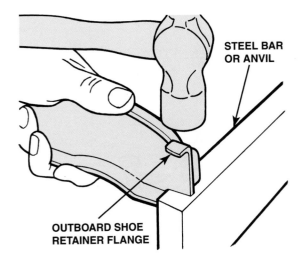

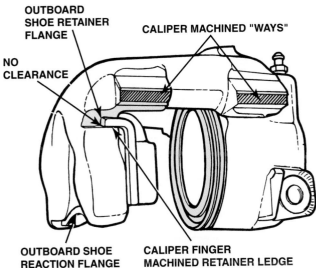

FIGURE 13-26 Often, a hammer is necessary to bend the retainer flange to make certain that the pads fit tightly to the caliper. If the pads are loose, a "click" may be heard every time the brakes are depressed. This click occurs when the pad(s) move and then hit the caliper or caliper mount. If the pads are loose, a clicking noise may be heard while driving over rough road surfaces. *(Courtesy of DaimlerChrysler Corporation)*

All braking force is transferred through the caliper to the mount. The places where the caliper contacts the caliper mount are called the **abutments, reaction pads,** or **ways.** The sliding surfaces of the caliper support should be cleaned with a wire brush and coated with a synthetic grease or anti-seize compound according to manufacturer's recommendations. See Figure 13-29.

As the vehicle ages and the brakes are used thousands of times, these abutments (pads) can wear, causing too much clearance between the caliper and the mounting. When this occurs, the caliper often rotates against the abutment when

FIGURE 13-27 A loaded caliper includes all hardware and shims with the correct pads all in one convenient package, ready to install on the vehicle.

the brakes are first applied, making a loud "knocking" noise. If this occurs, the service technician can repair this type of wear two ways:

Method 1   Replace the entire steering knuckle or caliper mount. This is the recommended method and also the most expensive. Replacement caliper mounts or knuckles may also be difficult to locate.

Method 2   Some aftermarket brake supply companies offer "abutment repair kits" that include oversize slides.

ROTATING PISTONS BACK INTO THE CALIPER

Many disc brake calipers used on the rear wheels require that the piston be rotated to reseat the pistons. When the parking brake is applied, the actuating screw moves the piston outward, forcing the pads against the disc brake rotor. The piston is kept from rotating because of an antirotation device or notches on the inboard pad and piston.

When the disc brake pads are being replaced, use a special tool to rotate the piston back into the brake calipers. Insert the tip of the tool in the holes or slots in the piston. Exert inward pressure while turning the piston. Make sure that the piston is retracting into the caliper and continue to turn the piston until it bottoms out.

NOTE: Some pistons are activated with left-handed threads.

After replacing the pads back into the caliper, check that the clearance does not exceed 1/16 in. (1.5 mm) from the rotor. Clearance greater than 1/16 in. may allow the adjuster to be pulled out of the piston when the service brake

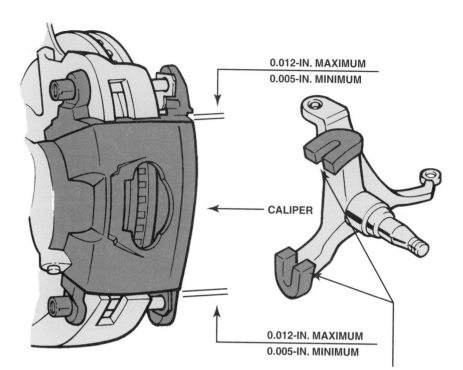

0.012-IN. MAXIMUM
0.005-IN. MINIMUM

CALIPER

0.012-IN. MAXIMUM
0.005-IN. MINIMUM

FILE ABUTMENTS (REACTION PADS)
IF NECESSARY TO OBTAIN CLEARANCE

FIGURE 13-28   Floating calipers must be able to slide during normal operation. Therefore, there must be clearance between the caliper and the caliper mounting pads (abutments). Too little clearance will prevent the caliper from sliding and too much clearance will cause the caliper to make a clunking noise when the brakes are applied.

(a)

(b)

FIGURE 13-29   (a) Using an air-powered sanding disc to clean the caliper mount pads. (b) Applying silicone brake grease to the slides assures proper caliper operation.

is applied. If the clearance is greater than 1/16 in., readjust by rotating the piston outward to reduce the clearance. See Figure 13-30.

Test Drive after Brake Replacement

After installing replacement disc brake pads or any other brake work, depress the brake pedal several times before driving the vehicle. This is a very important step! New brake pads are installed with the caliper piston pushed all the way into the

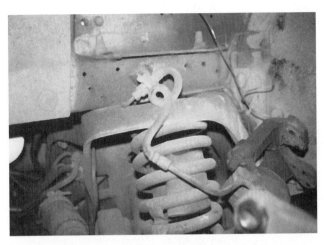

FIGURE 13-31   Note the twisted flexible brake line. This can cause brake hose failure if not corrected.

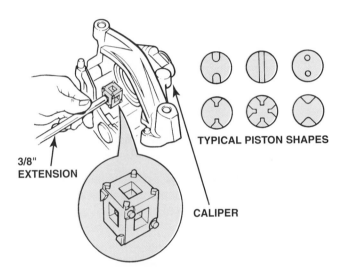

FIGURE 13-30   Determine which face of the special tool best fits the holes or slots in the piston. Sometimes needle-nose pliers can be used to rotate the piston back into the caliper bore.

ALWAYS DOUBLE-CHECK YOUR WORK

Whenever reassembling brakes, it is easy to twist the flexible brake hose as shown in Figure 13-31.

To prevent possible brake hose failure and possibly an accident, always double-check that the ribs on the brake hose are straight. The ribs allow the service technician to easily spot if the hose has been twisted.

caliper. The first few brake pedal applications usually result in the brake pedal going all the way to the floor. The brake pedal must be depressed ("pumped") several times before enough brake fluid can be moved from the master cylinder into the calipers to move the piston tight against the pads and the pads against the rotors.

CAUTION: Never allow a customer to be the first to test drive the vehicle after brake work has been performed.

Bedding-In Replacement Brake Pads

Some manufacturers recommend that their replacement brake pads be **bedded-in** or **burnished** before returning the vehicle to the owner. This break-in process varies with the manufacturer, but usually involves stopping the vehicle from 30 mph (48 km/h) up to 30 times, allowing the brakes to cool 2 to 3 minutes between stops. This break-in procedure helps the replacement pads to conform to the rotor and helps cure the resins used in the manufacture of the pads. Failure to properly break in new pads according to the manufacturer's recommended procedure could result in a hard brake pedal complaint from the driver and/or reduced braking effectiveness.

Even if the brake pad manufacturer does not recommend a break-in procedure, high speed stops and overheating of the brakes should be avoided as much as possible during the first 50 to 100 stops.

FOOT POWER IS STRONGER THAN AIR PRESSURE

Many times, a caliper piston becomes so stuck that normal shop air pressure is not powerful enough to pop the piston out of a caliper. Hydraulic pressure using the service brake pedal is often able to easily remove even the most corroded caliper piston.

If compressed air has been tried with the caliper off the vehicle, reattach the caliper to the brake line. Bleed the brakes by opening the bleeder valve as normal to rid the caliper of any trapped air. Use a wood board or shop rag in front of the caliper piston and apply the brake. Pump the brake pedal as necessary to force the piston out.

CAUTION: Pump the brake pedal *slowly*. The piston normally will be gently pushed from the caliper. If the pedal is pushed hard, the caliper piston could be forced out of the caliper bore with tremendous force. Position the caliper so that no damage will be done when the piston does pop free.

Some technicians will not try to overhaul a caliper, but simply replace it, if compressed air pressure will not remove the piston.

INCREASING PAD LIFE

Many vehicles seem to wear out front disc brakes more often than normal. Stop-and-go city-type driving is often the cause. Driving style, such as rapid stops, also causes a lot of wear to occur.

The service technician can take some actions to increase brake pad life that are easier than having to cure the driver's habits. These steps include the following:

1. Make sure the rear brakes are properly adjusted and working correctly. If the rear brakes are not functioning, all of the braking is accomplished by the front brakes alone.

NOTE: Remind the driver to apply the parking brake regularly to help maintain proper rear brake clearance on the rear brakes.

2. Use factory brake pads or premium brake pads from a known manufacturer. Tests performed by vehicle manufacturers show that many aftermarket replacement brake pads fail to deliver original equipment brake pad life.

DISC BRAKE SQUEAL

Causes

Disc brakes tend to create brake noise (squeal). The cause and correction of brake noise is a major concern for both the vehicle manufacturers and the service technicians. The greatest customer complaint about brake work involves brake noise. Noise is caused by moving air, which is moved by movement of the brake components.

Correcting Disc Brake Squeal

Brake squeal can best be *prevented* by careful attention to details whenever servicing any disc brake. Some of these precautions include the following.

Keeping the Disc Brake Pads Clean.   Grease on brake lining material causes the friction surface to be uneven. When

the brakes are applied, this uneven brake surface causes the brake components to move.

Use Factory-Type Clips and Antisqueal Shims.   The vehicle manufacturer has designed the braking system to be as quiet as possible. To assure that the brakes are restored to like-new performance, all of the original hardware should be used. Many original equipment brake pads use **constrained layer shims (CLS)** on the back of the brake pads. These shims are constructed with dampening material between two layers of steel. See Figure 13-32.

NOTE: Many aftermarket disc brake pads do *not* include replacement hardware that usually includes noise-reducing shims and clips. One of the advantages of purchasing original equipment (OE) disc brake pads is that they usually come equipped with all necessary shims and often with special grease that is recommended to be used on metal shims.

FIGURE 13-32   For best braking performance, purchase replacement disc brake pads that include all clips and shims specified by the vehicle manufacturer. Some pads even come with a package of the specified grease to use on the shims to reduce the possibility of brake noise.

Lubricate All Caliper Slide Points as per Manufacturer's Recommendation

Lubrication of moving or sliding components prevents noise from being generated as the parts move over each other. Many vehicle manufacturers recommend one or more of the following greases:

1. **Lithium-based brake grease**
2. **Silicone grease**
3. **Molybdenum disulfide (MOS$_2$) grease** ("Molykote") often referred to as "moly" grease

FIGURE 13-33   Most vehicle manufacturers recommend the use of silicone grease for brake lubrication. Silicone grease can be used to lubricate metal or rubber parts. Antiseize compound should only be used on metal-to-metal contacts.

4. **Synthetic grease** (usually **polyalphaolefin [PAO]**) sometimes mixed with graphite, Teflon, and/or MOS$_2$
5. **Antiseize compound**

The grease should be applied on both sides of shims used between the pad and the caliper piston. See Figure 13-33.

CAUTION: Grease should only be applied to the nonfriction (steel) side of the disc brake pads.

Machine the Brake Rotor as Little as Possible and with the Correct Surface Finish

Machining the brake rotor reduces its thickness. A thinner rotor will vibrate at a different frequency than a thicker rotor. See Chapter 15 for details on rotor machining and surface finish. Factors that can help or hurt brake squeal are referenced in the following chart.

Factor	Increase Noise	Reduce Noise
brake pad thickness	thinner (worn) pads	thicker (new) pads
rotor (disc) thickness	thinner (worn) rotor	thicker (new) rotor
brake pad material	harder	softer
lubrication of parts	dry—not lubricated	properly lubricated
dampening	no dampening	dampening material behind the pads
pad mounting	pad tabs not bent over	pad tabs securely crimped
antirattle clips	worn, defective, or not lubricated	new and properly lubricated

Vehicle manufacturers also change brake pad (lining) composition and the shape of the pads to help eliminate brake noise. The change of shape changes the frequency of the sound. Noise is vibration, but much of the vibration generated is not heard because the noise is beyond the normal frequency to be heard. Most people can hear from 20 to 20,000 cycles per second (called hertz). To stop brake noise, the manufacturer can change the frequency of the vibration to above or below the hertz range that can be heard. See Figure 13-34.

NOTE: All metal-to-metal contacts *must* be lubricated to help prevent brake noise.

DISC BRAKE SYMPTOM GUIDE

Pulls to One Side during Braking

Possible causes of this include the following:

1. Incorrect or unequal tire pressures
2. Front end out of alignment
3. Unmatched tires on the same axle
4. Restricted brake lines or hoses
5. Stuck or seized caliper or caliper piston
6. Defective or damaged shoe and lining (grease or brake fluid on the lining, or a bent shoe)
7. Malfunctioning rear brakes
8. Loose suspension parts
9. Loose calipers

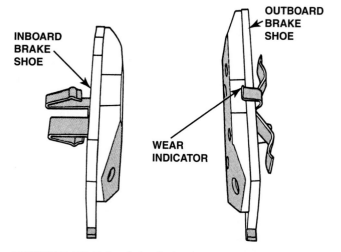

FIGURE 13-34 Notice the beveled pads. The shape of the pad helps determine the frequency of any vibration in the brakes. *(Courtesy of DaimlerChrysler Corporation)*

TECH TIP

THE SCREWDRIVER TRICK

A low brake pedal on GM vehicles equipped with rear disc brakes is a common customer complaint. Often the reason is a lack of self-adjustment that *should* occur whenever the brake pedal (or parking brake) is released. During brake release, the pressure is removed from the caliper piston and the spring inside the caliper piston is free to adjust. Often this self-adjustment does not occur and a low brake pedal results.

A common trick that is used on the vehicle assembly line is to use a screwdriver to hold the piston against the rotor while an assistant releases the brake pedal. See Figure 13-35.

As the brake pedal is released, the adjusting screw inside the caliper piston is free to move. Sometimes, it may be necessary to tap on the caliper itself with a dead-blow hammer to free the adjusting screw. Repeat the process as necessary until the proper brake pedal height returns. If this method does not work, replace the caliper assembly.

In summary, recall these steps.

Step 1   Have an assistant depress the brake pedal.
Step 2   Using a screwdriver through the hole in the top of the caliper, hold the piston against the rotor.

NOTE: Be careful not to damage the dust boot.

Step 3   While still holding the piston against the rotor, have the assistant release the brake pedal. The adjusting screw adjusts when the brake pedal is *released* and a slight vibration or sound will be noticed as the brake is released. This vibration or sound is created by the self-adjusting mechanism inside the caliper piston taking up the excess clearance.
Step 4   Repeat as necessary until normal brake pedal height is achieved.

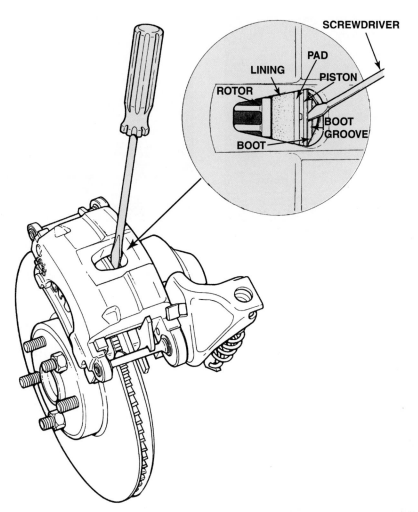

FIGURE 13-35   The screwdriver blade is used to keep the piston applied to allow self-adjustment to occur when the brake pedal is released.

Brake Roughness or Chatter (Pedal Pulsates)

Possible causes of this include the following:

1. Excessive lateral runout of rotor
2. Parallelism of the rotor not within specifications
3. Wheel bearings not adjusted correctly
4. Rear drums out-of-round
5. Brake pads worn to metal backing plate

Excessive Pedal Effort

Possible causes of this include the following:

1. Binding or seized caliper suspension
2. Binding brake pedal mechanism
3. Improper rotor surface finish
4. Malfunctioning power brake
5. Partial system failure
6. Excessively worn shoe and lining
7. Piston in the caliper stuck or sluggish
8. Fading brakes due to incorrect lining

Excessive Pedal Travel

Possible causes of this include the following:

1. Partial brake system failure
2. Insufficient fluid in the master cylinder
3. Air trapped in the system
4. Bent shoe and lining
5. Excessive pedal effort
6. Excessive parking brake travel (four-wheel disc brakes, except Corvette)

(a)

(b)

FIGURE 13-36   (a) A brake pressure tester. (b) The small "pads" can be placed between the caliper piston and the rotor to check for applied pressure and inserted between the caliper and the rotor on the outside of the rotor to test the pressure—the pressure should be the same if the caliper is able to slide on its pins or slides.

Dragging Brakes

Possible causes of this include the following:

1. Pressure trapped in the brake lines (to diagnose, momentarily open the caliper bleeder valve to relieve the pressure)
2. Restricted brake tubes or hoses
3. Improperly lubricated caliper suspension system
4. Improper clearance between the caliper and torque abutment surfaces
5. Check valve installed in the outlet of the master cylinder to the disc brakes

Front Disc Brakes Very Sensitive to Light Brake Applications

Possible causes of this include the following:

1. Metering valve not holding off the front brake application
2. Incorrect lining material
3. Improper rotor surface finish
4. Check other causes listed under "PULLS"

Rear Drum Brakes Skidding under Hard Brake Applications

Possible causes of this include the following:

1. Proportioning valve
2. Contaminated rear brake lining
3. Caliper or caliper piston stuck or corroded

TECH TIP

PRESSURE TESTING CAN HELP FIND PROBLEMS

A stuck caliper or caliper slide is often difficult to see or diagnose as a problem because the movement of the broken pads is so little. Using a pressure gauge between the caliper piston and the rotor (inboard) or between the rotor and the caliper (outboard) can tell the service technician if there is a difference between the left and the right side brakes. See Figure 13-36.

DISC BRAKE SERVICE   Step-by-Step

STEP 1
After properly setting the hoist pads under the vehicle, raise the vehicle to chest level and remove the lug nuts.

STEP 2
Remove the wheel/tire assembly and place it where it will not get in the way or be damaged.

STEP 3
It is recommended that the entire brake assembly be washed using a commercially available cleaner to avoid the possibility of allowing brake dust from becoming airborne.

STEP 4
If a commercial brake cleaning unit is not available, use brake cleaner from an aerosol or pressurized container.

STEP 5
To service the front disc brake pads on this vehicle, loosen the upper caliper retainer bolt and remove the lower bolt.

STEP 6
After the lower caliper bolt has been removed, the caliper assembly can be lifted upward by pivoting on the upper retaining bolt.

(continued)

DISC BRAKE SERVICE   continued

STEP 7   Use mechanic's wire to hold the caliper in the raised position to allow access to the disc brake pads.

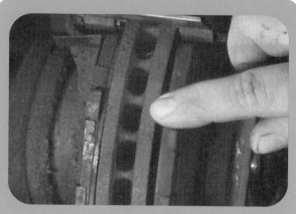

STEP 8   Notice that both the inboard and outboard pad remain attached to the steering knuckle. The pads and shims can be lifted off.

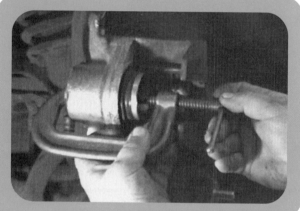

STEP 9   A C-clamp can be used to push the piston into the caliper, but be sure to open the bleeder valve first.

STEP 10   The bleeder valve should be opened to allow the old brake fluid to flow out of the caliper and not be forced up into the ABS hydraulic unit or master cylinder.

STEP 11   Often factory replacement disc brake pads include noise-dampening shims, antirattle clips, and special "moly" disc brake grease that is to be used on the shims.

STEP 12   All hardware, including this anchor shim, should be replaced.

DISC BRAKE SERVICE continued

STEP 13 Install new shims after thoroughly cleaning the steering knuckle area of any rust using a wire brush or other suitable tool.

STEP 14 The replacement disc brake pads are installed next to the rotor and held in place by the tension of the anchor shims.

STEP 15 After double-checking that all shims, clips, and spacers are correctly installed, lower the calipers and install this lower attaching bolt.

STEP 16 Torque the retaining bolts to factory specifications. Repeat the process on the other side and bleed the hydraulic system.

STEP 17 Reinstall the wheel/tire assembly.

STEP 18 Torque the lug nuts to factory specifications or use a torque-limiting adapter. Test drive the vehicle before returning it to the customer.

SUMMARY

1. Caliper pistons are either chrome-plated steel or plastic (phenolic). Any damaged piston must be replaced. Both the square-cut O-ring and the dust boot must be replaced when the caliper is disassembled.

2. All metal-to-metal contact points of the disc brake assembly should be coated with an approved brake lubricant such as synthetic grease, "moly" (molybdenum disulfide) grease, or antiseize compound.

3. After a brake overhaul, the brake pedal should be depressed several times until a normal brake pedal is achieved before performing a thorough test drive.

4. Many rear disc brake systems use an integral parking brake. Regular use of the parking brake helps maintain proper rear brake clearance.

REVIEW QUESTIONS

1. List what parts are included in a typical overhaul kit for a single piston floating caliper.

2. Describe how to remove caliper pistons and perform a caliper overhaul.

3. Explain what causes disc brake squeal and list what a technician can do to reduce or eliminate the noise.

CHAPTER QUIZ

1. Uneven disc brake pad wear is being discussed. Technician A says the caliper piston may be stuck. Technician B says the caliper may be stuck on the slides and unable to "float." Which technician is correct?
   a. Technician A only
   b. Technician B only
   c. Both Technicians A and B
   d. Neither Technician A nor B

2. A "chirping" noise is heard while the vehicle is moving forward, but stops when the brakes are applied. Technician A says that the noise is likely caused by the disc brake pad wear sensors. Technician B says the noise is likely a wheel bearing because the noise stops when the brakes are applied. Which technician is correct?
   a. Technician A only
   b. Technician B only
   c. Both Technicians A and B
   d. Neither Technician A nor B

3. Technician A says that disc brake pads should be replaced when worn to the thickness of the steel backing. Technician B says the pads should be removed and inspected whenever there is a brake performance complaint. Which technician is correct?
   a. Technician A only
   b. Technician B only
   c. Both Technicians A and B
   d. Neither Technician A nor B

4. A typical disc brake caliper overhaul (OH) kit usually includes what parts?
   a. Square-cut O-ring seal and dust boot
   b. Replacement caliper piston and dust boot
   c. Dust boot, return spring, and caliper seal
   d. Disc brake pad clips, dust boot, and caliper piston assembly

5. Technician A says that a lack of lubrication on the back of the disc brake pads can cause brake noise. Technician B says that pads that are not correctly crimped to the caliper housing can cause brake noise. Which technician is correct?
   a. Technician A only
   b. Technician B only
   c. Both Technicians A and B
   d. Neither Technician A nor B

6. Two technicians are discussing ways of removing a caliper piston. Technician A says to use compressed air. Technician B says to use large pliers. Which technician is correct?
   a. Technician A only
   b. Technician B only
   c. Both Technicians A and B
   d. Neither Technician A nor B

7. Which is *not* a recommended type of grease to use on brake parts?
   a. Silicone grease
   b. Wheel bearing (chassis) grease

c. Synthetic grease

d. Antiseize compound

8. Technician A says that many rear disc brake caliper pistons must be turned to retract before installing replacement pads. Technician B says that some vehicles equipped with rear disc brakes use a small drum brake as the parking brake. Which technician is correct?

a. Technician A only

b. Technician B only

c. Both Technicians A and B

d. Neither Technician A nor B

9. A vehicle is hoisted during routine service and the service technician discovers that the left front wheel does not turn when force is applied. Technician A says that the hoist (lift) pads could be against the left front tire. Technician B says that the disc brake caliper piston stuck in the bore is the most likely cause. Which technician is correct?

a. Technician A only

b. Technician B only

c. Both Technicians A and B

d. Neither Technician A nor B

10. Technician A says that a steel piston should be cleaned with sandpaper to remove rust. Technician B says that the brake assembly fluid or clean brake fluid should be used to lubricate the caliper pistons before installing in the caliper. Which technician is correct?

a. Technician A only

b. Technician B only

c. Both Technicians A and B

d. Neither Technician A nor B

PARKING BRAKE OPERATION, DIAGNOSIS, AND SERVICE

OBJECTIVES

After studying Chapter 14, the reader should be able to:

1. Prepare for the Brakes (A5) ASE certification test content area "E" (Miscellaneous Systems Diagnosis and Repair).

2. Describe what is required of a parking brake.

3. Describe the parts and operation of the parking brake as used on a rear drum brake system.

4. Describe how a parking brake functions when the vehicle is equipped with rear disc brakes.

5. Explain how to adjust a parking brake properly.

KEY TERMS

Application cables (p. 250)
Control cables (p. 250)
Equalizer (p. 251)

Intermediate lever (p. 251)
Red brake warning lamp (p. 249)
Vacuum servo (p. 249)

PARKING BRAKE

Before 1967, most vehicles had only a single master cylinder operating all four brakes. If the fluid leaked at just one wheel, the operation of all brakes was lost. This required the use of a separate method to stop the vehicle in case of an emergency. This alternative method required that a separate mechanical method be used to stop the vehicle using two of the four wheel brakes. After 1967, federal regulations required the use of dual or tandem master cylinders where half of the braking system has its own separate hydraulic system. In case one-half of the system fails, a dash brake warning lamp lets the driver know that a failure has occurred. The term *parking brake* has replaced the term *emergency brake* since the change to dual master cylinder design.

According to Federal Motor Vehicle Safety Standard (FMVSS) 135, the parking brake must hold a fully loaded (laden) vehicle stationary on a slope of 20% up or down grade. The hand force required cannot exceed 80 lb. (18 N) or a foot force greater than 100 lb. (22 N). See Figure 14-1 for a typical parking brake system.

PEDALS, LEVERS, AND HANDLES

Parking brakes are applied by a pedal, a lever, or a handle from inside the vehicle. Foot pedals and floor-mounted levers are the most common means of applying parking brakes. See Figures 14-2 and 14-3.

All parking brake controls incorporate a *ratchet* mechanism to lock the brake in the applied position. See Figure 14-4.

When service brake friction assemblies are used as the parking brakes, the service brake pedal should be depressed while the parking brake control is set. Applying the service brake increases parking brake holding power because the brake hydraulic system provides the actual application force, which

is far greater than the force that can be developed mechanically. The parking brake mechanism simply locks the brakes in position. If the parking brake is operated only by the pedal, lever, or handle, holding power will be reduced, and the cables in the linkage will tend to stretch.

All parking brakes are applied manually and the release procedure varies with the design of the parking brake control.

Parking Brake Pedals

A parking brake pedal is applied by depressing it with a foot. The ratchet engages automatically and the pedal remains in the depressed position. The pedal is released by a pull or a small T-handle or lever under the dash. This disengages the ratchet mechanism, and allows a return spring to move the pedal to the unapplied position. On some vehicles, the release lever is inte-

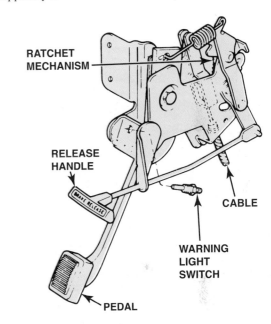

FIGURE 14-2   A typical parking brake pedal assembly.

FIGURE 14-1   Typical parking brake cable system showing the foot-operated parking brake lever and cable routing. *(Courtesy of DaimlerChrysler Corporation)*

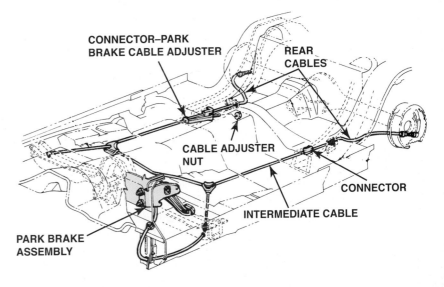

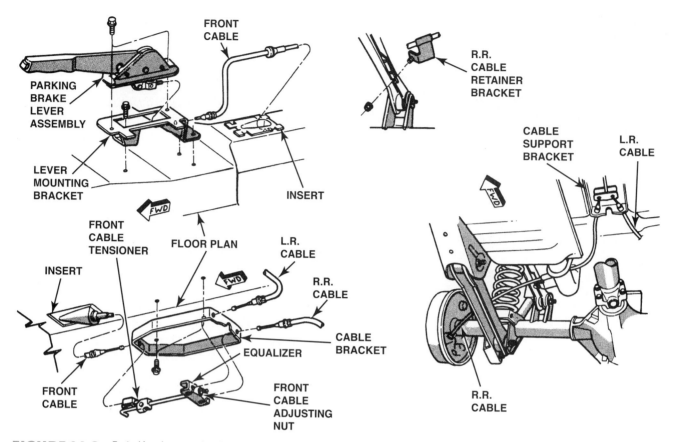

FIGURE 14-3 Typical hand-operated parking brake. Note that the adjustment for the cable is underneath the vehicle at the equalizer. *(Courtesy of DaimlerChrysler Corporation)*

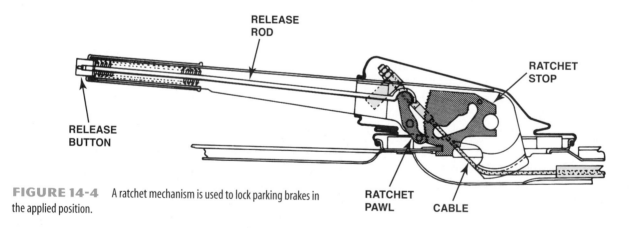

FIGURE 14-4 A ratchet mechanism is used to lock parking brakes in the applied position.

grated into the underside of the dash and connects to the release mechanism through a rod or cable. See Figure 14-5.

Some vehicles were equipped with a special pedal design that enabled them to meet federal regulations on parking brake holding power while keeping maximum pedal application force within legal limits. This type of pedal had a high leverage ratio and a special ratchet mechanism that locked the brake pedal in the applied position, but allowed the pedal to return after it had been depressed. Two full pedal strokes, or several partial strokes, were required to fully apply the parking brake. The brake was released by a single pull on a T-handle or release lever.

Some vehicles were equipped with a system that required the driver to depress the parking brake pedal to release the parking brake once it was set. The rubber pad on the parking brake pedal usually states "push to release."

Automatic Parking Brake Release

Some vehicles with pedal-operated parking brakes have an automatic release mechanism that disengages the parking brake using a **vacuum servo** controlled by an electrical solenoid. See Figure 14-6.

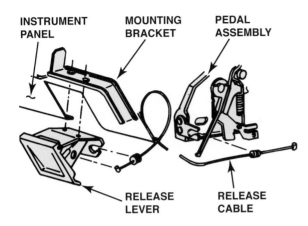

FIGURE 14-5   A remote-mounted parking brake release lever.

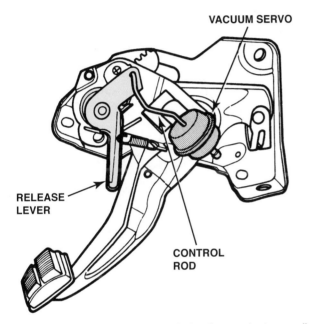

FIGURE 14-6   Automatic parking brake release mechanisms usually use a vacuum servo to operate the release lever.

REAL WORLD FIX

PUMP TO RELEASE?

A customer called and asked a dealer for help because the parking brake could not be released. The service technician discovered that the customer was attempting to release the parking brake by depressing the parking brake pedal, as was done on the customer's previous vehicle. The service technician simply pulled on the release lever and the parking brake was released.

A metal rod connects the vacuum servo to the upper end of the parking brake release lever. When the engine is running (to provide vacuum) and the shifter is placed in gear, an electrical contact closes to energize the solenoid and route vacuum to the servo. The servo diaphragm then retracts the rod, which releases the parking brake. See Figure 14-7.

PARKING BRAKE WARNING LAMP

Whenever the parking brake is engaged, a **red brake warning lamp** lights on the dash. On most vehicles, this is the same lamp that lights when there is a hydraulic or brake fluid level problem. The warning lamp for the parking brake warns the

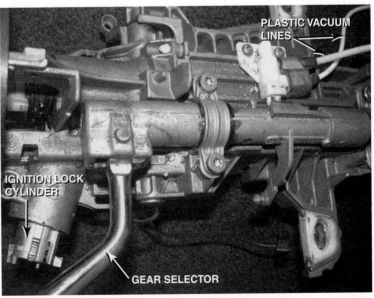

FIGURE 14-7   The two plastic vacuum tubes on the steering column are used to release the parking brake when the gear selector is moved from park into a drive gear.

driver that the parking brake is applied or partially applied. This warning helps prevent damage or overheating to the brake drums and linings that could occur if the vehicle was driven with the parking brake applied. If the red BRAKE warning lamp is on, check the parking brake to see if it is fully released. If the BRAKE lamp is still on, the parking brake switch may be defective, out of adjustment, or there may be a hydraulic problem.

PARKING BRAKE LINKAGES

Parking brake linkages transmit force from the pedal, lever, or handle inside the vehicle to the brake friction assemblies.

Linkage Rods

Parking brake linkage rods made from solid steel are commonly used with floor-mounted actuating levers to span the short distance to an intermediate lever or an equalizer.

Linkage Cables

The typical parking brake cable is made of woven-steel wire encased in a reinforced rubber or plastic housing. The housing is fixed in position at both ends, and is routed under the vehicle through mounting brackets that hold the cable in position, yet allow a small amount of movement. The cable slides back and forth inside the housing to transmit application force, and depending on the linkage design, the outer housing may play a part in parking brake application as well.

The ends of parking brake cables are fitted with a wide variety of connectors that attach to actuating devices, other linkage parts, or the wheel friction assemblies.

Parking brake linkages use control cables, transfer cables, and application cables. **Control cables** attach to the parking brake pedal, lever, or handle inside the vehicle, and transmit force to an intermediate lever or equalizer to the application cables. The **application cables** use the force passed through the linkage to apply the friction assemblies. See Figure 14-8.

Parking brake cables are subject to damage from water, dirt, and other debris thrown up under the vehicle by the tires. Most parking brake cables do not require lubrication because they are lined with nylon or Teflon, and any cable housing ends located under the vehicle are protected by rubber or nylon seals.

Linkage Levers

The rods and cables described in the previous section transmit application force in direct proportion. If 50 lbs of application force is delivered to one end of a rod or cable, 50 lbs of force will be available at the other end as well. Unfortunately, the

TECH TIP

LOOK FOR SWOLLEN PARKING BRAKE CABLES

Always inspect parking brake cables for proper operation. A cable that is larger in diameter in one section indicates that it is rusting inside and has swollen. See Figure 14-9.

A rusting parking brake cable can keep the rear brake applied even though the parking brake lever has been released. This can cause dragging brakes, reduced fuel economy, and possible vehicle damage due to overheated brakes.

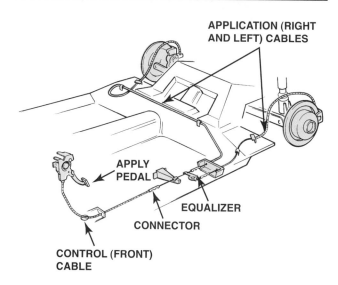

FIGURE 14-8 The cable from the activating lever to the equalizer is commonly called the control cable. From the equalizer, the individual brake cables are often called application cables. These individual cables can usually be purchased separately.

FIGURE 14-9 Notice how rust inside the covering of this parking brake cable has caused the cable to swell.

amount of physical force a driver can apply to the parking brake control is insufficient for effective parking brake operation. For this reason, all parking brake linkages contain one or more levers that increase application force.

The parking brake pedals, floor-mounted levers, and pivoting under dash handles described earlier are all types of levers used to increase parking brake application force. Straight-pull parking brake handles are not levers themselves, although they are commonly connected to other levers in the linkage.

A lever in the parking brake linkage under the vehicle is called an **intermediate lever.** See Figure 14-10.

To further increase parking brake application force, intermediate levers provide leverage in addition to that supplied by the parking brake control.

Linkage Equalizers

In some parking brake linkages, the rods or cables to the two friction assemblies are adjusted separately. If the adjustments are unequal, one brake will apply before the other, preventing full lining-to-drum contact at the opposite wheel and greatly reducing the holding power of the parking brake. To prevent unequal application, most parking brake linkages use an **equalizer** to balance the force from the parking brake control, and transmit an equal amount to each friction assembly.

Equalizers come in many shapes and sizes, but the simplest is the cable guide attached to a threaded rod. See Figure 14-11. This type of equalizer pivots or allows the inner cable to slide back and forth to even out application force.

Another type of equalizer installs in a long application cable that runs from the linkage at the front of the vehicle to one rear brake. See Figure 14-12.

A short application cable is routed from the equalizer to the other rear brake. When the parking brake is applied, the long cable actuates its brake directly. Once the shoes make contact with the drum, however, the inner cable cannot move any further so the entire cable assembly, along with the equalizer, is pulled toward the front of the vehicle. Movement of the equalizer then applies the other rear brake through the short cable.

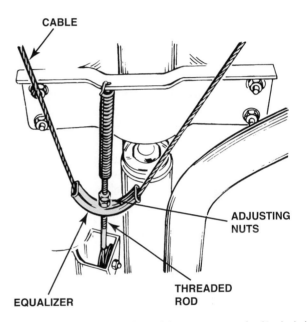

FIGURE 14-11   A cable guide is a common type of parking brake linkage equalizer.

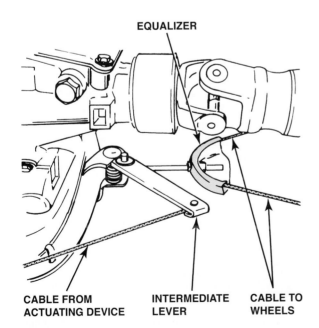

FIGURE 14-10   Intermediate levers in the parking brake linkage increase the application force.

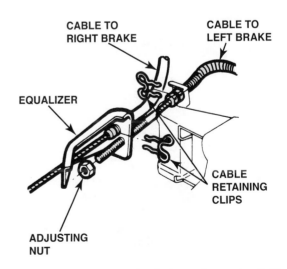

FIGURE 14-12   Some parking brake equalizers are installed in the brake cable.

Linkage Design

The number of different parking brake linkage designs is almost as great as the number of vehicle models on the road. Most linkages combine intermediate levers and equalizers in various ways and use from one to four cables to actuate the friction assemblies. See Figure 14-13.

FRONT AND REAR ENTRY PARKING BRAKE CABLES

The parking brake standard requires that the vehicle be held stationary on a 20% grade facing either uphill or downhill. Many drum parking brake systems attach the parking brake lever on the secondary (rearward) shoe and push the primary (forward facing) brake shoe against the drum. The parking brake cable enters the backing plate from the front of the vehicle (front entry). Because the primary shoe is attached to the secondary shoe on dual-servo brakes, any forward motion of the vehicle tends to wedge the primary shoe into the brake drum *and* force the rear secondary lining also against the drum.

Applying only the forward brake shoe tends to hold the vehicle best when the vehicle is being held on a hill with the front pointing downward. To help provide the same holding

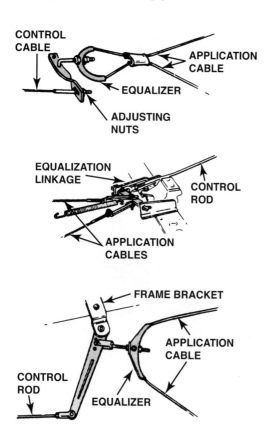

FIGURE 14-13   Many parking brake linkages use both an intermediate lever and an equalizer.

power for a vehicle being held from backing up, some vehicles reverse the parking brake arrangement for the right side. Instead of having the parking brake cable enter the backing plate from the front, this style has the cable entering from the rear (rear entry). In this case the right rear brake has the parking brake lever installed on the *primary* shoe.

NOTE: An easy way to remember how to reassemble a drum brake is to realize that the parking brake lever is usually attached to the secondary (rearward) brake shoe. The parking brake strut attaches between the shoes with the spring toward the front of the vehicle (remember, "spring forward").

DRUM PARKING BRAKES

Drum parking brakes are the most common types on vehicles and light trucks. Drum brakes make excellent parking brakes because they have a high static coefficient of friction combined with self-energizing action and, in the case of dual-servo brakes, servo action that increases their application force.

Integral Drum Parking Brakes

Integral drum parking brakes mechanically apply the rear drum service brakes to serve as the parking brakes. See Figure 14-14.

Integral drum parking brakes are the most common type not only because of their natural superiority in this application, but because it is simple and inexpensive to design a parking brake linkage into a drum brake.

The typical integral drum parking brake has a pivoting lever mounted on one brake shoe, and a strut placed between the lever and the other shoe. The strut may be fitted with a spring that takes up slack to prevent noise when the parking brake is not applied. The end of the lever opposite the pivot is moved by the parking brake cable, which enters through an opening in the backing plate. All integral drum parking brakes operate in essentially the same manner. See Figure 14-15.

When the parking brake control is operated, the cable pulls the end of the lever away from the shoe it is attached to. The lever pivots at the attaching point and moves the strut to apply the forward shoe. Once the forward brake shoe lining contacts the drum, the strut can travel no farther. The lever then pivots on the strut and forces the lining of the reverse shoe against the drum.

Rear Disc Auxiliary Drum Parking Brakes

Rear disc service brakes with fixed calipers commonly have a parking brake drum formed into the hub of the brake rotor. See Figure 14-16.

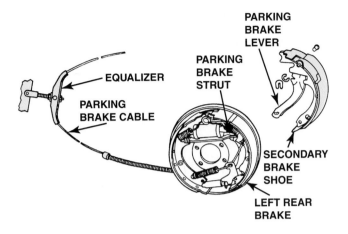

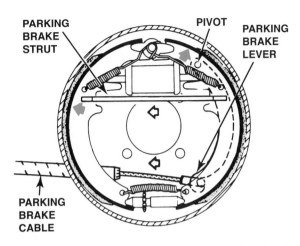

FIGURE 14-15 The parking brake cable pulls on the parking brake lever, which in turn forces the brake shoe against the drum.

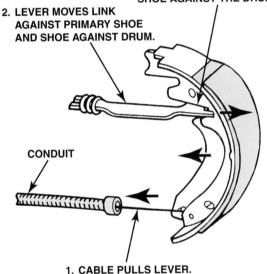

3. LEVER WORKS AGAINST LINK, AND PIVOT FORCES SECONDARY SHOE AGAINST THE DRUM.

2. LEVER MOVES LINK AGAINST PRIMARY SHOE AND SHOE AGAINST DRUM.

CONDUIT

1. CABLE PULLS LEVER.

FIGURE 14-14 Notice the spring at the end of the parking brake strut. This antirattle spring keeps tension on the strut. The parking brake lever is usually attached with a pin and spring (wavy) washer and retained by a horseshoe clip.

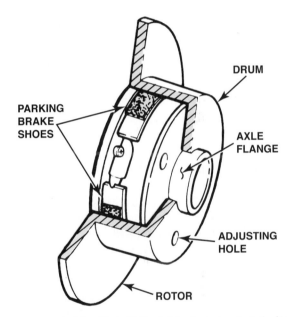

FIGURE 14-16 The inside "hat" of the disc brake rotor is the friction surface for the parking brake shoes.

Inside the drum is a small dual-servo drum brake friction assembly that serves as the parking brake. The rotor splash shield, or a special mounting bracket, provides the backing plate for the friction assembly. Rear disc auxiliary drum parking brakes use the dual-servo friction assembly design because it provides the most holding power, and does so equally in both forward and reverse directions. Dual-servo parking brake friction assemblies operate in essentially the same manner as service brakes except that the wheel cylinder is eliminated and the friction assembly is actuated mechanically. See Figure 14-17.

All rear disc auxiliary drum parking brakes are adjusted manually using a starwheel adjuster, which is reached through an opening in the outside of the drum.

CALIPER-ACTUATED DISC PARKING BRAKES

Caliper-actuated disc parking brakes are used on vehicles whose rear disc brakes are equipped with floating or sliding brake calipers. The single-piston construction of these calipers makes them easier to mechanically actuate than multiple-piston fixed calipers. In this design, a special mechanism in the caliper applies the caliper piston mechanically. The mechanism is operated by a parking brake cable attached to a lever that protrudes from the inboard side of the caliper.

FIGURE 14-17 A typical rear disc brake auxiliary drum brake friction assembly.

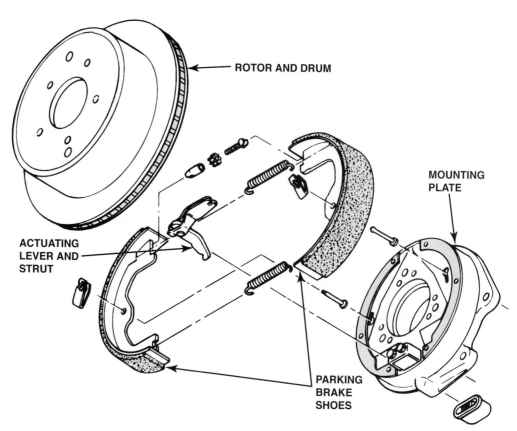

ROTOR AND DRUM

MOUNTING PLATE

ACTUATING LEVER AND STRUT

PARKING BRAKE SHOES

Ball and Ramp Actuation

The ball and ramp actuating system found in Ford rear brake calipers has three steel balls located in ramp-shaped detents between two plates. See Figure 14-18.

One plate has a thrust screw attached that is threaded into an adjuster mechanism in the caliper piston. The other

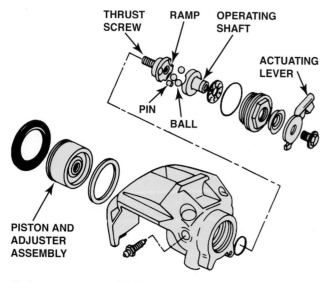

THRUST SCREW   RAMP   OPERATING SHAFT

ACTUATING LEVER

PIN

BALL

PISTON AND ADJUSTER ASSEMBLY

FIGURE 14-18 A Ford rear brake caliper ball and ramp-type apply mechanism.

plate is part of the operating shaft that extends out of the caliper. The actuating lever is mounted to the end of this shaft.

As the parking brake cable moves the lever and rotates the operating shaft, the balls ride up the ramps and force the two plates apart. The operating shaft plate cannot move because it butts against the caliper body. The thrust screw plate, which is pinned to the caliper body to prevent it from rotating, is driven away from the operating shaft and toward the rotor where the thrust screw moves the caliper piston to apply the brake. See Figure 14-19.

Adjustment of the ball and ramp linkage within the caliper is automatic, and takes place during service brake application. When the caliper piston moves away from the thrust screw, an adjuster nut inside the piston rotates on the thrust screw to take up any slack created by wear. See Figure 14-20.

A drive ring on the nut prevents it from rotating in the opposite direction when the parking brake is applied.

Screw, Nut, and Cone Actuation

General Motors' rear disc parking brake uses a screw, nut, and cone mechanism to apply the caliper piston. See Figure 14-21.

In this design, the actuator screw with the parking brake lever attached extends through the caliper body. The caliper piston contains a specially shaped nut that threads onto the actuator screw when the piston is installed in the bore. The nut butts against the backside of the cone, and is splined to the

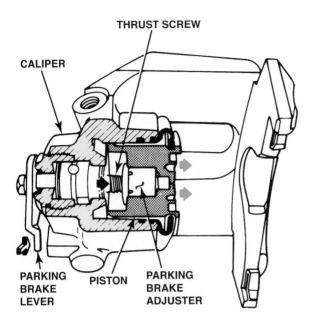

FIGURE 14-19   Operation of a ball and ramp-type rear disc brake caliper parking brake.

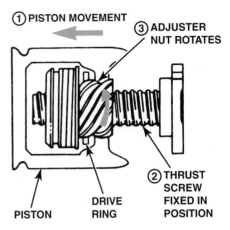

FIGURE 14-20   Automatic adjustment of a ball and ramp-type rear disc brake parking brake occurs when the service brakes are applied.

cone so that it cannot rotate unless the cone does so as well. The cone is a slip fit in the piston, and is free to rotate unless it is held tightly against a clutch surface located near the outer end of the piston bore.

When the parking brake is applied, the cable moves the lever and rotates the actuator screw. See Figure 14-22.

The nut then unthreads along the screw, and jams the cone against the clutch surface of the caliper piston. This prevents the cone from rotating because the caliper piston is keyed to the brake pad, which is fixed in the caliper. Because the cone cannot rotate, movement of the nut along the actuator thread forces the cone and piston outward against the inboard pad to apply the brake.

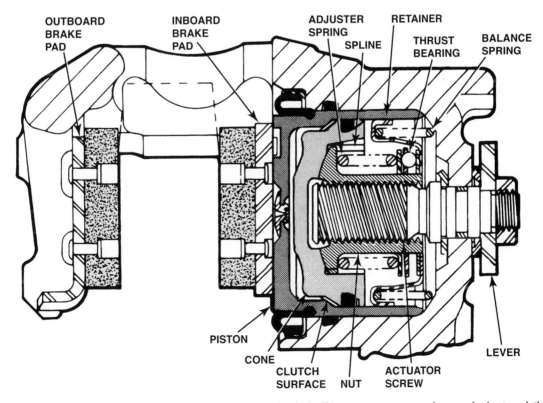

FIGURE 14-21   A typical General Motors rear disc brake with an integral parking brake. This type uses a screw, nut, and cone mechanism to apply the caliper piston.

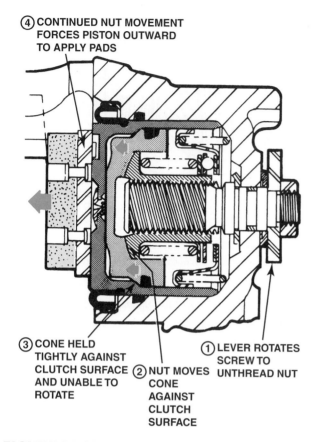

④ CONTINUED NUT MOVEMENT FORCES PISTON OUTWARD TO APPLY PADS

③ CONE HELD TIGHTLY AGAINST CLUTCH SURFACE AND UNABLE TO ROTATE

② NUT MOVES CONE AGAINST CLUTCH SURFACE

① LEVER ROTATES SCREW TO UNTHREAD NUT

FIGURE 14-22 Parking brake application of a General Motors rear drive brake caliper.

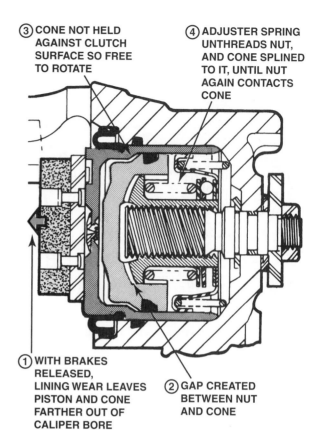

③ CONE NOT HELD AGAINST CLUTCH SURFACE SO FREE TO ROTATE

④ ADJUSTER SPRING UNTHREADS NUT, AND CONE SPLINED TO IT, UNTIL NUT AGAIN CONTACTS CONE

① WITH BRAKES RELEASED, LINING WEAR LEAVES PISTON AND CONE FARTHER OUT OF CALIPER BORE

② GAP CREATED BETWEEN NUT AND CONE

FIGURE 14-23 Automatic adjustment of a General Motors rear disc brake caliper.

Adjustment of the screw, nut, and cone mechanism occurs automatically during normal operation as the service brakes are released. See Figure 14-23.

When the service brakes are applied, the cone and piston move outward in the bore under hydraulic pressure. The nut, however, remains fixed because the actuator screw does not rotate. As long as there is brake application pressure, the cone is held tightly against the clutch surface of the piston, which prevents the cone, and the nut splined to it, from rotating.

The result of the above actions is that a gap develops between the outer end of the nut and the backside of the cone when the brakes are applied. If sufficient brake lining wear has occurred, a gap remains after seal deflection retracts the piston and cone when the brakes are released. Once the brakes are released, the cone is no longer held against the clutch surface, and becomes free to rotate in the piston. At this point, the adjuster spring, which exerts strong axial pressure on the nut, causes the nut and cone to unthread along the actuator screw and take up any clearance between the cone and piston.

The balance spring between the piston and the caliper bore has two purposes.

1. It prevents excessive piston retraction when the brakes are released.
2. It counterbalances the pressure of the adjuster spring.

Note that the outer end of the nut is in constant contact with the cone whenever the service brakes are not applied. If the automatic adjusting system fails, the tension of the adjustor spring against the thrust bearing at the back of the piston will retract the cone and piston from the rotor until the cone does contact the nut, resulting in a low brake pedal. See Figures 14-24 through 14-31.

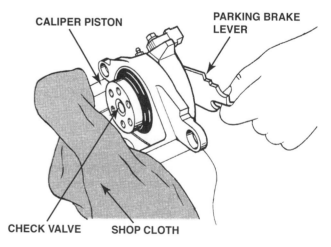

CALIPER PISTON

PARKING BRAKE LEVER

CHECK VALVE

SHOP CLOTH

FIGURE 14-24 Removing the piston from a typical General Motors rear disc brake caliper. *(Courtesy of Allied Signal Automotive Aftermarket)*

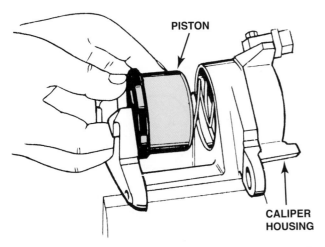

FIGURE 14-25   Installing the piston into a General Motors rear disc brake caliper.

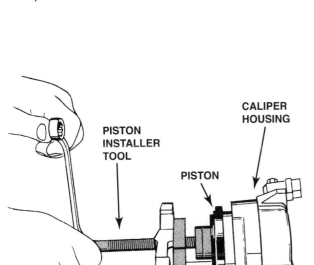

FIGURE 14-26   A piston installation tool is required to fully install the piston into a General Motors rear disc brake caliper.   *(Courtesy of Allied Signal Automotive Aftermarket)*

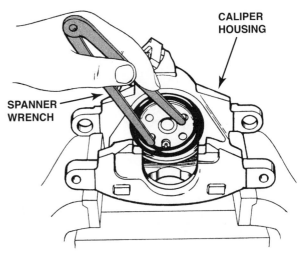

FIGURE 14-27   A spanner wrench (or needle-nose pliers) can be used to rotate the caliper piston prior to installing the disc brake pads. A notch on the piston must line up with a tab on the back of the brake pad to keep the piston from rotating when the parking brake is applied.   *(Courtesy of Allied Signal Automotive Aftermarket)*

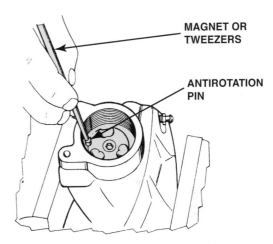

FIGURE 14-28   After removing the parking brake lever and thrust bearing, remove the antirotation pin.   *(Courtesy of Allied Signal Automotive Aftermarket)*

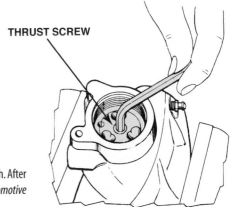

FIGURE 14-29   Unscrew the thrust screw from the piston with an Allen (hex) wrench. After removing the thrust screw, push the piston out of the caliper bore.   *(Courtesy of Allied Signal Automotive Aftermarket)*

FIGURE 14-30   To test the piston adjuster, thread the thrust screw into the piston. Hold the piston and pull the thrust screw outward 1/4 in. (6 mm). The adjuster nut should not turn when the thrust screw retracts. Replace the piston assembly if not functioning correctly.   *(Courtesy of Allied Signal Automotive Aftermarket)*

TECH TIP

THE PARKING BRAKE "CLICK" TEST

When diagnosing any brake problem, apply the parking brake and count the "clicks." This method works for both hand- and foot-operated parking brakes. Most vehicle manufacturers specify a maximum of 10 clicks. If the parking brake travel exceeds this amount, the rear brakes may be worn or out of adjustment.

CAUTION: Do not adjust the parking brake cable until the rear brakes have been thoroughly inspected and adjusted.

If the rear brake lining is usable, check for the proper operation of the self-adjustment mechanism. If the rear brakes are out of adjustment, the service brake pedal will also be low. This 10-click test is a fast and easy way to determine if the problem is due to rear brakes.

PARKING BRAKE CABLE ADJUSTMENT

Most manufacturers specify a minimum of 3 or 4, and a maximum of 8 to 10, clicks when applying the parking brake. Consult the service manual for the vehicle being serviced on the exact specification and adjustment procedures. Most vehicle manufacturers specify that the rear brakes be inspected and adjusted correctly before attempting to adjust the parking brake cable. Always follow the manufacturer's recommended procedure exactly.

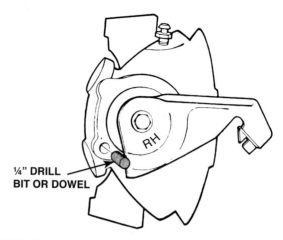

¼" DRILL BIT OR DOWEL

FIGURE 14-31   To adjust the parking brake cable on a Ford vehicle equipped with rear disc brakes, start by loosening the cable adjustment until the cables to the calipers are slack. Tighten until the caliper lever moves. Position a 1/4-in. drill bit or dowel into the caliper alignment hole. Adjustment is correct if the parking brake lever does not hit the 1/4-in. dowel.

Below is a general procedure for parking brake adjustment.

1. Make certain that the rear service brakes are adjusted correctly and the lining is serviceable.
2. With the drums installed, apply the parking brake 3 or 4 clicks. There should be a slight drag on both rear wheels.
3. Adjust the cable at the equalizer (equalizes one cable's force to both rear brakes) if necessary until there is a slight drag on both rear brakes. See Figures 14-32 and 14-33.
4. Release the parking brake. Both rear brakes should be free and not dragging. Repair or replace rusted cables or readjust as necessary to ensure that the brakes are not dragging.

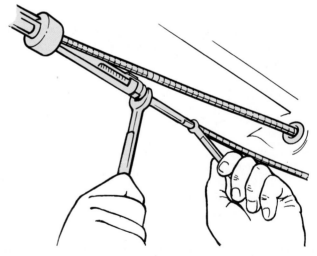

FIGURE 14-32   After checking that the rear brakes are okay and properly adjusted, the parking brake cable can be adjusted. Always follow the manufacturer's recommended procedure.

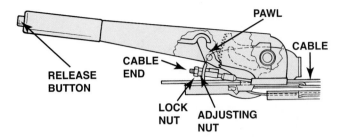

FIGURE 14-33 Many hand-operated parking brakes are adjusted inside the vehicle.

NOTE: The rear parking brake adjustment should always be checked whenever replacing the rear brake linings. It may be necessary to loosen the parking brake cable adjustment to allow clearance to get the drum over the new linings. This could happen because someone may have adjusted the parking brake cable during the life of the rear linings. See Figure 14-34.

With new thicker linings, the parking brake adjustment can keep the brake shoes pushed outward toward the drum.

To prevent possible parking brake cable adjustment problems when installing new rear brakes, always observe the following:

1. Both brake shoes should make contact with the anchor pin at the top. If not, check the parking brake cable for improper adjustment or improper installation of the brake shoes.
2. Feel the tension of the parking brake cable underneath the vehicle. It should be slightly loose (with the parking brake "off").

3. Lubricate the parking brake cable to ensure that water or ice will not cause rust or freezing of the cable. This is necessary because even though the parking brake lever is released inside the vehicle, a stuck parking brake cable could cause the linings to remain out against the drums.
4. If the parking brake needs to be adjusted (will not hold on a hill or requires excessive lever movement), always check and adjust the rear brake adjustment before adjusting the parking brake cable. See Figure 14-35.

NOTE: Some vehicles are equipped with an automatic adjusting parking brake lever/cable. Simply cycling the parking brake on/off/on three times is often all that is required to adjust the parking brake cable.

5. Replace any stuck, corroded, or broken parking brake cable.

TECH TIP

THE HOSE CLAMP OR WRENCH TRICK

It is often difficult to remove a parking brake cable from the backing plate due to the design of the retainer. The many fingers used to hold the cable to the backing plate can be squeezed all at once if a hose clamp is used to compress the fingers. A wrench as shown in Figure 14-36 can also be used.

FIGURE 14-34 Always check that the brake shoes contact the anchor pin.

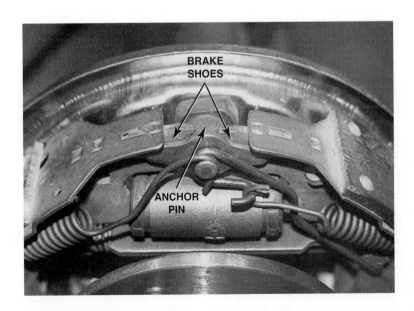

FIGURE 14-35 A 1/8-in. (3-mm) drill bit is placed through an access hole in the backing plate to adjust this General Motors leading-trailing rear parking brake. Adjust the parking brake cable until the drill can just fit between the shoe web and the parking brake lever.

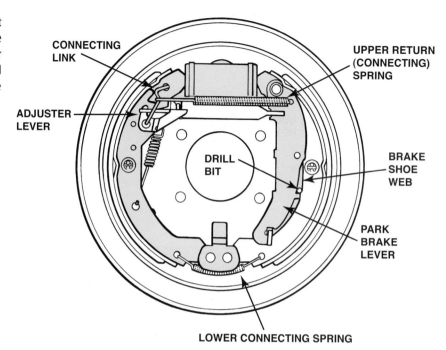

CONNECTING LINK

ADJUSTER LEVER

UPPER RETURN (CONNECTING) SPRING

DRILL BIT

BRAKE SHOE WEB

PARK BRAKE LEVER

LOWER CONNECTING SPRING

FIGURE 14-36 Many parking brake cables can be removed easily from the backing plate using a 1/2-in. (13-mm) box-end wrench. The wrench fits over the retainer finger on the end of the parking brake cable. *(Courtesy of DaimlerChrysler Corporation)*

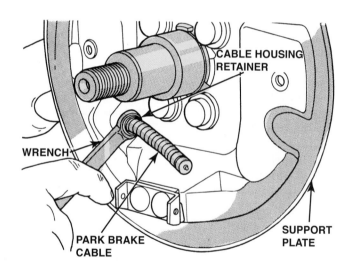

CABLE HOUSING RETAINER

WRENCH

PARK BRAKE CABLE

SUPPORT PLATE

SUMMARY

1. Government regulation requires that the parking brake be able to hold a fully loaded vehicle on a 20% grade.

2. The typical parking brake uses either a hand-operated lever or a foot-operated pedal to activate the parking brake.

3. On a typical drum brake system, the parking brake cable moves a parking brake lever attached to the secondary brake shoe. The primary shoe is applied through force being transferred through the strut.

4. All parking brake cables should move freely. The rear brakes should be adjusted properly before the parking brake is adjusted.

REVIEW QUESTIONS

1. Describe how a typical parking brake functions on a vehicle equipped with rear drum brakes.

2. Describe how a typical parking brake functions on a vehicle equipped with an integral rear disc brake system.

3. Explain how to adjust a parking brake properly.

CHAPTER QUIZ

1. Technician A says that the parking brake cable should be adjusted at each wheel. Technician B says that the parking brake cable adjustment is usually done after adjusting the rear brakes. Which technician is correct?
   a. Technician A only
   b. Technician B only
   c. Both Technicians A and B
   d. Neither Technician A nor B

2. Technician A says that the parking brake hand lever can turn on the red brake warning lamp. Technician B says that a foot-operated parking brake can turn on the red brake warning lamp. Which technician is correct?
   a. Technician A only
   b. Technician B only
   c. Both Technicians A and B
   d. Neither Technician A nor B

3. Technician A says that if the parking brake cable is adjusted too tight, the rear brakes may drag and overheat. Technician B says that the parking brake is adjusted properly if the cable is tight when in the released position. Which technician is correct?
   a. Technician A only
   b. Technician B only
   c. Both Technicians A and B
   d. Neither Technician A nor B

4. On most drum brake systems, the parking brake lever and strut transfer the pulling force of the parking brake cable against the _____.
   a. Primary shoe
   b. Secondary shoe

5. On most vehicles, the antirattle spring (strut spring) should be installed on the parking brake strut toward the _____ of the vehicle.
   a. Front
   b. Rear

6. In a typical integral rear disc brake caliper, the parking brake cable moves the _____.
   a. Caliper
   b. Actuator screw

   c. Auxiliary piston
   d. Rotor

7. The rear brakes should be inspected, and adjusted if necessary, if the parking brake requires more than _____.
   a. 5 clicks
   b. 10 clicks
   c. 15 clicks
   d. 20 clicks

8. A rear drum brake is being inspected. The primary shoe is not contacting the anchor pin at the top. Technician A says that this is normal. Technician B says that the parking brake cable may be adjusted too tight or is stuck. Which technician is correct?
   a. Technician A only
   b. Technician B only
   c. Both Technicians A and B
   d. Neither Technician A nor B

9. Technician A says that a hose clamp can be used to compress the retainer fingers of a parking brake cable in order to remove it from the backing plate. Technician B says a box-end wrench can be used instead of a hose clamp. Which technician is correct?
   a. Technician A only
   b. Technician B only
   c. Both Technicians A and B
   d. Neither Technician A nor B

10. The wrong replacement rear disc brake pads were installed on a vehicle that used an integral parking brake. The inboard pad did not have a pin that fit into a notch on the caliper piston. Technician A says that the brakes will likely overadjust. Technician B says that the parking brake will not work. Which technician is correct?
    a. Technician A only
    b. Technician B only
    c. Both Technicians A and B
    d. Neither Technician A nor B

MACHINING BRAKE DRUMS AND ROTORS

OBJECTIVES

After studying Chapter 15, the reader should be able to:

1. Prepare for the Brakes (A5) ASE certification test content area "E" (Miscellaneous Systems Diagnosis and Repair).
2. Discuss the construction of brake drums and rotors.
3. Explain the formation of hard spots in drums and rotors.
4. Describe how to measure and inspect drums and rotors before machining.
5. Discuss how surface finish is measured and its importance to satisfactory brake service.
6. Demonstrate how to machine a brake drum and rotor correctly.

KEY TERMS

Bellmouth (p. 266)
Chill spots (p. 265)
Composite rotors (p. 271)
Convection (p. 263)
Discs (disks) (p. 270)
Eccentric distortion (p. 267)
Elastic limit (p. 266)
Hard spots (p. 265)
Heat checking (p. 265)
Lateral runout (LRO) (p. 273)

Microinches (μin.) (p. 278)
Out-of-round (p. 266)
Parallelism (p. 274)
Ra (p. 278)
Root mean square (RMS) (p. 278)
Scoring (p. 264)
Scratch cut (p. 269)
Self-aligning spacer (SAS) (p. 269)
Thickness variation (TV) (p. 274)

BRAKE DRUMS

Brake drums are constructed of cast iron where the lining contacts the drum with mild steel centers. The drum is drilled for the lug studs. Cast iron contains approximately 3% carbon, which makes the drum hard, yet brittle. For this reason it is recommended that any pounding needed to remove drums be done on the center mild steel portion, which due to its material characteristics can take this force without damage. This 3% carbon content of the cast iron also acts as a lubricant, which prevents noise during braking. Also, the rubbing surface can be machined without the need of a coolant (as would be required if constructed of mild steel). Because of these properties, cast iron is used on the friction surface of all drums. See Figure 15-1.

Even aluminum brake drums use cast iron for the friction surface area. Besides saving weight, aluminum brake drums transfer heat to the surrounding air faster than cast iron or steel. Brake drums and rotors are the major energy-absorbing parts of the braking system. Friction between the friction material and the drum or rotor creates heat. This heat is absorbed by the drum or rotor and travels from the friction surface to the remainder of the drum or rotor by heat **convection.** As energy contin-

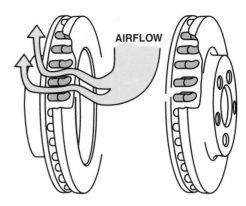

FIGURE 15-2   The airflow through cooling vents helps brakes from overheating.

ues to be absorbed, the drum or rotor increases in temperature. Airflow across the drum or rotor helps to dissipate the heat and keep the temperature rise under control. See Figure 15-2 through 15-4 for examples of how drums and rotors are cooled.

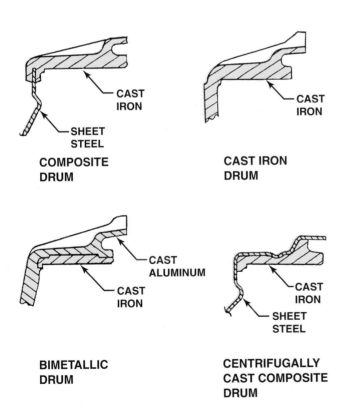

FIGURE 15-1   Types of brake drums. Regardless of the design, all types use cast iron as a friction surface.

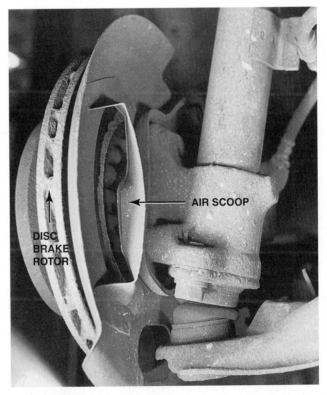

FIGURE 15-3   This air scoop is part of the water/dirt shield attached next to the rotor.

FIGURE 15-4   Most race cars are equipped with scoops to direct air past the brakes to dissipate the heat quickly. The cooler the air, the more efficient and effective the brakes.

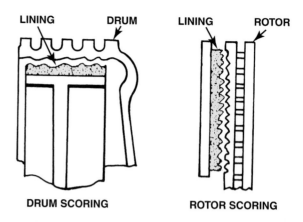

FIGURE 15-5   Scored drums and rotors often result in metal-to-metal contact.

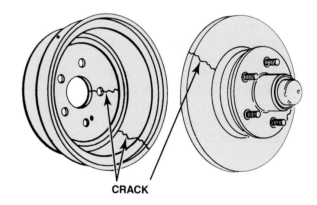

FIGURE 15-6   Cracked drums or rotors must be replaced.

BRAKE DRUM AND ROTOR DAMAGE

Besides wear, drums and rotors often experience damage to their friction surfaces. Because drum and rotor damage is caused by extremes of operation, it is most commonly found on front brakes, which experience more severe use than rear brakes.

Scoring

Scoring is an extreme form of drum and rotor wear consisting of scratches, deep grooves, and a generally rough finish on the friction surface. See Figure 15-5.

There are a number of causes for scoring, but the most common is brake linings that have worn to the point where a rivet, lining table, or pad backing plate contacts the drum or rotor. Certain friction materials are more likely to score drums and rotors than others, and glazed linings that have hardened from exposure to extreme heat can also cause scoring.

Drum brakes are more likely to become scored than disc brakes because their closed construction holds dirt, sand, and abrasive dust inside the friction assembly. This allows the con-

taminants to be scrubbed repeatedly between the linings and drum. Severe drum scoring often results when metal parts of the friction assembly fatigue, break loose, and are trapped between the linings and drum.

A scored drum or rotor will cause very rapid lining wear, often accompanied by a growling or grinding noise, particularly if there is metal-to-metal contact between the shoe and drum or pad and rotor. Scoring can be machined out of a drum or rotor so long as the amount of metal removed is within the allowable limits.

Cracking

Cracks in a brake drum or rotor are caused by the stress of severe braking or an impact during an accident. See Figure 15-6.

Generally, drums and rotors that have been previously machined are more susceptible to cracking than new parts. Cracks can appear anywhere on a drum or rotor, although on drums they are most often found near the bolt circle on the web, or at the open edge of the friction surface. Rotors generally crack first at the edge of their friction surfaces.

Heat Checking

A lesser form of drum and rotor cracking is called **heat checking,** which consists of many small, interlaced cracks on the friction surface. See Figure 15-7.

These cracks typically penetrate only a few thousandths of an inch into the metal and seldom pass through the structure of the drum or rotor. Heat checking is usually caused by a driver who leaves one foot on the brake pedal while applying the accelerator with the other. Heat checking can also be caused by repeated heavy braking or numerous panic stops made in rapid succession.

Light heat checking can often be machined away. In more severe cases the drum or rotor must be replaced.

Hard or Chill Spots

Earlier, it was stated that cast iron drums and rotors are durable because the friction, heat, and pressure of braking cause a tough "skin" to form on their friction surfaces. However, if brake temperatures become too great, localized impurities in the metal can be burned away, altering the structure of the metal and causing **hard spots,** also called **chill spots,** to appear. Hard spots are roughly circular, bluish/gold glassy appearing areas on the friction surface. See Figure 15-8.

Hard spots create a number of problems including the following:

- They are harder than surrounding areas of the friction surface, and do not wear at the same rate. Once the spots begin to stand out from the rest of the friction surface, they cause rapid brake lining wear.
- The friction coefficient of hard spots is less than that of surrounding areas so braking power is reduced or becomes uneven. This can cause the brakes to chatter, or result in a hard or pulsating brake pedal.
- A drum or rotor is more likely to crack in the area of hard spots than elsewhere.

Most vehicle manufacturers recommend that the drum or rotor should be replaced if hard spots are found.

BRAKE DRUM DISTORTION

To ensure smooth brake application without pedal pulsation or other problems, brake drum friction surfaces must remain in a fixed position in relation to the shoes. In some cases, a position variation of less than a thousandth of an inch will create

FIGURE 15-7   A heat-checked surface of a disc brake rotor.

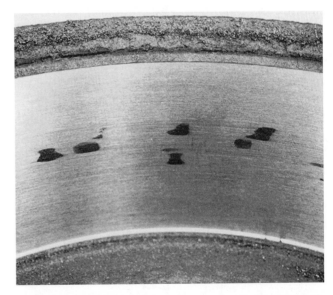

FIGURE 15-8   These dark hard spots are created by heat that actually changes the metallurgy of the cast iron drum. Most experts recommend replacement of any brake drum that has these hard spots.

STORING DRUMS AND ROTORS

A common cause of distortion in new brake drums and rotors is improper storage. Drums and rotors should always be stored lying flat; they should never be stood on edge. Distortion of new drums and rotors is common, so they should be routinely checked before installation.

braking problems. Distortion puts the drum friction surfaces out of proper alignment with the shoes.

Drum Distortion

The friction surface of a brake drum in perfect condition is parallel to the axis of the axle, and rotates in a precise circle centered on the axle or hub. All brake drums suffer from distortion during brake operation, but they usually return to their original shape once the brakes are released. When the friction surface does not return to its proper shape, is no longer parallel to the axle, or does not rotate in a precise circle around the axle, the drum is distorted.

Bellmouth Drums

When an open edge of a brake drum friction surface has a larger diameter than the closed edge, the drum is suffering from **bellmouth** distortion. See Figure 15-9. Bellmouth distortion is caused by poor drum rigidity combined with high heat and brake application force.

Bellmouth distortion occurs when a drum suffers mechanical fade and its open edge, unsupported by the drum web, expands more than its closed edge. When the brakes are applied harder to compensate for the fade, the shoes distort the open edge of the drum so far outward that the **elastic limit** of its metal is exceeded. Once this happens, the drum will not return to its original shape after it cools. Repeated occurrences of this process eventually cause the drum to take on a bellmouth shape.

Bellmouth distortion is especially common on wide drums and commonly occurs when a drum has had too much metal machined from it. If new shoes are installed in a bellmouthed drum, brake fade and unusual lining wear will result.

Out-of-Round Drums

Uneven heat distribution can sometimes cause **out-of-round** distortion in which the drum radius varies when measured at different points around its circumference. See Figure 15-10.

Out-of-round distortion can take place when a vehicle drives through a puddle after a series of hard stops and cold water splashed on the brakes causes rapid and uneven cooling of the drums. It can also result if the parking brake is firmly applied after a series of hard stops before the drums have had a chance to cool. In this case, the shoes extend out against the heat-expanded drum and prevent it from contracting to its original circular shape as it cools. Instead, the extended shoes force the drum into an out-of-round shape.

The most common symptom of an out-of-round drum is a pulsating brake pedal when the brakes are applied at all speeds. Out-of-round drums can also cause a vibration or brake chatter at speeds above approximately 40 mph (60 km/h). In more extreme cases, an out-of-round drum can re-

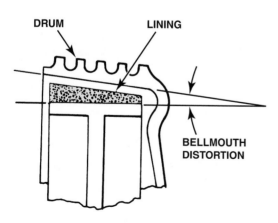

FIGURE 15-9   Bellmouth brake drum distortion.

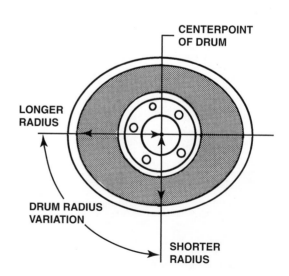

FIGURE 15-10   Out-of-round brake drum distortion.

THE PARKING BRAKE TRICK

Whenever attempting to diagnose a brake pedal pulsation, drive to a deserted area or parking lot and try stopping the vehicle using the parking brake. If a vibration occurs, the problem is due to a fault with the rear brakes. If a vibration does not occur except when using the service brakes, the problem is most likely due to a fault with the front brakes.

sult in erratic braking action, and possibly cause the brakes to grab with every revolution of the wheel.

Eccentric Drums

Eccentric distortion exists when the geometric center of the circle described by the brake drum friction surface is other than the center of the axle or the bolt circle of the drum web. See Figure 15-11. This type of distortion causes the drum to rotate with a cam-like motion. An eccentric drum will result in a pulsating brake pedal similar to that caused by an out-of-round drum.

Eccentric distortion is often caused by overtightened or unevenly tightened lug nuts or bolts. Not only will this cause an immediate problem, but it can lead to additional problems later. If a vehicle is driven for an extended time with an eccentric drum, the linings may slowly wear the friction surface "round" again. However, as soon as tension on the lug nuts or bolts is released, the drum will relax back to its original shape creating an out-of-round condition that was not apparent before the wheel was removed.

REMOVING DRUMS

Metal clips called tinnerman nuts are installed at the factory to keep the brake drums from falling off during vehicle assembly. These clips can be removed and do not need to be reinstalled since the wheel lug nuts hold onto the brake drum.

The first inspection step after removing a brake drum is to check it for warpage using a straightedge, as shown in Figure 15-12.

A warped drum is often a source of vibration. A brake drum that is out-of-round can cause a brake pedal pulsation during braking.

NOTE: To help diagnose if the front brakes or rear brakes are the cause of the vibration, try slowing the vehicle using the parking brake. If vibration occurs, the problem is due to the rear brakes.

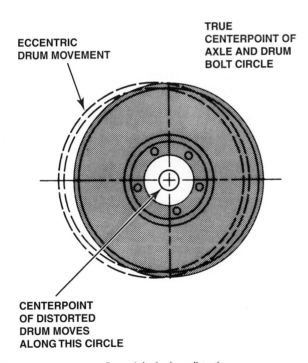

FIGURE 15-11 Eccentric brake drum distortion.

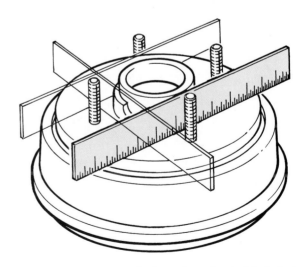

FIGURE 15-12 A straightedge can be used to check for brake drum warpage.

TECH TIP

MARK IT TO BE SURE

Most experts recommend that brake rotors, as well as drums and wheels, be marked before removing them for service. Many disc brake rotors are directional and will function correctly only if replaced in the original location. A quick-and-easy method is to use correction fluid. This alcohol-based liquid comes in small bottles with a small brush inside, making it easy to mark rotors with an "L" for left and an "R" for right. Correction fluid (also called "white-out" or "liquid paper") can also be used to make marks on wheel studs, wheels, and brake drums to help ensure reinstallation in the same location.

"MACHINE TO" VERSUS "DISCARD"

Brake drums can usually be machined a maximum of 0.060 in. (1.5 mm) oversize (for example, a 9.500-in. drum could wear or be machined to a maximum inside diameter of 9.560 in.) unless otherwise stamped on the drum. Most brake experts recommend that both drums on the same axle be within 0.010 in. (0.25 mm) of each other. *The maximum specified inside diameter (ID) means the maximum wear inside diameter.* See Figure 15-13.

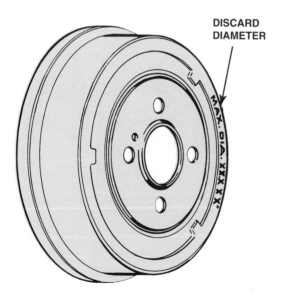

FIGURE 15-13 Discard diameter and maximum diameter are brake drum machining and wear limits.

Always leave at least 0.015 in. (0.4 mm) after machining (resurfacing) for wear. Many manufacturers recommend that 0.030 in. (0.8 mm) be left for wear.

REASONS FOR EQUAL DRUM INSIDE DIAMETER

There are several reasons why the service technician should check and make sure that both brake drums on the same axle are close to the same inside diameter (ID).

- **Reason 1.** Since heat is generated by braking, if there is less material (larger ID), the drum will tend to expand more rapidly than a drum with more material (smaller ID).
- **Reason 2.** If one drum expands more than the drum on the other side of the vehicle, unequal braking forces result.
- **Reason 3.** The drum that is larger in ID will expand away from the brake linings more than the other side.

For example:

Left Drum	Right Drum
9.500 in.	9.560 in.

In this example, when the drums get hot (heavy braking), the vehicle will tend to pull to the left.

TECH TIP

BRAKE DRUM CHAMFER

Look at the chamfer on the outer edge of most brake drums. When the chamfer is no longer visible, the brake drum is usually at or past its maximum ID. See Figure 15-14. Although this chamfer is not an accurate gauge of the ID of the brake drum, it still is a helpful indicator to the technician.

MEASURING AND MACHINING BRAKE DRUMS

Before measuring a brake drum, be sure it is not cracked by tapping it with a steel hammer. The brake drum should ring like a bell. If the brake drum makes a dull thud sound, discard the drum. Brake drums are usually measured using a micrometer especially designed for brake drums. See Figure 15-15.

FIGURE 15-14   Most brake drums have a chamfer around the edge. If the chamfer is no longer visible, the drum is usually worn (or machined) to its maximum allowable ID.

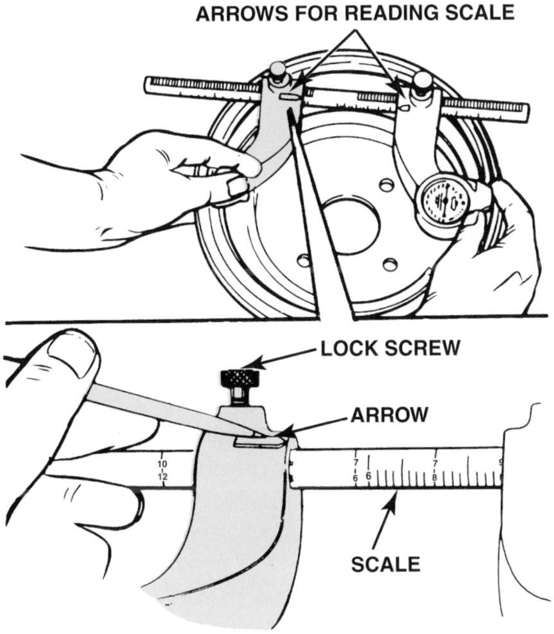

Use a **self-aligning spacer (SAS)** to be assured of even force being applied to the drum by the spindle nut. Always follow the instructions for the lathe you are using.

Hubless drums use a hole in the center of the brake drum for centering. Always check that the center hole is clean and free of burrs or nicks. Typical drum brake machining steps include the following:

Step 1   Mount the drum on the lathe and install the silencer band as shown in Figures 15-16 and 15-17.

Step 2   Turn the drum by hand before turning on the lathe to be sure everything is clean. Advance the tool bit manually until it just contacts the drum. This is called a **scratch cut**. See Figure 15-18.

FIGURE 15-15   Typical needle dial brake drum micrometer. The left movable arm is set to the approximate drum diameter and the right arm to the more exact drum diameter. The dial indicator (gauge) reads in thousandths of an inch.   *(Courtesy of Ammco Tools, Inc.)*

Compare the micrometer reading to the discard diameter. Both drums should be measured whenever they are removed for any brake service or inspection.

Always start any machining operation by making certain that the brake drum is clean and that excess grease is removed from the hub. If the drum has a hub with bearings, check the outer bearing races (cups) for wear and replace as necessary before placing the drum on the brake lathe. Also, carefully inspect and clean the lathe spindle shaft and cones before use.

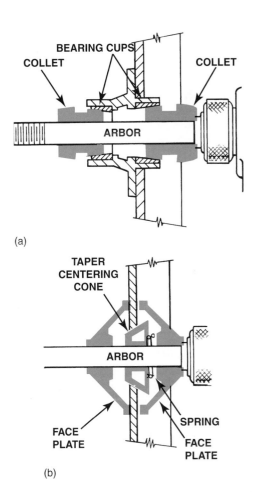

FIGURE 15-16   (a) A rotor or brake drum with a bearing hub should be installed on a brake lathe using the appropriate size collet that fit the bearing cups (races). (b) A hubless rotor or brake drum requires a spring and a tapered centering cone. A faceplate should be used on both sides of the rotor or drum to provide support.

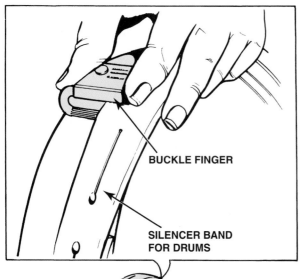

BUCKLE FINGER

SILENCER BAND
FOR DRUMS

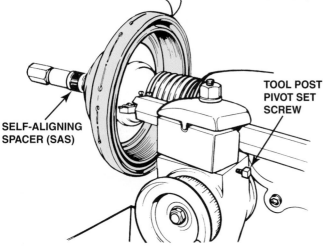

SELF-ALIGNING
SPACER (SAS)

TOOL POST
PIVOT SET
SCREW

FIGURE 15-17   A self-aligning spacer (SAS) should always be used between the drum or rotor and the spindle retaining nut to help ensure an even clamping force and to prevent the adapters and cone from getting into a bind. A silencer band should always be installed to prevent turning-tool chatter and to ensure a smooth surface finish.   *(Courtesy of Ammco Tools, Inc.)*

Step 3   Stop the lathe and back off the tool bit. Loosen the arbor nut, rotate the drum one-half turn (180°) on the arbor, and retighten the arbor nut. See Figure 15-19. Turn the lathe on and make a second scratch cut.
a. If the scratch cuts are side-by-side, the lathe is okay and machining can begin.
b. If the scratch cuts are opposite, remove the drum and check for nicks, burrs, or chips on the mounting surfaces.

Step 4   Start the lathe and set the depth of the cut. See Figures 15-20 and 15-21.
The maximum rough cut depends on the lathe type. The minimum cut is usually specified as no less than 0.002 in. (0.05 mm). A shallower cut usually causes the tool bit to slide over the surface of the metal rather than cut into the metal.

FIRST
SCRATCH
CUT

FIGURE 15-18   After installing a brake drum on the lathe, turn the cutting tool outward until the tool just touches the drum. This is called a scratch cut.   *(Courtesy of Ammco Tools, Inc.)*

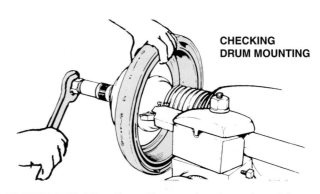

CHECKING
DRUM MOUNTING

FIGURE 15-19   After making a scratch cut, loosen the retaining nut, rotate the drum on the lathe, and make another scratch cut. If both cuts are in the same location, the drum is installed correctly on the lathe and drum machining can begin.   *(Courtesy of Ammco Tools, Inc.)*

See Figure 15-22 for an example of a drum machined without properly positioning the antichatter (vibration) strap.

DISC BRAKE ROTORS

Disc brake rotors use cast gray iron at the area that contacts the friction pad. Rotors, also called **discs** or **disks**, have mass (weight) that absorbs heat. The heavier the rotor, the more heat can be absorbed. Vehicle downsizing has resulted in the use of thinner- and lighter-weight rotors. As the weight of the rotor decreases, the less heat the rotor can "store" or absorb, resulting in the rotor getting hotter. As the rotor gets hotter, the rotor expands and "grows" larger where it is the hottest. If the rotor is allowed to cool gradually, the rotor simply returns to its original shape. If, however, the rotor is exposed to water, it may cool rapidly, causing the rotor to distort.

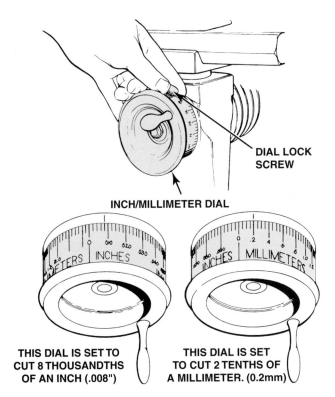

INCH/MILLIMETER DIAL

THIS DIAL IS SET TO CUT 8 THOUSANDTHS OF AN INCH (.008")

THIS DIAL IS SET TO CUT 2 TENTHS OF A MILLIMETER. (0.2mm)

FIGURE 15-20 Set the depth of the cut indicator to zero just as the turning tool touches the drum. *(Courtesy of Ammco Tools, Inc.)*

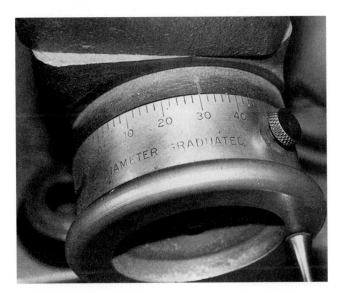

FIGURE 15-21 This lathe has a dial that is "diameter graduated." This means that a reading of 0.030 in. indicates a 0.015 in. cut that increases the inside diameter of the brake drum by 0.030 in.

Rotors are made in several styles, including the following:

1. **Solid.** These are used on the rear of many vehicles equipped with rear disc brakes and on the front of some small and midsize vehicles. Solid rotors are usually used on

FIGURE 15-22 Notice the chatter marks at the edge of the friction-area surface of the brake drum. These marks were caused by vibration of the drum because the technician failed to wrap the dampening strap (silencer band) over the friction-surface portion of the brake drum.

FIGURE 15-23 This excessively worn (thin) rotor was removed from the vehicle in this condition. It is amazing that the vehicle was able to stop with such a thin rotor.

the rear where only 20% to 40% of the braking occurs. Solid rotors are much thinner than vented rotors. See Figure 15-23 for an example of an excessively worn solid rotor.

2. **Vented.** These are used on the front of most vehicles. The internal vanes allow air to circulate between the two friction surfaces of the rotor. Rotors can either be straight vane design, as shown in Figure 15-24, or directional vane design, as shown in Figure 15-25.

Composite rotors use a steel center section with a cast iron wear surface. These composite rotors are lighter in weight than conventional cast iron rotors. See Figure 15-26.

The light weight of composite rotors makes them popular with vehicle manufacturers. However, technicians should be aware that full-contact adapters that simulate the actual wheel being bolted to the rotor must be used when machining composite rotors. If composite rotors are machined incorrectly, they must usually be replaced.

FIGURE 15-24   Severely worn vented disc brake rotor. The braking surface has been entirely worn away exposing the cooling fins. The owner brought the vehicle to a repair shop because of a "little noise in the front." Notice the straight vane design.

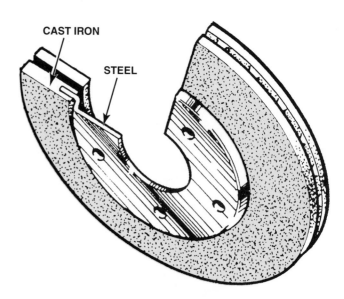

FIGURE 15-26   Typical composite rotor that uses cast iron friction surfaces and a steel center section.

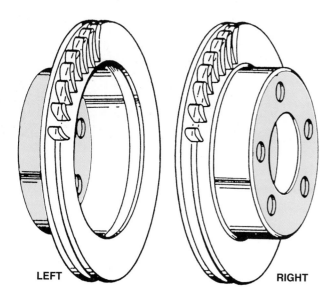

FIGURE 15-25   Directional vane vented disc brake rotors. Note that the fins angle toward the rear of the vehicle. It is important that this type of rotor be reinstalled on the correct side of the vehicle. *(Courtesy of Allied Signal Automotive Aftermarket)*

ALUMINUM METAL MATRIX COMPOSITE ROTORS

Some disc brake rotors are manufactured from an aluminum metal matrix composite alloy reinforced with 20% silicon carbide particulate. Aluminum composites combine the light weight and thermal conductivity of aluminum with the stiffness and wear resistance of a ceramic to create a disc brake rotor with excellent heat dissipation and service life.

These rotors can be distinguished from conventional cast iron rotors in several ways. At first glance the rotors are silver gray with a dark gray or black transfer layer (from the brake pad) on the rubbing surface. Unlike cast iron, these rotors will show no signs of rust and are nonmagnetic. When removed from the vehicle, the aluminum composite rotors can be further distinguished by their light weight, usually under 6 lb. (2.7 kg) versus over 12 lb. (5.4 kg) for cast iron rotors on the typical passenger vehicle. See Figure 15-27.

Servicing these rotors is slightly different from cast iron rotors. The dark transfer layer on the rubbing surface does not harm rotor performance and should not be removed unless the rotor needs to be machined due to being warped. *Aluminum composite disc brake rotors cannot be machined with steel cutting tools!* Carbide tools can be used to machine a single set of aluminum composite rotors. If a shop receives these rotors on a regular basis, a polycrystalline diamond (PCD), tipped tool is a good investment. Although more expensive initially, the PCD tool can last 100 times longer than a carbide tool.

Disc Brake Rotor Distortion

The friction surfaces of a rotor in perfect condition are perpendicular to the axle centerline, and have no side-to-side movement. Unlike brake drums, rotors do not suffer distortion as a routine part of brake operation. However, distortion can occur during braking if there is a problem with the friction assembly, such as a frozen caliper piston that creates unequal application force on the two sides of the rotor.

Friction surface distortion is much more significant in a disc brake rotor than in a brake drum because the design of the friction assembly magnifies the effect of any wear. The hydraulic principles dictate that small movements of the large

FIGURE 15-27   An aluminum metal matrix composite rear rotor for a Chrysler Plymouth Prowler. (Courtesy of Duralcan, USA)

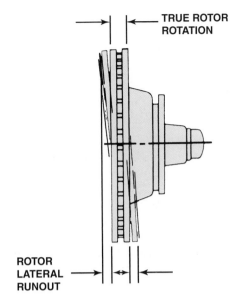

FIGURE 15-28   Brake rotor lateral-runout distortion.

pistons in the brake calipers are converted into large movements of the small pistons in the master cylinder. Even very small amounts of distortion in a disc brake rotor can cause large amounts of pedal pulsation.

Rotor Lateral Runout

Lateral runout, often abbreviated **LRO,** is side-to-side wobble of the rotor as it rotates on the spindle. See Figure 15-28. A small amount of runout provides caliper piston knockback that reduces drag when the brakes are not applied. However, if the

amount of runout is too great, excessive brake pedal travel and front-end vibration, felt in the steering wheel, will result. In cases of severe runout, a pulsating brake pedal may also be present.

Lateral runout can be caused by several factors. Overtightened or unevenly tightened lug nuts or bolts are a common source of runout on newer vehicles with downsized brake rotors. Extreme heat or rapid temperature variations also cause runout. Inaccurate machining at the factory or in the field is also a common cause of this distortion. Most maximum values range between .002 and .008 in. (0.05 and 0.20 mm). See Figures 15-29 and 15-30.

FIGURE 15-29   Before measuring lateral runout with a dial indicator (gauge), remove any wheel bearing end play by torquing the spindle nut to 10 to 20 ft-lb with a torque wrench. This step helps prevent an inaccurate reading. If the vehicle is to be returned to service, be sure to loosen the spindle nut and retighten to specifications (usually, finger tight) to restore proper bearing clearance.

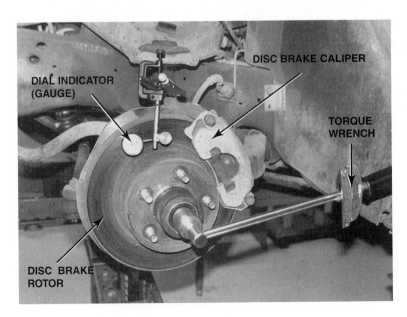

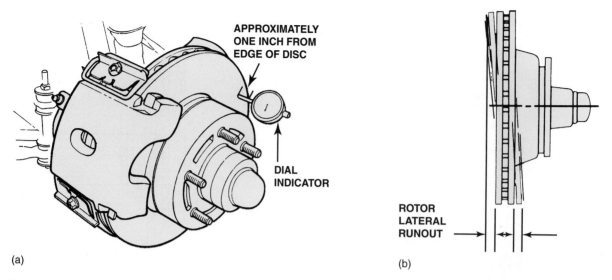

(a)

(b)

APPROXIMATELY
ONE INCH FROM
EDGE OF DISC

DIAL
INDICATOR

ROTOR
LATERAL
RUNOUT

FIGURE 15-30   (a) Rotate the disc brake rotor one complete revolution while observing the dial indicator (gauge). (b) Most vehicle manufacturers specify a maximum runout of about 0.003 in. (0.08 mm)   *((a) is Courtesy of DaimlerChrysler Corporation)*

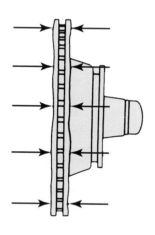

THICKNESS VARIATION
AT DIFFERENT POINTS
AROUND THE ROTOR

FIGURE 15-31   Brake rotor lack-of-parallelism distortion.

Rotor Lack of Parallelism

Lack of **parallelism,** also called **thickness variation (TV),** is a variation in the thickness of the rotor when it is measured at several places around its circumference. See Figure 15-31.

A rotor with friction surfaces that are not parallel is the most common disc brake cause of a pulsating brake pedal. A lack of rotor parallelism will cause a pedal pulsation when the brakes are applied at all speeds, and can also cause front-end vibration during braking. See Figure 15-32.

Lack of parallelism can be caused by a soft spot in the rotor casting that wears more rapidly than surrounding areas, but the most common cause is rust build-up on the rotor when

**TECH
TIP**

BRAKING VIBRATION COULD BE DUE TO THE TIRES

A vibrating condition (roughness) during braking is usually caused by disc brake rotor thickness variation or an out-of-round brake drum. Both conditions should be investigated. However, the tires and/or road conditions can also cause the same vibrations.

Tests performed by vehicle and tire-manufacturing engineers have shown that tires, and tires alone, could be the cause. If no other problem can be isolated, install a different brand of tire on the vehicle and retest. The cause of the tire vibration seems to be due to distortion or movement of the tire tread. A different brand of tires would have a different tread rubber compound, carcass body ply angles, or other factor that can contribute to a vibration during braking.

the vehicle is not driven for an extended period. The part of the friction surface protected by the brake pads does not rust as much as the rest of the rotor, and because the rusted areas wear faster, this results in a thickness variation when the vehicle is driven again.

Because parallelism variation is much more likely to cause a problem than lateral runout, the maximum amount allowed

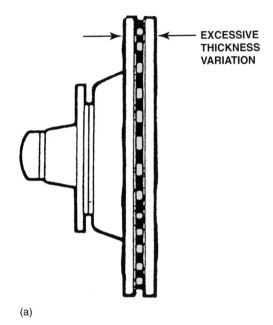

(a)

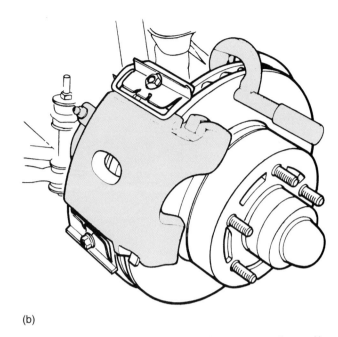

(b)

FIGURE 15-32   (a) Disc brake rotor thickness variation (parallelism). (b) The rotor should be measured with a micrometer at four or more equally spaced locations around the rotor. *(Courtesy of DaimlerChrysler Corporation)*

TECH TIP

THINK OF A HUMAN HAIR

Measurements and specifications do not seem to mean much unless you can visualize the size compared to something with which you are familiar. The diameter of a human hair is from 0.002 to 0.004 in. (2 to 4 thousandths of an inch).

The maximum lateral runout of a rotor is usually within this same dimension. The reason a dial indicator has to be used to measure runout, and a micrometer to measure parallelism, is that the dimensions involved are less than the diameter of a human hair. See Figure 15-33.

is much smaller than for runout. Most manufacturers specify that the two friction surfaces of a rotor must be parallel within half a thousandth of an inch, .0005 in. (0.013 mm), or less.

MINIMUM THICKNESS

Most rotors have a minimum thickness cast or stamped into the rotor. This thickness is minimum wear thickness. At least 0.015 in. (0.4 mm) must remain after machining to allow for wear. (Some vehicle manufacturers, such as General

Motors, specify that 0.030 in. [0.8 mm] be left for wear.) See Figure 15-34.

Whenever machining (resurfacing) a rotor, an equal amount of material must be removed from each side.

WHEN THE ROTORS SHOULD BE MACHINED

According to brake design engineers, a worn rotor has a very smooth friction surface that is ideal for replacement (new) disc brake pads. Often when the rotors are machined, the surface finish is not as smooth as specified. Therefore, a rotor should be machined only if one of the following conditions exists:

1. Deep grooves deeper than 0.060 in. (1.5 mm). This is the approximate thickness of a nickel! See Figure 15-35.
2. Thickness variation exceeding specifications and a brake pedal pulsation complaint.
3. Heavy rust that has corroded the friction surface of the rotor, as shown in Figure 15-36.

Therefore, if there is no complaint of a pulsating brake pedal during braking and the rotor is not deeply grooved or rusted, it should not be machined. New disc brake pads perform best against a smooth surface, and a used disc brake rotor is often smoother than a new rotor.

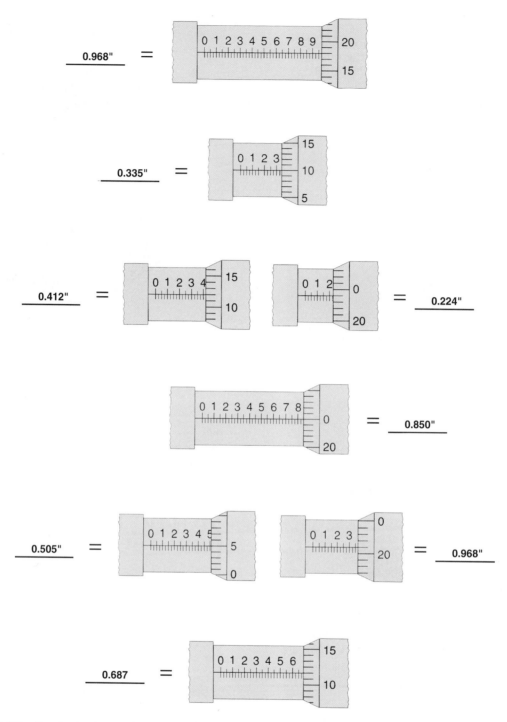

FIGURE 15-33   Sample micrometer readings. Each larger line on the barrel between the numbers represents 0.025″. The number on the thimble is then added to the number showing and the number of lines times 0.025″.

FIGURE 15-36   This rusted rotor should be machined.

FIGURE 15-37   The rotor on the left is shiny, indicating that non-metallic pads have been used, whereas the rotor on the right is brown, indicating that semimetallic pads have been used.

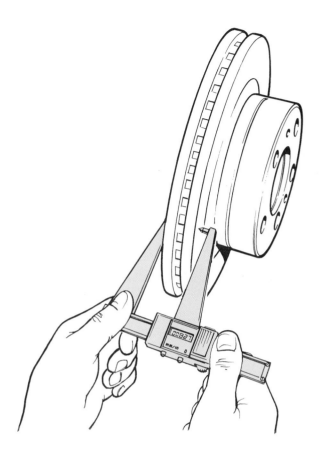

FIGURE 15-34   A digital readout rotor micrometer is an accurate tool to use when measuring a rotor. Both fractional inches and metric millimeters are generally available.

TECH TIP

BROWN = SEMIMETALLIC

Brake rotors that have used semimetallic brake pads during operation are brown on the friction surface. The reason for the brown color is the rust from the steel used in the manufacture of the pads. See Figure 15-37.

If the friction surface of the disc brake rotor is shiny, then organic (asbestos), nonasbestos organic (NAO), or nonasbestos synthetic (NAS) pads have been used on the rotor.

This information is helpful to know, especially if the vehicle being serviced is to be equipped with semimetallic pads as specified by the manufacturer and the rotors are shiny. In this case the incorrect lining may have been installed during a previous service. Friction surface color is a quick and easy way to determine whether or not semimetallic pads have been used.

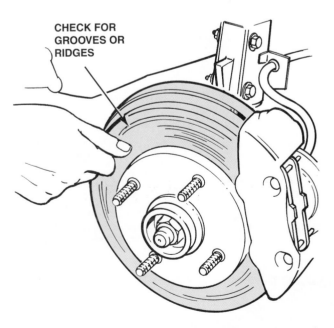

CHECK FOR GROOVES OR RIDGES

FIGURE 15-35   If a fingernail catches on a groove in the rotor, the rotor should be machined.

ROTOR FINISH

The smoothness of the rotor is called rotor finish or surface finish. Surface finish is measured in units called **microinches,** abbreviated **µin.,** where the symbol in front of "in." is the Greek lowercase letter µ (mu). One microinch equals 0.000001 in. (0.025 micrometer [mm]). The finish classification of microinch means the distance between the highest peaks and the deepest valley. The usual method of expressing surface finish is the arithmetic average roughness height, abbreviated **Ra,** which is the average of all peaks and valleys from the mean (average) line. This surface finish is measured using a machine with a diamond stylus, as shown in Figure 15-38.

Another classification of surface finish that is becoming obsolete is the **root mean square (RMS).** The RMS method gives a slightly higher number and can be obtained by multiplying Ra × 1.11 = RMS.

Often, a machined rotor will not be as smooth as a new rotor, resulting in a hard stopping complaint after new brakes have been installed. A rough rotor has less surface area touching the new brake pads, resulting in a hard brake pedal and reduced braking effectiveness. Most new rotors have a surface finish of 45 to 60 µin. Ra.

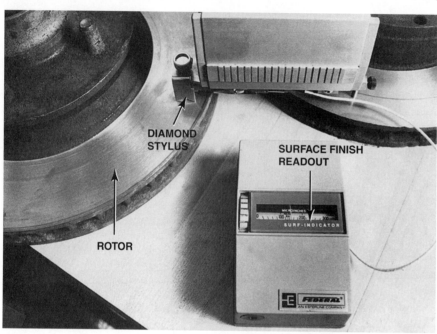

(a)

(b)

FIGURE 15-38 (a) Electronic surface finish machine. The reading shows about 140 µin. This is much too rough for use but is typical for a rough cut surface. (b) The stylus is moved over the surface by the machine and the readout gives the average of all the high and low ridges.

THE BALLPOINT PEN TEST

A smooth friction surface on a drum or rotor is necessary for proper brake operation. To quickly determine if the friction surface of a brake drum or rotor is not smooth enough, draw a ballpoint pen across the surface. If the surface is smooth enough, a solid ink line will be observed. If the line drawn by the pen is not solid, then the surface is not smooth enough.

POSITIVE RAKE VERSUS NEGATIVE RAKE BRAKE LATHES

Many lathes are capable of removing a large amount of material in one pass, thereby reducing the time necessary to refinish a drum or rotor. These lathes usually use a positive rake tool bit angle. See Figure 15-39.

Other lathes that use six-sided reversible tool bits usually use a negative rake tool bit angle. Ammco is an example of a negative rake lathe, whereas Perfect-Hofmann and Accu-turn are examples of positive rake lathes.

MACHINING A DISC BRAKE ROTOR

Before machining a rotor, be sure that it can be machined by comparing the minimum thickness specification and the measured thickness of the rotor.

CAUTION: Some original equipment and replacement disc brake rotors are close to the minimum allowable thickness when new. Often, these rotors cannot be safely machined at all!

Following is an example of the steps necessary to machine a disc brake rotor. Always follow the instructions for the equipment you are using.

Step 1   Mount the disc brake rotor to the spindle of the lathe using the cones and adapters recommended. See Figures 15-40 and 15-41 on page 281.

Step 2   Install a rotor damper and position the cutting tools close to the rotor surface as shown in Figure 15-42 on page 282.

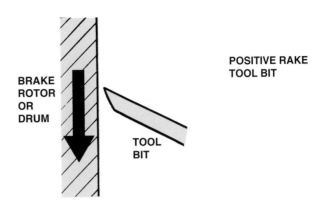

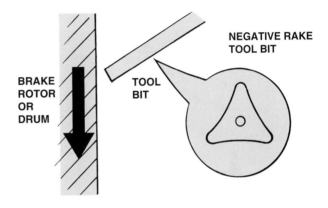

FIGURE 15-39   Most positive rake brake lathes can cut any depth in one pass, thereby saving time. A typical negative rake lathe uses a three-sided turning tool that can be flipped over, thereby giving six cutting edges.

NOTE: Failure to install the damper causes vibrations to occur during machining that create a rough surface finish.

Step 3   Make a scratch cut on the rotor face, as shown in Figure 15-43 on page 282.

Step 4   To check that the rotor is mounted correctly, loosen the retaining nut, turn the rotor one-half turn (180°), and retighten the nut. Make another scratch cut.

  a. The second scratch cut should be side-by-side with the first scratch cut if the rotor is properly installed, as shown in Figure 15-44 on page 282.

  b. If the second scratch cut is on the opposite side (180°) from the first scratch cut, the rotor may not be installed on the lathe correctly.

NOTE: The runout as measured with a dial indicator on the brake lathe should be the same as the runout measured on the vehicle. If the runout is not the same, the rotor is not installed on the brake lathe correctly.

TYPICAL ROTOR MOUNTING CONFIGURATIONS

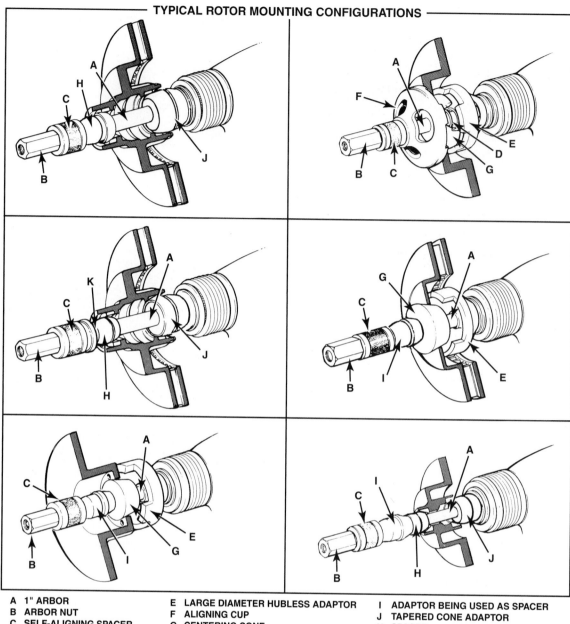

A 1" ARBOR	E LARGE DIAMETER HUBLESS ADAPTOR	I ADAPTOR BEING USED AS SPACER
B ARBOR NUT	F ALIGNING CUP	J TAPERED CONE ADAPTOR
C SELF-ALIGNING SPACER	G CENTERING CONE	K SPACER
D SPRING	H TAPERED CONE ADAPTOR	L SMALL DIAMETER HUBLESS ADAPTOR

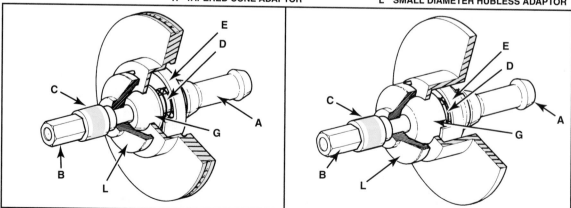

FIGURE 15-40   Recommended adapters and location for machining hubbed and hubless rotors.   *(Courtesy of Ammco Tools, Inc.)*

HUBLESS
ROTOR

(a)

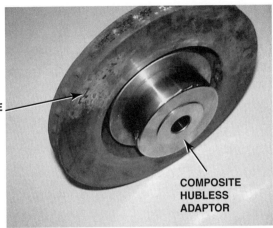

HUBLESS
DISC BRAKE
ROTOR

COMPOSITE
HUBLESS
ADAPTOR

(b)

SPINDLE
NUT

SELF-ALIGNING
SPACER

(c)

FIGURE 15-41   (a) Typical hubless adapters necessary to properly mount a composite rotor to a brake lathe. (b) Composite adapter fitted to a rotor. (c) Composite rotor properly mounted on a lathe.

After proper installation of the disc brake rotor on the brake lathe, proceed with machining the rotors. For best results do not machine any more material from the rotor than is absolutely necessary. Always follow the recommendations and guidelines as specified by the vehicle manufacturer.

ROUGH CUT

A rough cut on a lathe involves cutting 0.005 in. per side with a feed of 0.008 in. per revolution and 150 RPM spindle speed. This usually results in a very coarse surface finish of about 150 µin. Ra.

FINISH CUT

A finish cut means removing 0.002 in. per side with a feed of 0.002 in. per revolution and 150 RPM spindle speed. Although this cut usually looks smooth, the surface finish is about 90 to 100 µin. Ra. Even a typical finish cut is still not nearly as smooth as a new rotor.

NOTE: Measure the thickness of the rotor after the finish cut and compare with manufacturers' specifications. Be sure to allow for wear. See the chart in Figure 15-45 for a metric/fractional measurement chart.

Nondirectional Finish

Most vehicle and brake component manufacturers recommend a nondirectional finish to help prevent the grooves machined into the rotor from acting like record grooves that can force the pads to move outward while the rotor rotates.

CAUTION: Some nondirectional finish tools such as those that use Scotch Brite (a registered trademark) plastic pads often do not make the rotor as smooth as new, even though the finish has been swirled. See Figure 15-46.

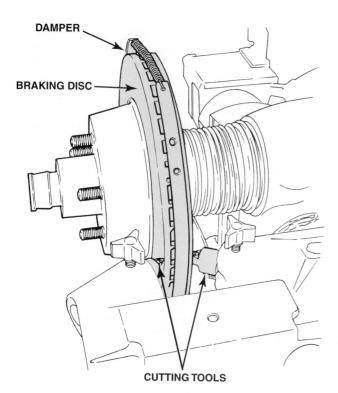

FIGURE 15-42   A damper is necessary to reduce cutting-tool vibrations that can cause a rough surface finish. *(Courtesy of DaimlerChrysler Corporation)*

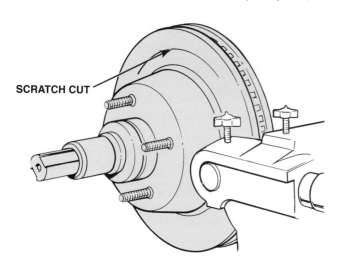

FIGURE 15-43   After installing the rotor on the brake lathe, turn the cutting tool in just enough to make a scratch cut.

Surface Finishing the Rotor

The goal of any brake repair or service should be to restore the braking effectiveness to match new vehicle brakes. This means that the rotor finish should be as smooth or smoother than a new rotor for maximum brake pad contact. Research conducted at Delphi has shown that like-new rotor finish can easily be accomplished by using a block and sandpaper. After completing the finish cut, place 150-grit aluminum oxide sandpaper on a block

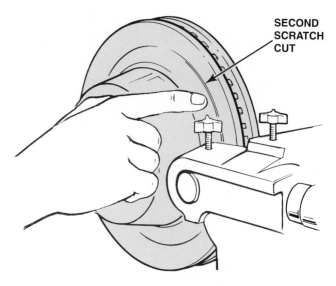

FIGURE 15-44   After making a scratch cut, loosen the retaining nut and rotate the rotor on the spindle of the lathe one-half turn. Tighten the nut and make a second scratch cut. The second scratch cut should be side-by-side with the first scratch if the rotor is installed correctly on the brake lathe.

and apply steady pressure against the rotor surface for 60 seconds on each side of the rotor. See Figure 15-47.

The aluminum oxide is hard enough to remove the highest ridges left by the lathe cutting tool. This results in a surface finish ranging from 20 to 80 µin. and usually less than 40 µin., which is smoother than a new rotor. See Figure 15-48 on page 284.

NOTE: Many commercial rotor-finish products may also give as smooth a surface finish. See Figures 15-49 and 15-50 on page 284. Always compare rotor finish to the rotor finish of a new rotor. Microinch finish is often hard to distinguish unless you have a new rotor with which to compare.

TECH TIP

TURN OR MACHINE?

When asked about what was done to their vehicle, a common response of customers is "They rotated my rotors." Many customers do not understand the terms that are commonly used in the vehicle service industry. Try to use terms that are technically correct and avoid slang when talking to customers. For example, the expression *machined the rotors* indicates an operation, whereas the expression *turned the rotors* may be misinterpreted by some customers as simply meaning using your hand and moving (rotating) the rotor. *Resurfacing, refinishing,* and *reconditioning* are other terms that could be used to describe a drum or rotor machining operation.

Inch	Decimal Inch	Millimeter
1/64	0.015625	0.396785
1/32	0.03125	0.79375
3/64	0.046875	1.190625
1/16	0.0625	1.5875
5/64	0.078125	1.984375
3/32	0.09375	2.38125
7/64	0.109375	2.778125
1/8	0.125	3.175
9/64	0.140625	3.571875
5/32	0.15625	3.96875
11/64	0.171875	4.365625
3/16	0.1875	4.7625
13/64	0.203125	5.159375
7/32	0.21875	5.55625
15/64	0.234375	5.953125
1/4	0.25	6.35001
17/64	0.265625	6.746875
9/32	0.28125	7.14375
19/64	0.296875	7.540625
5/16	0.3125	7.9375
21/64	0.328125	8.334375
11/32	0.34375	8.73125
23/64	0.359375	9.128125
3/8	0.375	9.525
25/64	0.390625	9.921875
13/32	0.40625	10.31875
27/64	0.421875	10.715625
7/16	0.4375	11.1125
29/64	0.453125	11.509375
15/32	0.46875	11.90625
31/64	0.484375	12.303125
1/2	0.50	12.7
33/64	0.515625	13.096875
17/32	0.53125	13.49375
35/64	0.546875	13.890625
9/16	0.5625	14.2875
37/64	0.578125	14.684375
19/32	0.59375	15.08125
39/64	0.609375	15.478125
5/8	0.625	15.875
41/64	0.640625	16.271875
21/32	0.65625	16.66875
43/64	0.671875	17.065625
11/16	0.6875	17.4625
45/64	0.703125	17.859375
23/32	0.71875	18.25625
47/64	0.734375	18.653125
3/4	0.75	19.05
49/64	0.765625	19.446875
25/32	0.78125	19.84375
51/64	0.796875	20.240625
13/16	0.8125	20.6375
53/64	0.828125	21.034375
27/32	0.84375	21.43125
55/64	0.859375	21.828125
7/8	0.875	22.225
57/64	0.890625	22.621875
29/32	0.90625	23.01875
59/64	0.921875	23.415625
15/16	0.9375	23.8125
61/64	0.953125	24.209375
31/32	0.96875	24.60625
63/64	0.984375	25.003125
1	1.00000	25.4

FIGURE 15-45   Metric/fractional chart.

FIGURE 15-46   A proper sanding disc for removing material and providing the proper surface finish.

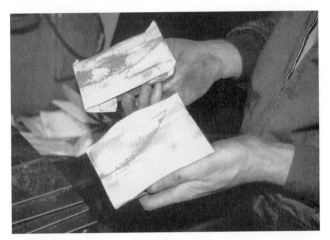

(a)

(b)

FIGURE 15-47   (a) This technician uses two sanding blocks each equipped with 150-grit aluminum-oxide sandpaper. (b) With the lathe turned on, the technician presses the two sanding blocks against the surface of the rotor after the rotor has been machined, to achieve a smooth microinch surface finish.

(a)

(b)

FIGURE 15-48   (a) After machining and sanding the rotor, it should be cleaned. In this case brake cleaner from an air pressurized spray can is used. (b) With the lathe turning, the technician stands back away from the rotor and sprays both sides of the rotor to clean it of any remaining grit from the sanding process. This last step ensures a clean, smooth surface for the disc brake pads and a quality brake repair. Sanding each side of the rotor surface for one minute using a sanding block and 150-grit aluminum-oxide sandpaper after a finish cut gives the rotor the proper smoothness and finish.

ON-THE-VEHICLE ROTOR MACHINING

Many vehicle manufacturers recommend on-the-vehicle machining for rotors if the disc brake rotor must be machined due to deep scoring or pulsating brake pedal complaint. This is especially true of composite rotors or for vehicles such as many Honda vehicles that require major disassembly to remove the rotors.

Caliper mount, on-the-vehicle lathes require that the disc brake caliper be removed. The cutter attaches to the steering knuckle or caliper support in the same location as the caliper. See Figure 15-51.

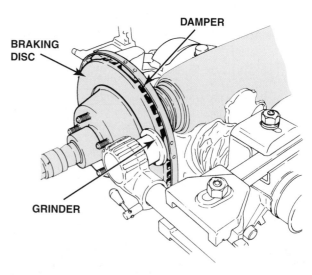

FIGURE 15-49   A grinder with sandpaper can be used to give a smooth nondirectional surface finish to the disc brake rotor. *(Courtesy of DaimlerChrysler Corporation)*

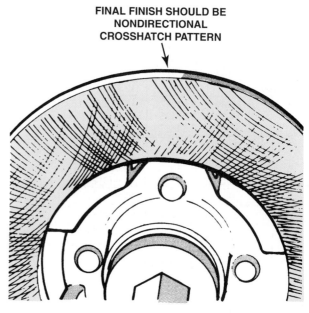

FIGURE 15-50   The correct final surface finish should be smooth and nondirectional. *(Courtesy of DaimlerChrysler Corporation)*

Hub mount, on-the-vehicle lathes attach to the hub using the lug nuts of the vehicle. To achieve a proper cut, the hub mount must be calibrated for any runout caused by the hub bearings and the outside surface face of the rotor. See Figures 15-52 and 15-53.

NOTE: All on-the-vehicle lathes require that the wheel be removed. For best results always use a torque wrench when tightening lug nuts or lathe adapters. Unequal torque on the bolts causes stress and distortion that can cause warped rotors and a pulsating brake pedal.

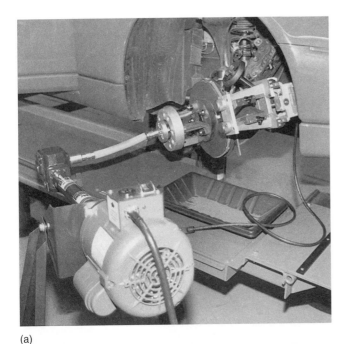

(a)

(b)

(c)

FIGURE 15-51 (a) Typical on-the-vehicle disc brake rotor lathe. (b) This lathe mounts to the steering knuckle in the same location as the caliper and is called a caliper mount lathe. (c) Close-up of the machining operation from below.

FIGURE 15-52 Rust should always be cleaned from both the rotor and the hub whenever the rotors are machined or replaced. An air-powered die grinder with a sanding disc makes quick work of cleaning this hub.

WHAT DOES "CROSS-DRILLED" AND "SLOTTED" MEAN?

The expression "cross-drilled" and "slotted" refers to two separate processes. The first procedure involves drilling rows of holes through the friction surfaces of the rotor. The second procedure refers to milling a series of specially machined grooves from the center of the disc toward the edge. When the friction surfaces of a rotor are smooth and flat, there is no means of escape for the gases and dust, which build up between pad and rotor. This is not a huge problem in normal driving, but is an important consideration in street performance applications.

The drill holes (which are sometimes called "gas relief openings") provide an exit route for the dust and gas. The holes are also commonly labeled "cooling holes" because of the improvements they make in this area. Better cooling means less fade during repeated heavy brake application. They also help dissipate water when driving in poor weather. See Figure 15-54.

Slotting increases the bite of the pads and is even more effective than cross-drilling in combating the problem known as "out-gassing." This is when, at very high braking temperatures, the bonding agents used in some brake pads produce a gas. Under extreme conditions, this gas can create a gas cushion between pad and rotor, giving a driver a normal pedal feel but reducing the amount of friction being generated. The slots pump away gas and restore full contact. The "microshaving" effect of the slots also serves to deglaze the pads and this is why the edges of the slots are not chamfered or "radiused." It also tends to even out the wear across the brake pad faces, increasing the effective contact area.

FIGURE 15-53   A typical hub-mount on-the-vechicle lathe. This particular lathe oscillates while machining the rotor, thereby providing a smooth and nondirectional finish at the same time.

FIGURE 15-54   A corvette equipped with high-performance brakes including cross-drilled brake rotors.

DRUM MACHINING Step-by-Step

STEP 1 Before starting to machine a brake drum, check the drum for any obvious damage such as heat cracks or hard spots.

STEP 2 Lightly tap the drum. It should ring like a bell. If a dull thud is heard, the drum may be cracked and should be discarded.

STEP 3 Use a drum micrometer to measure the inside diameter of the drum and compare this measurement to specifications to be sure that the drum can be safely machined.

STEP 4 Most brake drums have the maximum inside diameter cast into the drum as shown.

STEP 5 Thoroughly clean the outside and inside of the drum.

STEP 6 Be sure the center hole in the drum is clean and free from any burrs that could prevent the drum from being properly centered on the shaft of the brake lathe.

(continued)

DRUM MACHINING continued

STEP 7 A typical brake lathe used to machine drums.

STEP 8 Locate a tapered, centering cone that best fits inside the hole of the brake drum.

STEP 9 Slide the large face plate over the shaft of the brake lathe.

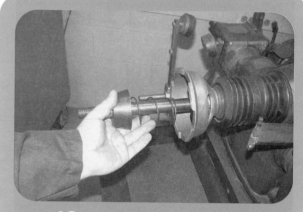

STEP 10 Slide the tapered centering cone onto the shaft with the spring between the face plate and the centering cone.

STEP 11 Slide the other face plate onto the shaft.

STEP 12 Install the self-aligning spacer (SAS) and left-hand-thread spindle nut.

DRUM MACHINING continued

STEP 13 Tighten the spindle nut.

STEP 14 Loosen the turning bar retainer.

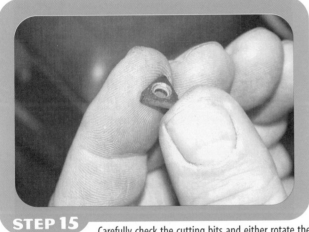

STEP 15 Carefully check the cutting bits and either rotate the bit to a new cutting point or replace it with a new part as necessary.

STEP 16 Turn the spindle control knob until the spindle is as short as possible (i.e., the drum as close to the machine as possible) to help reduce vibration as much as possible.

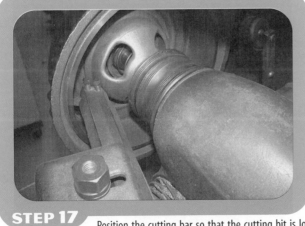

STEP 17 Position the cutting bar so that the cutting bit is located at the back surface of the drum.

STEP 18 Install the silencer band (vibration dampener strap).

(continued)

DRUM MACHINING continued

STEP 19 Be sure the tool bit and clothing are away from the drum and turn the brake lathe on.

STEP 20 Center the bit in the center of the brake surface of the drum and slowly rotate the control knob that moves the bit into contact with the drum friction surface. This should produce a light scratch cut. This step checks the setup for accuracy.

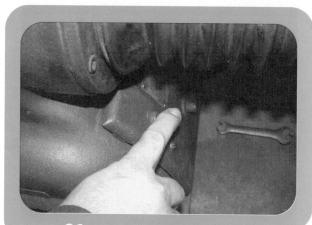

STEP 21 Turn the lathe off.

STEP 22 Observe the scratch cut.

STEP 23 Loosen the spindle nut.

STEP 24 Rotate the drum 180° (one-half turn) on the spindle.

DRUM MACHINING continued

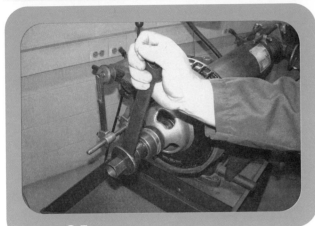

STEP 25 Tighten the spindle nut.

STEP 26 Turn the lathe on, rotate the control knob, and run the cutter into the drum for another scratch cut.

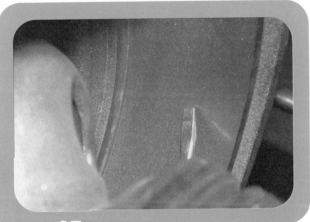

STEP 27 Observe the scratch cut. If the second scratch cut is in the same place as the first scratch cut or extends all the way around the drum, the drum is correctly mounted on the lathe and machining can continue.

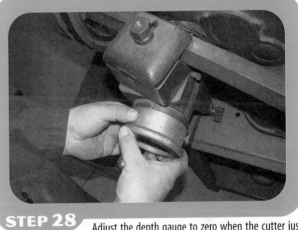

STEP 28 Adjust the depth gauge to zero when the cutter just touches the drum.

STEP 29 Run the cutter all the way to the back surface of the drum.

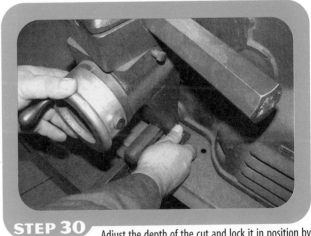

STEP 30 Adjust the depth of the cut and lock it in position by turning the lock knob. Most vehicle manufacturers recommend a rough cut depth should be 0.005–0.010 in. and a finish cut of 0.002 in.

(continued)

DRUM MACHINING continued

STEP 31 Select a fast-feed rate if performing a rough cut (0.006–0.016 in. per revolution) or 0.002 in. per revolution for a finish cut.

STEP 32 Turn the lock knob to keep the feed adjustment from changing.

STEP 33 Engage the automatic feed.

STEP 34 The drum will automatically move as the tool be remains stationary to make the cut.

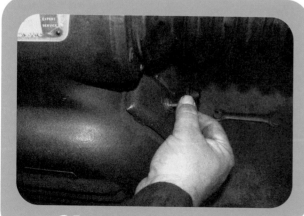

STEP 35 Turn the lathe off.

STEP 36 Observe the machined surface. If the feed rate was low and the surface is smooth on all portions of the friction surface, the drum can be removed. If additional material must be removed, proceed with the finish cut. Clean thoroughly before installing on a vehicle.

ROTOR MACHINING Step-by-Step

STEP 1 Before machining any rotor, use a micrometer and measure the thickness of the rotor.

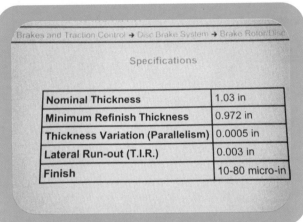

Brakes and Traction Control → Disc Brake System → Brake Rotor/Disc

Specifications

Nominal Thickness	1.03 in
Minimum Refinish Thickness	0.972 in
Thickness Variation (Parallelism)	0.0005 in
Lateral Run-out (T.I.R.)	0.003 in
Finish	10-80 micro-in

STEP 2 Check the specifications for the minimum allowable thickness.

STEP 3 Visually check the rotor for evidence of heat cracks or hard spots that would require replacement (rather than machining) of the rotor.

STEP 4 After removing the grease seal and bearings, remove the grease from the bearing races.

STEP 5 Clean and inspect the brake lathe spindle for damage or burrs that could affect its accuracy.

STEP 6 Select a tapered cone adapter that fits the inner bearing race.

(continued)

ROTOR MACHINING continued

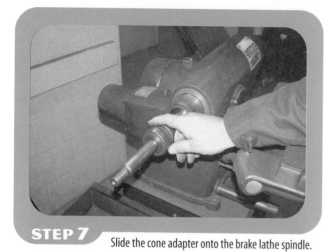

STEP 7 Slide the cone adapter onto the brake lathe spindle.

STEP 8 Select the proper size tapered cone adapter for the smaller outer wheel bearing race.

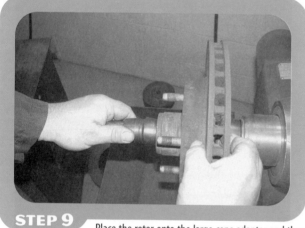

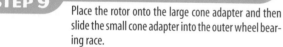

STEP 9 Place the rotor onto the large cone adapter and then slide the small cone adapter into the outer wheel bearing race.

STEP 10 Install the self-aligning spacer (SAS) and spindle nut.

STEP 11 Tighten the spindle nut (usually left-hand threads).

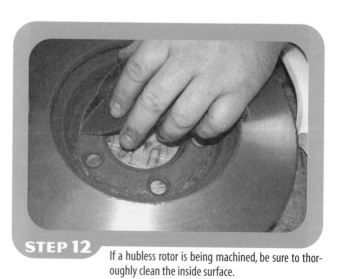

STEP 12 If a hubless rotor is being machined, be sure to thoroughly clean the inside surface.

ROTOR MACHINING   continued

STEP 13 Also remove all rust from the other side of the hubless rotor.

STEP 14 Select the proper centering cone for the hole in the center of the hub.

STEP 15 Select the proper size cone-shaped hubless adapter and the tapered centering cone with a spring in between.

STEP 16 After sliding the rotor over the centering cone, install the matching hubless adapter.

STEP 17 Install the self-aligning spacer (SAS) and spindle nut.

STEP 18 After the rotor has been secured to the brake lathe spindle, install the noise silencer band (dampener).

(continued)

ROTOR MACHINING continued

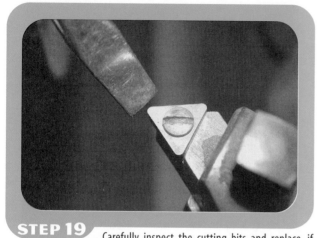

STEP 19 Carefully inspect the cutting bits and replace, if necessary.

STEP 20 Loosen the tool holder arm.

STEP 21 Adjust the twin cutter arm until the rotor is centered between the two cutting bits.

STEP 22 Turn the lathe on.

STEP 23 Move the cutter arm toward the center of the rotor, placing the cutting bits in about the center of the friction surface.

STEP 24 Turn one cutting bit into the surface of the rotor to make a scratch cut. This step checks the lathe setup for accuracy.

ROTOR MACHINING continued

STEP 25 Turn the lathe off.

STEP 26 Observe the first scratch cut.

STEP 27 Loosen the spindle retaining nut.

STEP 28 Rotate the rotor 180° (one-half turn) on the spindle of the brake lathe.

STEP 29 Tighten the spindle nut.

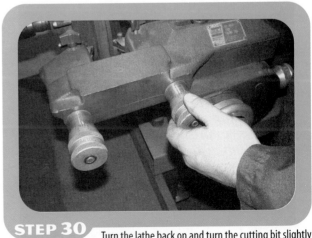

STEP 30 Turn the lathe back on and turn the cutting bit slightly into the rotor until a second scratch cut is made.

(continued)

ROTOR MACHINING continued

STEP 31 If the second scratch cut is in the same location as the first scratch cut or extends all around the surface of the rotor, then the rotor is properly installed on the lathe.

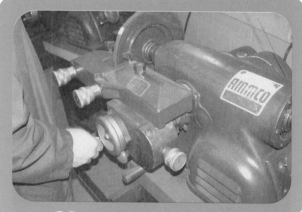

STEP 32 Start the machining process by moving the twin cutters to about the center of the rotor friction surface.

STEP 33 Turn the cutting bits inward until they touch the rotor and zero the depth adjustment.

STEP 34 Adjust the twin cutters, then dial in the amount of depth (0.005–0.010 in. per side for a rough cut or 0.002 in. for a finish cut) and lock the adjustment so that vibration will not change the setting.

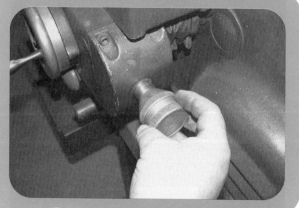

STEP 35 Turn the feed control knob until the desired feed rate is achieved for the first or rough cut (0.006–0.010 in. per revolution) or finish cut (0.002 in. per revolution).

STEP 36 Engage the automatic feed.

ROTOR MACHINING continued

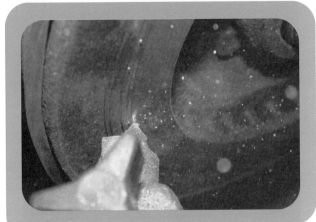

STEP 37 Observe the machining operation.

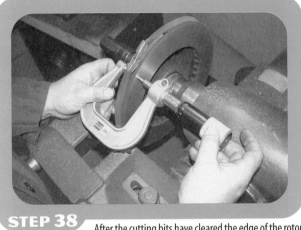

STEP 38 After the cutting bits have cleared the edge of the rotor, turn the lathe off and measure the thickness of the rotor.

STEP 39 Readjust the feed control to a slow rate (0.002 in. per revolution or less) for the finish cut.

STEP 40 Reposition the cutting bits for the finish cut.

STEP 41 Loosen the adjustment locks.

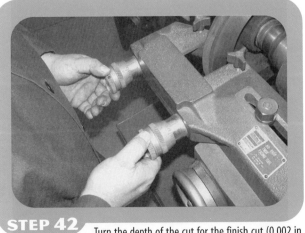

STEP 42 Turn the depth of the cut for the finish cut (0.002 in. maximum).

(continued)

ROTOR MACHINING continued

STEP 43 Lock the adjustment.

STEP 44 Engage the automatic feed.

STEP 45 After the last machining operation, use 150-grit aluminium-oxide sandpaper on a block of wood for 60 seconds per side or a grinder to give a nondirectional and smooth surface to both sides of the rotor.

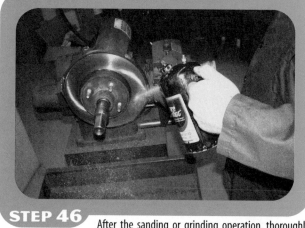

STEP 46 After the sanding or grinding operation, thoroughly clean the machined surface of the rotor to remove any and all particles of grit that could affect the operation and life of the disc brake pads.

STEP 47 Remove the silencer band.

STEP 48 Loosen the spindle retaining nut and remove the rotor.

ON-THE-VEHICLE LATHE Step-by-Step

STEP 1 Prepare to machine a disc brake rotor using an on-the-vehicle lathe by properly positioning the vehicle in the stall and hoisting the vehicle to a good working height.

STEP 2 Remove the wheels and place them out of the way.

STEP 3 Remove the disc brake caliper and use a wire to support the caliper out of the way of the rotor.

STEP 4 Measure the rotor thickness and compare it with factory specifications before machining. If a discard thickness is specified, be sure to allow an additional 0.015 in. for wear.

STEP 5 Install the hub adapter onto the hub and secure it using the wheel lug nuts.

STEP 6 Engage the drive unit by aligning the hole in the drive plate with the raised button on the adapter.

(continued)

ON-THE-VEHICLE LATHE continued

STEP 7 Use the thumb wheel to tighten the drive unit to the adapter.

STEP 8 Attach a dial indicator to a secure part on the vehicle and position the dial indicator on a flat portion of the lathe to measure the lathe runout.

STEP 9 Rotate the wheel or turn the lathe motor on and measure the amount of runout.

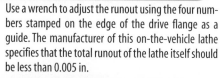

STEP 10 Use a wrench to adjust the runout using the four numbers stamped on the edge of the drive flange as a guide. The manufacturer of this on-the-vehicle lathe specifies that the total runout of the lathe itself should be less than 0.005 in.

STEP 11 After the hub runout is adjusted to 0.005 in. or less, remove the dial indicator from the vehicle.

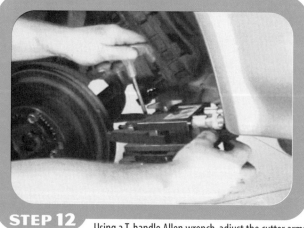

STEP 12 Using a T-handle Allen wrench, adjust the cutter arms until they are centered on the disc brake rotor.

ON-THE-VEHICLE LATHE continued

STEP 13 Move the cutters to the center of the rotor.

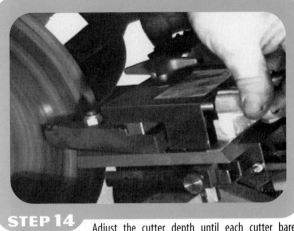

STEP 14 Adjust the cutter depth until each cutter barely touches the rotor.

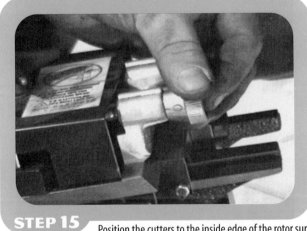

STEP 15 Position the cutters to the inside edge of the rotor surface and adjust the cutters to the desired depth of cut.

STEP 16 Adjust the automatic shut-off so the lathe will turn itself off at the end of the cut.

STEP 17 Turn the lathe on by depressing the start button.

STEP 18 Monitor the machining operations as the lathe automatically moves the cutters from the center toward the outside edge of the rotor.

(continued)

ON-THE-VEHICLE LATHE   continued

STEP 19   After the lathe reaches the outside edge of the rotor, the drive motor should stop.

STEP 20   Measure the thickness of the rotor after machining to be certain that the rotor thickness is within service limits.

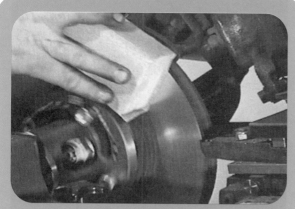

STEP 21   While this brand of on-the-vehicle lathe produces a nondirectional surface finish to the rotor, the technician is using 150-grit aluminium-oxide sandpaper and a wood block for 60 seconds on each side of the rotor to provide a smooth surface finish.

STEP 22   After completing the machining and resurfacing of the rotor unclamp the drive unit from the hub adapter and clean the rotor.

STEP 23   After the drive unit has been removed, remove the lug nuts holding the adapter to the rotor hub.

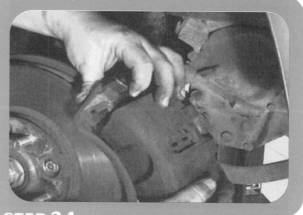

STEP 24   After removing the hub adapter, the caliper can be reinstalled.

ON-THE-VEHICLE LATHE continued

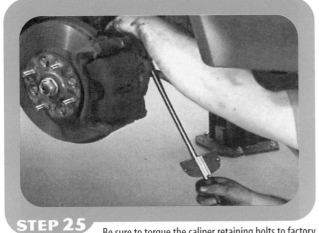

STEP 25 Be sure to torque the caliper retaining bolts to factory specifications.

STEP 26 Install the wheel and wheel cover. On this vehicle, the wheel cover must be installed before the lug nuts because the lug nuts hold the wheel cover on the wheel.

STEP 27 Always use a torque wrench or a torque-limiting adapter with an air impact wrench as shown here when tightening lug nuts.

STEP 28 Be sure to clean the wheel covers of any grease or fingerprints before returning the vehicle to the customer.

STEP 29 Pump the brake pedal several times to restore proper brake pedal height. Check and add brake fluid as necessary before moving the vehicle.

STEP 30 Carefully back out of the stall and test drive the vehicle to be assured of proper brake operation before returning the vehicle to the customer.

SUMMARY

1. Brake drums and rotors must absorb the heat generated by the friction of slowing and stopping a vehicle.
2. All rotors should be marked before removing them from the vehicle to assure that they will be reinstalled in the same position and on the same side of the vehicle.
3. All brake drums should be machined only enough to restore proper braking action. Brake drums should be the same size on the same axle to help prevent unequal braking.
4. Disc brake rotors should be machined and allow up to 0.030 in. (0.8 mm) for wear.
5. To assure proper braking, all rotors should be machined to a very smooth surface of less than 60 μin. finish.

REVIEW QUESTIONS

1. Explain the difference between "machine to" specifications and "discard."
2. List the steps for machining a brake drum.
3. Describe how to measure a disc brake rotor for lateral runout and thickness variation.
4. List the steps for machining a disc brake rotor.
5. Describe what is necessary to achieve "like new" disc brake rotor finish.

CHAPTER QUIZ

1. Technician A says that aluminum brake drums use cast iron friction surfaces. Technician B says that up to 0.030 in. (0.8 mm) should be left after machining a drum to allow for wear. Which technician is correct?
   a. Technician A only
   b. Technician B only
   c. Both Technicians A and B
   d. Neither Technician A nor B

2. Technician A says that hard spots in a brake drum should be removed using a carbide-tip machining tool. Technician B says that the drum should be replaced if hard spots are discovered. Which technician is correct?
   a. Technician A only
   b. Technician B only
   c. Both Technicians A and B
   d. Neither Technician A nor B

3. Technician A says that brake drums on the same axle should be close to the same inside diameter for best brake balance. Technician B says that a brake drum may be cracked if it rings like a bell when tapped with a light steel hammer. Which technician is correct?
   a. Technician A only
   b. Technician B only

   c. Both Technicians A and B
   d. Neither Technician A nor B

4. A hubless brake drum cannot be machined because it cannot be held in a lathe.
   a. True
   b. False

5. The major reason for brake pedal pulsation during braking is due to excessive rotor thickness variation.
   a. True
   b. False

6. Rotor finish is measured in _____.
   a. Millimeters
   b. Inches
   c. Microinches
   d. Centimeters

7. The lower the Ra of a rotor, the _____ the surface.
   a. Smoother
   b. Rougher
   c. Higher
   d. Lower

8. A disc brake rotor is being installed on a lathe for machining. During the setup a scratch test is performed. The scratch extended all the way around the rotor. Technician A says that the rotor should be loosened, rotated 180°, and retightened. Technician B says that the rotor is not warped. Which technician is correct?

   a. Technician A only

   b. Technician B only

   c. Both Technicians A and B

   d. Neither Technician A nor B

9. Typical maximum rotor runout specifications are _____.

   a. 0.0003 to 0.0005 in. (0.008 to 0.013 mm)

   b. 0.003 to 0.005 in. (0.08 to 0.13 mm)

   c. 0.030 to 0.050 in. (0.8 to 1.3 mm)

   d. 0.300 to 0.500 in. (8.0 to 13 mm)

10. Typical maximum rotor thickness variation (parallelism) specifications are _____.

   a. 0.0003 to 0.0005 in. (0.008 to 0.013 mm)

   b. 0.003 to 0.005 in. (0.08 to 0.13 mm)

   c. 0.030 to 0.050 in (0.8 to 1.3 mm)

   d. 0.300 to 0.500 in. (8.0 to 13 mm)

POWER BRAKE UNIT OPERATION, DIAGNOSIS, AND SERVICE

OBJECTIVES

After studying Chapter 16, the reader should be able to:

1. Prepare for the Brakes (A5) ASE certification test content area "D" (Power Assist Units Diagnosis and Repair).
2. List the parts of a vacuum brake booster.

3. Describe how a vacuum brake booster operates.
4. Explain how to test a vacuum brake booster.
5. Describe how a hydraulic or electrohydraulic brake booster operates.

KEY TERMS

Atmospheric pressure (p. 310)
Brake assist system (BAS) (p. 316)
Dual-diaphragm vacuum booster (p. 316)
inches of mercury (in. Hg) (p. 310)
millimeters of mercury (mm Hg) (p. 310)

Power chamber (p. 311)
Pressure differential (p. 309)
Tandem-diaphragm vacuum booster (p. 316)
Vacuum (p. 310)

THE NEED FOR POWER BRAKE ASSIST

To double the stopping power of a disc brake, the driver must double the force on the brake pedal. This is the reason that most vehicles equipped with disc brakes are power assisted, even on small, lightweight vehicles. The use of semimetallic brake pads also requires greater force. The most commonly used power-assisted units are vacuum operated.

When a power booster is fitted, the brake pedal ratio is decreased and the master cylinder bore size is increased. The combined effect of these changes is to reduce pedal effort, while greatly increasing pedal reserve. See Figure 16-1.

Power boosters do not alter the hydraulic system and they still allow braking even if the booster fails or its power supply is cut off. All boosters have a power reserve that provides assist for at least one hard stop, and sometimes several light brake applications, even after power is lost. However, because power brake systems are designed with the added force of the booster taken into account, the amount of brake pedal pressure required to slow or stop a vehicle is much higher than in a nonboosted system once the reserve is used up. For this reason, some vehicles with power brakes have a brake pedal that is wide enough to allow two-foot braking should the booster fail. See Figure 16-2.

PRINCIPLES OF VACUUM

Most vacuum-powered brake boosters get their vacuum supply from the engine intake manifold. An engine is essentially a big air pump because the pistons move up and down in the

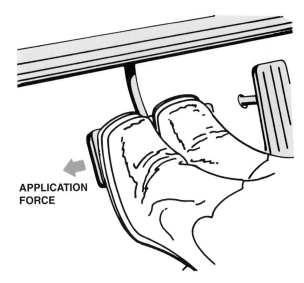

APPLICATION FORCE

FIGURE 16-2   A wide brake pedal allows two-foot braking if power assist is lost.

cylinders to pump in air and fuel, and pump out exhaust. They do this by creating differences in air pressure.

As a piston moves downward on an intake stroke with the intake valve open, it creates a larger area inside the cylinder for air to fill. This lowers the air pressure within the cylinder, and the higher-pressure air outside the engine flows in through the intake manifold in an attempt to fill the low-pressure area. Although it may seem as though the low pressure is pulling air into the engine, it is really the higher pressure outside that forces air in. The difference in pressure between two areas is called a **pressure differential.**

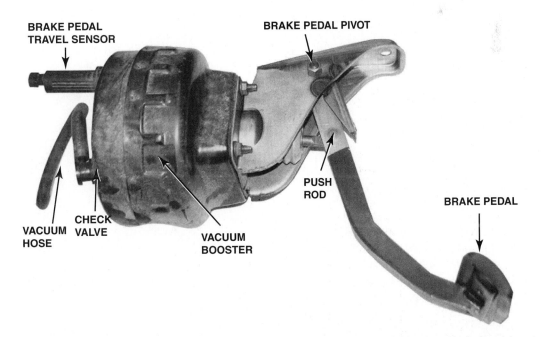

BRAKE PEDAL TRAVEL SENSOR

BRAKE PEDAL PIVOT

PUSH ROD

BRAKE PEDAL

VACUUM HOSE

CHECK VALVE

VACUUM BOOSTER

FIGURE 16-1   Typical vacuum brake booster assembly. The vacuum hose attaches to the intake manifold of the engine. The brake pedal travel sensor is an input sensor for the antilock braking system.

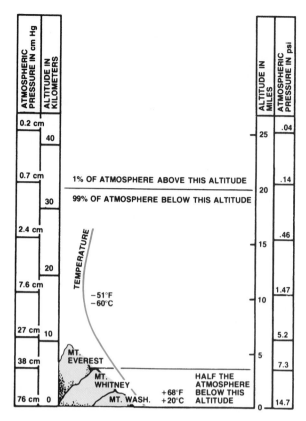

FIGURE 16-3 Atmospheric pressure varies with altitude.

varies with throttle position. The lowest manifold vacuum (highest pressure) occurs when the throttle is wide open with the engine under load. The highest manifold vacuum (lowest pressure) may be as much as 24 in. Hg (610 mm Hg) when the vehicle is rolling rapidly downhill in gear with the throttle closed. Manifold vacuum at idle typically falls between 15 and 20 in. Hg (381 and 508 mm Hg), and most vacuum brake boosters are designed to operate with vacuum levels in this range.

Booster Vacuum Supply

Vacuum boosters get their vacuum supply from the engine intake manifold. Diesel engines, however, run unthrottled (engine speed is controlled strictly by the amount of fuel injected) and have little or no intake manifold vacuum. If a vehicle with a diesel engine is equipped with a vacuum-powered brake booster, it must also be fitted with an auxiliary vacuum pump.

Some small gasoline-powered and diesel engines use a belt-driven add-on pump. See Figure 16-4.

An electrically powered vacuum pump is turned on and off by a pressure switch on the booster. This means they operate only when needed, and thus reduce power drain on the engine. See Figure 16-5.

Because throttle valves and manifold shape restrict intake airflow, high pressure air from outside the engine is almost never able to move into the cylinders fast enough to fill the space created. As a result, gasoline-powered internal-combustion engines normally operate with a low-pressure area, or partial vacuum, in the intake manifold. The term *vacuum* is used to refer to any pressure lower than **atmospheric pressure.** Atmospheric pressure varies with altitude, but is approximately 14.7 pounds per square inch (psi) at sea level. See Figure 16-3.

Measuring Vacuum

Vacuum is measured in **inches of mercury (in. Hg)** or in **millimeters of mercury (mm Hg),** a figure that indicates how far a column of mercury in a tube will rise when a vacuum is applied at one end, and atmospheric pressure at the other. Vacuum is a measurement of the pressure differential between the lower pressure inside the tube, and the higher pressure outside it.

A perfect vacuum is about 30 in. Hg (762 mm Hg). However, a perfect vacuum occurs only in space, and is never achieved in an engine's intake manifold. Manifold vacuum

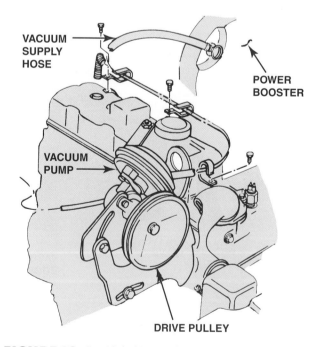

FIGURE 16-4 A belt-driven auxiliary vacuum pump.

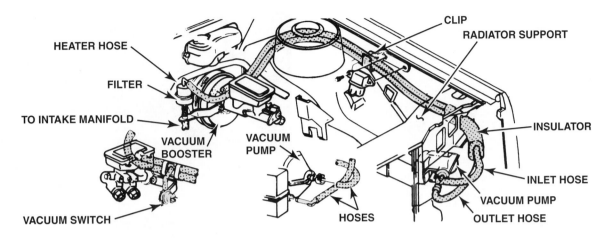

FIGURE 16-5   An electrically powered vacuum pump.

VACUUM BOOSTER THEORY

Vacuum boosters use the principle of pressure differential to increase brake application force. The typical vacuum booster has a **power chamber** separated into two smaller chambers by a flexible diaphragm. When air pressure is greater on one side of the diaphragm than the other, a pressure differential is created. In an attempt to equalize pressure in the two chambers, the higher pressure exerts a force that moves the diaphragm toward the lower pressure area. Rods attached to the diaphragm transmit this force, plus the force the driver exerts on the brake pedal, to the master cylinder.

The amount of force created in this manner is proportional to the difference in pressure between the two sides. In other words, the greater the pressure differential, the greater the force. To calculate the force, the pressure differential is multiplied by the diaphragm surface area. For example, if a power booster diaphragm has atmospheric pressure (14.7 psi) on one side, and a typical intake manifold vacuum of 20 in. Hg (10 psi of absolute pressure), the pressure differential acting on the diaphragm would be as follows:

$$14.7 \text{ psi} - 10 \text{ psi} = 4.7 \text{ psi}$$

If we once again multiply this times the area of the diaphragm, the result is as follows:

$$4.7 \text{ psi} \times 50 \text{ sq. in.} = 235 \text{ pounds of force}$$

Vacuum booster diaphragms are sized to fit specific applications and provide the necessary application force. Most vacuum boosters are capable of providing hundreds of pounds of application force. See Figure 16-6.

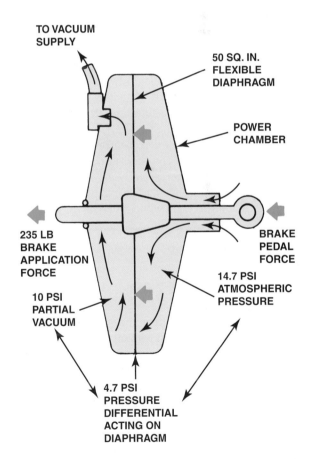

FIGURE 16-6   Vacuum brake boosters operate on the principle of pressure differential.

TECH TIP

CHECK THE VACUUM, THEN THE BRAKES

A customer complained of a very rough idle and an occasional pulsating brake pedal. The customer was certain that the engine required serious work since there were over 100,000 miles on the vehicle. During the troubleshooting procedure, a spray cleaner was used to find any vacuum (air) leaks. A large hole was found melted through a large vacuum hose next to the vacuum hose feeding the vacuum-operated power brake booster.

After repairing the vacuum leak, the vehicle was test driven again to help diagnose the cause of the pulsating brake pedal. The engine idled very smoothly after the vacuum leak was repaired and the brake pulsation was also cured. The vacuum leak resulted in lower-than-normal vacuum being applied to the vacuum booster. During braking, when engine vacuum is normally higher (deceleration), the vacuum booster would assist, then not assist when the vacuum was lost. This on-and-off supply of vacuum to the vacuum booster was noticed by the driver as a brake pulsation. Always check the vacuum at the booster whenever diagnosing any brake problems. Most vehicle manufacturers specify a maximum of 15 in. Hg of vacuum at the booster. The booster should be able to provide at least two or three stops even with no vacuum. The booster should also be checked to see if it can hold a vacuum after several hours. A good vacuum booster, for example, should be able to provide a power assist after sitting all night without starting the engine.

CHARCOAL FILTER

The vacuum hose leading from the engine to the power booster should run downward without any low places in the hose. If a dip or sag occurs in the vacuum hose, condensed fuel vapors and/or moisture can accumulate that can block or restrict the vacuum to the booster. Many manufacturers use a small charcoal filter in the vacuum line between the engine and booster, as shown in Figure 16-7.

The charcoal filter attracts and holds gasoline vapors and keeps fumes from entering the vacuum booster. Without this filter, gasoline fumes can enter the vacuum booster, where it can deteriorate the rubber diaphragm and other rubber components of the booster.

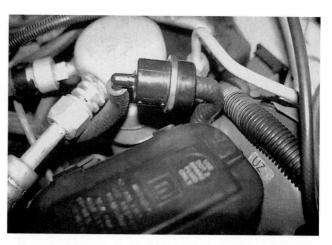

FIGURE 16-7   The charcoal filter traps gasoline vapors that are present in the intake manifold and prevents them from getting into the vacuum chamber of the booster.

VACUUM CHECK VALVE

All vacuum boosters use a one-way vacuum check valve. This valve allows air to flow in only one direction—from the booster toward the engine. This valve prevents loss of vacuum when the engine stops. Without this check valve, the vacuum stored in the vacuum booster would simply be lost through the hose and intake manifold of the engine. See Figures 16-8 and 16-9.

CAUTION: Sometimes an engine backfire can destroy or blow the vacuum check valve out of the booster housing. If this occurs, all power assist will be lost and a much greater-than-normal force must be exerted on the brake pedal to stop the vehicle. Be sure to repair the cause of the backfire before replacing the damaged or missing check valve. Normal causes of backfire include an excessively lean air/fuel ratio or incorrect firing order or ignition timing.

VACUUM BRAKE BOOSTER OPERATION

A vacuum power-brake booster contains a rubber diaphragm(s) connected to the brake pedal at one end and to the master cylinder at the other end. When the brakes are off or released, there is equal vacuum on both sides of the diaphragm.

The vacuum power unit contains the power-piston assembly, which houses the control valve and reaction mechanism, and the power-piston return spring. The control valve is composed of the air valve (valve plunger), the floating control-valve assembly, and the pushrod. The reaction mechanism consists of a hydraulic piston reaction plate and a series of reaction levers. An air filter, air silencer, and filter retainer are assembled around the valve operating rod, filling the cavity inside the hub of the power piston. The pushrod that operates the air valve projects out of the end. See Figure 16-10.

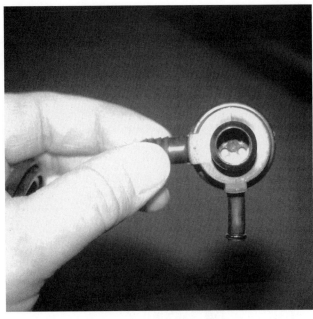

(a)   (b)

FIGURE 16-8 (a) Many vacuum-brake-booster check valves are located where the vacuum hose from the engine (vacuum source) attaches to the vacuum booster. (b) This one-way valve prevents the loss of vacuum when the engine is off. The diaphragm inside allows air to flow in one direction only.

FIGURE 16-9 Not all check valves are located at the vacuum line to the booster housing connection. This vehicle uses an in-line check valve located between the intake manifold of the engine and the vacuum brake booster.

Released-Position Operation

At the released position (brake pedal up), the air valve is seated on the floating control valve, which shuts off the air. The floating control valve is held away from the valve seat in the power-piston insert. Vacuum from the engine is present in the space on both sides of the power piston. Any air in the system is drawn through a small passage in the power piston, over the seat in the power-piston insert, and through a passage in the power-piston insert. There is a vacuum on both sides of the power piston, and it is held against the rear of the housing by the power-piston return spring. At rest, the hydraulic reaction plate is held against the reaction retainer. The air-valve spring holds the reaction lever against the hydraulic reaction plate and holds the air valve against its stop in the tube of the power piston. The floating control-valve assembly is held against the

FIGURE 16-10 Cross-sectional view of a typical vacuum
brake booster assembly.

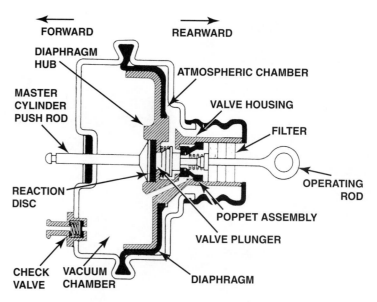

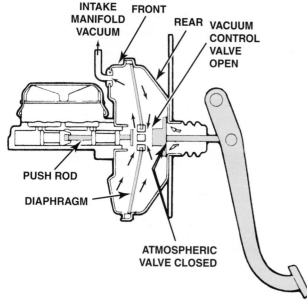

FIGURE 16-11 In the release position (brake pedal up), the vacuum is directed to both sides of the diaphragm. *(Courtesy of DaimlerChrysler
Corporation)*

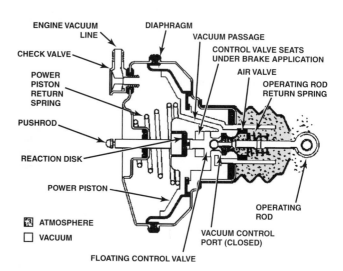

FIGURE 16-12 Vacuum booster in released position showing the
vacuum port open and the atmospheric port closed. The brake pedal is up and
no force is being applied to the master cylinder.

air-valve seat by the floating control-valve spring. See Figures
16-11 and 16-12.

Applied-Position Operation

As the brake pedal is depressed, the floating control valve is
moved toward its seat in the power piston, away from the rear
of the booster. The smaller air valve spring causes the air valve to
stretch out toward the retreating floating control valve until it
bottoms out on the lip of the power piston's vacuum passage.
This closes off the vacuum supply to the rear section of the hous-

ing. Since the floating control valve travels farther than the sealing end of the air valve, atmospheric air is allowed to enter between the air valve and the floating control valve pressurizing
the rear section of the housing. At this point, the rear section of
the housing is pressurized and the front section is under vacuum.
Atmospheric pressure can then force the power piston forward.

NOTE: This movement of air into the rear chamber of the brake booster
may be heard inside the vehicle as a hissing noise. The loudness of this airflow varies from vehicle to vehicle and should be considered normal.

As the power piston travels forward, the pushrod pushes against the hydraulic reaction plate in the master cylinder pushing the master cylinder primary and secondary pistons forward. As back-pressure builds up on the end of the master cylinder piston, the floating control valve is pushed back off of its seat in the power piston applying back pressure to the brake pedal. The power piston return spring also generates some brake pedal force. All in all, approximately 30% of the brake load is applied back to the brake pedal. This gives the driver a feel that is proportional to the degree of brake application (see Figures 16-13 and 16-14).

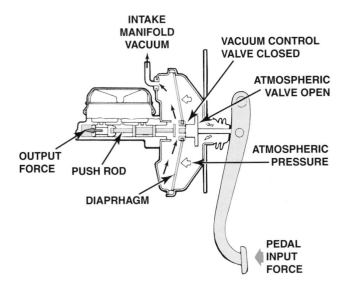

FIGURE 16-13   Simplified diagram of a vacuum brake booster in the apply position. Notice that the atmospheric valve is open and air pressure is being applied to the diaphragm.   *(Courtesy of DaimlerChrysler Corporation)*

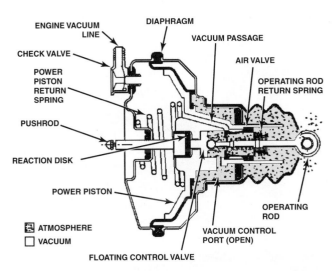

FIGURE 16-14   Cross-sectional view of a vacuum brake booster in the apply position, showing force being transferred and increased through the booster assembly.

Hold-Position Operation

When the desired brake pedal force is reached and there is balance between the opposing forces of the brake pedal and the master cylinder, the power piston moves forward "around" the floating control valve and reaction disc until the air valve sealing end "catches up" with the floating control valve. At this point, the air valve is once again sealed against the floating control valve and is no longer blocking the vacuum passage in the power piston. The floating control valve is again held away from its seat. Vacuum once again is present on both sides of the diaphragm and power piston. The status of the booster is almost exactly as it was in the released state except that the positions of the power piston and subsequently the master cylinder pistons are farther forward. Brake pedal force is keeping the power piston in its position. If additional braking is required (brake pedal pushed farther), the floating control valve moves away from the air valve permitting the power of atmospheric pressure to push the power piston and master cylinder pistons forward. If the pedal is released, since vacuum is then present on both sides of the diaphragm, the power piston return spring moves the power piston to its released state. See Figure 16-15.

Vacuum-Failure Mode

In case of vacuum source interruption, the brake operates as a standard brake as follows. As the pedal is pushed down, the operating rod forces the floating control valve against the power piston and reaction disc. This force is then applied to the pushrod and subsequently the hydraulic reaction plate fastened to the master cylinder piston rod, which applies pressure

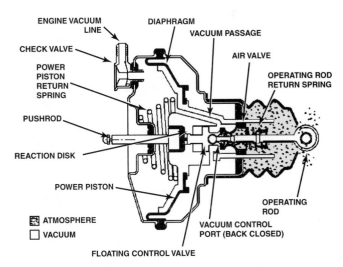

FIGURE 16-15   Cross section of a vacuum brake booster in the hold position with both vacuum and atmospheric valves closed. Note that the reaction force from the brake fluid pressure is transferred back to the driver as a reaction force to the brake pedal.

TECH TIP

A LOW, SOFT BRAKE PEDAL IS NOT A POWER BOOSTER PROBLEM

Some service technicians tend to blame the power brake booster if the vehicle has a low, soft brake pedal. A defective power brake booster causes a hard brake pedal, not a soft brake pedal. A soft or spongy brake pedal is usually caused by air being trapped somewhere in the hydraulic system.

Many times, the technician has bled the system and, therefore, thinks that the system is free of any trapped air. According to remanufacturers of master cylinders and power brake boosters, most of the returned parts under warranty are not defective. Incorrect or improper bleeding procedures account for much of the problem.

in the master cylinder. For safety in the event of a stalled engine and a loss of vacuum, a power brake booster should have adequate storage of vacuum for several power-assisted stops.

DUAL- (TANDEM-) DIAPHRAGM VACUUM BOOSTERS

To provide power assist, air pressure must work against a rubber diaphragm. The larger the area of the diaphragm, the more force can be exerted. The usual method of increasing the area of the vacuum diaphragm was to increase the diameter of the vacuum booster. However, a larger vacuum booster took up too much room under the hood of many vehicles. Instead of increasing the diameter, vacuum booster manufacturers used two smaller-diameter diaphragms and placed one in front of the other. These designs increased the total area without increasing the physical diameter of the booster. This style is called a **dual-diaphragm** or **tandem-diaphragm vacuum booster.** See Figure 16-16.

BRAKE ASSIST SYSTEM

Some vehicles are equipped with a **brake assist system (BAS)** that applies the brakes with maximum force if the system detects that the driver is making a panic stop. Tests performed by brake engineers have indicated that it is normal for a person to first apply the brakes rapidly during a panic situation. However, it was also found that the driver would tend to reduce the force applied to the brake pedal. As a result, the vehicle did not brake with the maximum effort.

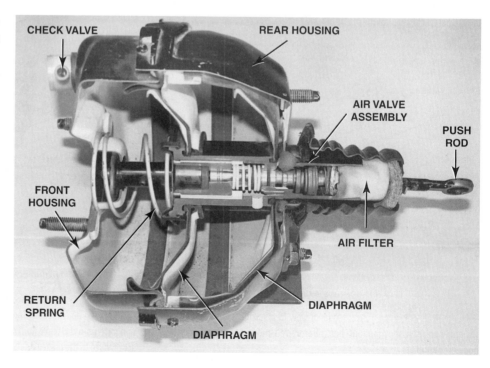

FIGURE 16-16 Cutaway showing a dual-diaphragm (tandem) vacuum brake booster.

Operation

The brake assist system opens an air valve on the rear part of the vacuum booster assembly. As a result, more air at atmospheric pressure can flow into the rear chamber of the vacuum booster, thereby increasing the force applied to the master cylinder. The BAS function works with the electronic stability control (ESC) system to ensure maximum braking efficiency during evasive or emergency situations.

If the speed of the brake pedal application exceeds a predetermined limit as determined by the brake pedal travel sensor, the ABS controller energizes the BAS solenoid valve. When the solenoid valve opens, additional air at atmospheric pressure enters the driver's side of the booster. The additional pressure applies the brakes faster and with more force. The BAS solenoid is de-energized when the brake pedal is released and normal braking returns. See Figures 16-17 and 16-18.

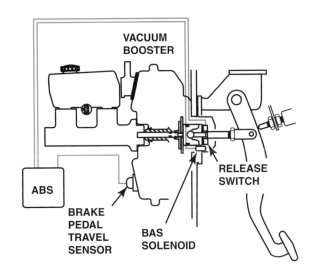

FIGURE 16-17   A typical brake assist system uses a brake pedal travel sensor and a BAS solenoid to apply the brakes during a panic condition.

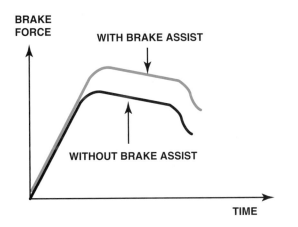

FIGURE 16-18   When the brake assist function operates, the brake force is much higher than normal.

VACUUM BOOSTER OPERATION TEST

With the engine "off," apply the brakes several times to deplete the vacuum. With your foot on the brake pedal, start the engine. The brake pedal *should* drop. If the brake pedal does *not* drop, check for proper vacuum source to the booster. If there is proper vacuum, repair or replacement of the power booster is required.

VACUUM BOOSTER LEAK TEST

To test if the vacuum booster can hold a vacuum, run the engine to build up a vacuum in the booster, then turn the engine off. Wait one minute, then depress the brake pedal several times. There should be two or more power-assisted brake applications.

If applications are not power assisted, either the vacuum check valve or the booster is leaking. To test the check valve, remove the valve from the booster and blow through the check valve. If air passes through, the valve is defective and must be replaced. If the check valve is okay, the vacuum booster is leaking and should be repaired or replaced based on the manufacturer's recommendations.

HYDRAULIC SYSTEM LEAK TEST

An internal or external hydraulic leak can also cause a brake system problem. To test if the hydraulic system (and not the booster) is leaking, depress and release the brake pedal (service brakes) several times. This should deplete any residual power assist. On some ABS units, this may require depressing the brake pedal twenty or more times!

After depleting the power-assist unit, depress and then hold the brake pedal depressed with medium force (20 to 35 lb. or 88 to 154 N). The brake pedal should *not* fall away. If the pedal falls, the hydraulic brake system is leaking. Check for external leakage at wheel cylinders, calipers, hydraulic lines, and hoses. If there is no external leak, there may be an internal leak inside the master cylinder. Repair or replace components as needed to correct the leakage.

PUSHROD CLEARANCE ADJUSTMENT

Whenever the vacuum brake booster or the master cylinder is replaced, the pushrod length should be checked. The length of the pushrod must match correctly with the master cylinder. See Figure 16-19.

If the pushrod is too long and the master cylinder is installed, the rod may be applying a force on the primary piston

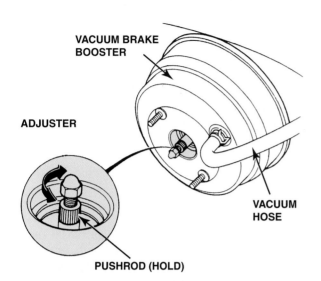

VACUUM BRAKE BOOSTER

ADJUSTER

VACUUM HOSE

PUSHROD (HOLD)

FIGURE 16-19 Typical adjustable pushrod. This adjustment is critical for the proper operation of the braking system. If the pushrod is too long, the brakes may be partially applied during driving. If the rod is too short, the brake pedal may have to be depressed farther down before the brakes start to work.

of the master cylinder even though the brake pedal is not applied. This can cause the brakes to overheat, causing the brake fluid to boil. If the brake fluid boils, a total loss of braking force can occur. Obviously, this pushrod clearance check and adjustment is very important. A gauge is often used to measure the position of the master cylinder piston, and then the other end of the gauge is used to determine the proper pushrod clearance. See Figure 16-20.

VACUUM BOOSTER DISASSEMBLY AND SERVICE

Some vehicle manufacturers recommend that the vacuum brake booster be disassembled and overhauled if defective.

CAUTION: Some vehicle manufacturers recommend that the vacuum brake booster be replaced as an assembly if tested to be leaking or defective. Always follow the manufacturer's recommendations.

A special holding fixture should be used before rotating (unlocking) the front and rear housing because the return spring is strong. See Figure 16-21.

Disassemble the vacuum brake booster according to the manufacturer's recommended procedures for the specific unit being serviced. See Figure 16-22.

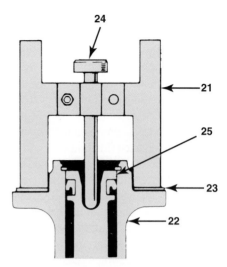

21. **GAGE J34873A**
22. **MASTER CYLINDER**
23. **GASKET**
24. **GAGE PIN**
25. **MASTER CYLINDER PISTON**

(a)

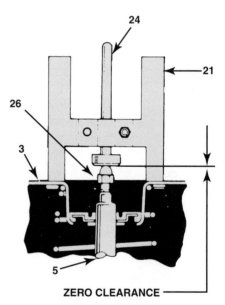

ZERO CLEARANCE

3. **FRONT HOUSING**
5. **PISTON ROD**
21. **GAGE J34873A**
24. **GAGE PIN**
26. **ADJUSTING BOLT**

(b)

FIGURE 16-20 Typical vacuum brake booster pushrod gauging tool. (a) The tool is first placed against the mounting flange of the master cylinder and the depth of the piston determined. (b) The gauge is then turned upside down and used to gauge the pushrod length. Some vacuum brake boosters do not use adjustable pushrods. If found to be the incorrect length, a replacement pushrod of the correct length should be installed.

FIGURE 16-21   A holding fixture and a long tool being used to rotate the two halves of a typical vacuum brake booster.

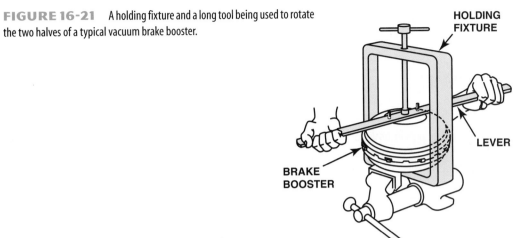

FIGURE 16-22   Exploded view of a typical dual diaphragm vacuum brake booster assembly.

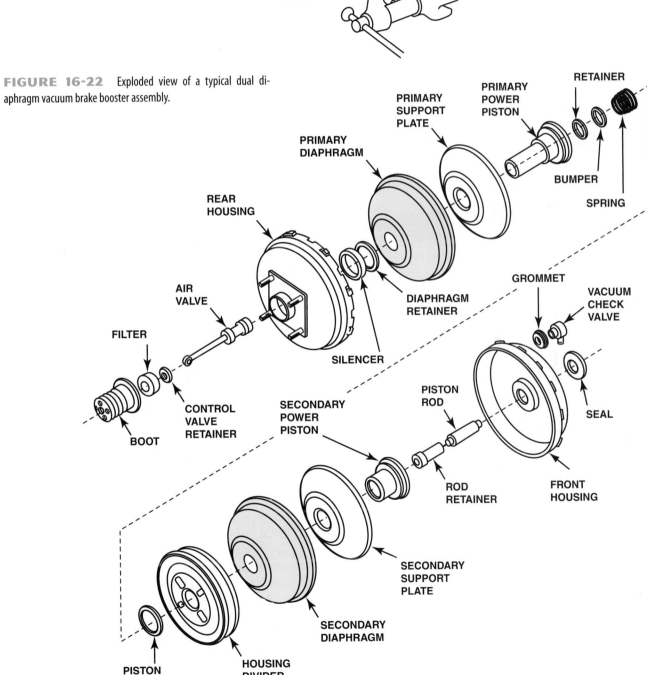

A rebuilding kit is available that includes all necessary parts and the proper silicone grease. The manufacturer warns that all parts included in the kit be replaced.

POWERMASTER POWER BRAKE UNIT

The Powermaster unit is a complete, integral power brake apply system. It combines the functions of the booster (vacuum or hydraulic) and master cylinder. The Powermaster uses brake fluid as its only fluid medium and eliminates dependence on external pumps, fluids, and vacuum sources.

The Powermaster consists of an electrohydraulic (E-H) pump, fluid accumulator, pressure switch, fluid reservoir, and a hydraulic booster with an integral dual master cylinder. See Figure 16-23.

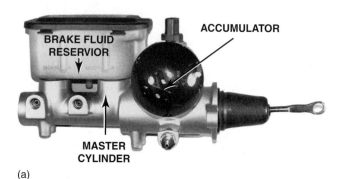

(a)

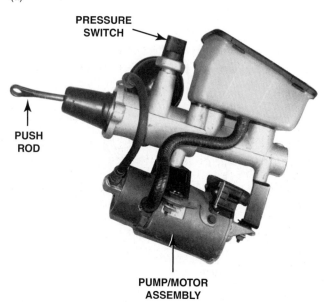

(b)

FIGURE 16-23   (a) A Powermaster power brake unit showing the location of the accumulator. (b) The pump and motor assembly supplies pressurized brake fluid to charge the accumulator.

Operation

The nitrogen-charged accumulator stores fluid at 510 to 685 psi (3500 to 4700 kPa) for hydraulic booster operation. The 12-volt E-H pump operates between pressure switch limits with the ignition "on." When the pressure switch senses accumulator pressure below 510 psi (3500 kPa), the E-H pump operates to increase accumulator pressure to 685 psi (4700 kPa). This is accomplished by transferring brake fluid from the pump reservoir into the accumulator, compressing the nitrogen, and causing the pressure to rise. When the brake pedal is depressed, pressurized fluid from the accumulator acts on the power piston to provide assist to the master cylinder, which functions in the same manner as a conventional dual master cylinder. When the brake pedal is released, this fluid is transferred back into the pump reservoir. Additional pedal applications will reduce the pressure in the accumulator to approximately 510 psi (3500 kPa). This will again cause the E-H pump to operate to increase the accumulator pressure.

Diagnosis

The first step in the diagnostic procedure is to discharge the accumulator fully by making 10 medium brake applications with the ignition "off." Inspect for fluid leakage at the brake pedal pushrod, reservoir cover, hose and pipe connections, reservoir attaching points, pressure switch, and

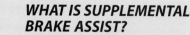

FREQUENTLY ASKED QUESTION

WHAT IS SUPPLEMENTAL BRAKE ASSIST?

Supplemental brake assist, SBA, is a motor-driven vacuum pump that can supplement engine vacuum to the vacuum brake booster. This unit is used on some General Motors vehicles. When a vehicle is driven under a heavy load, engine vacuum is low. To meet the brake standards, some vehicles are equipped with the brake assist system that consists of the following components:

- A pressure sensor that is used to measure the vacuum in the vacuum booster.
- An intake manifold check valve that is used to prevent vacuum from escaping the vacuum boost.
- A motor-driven vacuum pump.

The vacuum pump motor will start and run if the pressure sensor detects the vacuum in the booster is below 7 in. Hg and will shut off after the vacuum level increases to 9 in. Hg.

accumulator. The reservoir should be at least half full. Check for fluid leaks.

Remove the pressure switch from the Powermaster and install the pressure gauge and adapter in the pressure switch port. Reinstall the pressure switch in the test adapter. Close the bleed valve and route the tubing into the pump side of the reservoir.

Turn the ignition "on." The E-H pump should run and then shut off. (Do not allow the pump to run more than 20 seconds. Excess run time could severely damage the pump.)

HYDRO-BOOST HYDRAULIC BRAKE BOOSTER

Hydro-Boost is a hydraulically operated power-assist unit built by Bendix. The Hydro-Boost system uses the pressurized hydraulic fluid from the vehicle's power steering pump as a power source rather than using engine vacuum as is used with vacuum boosters. See Figures 16-24 and 16-25.

The Hydro-Boost unit is used on vehicles that lack enough engine vacuum, such as turbo-charged or diesel engine vehicles. During operation, diesel engines do not produce vacuum in the intake manifold. As a result, diesel engines must use accessory engine-driven vacuum pumps to operate vacuum accessories. Turbocharged and supercharged engines do not create engine vacuum during periods of acceleration. Even though vacuum is available when the engine is decelerating, some vehicle manufacturers elect to install a Hydro-Boost system rather than equip the vehicle with an accessory engine-driven vacuum pump.

Operation

Fluid pressure from the power steering pump enters the unit and is directed by a spool valve. See Figure 16-26.

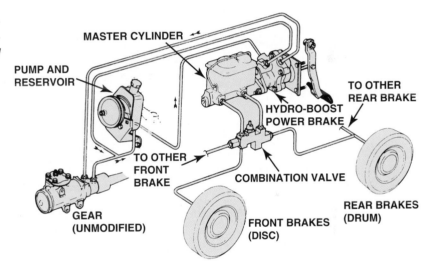

FIGURE 16-24   Hydro-boost unit attaches between the bulkhead and the master cylinder and is powered by the power steering pump. *(Courtesy of Allied Signal Automotive Aftermarket)*

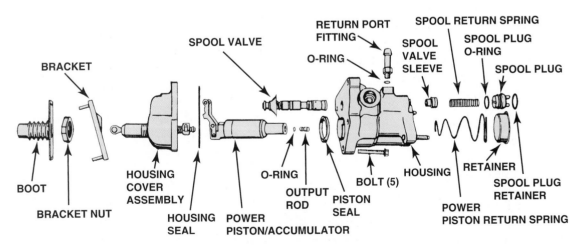

FIGURE 16-25   Exploded view of the hydro-boost unit. *(Courtesy of Allied Signal Automotive Aftermarket)*

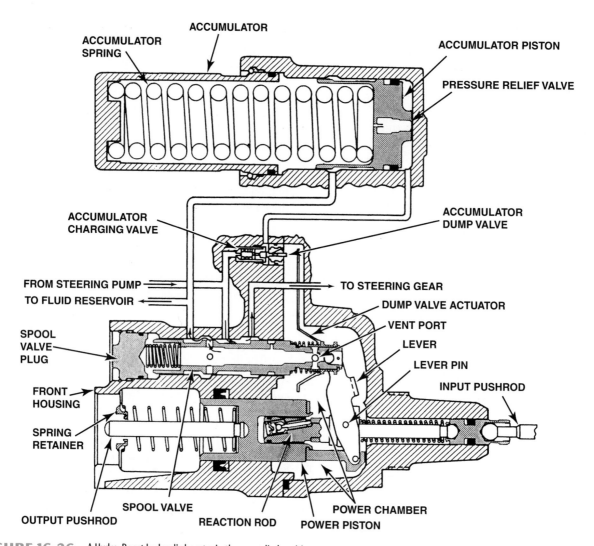

FIGURE 16-26   A Hydro-Boost hydraulic booster in the unapplied position.

When the brake pedal is depressed, the lever and primary valve are moved. The valve closes off the return port, causing pressure to build in the boost pressure chamber. The hydraulic pressure pushes on the power piston, which then applies force to the output rod that connects to the master cylinder piston. In the event of a power steering pump failure, power assist is still available for several brake applications. See Figure 16-27.

During operation, hydraulic fluid under pressure from the power steering pump pressurizes an accumulator. See Figure 16-28.

While some units use a spring inside the accumulator, most Hydro-Boost units use nitrogen gas. The fluid trapped in the accumulator under pressure is used to provide power-assisted stops in the event of a hydraulic system failure.

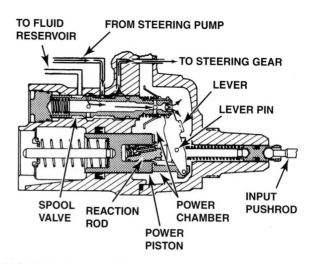

FIGURE 16-27   A Hydro-Boost hydraulic booster as the brakes are applied.

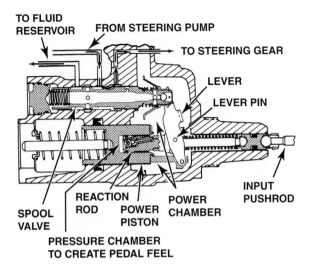

FIGURE 16-28   A Hydro-Boost hydraulic booster in the holding position.

Diagnosis

The power source for Hydro-Boost units comes from the power steering pump. The first step of troubleshooting is to perform a thorough visual inspection, including the following:

1. Checking for proper power steering fluid level
2. Checking for leaks from the unit or power steering pump
3. Checking the condition and tightness of the power steering drive belt
4. Checking for proper operation of the base brake system

After checking all of the visual components, check for proper pressure and volume from the power steering pump using a power steering pump tester, as shown in Figures 16-29 and 16-30.

The pump should be capable of producing a minimum of 2 gallons (7.5 liters) with a maximum pressure of 150 psi (1000 kPa) with the steering in the straight-ahead position. With the engine "off," the accumulator should be able to supply a minimum of two power-assisted brake applications.

HYDRO-BOOST FUNCTION TEST

With the engine off, apply the brake pedal several times until the accumulator is depleted completely. Depress the service brake pedal and start the engine. The pedal should fall and then push back against the driver's foot.

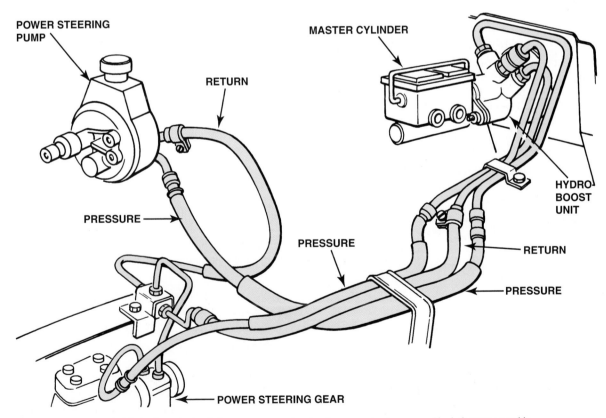

FIGURE 16-29   A typical Hydro-Boost hydraulic line arrangement showing the pump, steering gear, and brake booster assembly.

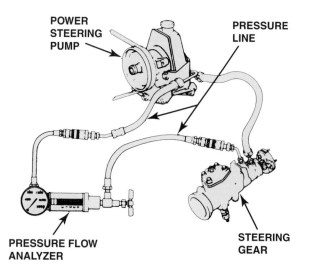

FIGURE 16-30 Pressure and flow analyzer installation to check the power steering pump output.

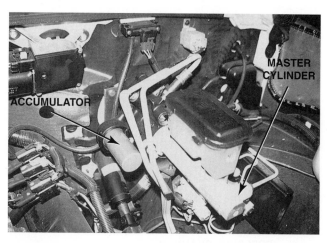

FIGURE 16-31 The accumulator should be able to hold pressure and feel tight when hand force is used to try to move it.

4. Leaks at tube fittings, power steering, booster, or accumulator connections
5. External leakage at the accumulator
6. Faulty booster piston seal, causing leakage at the booster flange vent
7. Faulty booster cover seal with leakage between the housing and cover
8. Faulty booster spool plug seal

Slow Brake Pedal Return

Possible causes for this include the following:

1. Excessive seal friction in the booster
2. Faulty spool action
3. Broken piston return spring
4. Restriction in the return line from the booster to the pump reservoir
5. Broken spool return spring

Grabby Brakes

Possible causes for this include the following:

1. Broken spool return spring
2. Faulty spool action caused by contamination in the system

Booster Chatters—Pedal Vibrates

Possible causes for this include the following:

1. Power steering pump belt slipping
2. Low fluid level in the power steering pump reservoir
3. Faulty spool operation caused by contamination in the system

TECH TIP

THE HYDRO-BOOST ACCUMULATOR TEST

The accumulator stores hydraulic fluid under pressure to provide a reserve in the event of a failure of the power steering system. The accumulator is designed to provide three or more power-assisted stops with the engine off. See Figure 16-31.

If the accumulator fails, it does not hold pressure. To easily check whether the accumulator has lost its charge, simply grasp the accumulator with your hand and try to twist or move it. The accumulator should have so much pressure on it that it should not move or wiggle. If the accumulator moves, it has lost its ability to hold pressure and the Hydro-Boost unit should be replaced.

HYDRO-BOOST SYMPTOM-BASED GUIDE

Excessive Brake Pedal Effort

Possible causes for this include the following:

1. Loose or broken power steering pump belt
2. No fluid in the power steering reservoir
3. Leaks in the power steering, booster, or accumulator hoses

SUMMARY

1. Vacuum brake boosters use air pressure acting on a diaphragm to assist the driver's force on the brake master cylinder.

2. At rest, there is vacuum on both sides of the vacuum booster diaphragm. When the brake pedal is depressed, atmospheric air pressure is exerted on the back side of the diaphragm.

3. The use of two diaphragms in tandem allows a smaller-diameter booster with the same area. The larger the area of the booster diaphragm, the more air pressure force can be applied to the master cylinder.

4. Hydraulic-operated brake boosters use either an electric motor-driven pump or the engine-driven power steering pump.

5. When replacing a vacuum brake booster, always check for proper pushrod clearance.

6. To be assured of power-assisted brake application in the event of failure, hydraulic power-assisted brake systems use an accumulator to provide pressure to the system.

REVIEW QUESTIONS

1. Describe the purpose and function of the one-way check valve used on vacuum brake booster units.

2. Explain how vacuum is used to assist in applying the brakes.

3. Describe how to perform a vacuum booster leak test and hydraulic system leak test.

4. Explain how a Hydro-Boost system functions.

CHAPTER QUIZ

1. Two technicians are discussing vacuum brake boosters. Technician A says that a low, soft brake pedal is an indication of a defective booster. Technician B says that there should be at least two power-assisted brake applications after the engine stops running. Which technician is correct?
   a. Technician A only
   b. Technician B only
   c. Both Technicians A and B
   d. Neither Technician A nor B

2. Technician A says that to check the operation of a vacuum brake booster, the brake pedal should be depressed until the assist is depleted and then start the engine. Technician B says that the brake pedal should drop when the engine starts, if the booster is okay. Which technician is correct?
   a. Technician A only
   b. Technician B only
   c. Both Technicians A and B
   d. Neither Technician A nor B

3. Brake pedal feedback to the driver is provided by the _____.
   a. Vacuum check-valve operation
   b. Reaction system

   c. Charcoal filter unit
   d. Vacuum diaphragm

4. The proper operation of a vacuum brake booster requires that the engine be capable of supplying at least _____.
   a. 15 in. Hg vacuum
   b. 17 in. Hg vacuum
   c. 19 in. Hg vacuum
   d. 21 in. Hg vacuum

5. The purpose of the charcoal filter in the vacuum hose between the engine and the vacuum brake booster is to _____.
   a. Filter the air entering the engine
   b. Trap gasoline vapors to keep them from entering the booster
   c. Act as a one-way check valve to help keep a vacuum reserve in the booster
   d. Direct the vacuum

6. A defective vacuum brake booster will cause a _____.
   a. Hard brake pedal
   b. Soft (spongy) brake pedal
   c. Low brake pedal
   d. Slight hiss noise when the brake pedal is depressed

7. An accumulator such as that used on electric or hydraulic brake boosters _____.
   a. Reduces brake pedal noise
   b. Provides higher force being fed back to the driver's foot
   c. Provides a reserve in the event of a failure
   d. Works against engine vacuum

8. The first step in diagnosing a Hydro-Boost problem is _____.
   a. A pressure test of the pump
   b. A volume test of the pump
   c. To tighten the power steering drive belt
   d. A thorough visual inspection

9. A brake pedal feels spongy when depressed. Technician A says that a defective hydraulic brake booster could be the cause. Technician B says that a defective vacuum brake booster could be the cause. Which technician is correct?
   a. Technician A only
   b. Technician B only
   c. Both Technicians A and B
   d. Neither Technician A nor B

10. If the engine stops running, the Hydro-Boost will not be able to provide any power assist for the brakes.
    a. True
    b. False

CHAPTER 17

REGENERATIVE BRAKING SYSTEMS

OBJECTIVES

After studying Chapter 17, the reader should be able to:

1. Describe how regenerative braking works.
2. Explain the principles involved in regenerative braking.
3. Discuss the parts and components involved in regenerative braking systems.
4. Describe the servicing precautions involved with regenerative brakes.

KEY TERMS

When test driving a hybrid vehicle the driver may notice that there is a slight surge or pulsation that occurs at lower speeds, usually about 5 to 20 mph (8 to 32 km/h). This is where the regenerative braking system stops regenerating electricity for charging the batteries and where the mechanical (friction) brakes take over. This chapter describes how this system works and how the various components of a hybrid vehicle work together to achieve the highest possible efficiency.

PRINCIPLES OF REGENERATIVE BRAKING

Inertia, Force, and Mass

If a moving object has a mass, it has **inertia.** Inertia is the resistance of an object to change its state of motion. In other words, an object in motion tends to stay in motion and an object at rest tends to stay at rest unless acted on by an outside force.

A hybrid electric vehicle reclaims energy by converting the energy of a moving object, called **kinetic energy,** into electric energy. According to basic physics:

A **force** applied to move an object results in the equation:

$$F = ma$$

where

F = force
m = mass
a = acceleration

The faster an object is accelerated, the more force that has to be applied. Energy from the battery (watts) is applied to the coil windings in the motor. These windings then produce a magnetic force on the rotor of the motor, which produces torque on the output shaft. This torque is then applied to the wheels of the vehicle by use of a coupling of gears and shafts. When the wheel turns, it applies a force to the ground, which due to friction between the wheel and the ground, causes the vehicle to move along the surface.

All vehicles generate **torque** to move the wheels to drive the vehicle down the road. During this time, it is generating friction and losses. When standard brakes are applied, it is just another friction device that has specially designed material to handle the heat from friction, which is applied to the drums and rotors that stop the wheel from turning. The friction between the wheel and the ground actually stops the vehicle. However, the energy absorbed by the braking system is lost in the form of heat and cannot be recovered or stored for use later to help propel the vehicle.

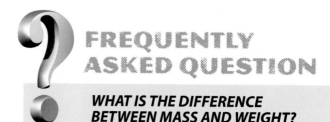

FREQUENTLY ASKED QUESTION

WHAT IS THE DIFFERENCE BETWEEN MASS AND WEIGHT?

Mass is the amount of matter in an object. One of the properties of mass is inertia. Inertia is the resistance to being put in motion and the tendency to remain in motion once it is set in motion. The weight of an object is the force of gravity on the object and may be defined as the mass times the acceleration of gravity.

Therefore, mass means the property of an object and weight is a force.

Reclaiming Energy in a Hybrid

On a hybrid vehicle that has regenerative brakes, the kinetic energy of a moving vehicle can be reclaimed that would normally be lost due to braking. Using the inertia of the vehicle is the key. Inertia is the kinetic energy that is present in any moving object. The heavier the object, and the faster it is traveling, the greater the amount of energy and therefore, the higher the inertia. It is basically what makes something difficult to start moving and what makes something hard to stop moving. Inertia is the reason energy is required to change the direction and speed of the moving object.

Transferring Torque Back to the Motor

Inertia is the fundamental property of physics that is used to reclaim energy from the vehicle. Instead of using 100% friction brakes (**base brakes**), the braking torque is transferred from the wheels back into the motor shaft. One of the unique things about most electric motors is that electrical energy can be converted into mechanical energy and also mechanical energy can be converted back into electrical energy. In both cases, this can be done very efficiently.

Through the use of the motor and motor controller, the force at the wheels transfers torque to the electric motor shaft. The magnets on the shaft of the motor (called the rotor—the moving part of the motor) move past the electric coils on the stator (the stationary part of the motor), passing the magnetic fields of the magnets through the coils, producing electricity. This electricity becomes electrical energy, which is directed to and recharges the high-voltage battery. This process is called **regeneration, regen** or simply "reclaiming energy."

Principles Involved

Brakes slow and stop a vehicle by converting kinetic energy, the energy of motion, into heat energy, which is then dissipated to the air. Fuel is burned in the internal combustion engine to make heat, which is then converted to mechanical energy and finally this is used to create kinetic energy in the moving vehicle. The goal of regenerative braking is to recover some of that energy, store it, and then use it to put the vehicle into motion again. It is estimated that regenerative braking can eventually be developed to recover about half the energy wasted as braking heat. Depending on the type of vehicle, this would reduce fuel consumption by 10% to 25% below current levels.

Regenerative braking can be extremely powerful and can recover about 20% of the energy normally wasted as brake heat. Regenerative braking has the following advantages:

- Reduces the drawdown of the battery charge
- Extends the overall life of the battery pack
- Reduces fuel consumption

All production hybrid electric vehicles use regenerative braking as a method to improve vehicle efficiency and this feature alone provides the most fuel economy savings. How much energy is reclaimed, depends on a many factors, including weight of the vehicle, speed, and the rate of deceleration. See Figure 17-1.

The amount of kinetic energy in a moving vehicle increases with the square of the speed. This means that at 60

FIGURE 17-2   A Toyota Prius hybrid electric vehicle. This sedan weighs more and therefore has greater kinetic energy than a smaller, lighter vehicle.

mph, the kinetic energy is four times the energy of 30 mph. The speed is doubled (times 2) and the kinetic energy is squared (2 times 2 equals four). See Figure 17-2.

The efficiency of the regenerative braking is about 80%, which means that only about 20% of the inertia energy is wasted to heat. There are losses when mechanical energy is converted to electrical energy by the motor/generator(s) and then some energy is lost when it is converted into chemical energy in the high-voltage batteries. Two different regeneration designs include:

- **Series regeneration.** In series regenerative braking systems, the amount of regeneration is proportional to the brake pedal position (BPP). As the brake pedal is depressed further, the controller used to regulate the regenerative braking system computes the torque needed to slow the vehicle as would occur in normal braking. As the brake pedal is depressed even further, the service brakes are blended into the regenerative braking to achieve the desired braking performance based on brake pedal force and travel. Series regenerative braking requires active brake management to achieve total braking to all four wheels. This braking is more difficult to achieve if the hybrid electric vehicle uses just the front or rear wheels to power the vehicle. This means that the other axle must use the base brakes alone whereas, the drive wheels can be slowed and stopped using a combination of regenerative braking and base brake action. All series regenerative braking systems use an electrohydraulic brake (EHB) system, which includes the hydraulic control unit that manages the brake cylinder pressures, as well as the front-rear axle brake balance. Most hybrid vehicles use this type of regenerative braking system. See Figure 17-3.

The regenerative braking system mainly uses the regenerative capability, especially at higher vehicle speeds,

FIGURE 17-1   This Honda Insight hybrid electric vehicle is constructed mostly of aluminum to save weight.

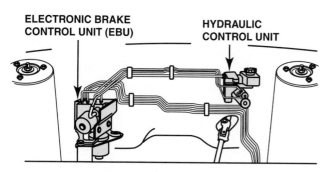

FIGURE 17-3 The electronic brake control unit (EBU) is shown on the left (passenger side) and the brake hydraulic unit is shown on the right (driver's side) on this Ford Escape system.

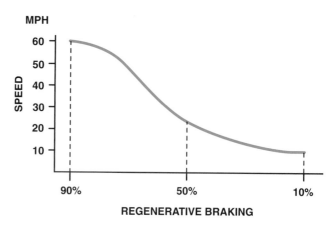

FIGURE 17-4 A typical brake curve showing the speed on the left and the percentage of regenerative braking along the bottom. Notice that the base brakes are being used more when the vehicle speed is low.

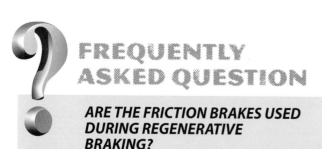

FREQUENTLY ASKED QUESTION

ARE THE FRICTION BRAKES USED DURING REGENERATIVE BRAKING?

Yes. Most hybrid vehicles make use of the base (friction) brakes during stopping. The amount of regenerative braking compared to the amount of friction braking is determined by the electronic brake controller. It is important that the base brakes be used regularly to keep the rotors free from rust and ready to be used to stop the vehicle. A typical curve showing the relative proportion of brake usage is shown in Figure 17-4.

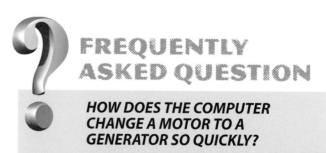

FREQUENTLY ASKED QUESTION

HOW DOES THE COMPUTER CHANGE A MOTOR TO A GENERATOR SO QUICKLY?

The controller of the drive motors uses a varying frequency to control power and speed. The controller can quickly change the frequency, and can therefore change the operation of a typical AC synchronous motor from propelling the vehicle (called motoring) to a generator. See Figure 17-5.

and then gradually increases the amount the base braking force at low vehicle speeds.

- Parallel regeneration. A parallel regenerative braking system is less complex because the base (friction) brakes are used along with energy recovery by the motors becoming generators. The controller for the regenerative braking system determines the amount of regeneration that can be achieved based on the vehicle speed. Front and rear brake balance is retained because the base brakes are in use during the entire braking event. The amount of energy captured by a parallel regenerative braking system is less than from a series system. As a result, the fuel economy gains are less.

Charging Batteries

Kinetic energy can be converted into electrical energy with a generator and it can be returned to the high-voltage batteries and stored for later use. Electric regenerative braking has its roots in the "dynamic brakes" used on electric trolley cars in the early twentieth century.

In the early electric trolley cars, the driver's control handle had a position that cut power to the electric motors and supplied a small, finely controlled excitation current to the motors' field windings. This turned the motors into generators that were driven by the motion of the trolley car. Increasing the magnetic field current increased the generating load, which slowed the trolley car, and the current being generated was routed to a set of huge resistors. These resistors converted the current to heat, which was dissipated through cooling fins. By the 1920s, techniques had been developed for returning that current to the power grid, making it available to all the other trolley cars in the system, reducing the load on the streetcar system's main generator by as much as 20%.

Regenerative braking systems are still being used in cities around the world. It is relatively easy to feed the current generated from braking into an on-board high-voltage battery system. The challenge was to make those components small enough to be practical, but still have enough storage capacity to be useful. A big breakthrough came with the development of the electronically controlled permanent-magnet motors.

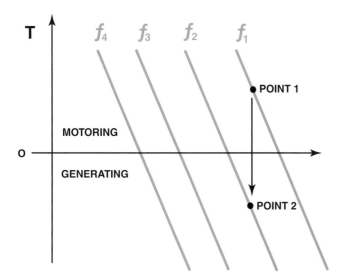

FIGURE 17-5 The frequency ("f") applied to the windings of an AC synchronous motor can be varied to create either forward torque ("T") or regenerative braking. If the frequency is changed from point 1 to point 2 as shown on the chart, the torque is changed from motoring (powering the vehicle) to generating and this change can be made almost instantly by the controller.

Motors work by activating electromagnets in just the right position and sequence. A conventional DC motor has groups of wire windings on the armature that act as electromagnets. The current flows through each winding on the armature only when the brushes touch its contacts located on the commutator. Surround the armature with a magnetic field and apply current to just the windings that are in the right position, and the resulting magnetic attraction causes the armature to rotate. The brushes lose contact with that set of windings just as the next set comes into the right position. Together, the brushes and rotation of the armature act like a mechanical switch to turn on each electromagnet at just the right position.

Another way to make a motor, instead of using electromagnets on the armature, is to use permanent magnets. Because it is impossible to switch the polarity of permanent magnets, the polarity of the field windings surrounding them needs to be switched. This is a brushless, permanent-magnet motor and the switching is only possible with the help of electronic controls that can switch the current in the field windings fast enough. The computer-controlled, brushless, permanent-magnet motor is ideal for use in electric vehicles. When connected to nickel-metal hydride (NiMH) batteries that can charge and discharge very quickly, the package is complete.

There are some limitations that will always affect even the best regenerative braking systems including:

- It only acts on the driven wheels.
- The system has to be designed to allow for proper use of the antilock braking system.

FREQUENTLY ASKED QUESTION

WHY ARE THE BATTERIES NOT KEPT 100 PERCENT CHARGED?

The batteries are commanded to be kept at a maximum of about 60%, plus or minus 20%, which is best for long battery life and to allow for energy to be stored in the batteries during regenerative braking. If the batteries were allowed to be fully charged, then there would no place for the electrical current to be stored and the conventional friction brakes alone have to be used to slow and stop and vehicle. Charging the batteries over 80% would also overheat the batteries.

So far its use is limited to electric or hybrid electric vehicles, where its contribution is to extend the life of the battery pack, as well as to save fuel.

REGENERATIVE BRAKING

The Toyota Prius is equipped with a center dash LCD that shows how many watt-hours of regeneration have occurred each 5 minutes. These are indicated by small "suns" that appear on the display and each sun indicates 50 watt-hours. When a sun appears, enough power has been put back into the battery to run a 50-watt light bulb for an hour. Depending on the driver and the traffic conditions, some drivers may not be seeing many suns on the display, which indicates that the regeneration is not contributing much energy back to the batteries. The battery level also gives an indication of how much regeneration is occurring. The battery level can be seen on the right in this display.

It is the ABS ECU that handles regenerative braking, as well as ABS functions, sending a signal to the hybrid ECU how much regeneration to impose. But how does the **ABS** ECU know what to do?

Rather than measuring brake pedal travel, which could vary with pad wear, the system uses pressure measuring sensors to detect master cylinder pressure. Some systems use a **brake pedal position (BPP)** sensor as an input signal to the brake ECU. The higher the master cylinder pressure, the harder the driver is pushing on the brake pedal.

If the driver is pushing only gently, the master cylinder piston displacement will be small and the hydraulic brakes will be only gently applied. In this situation, the ECU knows that the driver wants only gentle deceleration and instructs the hybrid ECU to apply only a small amount of regeneration. However, as master cylinder pressure increases, so does the amount of regeneration that can automatically be applied.

There are four pressure sensors in the braking system and two pressure switches. However, it is the master cylinder pressure sensor that is most important. See Figures 17-6 and 17-7.

FIGURE 17-6 The Toyota Prius regenerative braking system component showing the master cylinder and pressure switches.

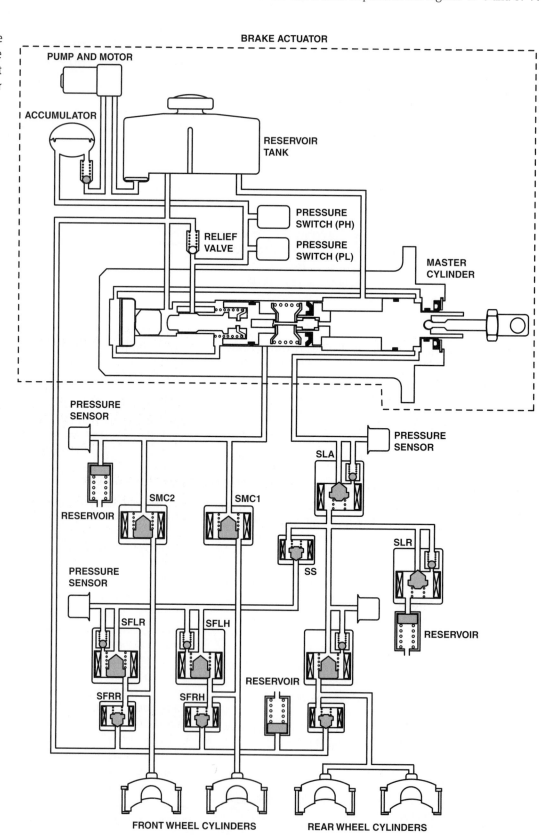

FIGURE 17-7 The Ford Escape regenerative braking system, showing all of the components. Notice the brake pedal position sensor is an input to the ECU, which controls both the brake and traction control systems.

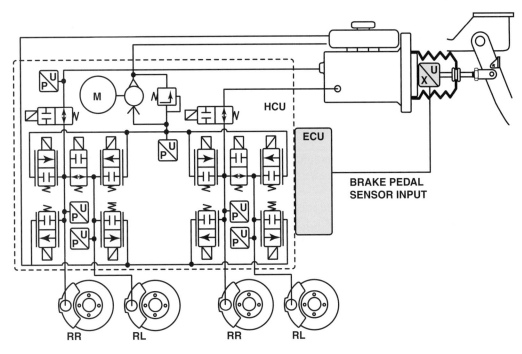

HCU

ECU

**BRAKE PEDAL
SENSOR INPUT**

RR   RL   RR   RL

TECH TIP

"B" MEANS BRAKING

All Toyota hybrid vehicles have a shift position marked "B." This position is to be used when descending steep grades and the regenerative braking is optimized. This position allows the safe and controlled decent without having the driver use the base brakes. Having to use the brakes only, wastes energy that could be captured and returned to the batteries. It can also cause the brakes to overheat. See Figure 17-8.

FIGURE 17-8 The "B" position on the shift display on this Lexus RX 400h means braking. This shifter position can be selected when descending long hills or grades. The regenerative braking system will be used to help keep the vehicle from increasing in speed down the hill without the use of the base brakes. *(Courtesy of Toyota Motor Sales U.S.A., Inc)*

HOW THE REGENERATION SYSTEM WORKS

To keep the hybrid electric vehicles feeling as much like other vehicles as possible, the hybrids from Toyota and Honda have both the regeneration and conventional brakes controlled by the one brake pedal. In the first part of its travel, the brake pedal operates the regenerative brakes alone, and then as further pressure is placed on the pedal, the friction brakes come into play as well. The current Honda Civic Hybrid mixes the two brake modes together imperceptibly, whereas the first model Toyota Prius, for example, has more of a two-stage pedal.

Regeneration also occurs only when the throttle has been fully lifted. In the Hybrid Civic, it is like decelerating in fourth gear (in a five- or six-speed transaxle), while in the Prius models it feels less strong.

The wear of the hydraulic brakes and pads will also be substantially lessened. The base brakes are still used when descending long hills, though as the battery becomes more fully charged, regeneration progressively reduces its braking action and the hydraulic brakes then do more and more of the work.

Regeneration switches off at low speeds, so the disc brake pads and rotors stay clean and fully functional.

NOTE: One of the major concerns with hybrid vehicles is rust and corrosion on the brake rotors and drums. This occurs on hybrids because the base brakes are usually only used at low vehicle speeds.

The amount of regeneration that occurs is largely dictated by the output of the master cylinder pressure sensor. The ECU looks at the brake pressure signal from the sensor when the brake pedal switch is not triggered and uses this as the starting value. When the brake pedal is pushed, it then checks the difference between the starting value and the "brake pedal on" value and sets the regeneration value, according to this difference.

The voltage output of the pressure sensor ranges from about 0.4 to 3.0 volts, rising with increasing pressure. Service information states that a fault will be detected if the voltage from the sensor is outside of the range of 0.14V to 4.4V, or if the voltage output of the sensor is outside a certain ratio to its nominally 5V supply voltage. See Figure 17-9.

DECELERATION RATES

Deceleration rates are measured in units of "feet per second per second." What it means is that the vehicle will change in

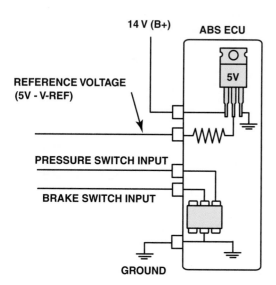

FIGURE 17-9 The ABS ECU on a Toyota Prius uses the brake switch and pressure sensor inputs to control the regenerative braking system. The circuit includes a voltage signal from the sensor, the regulated 5V supply to it, the input from the brake light switch (12V when the brakes are on), and the ground (labeled earth) connection.

FREQUENTLY ASKED QUESTION

CAN AN ON-VEHICLE BRAKE LATHE BE USED ON A HYBRID ELECTRIC VEHICLE?

Yes. When a brake rotor needs to be machined on a hybrid electric vehicle, the rotor is being rotated. On most hybrids, the front wheels are also connected to the traction motor that can propel the vehicle and generate electricity during deceleration and braking. When the drive wheels are being rotated, the motor/generator is producing electricity. However, unless the high-voltage circuit wiring has been disconnected, no harm will occur.

velocity during a certain time interval divided by the time interval. Deceleration is abbreviated "ft/sec²" (pronounced "feet per second per second" or "feet per second squared") or meters per sec² (m/s²) in the metric system. Typical deceleration rates include the following:

- Comfortable deceleration is about 8.5 ft/sec² (3 m/s²).
- Loose items in the vehicle will "fly" above 11 ft/sec² (3.5 m/s²).
- Maximum deceleration rates for most vehicles and light trucks range from 16 to 32 ft/sec² (5 to 10 m/s²).

An average deceleration rate of 15 ft/sec² (3 m/s²) can stop a vehicle traveling at 55 mph (88 km/h) in about 200 ft (61 m) and in less than 4 seconds. Deceleration is also expressed in units called a **g force**. One g is the acceleration of gravity, which is 32 ft/sec².

With a conventional hydraulic braking system, the driver can brake extremely gently, thereby only imperceptibly slowing the vehicle. A typical hybrid using regenerative braking will normally indicate a 0.1 g (about 3 ft/sec²) deceleration rate when the throttle is released and the brake pedal has not been applied. This rate is what a driver would normally expect to occur when the accelerator pedal is released. This slight deceleration feels comfortable to the driver, as well as the passengers, because this is what occurs in a nonhybrid vehicle that does not incorporate regenerative braking. When the brake pedal is pressed, the deceleration increases to a greater value than 0.1 g, which gives the driver the same feeling of deceleration that would occur in a conventional vehicle. Maximum deceleration rates are usually greater that 0.8 g and could exceed 1 g in most vehicles. See Figure 17-10.

FIGURE 17-10 This graph compares the figures: at the far left a throttle lift typically giving about 0.1 g deceleration; second from the left a minimum regenerative braking of about 0.1 g; second from the right, a moderate regenerative braking is about 0.2 g; and on the far right a hard emergency stop resulting in braking of (at least) 0.8 g, which uses both the regenerative braking system, as well as the base hydraulic brake system.

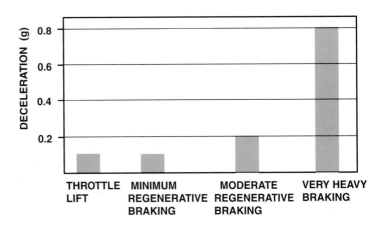

Engine Design Changes Related to Regenerative Braking

Some hybrid vehicles, such as the second generation Honda Civic and Accord, use a variation of the VTEC valve actuation system to close all of the valves in three cylinders in both the V-6 and the inline four cylinder engines during deceleration. This traps some exhaust in the cylinders and because no air enters the pistons, the cylinders do not have anything to compress. As a result, the engine does not cause any engine braking and therefore allows more of the inertia of the moving vehicle to be converted to electrical energy due to regenerative braking. See Figure 17-11.

FIGURE 17-11 This Honda valve train photo shows the small spring used to absorb the motion of the rocker arm when the cam is switched to a lobe that has zero lift. This action causes the valves to remain closed thereby reducing engine braking, which increases the amount of energy that can be captured by the regenerative braking system when the vehicle is slowing. The powertrain control module controls this valve action in response to inputs from the throttle position (TP) sensor and vehicle speed information.

Electric Motor Becomes a Generator

When a motor is used for regenerative braking, it acts as a generator and produces an alternating current (AC). The AC current needs to be rectified (converted) to DC current to go into the batteries. Each of the three main power wires coming out of the motor needs two large diodes. The two large diodes on each main wire do the job of converting the AC into DC.

Regenerative braking is variable. In the same way as the accelerator pedal is used to adjust the speed, the braking is varied by reducing the speed.

There are deceleration programs within the Powertrain Control Module (PCM), which vary the maximum deceleration rates according to vehicle speed and battery state-of-charge (SOC).

FREQUENTLY ASKED QUESTION

WHEN DOES REGENERATIVE BRAKING NOT WORK?

There is one unusual situation where regenerative braking will not occur. What happens if, for example, the vehicle is at the top of a long hill and the battery charge level is high? In this situation, the controller can only overcharge the batteries. Overcharging is not good for the batteries, so the controller will disable regenerative braking and use the base brakes only. This is one reason why the SOC of the batteries is kept below 80% so regenerative braking can occur.

SERVICING REGENERATIVE BRAKING SYSTEMS

On the Ford Escape hybrid system, the regenerative braking system checks the integrity of the brake system as a self-test. After a certain amount of time, the brake controller will energize the hydraulic control unit and check that pressure can be developed in the system.

- This is performed when a door is opened as part of the wake-up feature of the system.
- The ignition key does not have to be in the ignition for this self-test to be performed.
- This is done by developing brake pressure for short periods of time.

CAUTION: To prevent physical harm or causing damage to the vehicle when serving the braking system, the technician should do the following:

1. In order to change the brake pads, it is necessary to enter the "Pad Service Mode" on a scan tool and disable the self-test. This will prevent brake pressure from being applied.
2. Disconnect the wiring harness at the hydraulic control unit. See Figure 17-12.
3. Check service information regarding how to cycle the ignition switch to enter the Pad Service mode.

FIGURE 17-12   When working on the brakes on a Ford Escape or Mercury Mariner hybrid vehicle, disconnect the black electrical connector on the ABS hydraulic control unit located on the passenger side under the hood.

SUMMARY

1. All moving objects that have mass (weight) have kinetic energy.
2. The regenerative braking system captures most of the kinetic energy from the moving vehicle and returns this energy to high-voltage batteries to be used later to help propel the vehicle.
3. The two types of regenerative braking include parallel and series.
4. Brushless DC and AC induction motors are used in hybrid electric vehicles to help propel the vehicle and to generate electrical energy back to the batteries during braking.
5. Most hybrid electric vehicles use an electrohydraulic braking system that includes pressure sensors to detect the pressures in the system.
6. The controller is used to control the motors and turn them into a generator as needed to provide regenerative braking.

REVIEW QUESTIONS

1. What is inertia?
2. What is the difference between series and parallel regenerative braking systems?
3. What happens in the regenerative braking system when the high-voltage batteries are fully charged?
4. Describe what occurs when the driver first releases the accelerator pedal and then starts to brake on a hybrid electric vehicle equipped with regenerative braking.

CHAPTER QUIZ

1. Which type of regenerative braking system uses an electrohydraulic system?
   a. Series
   b. Parallel
   c. Both series and parallel
   d. Neither series nor parallel

2. Kinetic energy is_____.
   a. The energy that the driver exerts on the brake pedal
   b. The energy needed from the batteries to propel a vehicle
   c. The energy in any moving object
   d. The energy that the motor produces to propel the vehicle

3. Inertia is_____.
   a. The energy of any moving object that has mass (weight)
   b. The force that the driver exerts on the brake pedal during a stop
   c. The electric motor force that is applied to the drive wheels
   d. The force that the internal combustion engine and the electric motor together apply to the drive wheels during rapid acceleration

4. Technician A says that the powertrain control module (PCM) or controller can control the voltage to the motor(s) in a hybrid electric vehicle. Technician B says that the PCM or controller can control the electric motors by varying the frequency of the applied current. Which technician is correct?
   a. Technician A only
   b. Technician B only
   c. Both Technicians A and B
   d. Neither Technician A nor B

5. During braking on a hybrid electric vehicle equipped with regenerative braking system, what occurs when the driver depresses the brake pedal?
   a. The friction brakes are only used as a backup and not used during normal braking.
   b. The motors become generators.
   c. The driver needs to apply a braking lever instead of a depressing the brake pedal to energize the regenerative braking system.
   d. The batteries are charged to 100 percent SOC.

6. Technician A says that a front-wheel-drive hybrid electric vehicle can only generate electricity during braking from the front wheel motor(s). Technician B says that the antilock braking (ABS) is not possible with a vehicle equipped with a regenerative braking system. Which technician is correct?
   a. Technician A only
   b. Technician B only
   c. Both Technicians A and B
   d. Neither Technician A nor B

7. In a regenerative braking system, which part of the electric motor is being controlled by the computer?
   a. The rotor
   b. The stator
   c. Both the rotor and the stator
   d. Neither the rotor nor the stator

8. In a Toyota Prius regenerative braking system, how many pressure *sensors* are used?
   a. One
   b. Two
   c. Three
   d. Four

9. In a Toyota Prius regenerative braking system, how many pressure *switches* are used?
   a. One
   b. Two
   c. Three
   d. Four

10. Two technicians are discussing deceleration rates. Technician A says that a one "g" stop is a gentle slowing of the vehicle. Technician B says that a stopping rate of 8 ft/sec^2 is a severe stop. Which technician is correct?
    a. Technician A only
    b. Technician B only
    c. Both Technicians A and B
    d. Neither Technician A nor B

CHAPTER 18

ABS COMPONENTS AND OPERATION

OBJECTIVES

After studying Chapter 18, the reader should be able to:

1. Prepare for the Brakes (A5) ASE certification test content area "F" (Antilock Brake System Diagnosis and Repair).
2. Explain the reason for ABS.
3. Describe the purpose and function of the ABS components, such as wheel speed sensors, electrohydraulic unit, and electronic controller.
4. Discuss how the ABS components control wheel slippage.
5. Explain how the ABS components control acceleration traction control.

KEY TERMS

Antilock braking systems (ABS) (p. 339)
Accumulator (p. 347)
Active sensor (p. 345)
Air gap (p. 344)
Channel (p. 341)
Control module (p. 341)
Electronic stability control (p. 352)
Flash codes (p. 346)
Integral ABS (p. 342)
Isolation solenoid (p. 346)
Nonintegral ABS (p. 342)
Pressure decay stage (p. 347)
Pressure dump stage (p. 347)

Pressure increase stage (p. 347)
Pressure reduction stage (347)
Pressure release stage (347)
Rear Antilock Braking System (RABS) (p. 341)
Rear Wheel Anti-Lock (RWAL) (p. 341)
Release solenoid (p. 347)
Select low principle (p. 341)
Solenoid valves (p. 341)
Tire slip (p. 339)
Tone ring (p. 343)
Traction (p. 339)
Traction control (p. 349)
Wheel speed sensors (WSS) (p. 343)

ABS CHARACTERISTICS

Antilock braking systems (ABS) help prevent the wheels from locking during sudden braking, especially on slippery surfaces. This helps the driver maintain control.

Antilock brakes increase safety because they eliminate lockup and minimize the danger of skidding, allowing the vehicle to stop in a straight line. ABS also allows the driver to maintain steering control during heavy braking so the vehicle can be steered to avoid an obstacle or another vehicle.

ABS can optimize braking when road conditions are less than ideal, as when making a sudden panic stop or when braking on a wet or slick road. ABS does this by monitoring the relative speed of the wheels to one another. It uses this information to modulate brake pressure as needed to control slippage and maintain traction when the brakes are applied.

ABS and Tire Traction

Preventing brake lockup is important because of the adverse effect a locked wheel has on tire **traction**. The brakes slow the rotation of the wheels, but it is friction between the tire and road that stops the vehicle and allows it to be steered. If tire traction is reduced, stopping distances increase, and the directional stability of the vehicle suffers.

Traction is defined in terms of **tire slip,** which is the difference between the actual speed and the rate at which the tire tread moves across the road. A free-rolling wheel has nearly zero tire slip, while a locked wheel has 100% tire slip. See Figure 18-1.

When the brakes are applied, the rotational speed of the wheel drops, and tire slip increases because the tread moves across the road slower than the actual vehicle speed. This slip creates friction that converts kinetic energy into braking and cornering force.

Tire Slip and Braking Distance

On dry or wet pavement, maximum braking traction occurs when tire slip is held between approximately 15% and 30%. See Figure 18-2.

On snow- or ice-covered pavement, the optimum slip range is 20% to 50%. In each case, if tire slip increases beyond these levels, the amount of traction decreases. A skidding tire with 100% slip provides 20% to 30% less braking traction on dry pavement, and this is generally true on slippery roads as well. In nearly all cases, the shortest stopping distances are obtained when the brakes are applied with just enough force to keep the tire slip in the range where traction is greatest.

Tire Slip and Vehicle Stability

A tire's contact patch with the road can provide only a certain amount of traction. When a vehicle is stopped in a straight

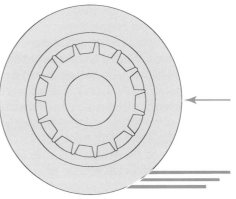

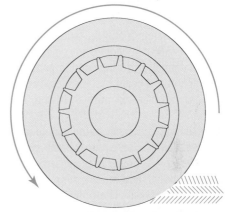

**VEHICLE MOVING-TIRE NOT
ROTATING — 100% SLIP**

TIRE ROTATING — 0% SLIP

FIGURE 18-1   Maximum braking traction occurs when tire slip is between 10% and 20%. A rotating tire has 0% slip and a locked-up wheel has 100% slip.

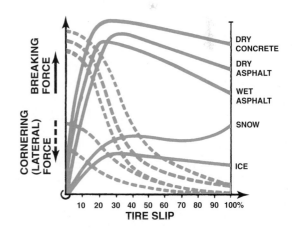

FIGURE 18-2   Traction is determined by pavement conditions and tire slip.

line, nearly all of the available traction can be used to provide braking force. Only a small amount of traction is required to generate lateral force that keeps the vehicle traveling in a straight line. However, if a vehicle has to stop and turn at the same time, the available traction must be *divided* to provide both cornering (lateral) and braking force.

No tire can provide full cornering power and full braking power at the same time. When a brake is locked and the tire has 100% slip, all of the available traction is used for braking, and none is left for steering. As a result, a skidding tire follows the path of least resistance. This means that if the rear brakes lock, the back end of the vehicle will tend to swing around toward the front causing a spin. If the front brakes lock, steering control will be lost and the vehicle will slide forward in a straight line until the brakes are released to again make traction available for steering.

ABS and Base Brakes

An antilock braking system is only an "add-on" to the existing base brake system. ABS only comes into play when traction conditions are marginal or during sudden panic stops when the tires lose traction and begin to slip excessively. The rest of the time ABS has no effect on normal driving, handling, or braking.

ABS also makes no difference in the maintenance, inspection, service, or repair of conventional brake system components. A vehicle with ABS brakes uses the same brake linings, calipers, wheel cylinders, and other system components as a vehicle without ABS brakes. The only exception being the master cylinder on certain applications.

All ABS systems are also designed to be as "fail-safe" as possible. Should a failure occur that affects the operation of the ABS system, the system will deactivate itself and the vehicle will revert to normal braking. Therefore, an ABS failure will not prevent the vehicle from stopping.

ABS Limitations

There are two situations in which an antilock brake system will *not* provide the shortest stopping distances. The first involves straight stops made on smooth, dry pavement by an *expert* driver. Under these conditions, a skilled driver can hold the tires consistently closer to the ideal slip rate than the ABS can. See Figure 18-3.

This is possible because current antilock braking systems may allow the amount of tire slip to drop as low as 5%, which is somewhat below the point where maximum tire traction is achieved. However, for the average driver, or under less than ideal conditions, antilock brakes will almost always stop the vehicle in a shorter distance.

The other situation in which antilock brakes will not provide the shortest stops is when braking on loose gravel or dirt, or in deep, fluffy snow. Under these conditions, a locked wheel will stop the vehicle faster because loose debris builds up and forms a wedge in front of the tire that helps stop the vehicle. See Figure 18-4.

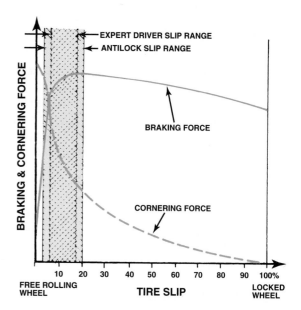

FIGURE 18-3 A good driver can control tire slip more accurately than an ABS if the vehicle is traveling on a smooth, dry road surface.

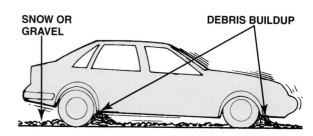

FIGURE 18-4 A wedge of gravel or snow in the front of a locked wheel can help stop a vehicle faster than would occur if the wheel brakes were pulsed on and off by an antilock braking system.

An antilock braking system will prevent this wedge from forming, so some vehicles with antilock brakes have a switch on the instrument panel that allows the system to be deactivated when driving on these kinds of road surfaces.

No ABS can overcome the laws of physics. The weight and speed of a moving vehicle give it a great deal of kinetic energy, and only so much of that energy can be converted into braking or cornering force at any given time. The limiting factor in this conversion is the traction between the tires and road.

Although a vehicle with four-wheel antilock brakes will stop in very nearly the shortest possible distance, this will still not prevent an accident if the brakes are applied too late to bring the vehicle to a complete stop before impact. However, because steering control is retained with four-wheel antilock brakes, it may be possible to drive the vehicle around a potential accident while in the process of braking.

Another situation where antilock brakes cannot defy the laws of physics occurs when a vehicle enters a corner traveling faster than it is physically possible to negotiate the turn. In

FIGURE 18-5 Being able to steer and control the vehicle during rapid braking is one major advantage of an antilock braking system.

this situation, antilock brakes will not prevent the vehicle from leaving the road. However, they will allow the vehicle to be slowed and steered in the process, thus lessening the severity of the eventual impact. See Figure 18-5.

ABS OPERATION

All ABS systems control tire slip by monitoring the relative deceleration rates of the wheels during braking. Wheel speed is monitored by one or more wheel speed sensors. If one wheel starts to slow at a faster rate than the others, or at a faster rate than that which is programmed in the antilock **control module,** it indicates a wheel is starting to slip and is in danger of losing traction and locking. The ABS responds by momentarily reducing hydraulic pressure to the brake on the affected wheel or wheels. This allows the wheel to speed up momentarily so it can regain traction. As traction is regained, brake pressure is reapplied to again slow the wheel. The cycle is repeated over and over until the vehicle stops or until the driver eases pressure on the brake pedal.

Electrically operated **solenoid valves** (or motor-driven valves in the case of Delphi ABS-VI applications) are used to hold, release, and reapply hydraulic pressure to the brakes. This produces a pulsating effect, which can be felt in the brake pedal during hard braking. The rapid modulation of brake pressure in a given brake circuit reduces the braking load on the affected wheel and allows it to regain traction to prevent lockup. The effect is much the same as pumping the brakes, except that the ABS system does it automatically for each brake circuit, and at speeds that would be humanly impossi-

ble—up to dozens of times per second depending on the system (some cycle faster than others). See Figure 18-6.

Once the rate of deceleration for the affected wheel catches up with the others, normal braking function and pressure resume, and antilock reverts to a passive mode.

SYSTEM CONFIGURATIONS

All ABS systems keep track of wheel deceleration rates with wheel speed sensors. The various ABS systems use a different number of sensors, depending on how the system is configured. See Figure 18-7.

Four-Channel ABS Systems

On some applications, each wheel is equipped with its own speed sensor. This type of arrangement is called a "four-wheel, four-channel" system since each wheel speed sensor provides input for a separate hydraulic control circuit or "channel."

The term **channel** always refers to the number of separate or individually controlled ABS hydraulic circuits in an ABS system, not the number of wheel speed sensor electrical circuits.

NOTE: For vehicle stability systems to function, there has to be four wheel speed sensors and four channels so the hydraulic control unit can pulse individual wheel brakes to help achieve vehicle stability.

Three-Channel ABS Systems

Some four-wheel ABS systems have a separate wheel speed sensor for each front wheel but use a common speed sensor for both rear wheels. These are called "three-channel" systems. The rear wheel speed sensor is mounted in either the differential or the transmission. The sensor reads the combined or average speed of both rear wheels. This type of setup saves the cost for an additional sensor and reduces the complexity of the system by allowing both rear wheels to be controlled simultaneously. This is known as the **select low principle.** Three-channel systems are the most common type of ABS setup used on rear-wheel-drive applications.

Single-Channel ABS Systems

The single-channel rear-wheel-only ABS system is used on many rear-wheel-drive pickups and vans. Ford's version is called **Rear Antilock Braking System (RABS),** while General Motors and DaimlerChrysler call theirs **Rear Wheel Anti-Lock (RWAL).** The front wheels have no speed sensors, and only a single speed sensor mounted in the differential or transmission is used for both rear wheels. Rear-wheel antilock

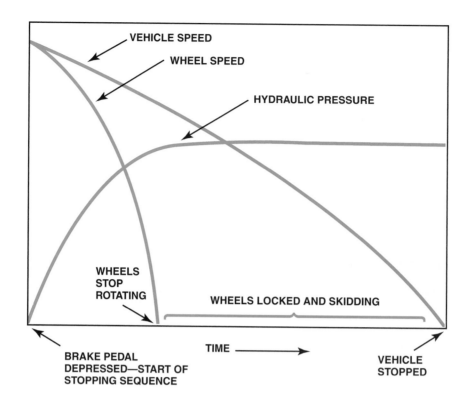

FIGURE 18-6 A typical stop on a slippery road surface without antilock brakes. Notice that the wheels stopped rotating and skidded until the vehicle finally came to a stop.

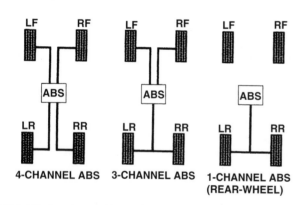

FIGURE 18-7 ABS configuration includes four-channel, three-channel, and single-channel.

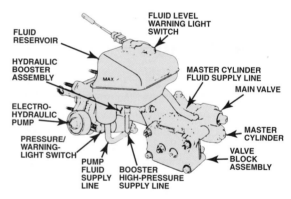

FIGURE 18-8 A typical integral ABS unit that combines the function of the master cylinder, brake booster, and antilock braking system in one assembly.

systems are typically used on applications where vehicle loading can affect rear wheel traction, which is why it is used on pickup trucks and vans. Because the rear-wheel antilock systems have only a single channel, they are much less complex and costly than their multichannel, four-wheel counterparts.

Integral and Nonintegral

Another distinction between ABS systems is whether they are **integral** or **nonintegral ABS.** Integral systems combine the brake master cylinder and ABS hydraulic modulator, pump, and accumulator into one assembly. See Figure 18-8.

Integral systems do not have a vacuum booster for power assist and rely instead on pressure generated by the electric pump for this purpose. Most of the older ABS applications are integral systems. Integral ABS systems include the Bendix 10 and Bendix 9 (Jeep) ABS systems, Bosch 3, Delco Moraine Powermaster III, and Teves Mark 2.

Nonintegral ABS systems, which are sometimes referred to as "add-on" systems, have become the predominant type of ABS system because of their lower cost and simplicity. See Figure 18-9.

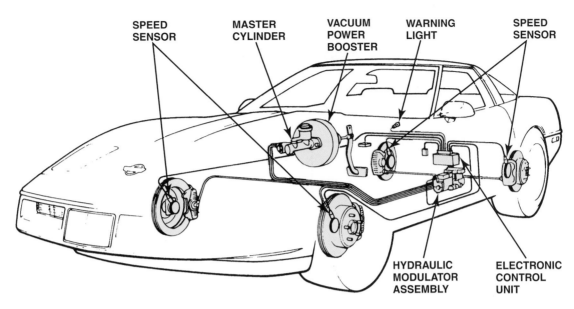

FIGURE 18-9   A typical nonintegral-type (remote) ABS system.

Nonintegral ABS systems have a conventional brake master cylinder and vacuum power booster with a separate hydraulic modulator unit. Some also have an electric pump for ABS braking (to reapply pressure during the ABS hold-release-reapply cycle), but do not use the pumps for normal power assist.

Nonintegral (add-on) systems include Bendix 3, Bendix 6, Bendix ABX-4, Bendix Mecatronic, Bosch 2, Bosch 2S Micro, Bosch 2U, Bosch 2E, Bosch 5, Delco Moraine ABS-VI, Kelsey-Hayes RABS/RWAL, 4WAL, EBC-5 and EBC-10, Sumitomo ABS, Teves Mark 4 ABS and MK20, and Toyota rear-wheel ABS.

ABS COMPONENTS

Basic components that are common to all antilock brake systems include the following:

- Wheel speed sensors
- Electronic control unit
- ABS warning lamp
- Hydraulic modulator assembly with electrically operated solenoid valves (or motor-driven valves in the case of Delphi ABS-VI)

Some systems also have an electric pump and accumulator to generate hydraulic pressure for power assist as well as ABS braking. See Figure 18-10.

Wheel Speed Sensors

The **wheel speed sensors WSS** consist of a magnetic pickup and a toothed sensor ring (usually called a **tone ring**). The sensor may be mounted in the steering knuckle, wheel hub, brake backing plate, transmission tailshaft, or differential housing. See Figure 18-11.

On some applications, the sensor is an integral part of the wheel bearing and hub assembly. The sensor rings may be mounted on the axle hub behind the brake rotors, on the brake rotors or drums, on the outside of the outboard constant velocity joints on a front-wheel-drive vehicle, on the transmission tailshaft, or inside the differential on the pinion gear shaft.

Sensor Operation

The sensor pickup has a magnetic core surrounded by coil windings. See Figure 18-12.

As the wheel turns, teeth on the sensor ring move through the pickup's magnetic field. This reverses the polarity of the magnetic field and induces an alternating current (AC) voltage in the sensor windings. The number of voltage pulses per second induced in the pickup changes frequency. See Figure 18-13.

The frequency of the signal is therefore proportional to wheel speed. The higher the frequency, the faster the wheel is turning.

The signals are sent to the ABS control module (or an intermediate module in some General Motors rear-wheel ABS applications), where the AC signal is converted into a digital signal for processing. The control module then monitors wheel speed by counting the pulses from each of the wheel speed sensors. If the frequency signal from one wheel starts to change abruptly with respect to the others, it tells the module that wheel is starting to lose traction. The module then applies antilock braking if needed to maintain traction.

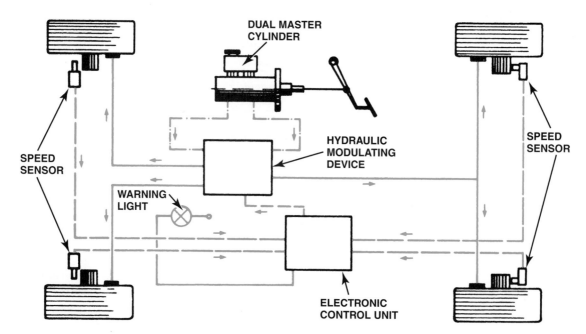

FIGURE 18-10   A schematic drawing of a typical antilock braking system.

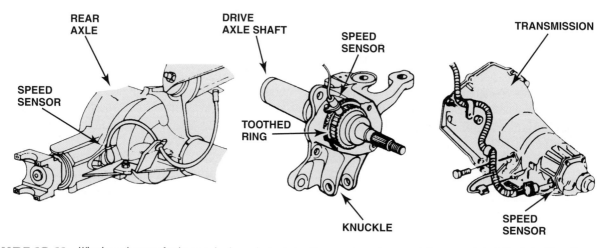

FIGURE 18-11   Wheel speed sensors for the rear wheels may be located on the rear axle, on the transmission, or on the individual wheel knuckle.

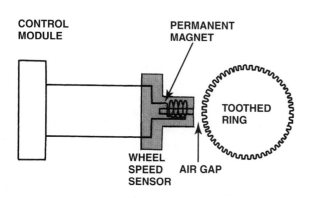

FIGURE 18-12   A schematic of a typical wheel speed sensor.

Sensor Air Gap

The distance or **air gap** between the end of the sensor and its ring is critical. A close gap is necessary to produce a strong, reliable signal. But metal-to-metal contact between the sensor and its ring must be avoided since this would damage both. The air gap must not be too wide or a weak or erratic signal (or no signal) may result. The air gap on some wheel speed sensors is adjustable, and is specified by the vehicle manufacturer.

Sensor Applications and Precautions

Wheel speed sensor readings are affected by the size of the wheels and tires on the vehicle. A tire with a larger overall di-

WHEEL SPEED SENSOR OUTPUT - LOW SPEED

WHEEL SPEED SENSOR OUTPUT - HIGHER SPEED
(FREQUENCY OF AC SIGNAL INCREASES
IN PROPORTION TO SPEED)

FIGURE 18-13   Wheel speed sensors produce an alternating current (AC) signal with a frequency that varies in proportion to wheel speed.

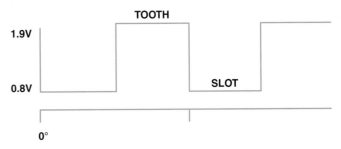

DIGITAL SIGNAL

FIGURE 18-14   A digital wheel speed sensor produces a square wave output signal.

ameter will give a slower speed reading than one with a smaller diameter. Because the ABS system is calibrated to a specific tire size, vehicle manufacturers warn against changing tire sizes. A different tire size or aspect ratio could have an effect on the operation of the ABS system.

Wheel speed sensors are also magnetic, which means they can attract metallic particles. These particles can accumulate on the end of the sensor and reduce its ability to produce an accurate signal. Removing the sensor and cleaning the tip may be necessary if the sensor is producing a poor signal.

Digital Wheel Speed Sensors

A conventional wheel speed sensor uses a permanent magnet with a surrounding coil of wire to produce an AC voltage signal that is proportional to wheel speed. The major problem with this type of sensor is that the voltage output and frequency are very low at slow speeds and therefore, cannot produce accurate wheel speed for ABS and traction control.

A digital wheel speed sensor, also called an **active sensor,** uses either a Hall-effect or a variable-reluctance circuit to produce a square waveform where the frequency is proportional to the wheel speed. A digital wheel speed sensor can also detect direction and can therefore be used by the controller for hill holding. The accuracy of these digital sensors also makes correlation to global positioning used in navigational systems more accurate, especially when the vehicle is being driven at slow speeds.

The typical digital wheel speed sensor uses two wires:

- A 12-volt supply
- A DC signal from the sensor

The sensor voltage toggles between about 0.8V and 1.9V. See Figure 18-14.

ABS Control Module

The ABS electronic control module, which may be referred to as an "electronic brake control module" (EBCM), "electronic brake module" (EBM), or "controller antilock brakes" (CAB) module, is a digital microprocessor that uses inputs from its various sensors to regulate hydraulic pressure during braking to prevent wheel lockup. The module may be located on the hydraulic modulator assembly (as it is on many of the newer compact ABS systems), or it may be located elsewhere in the vehicle, such as the trunk, passenger compartment, or under the hood.

Module Inputs

The key inputs for the ABS control module come from the wheel speed sensors and the brake pedal switch. See Figure 18-15.

The brake pedal switch signals the control module when the brakes are being applied, which causes it to go from a "standby" mode to an active mode. At the same time, the wheel speed sensors provide information about what is happening to the wheels while the brakes are being applied.

NOTE: A fault with the brake switch will not prevent ABS operation. The brake switch allows the controller to react faster to an ABS event.

Module Operation

If the control module detects a difference in the deceleration rate between one or more wheels when braking, or if the overall rate of deceleration is too fast and exceeds the limits programmed into the control module, it triggers the ABS control module to momentarily take over. The control module cycles the solenoid valves in the modulator assembly to pulsate hydraulic pressure in the affected brake circuit (or circuits) until sensor information indicates that the deceleration rates have returned to normal and braking is under control. Normal braking resumes. When the brake pedal is released or when the vehicle comes to a stop, the control module returns to a standby mode until it is again needed.

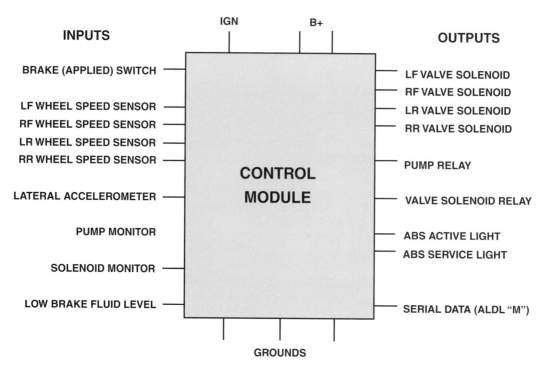

FIGURE 18-15   Typical inputs and outputs for brake control modules.

ABS Warning Lamp

Every ABS system has an amber indicator lamp on the instrument panel that warns the driver when a problem occurs within the ABS system. The lamp comes on when the ignition is turned on for a bulb check, then goes out after the engine starts. If the warning light remains on or comes on while driving, it usually indicates a fault in the ABS system that will require further diagnosis. On most applications, the ABS system disables if the ABS warning light comes on and remains on. This should have no effect on normal braking, unless the red brake warning lamp is also on. The ABS warning light is also used for diagnostic purposes when retrieving **flash codes** (trouble codes) from the ABS module.

Hydraulic Modulator Assembly

The modulator valve body is part of the master cylinder assembly in nonintegral antilock systems but separate in nonintegral systems. It contains solenoid valves for each brake unit (in Delphi ABS-VI applications, however, motor-driven valves are used instead of solenoids). The exact number of valves per circuit depends on the ABS system and the application. Some use a pair of on-off solenoid valves for each brake circuit while others use a single valve that can operate in more than one position.

ABS Solenoid

A solenoid consists of a wire coil with a movable core and a return spring. When current from the ABS control module ener-

gizes the coil, it pulls on the movable core. Depending on how the solenoid is constructed, this may open or close a valve that's attached to the movable core. When the control current is shut off, the solenoid snaps back to its normal or rest position.

Some solenoids are designed to do more than just switch on or off to open or close a valve. Some pull a valve to an intermediate position when a certain level of current is applied to the coil, then pull the valve to a third position when additional current is provided. See Figure 18-16.

This design allows a single solenoid to perform the same functions as two or even three single-position solenoids.

The solenoids in the hydraulic modulator assembly are used to open and close passageways between the master cylinder and the individual brake circuits. By opening or closing the modulator valves to which they're attached, brake pressure within any given circuit can be held, released, and reapplied to prevent lockup during hard braking.

ABS Control Pressure Strategy

The standard ABS control strategy that's used is a three-step cycle:

- The first step is to hold or isolate the pressure in a given brake circuit by closing an **isolation solenoid** in the modulator assembly. This solenoid is normally electrically and hydraulically opened. See Figure 18-17. When the solenoid is electrically closed, it becomes hydraulically closed, which blocks off the line and prevents any further pressure from the master cylinder reaching the brake. This is called the **pressure holding stage.**

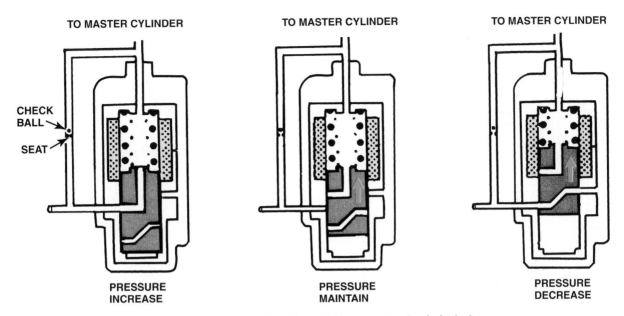

FIGURE 18-16   An ABS 3-way solenoid can increase, maintain, or decrease brake pressure to a given brake circuit.

- If the wheel speed sensor continues to indicate the wheel is slowing too quickly and is starting to lock, the same solenoid or a second **release solenoid** is energized to open a vent port that releases pressure from the brake circuit. See Figure 18-18. The fluid is usually routed into a spring-loaded or pressurized storage reservoir (called an **accumulator**) so it can be reused as needed. Releasing pressure in the brake circuit allows the brake to loosen its grip so the wheel can speed up and regain traction. This is called **pressure reduction, pressure release, pressure decay,** or **pressure dump stage.** The pressure reduction solenoid is normally hydraulically closed and electrically opened.

- The release and/or isolation solenoid(s) are then closed and/or the additional solenoid energized so pressure can be reapplied to the brake from the master cylinder or accumulator to reapply the brake. See Figure 18-19. This is called the **pressure increase stage.** During the pressure increase stages, the isolation solenoid is electrically and hydraulically opened. The pressure reduction solenoid is electrically opened and hydraulically closed.

The hold-release-reapply cycle repeats as many times as needed until the vehicle either comes to a halt or the driver releases the brake pedal. The speed at which this occurs depends on the particular ABS system that is on the vehicle, but can range from a few times per second up to dozens of times per second.

Pump Motor and Accumulator

A high-pressure electric pump is used in some ABS systems to generate power assist for normal braking as well as the reapplication of brake pressure during ABS braking. See Figure 18-20.

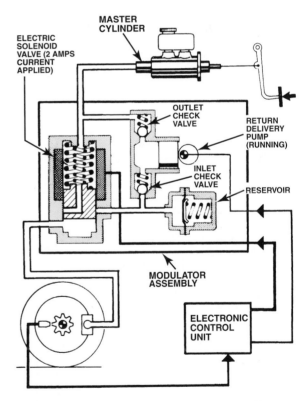

FIGURE 18-17   The isolation or hold phase of an ABS system on a Bosch 2 system.

In some systems, it is used only for the reapplication of pressure during ABS braking.

The pump motor is energized by a relay, which is switched on and off by the ABS control module. The fluid pressure generated by the pump is stored in the accumulator. Some

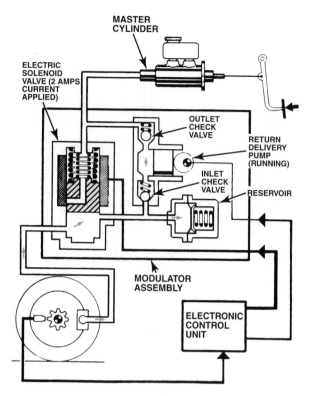

FIGURE 18-18 During the pressure reduction stage, pressure is vented from the brake circuit so the tire can speed up and regain traction.

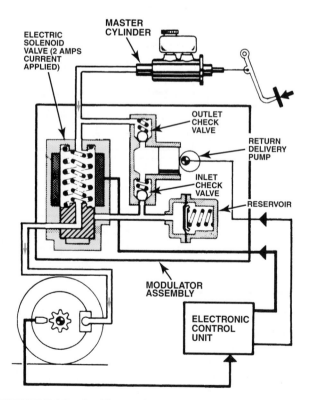

FIGURE 18-19 The control module reapplies pressure to the affected brake circuit once the tire achieves traction so that normal braking can continue.

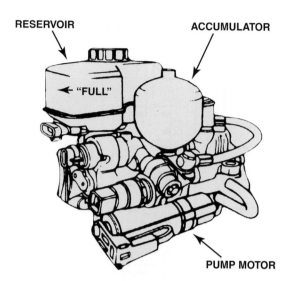

FIGURE 18-20 An integral ABS unit with a pump motor to provide power assist during all phases of braking and brake pressure during ABS stops.

ABS systems have more than one accumulator. The accumulator on ABS systems, where the hydraulic modulator is part of the master cylinder assembly, consists of a pressure storage chamber filled with nitrogen gas. A thick rubber diaphragm forms a barrier between the nitrogen gas and brake fluid. As fluid is pumped into the accumulator, it compresses the gas and stores pressure. When the brake pedal is depressed, pressure from the accumulator flows to the master cylinder to provide power assist.

A pair of pressure switches mounted in the accumulator circuit signals the ABS control module to energize the pump when pressure falls below a preset minimum, then to shut the pump off once pressure is built back up.

Should the pump fail (a warning lamp comes on when reserve pressure drops too low), there is usually enough reserve pressure in the accumulator for 10 to 20 power-assisted stops. After that, there is no power assist. The brakes still work, but with greatly increased effort.

On ABS systems that have a conventional master cylinder and vacuum booster for power assist, a small accumulator or pair of accumulators may be used as temporary storage reservoirs for brake fluid during the hold-release-reapply cycle. This type of accumulator typically uses a spring-loaded diaphragm rather than a nitrogen-charged chamber to store pressure.

Accumulator Precautions

A fully charged accumulator in an integral ABS system can store up to 2,700 psi (19,000 kPa) of pressure for power-assist braking and for reapplying the brakes during the hold-release-reapply cycle for antilock braking. This stored pressure represents a potential hazard for a brake technician who is servicing the brakes, so the accumulator should be depressurized prior to doing any type of brake service work by pumping the brake pedal 25 to 40 times with the ignition key off.

In nonintegral ABS systems where an accumulator is used to temporarily hold fluid during the release phase of the hold-release-reapply ABS cycle, the accumulator consists of a spring-loaded diaphragm. This type of accumulator does not have to be depressurized prior to performing brake service.

BRAKE PEDAL FEEDBACK

Many ABS units force brake fluid back into the master cylinder under pressure during an ABS stop. This pulsing brake fluid return causes the brake pedal to pulsate. Some vehicle manufacturers use the pulsation of the brake pedal to inform the driver that the wheels are tending toward lockup and that the ABS is pulsing the brakes.

NOTE: A pulsating brake pedal may be normal only during an ABS stop. It is not normal for a vehicle with ABS to have a pulsating pedal during normal braking. If the brake pedal is pulsating during a non-ABS stop, the brake drums or rotor may be warped.

Some manufacturers use an isolation valve that prevents brake pedal pulsation even during an ABS stop.

BRAKE PEDAL TRAVEL SWITCH (SENSOR)

Some ABS systems, such as the Teves Mark IV system, use a brake pedal travel switch (sensor). The purpose of the switch is to turn on the hydraulic pump when the brake pedal has been depressed to 40% of its travel. The pump runs and pumps brake fluid back into the master cylinder, which raises the brake pedal until the switch closes again, turning off the pump.

NOTE: Some early ABS systems did not use a brake switch. The problem occurred when the ABS could be activated while driving over rough roads. The brake switch can be the same as the brake light switch or a separate switch.

The brake pedal switch is an input for the electronic controller. When the brakes are applied, the electronic controller "gets ready" to act if ABS needs to "initialize" the starting sequence of events.

CAUTION: If the driver pumps the brakes during an ABS event, the controller will reset and reinitialization starts over again. This resetting process can disrupt normal ABS operation. The driver need only depress and hold the brake pedal down during a stop for best operation.

TECH TIP

KISS

KISS usually means *Keep It Simple, Stupid,* but can also mean *Keep It Stock, Stupid,* and it is important to remember when replacing tires. Vehicles equipped with antilock brakes are "programmed" to pulse the brakes at just the right rate for maximum braking effectiveness. A larger tire rotates at a slower speed and a smaller-than-normal tire rotates at a faster speed. Therefore, tire size affects the speed and rate of change in speed of the wheels as measured by the wheel speed sensors.

While changing tire size will not prevent ABS operation, it will cause less effective braking during hard braking with the ABS activated. Using the smaller spare tire can create such a difference in wheel speed compared with the other wheels that a false wheel speed sensor code may be set and an amber ABS warning lamp on the dash may light. However, most ABS systems will still function with the spare tire installed, but the braking performance will not be as effective. For best overall performance, always replace tires with the same size and type as specified by the vehicle manufacturer.

TRACTION CONTROL

Traction control allows an ABS system to control wheel lockup during deceleration can be adopted to control wheel spin during acceleration.

Low-speed traction control uses the braking system to limit positive slip up to a vehicle speed of about 30 mph (48 km/h). See Figure 18-21.

All speed traction control systems are capable of reducing positive wheel slip at all speeds. Most speed traction control systems use accelerator reduction and engine power reduction to limit slip. For example, if a vehicle were being driven on an icy or snow-covered road, the brakes may become overheated if heavy acceleration is attempted. To help take the load off the brakes, the acceleration and power output from the engine is reduced. Many systems use accelerator pedal reduction and fuel injector cutout or ignition timing retardation individually or in combination to help match engine power output to the available tire traction. Traction control is also called acceleration slip regulation (ASR). See Figures 18-22 and 18-23.

FIGURE 18-21 Typical low-speed traction control design that uses wheel speed sensor information and the application of the drive-wheel brakes to help reduce tire slippage during during acceleration.

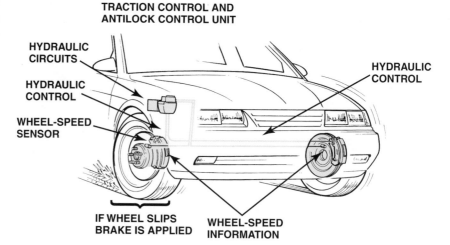

TRACTION CONTROL AND
ANTILOCK CONTROL UNIT

HYDRAULIC
CIRCUITS

HYDRAULIC
CONTROL

HYDRAULIC
CONTROL

WHEEL-SPEED
SENSOR

IF WHEEL SLIPS
BRAKE IS APPLIED

WHEEL-SPEED
INFORMATION

FIGURE 18-22 Typical all-speed traction control system that uses wheel speed sensor information and the engine controller to not only apply the brakes at lower speeds but also reduce engine power.

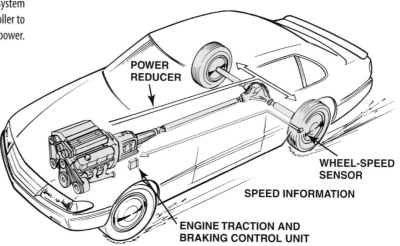

POWER
REDUCER

WHEEL-SPEED
SENSOR

SPEED INFORMATION

ENGINE TRACTION AND
BRAKING CONTROL UNIT

FIGURE 18-23 A cutaway of an ABS/traction control assembly used on a Honda.

NOTE: The ABS controller supplies to the wheel brake only the pressure that is required to prevent tire slipping during acceleration. The amount of pressure varies according to the condition of the road surface and the amount of engine power being delivered to the drive wheels. A program inside the controller will disable traction control if brake system overheating is likely to occur. The driver should either wait for the brakes to cool down or use less accelerator pedal while driving.

Inputs and Outputs

The input signals used for traction control include:

- Throttle position (TP) sensor—This indicates the position of the throttle.
- Wheel speed sensor (WSS)—The ABS controller (computer) monitors all four wheel speed sensors. If one wheel

FREQUENTLY ASKED QUESTION

I THOUGHT TRACTION CONTROL MEANT ADDITIONAL DRIVE WHEELS WERE ENGAGED

When the term *traction control* is used, many people think of four-wheel-drive or all-wheel-drive vehicles and powertrains. Instead of sending engine torque to other drive wheels, it is the purpose and function of the traction control system to prevent the drive wheel(s) from slipping during acceleration. A slipping tire has less traction than a non slipping tire—therefore, if the tire can be kept from slipping (spinning), more traction will be available to propel the vehicle. Traction control works with the engine computer to reduce torque delivery from the engine, as well as the ABS controller to apply the brakes to the spinning wheel if necessary to regain traction.

is rotating faster than the other, this indicates that the tire is slipping or has lost traction.

- Engine speed (RPM)—This information is supplied from the engine controller (Powertrain Control Module) and indicates the speed of the engine.
- Transmission range switch—Determines which gear the driver has selected so that the PCM can take corrective action.

The outputs of the traction control system can include one or more of the following:

- Retard ignition timing to reduce engine torque.
- Decrease the fuel injector pulse-width to reduce fuel delivery to the cylinder to reduce engine torque.
- Reduce the amount of intake air if the engine is equipped with an electronic throttle control. Reduced airflow will reduce engine torque.
- Upshift the automatic transmission/transaxle. If the transmission is shifted into a higher gear, the torque applied to the drive wheels is reduced.
- Lights a low traction or traction control warning light on the dash. See Figure 18-24.

Traction Control Operation

Traction control uses the same wheel speed sensors as ABS, but requires additional programming in the control module so

the system monitors wheel speed continuously, not just when braking. Traction control also requires additional solenoids in the hydraulic modulator so the brake circuits to the drive wheels can be isolated from the nondrive wheels when braking is needed to control wheel spin. An ABS system with traction control capability must also have a pump and accumulator to generate and store pressure for traction control braking. If a wheel speed sensor detects wheel spin in one of the drive wheels during acceleration, the control module energizes a solenoid that allows stored fluid pressure from the accumulator to apply the brakes on the wheel that is spinning. This slows the wheel that is spinning and redirects engine torque through the differential to the opposite drive wheel to restore traction. It works just as well on front-wheel-drive vehicles as it does rear-wheel-drive vehicles.

Traction Active Lamp

On most applications, a "TRAC CNTL" indicator light or "TRACTION CONTROL ACTIVE" message flashes on the instrumentation when the system is engaging traction control. This helps alert the driver that the wheels are losing traction. In most applications, the message does not mean there is anything wrong with the system—unless the ABS warning lamp also comes on, or the traction control light remains on continuously.

Traction Deactivation Switch

Many vehicles with traction control have a dash-mounted switch that allows the driver to deactivate the system when desired (as when driving in deep snow). An indicator light shows when the system is on or off, and may also signal the

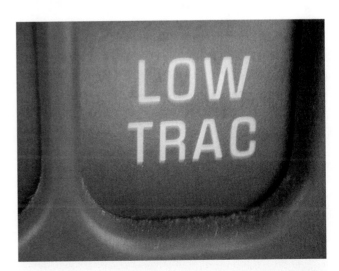

FIGURE 18-24   A traction control or low traction light on the dash is confusing to many drivers. When this lamp is on, the traction control system has either been turned off or a low traction condition is forcing the traction control system to take action.

driver when the traction control system is actively engaged during acceleration.

ELECTRONIC CONTROLLER OPERATION

The electronic controller is the computer in the system that controls all parts of ABS operation, including the following:

1. **A Self-Test.** The controller runs a self-test of all its components every time the ignition is turned on.

   > **NOTE:** Since an antilock braking system is a safety-related system, if it malfunctions, people can be injured. This is one reason why the system does a complete "system check" every time the ignition is cycled.

2. **The Wheel Hydraulic Controls.** The controller looks at the rate of wheel deceleration and compares it with normal stopping rates using an internal computer program that is based on vehicle weight, tire size, and so on. If a wheel is slowing down too fast, the controller activates the necessary hydraulic pressure controls.

TECH TIP

STOP ON A DIME?

Vehicles that are equipped with ABS help the driver avoid skidding and losing total control during braking. This is especially true for road surfaces that are slippery. However, vehicles equipped with ABS must still have traction between the tire and the road to stop.

This author had an experience with ABS on a snow-covered road. I applied the brakes while approaching a stop sign and the brake pedal started to pulsate, the electrohydraulic unit started to run, and the vehicle continued straight through the intersection! Luckily, no other vehicles were around. The vehicle did not stop for a long distance through the intersection, but it did stop straight—avoiding skidding. Because of the ice under the snow, the vehicle did not have traction between the tires and the road.

A common complaint is that the ABS did not stop the vehicle, while in reality, it did stop the vehicle from skidding or traveling out of control, even though short stops are not always possible. The service technician should explain the purpose and function of ABS before attempting to repair a problem that may be normal on the vehicle being inspected.

Remember – *The primary purpose of ABS is vehicle control—not short stopping distance!*

FREQUENTLY ASKED QUESTION

IS TIRE CHIRP NORMAL WITH ABS?

Some owners of vehicles complain that their ABS is not working correctly because their tires chirp and occasionally experience tire lockup during hard braking, especially at low speed. These conditions are perfectly normal because, for maximum braking, between 12% and 20% of slip means that the tire will slip or skid slightly during an ABS stop.

It is also normal for vehicles with ABS to have the tires lock and skid slightly when the speed of the vehicle is below 5 mph (8 km/h). This occurs because the wheel speed sensors cannot generate usable speed signals for the electronic controller. This low-speed wheel lockup seldom creates a problem.

Before attempting to troubleshoot or diagnose an ABS problem, be sure that the problem is not just normal operation of the system.

ELECTRONIC STABILITY CONTROL

Electronic Stability Control (ESC) uses the steering wheel position sensor and G-force and/or yaw sensor to determine if a vehicle is not under control. The ESC system, also called Electronic Stability Program (ESP), then applies individual wheel brakes to bring the vehicle under control. The following occurs if the vehicle is oversteering or understeering.

Oversteering

In this condition, the rear of the vehicle breaks loose resulting in the vehicle spinning out of control. This condition is also called *loose.* If the condition is detected during a left turn, the ESC system would apply the right front brake to bring the vehicle back under control.

Understeering

In this condition, the front of the vehicle continues straight ahead when turning, a condition that is also called *plowing* or *tight.* If this condition is detected during a right turn, the ESC system would apply the right rear wheel brake to bring the vehicle back under control. See Figure 18-25.

NOTE: When the brakes are applied during these corrections, a thumping sound and vibration may be sensed.

Stability control systems are offered under the following names:

- Acura: Vehicle Stability Assist (VSA)
- Audi: Electronic Stabilization Program (ESP)
- BMW: Dyanmic Stability Control (DSC), including Dynamic Traction Control
- Chrysler: Electric Stability Program (ESP)
- Dodge: Electronic Stability Program (ESP)
- DaimlerChrysler: Electronic Stability Program (ESP)
- Ferrari: Controllo Stabilita (CST)
- Ford: AdvanceTrac and Interactive Vehicle Dynamics (IVD)
- General Motors: StabiliTrak (Except Corvette – Active Handling)
- Hyundai: Electronic Stability Program (ESP)
- Honda: Electronic Stability Control (ESC), Vehicle Stability Assist (VSA), and Electronic Stability Program (ESP)
- Infiniti: Vehicle Dynamic Control (VDC)
- Jaguar: Dynamic Stability Control (DSC)
- Jeep: Electronic Stability Program (ESP)

- Kia: Electronic Stability Program (ESP)
- Land Rover: Dynamic Stability Control (DSC)
- Lexus: Vehicle Dynamics Integrated Management (VDIM) with Vehicle Stability Control (VSC) and Traction Control (TRAC) systems
- Lincoln: Advance Trak
- Maserati: Maserati Stability Program (MSP)
- Mazda: Dynamic Stability Control
- Mercedes: Electronic Stability Program (ESP)
- Mercury: AdvanceTrak
- Mini Cooper: Dynamic Stability Control
- Mitsubishi: Active Skid and Traction Control MULTIMODE
- Nissan: Vehicle Dynamic Control (VDC)
- Porsche: Porche Stability Management (PSM)
- Rover: Dynamic Stability Control (DSC)
- Saab: Electronic Stability Program (ESP)
- Saturn: StabiliTrak
- Subaru: Vehicle Dynamics Control Systems (VDCS)
- Suzuki: Electronic Stability Program (ESP)
- Toyota: Vehicle Dynamics Integrated Management (VDIM) with Vehicle Stability Control (VSC)
- Volvo: Dynamic Stability and Traction Control (DSTC)
- VW: Electronic Stability Program (ESP)

The purpose of the vehicle stability enhancement system along with the antilock brake system (ABS) is to provide vehicle stability enhancement during oversteer or understeer conditions.

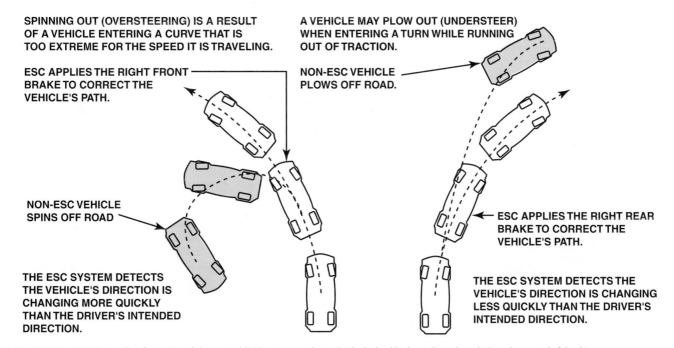

SPINNING OUT (OVERSTEERING) IS A RESULT OF A VEHICLE ENTERING A CURVE THAT IS TOO EXTREME FOR THE SPEED IT IS TRAVELING.

ESC APPLIES THE RIGHT FRONT BRAKE TO CORRECT THE VEHICLE'S PATH.

NON-ESC VEHICLE SPINS OFF ROAD

THE ESC SYSTEM DETECTS THE VEHICLE'S DIRECTION IS CHANGING MORE QUICKLY THAN THE DRIVER'S INTENDED DIRECTION.

A VEHICLE MAY PLOW OUT (UNDERSTEER) WHEN ENTERING A TURN WHILE RUNNING OUT OF TRACTION.

NON-ESC VEHICLE PLOWS OFF ROAD.

ESC APPLIES THE RIGHT REAR BRAKE TO CORRECT THE VEHICLE'S PATH.

THE ESC SYSTEM DETECTS THE VEHICLE'S DIRECTION IS CHANGING LESS QUICKLY THAN THE DRIVER'S INTENDED DIRECTION.

FIGURE 18-25   The electronic stability control (ESC) system applies individual wheel brakes to keep the vehicle under control of the driver.

WHEEL SPEED SENSOR Step-by-Step

STEP 1 A tone ring and a wheel speed sensor on the rear of a Dodge Caravan.

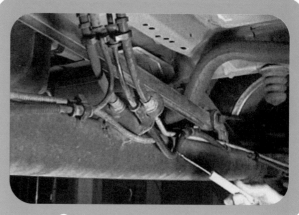

STEP 2 The wiring from the wheel speed sensor should be inspected for damage.

STEP 3 To test a wheel speed sensor, disconnect the sensor connector to gain access to the terminals.

STEP 4 Pulling down the rubber seal reveals the connector.

STEP 5 The ABS controller (computer) on this vehicle supplies a 2.5-volt reference signal to the wheel speed sensors.

STEP 6 The meter reads about 2.4 volts, indicating that the ABS controller is supplying the voltage to the wheel speed sensor.

WHEEL SPEED SENSOR continued

STEP 7 The test probes are touched to the terminals leading to the wheel speed sensor and the resistance is 1.1032 k ohms or 1,103.2 ohms.

STEP 8 The meter should (and does) read "OL," indicating that the wheel speed sensor and pigtail wiring is not shorted to ground.

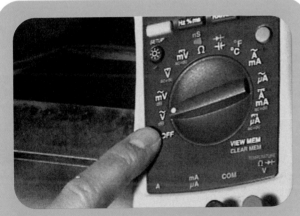

STEP 9 To measure the output of the wheel speed sensor, select AC volts on the digital multimeter.

STEP 10 Rotate the wheel and tire assembly by hand while observing the AC voltage output on the digital multimeter.

STEP 11 A good wheel speed sensor should be able to produce at least 100 mV (0.1 V) when the wheel is spun by hand.

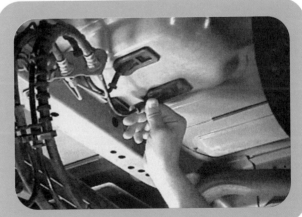

STEP 12 After testing, carefully reinstall the wiring connector into the body and under the rubber grommet.

SUMMARY

1. Antilock braking systems are designed to limit the amount of tire slip by pulsing the wheel brake on and off up to 20 times per second.

2. Steering control is possible during an ABS stop if the tires maintain traction with the road surface.

3. The three stages of ABS operation are pressure build-up, pressure holding, and pressure reduction.

4. The heart of an antilock braking system is the electronic controller (computer). Wheel speed sensors produce an electrical frequency that is proportional to the speed of the wheel. If a wheel is slowing down too fast, the controller controls the pressure of the wheel brake through an electrohydraulic unit.

5. Both integral and nonintegral antilock braking systems control the rear wheels only, both front wheels individually and the rear as one unit (three-channel), or all four wheel brakes independently (four-channel).

6. Antilock braking systems that control the drive-wheel brakes can be used for acceleration traction control.

REVIEW QUESTIONS

1. Describe how an antilock braking system (ABS) works.

2. List the three stages of ABS operation.

3. Explain how wheel speed sensors work.

4. Describe the difference between a three- and a four-channel system.

5. Explain how ABS can be used to prevent wheel slippage during acceleration.

CHAPTER QUIZ

1. Technician A says that the ABS system is designed so that the pressure to the wheel brakes is never higher than the pressure the driver is applying through the brake pedal. Technician B says that a pulsating brake pedal during normal braking is a characteristic feature of most ABS-equipped vehicles. Which technician is correct?

   a. Technician A only
   b. Technician B only
   c. Both Technicians A and B
   d. Neither Technician A nor B

2. The maximum traction between a tire and the road occurs when the tire is _____.

   a. Locked and skidding
   b. Rotating freely
   c. Slipping 10 to 20 percent
   d. Slipping 80 to 90 percent

3. Technician A says that ABS-equipped vehicles can stop quickly and without skidding on all road surfaces even if covered with ice. Technician B says that steering is possible during an ABS stop. Which technician is correct?

   a. Technician A only
   b. Technician B only
   c. Both Technicians A and B
   d. Neither Technician A nor B

4. A customer wanted the ABS checked because of tire chirp noise during hard braking. Technician A says that the speed sensors may be defective. Technician B says that tire chirp is normal during an ABS stop on dry pavement. Which technician is correct?

   a. Technician A only
   b. Technician B only
   c. Both Technicians A and B
   d. Neither Technician A nor B

5. Two technicians are discussing ABS wheel speed sensors. Technician A says that some ABS systems use a sensor located in the rear-axle pinion gear area. Technician B says that all ABS systems use a wheel speed sensor at each wheel. Which technician is correct?

   a. Technician A only
   b. Technician B only
   c. Both Technicians A and B
   d. Neither Technician A nor B

6. Technician A says that it may be normal for the hydraulic pump and solenoids to operate after the vehicle starts to move after a start. Technician B says that the ABS is disabled (does not function) below about 5 mph (8 km/h). Which technician is correct?

   a. Technician A only
   b. Technician B only

c. Both Technicians A and B

d. Neither Technician A nor B

7. Technician A says that a scan tool may be necessary to bleed some ABS hydraulic units. Technician B says that only DOT 3 brake fluid should be used with an ABS. Which technician is correct?

a. Technician A only

b. Technician B only

c. Both Technicians A and B

d. Neither Technician A nor B

8. Technician A says that many traction control systems reduce engine torque to help the drive wheels achieve traction. Technician B says that hydraulic pressure from the electrohydraulic unit supplies brake fluid pressure to the wheel brake that is spinning during a traction control event. Which technician is correct?

a. Technician A only

b. Technician B only

c. Both Technicians A and B

d. Neither Technician A nor B

9. The faster a wheel rotates, the higher the frequency produced by a wheel speed sensor.

a. True

b. False

10. Technician A says that some wheel speed sensors are enclosed in a wheel bearing assembly. Technician B says that some wheel speed sensors are exposed to possible damage from road debris. Which technician is correct?

a. Technician A only

b. Technician B only

c. Both Technicians A and B

d. Neither Technician A nor B

ANTILOCK
BRAKE SYSTEMS

OBJECTIVES

After studying Chapter 19, the reader should be able to:

1. Prepare for the Brakes (A5) ASE certification test content area "F" (Antilock Brake Systems Diagnosis and Repair).

2. Identify and describe Bendix antilock braking systems.

3. Explain the operation and components of Bosch antilock braking systems.

4. Describe the operation of Delphi antilock braking systems.

5. Identify and describe Kelsey-Hayes antilock braking systems.

6. Describe the operation and components of Teves antilock braking systems.

KEY TERMS

4WAL (Four-wheel antilock) (p. 379)
Antilock brake (ALB) (p. 385)
Acceleration slip regulation (ASR) (p. 370)
Brake pressure modulator (BPM) (p. 371)
Brake pressure modulator valve (BPMV) (p. 377)
Center valve (p. 365)
Controller antilock brake (CAB) (p. 365)
Electronic brake control module (EBCM) (p. 377)
Electronic brake traction control module (EBTCM) (p. 371)
Electrohydraulic control unit (EHCU) (p. 381)

High-pressure accumulator (HPA) (p. 383)
Hydraulic contorl unit (HCU) (p. 365)
Integrated control unit (ICU) (p. 389)
Low-pressure accumulator (LPA) (p. 382)
Pulse-width modulation (PWM) valve (p. 382)
Rear Anti-lock Braking System (RABS) (p. 379)
Rear-Wheel Anti-Lock (RWAL) (p. 379)
Select low principle (p. 368)
Tire pressure monitoring system (TPMS) (p. 378)
Vehicle speed sensor (VSS) (p. 381)

BENDIX 9 ABS

The Bendix ABS 9, which uses nine solenoids, was used in the late 1980s and early 1990s in Jeeps. The Bendix ABS 9 is an integral ABS system that combines the master brake cylinder with the hydraulic control modulator and two accumulators. See Figure 19-1.

The pump and motor are a separate assembly, but work with the master cylinder and hydraulic modulator assembly to provide power assist as well as antilock braking.

System Description

The Bendix 9 system is a four-wheel, three-hydraulic-channel ABS system. During normal braking, the vehicle's brake hydraulics are split front and rear. But during antilock braking, both front brakes are controlled separately while the rear brakes are controlled as a pair. The modulator assembly contains nine solenoid valves: an isolation valve, a decay valve, and a pressure build valve for each of the three ABS circuits.

Four-wheel speed sensors (one for each wheel) are used. Front sensors are on the steering knuckles with the sensor tone rings mounted on the axle shafts. Rear sensors are on the rear brake backing plates with the sensor rings mounted on the axles.

The Bendix 9 system control module is under the back seat attached to the floor pan. The mounting angle of the module is important because the module contains a mercury switch that monitors vehicle deceleration. This allows the module to adjust antilock braking to better suit slippery driving conditions when the vehicle is being operated in four-wheel drive.

Pressure Switches and Valves

The integral master cylinder, hydraulic control modulator, and accumulator assembly contain a boost pressure-differential switch mounted on the pressure modulator. It has a single terminal, is self-grounding, and is normally open. This switch functions the same as a differential pressure switch in a conventional brake system. It illuminates the BRAKE and ABS warning lights in the event of fluid loss from the brake on the driver's side of the engine compartment near the master cylinder/modulator assembly.

The modulator assembly also has a brake proportioning valve and switch, and an accumulator low-pressure switch for signaling the controller if accumulator pressure is lost. If pressure in the accumulator drops below 1,050 psi (7,240 kPa), the switch opens and the controller illuminates the amber ABS light. If accumulator pressure does not increase enough to

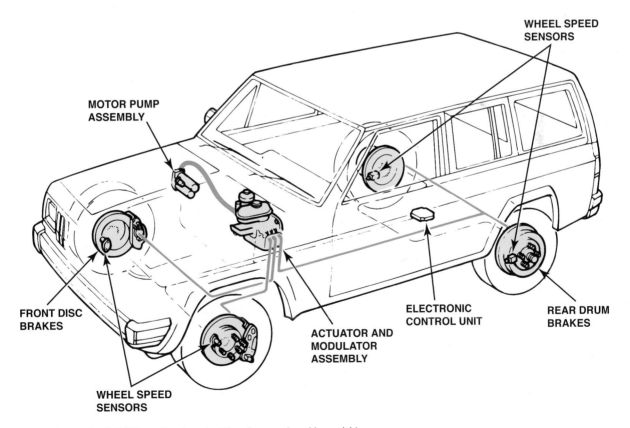

FIGURE 19-1   Bendix 9 ABS contains nine solenoids and was used on older model Jeeps.

close the switch within 20 seconds, the red BRAKE warning light will also come on.

Dual Accumulators

Bendix 9 uses two accumulators:

- A high-pressure accumulator, located on the master cylinder booster assembly, is nitrogen precharged to 1,000 psi (6,900 kPa), and capable of storing fluid at 1,700 to 2,000 psi (12,000 to 14,000 kPa).
- A low-pressure accumulator, precharged at 350 psi (2,400 kPa), but also capable of storing fluid at 1,700 to 2,000 psi, serves primarily as a fluid reservoir.

Both accumulators work together to provide additional fluid pressure during antilock braking, as well as power-assisted brake applications should the booster pump and motor fail.

The pressure switch is designed to keep the system operating pressure between 1,700 and 2,000 psi (12,000 to 14,000 kPa). When pressure drops below 1,700 psi, the switch closes and causes the pump to run until it builds sufficient pressure to recharge the accumulators. At 2,000 psi, the switch opens and the pump shuts off. Normal pump time for a completely discharged system (zero psi) is about 60 to 80 seconds. The pump runs only when the ignition is on.

System Operation

The Bendix 9 Jeep ABS system is unusual compared to other ABS systems because it does not become functional until vehicle speed reaches 12 to 15 mph (20 km/h). It is also designed to disengage at speeds below 3 to 5 mph (6 km/h), which may allow the wheels to chirp or skid slightly just before the vehicle completes an ABS stop. This is a normal condition for Bendix 9 systems and does not indicate a problem. It was designed to function this way to make it compatible with Jeep's Selec-Trac 4WD.

When the brake pedal is depressed, the brake pedal switch signals the ABS module to compare the relative deceleration rates of all four wheels. If ABS braking is needed, the module energizes the appropriate ABS isolation solenoid to seal off the affected wheel brake. If either rear brake needs ABS braking, a single solenoid isolates both lines simultaneously.

The system then releases pressure in the isolated brake circuit(s) by energizing the normally closed ABS decay solenoid. Pressure is reapplied by energizing the ABS build solenoid. This opens a passageway to allow pressure from the pump and accumulators to enter the line. Cycling of the decay and build solenoids continue until the vehicle slows to 3 to 5 mph, when the control module de-energizes the isolation so-

lenoid and discontinues antilock braking. The wheels may then lock up slightly or chirp as the vehicle comes to a complete stop.

BENDIX 10 ABS

DaimlerChrysler introduced the Bendix 10 ABS system, which uses 10 solenoids, in many early 1990s vehicles. Like the Bendix 9 system, it is an integral ABS system with a combined master cylinder and hydraulic modulator assembly and a separate pump and motor for power assist and antilock braking. See Figure 19-2.

There are four isolation solenoid valves (one for each wheel), a decay valve and build valve for each front brake, and a decay valve and build valve controlling the rear brake channel. The extra isolation solenoid in this system helps reduce pedal pulsation and feedback during antilock braking.

System Description

The Bendix 10 system uses a hydraulic booster rather than the conventional vacuum-assisted unit and functions normally with a diagonal split master cylinder. Bendix 10 ABS controls all four wheels but divides the brake system into three channels for antilock braking. The system controls the front brakes independently, and the rear brakes as a pair.

The system has four nonadjustable wheel-speed sensors. The sensor rings for the front-wheel speed sensors are located on the outboard constant velocity (CV) joint housings.

Dual Accumulators

The Bendix 10 has two accumulators. The high-pressure accumulator located on the master cylinder booster assembly is precharged with nitrogen to 1,000 psi (7,000 kPa) with a normal operating pressure range of 1,600 to 2,000 psi (11,000 to 14,000 kPa). See Figure 19-3.

The low pressure accumulators provide additional brake pressure during ABS braking as well as boost pressure for power-assisted normal stops.

Power Switches and Transducers

The modulator has a dual function pressure switch located on the bottom of the modulator. The switch maintains accumulator pressure by turning the pump on when pressure drops below 1,600 psi (12,000 kPa), and off when pressure reaches 2,000 psi (14,000 kPa). This switch also warns the control module if accumulator pressure drops below 1,000 psi (7,000 kPa). When the switch opens, the red brake and amber ABS warning lights are illuminated, and the ABS system is disabled.

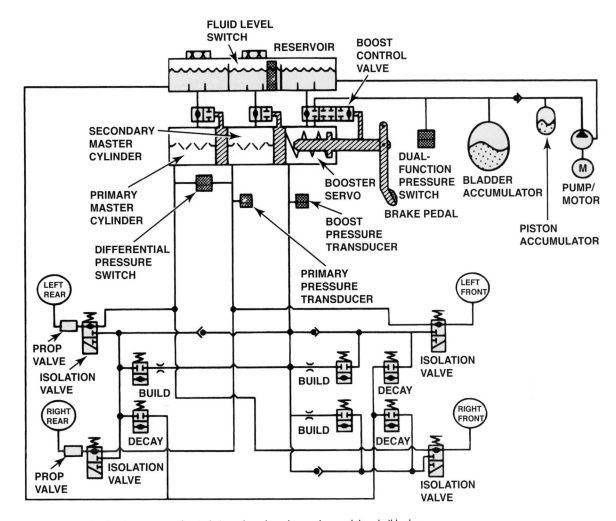

FIGURE 19-2   Bendix 10 systems use four isolation valves, three decay valves, and three build valves.

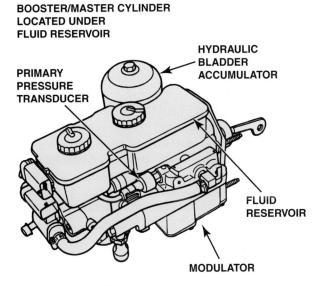

FIGURE 19-3   Bendix 10 hydraulic control unit.

A fluid level switch on the reservoir monitors the fluid level. The switch consists of a float and magnetic reed switch that closes when the fluid level is too low, illuminating both warning lights and disabling the ABS system.

BENDIX 6 ABS

The Bendix 6 system uses six solenoids and is used on many early 1990s DaimlerChrysler vehicles. The Bendix 6 system is a nonintegral ABS system with a conventional master brake cylinder and power booster. The hydraulic modulator, pump/motor, and accumulator assembly is located on the frame rail. See Figure 19-4.

System Description

Bendix 6 is a four-wheel, three-channel nonintegral ABS system with four nonadjustable wheel speed sensors. The sensor

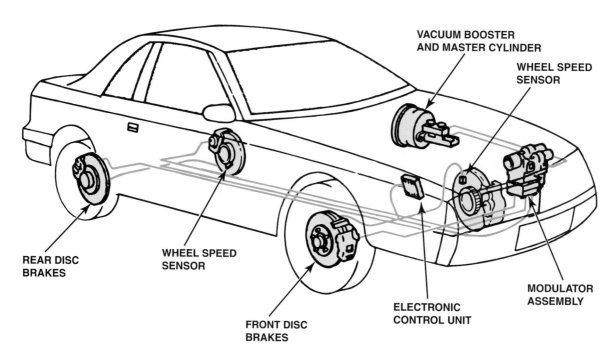

FIGURE 19-4   Bendix 6 ABS is a nonintegral system.

rings for the front-wheel speed sensors are located on the outboard CV joints. Rear sensors are located on the brake backing plates. See Figure 19-5.

There are two isolation solenoid valves: one for the primary side of the hydraulics and one for the secondary side. The control module activates the isolation valves when either front wheel needs antilock braking. The isolation valves are necessary for these applications because the vehicles are front-wheel drive with diagonally split brake hydraulics.

There are four combination build/decay solenoid valves (one for each wheel). These are two position solenoids that release fluid pressure from an affected wheel circuit in the decay mode, or increase it in the build mode. The front brakes are controlled individually while the build/decay solenoids for both rear brake circuits are controlled simultaneously as a pair, giving three-channel ABS braking.

The modulator also contains four shuttle orifice valves, one for each wheel. These are hydraulically actuated valves that restrict fluid flow in a circuit between the isolation valve and build/decay valve when the build/decay valve is in use. This provides a more gradual build rate during an antilock stop for smoother ABS operation. The shuttle orifice valve in the affected wheel circuit remains in the restricted position until the ABS stop has been completed. When the build/decay valve returns to its rest position, pressure equalizes in the circuit and spring pressure opens the shuttle orifice valves.

Dual Accumulators

The modulator assembly has two accumulators, one each for the primary and secondary sides. See Figure 19-6.

Both are piston and spring-type accumulators and do not have a gas precharge. Each accumulator also has a small fluid sump that holds fluid temporarily during an ABS stop as fluid returns through the build/decay valve from the brake circuit. The pressure within the sumps is typically about 50 psi (345 kPa). When the ABS function ceases, the fluid in the accumulators is pumped back to the master cylinder fluid reservoir.

Pressure Switch

A differential pressure switch, located inside the modulator assembly, illuminates the red BRAKE warning light if there is a difference of 70 to 225 psi (483 to 1,550 kPa) between the primary and secondary sides of the hydraulic system when the brake pedal is depressed, or if there is a pressure differential of more than 225 psi (1,550 kPa) at any other time.

Pump Motor and Control Module

The pump motor is part of the modulator assembly, and operates only during antilock stops. An electric motor drives two pistons, one for the primary side of the system and one for the secondary side. Each pump takes low-pressure brake fluid from its sump and delivers it at high pressure to one of the spring-loaded accumulators.

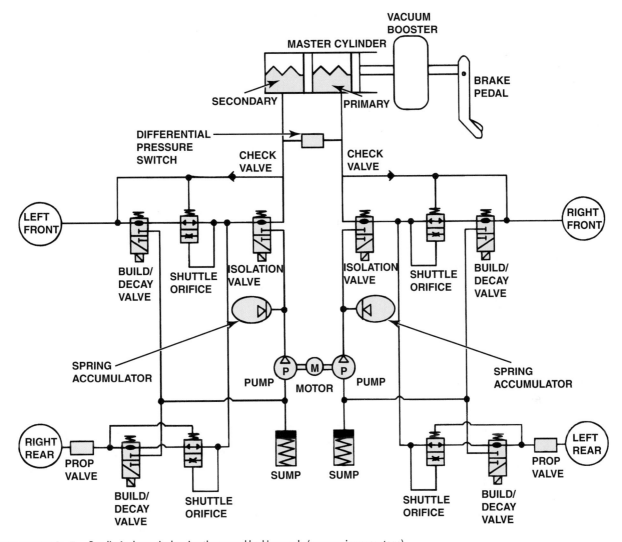

FIGURE 19-5   Bendix 6 schematic showing the normal braking mode (pressure increase stage).

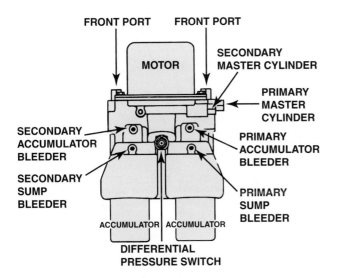

FIGURE 19-6   Bendix 6 modulator with dual accumulators.

BENDIX LC4 ABS

This system, which Bendix calls Bendix III but Daimler-Chrysler refers to as LC4 (for "Low Cost" system), is a lighter, more compact version of the Bendix 6 nonintegral ABS system it supercedes. LC4 is on 1994 and newer DaimlerChrysler vehicles. It is a nonintegral ABS system with a conventional master cylinder and vacuum booster, and is functionally similar to the Bendix 6 system.

System Description

LC4 is a four-wheel, four-channel ABS system with four-wheel speed sensors and four combination build/decay solenoid valves in the modulator assembly. See Figure 19-7.

Unlike Bendix 6, however, it uses no isolation solenoids because each brake is controlled separately. The brake system

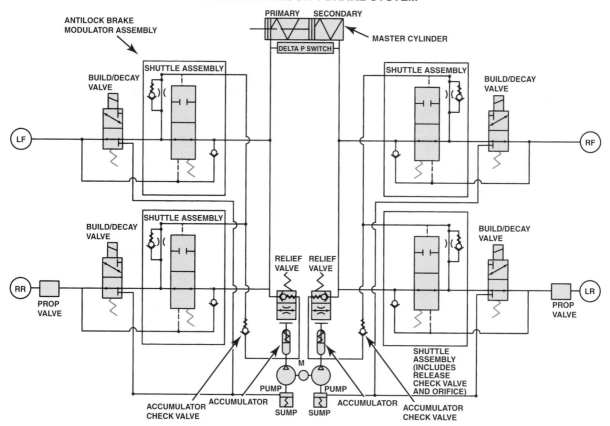

FIGURE 19-7 Bendix LC4 system schematic.

is split diagonally so the left front and right rear wheel are on the primary circuit while the right front and left rear wheels are on the secondary circuit.

System Operation

In the released position, the ABS build/decay solenoids provide a direct fluid path from the master cylinder to the brakes. In the actuated (decay) position, they allow fluid to flow from the brakes back to the fluid sumps in the hydraulic modulator assembly. There are two sumps, one for the primary and one for the secondary brake circuits. The build/decay valves are spring loaded in the normally released (build) position.

Like Bendix 6, the LC4 modulator contains shuttle orifice valves for each wheel circuit. These valves restrict fluid flow between the isolation valve and build/decay valve when the build/decay valve is in use.

Dual Accumulators

The LC4 modulator has two accumulators, one for the primary side and one for the secondary side. See Figure 19-8.

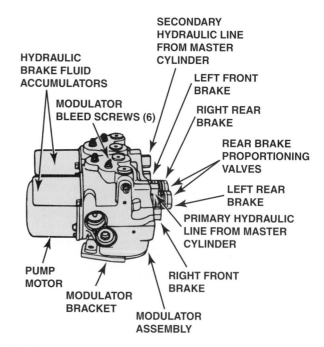

FIGURE 19-8 Bendix LC4 modulator and pump assembly.

Both are spring-loaded with no gas precharge. The accumulators store pressurized fluid during ABS braking only, and provide supplemental pressure when needed. During normal braking, no pressure is stored in the accumulators.

Each accumulator also has a small fluid sump that holds fluid temporarily during an ABS stop as fluid returns through the build/decay valve from the affected brake circuits. Pressure within the sumps is typically about 50 psi (345 kPa). When ABS ceases, the fluid is pumped back to the master cylinder fluid reservoir.

Pump Motor and Control Module

The modulator also has a pump motor with a dual-piston pump. Each piston pumps fluid from its respective sump to its accumulator as needed during ABS braking. The ABS control module energizes the pump motor relay.

BENDIX ABX-4

The Bendix ABX-4 antilock braking system is used on Dodge and Plymouth Neon models as well as on Chrysler Cirrus and Dodge Stratus. It is a four-wheel, four-channel ABS system with a more compact design than earlier Bendix systems.

On models with ABS, the master cylinder has only two outlets (one for the primary brake circuit and one for the secondary brake circuit). Both lines are routed to the hydraulic modulator assembly, which DaimlerChrysler refers to as the **hydraulic control unit (HCU).**

Inside the master cylinder are more differences. Those without ABS use a standard compensating port design with two screw-in proportioning valves. For those with ABS, the master cylinder has a **center valve** design and the proportioning valves are located on the hydraulic control unit rather than the master cylinder.

System Description

The ABX-4 system is functionally similar to the Bendix LC4 system, and consists of a compact hydraulic modulator and pump assembly. See Figures 19-9 and 19-10.

Inside the modulator are four ABS build/decay solenoids, one for each brake circuit. However, the system works like a three-channel system because both rear ABS solenoids are cycled simultaneously to improve vehicle stability.

As with Bendix 6 and LC4, shuttle orifice valves for each brake circuit restrict fluid flow between the pump and decay solenoid, providing a gradual build rate during an antilock stop for smoother ABS operation.

The **controller antilock brake (CAB)** receives inputs from four nonadjustable wheel speed sensors and the brake pedal switch. See Figure 19-11.

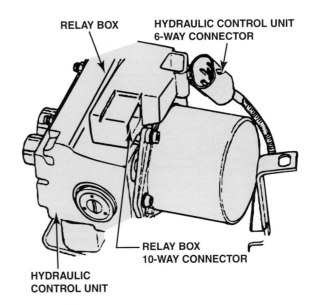

FIGURE 19-9   Bendix ABX-4 hydraulic control unit.

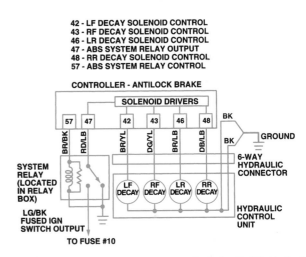

FIGURE 19-10   The wiring schematic for the Bendix ABX-4 hydraulic control unit.

The sensor rings for the front-wheel speed sensors are located on the outboard CV joints. The rear-wheel speed sensors bolt to the brake support plates and read sensor rings on the rear hubs.

No Accumulators

Unlike the Bendix systems previously described, ABX-4 has no accumulators. There are two fluid sumps in the hydraulic modulator for the primary and secondary hydraulic circuits. The fluid sumps temporarily store brake fluid vented from the brake circuits during ABS braking. The fluid is then delivered to the pump to provide additional build pressure. The typical pressure in the sumps is 50 psi (345 kPa) during ABS braking only.

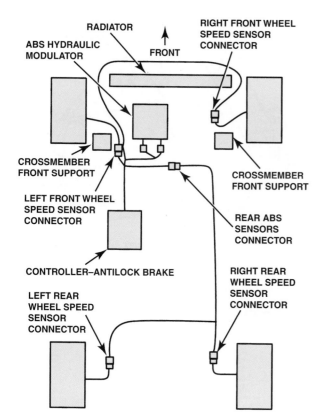

FIGURE 19-11   Bendix ABX-4 wiring harness and component locations.

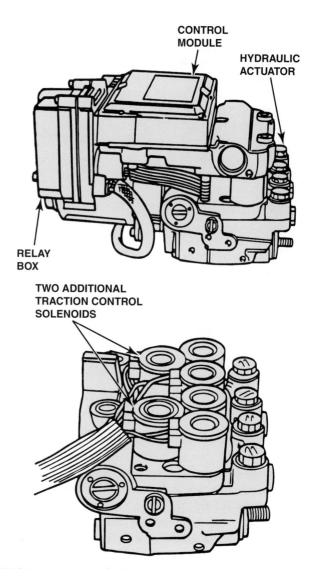

FIGURE 19-12   Bendix Mecatronic modulator controls ABS and drive wheel traction during acceleration.

A single electric pump motor drives a dual-piston pump (one piston for each hydraulic circuit). The motor runs only during ABS braking to provide build pressure. When the system needs additional build pressure, the control module grounds the pump motor relay, which is also mounted on the modulator, to start the pump.

BENDIX MECATRONIC II

The Ford Contour and Mercury Mystique use the Bendix Mecatronic II ABS system. It is a four-wheel, four-channel, nonintegral ABS system with four-wheel speed sensors and a conventional master cylinder and power booster.

The Mecatronic II ABS system also provides traction control. Below 31 mph (50 km/h), it uses braking alone to control wheel spin. Above 31 mph, a throttle relaxer backs off the throttle opening to reduce engine power. If the driver steps on the brake pedal while traction control is operating, the system uses the brake switch to deactivate traction control, causing the system to go into ABS brake mode.

System Description

The hydraulic modulator assembly has four ABS solenoids, plus two additional solenoids on models equipped with traction control. See Figure 19-12.

The control module, relay, and pump are also mounted on the compact "unitized" modulator assembly.

During ABS braking, Mecatronic II uses "closed-loop" hydraulic control. Fluid pressure relieved from the brake channels is held temporarily within an internal low-pressure reservoir in the modulator. Because there are no accumulators, the pump provides additional build pressure as needed. This system uses a single pump motor with a dual-piston pump that is capable of supplying hydraulic pressure to either brake circuit.

The front sensors attach to the knuckle assembly and read a sensor ring on the outboard CV joint. Rear sensors mount on the brake backing plates and read sensor rings on the rear hubs.

Dual Microprocessors

The Mecatronic control module contains two microprocessors. The first controls the function of the ABS solenoid and pump motor. The second monitors and compares inputs from the wheel speed sensors, overseeing the overall operation of the system.

The main ABS relay provides power to the ABS solenoids and the pump motor relay. The pump motor relay, however, is not activated by the control module until ABS braking is needed. If the main ABS relay fails, the ABS warning light comes on and deactivates the system.

Traction Control

Applications with traction control have two additional solenoids in the modulator. See Figure 19-13. These solenoids create a hydraulic path that allows the system to reverse the ABS control process. When the control module detects wheel spin during acceleration, it energizes the pump to create hydraulic pressure. At the same time, it energizes the appropriate ABS solenoid to route brake pressure to the spinning wheel. The appropriate traction control system (TCS) solenoid is also energized to prevent brake pressure from entering the brake reservoir. This isolates the spinning drive wheel brake so it is the only brake receiving hydraulic pressure during traction control.

A warning indicator on the instrument panel signals the driver when the traction control system is operating. The Mecatronic traction control system uses a throttle actuator to back off the throttle, reducing engine power to help control wheel spin. See Figure 19-14.

BOSCH 2 ABS

Bosch 2 ABS has been used on a wide variety of domestic and import brand vehicles, including Audi, BMW, Chevrolet Corvette, Infiniti, Lexus, Mercedes, Porsche, Mazda, Mitsubishi, Nissan, Rolls-Royce, Subaru, and Volvo.

Bosch 2 is a nonintegral ABS system with a conventional master brake cylinder and vacuum power booster. The hydraulic modulator assembly is a separate unit.

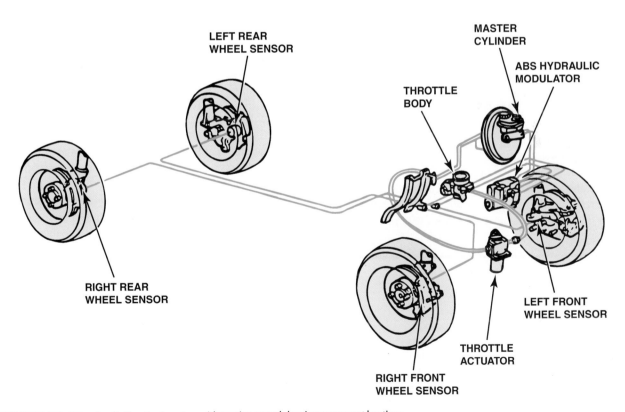

FIGURE 19-13   Bendix Mecatronic system with traction control showing component locations.

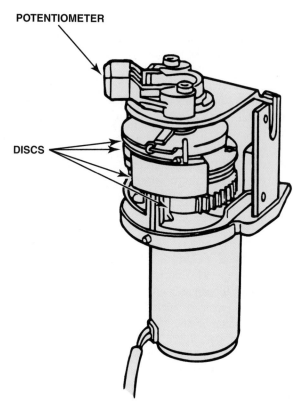

FIGURE 19-14 Bendix Mecatronic throttle actuator pushes back the throttle linkage to help reduce wheel spin by reducing engine torque.

TECH TIP

BRAKE, HOLD, AND STEER

When an ABS stop occurs, many drivers do not keep the brake pedal depressed, which can reduce the effectiveness of the antilock braking system. For maximum benefit from the ABS, the driver should brake firmly and keep the brake pedal depressed and at the same time try to steer around any object to avoid a collision.

System Description

Bosch 2 ABS provides four-wheel ABS braking with three control channels. The front wheels are controlled independently and the rear brakes share a common ABS circuit.

On most applications only three wheel speed sensors are used: one for each front wheel and a common sensor for both rear wheels. See Figure 19-15. On some applications, such as the Corvette, separate sensors are used for each rear wheel.

In applications where each rear wheel has its own speed sensor, the **select low principle** of control is used. The control module monitors the speed of both rear wheels and reacts to the one that is slowing (decelerating) the fastest. Consequently, if either rear wheel starts to lock up during a hard stop, the module activates the rear brake ABS circuit and cycles the pressure to both rear brakes to prevent wheel lockup.

The sensor rings for the wheel speed sensors may be mounted inside the front-wheel hub assembly, on the brake rotor or drum, on the axle shaft, or on the constant velocity joint housing. On applications where the rear wheels share a common sensor, the sensor ring is mounted on the pinion input shaft in the differential.

System Operation

The hydraulic modulator assembly has three, three-position ABS solenoids (one for each front brake and one for the combined rear brake circuit), a high-pressure return pump, two fluid accumulators, and pump and solenoid relays. See Figure 19-16.

Each of the ABS solenoid valves in the modulator is normally in the open position. Voltage is supplied through a relay on the modulator assembly. When a small current (1.9 to 2.3 amps) is applied to one of the ABS solenoids, it pulls the valve up to its second or intermediate position, which isolates the brake circuit and prevents any additional pressure from reaching the brake. When current to the solenoid is increased (4.5 to 5.7 amps), it pulls the valve to the third position, which opens a port and releases pressure from the brake circuit.

The fluid that flows back through the release port routes into a spring-loaded accumulator. There are two accumulators in the modulator, one for the front brakes and one for the rear brakes. The accumulators hold the fluid that is released from the brake circuits until the return pump can pump it back to the master cylinder (which produces the pulsations that are felt in the brake pedal during ABS braking).

The return pump receives its power through a pump relay mounted on the modulator. The ABS control module switches the pump relay on when the return pump is needed during ABS braking. The pump draws about 45 amperes and is capable of 2,900 psi (20,000 kPa). High pump pressure is needed to overcome brake pressure from the master cylinder.

Of all the components in the modulator assembly, only the relays and pump motor are serviceable. If one of the solenoid valves is defective or if the modulator assembly is leaking, the entire modulator assembly must be replaced.

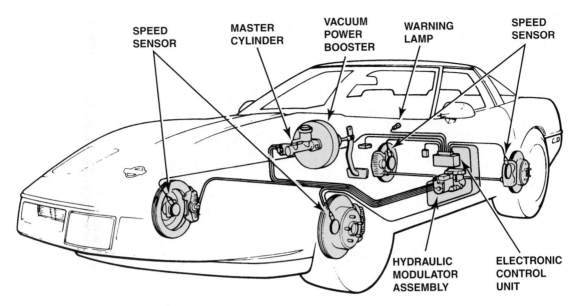

FIGURE 19-15 Bosch 2 ABS system showing the location of the components.

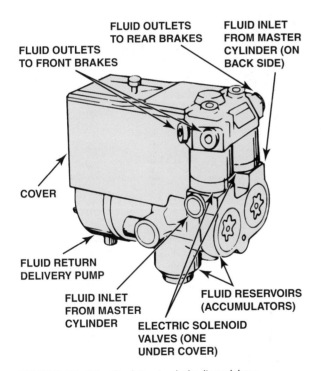

FIGURE 19-16 Bosch 2 system hydraulic modulator.

BOSCH 2E ABS

Bosch 2E is a variant of Bosch 2 and is also a nonintegral, four-wheel, three-channel ABS system with a conventional master cylinder and brake booster. It is used on many Daimler-Chrysler and Japanese import brands. Each wheel has its own adjustable wheel speed sensor.

The hydraulic modulator contains three, three-way ABS solenoids: one for each front brake and a common solenoid for both rear brakes. The control module governs the rear brakes with the select low principle. Relays for the pump motor and ABS solenoids are located on the modulator.

BOSCH 2U ABS

The Bosch 2U ABS system is functionally similar to the Bosch 2 and 2E systems used on many rear-wheel General Motors and Ford Motor Company vehicles. See Figure 19-17.

The differences that set this system apart from other Bosch 2 systems include the following:

1. The Bosch 2U modulator assembly has a different design and appearance but functions in exactly the same way as the one used in Bosch 2 applications. It contains three, three-way ABS solenoid valves, one for each of its three control channels (each front brake and a combined control channel for both rear brakes) and uses the select low principle for the rear brakes.

2. Bosch 2U in rear-wheel-drive applications uses only three wheel speed sensors. Front-wheel drive applications use four wheel speed sensors. The single wheel speed sensor for the rear brakes on the rear-wheel-drive General Motors applications is located in the differential, where it monitors the average speed of both rear wheels. Front-wheel-drive General Motors applications have a separate speed sensor at each rear wheel. The front sensors are mounted in the steering knuckles, and the sensor rings are pressed into the backs of the hub and rotor assembly. Rear sensors are mounted on the rear brake backing plates.

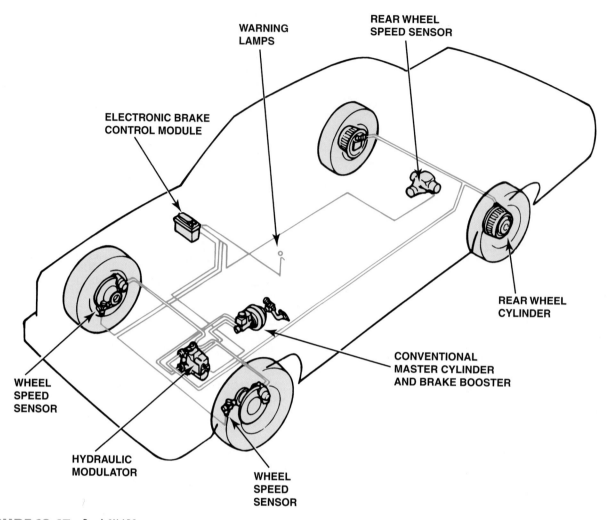

FIGURE 19-17   Bosch 2U ABS system components.

3. The Bosch 2U control module for General Motors applications has the ability to provide diagnostic fault codes. This eliminates the need for a special dedicated ABS tester and allows a technician to access the codes using either a manual flash code procedure or using a scan tool.

BOSCH ABS/ASR

The Bosch ABS/ASR system is used on many General Motors vehicles. See Figures 19-18 through 19-20.

This system adds traction control capability, which Bosch refers to as **acceleration slip regulation (ASR).** The ASR system uses both braking and engine torque management to limit wheel spin during acceleration.

The ABS/ASR system is a nonintegral, four-wheel, three-channel ABS system, but only in the antilock braking mode. The hydraulic modulator assembly contains an additional three-way solenoid valve so the ASR can operate the rear

brakes independently. The return pump is also used to provide hydraulic pressure for rear braking during ASR. The ABS/ASR modulator contains two other valves:

- Load Valve.   This is a hydraulically operated valve used to isolate the master cylinder prime pipe from the pump during brake apply and ABS control. The load valve is spring-loaded in the open position.
- Pilot Valve.   This is a two-way valve that is electronically operated to isolate the master cylinder from the pump when ASR is needed. When the normally open valve is closed, the pump routes fluid to the rear brake circuit. The control module also uses this valve to regulate fluid volume in the brake circuits when switching from ASR to ABS.

The ABS/ASR module is linked electronically to the powertrain control module (PCM) so it can reduce engine power if needed to control wheel spin during acceleration. This allows the ASR system to apply either rear brake as needed, or reduce

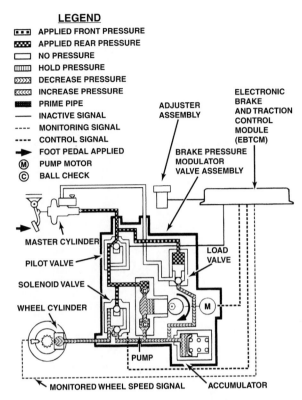

FIGURE 19-18 Bosch ABS/ASR system in normal braking mode.

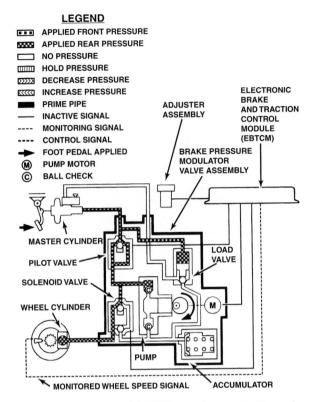

FIGURE 19-20 Bosch ABS/ASR system in the pressure decrease mode.

engine power by reducing the throttle opening (via a throttle relaxer on the throttle linkage), retarding ignition timing, and/or deactivating some of the fuel injectors depending on application.

BOSCH 5 SERIES

The Bosch 5.3 is used on 1998 and later Camaro, Firebird, Pontiac Grand Prix, Oldsmobile Intrigue, and Cadillac Catera. Another variant, the Delphi/Bosch hybrid, is found on 1996 and later Pontiac Bonneville, Buick Park Avenue, Buick LeSabre, Oldsmobile 98, and Oldsmobile 88.

The Bosch 5 series systems are nonintegral, four-wheel ABS with traction control. However, they are four-channel, rather than three-channel, systems with a compact "unitized" design. See Figure 19-21.

The hydraulic modulator or **brake pressure modulator (BPM)** valve body and control module are both part of the **electronic brake traction control module (EBTCM)** assembly. Wheel speed sensors at each wheel provide inputs to the control module.

System Operation

The brake pressure modulator valve assembly contains a pair of ABS valves for each brake circuit (one normally open inlet

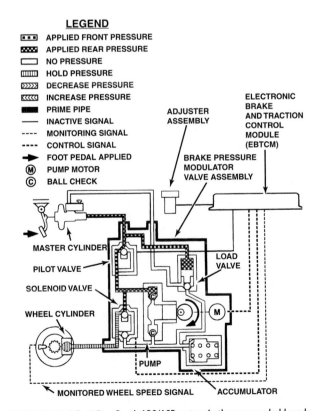

FIGURE 19-19 Bosch ABS/ASR system in the pressure hold mode.

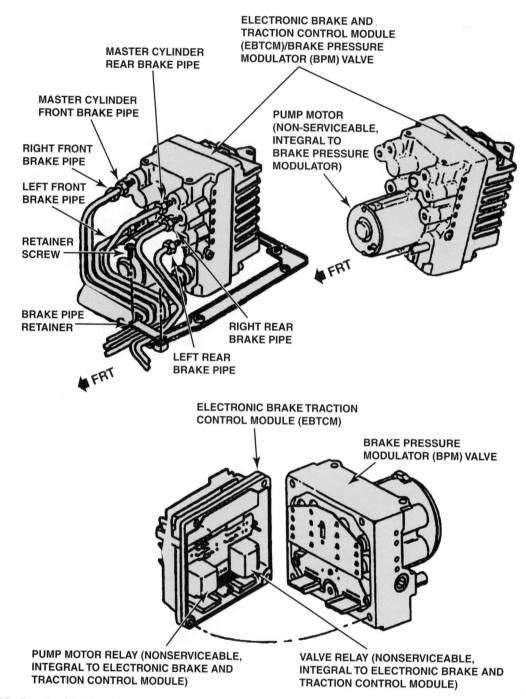

MASTER CYLINDER
REAR BRAKE PIPE

ELECTRONIC BRAKE AND
TRACTION CONTROL MODULE
(EBTCM)/BRAKE PRESSURE
MODULATOR (BPM) VALVE

MASTER CYLINDER
FRONT BRAKE PIPE

PUMP MOTOR
(NON-SERVICEABLE,
INTEGRAL TO
BRAKE PRESSURE
MODULATOR)

RIGHT FRONT
BRAKE PIPE

LEFT FRONT
BRAKE PIPE

RETAINER
SCREW

FRT

BRAKE PIPE
RETAINER

RIGHT REAR
BRAKE PIPE

LEFT REAR
BRAKE PIPE

FRT

ELECTRONIC BRAKE TRACTION
CONTROL MODULE (EBTCM)

BRAKE PRESSURE
MODULATOR (BPM) VALVE

PUMP MOTOR RELAY (NONSERVICEABLE,
INTEGRAL TO ELECTRONIC BRAKE AND
TRACTION CONTROL MODULE)

VALVE RELAY (NONSERVICEABLE,
INTEGRAL TO ELECTRONIC BRAKE AND
TRACTION CONTROL MODULE)

FIGURE 19-21   Bosch 5 ABS modulator.

solenoid) for a total of eight. When the control module senses wheel lockup, the inlet solenoid is energized to close and isolate the brake circuit. This prevents any further pressure increase to the brake. If wheel speed does not increase and match the reference speed of the other wheels, the control module energizes the outlet solenoid to open it so fluid pressure can escape the circuit. This relieves brake pressure and allows the wheel to regain traction. When the reference speed is obtained, the control module opens the inlet valve, allowing

pressure to be reapplied to the brake. The cycle is repeated continuously as long as needed or until the vehicle stops.

The EBTCM also contains the pump motor (used for fluid return during ABS braking and to generate rear brake pressure for traction control), pump motor relay, BPM valve relay (provides power to the ABS and traction control solenoids), and a pair of additional solenoid valves used for traction control.

The Bosch 5.3 system used in Camaro and Firebird applications does not have proportioning valves for the rear brakes. Instead, it uses computer control of the rear inlet valves to the brake pressure modulator valve. When the EBTCM detects that the rear wheels are decelerating just slightly faster than the front wheels, it pulses the rear brakes until the rear wheels' rate of deceleration matches the front wheels.

Traction Control

Bosch 5 also uses braking in conjunction with throttle reduction and spark retard to reduce wheel spin when traction control is needed. Braking is only used at speeds below 50 mph (80 km/h) and primarily at slow speeds when wheel spin is excessive.

When traction control braking is needed, the control module in the EBTCM energizes the pump and two solenoids:

1. Prime line solenoid valve. This opens a circuit that allows fluid to flow to the return pump so it can generate brake pressure.
2. Traction control solenoid. This closes to prevent pump pressure from returning to the master cylinder.

In addition to braking, a combination of spark retard and throttle reduction via a throttle adjuster assembly attached to

the throttle linkage allows the system to quickly and easily control engine torque as well as traction.

DELPHI ABS-VI

The Delphi (Delco Moraine) ABS-VI antilock braking system has been used on many General Motors vehicles since the early 1990s. It is a nonintegral ABS system with a conventional master brake cylinder and power booster. The brake systems on these applications are split diagonally so the primary (rear) master cylinder piston operates the right front and left rear brakes, and the secondary (front) piston operates the left front and right rear brakes.

System Description

Delphi ABS-VI is a four-wheel, three-channel ABS system. See Figure 19-22.

It controls the front brakes separately, but the rear brakes share a common ABS circuit. Each wheel, however, has its own nonadjustable wheel speed sensor. Front sensors are mounted on the steering knuckle assembly with the sensor rings located on the outside of the constant velocity (CV) joints. Front-wheel speed sensors are plastic rather than

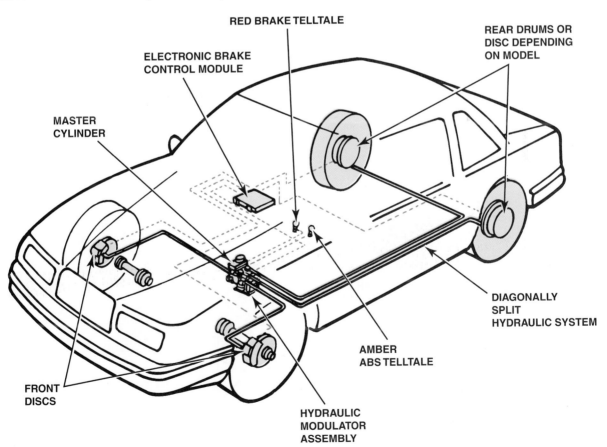

FIGURE 19-22   Delphi ABS VI components.

stainless steel, which improves corrosion resistance and lowers manufacturing costs. Rear-wheel speed sensors and sensor rings are located inside the rear wheel bearing and hub assemblies and must be replaced as a complete assembly.

Hydraulic Modulator and Motor Pack

The hydraulic modulator and motor pack assembly is next to the master cylinder. See Figure 19-23.

The modulator is held by two banjo bolts at the master cylinder's two upper outlet ports and two transfer tubes at the two lower outlet ports.

CAUTION: You must replace the two lower transfer tubes and O-rings if the master cylinder and modulator are disconnected from one another to prevent leaks that might result in brake failure.

The modulator, Figure 19-24, has fluid chambers for all four brakes, two ABS isolation solenoid valves, four check balls, and a motor pack. See Figure 19-25.

The motor pack contains three bidirectional direct current motors with electromagnetic brakes (EMBs) and/or expansion spring brakes (ESBs), three ball screw assemblies, four pistons, and a gear drive set and gear cover. See Figure 19-26. The modulator motor pack, isolation solenoid valves, gear cover, and individual gears are all serviceable parts and can be replaced separately.

The hydraulic modulator and motor pack assembly on the Delphi VI system is unique. The modulator contains two isolation solenoid valves to block off the front brake circuits when rear antilock braking is required. However, there is no isolation solenoid valve for the rear brakes. Isolation is provided by a check ball for each rear brake circuit.

In the Delphi ABS-VI system, brake pressure is modulated during antilock braking by positioning a small piston up and down inside a fluid chamber. The modulator is divided into three circuits. The right and left front brakes are controlled individually while the rear brakes are controlled as a pair. The system uses the select low principle of operation for the rear brakes. For each of the front brake circuits, there is an isolation solenoid valve, a check ball, a ball screw and piston, DC motor, gear drive, and electromagnetic motor brake (EMB). The EMBs are disc style brakes located on top of the front motor assemblies. When no voltage is applied to the EMB, a plate and spring pushes down against the pads, keeping the motor from turning.

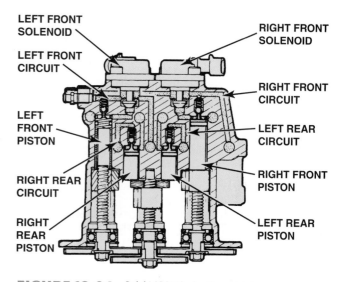

FIGURE 19-24   Delphi ABS VI hydraulic modulator.

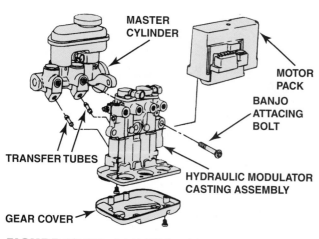

FIGURE 19-23   Delphi ABS VI modulator, motor pack, and master cylinder.

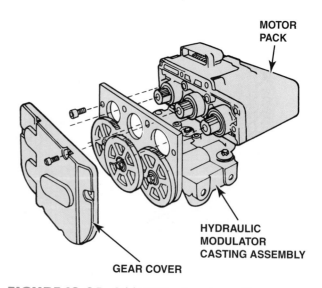

FIGURE 19-25   Delphi ABS VI motor pack assembly.

ESB OPERATION

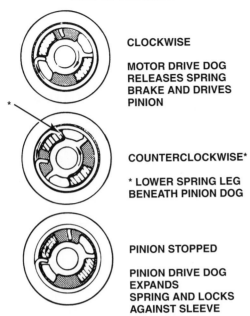

CLOCKWISE

MOTOR DRIVE DOG RELEASES SPRING BRAKE AND DRIVES PINION

COUNTERCLOCKWISE*

* LOWER SPRING LEG BENEATH PINION DOG

PINION STOPPED

PINION DRIVE DOG EXPANDS SPRING AND LOCKS AGAINST SLEEVE

ESB CONSTRUCTION

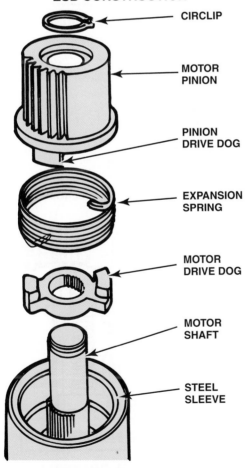

CIRCLIP

MOTOR PINION

PINION DRIVE DOG

EXPANSION SPRING

MOTOR DRIVE DOG

MOTOR SHAFT

STEEL SLEEVE

FIGURE 19-26 Delphi ABS VI expansion spring brake (ESB) construction and operation.

When voltage is sent to the EMB, the electromagnet pulls up on the plate, disengaging the brake. The motor is then free to turn.

During normal braking, fluid pressure from the master cylinder passes through the modulator and on to all four brakes. The ball screw piston in each circuit is at its highest or "home" position. This holds the check ball open so fluid can go through the upper passageways to the brakes. The ball screws and pistons for the front brake circuits are locked in this position to prevent the DC motors from turning. The two solenoid valves for the front brakes are also open when de-energized, which allows fluid to pass through their passageways in the modulator to the brakes. The front brakes provide about 80% of the total braking effort. The modulator is designed with two passageways to the front brakes in the event of a failure of either the isolation solenoid or ball screw assembly.

Each rear brake circuit also has its own piston chamber, but the two pistons share a common ball screw and motor. During normal braking, the ball screw for the rear circuit is also at its highest or "home" position. This holds each check ball for the rear brakes open so fluid can pass through to each rear brake. An expansion spring brake prevents the rear motor from turning during normal braking. The ESB will apply braking action to the rear motor assembly when current to the motor is removed. The ESB has no direct electrical connection to the controller. It is a mechanical brake that works similar to a window crank mechanism or overrunning clutch.

System Operation

When the ABS controller detects that a front or rear wheel is about to lock, it initiates ABS braking. If a front brake is involved, the first step is to energize the right or left isolation solenoid valve. This blocks the flow of fluid pressure through the isolation solenoid passage to the calipers. At the same time, the electromagnetic motor brake is energized to free up the motor and ball screw so they can turn. The motor will then draw the piston down by turning the ball screw, allowing the check ball to seat and isolate the brake circuit. This prevents any additional brake pressure from reaching the caliper.

As the motor continues to turn backward, the ball screw and piston move lower. This allows the volume area on top of the piston chamber to receive the corresponding drop in fluid pressure away from the caliper to prevent wheel lock. See Figure 19-27.

Pressure is then held or maintained when the force exerted by the motor against the ball screw and piston equals that in the brake circuit itself. When this point is reached, the piston stops moving downward and pressure is held steady. The controller provides current to the motor to accomplish this function. Pressure can then be reapplied as needed by running the piston back up. See Figure 19-28.

To do this, the controller increases current to the motor. This turns the ball screw in the opposite direction and reverses the direction of piston travel. This is the pressure increase

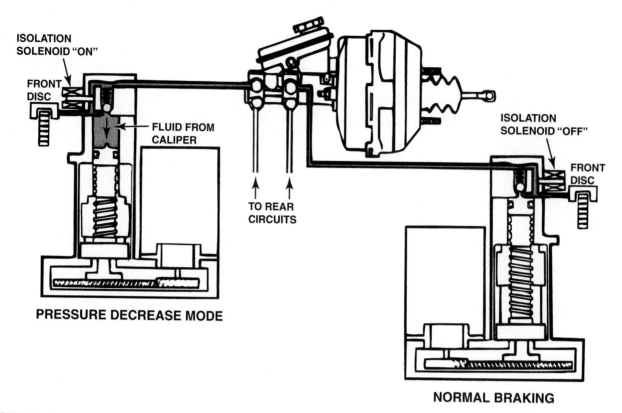

FIGURE 19-27 Delphi ABS VI system in pressure decrease mode for one front brake circuit.

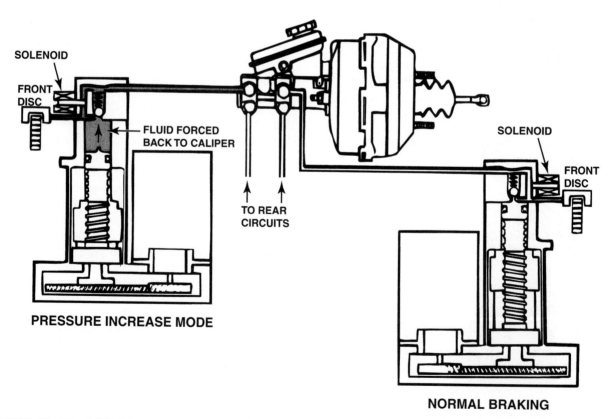

FIGURE 19-28 Delphi ABS VI system in the pressure increase mode for one front brake circuit.

phase. As the piston moves back up, it pushes fluid back into the caliper line and increases pressure at the brake. The piston can be moved upward and downward in the modulator bore and held in position at any point by applying current to the motor assembly.

When antilock braking is no longer needed, the motor is commanded to return the ball screw to its uppermost or "home" position. The EMB is de-energized and holds the motor, keeping it in the "home" position. The piston then returns to the top of the chamber and unseats the check ball, reopening that passageway for the brake fluid. The isolation solenoid valve is also de-energized and opens the second passageway to the calipers.

During antilock braking, the brake system is no longer split diagonally. The rear wheels are controlled together. The controller commands the rear motor to draw down the ball screw. See Figure 19-29. The rear ball screw now turns, allowing both rear pistons to back down the bore of the modulator. This seats the check balls for the rear brake circuits and isolates the lines from the master cylinder.

The Delphi ABS-VI system cannot increase brake pressure on its own above that which the driver's foot provides through the master cylinder because it has no high-pressure pump or accumulator.

Traction Control

On certain applications, ABS-VI also has added traction control capability, referred to as ABS-VI/TCS. ABS-VI/TCS uses a combination of braking and engine torque management to limit wheel spin at all speeds. Torque management involves retarding spark timing and/or shutting off up to half of the engine's injectors temporarily until traction is resumed.

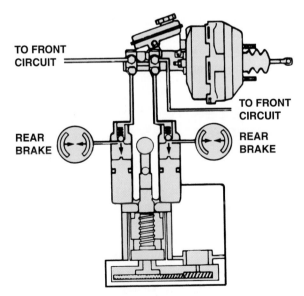

FIGURE 19-29 Delphi ABS VI system in pressure decrease for a rear brake.

The ABS-VI/TCS controller and engine powertrain control module (PCM) are interactive. Signals from the wheel speed sensors are fed to both the PCM and ABS-VI/TCS controller. When wheel spin is detected, the ABS-IV/TCS control module may apply braking to control wheel spin and/or the PCM may momentarily retard ignition timing to reduce engine torque to control wheel spin.

To generate brake pressure when traction control is needed, a TCS modulator is used instead of a pump and accumulator, as is the case with other ABS systems. Each of the two front brake circuits has its own separate TCS modulator, which is located in a separate add-on unit mounted on the frame rail. The TCS modulator/motor pack assembly is connected hydraulically to the ABS modulator with lines and has its own electrical connector.

Each traction control channel consists of a motor, piston, ball screw, spring, and poppet valve. Under normal operating conditions, the piston is located in the downward or home position, and the poppet valve is unseated. This is accomplished by turning the ball screw via the motor to drive the nut downward. Brake fluid enters the inlet port of the TCS modulator, flows past the unseated poppet valve, and goes out the outlet port to the brake. There are no solenoid valves or ESBs within the TCS modulator.

When traction control braking is needed, the ABS-IV/TCS control module energizes the appropriate TCS modulator. The motor drives the ball screws and pistons up from their home position. This unseats the poppet valve and isolates the circuit from the master cylinder. Now, running the bidirectional motor either way to change the volume within the TCS modulator piston chamber controls the amount of brake pressure applied to the drive wheel brake.

DELPHI DBC-7 ABS SYSTEM

Delphi Brake Control DBC-7 ABS system is the successor to the Delco ABS-VI system and is used on many General Motors vehicles.

System Components

The DBC-7 is a nonintegral system with the ABS valves and pump mounted in a valve block called the **brake pressure modulator valve** or **BPMV**. The solenoids that operate the ABS valves are combined with the controller into another unit called the **electronic brake control module** or **EBCM**. See Figure 19-30. On applications with traction control, it is referred to as the electronic brake traction control module or EBTCM.

The ABS relay controls power to the pump motor and solenoids, and is switched on (closed) by the controller when ABS braking is needed.

The BPMV contains six valves. There is one inlet (apply) valve and one outlet (release) valve for each brake channel,

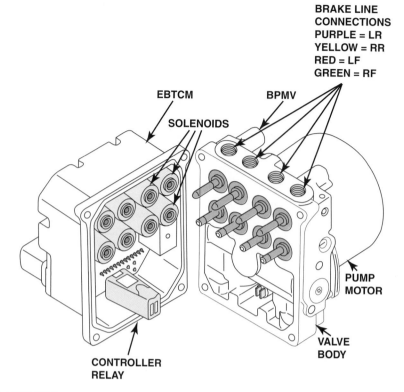

BRAKE LINE
CONNECTIONS
PURPLE = LR
YELLOW = RR
RED = LF
GREEN = RF

EBTCM

BPMV

SOLENOIDS

PUMP
MOTOR

VALVE
BODY

CONTROLLER
RELAY

FIGURE 19-30 Delphi DBC-7 ABS system.

plus two accumulators (one for each brake circuit) or 10 ABS valves if the vehicle has TCS traction control. The inlet valves are normally open, and the outlet valves are normally closed. The solenoid for each valve is energized when the EBCM provides a ground to complete the circuit.

All applications are four-channel ABS systems, so each of the four BPMV outlets is connected to the brake line for a separate wheel. The lines are color coded for identification:

Left rear is purple
Right rear is yellow
Left front is red
Right front is green

Additional system components include a brake pedal switch that closes when the pedal is depressed to signal the controller the brakes are being applied. Input from the brake pedal switch is not required to trigger an ABS stop, but if the switch is closed (pedal depressed), it will disengage traction control.

System Operation

The EBCM monitors wheel speed through four wheel speed sensors, which are part of the wheel bearing assembly and cannot be adjusted or serviced separately.

If wheel lockup is starting to occur, the ABS inlet valve for the affected brake circuit is energized to close off and isolate

the brake line. The *hold* or *isolate* phase prevents any further pressure from reaching the wheel. Next, the outlet valve is energized to release pressure from the brake line. Opening the valve begins the *pressure decrease* phase, and allows the wheel to speed up and regain traction. Pressure is vented back to the accumulator, while the pump runs to route the fluid back to the system. Finally, pressure is reapplied by de-energizing both the inlet and outlet solenoids, allowing pressure from the master cylinder to once again reach the wheel. The ABS inlet and outlet solenoids are cycled in rapid succession until wheel slip is within an acceptable range or the vehicle has stopped.

TIRE PRESSURE MONITORING SYSTEM (TPMS)

Tire pressure monitoring systems (TPMS) are required on all new vehicles. The type that uses the wheel speed sensor is called the *indirect* TPMS. The ability to compare wheel speeds also allows the DBC-7 ABS system to function as a low tire-pressure detection system. A tire that is underinflated will have a slightly smaller rolling radius than one that is properly inflated. This will create a difference in the wheel speed sensor reading if the difference in inflation pressure is 12 psi or more. The EBCM will then turn on the *low tire pressure* warning lamp to warn the driver that tires need attention. To help compensate for speed variation during cornering, an indirect tire pressure monitoring system checks the rotating speeds of diagonally opposed wheels. The system adds the speeds of the right front and left rear and then subtracts that value from the sum of the left front and right rear tires. If the total is less than or equal to a threshold value, no warning is given. However, if the total is greater than a predetermined value, the TPMS warning light is illuminated. The warning lamp will stay on until air is added to the tire and the ignition is cycled off and on.

NOTE: This system cannot detect if all of the tires are underinflated, only if one tire is underinflated.

ENHANCED TRACTION CONTROL SYSTEM

On applications with enhanced traction system (ETS), the EBTCM monitors the drive wheels for positive slip during acceleration. If wheel slip occurs, the EBTCM illuminates the *low trac* light and the powertrain control module (PCM) reduces engine power by retarding spark timing, disabling the spark to one or more cylinders, leaning the air/fuel mixture, and/or upshifting the transmission to a higher gear. No brake application is involved.

KELSEY-HAYES EBC2 RABS AND RWAL

Kelsey-Hayes EBC2 rear-wheel antilock braking systems have been in use since the late 1980s on Ford trucks and vans. Ford calls their version of EBC2, the **Rear-Wheel Antilock Braking System (RABS).** On General Motors truck and van applications, the EBC2 system is called **Rear-Wheel Anti-Lock (RWAL).**

Dodge has also used the RWAL system on its D and W 150-350, Dakota, and Ram pickups. Geo, Isuzu, Mazda, Nissan, and Subaru have used the system since 1991.

Rear-wheel only antilock braking cannot provide the same benefits as four-wheel ABS braking, but it is a major improvement over standard brakes on trucks and vans where vehicle loading has a major influence on brake balance and traction. In trucks and vans, the tendency of the rear wheels to lock up and skid is greatly influenced by the payload in the vehicle. The lighter the load over the rear wheels, the greater the tendency for the rear wheels to lock on wet surfaces or when braking hard. For this reason, rear-wheel antilock braking became standard on most pickups since the late 1980s.

System Description

The EBC2 RABS and RWAL systems are all nonintegral rear-wheel-only antilock braking systems. See Figure 19-31.

On four-wheel-drive applications, rear-wheel antilock braking is only used when in two-wheel-drive mode.

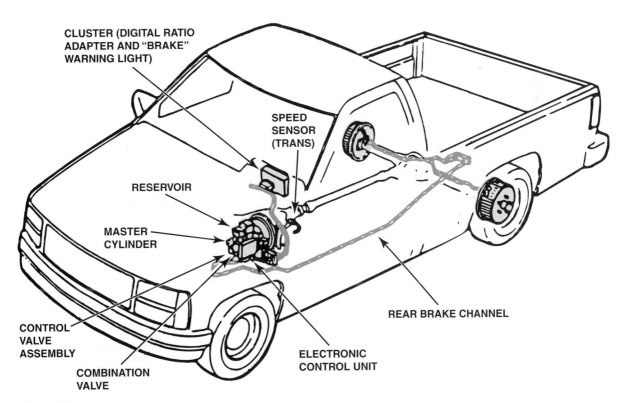

CLUSTER (DIGITAL RATIO ADAPTER AND "BRAKE" WARNING LIGHT)

SPEED SENSOR (TRANS)

RESERVOIR

MASTER CYLINDER

CONTROL VALVE ASSEMBLY

COMBINATION VALVE

ELECTRONIC CONTROL UNIT

REAR BRAKE CHANNEL

FIGURE 19-31 Kelsey-Hayes RWAL ABS system.

The conventional master brake cylinder and power booster supplies brake pressure to a dual solenoid control valve for the rear brakes. This unit contains only two solenoid valves:

1. A normally open isolation valve to block pressure from the master cylinder to the rear brakes during antilock braking.
2. A normally closed dump valve for relieving pressure in the rear brake circuits. See Figure 19-32.

The dual solenoid control valve also contains a pressure accumulator for storing fluid pressure during the dump or release phase of operation, and a reset switch which allows the system to maintain proper brake pressure.

When the ABS control module detects a difference in the average speed of the rear wheels compared to the vehicle's overall speed, it initiates antilock braking. The control module energizes the ABS isolation solenoid to prevent any further increase in brake pressure at the rear wheels. See Figure 19-33.

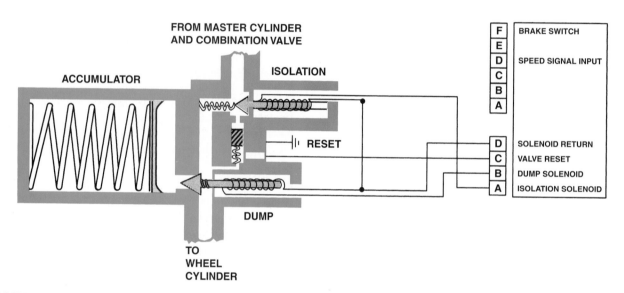

FIGURE 19-32   Kelsey-Hayes RWAL system modulator in the normal brake mode (pressure increase mode).

MAINTAIN PRESSURE—ANTILOCK BRAKING

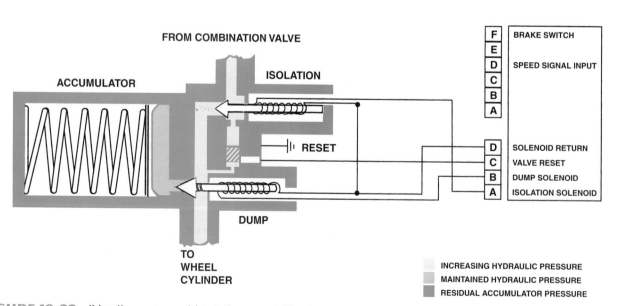

FIGURE 19-33   Kelsey-Hayes system modulator in the pressure hold mode.

Then, the ABS dump solenoid valve is opened to release pressure from the rear brake circuits so the wheels can regain speed and traction. See Figure 19-34.

Pressure is reapplied when both solenoids are de-energized and return to their normal positions. The cycle is repeated continuously for as long as ABS braking is needed or until the vehicle stops.

The control module receives a speed signal from a single **vehicle speed sensor (VSS).** On Ford and Dodge applications, the speed sensor is in the differential and the sensor ring is on the ring gear. On GM applications, the speed sensor is located in the transmission tailshaft, and the sensor ring is on the transmission output shaft.

KELSEY-HAYES EBC4 4WAL

The Kelsey-Hayes EBC4 four wheel antilock braking system is used on General Motors trucks and is called **4WAL.**

The 4WAL system is a nonintegral four-wheel, three-channel ABS system with a conventional master cylinder and brake booster. See Figure 19-35.

Each front brake circuit is controlled independently, but both rear brakes are controlled as a pair. The system remains active in four-wheel drive, unlike some earlier RWAL applications where ABS was deactivated in four-wheel drive.

System Description

Most 4WAL applications use four-wheel speed sensors, one for each wheel. A transmission-mounted vehicle speed sensor provides a common signal for both rear wheels.

The front wheel speed sensors on two-wheel-drive trucks are located on the splash shield behind the brake rotor, with the sensor ring behind the rotor. Four-wheel-drive trucks have the front sensors mounted behind the splash shield and can be replaced without having to pull the brake rotor. The tone ring, however, is part of the wheel bearing assembly. The rear wheel speed sensors are located on the rear brake backing plates with rings pressed onto the ends of the axle shafts. On most 4WAL applications, the signals from the wheel speed sensors go directly to the electronic control unit.

The ABS control module is mounted on the hydraulic modulator assembly, which General Motors calls the **electrohydraulic control unit (EHCU).** See Figure 19-36. The ABS control module receives input from the wheel speed sensors and a brake pedal switch. See Figure 19-37.

The 4WAL system also has a 4WD switch and indicator light. The 4WD switch changes the ABS control logic when the vehicle is shifted into four-wheel drive. The switch is closed in four-wheel drive and supplies 12 volts to the controller. The switch is part of the indicator light circuit and is mechanically operated by the shift linkage in the transfer case.

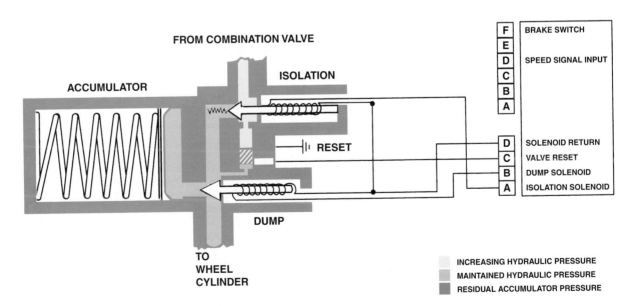

MAINTAIN PRESSURE—ANTILOCK BRAKING

FIGURE 19-34   Kelsey-Hayes system modulator in the pressure decrease mode (pressure dump mode).

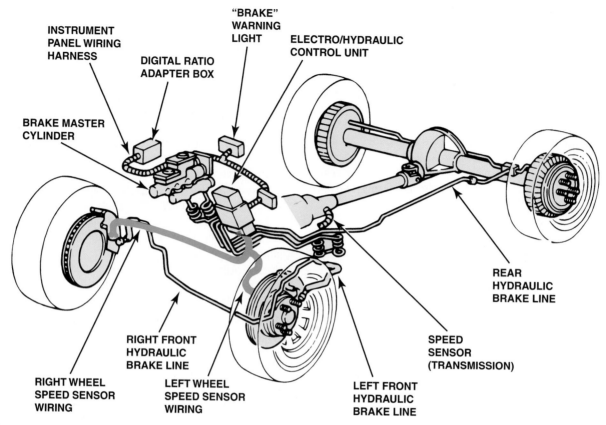

FIGURE 19-35 Kelsey-Hayes 4WAL ABS system.

For diagnostic purposes, there is both a red BRAKE and amber ANTILOCK warning light, instead of the single red BRAKE warning light on Kelsey-Hayes RWAL systems.

Electrohydraulic Control Unit (EHCU)

The EHCU contains six ABS solenoid valves: an isolation valve and a modulation valve for each of the three individual brake circuits. The EHCU also has a single pump motor that drives two separate pumps, one for the front brakes and one for the rear brakes. The relay for the pump motor is inside the EHCU. Also inside the EHCU are four pressure accumulators, one front and one rear low-pressure accumulator, and one front and one rear high-pressure accumulator. There are also three reset switches, one for each front brake and one for the combined rear brake circuit.

System Operation

During normal braking, fluid pressure from the master cylinder passes through the normally open isolation and modulation solenoid valves in the EHCU to the individual brakes. When the controller senses that wheel lockup is about to occur, it activates antilock braking.

The EHCU begins ABS operation in the usual way, by energizing the ABS isolation solenoid for the affected wheel to block any further pressure increase to the brake. At the same time, the pump motor relay is energized to start the pump, which builds pressure in the high-pressure accumulator for the pressure increase phase of antilock braking. Next, the system energizes the decay ABS solenoid, which is referred to as the **pulse-width modulation (PWM) valve,** to bleed pressure from the brake. The 4WAL control module can vary the amount of pressure decrease by varying the valve's open or "on" time. It does this by varying the "on" time or duration of voltage to the solenoid.

When the PWM valve is energized and closes, it opens a passage that allows pressure dumps into one of the two low-pressure accumulators. The spring-loaded **low-pressure accumulator (LPA)** serves as a temporary storage reservoir to hold the fluid until it can be rerouted back into the system. It also maintains sufficient fluid pressure in the EHCU to keep the high-pressure pump primed.

As the system reduces pressure in the affected brake circuit, the reset switch for that circuit may trip, signaling the ABS control module that fluid pressure has dropped to the point where additional pressure is needed to maintain proper braking action. At this point, the control module de-energizes the PWM valve and initiates the pressure increase mode.

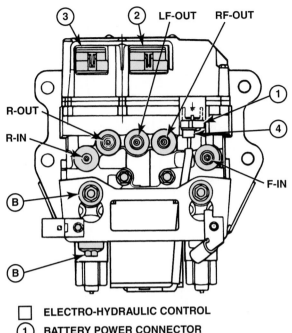

ELECTRO-HYDRAULIC CONTROL
1. BATTERY POWER CONNECTOR
2. SWITCH POWER/CIRCUIT CONNECTOR
3. WHEEL SPEED SENSOR CIRCUIT CONNECTOR
4. MOTOR CONNECTOR
☐ MOUNTING BRACKET FEATURES
B. ISOLATION GROMMETS (SIX)
R-IN   REAR INLET FITTING
R-OUT   REAR CHANNEL OUTLET FITTING
F-IN   FRONT INLET FITTING
LF-OUT   LEFT CHANNEL FITTING
RF-OUT   RIGHT CHANNEL OUTLET FITTING

FIGURE 19-36 Kelsey-Hayes 4WAL electrohydraulic control unit (EHCU).

When the PWM reopens, fluid pressure from the **high-pressure accumulator (HPA)** and high-pressure pump enters the brake circuit and builds brake pressure. This reapplies the brake as the wheel continues to decelerate. The reset switch also returns to its normal position as pressure is restored. The ABS controller then continues to cycle the PWM valve as needed to prevent wheel lockup for the duration of the stop.

During the pressure hold, decrease, and increase phases of antilock braking, the isolation valve for the brake circuit remains closed. This blocks brake pressure from the master cylinder so it cannot enter the brake circuit being controlled. The reapplication of brake pressure, therefore, must come from the high-pressure pump and accumulator.

After an ABS stop, the system de-energizes the isolation and PWM valves and normal braking resumes. The residual pressure that remains in the high-pressure accumulator bleeds into the master cylinder reservoir.

KELSEY-HAYES EBC5H

Later Kelsey-Hayes four-wheel ABS systems include the EBC5 and EBC10. The EBC5H system is on Dodge trucks and vans. It is a nonintegral, four-wheel hybrid three-channel system that uses a separate hydraulic modulator for the front wheels and a RWAL modulator for the rear wheels. See Figures 19-38 and 19-39.

This system uses three nonadjustable wheel speed sensors, one on the inboard side of each front disc brake rotor hub, and a common sensor for both rear wheels mounted on top of the differential housing. The signals route directly to the control module or controller antilock brakes (CAB), which is next to the ABS valve body on the driver-side fender panel.

The RWAL valve body for the rear wheels is the same as that used on rear-wheel ABS applications and contains two ABS solenoids: an isolation valve and a dump valve. The ABS modulator for the front brakes contains four ABS solenoid valves: an isolation solenoid and dump solenoid for each front brake circuit, and a pump to generate pressure as additional brake force is needed during ABS braking. The pump only runs if antilock braking occurs at either front wheel, and does not operate if the rear wheels only are involved.

The front modulator unit also contains a low-pressure accumulator (LPA) to temporarily store fluid under pressure during pressure release, and a high-pressure accumulator (HPA) to store hydraulic fluid under pressure for reapplying the front brakes. The LPA is normally empty and only fills when the brake fluid vents from either front brake as its dump valve opens. The HPA fills as soon as the pump starts to run.

A pump outlet check valve separates the master cylinder and pump, preventing unnecessary fluid flow to the HPA from the master cylinder during a high-pressure brake application. The valve is normally closed and opens only when pump pressure exceeds a certain value as pressure is reapplied to either front brake. This allows fluid to flow from the master cylinder reservoir to the pump, causing a slight drop in the brake pedal.

KELSEY-HAYES EBC5U

Ford Econoline vans use a different version of the EBC5 system named EBC5U for "unitized." This system has a single hydraulic modulator assembly for all four wheels instead of the separate front and rear ABS modulators used by Dodge. It is a nonintegral, four-wheel, three-channel system with the ABS control module mounted on the modulator.

The HCU has six ABS solenoids: three normally open isolation valves (one for each front brake circuit and one for the rear brakes), and three normally closed dump valves. An accumulator on the HCU temporarily stores fluid that is released from a brake circuit through its dump valve. A return pump routes fluid back to the main fluid reservoir. The valve body,

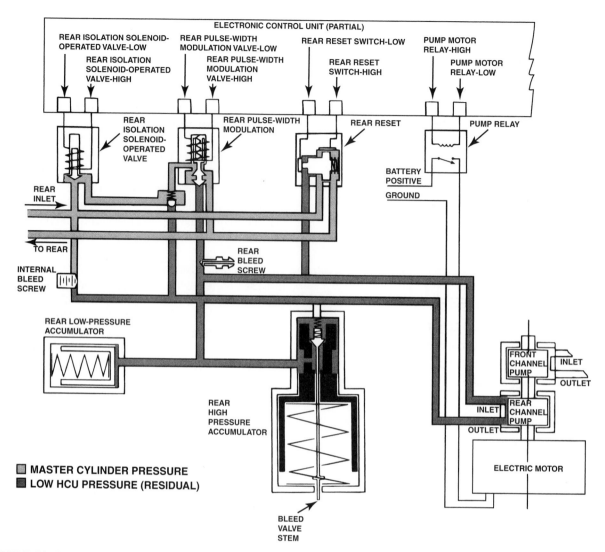

FIGURE 19-37   Kelsey-Hayes 4WAL system hydraulic schematic in the normal (pressure increase) mode.

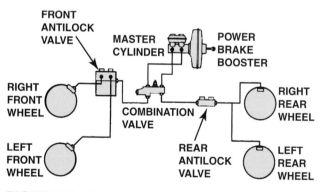

FIGURE 19-38   Kelsey-Hayes EBC5H four-wheel ABS system.

KELSEY-HAYES EBC310

The Kelsey-Hayes EBC310 is used on General Motors full-size pickup trucks. EBC310 is a nonintegral four-wheel, three-channel unitized system with the control module mounted on the modulator. The modulator contains six ABS valves: three isolation valves and three dump valves, plus a pump and accumulator. This system is functionally similar to the EBC5U system, but the parts are not interchangeable.

KELSEY-HAYES EBC410

Another Kelsey-Hayes ABS system, called EBC410, is used on Ford Windstar minivans. It is similar to the EBC310 system except the EHCU has eight ABS solenoids, and an isolation and dump valve for each brake circuit. The two extra solenoids allow the system to control each rear brake circuit separately,

pump, and pump motor are not serviceable separately. The module receives inputs from a brake pedal switch and three nonadjustable wheel speed sensors, one at each front wheel and a common sensor on the rear axle housing for the rear wheels.

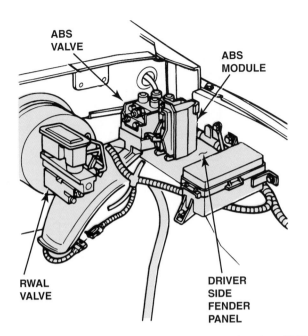

ABS
VALVE

ABS
MODULE

RWAL
VALVE

DRIVER
SIDE
FENDER
PANEL

FIGURE 19-39 Component location for the Kelsey-Hayes EBC5H four-wheel ABS system.

making it a four-channel system. See Figure 19-40. Independent control of the rear brakes is necessary on the Windstar because it has front-wheel drive and a diagonally split hydraulic system.

SUMITOMO ABS

Sumitomo ABS has been used on the Mazda RX7, 626, MX-6, and Ford Probe, and Honda offered it on the Prelude Si, and then the Accord EX and Civic EX in 1991, as well as the Acura NSX, Legend, Integra GS, and Vigor. The Sumitomo ABS system is a nonintegral, four-wheel, three-channel ABS system.

System Description

The three- and four-channel versions of the Sumitomo ABS system all have four wheel speed sensors. See Figure 19-41.

The modulator on three-channel systems contains three ABS solenoid valves as well as four modulator control pistons, one for each brake circuit. See Figure 19-42.

Honda versions use three pistons, one for each front brake and one for both rear brakes. Modulators for the later four-channel systems receive a fourth solenoid so the rear brakes can be controlled independently.

A pump and nitrogen-charged accumulator generate ABS brake pressure. On Hondas, the accumulator is also used for power-assisted normal braking. The pump and accumulator are part of the modulator assembly in all applications, except Honda where they are separate components mounted ahead of the modulator in the engine compartment.

ABS Operation

When ABS braking is needed, the control module, located under the dash or center console, energizes the normally open solenoid outlet valve in the modulator. This closes the reservoir outlet circuit valve in the modulator, which opens the pump supply to the modulator. Pump pressure enters the modulator and works against the control piston, which closes a cut-off valve in the brake circuit. Pressure is then released from the brake circuit so it can flow back to the reservoir, which also produces pedal feedback. Pressure is reapplied to the brake when the solenoid is de-energized. This allows the control piston to return to its normal position, opening the brake circuit cut-off valve.

HONDA

Honda **antilock brake (ALB)** versions use a conventional master cylinder with the Sumitomo ABS system. However, the brake booster is hydraulic rather than vacuum-assisted. The ABS pump generates pressure for normal power-assisted braking as well as ABS braking and stores it in the accumulator. Both pump and accumulator are located in the left front area of the engine compartment.

When the ignition is on, the ABS control module energizes the pump relay to start the pump if the accumulator pressure switch indicates low pressure, less than 1,720 psi (12,000 kPa). The pump draws fluid from the master cylinder reservoir and feeds it into the accumulator. When accumulator pressure reaches its maximum limit of 3,300 psi (23,000 kPa), the pump shuts off. The pressure stored in the accumulator is sufficient to provide several power-assisted stops or ABS applications should the pump fail. A pump failure will cause the ABS warning lamp to come on.

TEVES MARK IV

The Teves Mark IV is a nonintegral four-wheel ABS system that uses a standard master brake cylinder and booster with a separate hydraulic modulator and pump assembly. It is used on many General Motors, Ford, and DaimlerChrysler vehicles.

System Description

The Mark IV is a four-channel ABS system with individual wheel speed sensors and separate ABS solenoids for each brake circuit. See Figure 19-43.

It controls the front wheels independently, but both rear wheels are controlled as a single output with separate feed lines during ABS braking, similar to a three-channel ABS system. On applications with traction control, the rear brake circuit solenoid can provide independent braking for either rear wheel.

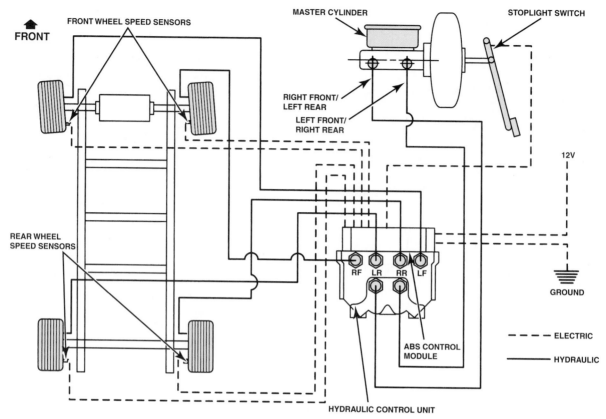

FIGURE 19-40 Hydraulic schematic of the Kelsey-Hayes EBC410 four-channel ABS system.

The cap on the fluid reservoir on Fords with Teves Mark IV contains a fluid level switch, which will illuminate the red BRAKE warning lamp if the level becomes too low. The reservoir also contains a low-pressure hose that supplies brake fluid to the hydraulic modulator mini reservoir. The valve body, pump and motor, and reservoir on the modulator assembly can all be serviced separately.

The hydraulic modulator is located in the front of the engine compartment. Ford service literature refers to the modulator as the hydraulic control unit (HCU), while General Motors calls it the pressure modulator valve (PMV) assembly. See Figure 19-44.

The modulator consists of a valve block manifold with four inlet and four outlet ABS solenoid valves, a pump and motor, and a "mini" fluid reservoir with a fluid level indicator. An indicator is needed because the reservoir is sealed and cannot be checked manually. If the fluid level is low for any reason, the amber ABS warning light will come on and the ABS system will be deactivated—but no fault code will set.

On applications with traction control, the modulator is larger and contains two additional isolation valves, one for each front wheel in rear-wheel-drive applications. The isolation valves close when the traction control function prevents application of the front brakes.

Control Module

The control module, which General Motors refers to as the EBCM and DaimlerChrysler calls the CAB, contains two microprocessors, receives identical inputs from the wheel speed sensors, and makes its own calculations. The results are then compared. If there is any disagreement, the controller disables the ABS/traction control system and illuminates the ABS and traction control warning lights. The EBCM monitors wheel speed continuously through its four wheel speed sensors, which are mounted in the front knuckles and rear brake rotor backing plates.

The control module also receives additional input from a switch mounted on the brake pedal, which provides pedal travel information. The switch is normally closed, but opens when the driver presses the brake pedal beyond 40% of its normal travel. This signals the control module to energize the pump in the modulator assembly, which then pumps brake fluid back to the master cylinder. The returning fluid causes the pedal to rise until the switch closes, at which point the pump is turned off. This maintains proper pedal feel during ABS stops and prevents the pedal from sinking too far toward the floor.

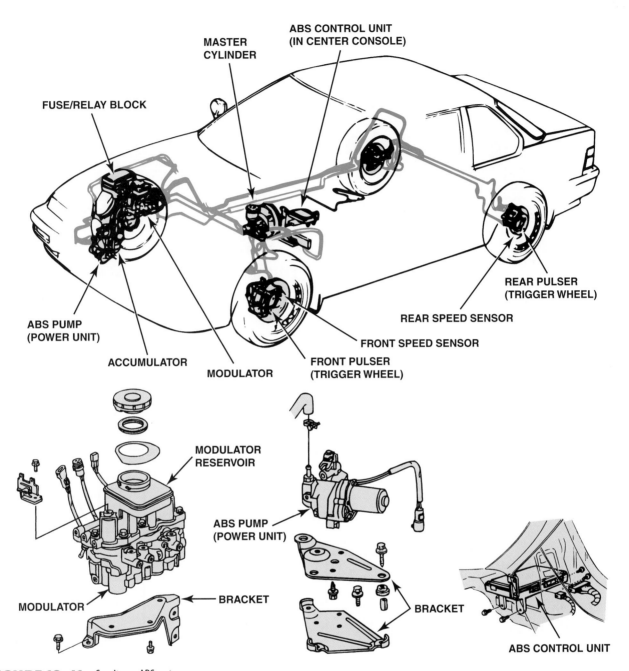

FIGURE 19-41   Sumitomo ABS system.

ABS Operation

During normal braking, fluid from the master cylinder enters the modulator assembly through two inlet ports located at the back of the modulator. The fluid then passes through four normally open isolation solenoid valves, one for each wheel, and passes into each of the four separate brake circuits.

If the control module senses that a wheel is about to lock, the control module energizes the isolation solenoid valve to close off the brake circuit and hold pressure in the line. If the wheel is still decelerating too rapidly, the control module opens the normally closed dump solenoid valve to release pressure in the circuit. The controller can then de-energize both solenoids, allowing pressure to be reapplied in the circuit. At the same time, the pump in the modulator is energized to build pressure in the system and to route fluid back to the master cylinder.

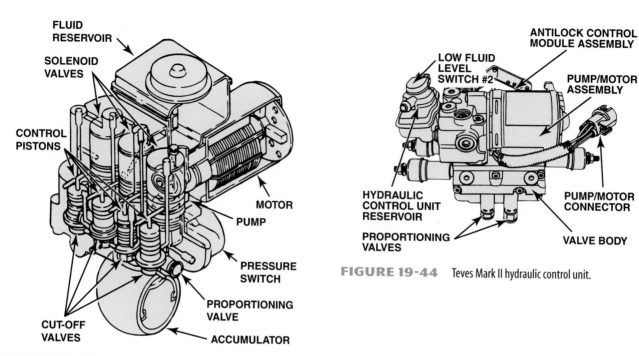

FLUID
RESERVOIR

SOLENOID
VALVES

CONTROL
PISTONS

MOTOR

PUMP

PRESSURE
SWITCH

PROPORTIONING
VALVE

CUT-OFF
VALVES

ACCUMULATOR

FIGURE 19-42 Sumitomo modulator.

ANTILOCK CONTROL
MODULE ASSEMBLY

LOW FLUID
LEVEL
SWITCH #2

PUMP/MOTOR
ASSEMBLY

HYDRAULIC
CONTROL UNIT
RESERVOIR

PUMP/MOTOR
CONNECTOR

PROPORTIONING
VALVES

VALVE BODY

FIGURE 19-44 Teves Mark II hydraulic control unit.

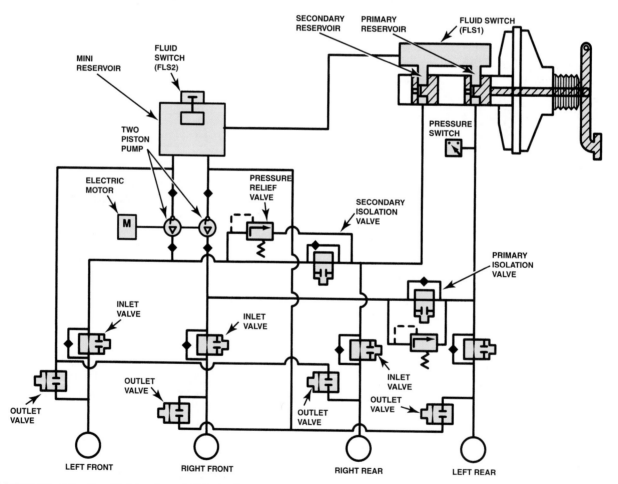

SECONDARY
RESERVOIR

PRIMARY
RESERVOIR

FLUID SWITCH
(FLS1)

MINI
RESERVOIR

FLUID
SWITCH
(FLS2)

TWO
PISTON
PUMP

ELECTRIC
MOTOR

PRESSURE
RELIEF
VALVE

SECONDARY
ISOLATION
VALVE

PRESSURE
SWITCH

PRIMARY
ISOLATION
VALVE

M

INLET
VALVE

INLET
VALVE

INLET
VALVE

OUTLET
VALVE

OUTLET
VALVE

OUTLET
VALVE

OUTLET
VALVE

LEFT FRONT

RIGHT FRONT

RIGHT REAR

LEFT REAR

FIGURE 19-43 Teves Mark II nonintegral ABS hydraulic circuit.

Traction Control

Mark IV traction control can be found on rear-wheel-drive Fords and front-wheel-drive General Motors and DaimlerChrysler applications. Traction control involves braking the drive wheels only and does not include reducing engine torque (no throttle relaxer, spark retard, or injector disabling functions).

When one or both drive wheels begin to spin while accelerating, the difference in wheel speed front-to-rear signals the control module to engage traction control. The control module does this by first closing the appropriate traction control isolation valve so pressure does not enter the wrong brake circuit when braking pressure is applied to the drive wheel. At the same time, the pump generates brake pressure, which the control module routes to the brake. A TRAC CNTL or TRACTION ASSIST indicator light illuminates to inform the driver that traction control is functioning.

On most Ford rear-wheel-drive and General Motors front-wheel-drive applications, traction control only functions at speeds of less than 25 miles per hour.

TEVES MARK 20 AND MARK IV G

The Teves Mark 20 is a nonintegral four-wheel ABS system and is used on many DaimlerChrysler vehicles. The hydraulic modulator and pump assembly, which DaimlerChrysler calls an **integrated control unit (ICU),** is separate from the master cylinder. A dual compensating port master cylinder is used on vehicles without traction control. A center valve master cylinder is used on vehicles with traction control.

DaimlerChrysler also refers to the Mark IV G as the "Mark 20 nonintegrated" system, which uses a separate controller (CAB) and hydraulic control unit (HCU) instead of the integrated Mark 20.

System Description

The Mark 20 has two different hydraulic circuits, depending on the application. Rear-wheel-drive vehicles separate the base brake system into front and rear hydraulic circuits. The ABS uses three channels and four-wheel sensors. See Figure 19-45.

The front wheels are controlled independently and the rear wheels are controlled together using the select low principle. Front-wheel-drive vehicles separate the base brake system into diagonally split circuits (right rear-left front and left rear-right front). The ABS uses four channels and four wheel sensors. See Figure 19-46 on page 391.

Like the rear-wheel-drive version, it controls the rear wheels together using the select low principle. On applications with traction control, the system applies braking force to the spinning drive wheel to slow it to approximately the same speed as the nonspinning drive wheel.

Master cylinder design differs according to whether the vehicle is equipped with traction control. On applications without traction control, a standard compensating port design is used. The compensating ports allow residual brake pressure to flow from the master cylinder bore to the reservoir when the pedal is released. The lip seals of the piston cups close off the compensating ports between the reservoir chambers and the master cylinder bore.

On applications with traction control, each master cylinder piston is equipped with a center valve. See Figure 19-47 on page 392.

The center valves open when the traction control system is in operation, allowing brake fluid to be drawn from the master cylinder reservoir. This protects the lip seals.

The solenoid valves are contained in a unit that incorporates the CAB on most models. See Figure 19-48 on page 392.

Control Module

The control module on most Mark 20-equipped vehicles includes the CAB, the hydraulic pump, its motor, and a valve block that contains the solenoid valves. On front-wheel-drive vehicles, which have a diagonally split base braking system, the valve block contains an inlet valve and an outlet valve for each wheel. The number of valves in the modulator varies according to application:

- Six for rear wheel drive (three channels)
- Eight for front wheel drive (four channels)
- Ten for traction control

The CAB receives two constant power inputs, one for the solenoids and one for the pump motor. When the ignition key is turned to RUN or START, a third power input causes the CAB to run a self-diagnostic check. If a problem is found, the CAB sets a code and disables the ABS.

On Jeep vehicles, the CAB also monitors signals from a *deceleration sensor,* also called a *G-switch,* to monitor deceleration in both forward and rearward braking. See Figure 19-49.

Three normally closed mercury switches contained in the switch housing open under the G-force of deceleration. There are two switches to measure forward deceleration and one for rearward deceleration. The forward switches are mounted at different angles in the housing, so they open at different G-forces. Under hard braking on a high-friction surface, such as dry pavement, the G-force from deceleration is enough to open both of the forward switches. Under hard braking on a medium-friction surface such as gravel, only forward switch G2 will open. On a slippery surface, neither of the switches will open. Switch G3 opens under hard braking when the vehicle is moving rearward.

ABS Operation

The Mark 20 ABS has one inlet valve and one outlet valve for each hydraulic channel (three channels with rear-wheel-drive

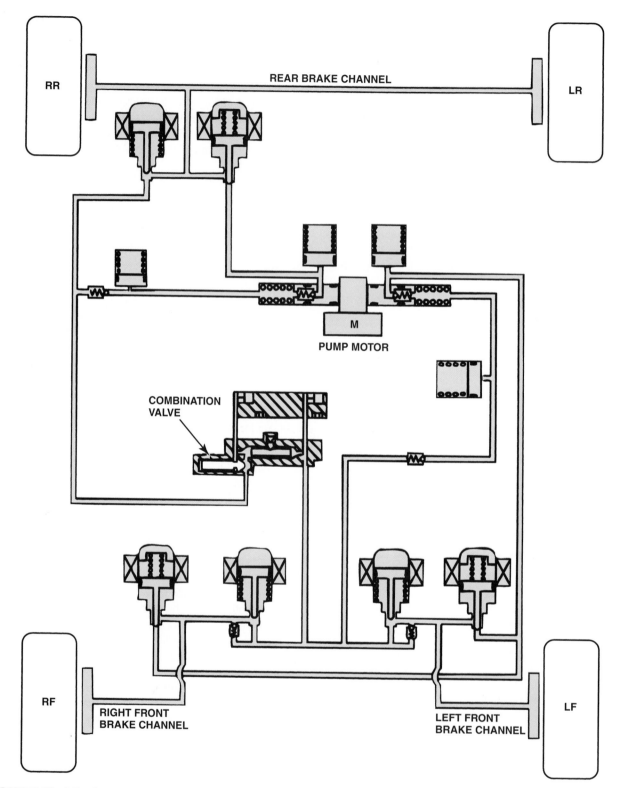

FIGURE 19-45   Teves Mark 20 ABS system on a typical rear-wheel-drive application.

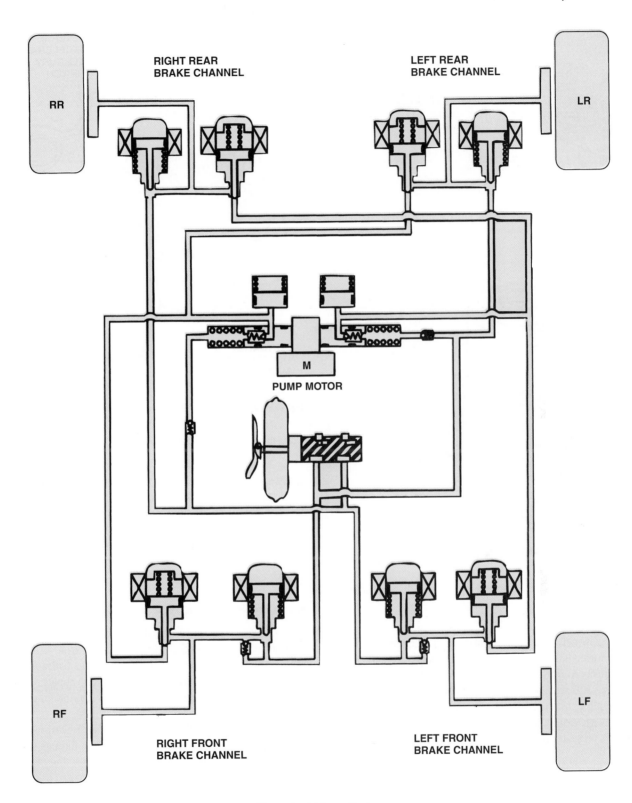

FIGURE 19-46   Teves Mark 20 ABS system on a typical front-wheel-drive application.

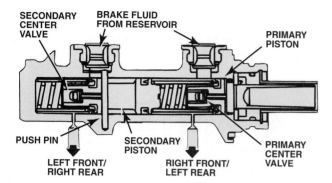

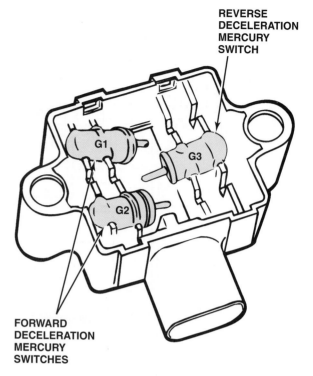

FIGURE 19-47 Teves Mark 20 ABS systems with traction control use a master cylinder that has center valves to allow the brake fluid to flow from the master cylinder reservoir.

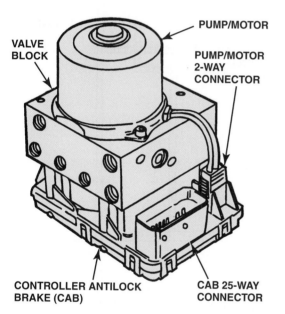

FIGURE 19-48 The integrated control unit (ICU) is used on most Mark 20 ABS applications.

FIGURE 19-49 The deceleration sensor in Teves Mark 20 ABS systems used on Jeep applications uses three mercury switches that open in response to forward and reverse deceleration forces.

and four channels with front-wheel-drive). During normal braking and during the pressure-build cycle of an ABS stop, the inlet valves are open and the outlet valves are closed. During the hold cycle of an ABS stop, both the inlet and outlet valves are closed, maintaining constant hydraulic pressure at the brake. During the decay cycle of an ABS stop, the outlet valve opens, releasing hydraulic pressure to a pair of accumulators for storage.

Traction Control Operation

The traction control system (TCS) operates at vehicle speeds up to 35 miles per hour. The system is automatically switched on whenever the ignition is turned on. On front-wheel-drive vehicles, the traction control system uses a pair of isolators to block pressure to the rear brakes so they will not be applied, then uses the pump and inlet and outlet valves to apply the brake pressure

at the spinning front wheel until it slows to the same approximate speed as the nonspinning wheel. A CAB thermal limiter function measures the number of times the brakes are applied within a given period of time, and uses this to calculate whether the brakes are overheating. When the CAB determines that the brakes are overheating, it disengages the traction control system for a predetermined period of time to promote cooling.

TOYOTA REAR-WHEEL ABS

Toyota's rear-wheel ABS system is different from other rear-wheel ABS systems. See Figure 19-50. It uses hydraulic pressure generated by the power steering pump to apply additional brake pressure to the rear wheels in the ABS braking mode. See Figure 19-51 on page 394.

All other rear-wheel ABS systems (Kelsey-Hayes) rely solely on brake pressure generated by the driver's foot through the master cylinder and vacuum power booster. Because the other rear-wheel ABS systems use no pump, brake pressure can bleed down rather quickly during an ABS stop. This, in turn, requires increased pedal effort by the driver and causes a drop in pedal height.

Toyota designed a system that uses a standard master cylinder and vacuum booster but functions much like an integral ABS system during the ABS mode by shunting hydraulic pressure from the power steering pump to generate braking without increased pedal effort or a loss of pedal height.

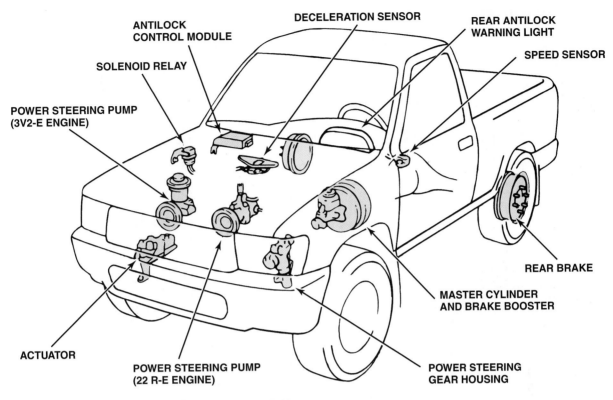

FIGURE 19-50　Component location of the Toyota rear-wheel ABS system.

The Toyota rear-wheel ABS system works only in two-wheel drive on trucks with 4WD. When driving in 4WD mode, the ABS system is disengaged and brake balance is controlled by a load sensing proportioning valve that prevents rear brake lockup.

System Components

Toyota's rear-wheel ABS system uses a single-speed sensor. It is a magnetic induction sensor that monitors rear-wheel speed by reading the ring gear in the rear differential. A deceleration sensor detects vehicle deceleration and is located inside the cab under the front center console.

The stop light switch, located on the brake pedal, signals the ABS control module when the brakes are applied. A REAR ANTILOCK warning light warns the driver if a problem occurs in the system.

An electronic control unit (ECU) monitors inputs from the sensors and brake switch and decides when ABS braking is needed. The ECU is also located inside the cab behind the glovebox.

The ABS solenoid relay routes voltage to the ABS solenoid in the hydraulic actuator. It contains a pressure regulator valve to control power steering pressure in relation to brake pressure, a bypass piston (opens and closes a bypass valve according to power steering pressure), a relief valve (relieves power steering pressure if the pressure in the actuator is too high), and a single ABS solenoid valve. The ABS solenoid valve is

controlled by the ECU via the ABS solenoid relay and performs the hold-release-reapply function that modulates pressure to the rear brakes.

System Operation

During normal braking, the rear-wheel ABS system does nothing unless the rear wheels start to slip, in which case the control module energizes the ABS solenoid relay, which passes current to the ABS solenoid in the actuator. The solenoid moves upward, isolating the rear brake circuit and releasing pressure at the same time to prevent wheel lockup. The control module then cycles the solenoid on and off to maintain pressure in the rear brake lines within a narrow range. If pressure needs to be increased, the control module alters the duty cycle or on/off ratio of the ABS solenoid. Increasing the percentage of "off time" to "on time" allows pressure from the power steering pump to increase pressure to the rear brakes.

TOYOTA FOUR-WHEEL ABS

The system uses three channels and four-wheel sensors in all models except the Supra, which has four channels. Three-channel applications control the rear wheels simultaneously and the four-channel system controls them independently. See Figure 19-52 on page 395.

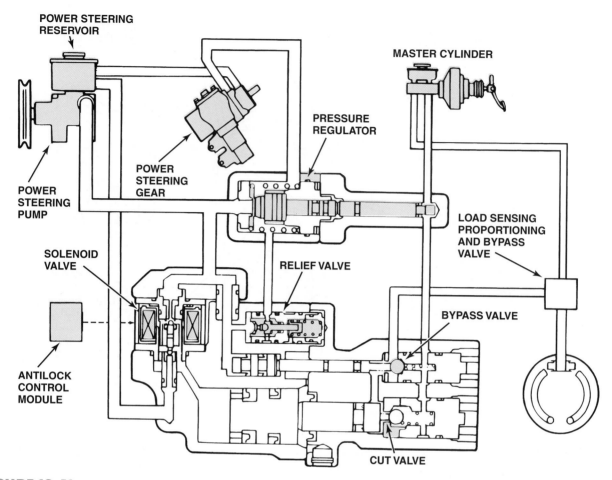

FIGURE 19-51   Toyota rear-wheel ABS hydraulic circuit.

There is a pair of solenoids in each channel, one for pressure hold and one for decay (six solenoids for three-channel versions and eight solenoids for four-channel applications).

The hold solenoids are normally open. During normal braking, hydraulic pressure from the master cylinder passes through the hold solenoids to the wheel brakes. See Figure 19-53.

When the pedal is released, a spring-loaded check valve in the hold solenoid opens to let hydraulic pressure return to the master cylinder. During an ABS stop, the hold solenoid closes, blocking hydraulic pressure from the master cylinder. The decay solenoid is also closed, holding hydraulic pressure constant. If the wheel still is approaching lockup, the decay solenoid opens, releasing hydraulic pressure to the reservoir. During the build cycle, the hold valve opens again and the pump supplies hydraulic pressure to the wheel brake. It also supplies pressure to the master cylinder, alerting the driver to ABS operation.

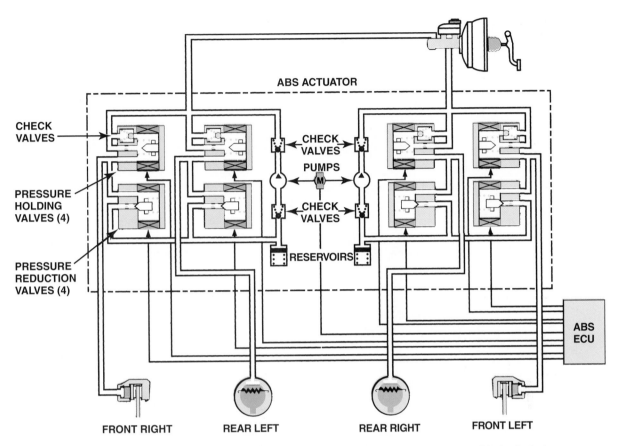

FIGURE 19-52   Toyota four-wheel ABS system uses a hold solenoid and decay (pressure reduction) solenoid in each hydraulic circuit.

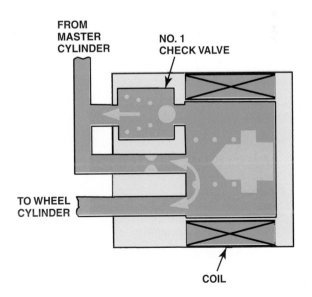

FIGURE 19-53   The normally open hold solenoid closes at the start of an ABS stop. The check valve allows fluid to flow to the master cylinder when the brake pedal is released.

SUMMARY

1. DaimlerChrysler used the nonintegral Bendix 6 ABS on many vehicles.
2. DaimlerChrysler used the Bendix LC4 ABS nonintegral ABS system on many vehicles as well as the Bendix ABX-4.
3. The Bendix Mecatronic II ABS system was used on Ford Contour and Mercury Mystique.
4. The Bosch 2E nonintegral ABS system was used on many DaimlerChrysler and Japanese import brand vehicles.
5. The Bosch 2U nonintegral ABS system was used on many General Motors and Ford Motor Company vehicles.
6. The Bosch 5 nonintegral ABS was used on many General Motors vehicles.
7. The Delphi ABS-VI nonintegral system has been used on many General Motors vehicles since the early 1990s.
8. Delphi DBC-7 replaced the Delphi ABS VI and is a non-integral four-channel ABS system with tire pressure monitoring system (TIMS) capability.
9. Kelsey-Hayes RABS, RWAL, and 4WAL have been used on most domestic pickup trucks since the late 1980s.
10. Sumitomo ABS is a nonintegral four-wheel, three-channel system used on many vehicles.
11. Teves Mark IV and Mark 20 are nonintegral ABS systems used on many domestic brand vehicles.
12. Toyota rear-wheel and four-wheel ABS are used in many Toyota vehicles.

REVIEW QUESTIONS

1. Why do some antilock braking systems use dual accumulators?
2. How many wheel speed sensors must an antilock braking system use for rear-wheel antilock to function?
3. How can an antilock braking system control rear brake proportioning?
4. How can an antilock braking system be used to determine tire inflation information?

CHAPTER QUIZ

1. Technician A says that General Motors manufactures all of the ABS units used on their vehicles. Technician B says that Ford manufactures all of the ABS units used on Ford vehicles. Which technician is correct?
   a. Technician A only
   b. Technician B only
   c. Both Technicians A and B
   d. Neither Technician A nor B

2. Most antilock braking systems do not function at speeds below about _____.
   a. 3 to 5 mph (5 to 8 km/h)
   b. 12 to 15 mph (19 to 24 km/h)
   c. 15 to 20 mph (24 to 32 km/h)
   d. Varies from type of unit from 10 to 25 mph (16 to 40 km/h)

3. A rear-wheel antilock braking system usually uses how many solenoids (valves)?
   a. 1
   b. 2
   c. 3
   d. 4

4. A four-channel ABS uses how many wheel speed sensors?
   a. 1
   b. 2
   c. 3
   d. 4

5. Which antilock braking system moves a small piston up and down inside a fluid chamber to control the wheel brakes during an ABS event?
   a. Bosch 2U
   b. Teves Mark IV
   c. Delphi VI
   d. Bendix 10

6. Technician A says a Kelsey-Hayes EBC4 is used on trucks. Technician B says that the unit controls only the rear wheel brakes. Which technician is correct?
   a. Technician A only
   b. Technician B only
   c. Both Technicians A and B
   d. Neither Technician A nor B

7. Which antilock braking system is rear wheel only?
   a. Delphi VI
   b. Bosch
   c. Kelsey-Hayes EBC2
   d. Teves Mark IV

8. Which antilock braking system can also detect tire pressure differences and warn the driver if the pressure drops more than 12 psi?
   a. Teves Mark IV
   b. Delphi DBC-7
   c. Bosch 2U
   d. Kelsey-Hayes EBC4

9. Which two antilock braking systems are almost the same, but are referred to by two different names?
   a. RWAL and RABS
   b. Bosch Delphi VI
   c. Teves Mark II and Teves Mark IV
   d. Bendix 9 ABS and Bendix 6 ABS

10. Some antilock braking systems use a deceleration sensor. Where is this sensor usually mounted?
    a. In the front of the vehicle near the radiator
    b. Attached to or near the brake pedal assembly
    c. On the master cylinder
    d. Inside the vehicle under a seat

ABS DIAGNOSIS AND SERVICE

OBJECTIVES

After studying Chapter 20, the reader should be able to:

1. Prepare for Brakes (A5) ASE certification test content area "F" (Antilock Brake System Diagnosis and Repair).
2. Describe normal ABS dash lamp operation.
3. Discuss visual inspection of the various types and brands of ABS.
4. Explain how to retrieve trouble codes.
5. List the methods used to clear trouble codes.
6. Explain the various methods for bleeding ABS systems.
7. Discuss methods and tools needed to diagnose an ABS-equipped vehicle.

KEY TERMS

Amber ABS warning lamp (p. 399)
Breakout box (BOB) (p. 409)

Red brake warning lamp (RBWL) (p. 399)

ABS DIAGNOSTIC PROCEDURE

Customer concerns about a fault with the antilock braking system can be best handled by performing the following:

Step 1   **Verify the customer concern.** This step is very important because often a problem with the base brakes is thought by the customer to be a fault with the antilock braking system. It is helpful for the owner to drive the vehicle with a service technician if the problem is not readily apparent.

Step 2   **Perform a visual inspection.** If both the red and the amber brake warning lights are on, look for a fault in the hydraulic system, including leaks at the following locations:
   - Master cylinder
   - Electrohydraulic control unit
   - Flexible brake hoses
   - Brake lines and fittings
   - Calipers and/or wheel cylinders

Step 3   **Check for stored diagnostic trouble codes (DTCs).** Use a scan tool or other necessary methods to retrieve diagnostic trouble codes. If found, follow the specified factory procedures to isolate and determine the cause.

Step 4   **Complete the repair.** This step may involve replacing a hydraulic component. If so, then the hydraulic system should be bled using the factory specified procedure. Clear all diagnostic trouble codes.

Step 5   **Verify the repair.** Always test drive the vehicle under the same conditions that were needed to verify the problem to be sure that the cause has been corrected.

BRAKE WARNING LAMP OPERATION

The first step in the visual diagnosis of an antilock braking system problem is to check the status of the brake warning lamps.

Red Brake Warning Lamp

A **red brake warning lamp** warns of a possible dangerous failure in the base brakes, such as low brake fluid level or low pressure in half of the hydraulic system. The red brake warning lamp will also light if the parking brake is applied and may light due to an ABS failure, such as low brake pressure on an integral system. See Figure 20-1.

Amber ABS Warning Lamp

The **amber ABS warning lamp** usually comes on after a start during the initialization or startup self-test sequence. The exact time the amber lamp remains on after the ignition is turned on varies with the vehicle and the ABS design. See Figure 20-2 for a typical example of a Teves Mark II integral ABS.

THOROUGH VISUAL INSPECTION

Many ABS-related problems can be diagnosed quickly if all the basics are carefully inspected. See Figure 20-3.

A thorough visual inspection should include the following items:

Brake fluid leaks	Check for cracks in flexible lines or other physical damage.
Fuses and fusible links	Check all ABS-related fuses.
Wiring and connections	Check all wiring, especially wheel speed sensor leads, for damage.
Wheel speed sensors	Check that the sensor ring teeth are not damaged. Clean debris from the sensor if possible.

NOTE: Most wheel speed sensors are magnetic and therefore can attract and hold metallic particles. Be sure to remove any metallic debris from around the magnetic wheel speed sensor.

Base brake components	All base brake components, such as disc brake calipers, drum brake wheel cylinders, and related components, must be in proper working condition.
Parking brake	Check that the parking brake is correctly adjusted and fully released.
Wheel bearings	All wheel bearings must be free of defects and adjusted properly.
Wheels and tires	Check for correct size, proper inflation, and legal tread depth.

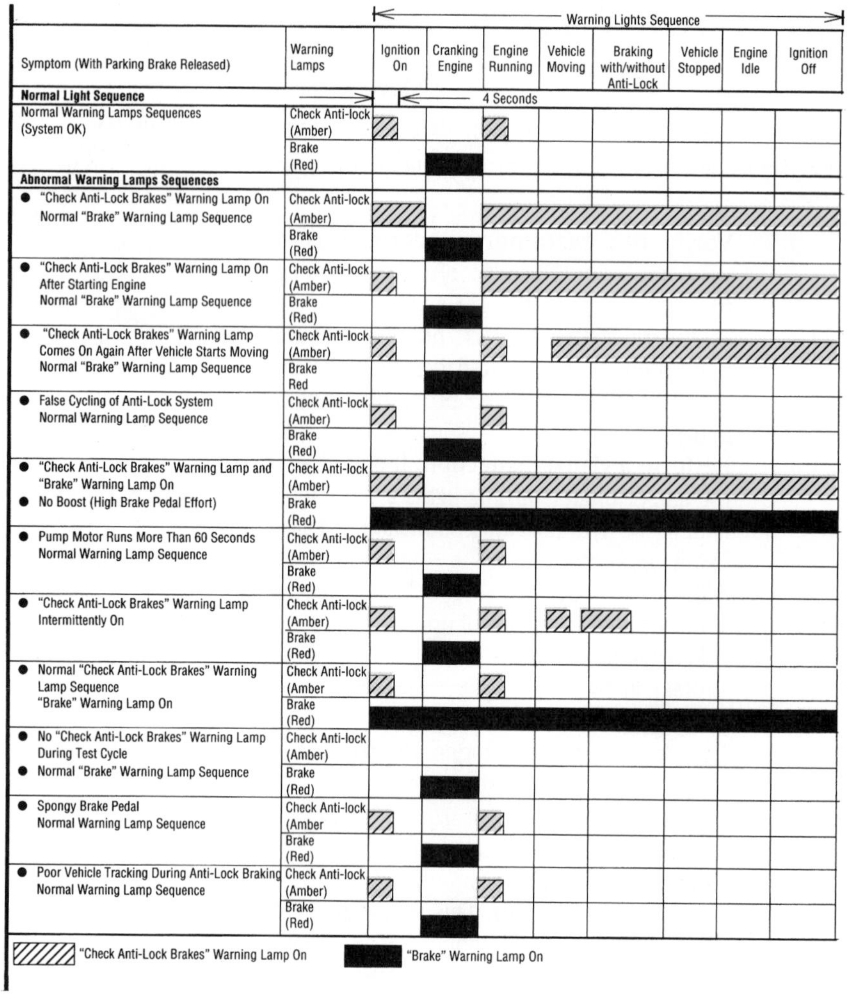

FIGURE 20-1 Typical brake warning lamp operation chart. Not all vehicles use the same light sequence. The top of the chart indicates normal warning lamp operation if the system is okay. *(Courtesy of Ford Motor Company)*

Symptom (With Parking Brake Released)	Warning Lamps	Ignition On	Cranking Engine	Engine Running	Vehicle Moving	Braking with/without Anti-Lock	Vehicle Stopped	Engine Idle	Ignition Off
Normal Light Sequence									
Normal Warning Lamps Sequences (System OK)	Check Anti-lock (Amber)	▨		▨					
	Brake (Red)		▬						
Abnormal Warning Lamps Sequences									
● "Check Anti-Lock Brakes" Warning Lamp On Normal "Brake" Warning Lamp Sequence	Check Anti-lock (Amber)	▨		▨▨▨▨▨▨▨▨					
	Brake (Red)		▬						
● "Check Anti-Lock Brakes" Warning Lamp On After Starting Engine Normal "Brake" Warning Lamp Sequence	Check Anti-lock (Amber)	▨		▨▨▨▨▨▨▨					
	Brake (Red)		▬						
● "Check Anti-Lock Brakes" Warning Lamp Comes On Again After Vehicle Starts Moving Normal "Brake" Warning Lamp Sequence	Check Anti-lock (Amber)	▨		▨	▨▨▨▨▨▨				
	Brake Red		▬						
● False Cycling of Anti-Lock System Normal Warning Lamp Sequence	Check Anti-lock (Amber)	▨		▨					
	Brake (Red)		▬						
● "Check Anti-Lock Brakes" Warning Lamp and "Brake" Warning Lamp On ● No Boost (High Brake Pedal Effort)	Check Anti-lock (Amber)	▨		▨▨▨▨▨▨▨					
	Brake (Red)	▬▬▬▬▬▬▬▬▬▬▬▬▬▬▬▬▬▬▬▬▬▬▬▬▬▬							
● Pump Motor Runs More Than 60 Seconds Normal Warning Lamp Sequence	Check Anti-lock (Amber)	▨		▨					
	Brake (Red)		▬						
● "Check Anti-Lock Brakes" Warning Lamp Intermittently On	Check Anti-lock (Amber)	▨		▨	▨ ▨				
	Brake (Red)		▬						
● Normal "Check Anti-Lock Brakes" Warning Lamp Sequence "Brake" Warning Lamp On	Check Anti-lock (Amber)	▨		▨					
	Brake (Red)	▬▬▬▬▬▬▬▬▬▬▬▬▬▬▬▬▬▬▬▬▬▬▬▬▬▬							
● No "Check Anti-Lock Brakes" Warning Lamp During Test Cycle ● Normal "Brake" Warning Lamp Sequence	Check Anti-lock (Amber)								
	Brake (Red)		▬						
● Spongy Brake Pedal Normal Warning Lamp Sequence	Check Anti-lock (Amber)	▨		▨					
	Brake (Red)		▬						
● Poor Vehicle Tracking During Anti-Lock Braking Normal Warning Lamp Sequence	Check Anti-lock (Amber)	▨		▨					
	Brake (Red)		▬						

▨▨▨ "Check Anti-Lock Brakes" Warning Lamp On   ▬▬▬ "Brake" Warning Lamp On

VEHICLE STATUS

INDICATOR STATUS	ENGINE STOPPED IGNITION ON	STARTER ENGAGED	ENGINE RUNNING (IMMEDIATELY AFTER START) TRANSMISSION IN "DRIVE"	VEHICLE BEING DRIVEN AT APPOX. 20 MPH TRANSMISSION IN "DRIVE"	NORMAL BRAKE APPLIED
ANTILOCK (AMBER)	1	2	3	4	4
BRAKE (RED)	4	2	4	4	4

1 WITH CHARGED ACCUMULATOR "ANTILOCK" LIGHT WILL COME ON FOR 3 - 5 SECONDS WITH IGNITION ON. IF ACCUMULATOR DISCHARGED, LAMP MAY STAY ON FOR UP TO 30 SECONDS.

2 "BRAKE" AND "ANTILOCK" LIGHTS WILL BOTH TURN ON DURING CRANKING.

3 IMMEDIATELY AFTER STARTING "ANTILOCK" LIGHT WILL TURN ON FOR 3 - 5 SECONDS.

4 BOTH LIGHTS SHOULD REMAIN OFF.

FIGURE 20-2 Another example of a normal warning lamp sequence chart during normal (no-fault) operation.

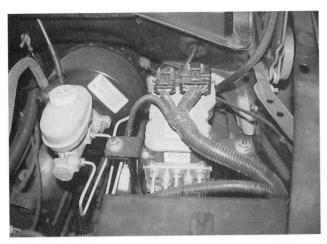
(a)

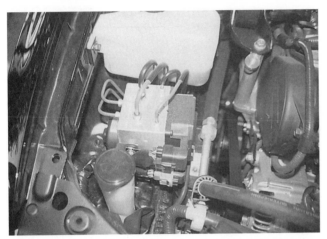
(b)

(c)

FIGURE 20-3 A thorough visual inspection should include carefully inspecting around the electro-hydraulic unit for signs of obvious problems or the installation of aftermarket devices such as alarm systems. (a) Dodge truck ABS hydraulic control unit. (b) Toyota Camry ABS hydraulic control unit. (c) Plymouth Prowler ABS hydraulic control unit. Note that the ABS hydraulic unit is underneath the vehicle as it is with the Dodge, Plymouth, and Chrysler minivans.

TECH TIP

QUICK AND EASY WHEEL SPEED SENSOR DIAGNOSIS

A fault in a wheel speed sensor (WSS) is a common ABS problem. A quick and easy test that works on most Bosch ABS systems (and perhaps others) involves the following steps:

Step 1 Hoist the vehicle safely.
Step 2 Turn the ignition on (engine off).
Step 3 Spin a tire by hand as fast as possible.
Step 4 The ABS amber warning light should come on, indicating that a speed was detected but not by all the wheel speed sensors.
Step 5 Turn the ignition off to reset the ABS warning light.
Step 6 Repeat the test on each of the remaining wheels.

If any wheel fails to turn on the ABS light, carefully inspect the wheel speed sensor for proper resistance and the tone ring and wiring. If the ABS light is on all the time and does not reset when the ignition is turned off, the problem is not caused by a wheel speed sensor.

TEST DRIVE AND VERIFY THE FAULT

A test drive is a very important diagnostic procedure. Many ABS systems and diagnostic trouble codes (DTCs) will not set unless the vehicle is moving. Often, the driver has noticed something like the self-test while driving and believed it to be a fault in the system.

NOTE: Some ABS units, such as the Delphi VI, will cause the brake pedal to move up and down slightly during cycling of the valves during the self-test. Each system has unique features. The service technician will have to learn to avoid attempting to repair a problem that is not a fault of the system.

Before driving, start the engine and observe the red and amber brake warning lamps. If the red brake warning lamp is on, the base brakes may not be functioning correctly. Do not drive the vehicle until the base brakes are restored to proper operation.

WHAT'S THAT NOISE AND VIBRATION?

Many vehicle owners and service technicians have been disturbed to hear and feel an occasional groaning noise. It is usually heard and felt through the vehicle after first being started and driven. Because it occurs when first being driven in forward or reverse, many technicians have blamed the transmission or related drive line components. This is commonly heard on many ABS vehicles as part of a system check. As soon as the ABS controller senses speed from the wheel speed sensors after an ignition cycles on, the controller will run the pump either every time or whenever the accumulator pressure is below a certain level. This can occur while the vehicle is being backed out of a driveway or being driven forward because wheel sensors can only detect speed—not direction. Before serious and major repairs are attempted to "cure" a noise, make sure that it is not the normal ABS self-test activation sequence of events.

General Motors ABS Diagnostic Guide

Type of ABS System	Code Clearing Procedure	Scan Tool* Code Retrieval
Teves IV Nonintegral	Yes	Yes
Bosch 2U Nonintegral	Yes	Yes
Delphi (Delco) VI	Yes	Yes
Bosch 2S	Yes	Yes
Delco Powermaster III	Yes	Yes
Kelsey-Hayes RWAL	Yes or disconnect the ABS fuse	Yes or flash codes
Kelsey-Hayes 4WAL	Yes	Yes

*A jumper key can be used for some systems. Not all scan tools can perform all functions.

NOTE: Some systems are diagnosed by "antilock" and "brake" warning lamps, vehicle symptoms, and the use of a breakout box.

Ford ABS Diagnostic Guide

Type of ABS System	Code Clearing Procedure	Scan Tool* Code Retrieval
Teves IV Nonintegral	Drive the vehicle after the repair.	Yes
Kelsey-Hayes RABS	Drive the vehicle after the repair.	Flash codes
Teves 4WABS	Drive the vehicle after the repair.	Yes

*A jumper wire can be used on some systems. Not all scan tools can perform all functions.

DaimlerChrysler ABS Diagnostic Guide

Type of ABS System	Code Clearing Procedure	Scan Tool* Code Retrieval
Bendix 6 Nonintegral	Yes or disconnect the battery	Yes
Bosch MMC	Yes	Yes
Bosch 2U Nonintegral	No codes available on this system	No codes available on this system
Teves Mark IV	Yes	Yes
Kelsey-Hayes RWAL	Disconnect the battery	Flash codes
.Kelsey-Hayes 4WAL	Yes	Yes

*A jumper wire can be used on some systems. Not all scan tools can perform all functions.

RETRIEVING DIAGNOSTIC TROUBLE CODES

After performing a thorough visual inspection and after verifying the customer's complaint, retrieve any stored ABS-related diagnostic trouble codes (DTCs). The exact procedure varies with the type of ABS and with the make, model, and year of the vehicle.

Always consult factory service information for the vehicle being diagnosed. Some systems can only display flash codes (flashing ABS or brake lamp in sequence), whereas other systems can perform self-diagnosis and give all information to the technician through a scan tool.

NOTE: With some antilock braking systems, the diagnostic trouble code is lost if the ignition is turned "off" before grounding the diagnostic connector.

KELSEY-HAYES ANTILOCK (NONINTEGRAL)

The Kelsey-Hayes rear-wheel antilock uses two solenoids and valves to control the rear-wheel brakes. Kelsey-Hayes four-wheel antilock uses the computer to pulse the valves rather than turning them on or off. The pulsing is called pulse-width modulated (PWM) and the valve is called a PWM valve.

Retrieving Diagnostic Trouble Codes

GM trucks' (RWAL) DTCs are retrieved by flash codes or scan data through the use of a scan tool or connect H to A at the data link connector (DLC). See Figure 20-4.

NOTE: Be sure that the brake warning lamp is on before trying to retrieve DTCs. If the lamp is not on, a false code 9 could be set.

Ford trucks' (RABS) DTCs are retrieved by jumper lead flash codes only. See Figure 20-5.
DaimlerChrysler light trucks' DTCs are retrieved by ground diagnostic connections. See Figure 20-6.

Kelsey-Hayes Diagnostic Trouble Codes

NOTE: If the ignition is turned off, the failure code will be lost unless it is a hard code that will be present when the ignition is turned back on.

RWAL Diagnostic Codes

Code	Description
2	Open isolation valve solenoid circuit or malfunctioning EBCM/VCM
3	Open dump valve solenoid circuit or malfunctioning EBCM/VCM
4	Grounded valve reset switch circuit
5	Excessive actuations of dump valve during antilock braking
6	Erratic speed signal
7	Shorted isolation valve circuit or faulty EBCM/VCM
8	Shorted dump valve circuit or faulty EBCM/VCM
9	Open or grounded circuit to vehicle speed sensor
10	Brake switch circuit
12 to 17	Computer malfunction

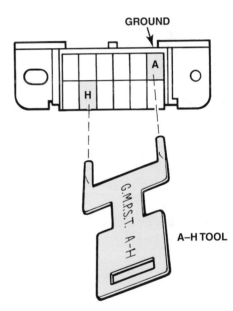

FIGURE 20-4 General Motors diagnostic connector. Flash codes are available by using a jumper wire to ground (terminal A) to terminal H. This connector is located under the dash near the steering column on most General Motors vehicles.

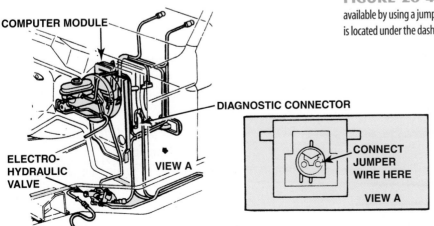

FIGURE 20-5 Connecting a jumper wire from the diagnostic connector to ground. The exact location of this diagnostic connector varies with the exact vehicle model and year. *(Courtesy of Ford Motor Company)*

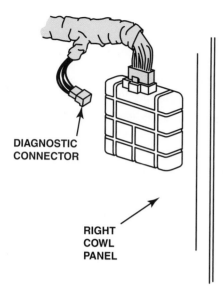

DIAGNOSTIC CONNECTOR

RIGHT COWL PANEL

FIGURE 20-6 Chrysler diagnostic connector location varies with the model and year.

REAL WORLD FIX

RWAL DIAGNOSIS

The owner of an S-10 pickup truck complained that the red brake warning lamp on the dash remained on even when the parking brake was released. The problem could be one of the following:

1. A serious hydraulic problem
2. Low brake fluid
3. A stuck or defective parking brake switch
4. If the brake lamp is dim, RWAL trouble is indicated.

The technician found that the brake lamp was on dimly, indicating that an antilock braking problem was detected. The first step in diagnosing an antilock braking problem with a dash lamp on is to check for stored trouble codes. The technician used a jumper between terminals A and H on the DLC (ALCL), and four flashes of the brake lamp indicated a code 4.

Checking a service manual, code 4 was found to be a grounded switch inside the hydraulic control unit. The hardest part about the repair was getting access to, and the replacement of, the defective (electrically grounded) switch. After bleeding the system and a thorough test drive, the lamp sequence and RWAL functioned correctly.

NOTE: A scan tool may or may not be able to retrieve or display diagnostic trouble codes. Check with the technical literature for the specific vehicle being scanned.

4WAL Diagnostic Trouble Codes

Code	Description
12	System normal (2WD applications)
13	System normal – brake applied (2WD applications)
14	System normal (4WD/AWD applications)
15	System normal – brake applied (4WD/AWD applications)
21 RF	Speed sensor circuit open
25 LF	
31 RR	
35 LR	
35	VSS circuit open
22 RF	Missing speed sensor signal
26 LF	
32 RR	
36 LR	
36	Missing VSS signal
23 RF	Erratic speed sensor signal
27 LF	
33 RR	
37 LR	
37	Erratic VSS signal
28	Simultaneous dropout of front-wheel speed sensors
29	Simultaneous dropout of all speed sensors
35	Vehicle speed sensor circuit open
36	Missing LR or vehicle speed sensor signal
37	Erratic LR or vehicle speed sensor signal
38	Wheel speed error
41 to 66	Malfunctioning BPMV/EHCU
67	Open motor circuit or shorted EBCM output
68	Locked motor or shorted motor circuit
71 to 74	Memory failure
81	Open or shorted brake switch circuit
86	Shorted ABS warning lamp
88	Shorted red brake warning lamp (RBWL)

BOSCH 2 ABS (NONINTEGRAL)

The Bosch 2U/2S ABS is used on many domestic and imported brands of vehicles.

Retrieving Diagnostic Trouble Codes

On General Motors vehicles, DTCs can be retrieved by connecting A to H at the data link connector (DLC). On most Bosch 2 systems, a scan tool can and should be used if available to retrieve DTC.

Bosch 2U/2S ABS Diagnostic Trouble Codes

Code	Description
12	Diagnostic system operational
21 RF	Wheel speed sensor fault
25 LF	
32 RR	
35 LR	
35	Rear-axle speed sensor fault
22 RF	Toothed wheel frequency error
26 LF	
32 RR	
36 LR	
36	Rear-axle toothed wheel frequency error
41 RF	Valve solenoid fault
45 LF	
55	Rear valve solenoid fault
61	Pump motor or motor relay fault
63	Solenoid valve relay fault
71	Electronic brake control module (EBCM) fault
72	Serial data link fault
74	Low voltage
75	Lateral acceleration sensor fault
76	Lateral acceleration sensor fault

TEVES MARK IV

The Teves Mark IV is a nonintegral (remote) ABS system.

Retrieving Diagnostic Trouble Codes

Trouble codes are accessed only by a bidirectional scan tool connected to the data link connector (DLC). See Figure 20-7.

Teves Mark IV ABS Diagnostic Trouble Codes

Code	Description
21	RF speed sensor circuit open
22	RF speed sensor signal erratic
23	RF wheel speed is 0 mph
25	LF speed sensor circuit open
26	LF speed sensor signal erratic
27	LF wheel speed is 0 mph
31	RR speed sensor circuit open
32	RR speed sensor signal erratic
33	RR wheel speed is 0 mph
35	LR speed sensor circuit open
36	LR speed sensor signal erratic
37	LR wheel speed is 0 mph
41	RF inlet valve circuit
42	RF outlet valve circuit
43	RF speed sensor noisy
45	LF inlet valve circuit
46	LF outlet valve circuit
47	LF speed sensor noisy
51	RR inlet valve circuit
52	RR outlet valve circuit
53	RR speed sensor noisy
55	LR inlet valve circuit
56	LR outlet valve circuit
57	LR speed sensor noisy
61	Pump motor test fault
62	Pump motor fault in ABS stop
71	EBCM check sum error
72	TCC/antilock braking switch circuit
73	Fluid level switch circuit

Clearing Diagnostic Trouble Codes

A scan tool is required to clear DTCs on some vehicles. Driving the vehicle over 20 mph (32 km/h) will clear the codes on some vehicles. Disconnecting the battery will also clear the codes but will cause other "keep-alive" functions of the vehicle to be lost.

DELPHI (DELCO) ABS VI (NONINTEGRAL)

The Delphi (Delco) ABS VI is unique from all other antilock systems because it uses motor-driven ball screws and pistons for brake pressure to reduce, hold, and apply. See Figures 20-8, 20-9, and 20-10.

REAL WORLD FIX

THE NERVOUS TAURUS

A customer complained that, sometimes during normal braking, the ABS would be activated just before coming to a stop. However, the ABS light would not come on. The service technician was able to duplicate the condition and there were no DTCs stored. Using a scan tool to monitor the wheel speed sensors, the technician discovered that the left front wheel speed was slightly different than the others. A thorough visual inspection revealed that the tone wheel (sensor ring) was cracked. This crack created a different wheel speed signal to the ABS controller than the other wheels and the controller activated the ABS as it would normally—that was why there were no DTCs.

Other things that could have caused this problem, which is often called "false modulation," include a bent wheel, mismatched tire sizes, or metal debris around the sensor.

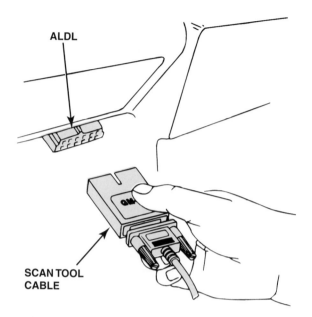

FIGURE 20-7   A scan tool is the recommended method to use to access General Motors Teves Mark IV systems.

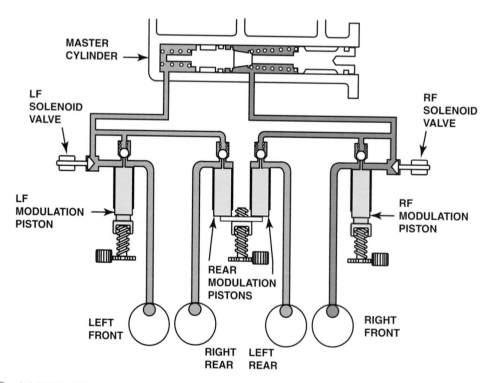

FIGURE 20-8   Delphi (Delco) VI system components. Notice that each front brake is controlled by a separate piston, whereas the rear brakes are controlled by the same piston.

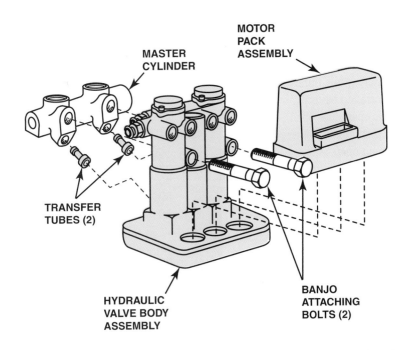

FIGURE 20-9   The Delphi (Delco) VI attaches to the side of the master cylinder and connects hydraulically through transfer tube assemblies.

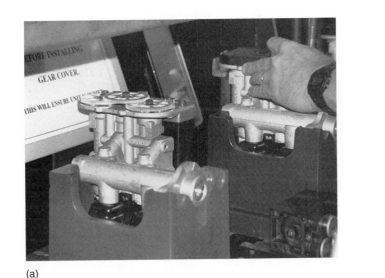

(a)

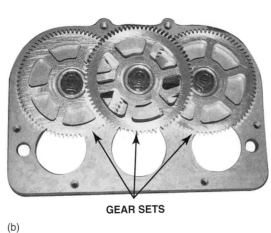

(b)

FIGURE 20-10   (a) Delphi (Delco) ABS VI units being assembled at the Delphi (Delco) chassis assembly plant in Dayton, Ohio. (b) These gears are turned by high-speed electric motors and move pistons up and down to control braking during an ABS stop.

Retrieving Diagnostic Codes

The Delphi (Delco) VI antilock braking system has extensive self-diagnostic capability. Access to this vast amount of infor- mation requires the use of a scan tool designed to interface (work) with the Delphi VI system.

Delphi (Delco) ABS VI Diagnostic Trouble Codes

Code	Description
11	ABS lamp open or shorted to ground
13	ABS lamp circuit shorted to battery
14	Enable relay contacts open, fuse open
15	Enable relay contacts shorted to battery
16	Enable relay coil circuit open
17	Enable relay coil shorted to ground
18	Enable relay coil shorted to B1 or 0 ohms
21	Left-front wheel speed
23	Left-rear wheel speed
24	Right-rear wheel speed
25	Excessive left-front wheel acceleration
26	Excessive right-front wheel acceleration
27	Excessive left-rear wheel acceleration
28	Excessive right-rear wheel acceleration
31	Two-wheel speed sensors open
36	System voltage is low
37	System voltage is high
38	Left-front EMB will not hold motor
41	Right-front EMB will not hold motor
42	Rear-axle ESB will not hold motor
44	Left-front EMB will not release motor, gears frozen
45	Right-front EMB will not release motor, gears frozen
46	Rear-axle ESB will not release motor, gears frozen
47	Left-front nut failure (motor free-spins)
48	Right-front nut failure (motor free-spins)
51	Rear-axle nut failure (motor free-spins)
52	Left-front channel in release too long
53	Right-front channel in release too long
54	Rear axle in release too long
55	Motor driver interface (MDI) fault detected
56	Left-front motor circuit open
57	Left-front motor circuit shorted to ground
58	Left-front motor circuit shorted to battery
61	Right-front motor circuit open
62	Right-front motor circuit shorted to ground
63	Right-front motor circuit shorted to battery
64	Rear-axle motor circuit open
65	Rear-axle motor circuit shorted to ground
66	Rear-axle motor circuit shorted to battery
67	Left-front EMB release circuit open or shorted to ground
68	Left-front EMB release circuit shorted to battery or driver open
71	Right-front EMB release circuit open or shorted to ground
72	Right-front EMB release circuit shorted to battery or driver open

Code	Description
76	Left-front solenoid circuit open or shorted to battery
77	Left-front solenoid circuit shorted to ground or driver open
78	Right-front solenoid circuit open or shorted to battery
81	Right-front solenoid circuit shorted to battery or driver open
82	Calibration memory failure
86	ABS controller turned "on"; red brake telltale
87	Red brake telltale circuit open
88	Red brake telltale circuit shorted to battery or driver open
91	Open brake switch contacts (deceleration detected)
92	Open brake switch contacts
93	Test 91 or 92 failed last or current ignition cycle
94	Brake switch contacts shorted
95	Brake switch circuit open
96	Brake lamps open, brake lamp ground open, center high-mounted stop lamp open during four-way flasher operations

TECH TIP

SOMETIMES IT PAYS TO LOOK AT THE ENTIRE VEHICLE

There are often strange electrical problems that can occur including false DTCs or intermittent operation of electrical sensors, ABS, accessories, or gauges. Sometimes the root of these problems is due to rust and corrosion after a vehicle is involved in a flood. Here are some telltale signs that a vehicle may have been in a flood or in deep water.

- Mud, silt, or caked dust under the dash and inside the doors
- Corroded electrical connectors at the computer, fuse box, or ABS controller (computer)
- Visible water line in the doors or behind panels
- Rust in abnormal places such as seat springs or brackets behind the dash
- Moisture in lenses
- Musty smell and/or strong air freshener smell
- Powdery corrosion on aluminum parts such as intake manifold and inside the throttle bore
- Rust or moisture inside electrical switches or relays
- Areas that are normally dusty such as an ashtray or glove box are very clean

REAL WORLD FIX

THE MYSTERY ABS AMBER WARNING LIGHT

The owner of an Acura Legend complained to a service technician that the ABS warning light would come on but only while driving down from a parking garage. When the driver turned off the ignition and restarted the engine, the ABS amber light was not on and did not come on again until the vehicle was again driven down the spiral parking garage ramp. The service technician used a scan tool and found that no DTCs had been stored.

NOTE: Some ABS systems will not retain a DTC unless the problem is currently present and the ABS amber warning light is on.

All of the brakes were in excellent condition, but the brake fluid level was down a little. After topping off the master cylinder with clean DOT 3 brake fluid, the vehicle was returned to the customer with the following information:

- The ABS amber warning light may have been triggered by the brake fluid level switch. While driving down the steep parking garage ramp, the brake fluid moved away from the fluid level sensor.

NOTE: While the brake fluid level sensor normally would turn on the red brake warning light, in some systems it turns on the amber ABS light if the brake fluid falls below a certain level in the ABS reservoir.

- The difference in wheel speed between the outboard and the inboard wheels could have triggered a fault code for a wheel speed sensor during the drive down the spiral parking garage ramp.

WHEEL SPEED SENSOR DIAGNOSIS

Wheel speed sensor (WSS) circuits are often the cause of many ABS problems. See Figure 20-11. These components may suffer from physical damage, build-up of metallic debris on the sensor tip, corrosion, poor electrical connections, and damaged wiring.

Test a WSS by measuring its output voltage and circuit continuity. A **breakout box (BOB)** cable connects to the ABS harness near the ABS module. All WSS resistance checks, including the wiring to the sensors, can be measured at one location. See Figure 20-12. Follow the equipment manufacturer's instructions for connecting the breakout box to the vehicle, and for probing the appropriate pins on the breakout box.

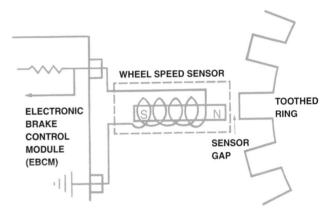

FIGURE 20-11   Typical wheel speed sensor. When a tooth on the sensor ring is close to the sensor, the strength of the magnetic field is stronger because the metal of the tooth conducts magnetic lines of force better than air. When the tooth moves away, the magnetic field strength is reduced. It is this changing magnetic field strength that produces the changing voltage. Frequency of the signal is determined by the speed of the rotating sensor.

(a)

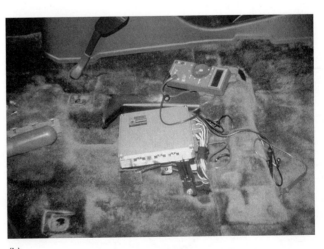
(b)

FIGURE 20-12   (a) A breakout box is being used to diagnose an ABS problem. The controller (computer) is located in the trunk of this vehicle, and a digital multimeter is being used to measure resistance and voltage at various points in the system, following the service manual procedure. (b) Another vehicle being tested for an ABS fault. In this vehicle, the computer is located under the passenger seat, which has been removed to gain better access to the wiring and terminals.

Resistance Measurement

The resistors of most WSS range from 800 Ω to 1,400 Ω. Therefore, a reading of about 1,000 ohms or 1 KΩ would indicate proper sensor coil resistance. See Figure 20-13.

Checking for Short-to-Ground

Connect either lead of the ohmmeter to one of the WSS wires and the other to a good, clean chassis ground. The resistance should be infinity (OL). If a low resistance reading is obtained, the sensor or sensor wiring is shorted-to-ground and must be replaced.

AC Voltage Check

Connect a digital meter to the WSS terminals or input to the controller in the breakout box and set the meter to read AC volts. Rotate the wheel by hand at a rate of one revolution per second. A good WSS should produce voltage of at least 0.1 volt (100 mV). A sensor voltage of lower than 0.1 volt (100 mV) may be caused by three things.

1. Excessive clearance between the sensor and the tone ring.
2. Build-up of debris on the end of the sensor. Most WSSs are magnetic and can attract metallic particles, which can affect the operation of the sensor.
3. Excessive resistance in the sensor or sensor wiring, which can also cause a weak signal to be produced by the WSS.

Scope Testing

Attach the scope leads to the sensor terminals or to the input connector on the breakout box. Rotate the wheel by hand or by using engine power with the vehicle safely hoisted with all four wheels off the ground. A good WSS should produce an alternating current (AC) sine wave signal that increases in frequency and amplitude with increasing wheel speed. See Figure 20-14.

Damaged or missing teeth on the tone ring will cause flat spots or gaps in the sine wave pattern. See Figure 20-15.

A bent axle or hub will produce a wavelike pattern that fluctuates as the strength of the sensor signal changes with each revolution.

Scan Tool Testing

A scan tool can be used to check for the proper operation of the WSS. As an assistant drives the vehicle, connect the scan tool and monitor the speed of all of the sensors. All of the sensors should indicate the same speed. If a sensor shows a slower or faster speed than the others, carefully check the tone ring for damage such as a crack.

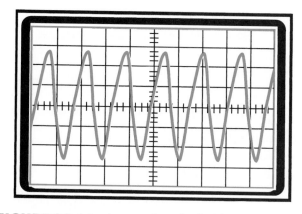

FIGURE 20-14   A scope can be used to check for proper operation of a wheel speed sensor.

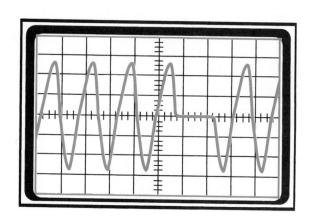

FIGURE 20-15   A broken tooth on a wheel speed sensor tone ring shows on the scope trace as a missing wave.

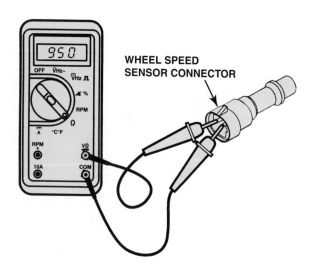

FIGURE 20-13   Measuring the resistance of a wheel speed sensor.

WHEEL SPEED SENSOR ADJUSTMENT

Some ABS applications use adjustable WSSs. Most sensors adjust by first loosening a set screw, then inserting a nonmagnetic brass or plastic feeler gauge between the tip of the sensor and a high point on the tone ring. See Figure 20-16. Adjust the position of the sensor so there is a slight drag on the feeler gauge, and then tighten the setscrew to lock the sensor in place.

When installing new sensors, look for a piece of paper or plastic on the tip end of the unit. This is more than a protective covering and must be left in place during installation. The paper or plastic is the precise thickness to guarantee a correct air gap between the tip of the sensor and the tone ring. Adjust the sensor so the tip just touches the tone ring and you can slip the paper or plastic out without ripping it. Tighten the setscrew and the air gap is properly set. See Figure 20-17.

Some manufacturers recommend leaving a paper covering in place. The motion of the tone ring removes it after the vehicle is driven for several miles.

Digital Wheel Speed Sensor Diagnosis

Test a digital WSS by first checking that battery voltage is available at the sensor with the key on, engine off. If the sensor does not have 12 volts, then the problem is most likely in the ABS controller or the wiring between the controller and the sensor.

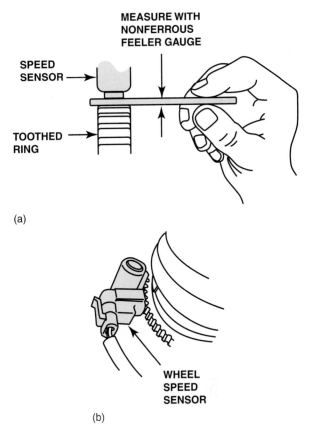

(a)

(b)

FIGURE 20-17   (a) Always use a nonferrous (brass or plastic) feeler (thickness) gauge when measuring the gap between the toothed ring and the wheel speed sensor. (b) Sometimes a sensor is equipped with a paper spacer that is the exact thickness of the spacing required between the toothed ring and the sensor. If equipped, the sensor is simply installed with the paper touching the toothed wheel. A typical gap ranges from 0.020 to 0.050 in. (0.5 to 1.3 mm).

If there are 12 volts at the sensor, measure the signal voltage. The voltage should switch from about 0.8V to about 1.9V as the wheel is rotated by hand.

HYDRAULIC ABS SERVICE

Before doing any brake work on a vehicle equipped with antilock brakes, always consult the appropriate service information for the exact vehicle being serviced. For example, some manufacturers recommend discharging the hydraulic accumulator by depressing the brake pedal many times before opening bleeder valves. Many service checks require that a pressure gauge be installed in the system.

Air can easily get trapped in the ABS electronic-hydraulic (E-H) assembly whenever the hydraulic system is opened. Even though the master cylinder and all four wheel cylinders/calipers have been bled, sometimes the brake pedal will still feel spongy. Some E-H units can be bled through the use of a scan tool where the valves are pulsed in

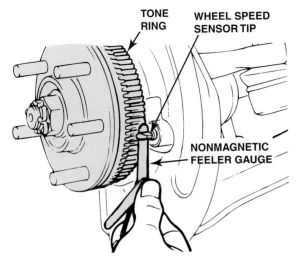

FIGURE 20-16   Use a nonmagnetic brass or plastic feeler gauge to check wheel speed sensor gap. A steel gauge would be attracted by the magnet in the sensor and would produce a drag on the gauge as it is moved between the sensor and the tone ring. This drag could be interpreted as a correct clearance reading.

sequence by the electronic brake controller (computer). Some units are equipped with bleeder valves while others must be bled by loosening the brake lines. Bleeding the E-H unit also purges out the older brake fluid, which can cause rust and corrosion damage. Only DOT 3 brake fluid is specified for use in an antilock braking system. Always check the label on the brake fluid reservoir and/or service manual or owner's manual.

CAUTION: Some ABS units require that the brake pedal be depressed as many as 40 times to discharge brake fluid fully from the accumulator. Failure to discharge the accumulator fully can show that the brake fluid level is too low. If additional brake fluid is added, the fluid could overflow the reservoir during an ABS stop when the accumulator discharges brake fluid back into the reservoir.

Bleeding ABS

During routine brake service, attempt to keep the air from entering the hydraulic system by doing the following:

1. Do not allow the brake system to run dry. Use a brake pedal depressor or plug any open brake line to keep brake fluid from flowing out of the brake master cylinder reservoir.
2. Do not allow the master cylinder to run dry during the bleeding operation. Check the master cylinder reservoir often and keep it filled with fresh brake fluid from a sealed container.
3. Always bench bleed a replacement master cylinder to help prevent against introducing air into the hydraulic system.

After depressing the unit as per manufacturer's recommended procedures, the brakes can be bled using the same procedure as for a vehicle without ABS. Air trapped in the ABS hydraulic unit may require that a scan tool be used to cycle the valves. See Figures 20-18 and 20-19.

The bleeding procedure for vehicles equipped with antilock brakes is often different than vehicles without ABS.

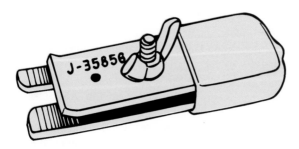

FIGURE 20-18   Special bleed valve tools are often required when bleeding some ABS units such as the Kelsey-Hayes 4WAL system.

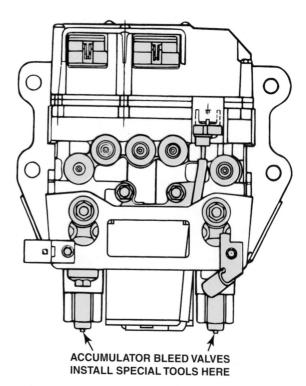

ACCUMULATOR BLEED VALVES
INSTALL SPECIAL TOOLS HERE

FIGURE 20-19   Two bleed valve tools are needed to bleed the Kelsey-Hayes 4WAL system, which attaches to the bleed valves on the accumulator.

Consult the service information for the specified bleeding procedure and sequence.

NOTE: To avoid having to bleed the hydraulic unit, use a brake pedal depressor during brake service to avoid losing brake fluid. This simple precaution keeps air from getting into the hard-to-bleed passages of the hydraulic unit.

ABS SAFETY PRECAUTIONS

1. Avoid mounting the antenna for the transmitting device near the ABS control unit. Transmitting devices include cellular (cell) telephones, citizen-band radios, and so on.
2. Avoid mounting tires of different diameter than that of the original tires. Different size tires generate different wheel speed sensor frequencies which may not be usable by the ABS controller.
3. Never open a bleeder valve or loosen a hydraulic line while the ABS is pressurized. The accumulator must be depressurized according to the manufacturer's recommended procedures.
4. If arc welding on a vehicle, disconnect all computers (electronic control modules) to avoid possible damage due to voltage spikes.
5. Do not pry against or hit the wheel speed sensor ring.

ABS BLEEDING   Step-by-Step

STEP 1   Prepare to bleed the brake hydraulic system by checking the hydraulic system, including the master cylinder.

STEP 2   Always use DOT 3 brake fluid in any vehicle equipped with ABS.

STEP 3   Be sure the brake fluid level in the reservoir is filled to the maximum line. Do not overfill.

STEP 4   Hoist the vehicle safely and raise to a good working level to service the wheel brakes.

STEP 5   Remove the wheels.

STEP 6   The Chrysler service manual specifies that the base brakes be manually bled before using the scan tool to bleed the air in the hydraulic unit. Tapping on the bleeder valve helps break the taper of the bleeder valve.

(continued)

ABS BLEEDING continued

STEP 7 Use a 6-point wrench or socket and loosen the bleeder valve.

STEP 8 Have an assistant depress the brake pedal slowly to bleed the air from each wheel, starting at the right rear then the left rear, right front, and finally the left front wheel.

STEP 9 After manually bleeding all four wheels, connect the Chrysler DRB III scan tool to the data link connector (DLC) located under the dash.

STEP 10 Turn the scan tool on and follow the directions on the display.

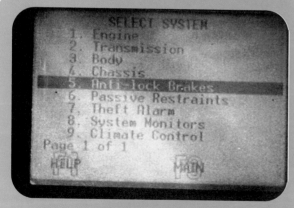

STEP 11 Select "antilock" brakes from the menu.

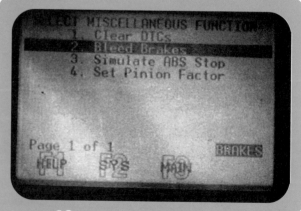

STEP 12 Select "bleed brakes" from the selection menu.

ABS BLEEDING continued

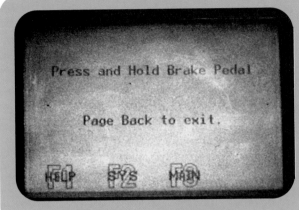

STEP 13 The scan tool now instructs the service technician to press and hold the brake pedal.

STEP 14 With the brake pedal depressed, the scan tool commands the ABS pump motor to operate.

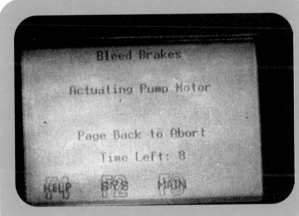

STEP 15 The pump motor will run until the countdown on the display reads zero.

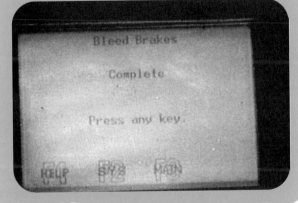

STEP 16 Finally, the scan tool display indicates that the brake bleeding process is complete.

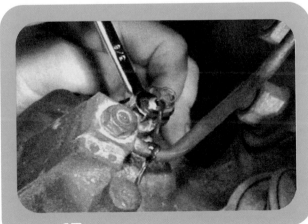

STEP 17 After the scan tool bleeding is complete, fill the master cylinder if necessary and bleed the base brakes again.

STEP 18 Install all four wheels and torque the lug nuts to factory specifications.

ABS DIAGNOSIS Step-by-Step

STEP 1 A Chevrolet pickup truck is being driven into the shop with an antilock brake system (ABS) problem.

STEP 2 The amber ABS warning light remains on whenever the ignition is on.

STEP 3 The first step of almost any diagnostic procedure is to perform a thorough visual inspection, including checking the level and condition of the brake fluid in the master cylinder reservoir.

STEP 4 A visual inspection should also include an inspection of the wiring and all hydraulic components under the hood.

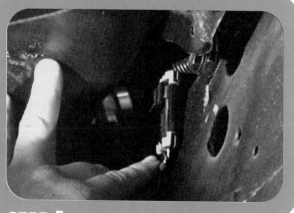

STEP 5 A thorough visual inspection should also include checking all wheel speed sensor wiring and connectors.

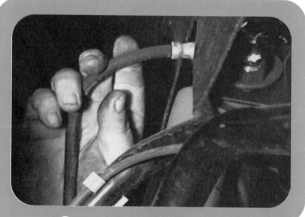

STEP 6 The hydraulic system should also be inspected for obvious faults or damage that could have been caused by road debris such as a cut flexible brake line.

ABS DIAGNOSIS continued

STEP 7 After a thorough visual inspection, a scan tool should be used to retrieve any stored diagnostic trouble codes (DTCs). A Tech 2 is being used on this Chevrolet truck.

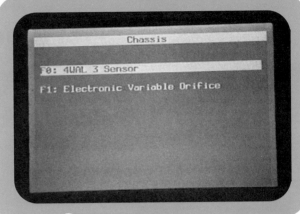

STEP 8 From "chassis" select "4WAL, 3 sensor" ABS on the Tech 2 scan tool.

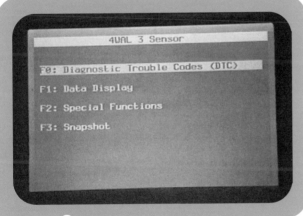

STEP 9 Select "diagnostic trouble codes (DTC)" from the selection menu.

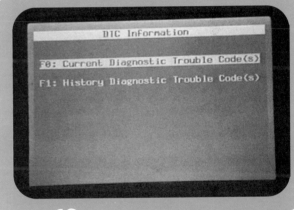

STEP 10 Select "current diagnostic trouble code(s)" from the selection menu.

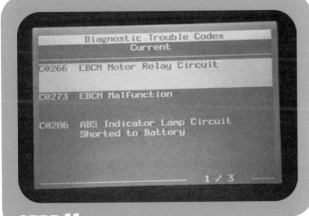

STEP 11 There are three DTCs stored, including C0266. The "C" means that it is a chassis code and the "0" indicates that this is an SAE-specified OBD II DTC.

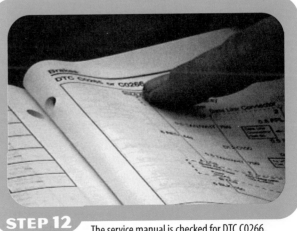

STEP 12 The service manual is checked for DTC C0266.

(continued)

ABS DIAGNOSIS continued

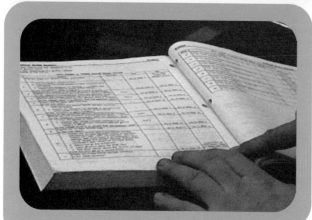

STEP 13 By following the service manual test procedure, the technician is led to the conclusion that the fault is due to a defective ABS controller (computer).

STEP 14 The technician disconnected the battery before replacing the ABS computer.

STEP 15 The Tech 2 was connected again. If another fault had been found, the scan tool should be used to clear the stored DTC and the vehicle driven to confirm that the problem has been corrected.

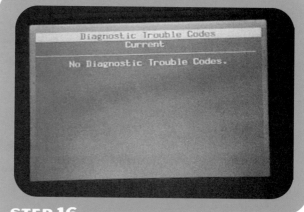

STEP 16 After test driving the vehicle, a quick check using the Tech 2 indicates no stored DTCs.

STEP 17 Snap-On or similar scanner can also be used on this vehicle to retrieve and clear ABS DTCs.

STEP 18 After double-checking that everything is okay with the antilock braking system, the vehicle can be driven out of the stall and returned to the customer.

SUMMARY

1. ABS diagnosis starts with checking the status of both the red brake warning lamp and the amber ABS warning lamp.
2. The second step in diagnosis of an ABS problem is to perform a thorough visual inspection.
3. The third step in diagnosis of an ABS problem is to test drive the vehicle and verify the fault.
4. Always consult the factory service information for the specific vehicle being serviced for the proper procedure

to use to retrieve and clear diagnostic trouble codes (DTCs).
5. A breakout box is used with a digital multimeter to diagnose electrical ABS components.
6. Hydraulic service on most integral ABS units requires that the brake pedal be depressed as many as 40 times with the ignition key "off" to depressurize the hydraulic system.

REVIEW QUESTIONS

1. Describe the proper operation of the red and amber brake warning lamps.
2. List the items that should be checked as part of a thorough visual inspection.
3. Explain how to retrieve a diagnostic trouble code from a General Motors vehicle equipped with Kelsey-Hayes RWAL ABS.
4. Describe how to use a breakout box to check for proper wheel speed sensor operation.

CHAPTER QUIZ

1. The red brake warning lamp is on and the amber ABS lamp is off. Technician A says that a fault is possible in the base brake system. Technician B says that the red brake warning lamp can be turned on by a low brake fluid level in the master cylinder. Which technician is correct?
   a. Technician A only
   b. Technician B only
   c. Both Technicians A and B
   d. Neither Technician A nor B

2. Two technicians are discussing magneto-type wheel speed sensors. Technician A says that wheel speed sensors are magnetic. Technician B says that the toothed sensor ring is magnetic. Which technician is correct?
   a. Technician A only
   b. Technician B only
   c. Both Technicians A and B
   d. Neither Technician A nor B

3. Technician A says that using the space-saving small spare tire may trigger an ABS amber warning lamp. Technician B says the use of the small spare tire may trigger the red brake warning lamp. Which technician is correct?
   a. Technician A only
   b. Technician B only
   c. Both Technicians A and B
   d. Neither Technician A nor B

4. Technician A says that, with some antilock braking systems, the diagnostic trouble code may be lost if the ignition is turned off before retrieving the code. Technician B says that some antilock braking systems require that a terminal be grounded to cause the amber ABS warning lamp to flash diagnostic trouble codes. Which technician is correct?
   a. Technician A only
   b. Technician B only
   c. Both Technicians A and B
   d. Neither Technician A nor B

5. Technician A says that a scan tool may be required to retrieve data and diagnostic trouble codes from some antilock braking systems. Technician B says that a jumper wire can be used to retrieve diagnostic trouble codes on some antilock braking systems. Which technician is correct?
   a. Technician A only
   b. Technician B only
   c. Both Technicians A and B
   d. Neither Technician A nor B

6. Technician A says that a breakout box is sometimes required to diagnose an antilock braking system. Technician B says that a breakout box requires the use of a digital multimeter. Which technician is correct?
   a. Technician A only
   b. Technician B only

   c. Both Technicians A and B

   d. Neither Technician A nor B

7. Technician A says that a dim red brake warning lamp could indicate a fault in the antilock braking system on some vehicles. Technician B says that the ABS fuse may have to be removed to erase some ABS diagnostic codes if a scan tool is not used. Which technician is correct?

   a. Technician A only

   b. Technician B only

   c. Both Technicians A and B

   d. Neither Technician A nor B

8. The ABS computer uses what signal characteristic from a wheel speed sensor?

   a. Voltage

   b. Frequency

   c. Resistance

   d. Electromagnetic

9. Most wheel speed sensors should measure how much resistance?

   a. 800 to 1,300 ohms

   b. 100 to 300 ohms

   c. 1 to 3 ohms

   d. 0.1 to 1 ohm

10. Technician A says that the ABS electrohydraulic unit can be bled using bleeder screws and the manual method. Technician B says that a scan tool is often required to bleed the ABS electrohydraulic unit. Which technician is correct?

   a. Technician A only

   b. Technician B only

   c. Both Technicians A and B

   d. Neither Technician A nor B

SAMPLE BRAKES (A5) ASE CERTIFICATION TEST WITH ANSWERS

1. Technician A says that the more lines on the head of a bolt, the higher the grade. Technician B says that nongraded hardware store bolts can be used in the place of a missing brake bolt. Which technician is correct?
   a. Technician A only
   b. Technician B only
   c. Both Technicians A and B
   d. Neither Technician A nor B

2. When working on a vehicle, safety experts recommend that the technician _____.
   a. Wears safety glasses
   b. Wears a bump cap
   c. Wears gloves
   d. All of the above

3. A 6 mm diameter bolt requires a _____ wrench.
   a. 6 mm
   b. 8 mm
   c. 10 mm
   d. 12 mm

4. A vehicle component interchange manual is usually called _____.
   a. Vehicle interchange manual
   b. Hollander interchange manual
   c. Lester's interchange manual
   d. SAE interchange manual

5. Rear brakes tend to lockup during hard braking before front brakes because _____.
   a. The rear brakes are larger
   b. The vehicle weight transfers forward
   c. The tires have less traction
   d. Both b and c are correct

6. Most vehicle manufacturers recommend using _____ brake fluid.
   a. DOT 2
   b. DOT 3

   c. DOT 4
   d. DOT 5

7. Used brake fluid should be disposed of _____.
   a. According to local, state, or federal regulations
   b. As hazardous waste
   c. By burning in an EPA-certified facility
   d. By recycling

8. The rubber used in most brake system components will swell if exposed to _____.
   a. Engine oil or ATF
   b. Moisture in the air
   c. DOT 5 brake fluid
   d. Water

9. The edge code lettering on the side of friction material tells the technician _____.
   a. The coefficient of friction code
   b. The quality of the friction material
   c. The temperature resistance rating
   d. All of the above

10. Technician A says that linings with asbestos can be identified by the dark gray color. Technician B says that all brake pads and linings should be treated as if they do contain asbestos. Which technician is correct?
    a. Technician A only
    b. Technician B only
    c. Both Technicians A and B
    d. Neither Technician A nor B

11. Technician A says brake fluid should be filled to the top of the reservoir to be assured of proper brake pressure when the brakes are applied. Technician B says that the brake fluid level should be filled only to the maximum level line to allow for expansion when the brake fluid gets hot during normal operation. Which technician is correct?
    a. Technician A only
    b. Technician B only

    c. Both Technicians A and B

    d. Neither Technician A nor B

12. Self apply of the brakes can occur if _____.

    a. The master cylinder is overfilled

    b. The vent port is clogged or covered

    c. The replenishing port is clogged or covered

    d. Both a and b

13. Technician A says that the brake pedal height should be checked as part of a thorough visual inspection of the brake system. Technician B says the pedal free play and pedal reserve should be checked. Which technician is correct?

    a. Technician A only

    b. Technician B only

    c. Both Technicians A and B

    d. Neither Technician A nor B

14. Two technicians are discussing overhauling master brake cylinders. Technician A says that the bore of an aluminum master cylinder cannot be honed because of the special anodized surface. Technician B says that many over (OH) kits include replacement piston assemblies. Which technician is correct?

    a. Technician A only

    b. Technician B only

    c. Both Technicians A and B

    d. Neither Technician A nor B

15. Technician A says the red brake warning lamp on the dash will light if there is a hydraulic failure or low brake fluid level. Technician B says the red brake warning lamp on the dash will light if the parking brake is on. Which technician is correct?

    a. Technician A only

    b. Technician B only

    c. Both Technicians A and B

    d. Neither Technician A nor B

16. A vehicle tends to lock up the *front* wheels when being driven on slippery road surfaces. Technician A says that the metering valve may be defective. Technician B says the proportioning valve may be defective. Which technician is correct?

    a. Technician A only

    b. Technician B only

    c. Both Technicians A and B

    d. Neither Technician A nor B

17. A vehicle pulls to the left during braking. Technician A says that the metering valve may be defective. Technician B says the proportioning valve may be defective. Which technician is correct?

    a. Technician A only

    b. Technician B only

    c. Both Technicians A and B

    d. Neither Technician A nor B

18. A vehicle tends to lock up the rear wheels during hard braking. Technician A says that the metering valve may be defective. Technician B says the proportioning valve may be defective. Which technician is correct?

    a. Technician A only

    b. Technician B only

    c. Both Technicians A and B

    d. Neither Technician A nor B

19. Two technicians are discussing loosening a stuck bleeder valve. Technician A says to use a 6-point wrench and simply pull on the wrench until it loosens. Technician B says that a shock is usually necessary to loosen a stuck bleeder valve. Which technician is correct?

    a. Technician A only

    b. Technician B only

    c. Both Technicians A and B

    d. Neither Technician A nor B

20. The proper brake bleeding sequence for a front/rear split hydraulic system is _____.

    a. Right front, right rear, left front, left rear

    b. Right rear, left front, right front, left rear

    c. Left front, left rear, right front, right rear

    d. Right rear, left rear, right front, left front

21. Two technicians are discussing bleeding air from the brake hydraulic system. Technician A says to depress the brake pedal slowly and not to the floor to prevent possible seal damage inside the master cylinder. Technician B says to wait 15 seconds between strokes of the brake pedal. Which technician is correct?

    a. Technician A only

    b. Technician B only

    c. Both Technicians A and B

    d. Neither Technician A nor B

22. Two technicians are discussing wheel bearings. Technician A says that conventional tapered roller bearings as used on the front of most rear-wheel drive vehicles should be slightly loose when adjusted properly. Technician B says that the spindle nut should not be tightened more than finger tight as the final step. Which technician is correct?

    a. Technician A only

    b. Technician B only

    c. Both Technicians A and B

    d. Neither Technician A nor B

23. Wheel bearings are being packed with grease. Technician A says to use grease that is labeled "GC." Technician B says to use grease with a NLGI number of 2. Which technician is correct?

    a. Technician A only

    b. Technician B only

    c. Both Technicians A and B

    d. Neither Technician A nor B

24. Technician A says that brake drums should be labeled left and right before being removed from the vehicle so that they can be reinstalled in the same location. Technician B says that the hold-down pins may have to be cut off to remove a worn brake drum. Which technician is correct?

    a. Technician A only
    b. Technician B only
    c. Both Technicians A and B
    d. Neither Technician A nor B

25. Technician A says that the backing plate should be lubricated with chassis grease on the shoe pads. Technician B says that the brakes will squeak when applied if the shoe pads are not lubricated. Which technician is correct?

    a. Technician A only
    b. Technician B only
    c. Both Technicians A and B
    d. Neither Technician A nor B

26. Technician A says that most experts recommend replacing all drum brake hardware including the springs every time the brake linings are replaced. Technician B says that the starwheel adjuster must be cleaned and lubricated to assure proper operation. Which technician is correct?

    a. Technician A only
    b. Technician B only
    c. Both Technicians A and B
    d. Neither Technician A nor B

27. New brake shoes are being installed and they do not touch the anchor pin at the top. Technician A says the brake shoes are not the correct size. Technician B says the parking brake cable may need to be loosened. Which technician is correct?

    a. Technician A only
    b. Technician B only
    c. Both Technicians A and B
    d. Neither Technician A nor B

28. A starwheel adjuster is installed on the wrong side of the vehicle. Technician A says that the adjuster cannot operate at all if installed on the wrong side. Technician B says the adjuster would cause the clearance to increase rather than decrease when activated. Which technician is correct?

    a. Technician A only
    b. Technician B only
    c. Both Technicians A and B
    d. Neither Technician A nor B

29. Technician A says to use synthetic grease to lubricate the backing plate. Technician B says to use special lithium-based brake grease. Which technician is correct?

    a. Technician A only
    b. Technician B only
    c. Both Technicians A and B
    d. Neither Technician A nor B

30. One disc brake pad is worn more than the other. Technician A says that the caliper piston may be stuck in the caliper bore. Technician B says that the caliper slides may need to be cleaned and lubricated. Which technician is correct?

    a. Technician A only
    b. Technician B only
    c. Both Technicians A and B
    d. Neither Technician A nor B

31. Technician A says that all metal-to-metal contact areas of the disc brake system should be lubricated with special brake grease for proper operation. Technician B says that the lubrication helps reduce brake noise (squeal). Which technician is correct?

    a. Technician A only
    b. Technician B only
    c. Both Technicians A and B
    d. Neither Technician A nor B

32. After a disc brake pad replacement, the brake pedal went to the floor the first time the brake pedal was depressed. The most likely cause was _____.

    a. Air in the lines
    b. Improper disc brake pad installation
    c. Lack of proper lubrication of the caliper slides
    d. Normal operation

33. Technician A says the parking brake cable adjustment should be performed before adjusting the rear brakes. Technician B says the parking brake cable should allow for about 15 "clicks" before the parking brake holds. Which technician is correct?

    a. Technician A only
    b. Technician B only
    c. Both Technicians A and B
    d. Neither Technician A nor B

34. Technician A says that rotor thickness variation is a major cause of a pulsating brake pedal. Technician B says that at least 0.015 in. (0.4 mm) should be left on a rotor after machining to allow for wear. Which technician is correct?

    a. Technician A only
    b. Technician B only
    c. Both Technicians A and B
    d. Neither Technician A nor B

35. The brake pedal of a vehicle equipped with ABS pulsates rapidly during hard braking on a slippery road surface. Technician A says that the rotor may require machining. Technician B says the lateral runout of the disc brake rotors may be excessive. Which technician is correct?

    a. Technician A only
    b. Technician B only
    c. Both Technicians A and B
    d. Neither Technician A nor B

36. Two technicians are discussing hard spots in brake drums. Technician A says the drum should be replaced. Technician B says the hard spots are caused by using riveted rather than bonded brake shoes. Which technician is correct?

a. Technician A only

b. Technician B only

c. Both Technicians A and B

d. Neither Technician A nor B

37. Disc brake rotors should be machined if rusted.

a. True

b. False

38. Before checking the brake fluid level in a typical integral ABS, the technician should pump the brake pedal _____.

a. 2 or 3 times

b. 3 or 4 times

c. 5 to 10 times

d. 25 times or more

39. Technician A says that wheel speed sensors should be cleaned regularly as part of normal vehicle service. Technician B says that wheel speed sensors are magnetic and can attract metal particles. Which technician is correct?

a. Technician A only

b. Technician B only

c. Both Technicians A and B

d. Neither Technician A nor B

40. Technician A says that a jumper wire or key can be used to retrieve diagnostic trouble codes. Technician B says that some ABS trouble codes can be erased simply by driving the vehicle over a certain speed. Which technician is correct?

a. Technician A only

b. Technician B only

c. Both Technicians A and B

d. Neither Technician A nor B

ANSWERS TO THE SAMPLE BRAKES (A5) ASE CERTIFICATION TEST

1. a	11. b	21. c	31. c
2. d	12. d	22. c	32. d
3. c	13. c	23. c	33. d
4. b	14. c	24. c	34. c
5. d	15. c	25. b	35. d
6. b	16. a	26. c	36. a
7. a	17. d	27. c	37. a
8. a	18. b	29. b	38. d
9. a	19. b	29. c	39. c
10. b	20. d	30. c	40. c

ASE CERTIFICATION TEST CORRELATION CHART

Brakes (A5) ASE Task List

Content Area	Textbook Page #
A. Hydraulic System Diagnosis and Repair (1) Master Cylinder	
1. Diagnose poor stopping or dragging, high or low pedal, hard or spongy pedal caused by problems in the master cylinder; determine needed repairs.	85–132
2. Diagnose problems in the step bore master cylinder and internal valves (e.g., volume control devices, quick take-up valve, fast-fill valve, pressure regulating valve); determine needed repairs.	92–96
3. Measure and adjust master cylinder pushrod length.	95–96, 318–322
4. Check master cylinder for failures by depressing brake pedal; determine needed repairs.	95–96, 317
5. Diagnose the cause of master cylinder external fluid leakage.	95
6. Remove and replace master cylinder; bench bleed and test operation and install master cylinder; verify master cylinder function.	96–98
A. Hydraulic System Diagnosis and Repair (2) Lines and Hoses	
1. Diagnose poor stopping, pulling, or dragging caused by problems in lines and hoses; determine needed repairs.	125–128
2. Inspect brake lines and fittings for leaks, dents, kinks, rust, cracks, or wear; inspect for loose fittings and supports; determine necessary action.	122–127
3. Inspect flexible brake hoses for leaks, kinks, cracks, bulging, wear, or corrosion; inspect for loose fittings and supports; determine necessary action.	127–128
4. Replace brake lines, hoses, fittings, and supports; fabricate brake lines using proper material and flaring procedures (double flare and ISO types).	122–125
5. Inspect brake lines and hoses for proper routing and support.	125–126
A. Hydraulic System Diagnosis and Repair (3) Valves and Switches	
1. Diagnose poor stopping, pulling, or dragging caused by problems in the hydraulic system valve(s); determine needed repairs.	105–112
2. Inspect, test, and replace metering, proportioning, pressure differential, and combination valves.	102–112
3. Inspect, test, replace, and adjust load or height sensing-type proportioning valve(s).	108–109
4. Inspect, test, and replace brake warning light, switch, sensor and circuit.	102–105

Content Area	Textbook Page #
A. Hydraulic System Diagnosis and Repair (4) Bleeding, Flushing, and Leak Testing	
1. Diagnose poor stopping, pulling, or dragging caused by problems in the brake fluid; determine needed repairs.	116–121
2. Bleed and/or flush hydraulic system (manual, pressure, vacuum, or surge method).	132–143
3. Pressure test brake hydraulic system.	108–109
4. Select, handle, store, and install proper brake fluids (including silicone fluids).	121
B. Drum Brake Diagnosis and Repair	
1. Diagnose poor stopping, pulling, or dragging caused by drum brake hydraulic problems; determine needed repairs.	191–194
2. Diagnose poor stopping, noise, pulling, grabbing, dragging, or pedal pulsation caused by drum brake mechanical problems; determine needed repairs.	187–191
3. Remove, clean, inspect, and measure brake drums; follow manufacturers' recommendations in determining need to machine or replace.	264–267
4. Machine drums according to manufacturers' procedures and specifications.	268–270
5. Using proper safety procedures, remove, clean, and inspect brake shoes/linings, springs, pins, self-adjusters, levers, clips, brake backing (support) plates and other related brake hardware; determine needed repairs.	189–191
6. Lubricate brake shoe support pads on backing (support) plate, self-adjuster mechanisms, and other brake hardware.	194–195
7. Install brake shoes and related hardware.	195–197
8. Pre-adjust brake shoes and parking brake before installing brake drums or drum/hub assemblies and wheel bearings.	195–196
9. Reinstall wheel, torque lug nuts, and make final checks and adjustments.	243
C. Disc Brake Diagnosis and Repair	
1. Diagnose poor stopping, pulling, or dragging caused by disc brake hydraulic problems; determine needed repairs.	225–229
2. Diagnose poor stopping, noise, pulling, grabbing, dragging, pedal pulsation or pedal travel caused by disc brake mechanical problems; determine needed repairs.	229–238
3. Retract integral parking brake caliper piston(s) according to manufacturers' recommendations.	235, 253–258
4. Remove caliper assembly from mountings; inspect for leaks and damage to caliper housing.	225–227
5. Clean, inspect, and measure caliper mountings and slides/pins for wear and damage.	233–234
6. Remove, clean, and inspect pads and retaining hardware; determine needed repairs, adjustments, and replacements.	229–234
7. Clean caliper assembly; inspect external parts for wear, rust, scoring, and damage; replace any damaged or worn parts; determine the need to repair or replace caliper assembly.	227–233
8. Clean, inspect, and measure rotor with a dial indicator and a micrometer; follow manufacturers' recommendations in determining the need to index, machine, or replace the rotor.	272–275
9. Remove and replace rotor.	273, 285
10. Machine rotor, using on-car or off-car method, according to manufacturers' procedures and specifications.	275–285, 293–305
11. Install pads, calipers, and related attaching hardware; lubricate components following manufacturers' procedures and specifications; bleed system.	229–238, 133–140
12. Adjust calipers with integrated parking brakes according to manufacturers' recommendations.	139, 257–258
13. Fill master cylinder to proper level with recommended fluid; inspect caliper for leaks.	235
14. Reinstall wheel, torque lug nuts, and make final checks and adjustments.	243

Content Area	Textbook Page #
D. Power Assist Units Diagnosis and Repair	
1. Test pedal free travel with and without engine running to check power booster operation.	317–318
2. Check vacuum supply (manifold or auxiliary pump) to vacuum-type power booster.	310–317
3. Inspect the vacuum-type power booster unit for vacuum leaks and proper operation; inspect the check valve for proper operation; repair, adjust, or replace parts as necessary.	312–313
4. Inspect and test hydro-boost system and accumulator for leaks and proper operation; repair or replace parts as necessary; refill system.	321–324
E. Miscellaneous Systems (Pedal Linkage, Wheel Bearings, Parking Brakes, Electrical, etc.) Diagnosis and Repair	
1. Diagnose wheel bearing noises, wheel shimmy and vibration problems; determine needed repairs.	152–153
2. Remove, clean, inspect, repack wheel bearings, or replace wheel bearings and races; replace seals; replace hub and bearing assemblies; adjust wheel/hub bearings according to manufacturers' specifications.	151–155
3. Check parking brake system; inspect cables and parts for wear, rust, and corrosion; clean or replace parts as necessary; lubricate assembly.	247–252, 258–259
4. Adjust parking brake assembly; check operation.	258–259
5. Test the parking brake indicator light, switch, and wiring.	247
6. Test, adjust, repair or replace brake stop light switch, lamps, and related circuits.	247
7. Inspect and test brake pedal linkage for binding, looseness, and adjustment; determine needed repairs.	247–253
F. Electronic Brake Control Systems; Antilock Brake System (ABS) and Traction Control Systems (TCS) Diagnosis and Repair	
1. Follow accepted service and safety precautions when inspecting, testing, and servicing ABS/TCS hydraulic, electrical, and mechanical components.	399–418
2. Diagnose poor stopping, wheel lock up, pedal feel and travel, pedal pulsation, and noise concerns associated with the ABS/TCS; determine needed repairs.	399–411
3. Observe ABS/TCS warning light(s) at startup and during road test; determine if further diagnosis is needed.	399–401
4. Diagnose ABS/TCS electronic control(s), components, and circuits using on-board diagnosis and/or recommended test equipment; determine needed repairs.	399–411
5. Bleed and/or flush the ABS/TCS hydraulic system following manufacturers' procedures.	413–415
6. Remove and install ABS/TCS components following manufacturers' procedures and specifications; observe proper placement of components and routing of wiring harness.	411–413
7. Test, diagnose, and service ABS/TCS speed sensors (digital or analog), toothed ring (tone wheel), magnetic encoder, and circuits following manufacturers' recommended procedures (includes output signal, resistance, shorts to voltage/ground, and frequency data).	411–412
8. Diagnose ABS/TCS braking concerns caused by vehicle modifications (wheel/tire size, curb height, final drive ratio, etc.) and other vehicle mechanical and electrical/electronic modifications (communication, security, and radio, etc.).	409
9. Repair wiring harness and connectors following manufacturers' procedures.	416–418

NATEF TASK CORRELATION CHART

For every task in Brakes, the following safety requirement must be strictly enforced:

Comply with personal and environmental safety practices associated with clothing; eye protection; hand tools; power equipment; proper ventilation; and the handling, storage, and disposal of chemicals/materials in accordance with local, state, and federal safety and environmental regulations.

Brakes (A5) NATEF Task List

Task	Textbook Page #	Worktext Page #
A. General Brake Systems Diagnosis		
1. Complete work order to include customer information, vehicle identifying information, customer concern, related service history, cause, and correction. (P-1)	2–5	4
2. Identify and interpret brake system concern; determine necessary action. (P-1)	186–199 224–240	9
3. Research applicable vehicle and service information, such as brake system operation, vehicle service history, service precautions, and technical service bulletins. (P-1)	2–5	5–6
4. Locate and interpret vehicle and major component identification numbers (VIN, vehicle certification labels, calibration decals). (P-1)	2–5	7
B. Hydraulic System Diagnosis and Repair		
1. Diagnose pressure concerns in the brake system using hydraulic principles (Pascal's Law). (P-1)	20–77	13
2. Measure brake pedal height; determine necessary action. (P-2)	94–96	14
3. Check master cylinder for internal and external leaks and proper operation; determine necessary action. (P-2)	94–96	15
4. Remove, bench bleed, and reinstall master cylinder. (P-1)	97–98	16
5. Diagnose poor stopping, pulling, or dragging concerns caused by malfunctions in the hydraulic system; determine necessary action. (P-1)	80–127	17
6. Inspect brake lines, flexible hoses, and fittings for leaks, dents, kinks, rust, cracks, bulging, or wear; tighten loose fittings and supports; determine necessary action. (P-2)	122–127	24
7. Fabricate and/or install brake lines (double flare and ISO types); replace hoses, fittings, and supports as needed. (P-2)	122–125	25
8. Select, handle, store, and fill brake fluids to proper level. (P-1)	116–121	26
9. Inspect, test, and/or replace metering (hold-off), proportioning (balance), pressure differential, and combination valves. (P-2)	105–112	18, 19, 20
10. Inspect, test, and adjust height (load) sensing proportioning valve. (P-3)	108–109	21
11. Inspect, test, and/or replace components of brake warning light system. (P-3)	102–105	22
12. Bleed (manual, pressure, vacuum, or surge) brake system. (P-1)	131–143	27, 28, 29, 30, 31
13. Flush hydraulic system. (P-3)	140–141	32

Task	Textbook Page #	Worktext Page #
C. Drum Brake Diagnosis and Repair		
1. Diagnose poor stopping, noise, vibration, pulling, grabbing, dragging, or pedal pulsation concerns; determine necessary action. (P-1)	186–198	39
2. Remove, clean (using proper safety procedures), inspect, and measure brake drums; determine necessary action. (P-1)	186–188 264–269	59
3. Refinish brake drum. (P-1)	268–270	59
4. Remove, clean, and inspect brake shoes, springs, pins, clips, levers, adjusters/self-adjusters, other related brake hardware, and backing support plates; lubricate and reassemble. (P-1)	188–197	40, 41, 42, 43
5. Remove, inspect, and install wheel cylinders. (P-2)	191–194	44
6. Pre-adjust brake shoes and parking brake before installing brake drums or drum/hub assemblies and wheel bearings. (P-1)	195, 200	45
7. Install wheel, torque lug nuts, and make final checks and adjustments. (P-1)	243	46
D. Disc Brake Diagnosis and Repair		
1. Diagnose poor stopping, noise, vibration, pulling, grabbing, dragging, or pedal pulsation concerns; determine necessary action. (P-1)	224–240	48
2. Remove caliper assembly from mountings; clean and inspect for leaks and damage to caliper housing; determine necessary action. (P-1)	225–229	49
3. Clean and inspect caliper mounting and slides for wear and damage; determine necessary action. (P-1)	231–235	50
4. Remove, clean, and inspect pads and retaining hardware; determine necessary action. (P-1)	224–225	51
5. Disassemble and clean caliper assembly; inspect parts for wear, rust, scoring, and damage; replace seal, boot, and damaged or worn parts. (P-2)	225–231	52
6. Reassemble, lubricate, and reinstall caliper, pads, and related hardware; seat pads, and inspect for leaks. (P-1)	230–235	53
7. Clean, inspect, and measure rotor with a dial indicator and a micrometer; follow manufacturer's recommendations in determining need to machine or replace. (P-1)	264–265 273–277	61
8. Remove and reinstall rotor. (P-1)	285	62
9. Refinish rotor on vehicle. (P-1)	284–286	63
10. Refinish rotor off vehicle. (P-1)	275–284	64
11. Adjust calipers equipped with an integrated parking brake system. (P-3)	238–239 253–259	55
12. Install wheel, torque lug nuts, and make final checks and adjustments. (P-1)	243	54
E. Power Assist Units Diagnosis and Repair		
1. Test pedal free travel with and without engine running; check power assist operation. (P-2)	317–318	66
2. Check vacuum supply (manifold or auxiliary pump) to vacuum-type power booster. (P-2)	317	67
3. Inspect the vacuum-type power booster unit for vacuum leaks; inspect the check valve for proper operation; determine necessary action. (P-2)	317	68
4. Inspect and test hydraulically assisted power brake system for leaks and proper operation; determine necessary action. (P-3)	317	69
5. Measure and adjust master cylinder pushrod length. (P-3)	317–318	69

Task	Textbook Page #	Worktext Page #
F. Miscellaneous (Wheel Bearings, Parking Brakes, Electrical, etc.) Diagnosis and Repair		
1. Diagnose wheel bearing noises, wheel shimmy, and vibration concerns; determine necessary action. (P-1)	151–153	33
2. Remove, clean, inspect, repack, and install wheel bearings and replace seals; install hub and adjust wheel bearings. (P-1)	151–155	34
3. Check parking brake cables and components for wear, rusting, binding, and corrosion; clean, lubricate, or replace as needed. (P-2)	250–252	56
4. Check parking brake operation; determine necessary action. (P-1)	258–259	57
5. Check operation of parking brake indicator light system. (P-3)	249–250	58
6. Check operation of brake stop light system; determine necessary action. (P-1)	249–250	23
7. Replace wheel bearing and race. (P-1)	254	35
8. Inspect and replace wheel studs. (P-1)	243	36
9. Remove and reinstall sealed wheel bearing assembly. (P-2)	248–249	37
G. Antilock Brake and Traction Control Systems		
1. Identify and inspect antilock brake system (ABS) components; determine necessary action. (P-1)	399–403	73, 74
2. Diagnose poor stopping, wheel lock-up, abnormal pedal feel or pulsation, and noise concerns caused by the antilock brake system (ABS); determine necessary action. (P-2)	401–412	75
3. Diagnose antilock brake system (ABS) electronic control(s) and components using self-diagnosis and/or recommended test equipment; determine necessary action. (P-1)	402–411	76, 77
4. Depressurize high-pressure components of the antilock brake system (ABS). (P-3)	411–412	78
5. Bleed the antilock brake system's (ABS) front and rear hydraulic circuits. (P-2)	412	79
6. Remove and install antilock brake system (ABS) electrical/electronic and hydraulic components. (P-3)	412–413	80
7. Test, diagnose, and service ABS speed sensors, toothed ring (tone wheel), and circuits using a graphing multimeter (GMM)/digital storage oscilloscope (DSO) (includes output signal, resistance, shorts to voltage/ground, and frequency data). (P-1)	409–412	81
8. Diagnose antilock brake system (ABS) braking concerns caused by vehicle modifications (tire size, curb height, final drive ratio, etc.). (P-3)	409–412	82
9. Identify traction control/vehicle stability control system components. (P-3)	359–395	71, 84

ENGLISH GLOSSARY

μ in.   Microinches; a millionth of an inch.

4 WAL   An abbreviation for four-wheel antilock. The Kelsey-Hayes EBC4 braking system used on General Motors trucks.

ABS   See *Antilock braking system.*

Acceleration slip regulation (ASR)   A name for traction control system used on some General Motors vehicles.

Accumulator   A temporary location for fluid under pressure.

Active sensor   A type of wheel speed sensor that produces a digital output signal.

Adjustable wrench   A wrench that has a moveable jaw to allow it to fit many sizes of fasteners.

AGST   Abbreviation for above ground storage tank.

Air gap   The distance between the wheel speed sensor and the reluctor wheel.

ALB   Abbreviation for antilock brakes. See also *Antilock braking system.*

Align   To bring the parts of a unit into the correct position with respect to each other.

Amber ABS warning lamp   The dash warning lamp that lights (amber color) if a fault in the antilock braking system (ABS) is detected.

Anchor   The curved end of a brake shoe where it contacts the anchor pin.

Anchor pin   A steel stud firmly attached to the backing plate. One end of the brake shoes is either attached to or rests against it.

Anchor plate   The support for the anchor pin on a drum brake backing plate.

Antifriction bearings   Bearings that use steel balls or rollers to reduce friction.

Antilock braking system (ABS)   A system that is capable of pulsing the wheel brakes if lockup is detected to help the driver maintain control of the vehicle.

Antirattle clips   Metal clips used to eliminate or dampen noise in a brake system.

Apply system   The part of a brake system that starts the operation of the brakes, including the brake pedal and levels, as well as the parking brake.

Aramid fiber   Generic name for aromatic polyamide fibers developed in 1972. Kevlar is the Dupont brand name for aramid.

Armored brake line   Steel brake line that has wire wrapped around it to provide protection against stones and other debris.

Asbestosis   A health condition where asbestos causes scar tissue to form in the lungs causing shortness of breath.

ASR   See *Acceleration slip regulation.*

ATE   Alfred Teves Engineering, a manufacturer of brake system components and systems.

Atmospheric pressure   Pressure exerted by the atmosphere on all things. (14.7 pounds per square inch at sea level)

Automatic adjusters   Drum brake adjusters that work to keep the proper clearance between the shoe lining and the brake drum.

Axial load   A force in line (same axis) as the centerline of the bearing or shaft.

Backing plate   A steel plate upon which the brake shoes are attached. The backing plate is attached to the steering knuckle or axle housing.

Ball bearings   An antifriction bearing that uses steel balls between the inner and outer race to reduce friction.

Barrel shaped   A brake drum having a frictional surface that is larger in the center than at the open end or at the rear of the drum.

Base brakes   The standard four-wheel brake system. See also *Service brakes.*

BCI (Battery Council International)   A trade organization of battery manufacturers.

Bearingized   A hard surface created inside a wheel cylinder or master cylinder by forcing a hardened steel ball through the bore.

Beehive hold-down   A type of hold-down spring used on drum brakes and shaped like a beehive.

Bellmouth   A brake drum with a frictional surface larger at the open end of the drum than at any other point toward the rear of the drum.

Bleeder screw   A valve in wheel cylinders (and other locations) for bleeding air from the hydraulic system.

Bleeder valve   A threaded valve used to bleed air from a brake hydraulic system. Also called a bleed valve.

BOB   See *Breakout box.*

Bonded linings   Brake linings that are glued or bonded to the brake shoes.

Boost system   The component in the brake system used to increase the brake pedal force.

Boots   Rubber dust protectors on the ends of wheel or caliper cylinders.

BPM (brake pressure modulator)   A part of the Bosch ABS hydraulic control unit.

BPMV (brake pressure modulator valve)   A part of the hydraulic control unit used in a Delphi DBC-7 ABS system.

BPP (brake pedal position)   A sensor used to detect the position of the brake pedal. Used in most regenerative braking systems.

Brake balance control system   The component in a brake system that ensures that the wheel brakes are applied quickly and balanced among all four wheels for safe operation.

Brake bleeding   A process of removing air from the brake hydraulic system.

Brake block   Brake pad material is pressed into a brake block before being heated to become a brake pad.

Brake fade   A result of heat buildup. It is the reduction in braking force due to loss of friction between the brake shoes and the drum.

Brake fluid   A non-petroleum-based fluid called polyglycol used in hydraulic brake systems.

Brake fluid level sensor   A sensor used in the brake fluid reservoir to detect when brake fluid is low and turns on the red brake warning light on the dash.

Brake hardware kit   Springs, clips, and other hardware items to replace the original items when the brake lining or pads are replaced.

Brake light switch   A switch located on the brake pedal linkage used to turn on the rear brake lights.

Brake lines   Steel tubes used to transmit brake fluid pressure.

Brake lining   A friction material fastened to the brake shoes. It is pressed against the rotating brake drum to accomplish braking.

Brake pad   The brake friction material used in disc brakes.

Brake pedal   The pedal depressed by the driver to operate the wheel brakes.

Brake pipes   Lines that carry brake fluid from the master cylinder to the wheel brakes.

Brake shoe holddown   Springs or clips used to hold brake shoes against the backing plate.

Brake shoe return springs   The springs used on a drum brake to retract the linings away from the drum when the brakes are released.

Brake shoes   The part of the brake system upon which the brake lining is attached.

Brake tubing   Pipes used to carry brake fluid from the master cylinder to the wheel brakes.

Brake warning lights   Include the red brake warning light and the amber ABS warning light.

Breaker bar (flex handle)   A long-handled socket drive tool.

Breakout box (BOB)   A piece of test equipment that installs between an electrical/electronic component, such as a controller, and the wiring harness.

Breather port   Another name for the master cylinder replenishing port (rearward port).

BTU (British Thermal Unit)   A unit of heat measurement.

Bump cap   A hat that is plastic and hard to protect the head from bumps.

Bypass port   Another name for the master cylinder vent port (forward port).

Bypassing   A type of fault when brake fluid flows past cup seals and enters another chamber.

CAA (Clean Air Act)   A federal law passed in 1970 and updated in 1990.

CAB   See *Controller antilock brake.*

Cage   The support for rollers or ball bearings.

Calibration codes   Codes used on many powertrain control modules.

Caliper   The U-shaped housing that contains the hydraulic cylinders and holds the pads on disc brake applications.

Campaign   A recall where vehicle owners are contacted to return a vehicle to a dealer for corrective action.

Cap screw   A capped fastener that is threaded into a casting. Often called *bolts.*

Casting number   An identification code cast into an engine block or other large cast part of a vehicle.

Castle nut   A nut with notches cut out around the top to allow the installation of a cotter key to keep the nut from loosening.

Center valve   A valve used in some master cylinders that allows brake fluid to flow into and out of the reservoir without causing harm to lip seals.

CFR (Code of Federal Regulations)   A compilation of the general and permanent rules published in the federal register by the executive departments and agencies of the federal government.

CFRC (carbon fiber reinforced carbon)   A type of friction material.

Channel   A term used to describe a wheel brake being controlled by the antilock brake system controller.

Chatter   Sudden grabbing and releasing of the drum when brakes are applied.

Cheater bar   A bar used on a wrench to increase the amount of torque that can be applied to a fastener. Not recommended.

Chill spots   Hard stops on a brake rotor or brake drum.

C-lock axle   A type of rear differential that uses a C-lock to retain the axles.

Close end   An end of a wrench that grips all sides of the fastener.

Coefficient of friction   A method of expressing friction between two bodies in mathematical terms.

Combination valve   A valve used in the brake system that performs more than one function, such as a pressure differential switch, metering valve, and/or proportioning valve.

Combination wrench   A type of wrench that has an open end at one end and a closed end at the other end of the wrench.

Compensating port   The port located in the master cylinder that allows excess fluid to return to the reservoir. See vent port.

Concentric   Perfectly round—the relationship of two round parts on the same center.

Cone   A tapered metal cone with a hole in the center. Used to center a hubless brake drum or rotor on a brake lathe.

Control module   An electronic device used to control the operation of actuators.

Controller antilock brake (CAB)   The term used by DaimlerChrysler for their ABS.

Convection   The movement of heat from the friction surface of a brake drum or rotor to the cooler part of the drum or rotor.

Core charge   An amount of money paid when a rebuildable part is purchased and refunded when the worn or defective part is returned to the parts store.

Crest   The outside diameter of a bolt measured across the threads.

Cup   Rubber seals that have a lip that forces outward when pressure is applied.

Cylinder hone   A tool that uses an abrasive to smooth out and bring to exact measurement such things as wheel cylinders.

Deflection   A bending or distorting motion. Usually applied to a brake drum when it is forced out-of-round during brake application.

Department of Transportation (DOT)

Diagonal split master cylinder   A master cylinder for front-wheel vehicles that contains two circuits—one for the LF and LR wheel brakes and the other for the RF and LR wheel brakes.

Diaphragm   A flexible cloth/rubber sheet that is stretched across an area, separating two different compartments.

Disc brakes   A type of wheel brake that squeezes two brake pads on both sides of a rotor or disc.

Discs   Another name for brake rotors. Also spelled *disks*.

DOT 3   Rating of the most commonly specified brake fluid.

DOT 4   A brake fluid rating for polyglycol.

DOT 5   Silicone brake fluid rating.

DOT 5.1   The highest rated polyglycol brake fluid.

Double flare   A tubing end made such that the flare area has two wall thickness.

Double-trailing shoe   A type of non-servo drum brake when both shoes are the same size that are applied with equal force by a pair of wheel cylinders.

Drive size   The size in fractions of an inch of the square drive for sockets.

Drum brakes   A type of wheel brake that uses expanding brake shoes inside a brake drum.

Dual diameter bore master cylinder   A master cylinder designed to work with low-drag calipers that uses two different bore sizes.

Dual-diaphragm vacuum booster   A type of vacuum booster that uses two parallel diaphragms.

Dual master cylinder   A two-compartment master cylinder.

Dual-servo brake   A drum brake design where the primary (forward facing) brake shoe exerts force against the secondary (rearward facing) brake shoe during braking while the vehicle is traveling forward.

Dual split master cylinder   A tapered master cylinder for a rear-wheel drive vehicle that has two different portions—one for the front wheel brakes and the other for the rear wheel brakes.

Duo-Servo   Brand name of a Bendix dual-servo drum brake.

Dynamic balance   When the weight mass centerline of a tire is in the same plane as the centerline of the object.

Dynamic seals   Seals used between two surfaces where there is movement.

EBCM (electronic brake control module)   The name Cadillac uses to describe the control module used on the Bosch 3 ABS unit.

EBTCM (electronic brake traction control module)   The term used to describe the valve body and control module of a Bosch 5 ABS unit.

Eccentric   The relationship of two round parts having different centers. A part, which contains two round surfaces, not on the same center.

Eccentric distortion   A fault with brake drums where the geometric centerline of the drum is different from the centerline of the axle.

EHCU (electrohydraulic control unit)   General Motors ABS control module for four-wheel antilock braking systems.

Elastic limit   The limit of movement of brake shoes due to the metal not being able to return to its original dimensions.

Elastomer   Another term used to describe rubber.

Electronic brake proportioning   The control of the rear brakes during heavy braking is controlled by the ABS controller instead of using a proportioning valve.

Emergency brake   See *Parking brake*.

Energized shoe   A brake shoe that receives greater applied force from wheel rotation.

Energy   A term used to describe the capacity for performing work.

EPA (Environmental Protection Agency)   A federal agency created by the Clean Air Act of 1970.

EPR   Abbreviation for ethylene propylene rubber.

Equalizer   A bracket used in a parking brake cable system to balance the force and transmit an equal amount to each rear brake assembly.

Expander   A spring used inside a sealing cup in a wheel cylinder to help prevent the lip from deforming when the brakes are rapidly released.

Extension   A socket wrench tool used between a ratchet or breaker bar and a socket.

Eye wash station   A water fountain designed to rinse the eyes with a large volume of water.

F = MA   A formula for inertia. The force (F) of an object in motion is equal to the mass (M) times the acceleration (A).

Fade   To grow weak; brakes becoming less effective.

Fast-fill master cylinder   Another name for a quick-take-up master cylinder used with low-drag calipers.

Filler port   A term sometimes used to identify the replenishing port (rear port) of a master cylinder.

Filler vent   A breather hole in the filler cap on the master cylinder.

Fire blanket   A fire-proof wool blanket used to cover a person who is on fire in order to smother the fire.

Fire extinguisher classes   The classification of fire extinguishers by the type of fires they are designed to handle.

First-class lever   A type of lever where the fulcrum is between the weight and the force.

Fixed brake caliper   A type of disc brake caliper that has pistons on both sides of the rotor.

Flare nut wrench   A type of wrench used to remove brake lines. Also called *line wrench, fitting wrench,* and *tube-nut wrench.*

Flash codes   Diagnostic trouble codes that are retrieved using a jumper wire and watching the flashing of a light.

Flex handle   A long-handled socket drive tool, also called a breaker bar.

Flexible brake hoses   Brake hoses between the body or frame of a vehicle and the caliper or axle.

Floating caliper   A type of caliper used with disc brakes that moves slightly to ensure equal pad pressure on both sides of the rotor.

FMSI   Abbreviation for Friction Materials Standards Institute.

FMVSS   Federal Motor Vehicle Safety Standard.

Force   Energy applied to an object.

Foundation brakes   See *Service brakes*.

Fulcrum   A pivot point of a lever.

G force   The force of gravity.

Garter spring   A spring used around the lip of a seal.

Gas fade   A type of brake fade where the lining materials are heated enough to emit gas. The gas between the pads and the rotor result in a loss of braking force.

GAWR   Abbreviation for gross axle weight rating.

GC-LB   A grease rating for GC is the highest rating for wheel bearing grease and LB is the highest rating for chassis grease. A GC-LB grease, therefore, can be used.

Glazed drum   A drum surface hardened excessively by intense heat.

Grab   Seizure of the drum on linings when brakes are applied.

Grade   The strength rating of a bolt.

Gravity bleeding   Removing air from a hydraulic brake system by opening the bleeder valve and allowing the brake fluid to flow downward and out the bleeder taking any trapped air with it.

Grease Oil with thickener.

Grease seal A rubber seal with a steel backing used to keep grease in a bearing assembly from leaking.

GVWR Abbreviation for gross vehicle weight rating.

Hand brake See *Parking brake.*

Hard spots Formed in brake drums or rotors due to high heat.

HCU See *Hydraulic control unit.*

Heat checked Cracks in the braking surface of a drum caused by excessive heat.

Heat checking Cracks (checking) of a brake drum or rotor caused by excessive heat.

Height-sensing proportioning valve A valve connected to the rear suspension that limits the brake pressure sent to the rear brakes if the rear of the vehicle is high (unloaded).

HEPA Abbreviation for High Efficiency Particulate Air filter.

HEPA vacuum High efficiency particulate air filter (HEPA) vacuum used to clean brake dust.

HPA (high pressure accumulator) A brake fluid storage container, which is part of the electrohydraulic control unit of a Kelsey-Hayes EBC4 4WAL antilock braking system.

HSMO Abbreviation for hydraulic system mineral oil.

Hydraulic control unit (HCU) A mechanical assembly that controls hydraulic pressure to wheel brakes. Used in ABS and traction control systems.

Hydraulic system The base brake system containing the master cylinder, wheel cylinders, calipers, and brake fluid lines.

Hygroscopic Ability of brake fluid to absorb moisture from the air.

ICU (Integrated control unit) DaimlerChrysler's name for the hydraulic modulator and pump assembly used in the Teves Mark 20 nonintegral four-wheel ABS system.

In. Hg Abbreviation for inches of mercury—a unit of measure for vacuum.

Inches of Mercury A measurement of vacuum; pressure below atmospheric pressure.

Inertia Energy in a moving object.

Inlet port See *Replenishing port.*

Integral ABS An antilock braking system that includes the master cylinder, booster, ABS solenoids, and accumulator(s) all in one unit.

Integrally molded Disc brake pads where the friction material is molded and locked into holes in the steel backing plate.

Intermediate lever A lever used as part of the parking brake cable system.

ISO Abbreviation for International Standard Organization.

Isolation solenoid A solenoid used in an antilock braking system to isolate the master cylinder from the wheel brakes.

Kevlar Dupont brand name of aramid fibers.

Kinetic energy The energy in any moving object. The amount of energy depends on the weight (mass) of the object and the speed of the object.

Kinetic friction Friction between two surfaces that are moving against each other.

Labyrinth seal A water seal formed by the curved area at the lip of the backing plate and the notch in the brake drum.

Lateral runout (LRO) The side-to-side wobble of a disc brake rotor as it rotates on the spindle.

Leading shoe The forward facing brake shoe on a leading/trailing type of drum brake.

Leading-trailing brakes A type of drum brake design that anchors the bottom of both shoes to the backing plate.

Ledges A raised support on the backing plate against which the shoe edge rests where the brake lining controls the backing plate; also called shoe pads.

Leverage The ability of a lever or other mechanical device used to increase force.

Lining edge codes Letters and numbers that indicate the friction code cold and hot, as well as the manufacturer and details about the lining.

Lining fade A condition where the brake lining overheats, reducing the coefficient of friction.

Lining table The part of a drum brake shoe where the lining is attached.

LLVW Lightly loaded vehicle weight.

LMA Low moisture absorption type of brake fluid (D.O.T. 4).

Low-drag caliper A type of disc brake caliper where the piston retracts more than usual, reducing the brake drag between the pad and the rotor.

LPA (low pressure accumulator) A spring-loaded temporary storage reservoir used to hold brake fluid. Part of the electrohydraulic control unit of a Kelsey-Hayes EBC4 4WAL antilock brake system.

LRO An abbreviation for lateral runout. See *Lateral runout.*

μ The Greek letter that represents the coefficient of friction.

Mass The weight of an object.

Master cylinder The part of the brake hydraulic system where the pressure is generated.

Mechanical advantage   The use of levers, such as a brake pedal to increase the force applied by the driver.

Mechanical brakes   Brakes that are operated by a mechanical linkage or cable connecting the brakes to the brake pedal.

Mechanical fade   Braking reduction caused by the heat expansion of the brake drum away from the brake lining.

Mercury   A heavy metal that is liquid at room temperature and is hazardous to health.

Mesothelioma   A fatal type of cancer of the lining of the chest or abdominal cavity, which can be caused by asbestos inhalation.

Metering valve   A hold-off valve installed between the master cylinder and front disc brakes, which prevents operation of front disc brakes until 75–125 psi is applied to overcome rear drum brake return spring pressure.

Metric bolts   Bolts manufactured and sized in the metric system of measurement.

Microinches (M in.)   One-millionth of an inch; a unit of measure of surface finish. The lower the number, the smoother the surface.

Mm Hg   Abbreviation for millimeters of mercury. A metric measure of vacuum.

Mold bonded lining   A design of disc brake pads where the lining material is molded into holes in the steel backing plate.

MSDS (Material Safety Data Sheets)   A listing of all materials used in a building with a description and the hazards associated with it.

NAO (nonasbestos organic)   A type of brake lining that does not include asbestos.

NAS (nonasbestos synthetic)   A type of brake lining that does not include asbestos but uses other synthetic fibers.

Natural frequency   The frequency where the brake pads tend to vibrate.

Nibs   Small V-shaped notches on the side of brake shoes where they rest against the backing plate.

Nitrile   A type of rubber that is okay for use with petroleum.

NLGI   Abbreviation for National Lubricating Grease Institute.

Nonasbestos   Brake linings or pads that do not contain asbestos.

Nonhygroscopic   Brake fluid, such as DOT 5 that does not absorb moisture from the air.

Nonintegral ABS   An antilock braking system (ABS) that uses a conventional master cylinder and power brake booster.

Non-servo brakes   A drum brake design where the primary lining (forward facing) does not control or transmit a force to the secondary (rearward facing) brake shoe.

Open end   The end of a wrench that is open to allow the wrench to be inserted onto a fastener from the side.

OSHA (Occupational Safety and Health Administration)   An organization formed in 1970 to assist and encourage safe working conditions.

Out-of-round   A fault with a brake drum that is not perfectly round.

Over-travel spring   A spring used as part of the self-adjusting components that allow normal operation even if the star wheel adjuster does not move.

Pad wear indicators   A metal strap or notch in the disc brake pad to indicate that the pads are worn to the point of needing replacement.

Parallelism   A measurement of a brake rotor to determine that both sides of the rotors are perfectly parallel.

Parking brake   Components used to hold a vehicle on a 30° incline. Formerly called an emergency brake before 1967 when dual master cylinders and split braking systems became law; also called the hand brake.

Pascal's law   A law of hydraulics named for the person who developed it, Blaise Pascal (1632–1662).

Pawl   A lever for engaging in a notch. Used to rotate the notched starwheel on self-adjusting brakes.

Pedal free play   The amount of brake pedal movement where no pressure is built up in the master cylinder.

Pedal height   The height of the brake pedal measured from the floor to the top of the pedal.

Pedal ratio   The mechanical advantage of the brake pedal due to the location of the fulcrum and the length of the pedal arm.

Pedal reserve distance   A measurement from the floor to the top of the brake pedal when the brakes are applied.

Personal protective equipment (PPE)   Items worn or used by workers to protect them from hazards of the work place, including safety glasses, gloves, and eye protection.

Phenolic brake pistons   Hard type of plastic disc brake caliper pistons which do not rust or corrode.

Pinch weld seam   A strong section under a vehicle where two body panels are welded together.

Pin-slider caliper   A disk brake caliper design that uses guide pins and is able to move slightly during a brake application.

Piston assemblies   A part of a master cylinder where the sealing cups and the piston are replaceable as an assembly.

Piston stops   Metal tangs next to drum brake wheel cylinders used to prevent cylinder pistons from coming out of their bores when the brake lining is removed.

Pitch   The number of threads per inch of a threaded fastener.

Platform   The basic structure of a vehicle, such as the axles, brakes, and other structural parts.

Polyglycol   The chemical name for conventional (nonsilicon) brake fluid, which means that it contains a polyalkylene-glycol-ether mixture.

Power bleeding   See *Pressure bleeding*.

Power chamber   The enclosure of a vacuum brake booster assembly that is separated into the vacuum side and the atmospheric air pressure side by a flexible diaphragm.

PPE   See *Personal protective equipment*.

Pressure bleeder   A device that forces pressure into the master cylinder, so that when the bleeder screws are opened at the wheel cylinder, air will be forced from the system.

Pressure bleeding   A method used to bleed air out of a brake hydraulic system using compressed air above the master cylinder reservoir. Also called *power bleeding*.

Pressure decay stage   A stage during ABS operation where the pressure of the brake fluid at a wheel brake is reduced.

Pressure differential   A difference in pressure from one brake circuit to another.

Pressure-differential switch   Switch installed between the two separate braking circuits of a dual master to light the dash board "brake" light in the event of a brake system failure, causing a *difference* in brake pressure.

Pressure dump stage   See *Pressure decay stage*.

Pressure holding stage   A stage during ABS operation where the pressure of the brake fluid at a wheel brake is held at the correct level.

Pressure increase stage   A stage during ABS operation where the pressure of the brake fluid at a wheel brake is increasing due to a driver brake application.

Pressure reduction stage   See *Pressure decay stage*.

Prevailing torque nut   A type of nut that holds torque; also called a *lock nut*.

Primary shoe   A brake shoe installed facing the front of the vehicle.

Proportioning valve   Valve installed between the master cylinder and rear brakes that limits the amount of pressure to the rear wheels to prevent rear wheel lock-up.

Push rod   The link rod connecting the brake pedal to the master cylinder piston.

PWM (pulse-width modulation)   The control of a solenoid or actuator using an electronic controller to pulse the unit on and off for various percentages of time to control the ouput of the device.

Quick take-up master cylinder   A type of master cylinder that uses a large and small diameter bore for use with a low-drag caliper.

Ra   Roughness average; a measurement of surface finish. The lower the number, the smoother the surface.

RABS (Rear Antilock Braking System)   Ford's version of a single-channel rear-wheel-only antilock braking system used on many rear-wheel-drive pickups and vans.

Race   Inner and outer machined surface of a ball or roller bearing.

Radial load   The load applied to a bearing 90 degrees from the axis. The weight of the vehicle applies a radial load to the wheel bearing.

Ratchet   A hand tool used to drive a socket wrench that is capable of being changed to tighten or loosen a fastener.

RBWL (red brake warning lamp)   This dash-mounted warning light is used to notify the driver in the event of a hydraulic base brake problem, such as low brake fluid level or a loss of hydraulic pressure.

RCRA   Resource Conservation and Recovery Act.

Reaction Disc   A feature built into a power brake unit to provide the driver with a "feel" of the pedal.

Recall   A notification to the owner of a vehicle that a safety issue needs to be corrected.

Red brake warning lamp   The dash-mounted warning lamp that lights if a hydraulic system fault is detected.

Regen   An abbreviation for regenerative braking.

Regeneration   A process of taking the kinetic energy of a moving vehicle and converting it to electrical energy and storing it in a battery.

Release solenoid   A solenoid used to open a vent port to release pressure from a brake circuit.

Replenishing port   The Society of Automotive Engineers (SAE) term for the rearward low pressure master cylinder port. Also called inlet port, bypass port, filler port, or breather port.

Residual check valve   A valve in the outlet end of the master cylinder to keep the hydraulic system under a light pressure on drum brakes only.

Retainer plate-type rear axles   A type of rear axle that uses a retainer plate instead of a C-clip to keep the axle retained to the axle housing.

Reverse fluid injection   A hand-operated device used to inject brake fluid into the bleeder valves at the wheel brake.

Right-to-know laws   Laws that state that employees have a right to know when the materials they use at work are hazardous.

Riveted linings   Brake lining that is held to the brake shoe using rivets.

RMS (root mean square)   A method of calculating surface roughness using the square root of the average readings squared.

Roller bearings Antifriction bearings that use hardened steel rollers between the inner and outer races.

RWAL Rear Wheel Anti-Lock. General Motors and DaimlerChrysler's version of a single-channel rear-wheel-only antilock braking system used on many rear-wheel-drive pickups and vans.

SAE Society of Automotive Engineers.

SAS (self-aligning spacer) A double-cone device used to ensure proper torque is applied to a brake drum or rotor when installed on a brake lathe.

SBR Abbreviation for styrene butadiene rubber.

Scoring Grooves worn into the drum or disc braking surface.

Second class lever A type of lever where the fulcrum is at one end of the lever and the applied force is at the other end of the lever with the load in the center.

Secondary shoe The brake shoe installed facing the rear of the vehicle.

Select low principle The principle where during an ABS stop, the wheel on the same axle that is slowing the fastest is the one which determines when to increase, hold, or decrease pressure to both wheel brakes.

Self-adjusting brakes Brakes that maintain the proper lining-to-drum clearance by automatic adjusting mechanism.

Self-apply A condition where the brakes apply without the driver depressing the brake pedal.

Self-aligning spacer A double cone used to spread the force of the retaining nut on the spindle of a brake lathe.

Self-energizing action A brake shoe, that when applied, develops a wedging action that assists the braking force applied by the wheel cylinder.

Semimets Semimetallic brake linings.

Service brakes The main driver-operated vehicle brakes.

Servo action Brake construction having the end of the primary shoe bear against the secondary shoe. When the brakes are applied, the primary shoe applies force to the secondary shoe.

Servo brake A type of drum brake that uses the primary (forward facing) brake shoe to increase the application force to the rear facing brake shoe.

Shimmy A type of tire vibration usually noticed as a rapid back and forth motion in the steering wheel. Usually caused by dynamic out-of-balance or a bent wheel.

Shoe anchors A round part at the top of most backing plates used to prevent the brake shoes from rotating with the drum during a brake application.

Shoe contact areas Raised areas on the backing plate of a drum brake where the brake shoes contact.

Shoe pad A raised support on the backing plate against which the shoe edge rests where the brake lining controls the backing plate; also called a *shoe ledge*.

Shoe rim Another name for the lining table where the brake lining is attached to the brake shoe.

Shoe support pads Six areas on the backing plate of a drum brake where the lining makes contact.

Shoe web The support under the shoe table on a drum brake shoe.

Silicone brake fluid A type of brake fluid that is purple and does not absorb moisture.

Single stroke bleeding method A method of manual brake bleeding where the brake pedal is depressed one time, held until the bleeder is closed and then released.

Sintered metal See *Sintering*.

Sintering A process where metal particles are fused together without melting.

Sliding caliper A type of disc brake caliper that is free to move within a limited range.

Slope The ratio of front to rear brake pressure by a proportioning valve.

Snub One brake application.

Socket A type of tool used to remove threaded fasteners that fits over the top.

Socket adapter An adapter that allows the use of one size of driver (ratchet or breaker bar) to rotate another drive size of socket.

Solenoid valves Valves that are opened and closed using an electromagnetic solenoid.

Solvent Usually colorless liquids that are used to remove grease and oil.

Special service tools (SST) Tools specified by the vehicle manufacturer to be used to remove/install or disassemble/assemble vehicle components.

Speed nuts Used to keep the brake drum on at the assembly plant. Can be removed and discarded when servicing drum brakes for the first time; also called *Tinnerman nuts*.

Split μ A term used to describe two different friction (μ) surfaces under the wheels of a vehicle. Mu (μ) is the Greek letter for coefficient of friction.

Split point The pressure point where reduction of pressure to the rear brake begins in a proportioning valve.

Split system A divided hydraulic brake system.

Spongy pedal When there is air in the brake lines, the pedal will have a springy or spongy feeling when applied.

Spontaneous combustion Ignition of oily rags without the use of an ignition source.

Squeal   A high pitched noise caused by high-frequency vibrations when brakes are applied.

SST   See *Special service tools*.

Stabilitrack   A brand name of the General Motors Corporation electronic stability control (ESC) system.

Starwheel   A notched wheel with a left or right-hand threaded member for adjusting brake shoes.

Static balance   The balance of a tire with even distribution of weight about its axis.

Static friction   The friction between two surfaces at rest (not moving).

Static seal   A seal used between two surfaces that are not moving.

Step-bore master cylinder   A wheel cylinder having a different diameter at each end.

Stud   A short rod with threads on both ends.

Swept area   The amount of brake drum or rotor friction surface that moves past the brake linings every time the drum or rotor completes a rotation.

Table   The portion of the shoe to which the lining is attached.

Tandem cylinder   A master cylinder with two pistons arranged one ahead of the other. One cylinder operates rear brakes and the other front brakes.

Tandem-diaphragm vacuum booster   A type of vacuum brake booster that uses two diaphragms.

Tapered roller bearings   A type of antifriction bearing that uses tapered rollers between the inner and outer races.

TC   See *Traction control*.

Technical service bulletins (TSB)   A written notification published by a vehicle manufacturer regarding the diagnosis and correction of a problem affecting certain years or models of vehicles.

Tensile strength   The maximum stress used under tension (lengthwise force) without causing failure.

Thickness variation (TV)   A term used to describe a brake rotor dimension. Both sides of the rotor must be parallel and the distance between the surfaces must not vary by more than about a half of a thousandth of an inch, according to most vehicle manufacturer's specifications.

Third-class lever   A type of lever where the fulcrum is located at the end of the lever and the force is applied to the middle of the lever.

Tinnerman nuts   Used to keep the brake drums on at the assembly plant. Can be removed and discarded when servicing the drum brake for the first time; also called speed nuts.

Tire pressure monitoring system (TPMS)   A system of sensors or calculations used to detect a tire that has low tire pressure.

Tire slip   The difference between the actual speed and the rate at which the tire tread moves across the road surface.

Tone ring   A notched wheel used as a reluctor for the wheel speed sensor.

Torque   A twisting force.

Torque wrench   A wrench that registers the amount of applied torque.

TPMS   See *Tire pressure monitoring system*.

Traction   The friction (traction) between tires and the pavement.

Traction control (TC)   The electromechanical parts used to control wheel slip during acceleration.

Trailing shoe   The rear facing drum brake shoe on a leading/trailing type of drum brake.

Tramp   An up and down vibration of a tire/wheel assembly usually due to out-of-round tire or out-of-balance condition.

TSB   See *Technical service bulletin*.

UGST   Abbreviation for underground storage tank.

UNC (Unified National Coarse)   A standard for coarse threads used on fractional sized fasteners.

UNF (Unified National Fine)   A standard for fine threads used on fractional sized fasteners.

Universal joint   A joint in a steering or drive shaft that allows torque to be transmitted at an angle.

Used oil   Any petroleum-based or synthetic oil that has been used.

Vacuum   Any pressure less than atmospheric pressure (14.7 psi).

Vacuum bleeding   Using a vacuum source to draw air from a brake hydraulic system.

Vacuum booster   A vacuum power brake unit.

Vacuum power unit   A device utilizing engine manifold vacuum to assist application of the brakes, reducing pedal effort.

Vacuum servo   A vacuum-controlled parking brake release mechanism controlled by an electrical solenoid.

VECI (vehicle emission control information)   This underhood label shows settings and emission hose routing information and other emission control information.

Vehicle Identification Number (VIN)   A unique 17 character string of numbers and letters that identify most major systems of the vehicle, as well as the serial number.

Vent port The Society of Automotive Engineers (SAE) term for the front port of a master cylinder, also called the *compensating port* or *bypass*.

VIN See *Vehicle identification number.*

VSES (Vehicle Stability Enhancement System) A General Motors term used to describe one type of electronic stability control system.

VSS (vehicle speed sensor) This sensor, usually located at the extension housing of the transmission/transaxle is used by the electronic control module for vehicle speed.

Warning light A light on the instrument panel to alert the driver when one half of a split hydraulic system fails as determined by the pressure-differential switch.

Water fade A lack of braking caused by water getting between the friction material and the brake drum or rotor.

Ways Places where the disc brake caliper contacts on a sliding-type caliper design.

Web The stiffening member of the shoe to which the shoe table is attached.

Weight bias The amount of weight on the front compared with the rear of a vehicle.

Weight transfer The movement of weight forward during braking.

Wheel brakes Brakes at each wheel of a vehicle that slows and stops the rotation of that wheel.

Wheel cylinder The part of the hydraulic system that receives pressure from the master cylinder and applies the brake shoes to the drums.

Wheel speed sensors (WSS) Sensors used to detect the speed of the wheels. Used by an electronic controller for antilock brakes and/or traction control.

WHMIS Workplace Hazardous Materials Information Systems.

Work The transfer of energy from one physical system to another. Actually moving an object is work.

Wrench A hand tool used to grasp and rotate a threaded fastener.

Zerk fitting A name for a chassis grease fitting, also known as an alemite fitting (named for Oscar U. Zerk).

SPANISH GLOSSARY

"Snub"   Una sola frenada.

µ in.   Micro-pulgada; una millonésima parte de una pulgada.

4WAL   Abreviación en inglés para antibloqueo en las cuatro ruedas. El sistema Kelsey-Hayes EBC4 utilizado en camiones de General Motors.

Abaniqueo o bamboleo   Un tipo de vibración de la rueda que usualmente se reconoce mediante una oscilación rápida del volante. Usualmente causado por desequilibrio dinámico de la rueda o alabeo de la llanta (rueda "torcida").

Abrazadera o caliper   La caja en forma de U que contiene los cilindros hidráulicos y sostiene las pastillas en las aplicaciones de disco de frenos.

ABS   Véase *sistema de frenos antibloqueo*.

Acción auto-activante   Una Zapata que al accionarse desarrolla una acción acuñante que ayuda a la fuerza de frenada aplicada por los cilindros de las ruedas.

Aceite usado o reciclado   Cualquier aceite sintético o en base a petróleo que ya ha sido utilizado previamente.

Acumulador   Un depósito o recipiente temporal para fluidos bajo presión.

Adaptador de cubos o dados   Un adaptador que permite que se utilice un tamaño de cubo o dado (matraca o mango articulado) para rotar otro tipo de tamaño de cubo o dado.

Afilador de cilindro   Una herramienta que utiliza un abrasivo para suavizar y conseguir la medida exacta de cosas tales como los cilindros de las ruedas.

Agarrotamiento   Problema en el cual el embrague se aplica repentinamente, más rápido de lo esperado.

AGST   Abreviación en inglés de depósito de almacenamiento no subterráneo.

Ajustadores o reguladores automáticos   Dispositivos graduadores o reguladores ubicados en el tambor de frenos cuya función consiste en mantener el espacio u holgura apropiada entre el forro de la zapata y el tambor del freno.

ALB   Abreviación en inglés de frenos antibloqueo. Véase también *sistema de frenos antibloqueo*.

Alinear   Poner una parte de una unidad en la posición correcta con las demás partes.

Almohadilla de la zapata   Un material de apoyo elevado ubicado en el plato de anclaje sobre el cual la punta de la zapata descansa donde el forro de frenos controla el plato de anclaje; también llamado forro del freno o de la zapata.

Altura del pedal   La altura del pedal de freno medida desde el piso hasta la parte superior del pedal.

Ancla   El extremo curvado de una zapata o banda de freno donde entra en contacto con el perno o pasador de anclaje.

Anclas de Zapata   Un pivote esférico ubicado en la parte superior de la mayoría de las placas de los platos de anclaje utilizado para prevenir que las zapatas roten al interior del tambor de freno durante una frenada.

Anillo de tono   Una rueda con ranuras utilizada como un reluctor para el sensor de velocidad de las ruedas.

Apalancamiento   La habilidad de una palanca u otro instrumento mecánico utilizado para incrementar la fuerza.

Apertura doble   Un extremo de tubería fabricado de tal manera que la zona de apertura tiene un ancho que es el doble de una barrera.

Área barrida   La cantidad de superficie de tambor de freno o de fricción de rotor que se mueve más allá del revestimiento de los frenos cada vez que el rotor completa una rotación.

Áreas de contacto de la zapata   Áreas de contacto elevadas ubicadas en el plato de anclaje en el punto donde las zapatas se unen.

Asbestosis   Condición médica en la que la asbestos produce la formación de cicatrices en los pulmones, lo cual conduce a la falta de aliento.

ASR   Véase *regulación del deslizamiento de la aceleración*.

ATE   Sigla o nombre comercial de Alfred Teves Engineering, empresa fabricante de componentes y sistemas de frenos.

Autofrenado   Una condición en la cual los frenos actúen sin que el conductor presione el pedal de freno.

Balance estático   Cuando una rueda presenta una distribución pareja del peso en su eje, se dice que tiene un balance estático.

Bandas   Seis puntos en la placa de soporte de un tambor de freno donde el forro hace contacto.

Barra articulada (mango articulado)   Una herramienta de mango largo, para la propulsión del dado.

Barra de alargue   Una barra utilizada en una llave para incrementar el monto de torción que se puede aplicar a un sujetador. No se recomienda.

BOB   Véase caja de desconexión.

Boletín de servicios técnicos (TBS por sus siglas en inglés)   Una notificación escrita publicada por un fabricante de vehículos acerca del diagnostico y corrección de problemas mecánicos que afectan a los vehículos de determinado año y modelo.

BPM (Siglas en inglés para modulador de presión de los frenos)   Un componente de la unidad de control hidráulica de frenos antibloqueo Bosch.

BPMV (Siglas en inglés para válvula de modulador de presión de los frenos)   Un componente de la unidad hidráulica de control utilizada en un sistema de frenos antibloqueo Delphi DBC-7.

BPP (Siglas en inglés para posición del pedal de frenos)   Un sensor utilizado para detectar la posición del pedal de freno. Utilizado en la mayoría de sistemas de frenos regenerativos.

BTU (*British Thermal Unit* o Unidad Térmica Británica)   Una unidad de medida de calor.

CAA (Siglas en inglés para la Ley de Aire Limpio)   Una ley federal promulgada en 1970 y actualizada en 1990.

Cabezal de Zerk   Un nombre utilizado para un cabezal de pistola de grasa, también llamado un cabezal alemite (nombrado por Oscar U. Zerk).

CAB   Véase *controlador de freno antibloqueo.*

Caja de desconexión (BOB por sus siglas en inglés)   Una parte de un equipo de prueba que se instala entre un componente eléctrico / electrónico, tal como un controlador, y el arnés de cableado.

Caliper con pasador de pistón deslizante   Un diseño de calibrador de freno de disco que utiliza pasadores o pivotes de pistón y que puede moverse ligeramente durante una aplicación de frenos.

Caliper de bajo arrastre   Un tipo de calibrador de freno de disco donde el pistón se retrae más de lo usual, reduciendo el arrastre del freno entre el relleno y el rotor.

Caliper flotante   Un tipo de calibrador utilizado con los frenos de disco, el cual se mueve levemente para asegurar que se aplica una presión igual de los rellenos de frenos en ambos lados del rotor.

Caliper, pinza o mordaza de freno fijo   Un tipo de calibrador de freno de disco que tiene pistones a ambos lados del rotor.

Cámara de poder   El espacio circundado por el ensamblaje de un reforzador de frenos al vacío o "boster", el cual es dividido entre el lado del vacío y el de la presión de aire atmosférica por un diafragma flexible.

Campaña   Una llamada efectuada cuando los dueños de un vehículo son contactados para devolver el vehículo a la empresa donde lo compraron para que el mismo pueda someterse a una acción correctiva.

Carga axial   Una fuerza alineada (sobre el mismo eje) con la línea central de un cojinete.

Carga radial   La carga aplicada a un cojinete a 90 grados del eje. El peso del vehículo aplica una carga radial al cojinete de la rueda.

CFR (Siglas en inglés para el Código de Regulaciones Federales)   Una compilación de reglas permanentes y generales publicada en el registro federal por las agencias y departamentos ejecutivos del gobierno federal.

CFRC (Siglas en inglés para carbono reforzado con fibra de carbono)   Un tipo de material de fricción.

Cilindro de rueda   La parte del sistema hidráulico que recibe presión de un cilindro principal y aplica las zapatas de frenos a los tambores de freno.

Cilindro de ruedas maestro diferenciado   Un cilindro de ruedas que tiene un diámetro diferente en cada salida o extremo.

Cilindro de tensión rápida   Un tipo de cilindro principal que utiliza un barreno de diámetro grande y pequeño para su uso con un calibrador de bajo arrastre.

Cilindro doble o tandem   Un cilindro principal con dos pistones colocados uno delante del otro. Un cilindro opera los frenos traseros y el otro opera los frenos delanteros.

Cilindro maestro con diámetro doble   Un cilindro principal diseñado para trabajar con calipers o mordazasde bajo arrastre y que utiliza dos diferentes tamaños de diámetro.

Cilindro maestro con división doble   Un cilindro principal que acaba en punta para un vehículo con tracción en las ruedas traseras, que tiene dos diferentes porciones—una para los frenos de las ruedas delanteras y otro para los frenos de las ruedas traseras.

Cilindro maestro doble   Un cilindro principal con dos compartimientos.

Cilindro principal con división diagonal   Un cilindro principal para los vehículos de tracción delantera que incluye dos circuitos—uno para los frenos de las ruedas izquierda delantera e izquierda trasera y el otro para los frenos de ruedas derecha delantera y derecha trasera.

Cilindro principal de llenado rápido Otro nombre para un cilindro principal de ajuste rápido utilizado con calibradores de bajo arrastre.

Cilindro principal o maestro Pieza de un sistema de frenos hidráulicos donde se genera la presión.

Cobro principal Un monto de dinero pagado cuando una parte que se puede reconstruir es adquirida y luego reembolsada cuando la parte gastada o defectuosa se devuelve a la tienda de partes de automóviles.

Códigos de calibración Los códigos utilizados en muchos módulos de control del tren de fuerza.

Códigos de luz parpadeante Códigos de problemas de diagnóstico que se solucionan utilizando un cable de cierre y observando una luz parpadeante.

Códigos de revestimiento en el reborde Letras y números que indica el código de fricción tanto en frío como caliente, así como el fabricante y detalles acerca del revestimiento.

Coeficiente de fricción Un método de expresar la fricción entre dos cuerpos en términos matemáticos.

Cojinetes de bolas Un tipo de cojinete antifricción que utiliza bolas de rodamiento entre el anillo de rodadura interior y el exterior a fin de reducir la fricción.

Combustión espontánea Un incendio que se produce espontáneamente en trapos llenos de aceite o grasa a pesar de la ausencia de una fuente de ignición.

Compensador Un soporte utilizado en un sistema de cableado del freno de estacionamiento para equilibrar la fuerza y transmitir un monto igual a cada ensamblaje de frenos traseros.

Concéntrico Perfectamente circular—la relación de dos partes redondas al mismo centro.

Conductos Lugares donde el caliper del disco de freno hace contacto con un diseño de tipo deslizante.

Conjunto de ensamblaje de frenos Resortes, sujetadores y otros repuestos utilizados para reemplazar las piezas originales cuando se reemplazan las pastillas o el forro de los frenos.

Cono Un cono de metal que acaba en punta con un orificio en el centro. Utilizado para centrar el tambor de freno sin maza o el rotor en un torno de freno.

Consejo Internacional de Baterías o BCI por sus siglas en inglés Una organización comercial de fabricantes de baterías.

Control de tracción (TC por sus siglas en inglés) Las partes electromecánicas utilizadas para controlar el deslizamiento de los neumáticos durante la aceleración.

controlador de freno antibloqueo (CAB por sus siglas en inglés) El termino utilizado por la compañía Daimler/Chysler para sus sistemas de frenos antibloqueo.

Convección El movimiento del calor de la superficie de fricción de un tambor de freno o rotor a la parte más fría del motor o rotor.

Cresta El diámetro exterior de un tornillo medido a lo largo de sus roscas.

Dado o cubo Un tipo de instrumento utilizado para retirar los sujetadores enroscados que encajan mediante su parte posterior.

Derivación Un tipo de falla donde el fluido de los frenos fluye pasando los sellos e ingresa a otra cámara.

Desalineado o desbalanceado Una falla con el tambor de frenos, el cual no es perfectamente redondo.

Descentramiento lateral (LRO pos sus siglas en inglés) El bamboleo de lado a lado de un rotor del freno de disco a medida que rota en el huso.

Deslizamiento de neumático La diferencia entre la velocidad actual y el índice con el cual la banda de rodamiento del neumático se mueve a lo largo de la superficie del camino.

Desvanecimiento de frenos en material gaseoso Un tipo de desvanecimiento de frenos que ocurre a causa de que los forros o pastillas se calienten a tal punto que ocurre la agregación del material en estado gaseoso.

Desvanecimiento del freno, "perdida de fuerza de roce del freno" o "fading" de frenos Un resultado del incremento de la temperatura en el vehículo. Se refiere a la reducción de la fuerza de frenado debido a la perdida de fricción entre las zapatas y el tambor.

Desvanecimiento mecánico Reducción de la frenada causada por la expansión del calor en el tambor de frenos lejos del pedal de freno.

Desvanecimiento o debilitamiento del revestimiento Una condición donde el revestimiento de los frenos se sobrecaliente, reduciendo el coeficiente de fricción.

Desviación Un movimiento que dobla o distorsiona. Por lo general se aplica al tambor de frenos cuando el mismo se fuerza fuera de ciclo durante la aplicación de los frenos.

Diafragma Una placa de tela o goma flexible que se estira a lo largo de un área, a fin de crear dos compartimientos diferentes.

Diferencial de presión Una diferencia en la presión de un circuito de frenos a otro.

Disco de reacción Una característica incorporada a la unidad de potencia de frenos para proporcionarle al conductor con la "sensación" del pedal.

Discos Otro nombre para los rotores de los frenos. Termino que se escribe *disks* o *discs* en inglés.

Disminución de capacidad o desvanecimiento de frenos Debilitación; los frenos se vuelven menos efectivos.

Disminución de capacidad por agua   Una falla en el frenado ocasionada por agua se que infiltró entre el material de fricción y el tambor de freno o rotor.

Disolvente   Líquido que disuelve grasa u otras sustancias.

Distancia de reserva del pedal   Una medida desde el piso hasta la parte superior del pedal de freno cuando se aplican los frenos.

Distancia entre roscas   El número de roscas por pulgada de un sujetador enroscado.

Distorsión excéntrica   Una falla con los tambores de frenos donde la línea de centro geométrica del tambor es diferente de la línea de centro del eje.

DOT 3   La calificación del fluido de frenos más comúnmente especificado.

DOT 4   Una calificación de fluido de frenos para poliglicol.

DOT 5.1   El fluido de frenos de poliglicol con la calificación más alta.

DOT 5   Calificación para fluido de frenos de silicona.

DOT   *Siglas en inglés de* Departamento o Ministerio de Transporte.

Duo-servo   Nombre de marca de un tambor de frenos Bendix de servodirección doble.

EBCM (Siglas en inglés para módulo de control de frenos electrónico)   El nombre que la empresa Cadillac utiliza para describir el módulo de control utilizado en las unidades Bosch 3 ABS.

EBTCM (Siglas en inglés para módulo de control electrónico de tracción de frenos)   El término utilizado para describir el cuerpo de la válvula y el módulo de control de una unidad Bosch 5 ABS.

ECU (Siglas en inglés para unidad de control electrohidráulica)   La unidad de control ABS para sistemas de antibloqueo en las cuatro ruedas de la empresa General Motors.

Eje de bloqueo tipo C   Un tipo de diferencial trasero que utiliza un bloqueo de tipo C para sujetar los ejes.

Ejes traseros de placa de tipo retenedor   Un tipo de eje trasero que utiliza una placa de retenedor en vez de clips en forma de C para mantener el eje sujetado a la caja del eje.

Elastómero   Otro término utilizado para designar el hule o la goma.

Elevador de presión de diafragma doble o de tandem   Un tipo de propulsor de frenos al vacío que utiliza dos diafragmas.

Elevador de presión de diafragma doble   Un tipo de elevador de presión al vacío que utiliza dos diafragmas paralelos.

Encauzar   Un término utilizado para describir el freno de una rueda y cómo éste es controlado por el controlador del sistema antibloqueo de frenos.

Energía cinética   La energía en cualquier objeto en movimiento. La cantidad de energía depende del peso (masa) del objeto y de la velocidad del objeto.

Energía   Un término utilizado para describir la capacidad para llevar a cabo trabajos que requieren esfuerzo.

Ensamblajes de pistón   Una parte de un cilindro principal donde los bordes de o tapas de sello y el pistón se reemplazan como un ensamblaje.

Entretuerca   Un tipo de tuerca que tiene fuerza de torsión; también llamada una tuerca de seguridad.

EPA (Siglas en inglés para Agencia de Protección Ambiental)   Una agencia federal creada por la Ley de Aire Limpio de 1970.

EPR   Abreviación en inglés de goma de etileno propileno.

Equilibrio dinámico   Cuando el peso de la masa de la línea de centro de un neumático se encuentra en el mismo plano que la línea de centro del objeto.

Equipo de protección personal (PPE por sus siglas en inglés)   Prendas que los trabajadores llevan o utilizan a fin de protegerse de peligros en el lugar de trabajo, incluyendo los anteojos de seguridad, los guantes y los elementos de protección de la vista.

Espaciador auto-alineante   Un doble cono utilizado para espaciar o dispersar la fuerza de la tuerca de retención del husillo o huso de un torno de freno.

Estación de lavado de ojos   Una unidad dispensadora de agua diseñada para enjuagar los ojos con un gran volumen de agua.

Etapa de descarga de presión   Véase *desgaste de presión.*

Etapa de desgaste de presión   Una etapa durante la operación del sistema de frenos antibloqueo donde se reduce la presión del fluido de frenos de un freno de ruedas.

Etapa de disminución de presión   *Véase* etapa de desgaste de presión.

Etapa de incremento de presión   Una etapa durante la operación del sistema de frenos antibloqueo donde la presión del fluido de frenos en un freno de rueda incrementa debido a la aplicación de los frenos por el conductor.

Etapa de mantenimiento de presión   Una etapa durante la operación del sistema de frenos antibloqueo donde la presión del fluido de frenos en un freno de rueda se mantiene en el nivel adecuado.

Excéntrico   La relación entre dos partes redondas que tienen centros diferentes. Una parte, que contiene dos superficies redondas, que no se encuentran en el mismo centro.

Extensión   Un herramienta de llave de cubo o dado utilizada entre una matraca o mango articulado (maneral) y un dado o cubo.

Extinguidor, tipos de incendios Tipos de incendios que un extinguidor de fuego está diseñado para manejar, se refiere como una clasificación de incendios.

Extremo abierto El extremo de una llave que es abierto para permitir que la llave se inserte en un sujetador del otro lado.

Extremo cerrado Un extremo de una llave que aprieta todos los lados de un sujetador.

Extremos o "nibs" Pequeñas ranuras en forma de V en los bordes de las zapatas de frenos, en el lugar donde se apoyan contra la placa de soporte.

F = MA La fórmula para la inercia. La fuerza (F) de un objeto en movimiento es igual a la masa (M) por la aceleración (A).

Fibra aramida Nombre genérico de las fibras de poliamida aromática desarrolladas en 1972. El nombre de la marca de fibra aramida de Dupont es Kevlar.

Fluido para frenos hidráulicos Un fluido sintético, no mineral, llamado poliglisol utilizado en los sistemas hidráulicos de frenos.

FMSI Abreviación en inglés para Instituto de Estándares para Materiales de Fricción.

FMVSS Siglas en inglés para Estándar Federal de Seguridad de Vehículos Automotrices.

Forro de frenos adherido Forro de los frenos pegado o enlazado a las zapatas de los frenos.

Forro de frenos Un material friccionable acoplado a las zapatas de los frenos. Se presiona contra el tambor de frenos rotatorio a fin de lograr la acción del frenado.

Frazada antiincendios Una frazada de lana a prueba de incendios que se utiliza para cubrir a una persona que se esta quemando a fin de apagar el fuego.

Frecuencia natural La frecuencia con la que las pastillas o balatas de frenos tienden a vibrar.

Freno con doble servodirección Un diseño de freno de tambor donde la zapata de freno primaria (delantera) ejerce fuerza contra la zapata de freno secundaria (trasera) durante el proceso de frenado, a medida que el vehículo avanza.

Freno de emergencia *Véase* freno de estacionamiento.

Freno de estacionamiento Componentes utilizados para sostener a un vehículo en un ángulo de inclinación de 30°. Conocido como un freno de emergencia antes de 1967 cuando los cilindros principales dobles y los sistemas de frenos divididos se volvieron obligatorios por ley. El freno de estacionamiento también es conocido como el freno de mano.

Freno de mano *Véase* freno de estacionamiento.

Frenos auto regulantes Frenos que mantienen la holgura correcta entre el forro y el tambor mediante una regulación mecánica automática.

Frenos base o básicos El sistema de frenos estándar de un sistema de frenos en las cuatro ruedas.

Frenos de arrastre delanteros Un tipo de diseño de tambor de freno el cual ancla la parte inferior de ambas zapatas a la placa de soporte.

Frenos de base *Véase* frenos de servicio.

Frenos de disco Un tipo de freno de rueda que estruja dos pastillas desde ambos lados de un rotor o disco.

Frenos de ruedas Los frenos en cada rueda de un vehículo que disminuyen y detienen la rotación de esa rueda.

Frenos de servicio Los frenos principales del vehículo que son operados por el conductor.

Frenos de tambor Un tipo de freno de rueda que utiliza zapatas de frenos que se expanden dentro de un tambor de freno.

Frenos mecánicos Frenos operados por un varillaje mecánico o cable que conecta los materiales de fricción.

Frenos no servodireccionales Un diseño de tambor de freno donde el revestimiento de la zapata primaria (delantera) no controla ni transmite una fuerza a la zapata de freno secundaria (trasera).

Fricción cinética La fricción entre dos superficies las cuales se mueven la una contra la otra.

Fricción estática La fricción entre dos superficies en reposo (sin movimiento).

Fuelles / Botas / Cubrepolvos Protectores de goma que se ubican en los extremos de un cilindro de rueda o de pinza (caliper) de frenos.

Fuerza de tensión La resistencia máxima utilizada bajo tensión (fuerza longitudinal) sin causar un fallo.

Fuerza G La fuerza de la gravedad.

Fuerza La energía aplicada a un objeto.

Fuga de fuerza *Véase* Sangrado de presión.

Fuga por gravedad Método para retirar aire del sistema hidráulico abriendo la válvula de purgado o sangrado y permitiendo que el fluido de los frenos fluyan hacia abajo con la fuerza de la gravedad y se purguen a través del purgador llevando consigo cualquier aire atrapado.

GAWR Abreviación en inglés para Peso bruto nominal por eje.

GC-LB Un calificación o clasificación de la grasa de GC es la calificación más alta para grasa de los cojinetes de las ruedas y LB es la calidad más alta de grasa de chasis. Por lo tanto, un tipo de grasa GC-LB es un lubricante funcional que puede aplicarse.

Gorra de seguridad Una gorra de plástico duro para proteger la cabeza de golpes.

Grasa Aceite con un agente espesador.

GVWR   Abreviación en inglés para nivel de peso total del vehículo.

HCU   Véase *unidad de control hidráulico.*

HEPA   Abreviación en inglés de filtro de aire particulado de eficiencia elevada.

Herramientas especiales de servicio (o SST por sus siglas en inglés)   Herramientas especificadas por el fabricante del vehículo para ser usadas para instalar/desinstalar o ensamblar/desensamblar componentes vehiculares.

Higroscópico   La habilidad de un fluido de frenos de absorber la humedad del aire.

HPA (Siglas en inglés para acumulador de alta presión)   Un recipiente de almacenamiento de líquido de frenos, que es parte de la unidad de control electro-hidráulica de un sistema de frenos antibloqueo tipo Kelsey-Hayes EBC4 4WAL.

HSMO   Abreviación en inglés para aceite mineral para sistemas hidráulicos.

ICU (Siglas en inglés para unidad de control integrada)   El nombre con el cual la empresa Daimler-Chrysler designa a un modulador hidráulico y ensamblaje de bomba utilizado en el sistema ABS no-integrado de cuatro ruedas de tipo Teves Mark 20.

Inclinación   La relación de presión de frenos delantera y trasera por válvula proporcionante.

Indicadores de desgaste de relleno   Una cinta o ranura de metal en el relleno de disco de frenos que indica que las pastillas están desgastadas al punto de requerir su reemplazo.

Inercia   La energía que reside en un objeto en movimiento.

Integralmente moldeado   Pastillas de disco de freno donde el material de fricción es moldeado y fijado a los orificios de la placa de apoyo.

Interruptor de diferencial de presión   Interruptor instalado entre los dos circuitos de frenos separados de un circuito maestro doble, para iluminar la luz de "freno" del tablero de instrumentos, en caso de una falla en el sistema de frenos, la cual causaría una *diferencia* en la presión de los frenos.

Interruptor de la luz del freno   Un interruptor ubicado en el varillaje del pedal de frenos utilizado para encender la luz de freno trasera.

Intervalo de aire   La distancia entre el sensor de velocidad de la rueda y la rueda del reluctor.

Inyección de fluido de reversión   Un mecanismo operado manualmente y utilizado para inyectar fluido de frenos a las válvulas de descarga en el freno de rueda.

ISO   Abreviación de la Organización Internacional para la Estandarización.

Jaula   El soporte para los rodillos o cojinetes de bolas.

Juego de pedal libre   El movimiento de pedal de freno disponible cuando no se ha producido ninguna presión en el cilindro principal.

Kevlar   Nombre de marca de Dupont de fibras aramidas.

Lámpara de advertencia amarilla del sistema ABS o luz ámbar ABS   La lámpara de advertencia o luz de aviso en el tablero de instrumentos que se activa (de un color amarillo) si se detecta una falla en el sistema de frenos antibloqueo (ABS).

Ley de Pascal   Una ley o principio científico de hidráulica que toma su nombre de la persona que la desarrolló, Blaise Pascal (1623–1662).

Leyes del derecho de saber   Leyes que estipulan que los empleados tienen el derecho a saber cuando los materiales que utilizan en su trabajo son peligrosos.

Límite elástico   El límite de movimiento de las zapatas de freno debido a que el metal no puede volver a sus dimensiones originales.

Líneas del sistema de frenos   Tubos o mangueras de acero utilizados para transmitir la presión del fluido de frenos.

Líquido de frenos con base de silicona   Un tipo de líquido o fluido de frenos higroscópico de color púrpura.

Llave combinada   Un tipo de llave que tiene un extremo abierto y el otro en forma de estría.

Llave de boca ajustable   Llave con una quijada móvil que le permite adaptarse a diferentes tipos de medida de sujetadores de tuerca.

Llave de torsión   Una llave que registra la cantidad de torsión aplicada.

Llave de tuerca de apertura   Un tipo de llave utilizada para retirar líneas de frenos. También denominada una *tuerca de orejetas, tuerca de empalme* y *tuerca de mariposa.*

Llave   Una herramienta manual utilizada para sostener y rotar un sujetador enroscado.

LLVW   Siglas en inglés para peso de vehículo con carga liviana.

LMA   Siglas en inglés para tipo de fluido de frenos (DOT 4) con baja absorción de humedad.

LPA (Siglas en inglés para acumulador de presión baja)   Un depósito de almacenamiento temporal accionado por resortes utilizado para retener líquidos de freno. Parte de una unidad electrohidráulica de un sistema de frenos antibloqueo tipo Kelsey-Hayes EBC4 4WAL.

LRO   Siglas en inglés que representan una abreviación de descentramiento lateral. Véase *descentramiento lateral.*

Luces de advertencia de los frenos   Incluyen la luz de advertencia de frenos roja y la luz amarilla de advertencia del ABS.

Luz de advertencia   Una luz en el panel de instrumentos para alertar al conductor cuando la mitad de un sistema hidráulico dividido falla, lo cual es determinado por el interruptor diferencial de presión.

Luz roja de advertencia de frenos   La luz de advertencia montada en el tablero de instrumentos que se ilumina si se detecta una falla con el sistema hidráulico.

Mango articulador   Una herramienta de asa larga, para la propulsión del dado, también llamado una barra articuladora.

Mangueras flexibles de freno   Mangueras de freno entre el cuerpo o armazón de un vehículo y el calibrador o eje.

Marcas de frío   Marcas endurecidas por el frío en el rotor de un freno o en el tambor de freno.

Masa   El peso de un objeto.

Matraca o maneral   Un instrumento manual utilizado para propulsar una llave de cubo capaz de ser modificada a fin de soltar o ajustar un sujetador de tuerca o perno.

Mecanismo de expansión, expansor   Un resorte utilizado dentro de un sello de campana en un cilindro de rueda para ayudar a prevenir que el borde del labio del sello se deforme cuando los frenos se sueltan abruptamente.

Mercurio   Un metal pesado que a temperatura ambiente se encuentra en estado líquido y es dañino para la salud.

Mesotelioma   Tipo fatal de cáncer del tejido que recubre el pecho o la cavidad abdominal, el cual puede ser ocasionado por la inhalación de asbestos.

Metal sinterizado   Véase *sinterización*.

Micro pulgadas (M pulgada)   Una millonésima parte de una pulgada; una unidad de medida del acabado o retocado de una superficie. Cuanto más bajo sea el número, más suave será la superficie.

Mm Hg   Abreviación de milímetros de mercurio. Una medida métrica de un vacío.

Módulo de control   Un mecanismo electrónico utilizado para controlar la operación de actuadores.

MSDS (Siglas en inglés para hoja de datos de seguridad física)   Una lista de todos los materiales utilizados en una construcción incluyendo su descripción y los peligros asociados a la misma.

Muelle toroidal   Un muelle o resorte utilizado alrededor del borde de un sello.

NAO (Siglas en inglés para no asbesto orgánico)   Un tipo de forro de frenos que no incluye asbestos.

NAS (Siglas en inglés para no asbesto sintético)   Un tipo de forro de frenos que no incluye asbestos pero que utiliza otro tipo de fibras sintéticas.

Nervaduras   El punto de apoyo bajo la mesa o plancha de revestimiento de la zapata en una zapata de freno de tambor.

Nitrilo   Un tipo de goma que sí se puede utilizar con petróleo.

NLGI   Abreviación en inglés de instituto Nacional de Grasas Lubricantes.

No asbesto   Revestimientos o pastillas de frenos que no contienen asbesto.

No higroscópico   Fluido de frenos, tal como un DOT 5, que no absorbe humedad del aire.

Número de identificación del vehículo o de bastidor (VIN por sus siglas en inglés)   Una serie de caracteres y números única que identifica la mayoría de los sistemas y componentes del vehículo así como el número de serie.

Número de metal moldeado   Un código de identificación moldeado en un bloque del motor o en algún otro componente principal moldeado de un vehículo.

Orifico de escape de gases   Un orificio de ventilación en la tapa de reabastecimiento del cilindro maestro.

OSHA (Siglas en inglés para Administración de la Salud y Seguridad Ocupacionales)   Una organización establecida en 1970 para asistir e incentivar la creación de condiciones de seguridad en el trabajo.

Palanca de primera clase   Un tipo de palanca donde el punto de apoyo se encuentra entre el peso y la fuerza.

Palanca de segundo género   Un tipo de palanca donde el punto de apoyo se encuentra en un extremo y la fuerza aplicada se encuentra al otro extremo mientras que la carga o resistencia se encuentra en el centro.

Palanca de tercer genero   Un tipo de palanca donde el punto de apoyo está ubicado en el extremo de la palanca y la fuerza se aplica en el medio de la palanca.

Palanca intermedia   Una palanca utilizada como parte de un sistema del cable del freno de estacionamiento.

Paralelismo   Una medida de un rotor de frenos para determinar que ambos lados de los rotores sean perfectamente paralelos.

Pasador o perno del ancla   Varilla o clavo de acero que se sujeta firmemente al plato de soporte o placa de apoyo. Un extremo de las zapatas se fija o descansa, afianzado, sobre dicho plato o placa.

Pastilla de freno   El material friccionable de frenos utilizado en los discos de frenos.

Pedal de freno   El pedal que presiona el conductor a fin de activar los frenos de ruedas.

Pedal esponjoso   Cuando existe aire en el revestimiento de los frenos, el pedal se sentirá esponjoso cuando se presiona.

Perno Métrico   Un perno que se fabrica y diseña en base al sistema métrico.

Perno prisionero o espárrago   Una varilla o barra corta con ranuras en ambos extremos.

Pista   Superficie interior y exterior maquinada de un cojinete de rótula o bola.

Pistones de frenos fenólicos   Pistones calibradores de discos de frenos fabricados de un tipo duro de plástico que no se herrumbra ni corroe.

Placa de apoyo o plato de soporte   Una placa de acero donde se acoplan las zapatas. La placa de apoyo está acoplada al muñón de la dirección o a la caja del eje.

Plancha de la zapata   La porción de la zapata de frenos a la cual se sujeta el revestimiento.

Plancha de revestimiento   La parte de una zapata de tambor de freno donde se sujeta el revestimiento.

Plataforma   La estructura básica de un vehículo, tal como los ejes, frenos y otras partes estructurales.

Plato de anclaje   La pieza donde se apoya el pasador del ancla en el plato de soporte de un tambor de freno.

Poliglicol   El nombre químico utilizado para designar el fluido de frenos convencional (no a base de silicona), es decir que contiene una mezcla de éter polialkileno glicol.

Portazapata de freno   El material de relleno de frenos es moldeado en la forma de un portazapata de freno antes de ser recalentado para convertirlo en un revestimiento de frenos.

PPE   Véase *equipos de protección personal*.

Presión atmosférica   Presión que la atmósfera ejerce sobre todas las cosas. (14,7 libras por pulgada cuadrada al nivel del mar.)

Principio de selección baja   Véase selección baja.

Proceso de purga continuo   Un tipo de método o proceso de purga manual donde el pedal de frenos se presionara una sola vez y el conductor mantendrá esta posición de forma continua hasta que el purgador este cerrado y sólo entonces liberara el pedal de freno.

Proporcionamiento electrónico de frenos   El control de los frenos traseros durante el frenado con fuerza se controla por medio del controlador del sistema de frenos antibloqueo en vez de utilizar una válvula de proporcionamiento.

Puerto de compensación   El puerto ubicado en el cilindro principal que permite que el fluido excedentario retorne a la reserva. *Véase* puerto de ventilación.

Puerto de derivación   Otro nombre para el puerto de emisión del cilindro principal (puerto anterior).

Puerto de llenado   Un término a veces utilizado para identificar el puerto u orificio de reabastecimiento (puerto trasero) de un cilindro principal.

Puerto de restauración   El término utilizado por la Sociedad de Ingenieros Automotrices (SAE por sus siglas en inglés) para el puerto de baja presión trasero del cilindro principal. También llamado puerto u orificio de ingreso, puerto de desviación, puerto de relleno o puerto u orificio de alivio.

Puerto de ventilación   El término de la Sociedad de Ingenieros Automotrices (SAE) para el puerto frontal de un cilindro principal, también llamado el puerto de compensación o puerto de derivación.

Puerto de ventilación   Otro nombre para el cilindro principal del puerto de entrada de aire (puerto del extremo posterior).

pulg. Hg.   Abreviación de pulgadas de mercurio—una unidad de medidas utilizada para medir un vacío.

Pulgadas de mercurio   Una unidad de medida de un vacío; cantidad de presión por debajo de la presión atmosférica.

Pulido en fino   Una superficie dura creada al interior de un cilindro maestro o de rueda por efecto de forzar una bola de acero endurecida a través de su superficie interior.

Punto de apoyo   Un punto de pivote de una palanca.

Punto de quiebre   El punto donde la reducción de la presión a la rueda trasera comienza en una válvula proporcionante.

Puntos de contacto de las zapatas   Véase *Bandas*.

Puntos duros   Formados en los tambores de frenos o rotores a causa del calor excesivo.

PWM (Siglas en inglés para modulación de la amplitud del pulso)   El manejo de un solenoide o actuador a través de la utilización de un controlador electrónico que prende y apaga la unidad a diferentes ritmos de tiempo a fin de controlar el mecanismo de salida.

RABS (Siglas en inglés para sistema de frenos de antibloqueo trasero)   La versión de la empresa Ford de un sistema de frenos antibloqueo mono-encauzado de ruedas traseras utilizado en varias camionetas y furgonetas.

Rajamiento por calor   Rayas (rajaduras) en la superficie de fricción de un tambor de freno causadas por calor excesivo.

Ranura de soldadura de pinza   Una sección fuerte en la parte inferior del vehículo donde dos paneles del cuerpo del automóvil se soldan juntos.

Ranuración   Ranuras o grietas erosionadas en la superficie de contacto de un tambor o disco de freno.

Ra   Siglas en inglés para promedio de aspereza; una medida del acabado de una superficie. Cuanto más bajo el número, menos áspera la superficie.

Rayas de calor   Rayas en la superficie de fricción de un tambor de freno causadas por calor excesivo.

RBWL (Siglas en inglés para luz roja de advertencia de frenos)   Esta luz de advertencia montada en el tablero es utilizada para alertar al conductor si existe un problema con la base de freno hidráulica, tal como la existencia de bajos niveles de fluidos de frenos o la perdida de la presión hidráulica.

RCRA   Siglas para *Resource Conservation and Recovery Act* (Ley de Conservación y Recuperación de Recursos).

Rebotar   Una vibración usualmente causada por el movimiento horizontal de un ensamblaje de ruedas no balanceado o desalineado.

Rechinar   Un sonido alto y agudo causado por las vibraciones de alta frecuencia que se producen cuando se aplican los frenos.

Reforzador de potencia al vacío   Una unidad de frenos de propulsión al vacío.

Refuerzo   El brazo endurecido de la zapata de freno a la cual se sujeta la tabla de la zapata.

Regeneración   Un proceso que toma la energía cinética de un vehículo en movimiento y la convierte en energía eléctrica que la almacena en una batería.

Regen   Una abreviación para frenado regenerativo.

Regulación del deslizamiento de la aceleración o ASR por sus siglas en inglés   El nombre con el que se designa un sistema de control de tracción utilizado en algunos vehículos de General Motors.

Relación de pedal   La ventaja mecánica del pedal de freno debido a la ubicación del punto de apoyo y el largo del brazo del pedal.

Remaches del revestimiento   Revestimiento de frenos que se sostiene en la zapata de frenos utilizando remaches.

Resistencia   La calificación de fuerza de una tuerca.

Resorte de retención tipo colmena   Un tipo de resorte o muelle de retención utilizado en un tambor de frenos que tiene la forma de una colmena.

Resorte o muelle de retorno de los frenos   Los resortes utilizados en un tambor de freno para retraer los forros alejándolos del tambor, cuando se sueltan los frenos.

Resorte para sobre trayectoria   Un resorte utilizado como parte de los componentes de auto ajuste que permiten una operación normal, aún si el ajustador estrella de la rueda no se mueve.

Retiro   Una notificación al dueño de un vehículo de que un problema de seguridad debe ser corregido.

Revestimiento de frenos adherido y moldeado   Un diseño de pastillas de discos de frenos donde el revestimiento esta moldeado en los orificios de la placa de acero de la placa de apoyo.

Rin de la zapata   Otro nombre para la mesa o plancha de revestimiento de la zapata donde se fija el revestimiento de frenos a la zapata.

RMS (Siglas en inglés para raíz cuadrada promedio al cuadrado)   Un método para calcular la aspereza o rugosidad de una superficie utilizando la raíz cuadrada del promedio de las lecturas cuadradas.

Rodamientos antifricción   Rodamiento que usa bolas o rodillos para reducir la fricción.

Rodillos cónicos   Cojinetes antifricción que utilizan rodillos de acero endurecido entre las pistas interiores y exteriores.

Rodillos cónicos   Un tipo de cojinete antifricción que utiliza rodillos cónicos entre las pistas internas y externas.

Rueda Estrellada   Una rueda ranurada con un accesorio enroscado zurdo o derecho utilizado para ajustar las zapatas.

RWAL (Siglas en inglés para frenos antibloqueo de las ruedas traseras)   La versión de las empresas General Motors y Daimler-Chrysler de un sistema de frenos antibloqueo utilizado en muchas camionetas o furgonetas de tracción trasera.

SAE   Siglas en inglés para Sociedad de Ingenieros Automotrices.

Salientes   Un soporte elevado en la placa de apoyo contra la cual descansa la zapata donde el relleno de los frenos controla la placa de apoyo o plato de soporte; también llamadas pastillas.

Sangrado de presión   Un método utilizado para expulsar o purgar el aire de un sistema de frenos hidráulicos, utilizando aire comprimido colocado encima de la reserva del cilindro maestro. También conocido como Fuga de fuerza.

Sangrado o purgado de Frenos   El proceso que consiste en purgar aire del sistema hidráulico de los frenos.

Sangrado o purgado de vacío   Acción que consiste en utilizar una fuente de vacío para retirar aire de un sistema hidráulico de frenos.

Sangrador o purgador de presión   Un mecanismo que fuerza la presión al cilindro principal, de tal manera que cuando los tornillos purgadores se abren en el cilindro de rueda, se forzará una fuga de aire del sistema.

SAS (Siglas en inglés para espaciador auto-alineante)   Un mecanismo de doble cono utilizado para garantizar la aplicación de la torción correcta a un rotor o tambor de frenos cuando este se instala en un torno de freno.

SBR   Abreviación en inglés de hule butadieno-estireno.

Selección baja   El principio mediante el cual la rueda sobre el eje que desacelera más rápidamente durante una frenada ABS, es la que determina cuando incrementar, retener, o disminuir la presión a los frenos de las ruedas.

Sello de grasa   Un sello de goma con un tope utilizado para evitar la fuga de la grasa o lubricante de un conjunto de rodamiento de rueda.

Sello estático   Un tipo de sellante hermético que no admite movimiento entre las partes selladas.

Sello laberíntico   Un sello de agua formado por el área curvada en el borde de la placa apoyo o plato de soporte y la ranura en el tambor del freno.

Sellos de campana para frenos   Sellos de goma que tienen un borde que empuja hacia afuera cuando se le aplica presión.

Sellos dinámicos   Sellos utilizados entre dos superficies cuando existe movimiento.

Semi mets   Abreviación en inglés de forros de freno semi-metálicos.

Sensor activo   Tipo de sensor de velocidad de rueda que produce una señal digital de salida.

Sensor de nivel de fluidos de freno   Un sensor utilizado en el depósito de fluidos para frenos que al detectar los bajos niveles de fluidos activa la luz roja de alerta para frenos ubicada en el tablero de instrumentos.

Sensores de velocidad de las ruedas (WSS por sus siglas en inglés)   Sensores utilizados para detectar la velocidad de las ruedas. Utilizado por un controlador electrónico para el sistema antibloqueo de frenos y / o para los frenos que utilizan control de tracción.

Servodireccional al vacío   Un mecanismo de liberación del freno de estacionamiento controlado por una fuerza al vacío, a su vez controlado por un solenoide eléctrico.

Servo-frenos o servoaccionado   Diseño de construcción de frenos en el cual el puntal de la zapata primaria empuja la zapata secundaria. Cuando se aplican los frenos, la zapata principal aplica fuerza a la zapata secundaria.

Servofrenos   Un tipo de tambor de freno que utiliza la zapata primaria (delantera) a fin de incrementar la fuerza aplicada a la zapata secundaria o trasera.

Sinterización   Un proceso mediante el cual las partículas metálicas son agregadas o fusionadas prescindiendo del proceso de fundición.

Sistema antibloqueo de frenos integral   Un sistema de antibloqueo de frenos que incorpora el cilindro de frenos principal o maestro, los solenoides ABS y el acumulador en una sola pieza.

Sistema de aplicación de frenos   El componente de un sistema de frenos que hace que los frenos comiencen a operar. Incluye el pedal y las palancas de freno, así como el freno de mano.

Sistema de control de maniobra de frenos   El componente en un sistema de frenos que se asegura que los frenos sean aplicados y, al mismo tiempo, balanceados rápidamente entre todas las cuatro ruedas a fin de asegurar el control de la maniobrabilidad del vehículo.

Sistema de frenos antibloqueo no integral   Un sistema de frenos antibloqueo (ABS) que utiliza un cilindro maestro convencional como reforzador de potencia de frenos o "booster".

Sistema de frenos antibloqueo o ABS por sus siglas en inglés   Sistema que puede dar impulsos breves a los frenos de las ruedas si se detecta que estos están bloqueados, para ayudar al conductor a mantener el control sobre el vehículo.

Sistema de monitoreo de la presión neumática (TPMS por sus siglas en inglés)   Un sistema de sensores o cálculos utilizados para detectar un neumático con baja presión de aire.

Sistema de reforzadores de freno   El componente del sistema de frenos utilizado para incrementar la fuerza en el pedal de frenos.

Sistema hidráulico dividido   Un sistema de frenos hidráulico dividido.

Sistema hidráulico   El sistema de frenos que contiene el cilindro de freno principal, los cilindros de ruedas, las mordazas de frenos y las tuberías de fluidos de freno.

Solenoide aislante   Un solenoide utilizado en un sistema antibloqueo de frenos para aislar el cilindro maestro de frenos de las ruedas.

Solenoide de liberación   Un solenoide utilizado para abrir un puerto de ventilación para aliviar la presión de un circuito de frenos.

Split μ   Termino técnico del campo de la ingeniería que describe un escenario de adherencia desigual, con diferentes coeficientes de fricción bajo las ruedas de un vehículo. Mu corresponde al símbolo griego de coeficiente de fricción.

SST   Véase *herramientas especiales de servicio*.

Stabilitrack   El nombre de la marca de un tipo de sistema de control de suspensión electrónica.

Sujetador o retenedor de la zapata de frenos   Resortes o clips utilizados para sujetar o retener las zapatas de freno contra la placa de soporte.

Sujetadores anti-traqueteo   Sujetadores de metal que se usan para eliminar o reducir el ruido en un sistema de frenos.

Tamaño del mando   El tamaño en fracciones de pulgada del mando cuadrado para dados o cubos.

Tambor de Freno Abocardado   Un tambor de freno cuya superficie friccional en el extremo abierto es mayor que otra en cualquier punto a lo largo de la parte trasera del tambor.

Tambor de Freno tipo barril   Un tambor de freno que tiene una superficie friccional de mayores proporciones en su centro que en el extremo abierto o la parte posterior del tambor.

Tambor de frenos vitrificado o acristalado   La cubierta de un tambor de frenos excesivamente endurecido por efecto de la aplicación de altas temperaturas a su superficie.

TC   Véase *control de tracción*.

Tendencia de peso   La cantidad de peso en la parte frontal del vehículo comparada con aquella en la parte trasera del vehículo.

Topes de pistón   Lengüetas de metal junto a los cilindros de ruedas del tambor de freno, utilizadas para prevenir que los pistones del cilindro salgan de su paredes interiores cuando se retira el revestimiento de frenos.

Tornillo de purga   Válvula que se ubica en los cilindros de rueda (y otros lugares) para purgar aire del sistema hidráulico.

Tornillo de tope   Un sujetador coronado o tapado que se enrosca a una pieza moldeada. A menudo se llaman *pernos*.

Torsión   Una fuerza de torsión.

TPMS   Véase *sistema de monitoreo de presión neumática*.

Trabajo   La transferencia de energía de un sistema físico a otro. El mover un objeto en realidad es considerado como trabajo.

Tracción   La fricción (tracción) entre los neumáticos y el pavimento.

Transferencia de peso   El movimiento de transferencia de peso hacia adelante durante el frenado.

Traqueteo / Vibración   Repentino asirse y soltarse del tambor del freno cuando se aplican los frenos.

Trinquete   Una palanca que se inserta en una ranura. Utilizado para rotar la rueda estrella con ranuras en los frenos auto-ajustantes.

TSB   Véase *boletín de servicios técnicos*.

Tubería alambrada del sistema de frenos   Tubería de acero del freno envuelta en un alambre que la protege contra piedras y otros escombros.

Tubería de frenos   Tubería utilizada para transportar el fluido de frenos desde el cilindro principal hasta los frenos de las ruedas.

Tubos del sistema de frenos   Líneas de frenos que llevan los fluidos desde el cilindro maestro a los frenos de ruedas.

Tuerca almenada   Una tuerca con incisiones talladas alrededor de la parte superior para permitir la instalación de un pasador de chaveta, con el propósito de prevenir que la tuerca se suelte.

Tuercas de sujeción del tambor   También conocidas como tuercas "tinnerman". Utilizadas para sujetar el tambor de freno a los cojinetes del buje. Dicha tuerca puede ser retirada y descartada cuando se lleva a cabo el mantenimiento de los frenos la primera vez.

Tuercas Tinnerman   Utilizadas para mantener los tambores de frenos aplicados en la planta de ensamblaje. Pueden ser retiradas y desechadas cuando se lleva a cambo el mantenimiento del tambor de freno por primera vez; también conocidas como tuercas de sujeción del tambor.

UGST   Siglas en inglés para *depósito de almacenamiento subterráneo*.

UNF (Siglas en inglés para estándar nacional de roscas o ranuración gruesa de tornillo)   Un estándar para roscas o ranuras gruesas de tornillos ubicadas en sujetadores de tuerca o tornillos de grosores menores a una pulgada.

UNF (Siglas en inglés para estándar nacional de roscas o ranuración fina)   Un estándar para roscas o ranuras delgadas de tornillos ubicadas en sujetadores de tuerca o tornillos de grosores menores a una pulgada.

Unidad de control hidráulico (HCU por sus siglas en inglés)   Un ensamblaje mecánico que controla la transmisión de la presión hidráulica a los frenos de las ruedas. Utilizado en los sistemas de control de frenos ABS y de tracción.

Unidad de potencia de vacío   Un mecanismo que utiliza el vacío múltiple de un motor para reforzar la aplicación de los frenos a fin de reducir el esfuerzo ejercido sobre el pedal.

Unión universal   Una unión o junta en un eje de propulsión o transmisión que permite que se transmita fuerza de torsión en un ángulo.

Vacío APEE o HEPA   Un vacío equipado con un filtro (tipo HEPA) de aire particulado de eficiencia elevada.

Vacío   Cualquier presión menor a la presión atmosférica (de 14.7 psi).

Válvula central   Una válvula utilizada en algunos cilindros principales que permite que el fluido de frenos fluya hacia y desde la reserva sin ocasionar daños a los bordes de los sellos.

Válvula combinada   Una válvula utilizada en el sistema de frenos que ejecuta más de una función, tal como el interruptor de la presión diferencial, la válvula de medición, y / o la válvula de proporcionamiento.

Válvula de nivelación de sensor de altura   Una válvula conectada a la suspensión trasera que limita la presión transmitida a los frenos traseros si la parte posterior del vehículo esta muy alta (descargada).

Válvula de proporcionamiento   Válvula instalada entre el cilindro maestro y los frenos traseros la cual limita el monto de presión que reciben las ruedas traseras para prevenir que las ruedas traseras se inmovilicen.

Válvula de purga   Válvula enroscada que se utiliza para purgar el aire del sistema hidráulico de los frenos. También conocida como una válvula de sangrado.

Válvula de verificación residual   Una válvula en el extremo de salida del cilindro principal, utilizada para mantener una presión suave del sistema hidráulico en los tambores de freno solamente.

Válvula dosificadora   Una válvula de control o retención instalada entre el cilindro maestro y los discos de freno delanteros, que previene la operación de los discos de frenos delanteros hasta que se haya aplicado entre 75–125 psi a fin de sobreponerse a la presión del resorte de retorno del tambor de frenos trasero.

Válvulas de solenoide   Válvulas que se abren y cierran usando un solenoide electromagnético.

Variación de grosor (TV por sus siglas en inglés)   Un término utilizado para describir las dimensiones de un rotor de frenos. Ambos lados del rotor deben ser paralelos y la distancia entre una y otra superficie no debe variar más de aproximadamente media milésima de pulgada, de acuerdo a las especificaciones de la mayoría de los fabricantes de vehículos.

Vástago   La varilla de conexión que conecta el pedal de freno con el pistón del cilindro principal.

VECI (Siglas en inglés para información de control de emisiones de vehículos)   Esta etiqueta bajo el capo detalla la información de ruta del cableado y otra información relativa al control de emisiones.

Ventaja mecánica   El uso de palancas, tal como un pedal de frenos a fin de magnificar la fuerza aplicada por el conductor.

Vernier deslizante   Un tipo de calibrador de discos de frenos que tiene una libertad de movimiento de rango limitado.

VIN   Véase *número de identificación del vehículo.*

VSES (Siglas en inglés para sistema de aumento de estabilidad vehicular)   Un término de la empresa General Motors utilizado para describir un tipo de sistema de control de suspensión electrónica.

VSS (Siglas en inglés para sensor de velocidad del vehículo)   Este sensor, usualmente ubicado en la carcasa o caja de extensión del eje transversal / transmisión, es utilizado por el módulo de control electrónico en relación a la velocidad vehicular.

WHMIS   Siglas en inglés de Sistema de Información sobre Materiales Peligrosos en el Lugar de Trabajo.

WSS   Siglas en inglés para sensor de velocidad de rueda.

Zapata de doble arrastre   Un tipo de tambor de frenos no servodireccional donde ambas zapatas son del mismo tamaño y se aplican con la misma fuerza por un par de cilindros de ruedas.

Zapata delantera   La zapata de freno que mira hacia la parte delantera en un tambor de freno de tipo delantero / de arrastre.

Zapata energizada   Una zapata de freno que recibe una mayor fuerza aplicada de la rotación de las ruedas.

Zapata principal   Una zapata de frenos instalada mirando hacia la parte delantera del vehículo.

Zapata reactora   La zapata del tambor de frenos que mira hacia la parte posterior del vehículo en un tipo de tambor de freno delantero / de arrastre.

Zapata secundaria   La zapata instalada en la parte posterior del vehículo.

Zapatas de frenos   La parte del sistema de frenos sobre la cual se sujeta el forro de los frenos.

INDEX